ANNUAL EGYPTOLOGICAL BIBLIOGRAPHY
BIBLIOGRAPHIE ÉGYPTOLOGIQUE ANNUELLE

INTERNATIONAL ASSOCIATION OF EGYPTOLOGISTS
ASSOCIATION INTERNATIONALE DES ÉGYPTOLOGUES

ANNUAL EGYPTOLOGICAL BIBLIOGRAPHY

BIBLIOGRAPHIE ÉGYPTOLOGIQUE ANNUELLE

1977

Compiled by / Composée par

JAC. J. JANSSEN

with the collaboration of / avec la collaboration de

INGE HOFMANN

and / et

L. M. J. ZONHOVEN

ARIS & PHILLIPS LTD

British Library Cataloguing in Publication Data

Annual Egyptological bibliography = Bibliographie
Egyptologique annuelle. - 1977
1. Egyptology - Bibliographies
016.932'007'2   DT60

ISBN 0-85668-186-5

© Jac. J. Janssen 1981. No part of this publication may be reproduced, stored in a retrieval system, or transmitted in any form by any means without the prior written permission of the publishers.

Printed in England by BIDDLES LTD, Guildford, Surrey.

Published by ARIS & PHILLIPS LTD, Warminster, Wilts., England.

TABLE OF CONTENTS

Acknowledgments	vi
List of Abbreviations	vii
Alphabetical List of Authors and Titles	1
Necrologies	268

ACKNOWLEDGEMENTS

The editor acknowledges the financial assistance of UNESCO in collecting the material for this volume; subvention UNESCO 1978 (CA.2/9) under the auspices of the International Council for Philosophy and Humanic Studies (ICPHS).

Other grateful acknowledgment must be made of the financial contributions for the same purpose kindly given by the following institutions:

Ægyptologisk Institut, Københavns Universitet,
Deutsches Archäologisches Institut, Berlin-Cairo,
Durham University, Durham,
Egypt Exploration Society, London,
The Griffith Institute, Oxford,
Heidelberger Akademie der Wissenschaften, Heidelberg,
The Metropolitan Museum of Art, New York,
Museum of Fine Arts, Boston, Mass.,
Oosters Genootschap in Nederland, Leiden,
The Oriental Institute, The University of Chicago, Chicago, Ill.,
Royal Ontario Museum, Toronto,
Schweizerisches Institut für Ägyptische Bauforschung und Altertumskunde, Cairo,
Société française d'Égyptologie, Paris,
University of Liverpool, Liverpool,
The University Museum, The University of Pennsylvania, Philadelphia, Pa.,
Kon. Vitterhets-, Historie- och Antikvitetsakademien, Stockholm.

Adres van de redacteur / Editor's address
Adresse du rédacteur / Anschrift des Schriftleiters:

Dr. Jac. J. JANSSEN
Nederlands Instituut voor het Nabije Oosten
Noordeindsplein 4-6
LEIDEN

LIST OF ABBREVIATIONS

1) *periodicals,* Festschriften *and serials:*

Ägypten und Kusch: Ägypten und Kusch. Zusammengestellt und herausgegeben von Erika Endesfelder, Karl Heinz Priese, Walter-Friedrich Reineke und Steffen Wenig, Berlin, Akademie Verlag, 1977 = Schriften zur Geschichte und Kultur des Alten Orients, 13; at head of title: Akademie der Wissenschaften der DDR. Zentralinstitut für alte Geschichte und Archäologie; rev. *BiOr* 35 (1978), 31 (P.L. Shinnie); *CdE* LIII, No. 106 (1978), 254-255 (Herman de Meulenaere); *JNES* 38 (1979), 302-303 (Bruce Williams).

Aegyptus: Aegyptus. Rivista Italiana di Egittologia e di Papirologia, Milano 57 (1977).
Address: Università Cattolica (Scuola di Papirologia), Largo A. Gemelli 1, 20123 Milano, Italia.

Aegyptus Antiquus: Aegyptus Antiquus, Buenos Aires 2 (1977) = In Memoriam: Jean Capart 1877-1947.
Address: Mr. Jorge R. Ogdon, General Secretary, Instituto de Egiptología de la Argentina, Arribeños 2350 Casa I, 1428 Buenos Aires, Argentina.

AfO: Archiv für Orientforschung, Horn 25 (1974/1977) = Ernst Weidner-Gedenkband.
Address: Verlag Ferdinand Berger & Söhne OHG, Wiener Strasse 21, A-3850 Horn, NÖ., Österreich.

AJA: American Journal of Archaeology, [New York] 81 (1977).
Address: General Secretary, Archaeological Institute of America, 260 West Broadway, New York. N.Y. 10012. U.S.A.

Antiquity: Antiquity. A Quarterly Review of Archaeology. [Cambridge] 51 (1977).
Address: Heffers Printers Ltd, 104 Hills Road, Cambridge, CB2 1LW, Great Britain.

Archaeology: Archaeology. A Magazine Dealing with the Antiquity of the World, [New York] 30 (1977).
Address: Archaeology, 260 West Broadway, New York, N.Y. 10013, U.S.A.

ASAE: Annales du Service des Antiquités de l'Égypte, Le Caire 62 (1977) = Mélanges Selim Hassan I.
Address: Service des Antiquités de l'Égypte, Le Caire, Egypte (R.A.U.).

BASOR: Bulletin of the American Schools of Oriental Research Number 225 (February, 1977), 226 (April, 1977), 227 (October, 1977) and 228 (December, 1977).
Address: American Schools of Oriental Research, Publications Office, 126 Inman Str., Cambridge, Massachusetts 02139, U.S.A.

BIFAO: Bulletin de l'Institut français d'Archéologie orientale, Le Caire 77 (1977) = Volume dediée à la mémoire de Serge Sauneron.
Address: Imprimerie de l'Institut français d'Archéologie orientale, 37 Rue el-Cheikh Aly Youssef (ex-rue Mounira), Le Caire, Egypte (R.A.U.).

BiOr: Bibliotheca Orientalis, Leiden 34 (1977).
Address: Noordeindsplein 4-6, Leiden, Nederland.

BSFE: Bulletin de la Société française d'Égyptologie. Reunions trimestrielles. Communications archéologiques Nos 77-78 (Octobre 1976 et mars 1977); No. 79 (juin 1977); No. 80 (octobre 1977).
Address: Mme. F. Le Corsu. Cabinet d'Égyptologie, Collège de France, 11 Place Marcelin-Berthelot, Paris 5e, France.

CdE: Chronique d'Égypte. Bulletin périodique de la Fondation égyptologique Reine Elisabeth. Bruxelles LII Nos. 103-104 (1977).
Address: Fondation égyptologique "Reine Elisabeth". Musées Royaux d'Art et d'Histoire, Parc du Cinquantenaire, B 1040 - Bruxelles. Belgique.

Enchoria: Enchoria. Zeitschrift für Demotistik und Koptologie. Herausgegeben von E. Lüddeckens, H.-J. Thissen. K.-Th. Zauzich, in Kommission bei Otto Harrassowitz, Wiesbaden 7 (1977).
Address: Otto Harrassowitz, Taunusstrasse 5, Postfach 349, 6200 Wiesbaden, Bundesrepublik Deutschland.

Forschungen und Berichte: Forschungen und Berichte. Archäologische Beiträge, Berlin 18 (1977).
Address: Staatliche Museen zu Berlin, Bodestr. 1-3, 102 Berlin.

Fragen an die altägyptische Literatur: Fragen an die altägyptische Literatur. Herausgegeben von Jan Assmann, Erika Feucht, Reinhard Grieshammer. Studien zum Gedenken an Eberhard Otto, Wiesbaden, Dr. Ludwig Reichert Verlag, 1977 (17.1 x 24.1 cm; VII + 529 p.).   Pr. DM 72

GM: Göttinger Miszellen. Beiträge zur ägyptologischen Diskussion, Göttingen Hefte 23-26 (1977) [Heft 25 = Siegfried Schott (20.8.1897 - 29.10.1971) zum Gedächtnis. Ordentlicher Professor für Ägyptologie an der Georg-August-Universität Göttingen (1952-1966)].
Address: Seminar für Ägyptologie der Universität, 34 Göttingen, Prinzenstrasse 21, Bundesrepublik Deutschland.

JAOS: Journal of the American Oriental Society, New Haven, Connecticut 97 (1977).
Address: American Oriental Society, 329 Sterling Memorial Library, Yale Station, New Haven, Connecticut 06250, U.S.A.

JARCE: Journal of the American Research Center in Egypt, Princeton, New Jersey 14 (1977).
Address: J.J. Augustin Publisher, Locust Valley, New York 11560, U.S.A.

JEA: The Journal of Egyptian Archaeology, London 63 (1977).
Address : Honorary Treasurer of the Egypt Exploration Society, 2-3 Doughty Mews, London WC1N 2PG, Great Britain.

JNES: Journal of Near Eastern Studies, Chicago, Illinois 36 (1977).
Address: University of Chicago Press, 5801 Ellis Avenue, Chicago, Illinois 60637, U.S.A.

MDAIK: Mitteilungen des Deutschen Archäologischen Instituts Abteilung Kairo, Wiesbaden 33 (1977)

Address: Verlag Philipp von Zabern, P.O.B. 4065, Mainz/Rhein, Bundesrepublik Deutschland.

Мероэ: Мероэ. История, история культуры, язык древнего Судана, Москва, Издательство "Наука". Главная редакция восточной литературы, 1977; at head of title: Академия Наук СССР. Институт востоковедения.

MNL: Meroitic Newsletter. Bulletin d'Informations meroitiques, [Paris] No. 18 (Octobre 1977).
Address; Jean Leclant, 77 rue Georges Lardennois, F-75019 Paris, France.

Mundus: Mundus. A Quarterly Review of German Research Contributions on Asia, Africa and Latin America. Arts and Science, Stuttgart.
Address: Wissenschaftliche Verlagsgesellschaft mbH, Postfach 40, 7000 Stuttgart 1, Bundesrepublik Deutschland.

Newsletter ARCE: Newsletter of the American Research Center in Egypt, Princeton, N.J. Nos. 99/100 (Winter-Spring 1977); Nos. 101-102 (Summer-Fall 1977).
Address: 20 Nassau Street, Princeton, N.J. 08540, U.S.A.

Newsletter SSEA: Newsletter (of) The Society for the Study of Egyptian Antiquities, Toronto Vol. 7, No. 2 (March 1977); No. 3 (May 1977); No. 4 (August 1977).
Address: 30 Chestnut Park, Toronto, Ontario M4W 1W6, Canada.

XIX. Deutscher Orientalistentag: XIX. Deutscher Orientalistentag vom 28. September bis 4. Oktober 1975 in Freiburg im Breisgau. Vorträge herausgeben von Wolfgang Voigt, Wiesbaden, Franz Steiner Verlag GmbH, 1977 = Zeitschrift der Deutschen Morgenländischen Gesellschaft. Supplement III, 1-2.

OLZ: Orientalistische Literaturzeitung, Berlin.
Address: Akademie-Verlag GmbH, Leipzigerstrasse 3-4, 108 Berlin.

OMRO: Oudheidkundige Mededelingen uit Rijksmuseum van Oudheden te Leiden (Nuntii ex museo antiquario Leidensi), Leiden 58 (1977).
Address: Rijksmuseum van Oudheden, Rapenburg 28, Leiden, Nederland.

Oriens Antiquus: Oriens Antiquus. Rivista del Centro per le Antichità e la Storia dell' Arte del Vicino Oriente, Roma 16 (1977).
Address: Centro per le Antichità e la Storia dell' Arte del Vicino Oriente, Via Caroncini 27, 00197 Roma, Italia.

Orientalia: Orientalia. Commentarii trimestres a facultate studiorum orientis antiqui pontificii instituti biblici in lucem editi in urbe, [Rome] Nova Series 46 (1977).
Address: Pontificium Institutum Biblicum, Piazza della Pilotta 35, 1-00187 Roma, Italia.

RdE: Revue d'Égyptologie, Paris 29 (1977).
Address: Librarie C. Klincksiek, 11 rue de Lille, Paris 7e, France.

Rivista: Rivista degli Studi Orientali, Roma 51 (1977).
Address: Dott. Giovanni Bardi editore, Salita de crescenzi 16, Roma, Italia.

SAK: Studien zur Altägyptischen Kultur, Hamburg 5 (1977).
Address: Helmut Buske Verlag, Hamburg, Bundesrepublik Deutschland.

Studia aegyptiaca: Studia aegyptiaca, Budapest 3 (1977) = Az Eötvös Loránd Tudományegyetem ókori történeti tanszékeinek kiadváyai, 21.

ВДИ: Вестник Древней Истории, Москва 1 (139)-4 (142), 1977.
Address: Москва В-36, ул. Дмитрия Ульнова. Д. 19, Комн. 237, Институт всеобщей Истории, АН СССР.

WZKM: Wiener Zeitschrift für die Kunde des Morgenlandes, Wien 69 (1977).
Address: Selbstverlag der Wiener Zeitschrift für die Kunde des Morgenlandes, Universitätsstrasse 7 V, A-1010 Wien 1. Österreich.

ZÄS: Zeitschrift für ägyptische Sprache und Altertumskunde, Berlin 104 (1977).
Address: Akademie-Verlag GmbH, Leipzigerstrasse 3-4, 108 Berlin.

ZAW: Zeitschrift für die alttestamentliche Wissenschaft, Berlin 89 (1977).
Address: Walter de Gruyter & Co., Postfach 110240, 1000 Berlin 11.

ZDMG: Zeitschrift der Deutschen Morgenländischen Gesellschaft, Wiesbaden 127 (1977).
Address: Franz Steiner Verlag GmbH, Bahnhofstrasse 39, Postfach 743, 62 Wiesbaden, Bundesrepublik Deutschland.

2) *other abbreviations:*

AEB:	*Annual Egyptological Bibliography/Bibliographie égyptologique annuelle.*	M.K.:	Middle Kingdom
		N.K.:	New Kingdom
		O.Eg.:	Old Egyptian
B.D.:	Book of the Dead	O.K.:	Old Kingdom
cfr:	*confer,* compare	O.T.:	Old Testament
cm:	centimetre(s)	p.:	page(s)
col.:	column	pl.:	plate(s)
C.T.:	Coffin Texts.	pr.:	price
etc.:	*et cetera*	P.T.:	Pyramid Texts
fig.:	figure(s)	publ.:	publication(s)
F.I.P.:	First Intermediate Period	rev.:	review *or* summary
ill.:	illustration(s)	S.I.P.:	Second Intermediate Period
km:	kilometre(s)	T.I.P.:	Third Intermediate Period
L.Eg.:	Late Egyptian	Urk.:	Urkunden
L.Z.:	L. Zonhoven	𓏺	above a numeral, this hieroglyph indicates a monograph
m:	metre(s)		
M.Eg.:	Middle Egyptian		

ALPHABETICAL LIST OF AUTHORS AND TITLES

77001   ᶜABD EL ᶜAL, A. Hafeez, An Enigmatic Wooden Object Discovered Beside the Southern Side of the Giza Second Pyramid, *ASAE* 62 (1977), 103-120, with 22 pl.
During the process of removing debris and sand E. of the Chephren pyramid a steep sloping passage was discovered, obstructed by heavy stone blocks. At the bottom, in a niche, a wooden box was found containing three layers of 56 pieces of wood. The pieces are described by Ahmed Youssef (p. 107-116), who also succeeded in restoring the object. It was evidently intentionally broken and consisted of four cylindrical columns, a corniche and a base (see pl. XIV a-b). Its meaning is quite obscure.
An addition containing 3 pl. relating to the enigmatic box is to be found in *ASAE* 63 (1979), at the end.

77002   ABDALLA, Abdelgadir M., Some Examples of Incremental Repetition in Meroitic Personal Names, *in: Ägypten und Kusch*, 17-40.
Unter "Incremental Repetition" wird die Anfügung einer oder mehrerer Komponenten an einen bereits bekannten Komplex verstanden, der als Einheit gewonnen wurde. In einigen Fällen werden zwei einheitliche Komplexe zu einem dritten verbunden; diese werden vom Verfasser als "Kombination von Komplexen" bezeichnet. Die "Incremental Repetition" wird einer Untersuchung über zusammengesetzte meroitische Personennamen zugrunde gelegt. Eine Zusammensetzung von Personennamen läßt sich bereits für die Napata-Zeit nachweisen. Abschließend wird auf abgekürtze meroitische Personennamen hingewiesen.   *Inge Hofmann*

77003   ABOU-GHAZI, Dia' M., Finds by Selim Hassan in the Egyptian Museum (Cairo). IInd Section, *ASAE* 62 (1977), 1-83, with 20 pl.
A list of objects discovered by Selim Hassan during his ten excavation seasons at Gîza and at present in the Cairo Museum. The list consists

of 87 objects: 63 statues and fragments of statues, 10 vessels and 14 miscellaneous objects, among which stelae, a set of model tools, etc. Of each various numbers, provenance and present place in the museum, references to literature and a short description (under the heading "observations") are noted.

77004 ACQUARO, Enrico, Amuleti egiziani ed egittizanti del Museo Nazionale di Cagliari, Roma, Consiglio Nazionale delle Ricerche, 1977 (20 × 28 cm; 158 p., 61 pl.) = Collezione di studi fenici, 10; at head of title: Consiglio Nazionale delle Ricerche. Centro di studio per la civiltà fenicia e punica presso l'istituto di studi del Vicino Oriente dell'Università di Roma; rev. *Aegyptus* 58 (1978), 292-295 (Sergio Pernigotti).

After the publication of the scarabs and scaraboids preserved in the museum of Cagliari by Mme Matthiae Scandone (our number 76530) this volume deals with the amulets.

The catalogue proper (p. 39-150) lists 1271 pieces. Of each of them the data (inventory number, material, present condition, measurements and type) are noted, while all are represented by a small photograph on the plates.

The pages preceding the catalogue deal in three chapters with: the history of the collection, a typology of the objects, and their iconography. In the latter chapter three subjects are briefly discussed: monstruosity (change in the outer appearance of a figure and juxtaposition of elements which do not belong together in reality), vulgarization of cultic themes in amulets, and the reduction in size of larger representations they show.

After the catalogue indices of provenance of the objects and concordances between catalogue and inventory numbers.

77005 ADAMS, Barbara, Egyptian Objects in the Victoria and Albert Museum, Warminster, Aris & Phillips Ltd, 1977 (21 × 29.5 cm; [IV +] 61 p., 15 ill., ill. on cover) = Egyptology Today No. 3; rev. *CdE* LIII, No. 106 (1978), 291-292 (C. Vandersleyen).   Pr. £7.50

The catalogue begins with a description of the XVIIIth Dynasty sculpture and relief fragments from Theban mortuary temples at present in the Victoria and Albert Museum. They come from Petrie's excavations at Thebes in 1896 and have only recently been retraced, so that they are not yet in *Porter-Moss II*[2]. The twelve pieces are minutely described and represented by photographs. Among them are a black granite head of Amenophis III (V & A 917.1896), three fragments of a sandstone Osiride statue of the same king (V & A

914.1896, 915.1896 and 916.1896), the upper part of a colossal sandstone jackal paw (its head may be Cairo Ent. 31412), and two sandstone relief heads of Tuthmosis IV (V & A 911.1896 and 912.1896).
In the appendix a register of the Egyptian objects in the V & A Museum, at present in various departments. They come partly from Petrie's excavations and partly from those of the EES. Objects from other sources are not included.

77006 ADAMS, William Y., Nubia. Corridor to Africa, [London], Allen Lane, [1977] (14.5 × 23 cm; XXVI + 797 p., 32 maps, 29 plans, 26 fig., 24 pl.); rev. *American Historical Review* 83 (1978), 1233-1234 (Gerald E. Kadish); *JNES* 38 (1979), 299-302 (Bruce Williams).
Pr. £17.50
In einem einführenden Kapitel werden Geographie und Ökologie Nubiens, seine Bewohner und Sprache dargestellt, sowie ein Überblick über die historischen und archäologischen Quellen gegeben. Der erste große Teil behandelt die "Tribal Beginnings", angefangen mit den steinzeitlichen Perioden über die A-Periode bis zur C-Kultur und dem Beginn des ägyptischen Imperialismus während des Alten und Mittleren Reiches. Im 2. Teil "Dynasties and Empires" werden behandelt: das nubische Reich von Kerma, das Vizekönigtum von Kusch während des Neuen Reiches, das "heroische" Zeitalter während der Napata-Epoche, die meroitische Zivilisation der Steppen, der nubische Nordteil unter ptolemäischer, römischer und schließlich meroitischer Herrschaft und der nubische X-Horizont als Abschluß des Reiches. Teil 3 schließlich, "Medieval Civilizations", führt vom Beginn der Christianisierung bis zur Mahdiya. Ein abschließender Teil behandelt Nubien im 20. Jahrundert.
There has also appeared an American edition: Princeton, N.J., Princeton University Press, 1977 ($35). *Inge Hofmann*

77007 ADAMS, William Y., Reflections on the Archaeology of Kerma, *in: Ägypten und Kusch,* 41-51.
Die Epoche der Kerma-Kultur in Obernubien ist eine der wichtigsten Phasen der nubischen Geschichte. Fünf Problemkreise werden untersucht: die Struktur der Deffufas, die Funktion der Deffufas, der Ursprung und die Datierung der in Kerma gefundenen Handelsgüter und die relative Chronologie des Kerma-Friedhofs. Die Kerma-Kultur wird als zentralisierte und autokratische Monarchie (im Gegensatz zu der relativ demokratischen Gesellschaftsstruktur der A- und C-Gruppe) verglichen mit dem frühen Königreich von Napata und

westafrikanischen Königreichen des Mittelalters.
Vgl. jetzt: Brigitte Gratien, Les cultures Kerma. Essai de classification, [Lille], Publications de l'Université de Lille III, [1978].

Inge Hofmann

ADAMS, William Y., see also our numbers 77346 and 77601.

77008 ADEMOLLO, Aldo, I morbi nel racconto biblico delle piaghi d'Egitto e nella loro rispondenza scientifica, *Rivista di Storia della Medicina*, Roma 20 (1976), 137-167.

Medical comment on some of the Ten Plagues of Egypt (Ex. 8-12) using i.a. evidence from ancient Egypt.

ADRIANI, Achille, see our number 77586.

77009 Ägypten. Das alte Kulturland am Nil auf dem Weg in die Zukunft. Raum-Gesellschaft-Geschichte-Kultur-Wirtschaft. Herausgegeben von Heinz Schamp, Tübingen und Basel, Horst Erdmann Verlag, 1977 (14.9 × 23.2 cm; VIII + 727 p., 10 maps, 15 plans, 22 fig., 5 ill., 24 pl. [4 in colour], many tables) = Buchreihe Ländermonographien, 9.
Pr. DM 54

In this book on modern Egypt the sections of which are written by various authors attention is paid as well to the historical developments. In the second chapter, on history, the section on pre-islamic Egypt is written by Wolfgang Helck, while that on the ancient art in the third chapter (on art) is written by Hartwig Altenmüller. In the section on music in the same chapter, by Jürgen Trautmann, ancient Egyptian music is also discussed.

The book is concluded by an extensive systematic bibliography and an index.
L.Z.

77010 Ägyptische Altertümer aus der Skulpturensammlung Dresden. Staatliche Kunstsammlungen Dresden. Ausstellung im Albertinum. Mai 1977, [Dresden, 1977] (17 × 23 cm; 79 p., 48 pl. [8 in colour], 96 ill., colour ill. on cover).
Pr. DM 30

This is the catalogue, written by Steffen Wenig, of an exhibition of Egyptian antiquities preserved in the sculpture collection at Dresden, to which have been added a few objects from the East Berlin collection (mentioned on a loose sheet).

In the introduction Martin Raumschüssel briefly describes the history of the collection, part of which came from the collection of Ricci, one of the companions of Champollion. There follow surveys of the history and art of ancient Egypt.

The catalogue itself comprises 337 numbers, divided into categories, e.g. funerary equipment, shawabtis, bronze figurines, vessels, scarabs, etc. The most important is the first group, consisting of statues, relief fragments and stelae. Of each object the data (inventory number, material, measurements, provenance and date) are given, and bibliographical references, if available. Most of them are also very briefly described.

From the more important objects we mention: fragments from the Sun-temple of Abû Ghurâb and of paintings from an XVIIIth Dynasty tomb at Thebes, a fragmentary F.I.P. stela (unpublished), a copy of the *B.D.* and another of the *Book of Amduat* (both XXth - XXIst Dynasty).

On p. 67-79 a glossary. The 96 photographs represent the more important pieces.

77011   AFANASSJEWA, W. — W. LUKONIN — N. POMERANZEWA, Kunst in Altvorderasien und Ägypten, Dresden, VEB Verlag der Kunst/Moskau, Verlag Iskusstwo, 1977 (13.5 × 19 cm; 384 p., 2 maps, 20 fig., 178 ill., 45 colour ill., colour ill. on cover); series: Kleine Geschichte der Kunst.

This paperback publication on the art of the ancient Near East and Egypt is intended for the general public. Egypt is dealt with on p. 199-340. Apart from an introduction the development of the Egyptian art is discussed in eight chapters, in a historical order from the Prehistory to the Late Period, which here includes the time from the end of the N.K. to the Roman Empire. Text and illustration are of the traditional type.

Glossary on p. 343-350; synoptic tables p. 351-372; bibliography p. 373-383.

The Russian version has been published in the same year.

77012   AFFUSO, Egidio, I pronomi di I e II persona in semitico, egiziano e berbero, *Annali. Istituto Orientale di Napoli*, Napoli 37 (1977), 249-281.

The author studies the personal pronouns for the 1st and 2nd pers. sing. and plur., used either as subject or as complement, in Semitic, Egyptian and Berber languages. He points out the irregularities in the system and attempts to reconstruct three stages: prae-hamito-semitic, prehistorical and historical hamito-semitic.

77013   L'Alba della civiltà. Società, economia e pensiero nel vicino oriente antico. Volume primo. La Società. A cura di Paolo Matthiae, F.

Mario Fales, Mario Liverani, Franco Pintore. Direzione e coordinamento di Sabatino Moscati, [Torino], UTET, [1976] (17 × 25 cm; XX + 511 p., 68 pl. [10 in colour], 17 plans, 4 fig.); rev. *Journal of Biblical Literature* 98 (1979), 411-414 (William L. Moran); *Revue Biblique* 84 (1977), 456-458 (R. T[ournay]).

Pr. 3 vols. L.54,000

In three volumes (see our following numbers) a group of Italian scholars present their views on society (vol. I), economy (vol. II), and mental structure (vol. III) of the Ancient Near East, including ancient Egypt.

The subjects discussed in the present volume are: man and his environment, the social structure (particularly the family system), the political structure and the juridical structure. As in all three volumes, it is difficult to find the places where Egypt is dealt with since a subject index is lacking. The authors conceive the Ancient Near East as a unity, a stage in the development of human society, although regional differences are not neglected. Since some of them feel more at home in the Near East than in Egypt, Egyptian evidence plays a minor role in their argument. In some chapters this may reflect the lower level of knowledge about the subject compared with that of other regions, however.

77014   L'Alba della civiltà. Società, economia e pensiero nel vicino oriente antico. Volume secondo. L' Economia. A cura di Mario Liverani, F. Mario Fales, Carlo Zaccagnini. Direzione e coordinamento di Sabatino Moscati, [Torino], UTET, [1976] (17 × 25 cm; XV + 582 p., 50 pl. [10 in colour], 40 fig.); rev. *Journal of Biblical Literature* 98 (1979), 411-414 (William L. Moran); *Revue Biblique* 84 (1977), 456-458 (R. T[ournay]).

Pr. 3 vols. L.54,000

Sequel to our preceding number.

The four chapters are devoted to: the mode of production (the economic structure in general), the primary production (including a section on food), techniques and sciences, and the circulation of goods (roads, transport, gift-exchange, trade, credit, measures of value, etc.). Like in volume I, references to ancient Egypt occur throughout the chapters: they are particularly numerous in chapter I (by Mario Liverani).

77015   L' Alba della civiltà. Società, economia e pensiero nel vicino oriente antico. Volume terzo. Il Pensiero. A cura di Pelio Fronzaroli, Sabatino Moscati, Giovanni Garbini, Mario Liverani. Direzione e coordinamento di Sabatino Moscati, [Torino], UTET, [1976] (17 ×

25 cm; XV + 555 p., 94 pl. [10 in colour], 31 fig., 5 plans, 1 folding map, 5 tables).; rev. *Journal of Biblical Literature* 98 (1979), 411-414 (William L. Moran); *Revue Biblique* 84 (1977), 456-458 (R. T[ournay]). Pr. 3 vols. L.54,000

Sequel to our preceding numbers.

In five chapters, on the transmission of culture, the literary and the artistic expression, religiosity and cult, and the concept of the universe, the authors present their view on the mental culture of the Ancient Near East. Once more numerous mentions of Egyptian evidence are included, although the unity of the area is stressed against regional peculiarities.

The volume contains indexes to the entire series (p. 533-555), but only to ancient proper names.

77016 ALDRED, Cyril, The Sheyba in Ancient Egypt, *JEA* 63 (1977), 176-177.

The writer identifies the white collars worn by negro prisoners shown in the tomb of Huy, no. 40, with the slave-yokes used in Africa quite recently. *E. Uphill*

ALDRED, Cyril, see also our number 77024.

77017 ALING, Charles Frederick, A Prosopographical Study of the Reigns of Tuthmosis IV and Amenhotep III, *Dissertation Abstracts International,* Ann Arbor, Mich. 37, No. 12 (June 1977), 7896/7-A.

Abstract of a thesis University of Minnesota, 1976 (Order No. 77-12,775; 302 p.).

The purpose of the thesis is to consider the careers of the royal family members and selected notables during the reigns of Tuthmosis IV and Amenhotep III, in order to shed light on the roots and causes of the Amarna revolution, which appears to have been a calculated attempt to diminish the power of the priesthood. *L.Z.*

77018 ALLAM, S. Les obligations et le famille dans la société égyptienne ancienne, *Oriens Antiquus* 16 (1977), 89-97.

The author first deals with instances from which appears that the state held the entire nuclear family responsible for actions of one member. The same collective responsibility appears to exist in matters of civil law, not only according to Demotic documents but also in Pharaonic times. The reason is that the nuclear family possessed rights in the family properties, which could remain undivided after the death of the parents.

ALLARD, Léone, see our number 77369.

77019 ALMAGRO BASCH, M. et M. HAINSWORTH, Inscripciones de la Necropolis Meroitica de Nag Gamus—Masmas, *MNL* No.18 (Octobre 1977), 3-14, with 2 fig. and 3 ill. on a pl.

Es werden zwei neue meroitische Inschriften aus Nag Gamus vorgestellt (Nag Gamus 18 und 19 = REM 1149 und 1150) und auf Besonderheiten der übrigen 17 bisher eruierten Inschriften hingewiesen.
Inge Hofmann

77020 ALTENMÜLLER, Hartwig, Bemerkungen zum Kannibalenspruch, in: *Fragen an die altägyptische Literatur*, 19-39.

The author translates and discusses the Cannibal Hymn (P.T.§ 393-414, Spell 273/4), and its changed and corrupted form in C.T. Spell 573 (VI, 177a-183e). The older and ruder Unas version is to be connected with rituals for the royal statue, while the younger and milder Teti version and the C.T. Spell belong to the magical spells for the glorification of the deceased. Magical powers are acquired as food by recitation during offerings, possibly slaughterings, by which the deceased identifies himself with the Heliopolitan sun god, and procures the maintenance of his life in the hereafter. Since human offerings for the sun god are not probable, this slaughtering of gods and men was carried out on animals as substitutes. The author adduces some evidence from scenes in mastabas which may support the passage on the food for the various meals. *L.Z.*

ALTENMÜLLER, Hartwig, see also our numbers 77009, 77449 and 77542.

77021 ALTHERR-CHARON, Antoinette, Origine des temples à trois *cellae* du bassin méditerranéen est: état de la question, *L'Antiquité Classique*, Bruxelles 46 (1977), 389-440, with 18 pl. containing plans.

In this broad study on the tripartite temple in the Eastern Mediterranean a complete section is devoted to Egypt (p. 392-8). The author traces the history of the type in temple and funerary architecture up to the Ptolemaic Period. The tripartite pattern does in her opinion not originate from cellae for divine triads, but rather from a typically Egyptian esthetical architectural conception.

Dealing with tripartite edifices of Phoenicia and Punia she concludes that Egyptian influence is very probable.

Conclusion on p. 431-3. *L.Z.*

77022 ALTMAN, Amnon, The fate of Abdi-Ashirta, *Ugarit-Forschungen*, Kevelaer/Neukirchen-Vluyn, 9 (1977), 1-10.

The author, dealing with the evidence in the Amarna letters on the fate of Abdi-Ashirta, ruler of Amurru, discusses several scholarly opinions and reaches the conclusion that Abdi-Ashirta was not murdered by his own people, as must be concluded from the absence of any mention of murder in the Amarna letters of his opponent Rib-Addi, ruler of Byblos, but that he was taken to Egypt where apparently his life ended shortly after his arrest. L.Z.

77023 ALVAREZ, Luis W., Search for Hidden Chambers in the Pyramids, in: *Research Reports. National Geographic Society*. Abstracts and reviews of research and exploration authorized under grants from the National Geographic Society during the year 1968, Washington D.C., National Geographic Society, [1976], 1-17, with 9 fig. and 2 ill.

Technical report on the work done on the Chephren pyramid in order to detect hidden cavities. 19 percent of the volume of the pyramid having been explored now, the results are so far negative. Compare our number 70010. L.Z.

77024 Ancient Egypt in the Metropolitan Museum Journal, Volumes 1-11 (1968-1976). Articles by Cyril Aldred, Henry G. Fischer, Herman de Meulenaere, Birgit Nolte, Edna R. Russmann, [New York], The Metropolitan Museum of Art, 1977 (21 × 28 cm; [VIII+] 201 p., 122 ill., 106 fig.). Pr. $15

The volume contains reprints of 13 articles on egyptological subjects which have been published in the *Metropolitan Museum Journal*. Apart from one by Aldred, Nolte, de Meulenaere and Russmann each they are by the hand of Fischer. Of all of them abstracts have been given in the *AEB;* the numbers are: 71010 (Aldred), 71429 (Nolte), 73239, 73236, 73240, 73235, 74195 (Fischer), 74499 (de Meulenaere), 74625 (Russmann), 75217, 75220, 76252 and 76254 (Fischer).
On p. 181-184 some addenda, all to the articles by Fischer. On p. 185-201 indexes by Edna Russmann.

77025 Ancient Glass. The Bomford Collection of Pre-Roman & Roman Glass on Loan to the City of Bristol Museum & Art Gallery, City of Bristol, Museum & Art Gallery, [1976] (21 × 29.7 cm; II + 48 p., 48 colour ill., 3 fig., 1 ill., colour ill. on cover).

The catalogue, by the director of the museum Nicholas Thomas, consists of 175 items, all presented in colour photographs (three or more in one ill.) accompanied by captions containing the data. Eleven

of the objects came from Egypt, the numbers 2-3, 20-22, 27, 37, 79-80, 89 and 99, mostly dating from the Graeco-Roman period.
To the catalogue proper are added forewords, i.a. by the owner of the collection, a chapter on the history and technology of ancient glass, and a classification of the objects after their techniques, areas of manufacture, and shapes. Bibliography on p. 45-47.

77026 ANDERSON, Ann Stewart, Photographic Documentation of the Life Activities of the Contemporary Egyptian as they Reflect Those Shown in Pharaonic Tombs: Agriculture and Preparation of Food, *Newsletter ARCE* Nos. 99/100 (Winter/Spring), 18.
Abstract of a paper.

77027 ANDREU, G., Un fragment d'ouchebti au nom de Nectanébo Ier, *RdE* 29 (1977), 225-226, with 1 ill.
Doublet vraisemblablement de CGC 48538. *Ph. Derchain*

77028 ANDREU, Guillemette et Sylvie CAUVILLE, Vocabulaire absent du *Wörterbuch* (I), *RdE* 29 (1977), 5-13.
Premier article d'une série de compléments au *WB*. Les auteurs ont dépouillé les indices d'ouvrages égyptologiques antérieurs à 1965 et exclu de leur choix les mots qui, absents du *WB*, figurent soit dans le Concise Dictionary de Faulkner, soit dans quelque liste de mots nouveaux dont on trouvera l'énumération p. 5 n. 4. *Ph. Derchain*.

ANDREWS, Carol A.R., see our number 77566.

77029 Les animaux dans l'Égypte ancienne. Le Louvre présente au Muséum de Lyon. Du 6 novembre 77 au 31 janvier 78, [Lyon, 1977] (19.2 × 22 cm; 123 p., 68 ill., 8 colour pl., colour ill. on cover).
Catalogue of an exhibition of objects from the Louvre Museum, held in the Musée d'Histoire Naturelle in Lyon.
Apart from prefaces and an introduction by Chr. Desroches Noblecourt about the fauna of ancient Egypt the catalogue (by Bernadette Letellier and Christiane Ziegler) consists of two parts: short introductions to a large number of animals as represented in two- or three-dimensional objects from ancient and Hellenistic Egypt, and some general subjects: the animal in hieroglyphic writing, in offerings, in the decoration, in magic and in fables. To each subject one or more objects are added, of which the data are mentioned. All together the exhibition comprises 147 objects, many of which illustrated.
Several items are remarkable, e.g.: No. 6 (the representation on a

coffin from the F.I.P. of a mummy on the back of an Apis bull = E 5534); No. 15 (a limestone statuette of a goddess with cows' feet from the Late Period = E 17234); No. 27 (the figure of an elephant on a Roman faience vessel = E 22582); No. 45 (a faience cat with five kittens = E 8391); No. 177 (a bronze rhinoceros-scarab on a sarcophagus = N 3357).

77030 Anonymous, Die Ägyptologie an der Universität Würzburg, *Information*. Mitteilungsblatt der Bayerischen Julius-Maximilians-Universität Würzburg 11, Nr. 2 (1977), 25-29, with 1 ill.

Defence of a place for the Egyptology among the smaller subjects at the University and survey of the special activities of the Egyptologists at Würzburg.

77031 Anonymous, Department of Egyptian and Near Eastern Art, *Annual Report of the Museum of Fine Arts*, Boston 102 (1976-77), 42, with 2 ill. on p. 28-29.

A list of acquisitions, among which a bronze statuette of a kneeling king from the Late Period (Inv. No. 1977.16) and a fragmentary limestone head from the Amarna Period (Inv. No. 1976.602). *L.Z.*

77032 Anonymous, Jahresbericht 1976 des Deutschen Archäologischen Instituts. Abteilung Kairo, *Archäologischer Anzeiger*, Berlin, 1977, 639-642.

Yearly report of the activities of the German Archaeological Institute, with very short sections on the excavations at Elephantine, Thebes-West and Dashûr. *L.Z.*

77033 Anonymous, King Tut Rises Again, *Horizon*, New York 19, No. 3 (May 1977), 12-15, with 6 ill. (4 in colour).

Short note on the Tutankhamon exhibition traveling through the USA. *L.Z.*

77034 Anonymous, The Lady Wallis Budge Fellowships in Egyptology, *JEA* 63 (1977), 131-136.

A list of holders of Lady Wallis Budge Fellowships in Egyptology at Christ's College, Cambridge and University College, Oxford. *L.Z.*

77035 Anonymous, Primer Congreso Internacional de Egiptologia — el Cairo — 1976, *Aegyptus Antiquus* 2 (1977), VII.

Short note to the First International Congress of Egyptology in Cairo, 1976.

77036   Anonymous, Pyramiden-Baubüro entdeckt, *Antike Welt*, Feldmeilen 8, Heft 3 (1977), 60.

Short note on the discovery of the model of a so far unknown pyramid at Dashûr.

77037   Anonymous, Third International Meroitic Conference, Toronto, 11-15 Octobre 1977, *MNL* No. 18 (Octobre 1977), 33-34.

Zusammenfassender Bericht über die dritte meroitische Konferenz in Toronto, über die Hauptreferate und die Themen der Beiträge.

Inge Hofmann

77038   Anonymous, Tutankhamon Treasures, *The Connoisseur*, London 194, No. 782 (April 1977), 290, with 1 ill.

Note on the Tutankhamon exhibition travelling through the USA from 1977-1979.

77039   ANTHES, Rudolf, Mytologie ve Starém Egyptě, *in: Mytologie staroveku*. Vybral a předmluvou opatřil Samuel Noah Kramer, Praha, Orbis, [1977], 13-78, with 3 fig. and 2 pl.

Czech version of our number 61027.

77040   ANTHES, R., Мифология в Древнем Египте, *in:* Мифологии Древнего Мира. Перевод с английского, Москва, Издательство "Наука". Главная редакция Восточной Литературы, 1977, 55-121.

"Mythology in Ancient Egypt".
Russian translation of our number 61027 (by O.D. Berlev).

77041   ANTHES, Rudolf, Zur Echtheit der Lehre des Amenemhet, *in: Fragen an die altägyptische Literatur*, 41-54.

In his first item, the author defends his earlier refuting of *ir sdm.n.i* as irrealis in the Teaching of Amenemhet (our number 57022) on account of the reading *ir šsp.i* by Lopez in P. Millingen 2,3 (our number 63334) instead of the proposed *ir šsp.n.i* known from Ramesside variants. The second item is concerned with the consequence of the above for the question of the commonly accepted posthumous and falsified character of the teaching, and the additions of *m3ᶜ ḥrw* in P. Mill. 1 and *ᶜ.w.s.* in P. Chester Beatty IV, 6, 14 after the name of the king which cannot be taken as evidence for his death. Because of the weakness of old age felt by Amenemhat at the time of the assault, Sesostris may have been made his coregent. The third item contains a translation and discussion of P. Mill. 1,1-3 and 1,11-2,6.   *L.Z.*

ANUS, Pierre, see our number 77315.

77042 ARKELL, Anthony J., Dating "Early Khartoum", *in: Ägypten und Kusch*, 53-55, with 1 map.

Südlich von Shabona am Weißen Nil fand Clark u.a. Fragmente von Knochenspitzen mit Widerhaken in einer Schicht, die gemäß Radiokarbon-Datierung in die Zeit $\pm$ 6000 v.Chr. gehört. Ein anderes Fragment einer Knochenspitze mit Widerhaken stammt von einer kleinen Nilinsel in der Nähe von Guli; Radiokarbonuntersuchungen der gleichen Schicht ergaben als Datum 3530 $\pm$ 90 v.Chr.; Guli ist daher zeitgleich mit dem Khartumer Neolithikum von Shaheinab. Die Keramik von Guli läßt sich vergleichen mit der Khartumer Variante des 2. Kataraktes und von Khashm el Girba am Atbara.

Inge Hofmann

77043 ARMAYOR, O. Kimball, Herodotus and Egyptology on Lake Moeris and the Labyrinth, *Newsletter ARCE* Nos. 99/100 (Winter/Spring 1977), 12-13.

Abstract of a paper.

77044 ARMELAGOS, George J., Disease in Ancient Nubia, *in: Culture, Disease and Healing*. Studies in Medical Anthropology. Edited by David Landy, New York, Macmillan Publishing Co., Inc./London, Collier Macmillan Publishers, [1977], 77-83, with 1 map and 4 fig.

Abridged edition of our number 69040.

ARMELAGOS, George J., see also our number 77255.

77045 ARNOLD, Dieter, Rituale und Pyramidentempel, *MDAIK* 33 (1977), 1-14, with 2 plans (1 on a folding pl.).

The author rejects the thesis of Ricke and Schott (cfr our number 1499) that the pyramid temple was the stage on which the burial ritual was enacted, a "play" derived from the P.T. On account of various arguments he suggests that no ritual at all was enacted here, except for the service in front of the false door and the statues of the king in the Western part, and a victory play in the front part, particularly in the *pr-wrw*. The function of the various rooms is discussed. That of the square anteroom was connected with the *Sed* festival that was celebrated by the deceased ruler in the netherworld. The storehouses may have mostly contained imitations of vessels and weapons for the dead; they were funerary palace storehouses. The function of the valley temple (very probably not a purification tent) is still obscure. In general, the pyramid temple constitutes, like the Djoser complex, a palace for the hereafter, containing installations for the role of the king as ruler after his death.

77046 ARNOLD, Dieter und Rainer STADELMANN, Dahshur. Zweiter Grabungsbericht, *MDAIK* 33 (1977), 15-20, with 1 fig., 2 plans (1 folding) and 4 pl.

Sequel to our number 75024.

During the second campaign the following points were studied: the tunnel-like construction in the road near the Valley temple, the Valley temple itself, a house from the XIIth Dynasty N. of the causeway near the pyramid, the entrance to the pyramid.

Among the finds we mention a limestone model of the subterranean rooms of a royal tomb and an inscribed limestone shawabti from the M.K. The human remains found during the first campaign consist of bones of two women, one 50-70 and the other 25-30 years old; the connection with the pyramid is still uncertain.

ARNOLD, Dieter, see also our number 77056.

77047 ARNOLD, Dorothea, Zur Keramik aus dem Taltempelbereich der Pyramide Amenemhets III. in Dahshur, *MDAIK* 33 (1977), 21-26, with 2 fig.

Study of pottery found during the excavation in the valley temple of Amenemhet III, with a systematic description of the types. Two traditions, that of the XIIth Dynasty and that of the S.I.P., are both represented, pointing at a date of c. 1760-1730 B.C. The pottery came from houses of the XIIIth Dynasty which may have stood in or near the W. court of the valley temple.

77048 ASPESI, Francesco, La distinzione dei generi nel nome antico-egiziano e semitico, Firenze, La Nuova Italia Editrice, [1977] (16.2 × 24 cm; XII + 76 p.) = Pubblicazioni della facoltà di lettere e filosofia dell' Università di Milano, 80 = Sezione a cura dell' Istituto di glottologia, 3; rev. *Aegyptus* 58 (1978), 295-300 (Paolo Marassini); *BiOr* 35 (1978), 41-42 (E. Lipiński); *Oriens Antiquus* 17 (1978), 304-308 (Antonio Loprieno); *ZDMG* 129 (1979), 159 (J[ürgen] v. B[eckerath]). Pr. L.5,500

In chapter 1 the author presents a survey of the problem: the origin and nature of the distinction in two genders in Semitic languages. The older explications, e.g.: that feminine indicates inferiority (Brockelmann) or intensity (Wensinck) appear to be incorrect, while Meillet's theories about the genders in Indo-European languages are not applicable to the Semitic. The best approach appears to be that of Féghali and Cuny ("Du genre grammatical en sémitique", Paris, 1924), who state that the feminine ending was originally an element of opposition.

In the second chapter the author points out the significance of ancient Egyptian for the study of the problem. It is important because of the age and quantity of the evidence and because of its central position among the Hamito-Semitic languages.

Chapter 3 presents the Egyptian material, mainly from the O. and M.K. The author mainly discusses three groups of feminines: "natural" feminines indicating female beings, abstracts, particularly those derived from qualitative verbs, and collectives. Other categories such as the fem. infinitives and pairs of words one of which ends in a -t without any apparent semantic difference (e.g., ḥw-ḥwt), are briefly discussed.

In the last chapter the author draws his conclusions and compares the results with the situation in Semitic languages. He suggests that in Egyptian as in other Hamito-Semitic languages there has been an early stage in which derivation of nouns from verb-stems and systematization in the connotation of the gender was less general than in later times. In Semitic this stage is still clearly visible, for instance in the word *ummu,* "mother" (Eg. *mwt,* with later "feminization"). The combination in a class of "feminines" of words derived from "masculine" corresponding words, collectives and part of the abstracts is due to the formal aspect, the ending in -t. Opposition between names in -(w)t and others without the ending is thus a secondary phenomenon.

77049 ASSMANN, Jan, Das ägyptische Zweibrüdermärchen (Papyrus d' Orbiney). Eine Textanalyse auf drei Ebenen am Leitfaden der Einheitsfrage, *ZÄS* 104 (1977), 1-25, with 3 tables.

Mit den im Untertitel erwähnten Ebenen sind die sprachliche Formulierung und graphische Einrichtung, der Handlungsaufbau der Geschichte und die thematische Kohärenz gemeint.

Verfasser betrachtet die thematischen Komponenten der Erzählung auf dem Hintergrund des Initiationsmodells, wie von Propp and Eliade ausgearbeitet. Damit erreicht er eine Einteilung in drei Stadien, die der äusseren Gliederung in drei Bücher zu je acht Kapiteln genau entspricht.

Ergänzende Bemerkungen in unserer Nummer 77052.

M. Heerma van Voss

77050 ASSMANN, Jan, Fest des Augenblicks — Verheissung der Dauer. Die Kontroverse der ägyptischen Harfnerlieder, in: Fragen an die altägyptische Literatur, 55-84.

After translating the Antef harper's song, the author poses the central problem of the contrast between the harper's songs and the normal Egyptian attitude, and of their almost exclusive presence in just the tombs, where the scene of the harper is the typical recording form, which fact must also be taken into account apart from the "Sitz im Leben" and the genres.

Then the author turns to the songs themselves, which are to be divided according to form and contents: the Antef song type propagating the feast of the moment and the other promising duration and glorification for the deceased ($s3\underline{h}w$), which difference is even explicitly stated in Theban Tomb No. 50. Since both types existed side by side and the Antef song criticizes the promises for the hereafter expressed in the other type, there is no question of transition. After refuting Lorton's interpretation of the Antef song (see our number 68386 on $šms-\hat{i}b$, and 75463 on $\hat{i}r\hat{i}\ hrw\ nfr$) the author argues that the real world of the $\hat{i}b$, of active life, in contrast to afterlife notions as $wr\underline{d}-\hat{i}b$ and $\underline{h}d-\hat{i}b$, expressing the absence of activity, is stressed in the Antef song type. That this philosophy of the feast, introduced in the tomb in the Amarna Period, has maintained itself in the Ramesside period, stressing the promise of duration in the afterlife, may be explained from hope being less an illusion, if there is place for doubt.   L.Z.

77051 ASSMANN, Jan, Das Grab der Mutirdis. Mit Beiträgen von Aleida Assmann. Photos von Dieter Johannes u.a. Zeichnungen und Malereien von Aleida Assmann u.a., Mainz am Rhein, Verlag Philipp von Zabern, [1977] (27 × 36 cm; 102 p., 42 fig., 3 colour pl., 46 pl. including 1 folding plan) = Grabung im Asasif 1963-1970, 6 = Archäologische Veröffentlichungen. Deutsches Archäologisches Institut Abteilung Kairo, 13.   Pr. DM 150

Mutirdis, Obergefolgsdame der Gottesanbeterin unter Nitokris und Psammetichos I., ließ ihr Grab im Vorhof-Bereich des Intef-Grabes errichten, bei dessen Säuberung es 1963 entdeckt wurde. Architektonisch bescheidener als das gleichzeitig angelegte Grab des Basa, dafür im Bild- und Textprogramm reichhaltiger, weniger konventionell, verdient besonders die Sargkammer wegen ihres guten Erhaltungszustandes Beachtung. Bei den relativ aufwendigen Oberbauten aus luftgetrockneten Schlammziegeln, die die Pfeilerhalle des Intef-Grabes einbeziehen, ist das Fehlen von Kulträumen bemerkenswert. Vier unterirdische Kammern vervollständigen die

Anlage. Von den beiden Pylonen mit Texten an die Lebenden gelangt man durch einen Treppengang mit der Darstellung der Unterweltstore (TB. Kap. 145/146) in den Lichthof mit Szenen der Reinigung und Einführung bei den Göttern. In den Kammern I bis IV sind solare und osirianische Texte, meist aus den Unterweltsbüchern des Neuen Reiches (Amduat, Pfortenbuch, TB. Kap. 125) angebracht, die durch astronomische Decken in zwei Räumen ergänzt werden. Die übrigen Decken tragen florale Ornamente. Die "Verklärungen" an den Wänden der Sargkammer beziehen sich auf das Ritual der Balsamierung und den Schutz der Götter bei den Stundenwachen.
E.M. Wolf-Brinkmann

77052 ASSMANN, Jan, Textanalyse auf verschiedenen Ebenen: zum Problem der Einheit des Papyrus d' Orbiney, *in: XIX. Deutscher Orientalistentag,* 1-15.
This paper has appeared in a more elaborate form in our number 77049.
L.Z.

77053 ASSMANN, Jan, Die Verborgenheit des Mythos in Ägypten, *GM* Heft 25 (1977), 7-43.
Es wird der Frage nach der Entstehungszeit der ägyptischen Mythen nachgegangen, und dabei die Möglichkeit näher ins Auge gefaßt und untersucht, daß die Mythen selbst sich nach langen, latenten Vorstufen erst in der Zeit der ersten mythologischen Texte, im M.R. und vor allem im N.R. und in der Spätzeit herauskristallisiert hätten. Dabei wird der Weg einer begrifflichen Klärung beschritten, indem der Begriff Mythos mit verschiedenen von ihm zu unterscheidenden Begriffen konfrontiert wird: Mythos versus Götterwelt; Mythos versus Ritus (Verklärung versus Erzählen: Mythologisierung als sakramentale Ausdeutung; Wiederholung versus Vergegenwärtigung); Mythos versus mythische Aussage (Handeln und Wissen; Mythos als "Geno-Text"). Es ergibt sich, daß zwischen Mythos und mythischer Aussage unterschieden werden muß. Der Mythos entspringt dem Streben, den Abgrund zwischen der schlechteren Gegenwart und den Anfängen der Geschichte zu überbrücken. Er beginnt in Ägypten im M.R. und läßt sich aus der Situation dieser Zeit erklären. Der Götterwelt der Pyramidentexte wird der Charakter des Mythischen im engeren Sinne noch abgesprochen.
Inge Hofmann

77054 A[SSMANN], J[an], E[rika] F[EUCHT], and R[einhard] G[RIESHAMMER], Vorwort, in: Fragen an die altägyptische Literatur, I-III.

The preface contains a tribute to Eberhard Otto. Compare also our number 74845.

77055 ASTOUR, Michael C., The Cambridge Ancient History: History of the Middle East and the Aegean region c. 1380-1000 B.C., *BASOR* No. 227 (October 1977), 66-69.

Review article of our number 75126.

77056 [Ausgrabungen in] Ägypten, *AfO* 25 (1974/77), 310-336, with 12 ill., 3 plans, and 1 folding pl. = plan.

In this article on recent excavations in Egypt, to which several authors contributed we mention: those at Kom Abu Billu-Terenuthis, Merimde, Mendes, Tell ed-Dabʿa, Saqqâra and its pyramids, West Thebes (tombs of Anch-Hor and of others from the Saite period), Elephantine and Wadi Gawâsîs, as well as the introduction and the sections on Early Dynastic finds in the Eastern Delta, on finding places of the Syro-Palestinian M.B. culture in the Delta, on the Cairo Museum, and on a Prehistoric Survey in the Western Desert, by Manfred Bietak. Dieter Arnold devotes a section to Dahshûr, Jean Lauffray one to Karnak, Rainer Stadelmann one to the Sethos temple at Qurna (West Thebes), and lastly Horst Jaritz a retrospect to Philae.

L.Z.

77057 AVDIEV, V.I., Египетская традиция в труде Геродота, ВДИ 1 (139), 1977, 184-189, with an English summary on p. 189.

"Egyptian Traditions in Herodotus".

77058 BADAWY, Alexander, L' art au tombeau de 'Ankhm'ahor, au beau nom de Sesi, *Gazette des Beaux-Arts,* Paris 89 (1977), 113-120, with 1 plan and 16 ill.

The author describes the tomb of the architect and physician ᶜAnkhmaᶜhor at Saqqâra, which shows several interesting details in various scenes such as those on medical treatment and physical anomalies and two representations of hyenas being modified into a calf and an antelope. The composition of the wall scenes, compository technique and the cooperation of various artists are discussed. Compare our number 75032.

L.Z.

77059   BADAWY, Alexander, The Periodic System of Building a Pyramid, *JEA* 63 (1977), 52-58, with 3 fig.
The writer discusses the question of the ramps used in building a pyramid, cosmic orientation and the avoidance of twist in setting out, as well as maintaining the correct angle of incline. The use of layers slanting at an angle of 75% may have helped in this. A sighting device to control this batter of 1:4 is suggested, i.e. the use of vertical corner walls as found by Petrie in a mastaba at Maidûm. Such walls at Maidûm would have varied from 14.5 m to 8 m.   *E. Uphill*

77060   BAKR, Mohamed I., Der Ohrschmuck in den antiken Kulturen des Niltals, *in: Ägypten und Kusch,* 57-62, with 6 ill. on 4 pl.
Der Ohrschmuck taucht in Ägypten erst mit dem Neuen Reich auf, ist dann aber in den oberen Schichten sehr beliebt, wird aber niemals Bestandteil der ägyptischen Königstracht. Im Gegensatz dazu ist der Ohrschmuck ein fester Bestandteil der Trachten der C- und Kerma-Kultur. Die ägyptischen Darstellungen des N.R. zeigen daher die Bewohner von Kusch oft mit diesem Schmuck. Der Schmuck wird von der Napata-Kultur übernommen und wurde zum Bestandteil der Könige der 25. Dynastie auch dann, wenn sie einen rein ägyptischen Ornat trugen. Noch in meroitischer Zeit ist der Ohrschmuck für die Königsfamilie typisch. Somit wird man für Ägypten eine Herkunft der Ohrrings aus dem Süden annehmen dürfen.   *Inge Hofmann*

77061   BALL, E.,, The Coregency of David and Solomon (1 Kings 1), *Vetus Testamentum,* Leiden 27 (1977), 268-279.
Proceeding the discussion about the elements the Davide monarchy derived from Egypt (see, e.g., our numbers 71405, 74298 and 75809) the author deals with the coregency between David and Solomon mentioned in I Kings 1. He lists and briefly discusses the possible, probable and certain instances of coregency in Egypt suggesting that the Israelite instance was based on the Egyptian model. The author has not yet been able to consult Murnane's study, our number 77549.

77062   BAQUÉS ESTAPÉ, Lorenzo, Sobre un fragmento de vaso ceramico con inscripcion hieratica, *Boletin de la Asociacion Española de Orientalistas,* Madrid 13 (1977), 254-264, with 1 ill.
Note on a pottery fragment in the Museo del Oriente Bíblico de Montserrat, bearing in hieratic the word *srmt,* the identification of which liquid is discussed.   *L.Z.*

77063 BAQUÉS ESTAPÉ, Lorenzo and Jorge R. OGDON, Un ataud en el Museo del Oriente Bíblico de Monserrat — España, *Aegyptus Antiquus* 2 (1977), 1-31, with 15 ill. and 1 diagram.

After preliminary notes on the Egyptian collection in the Museo del Oriente Bíblico at Montserrat, Spain, the authors study a F.I.P. or M.K. rectangular sarcophagus in the museum, which is first generally described. Then follows a study of the texts on its four sides, which are presented in hieroglyphs with translation and comments, while in an excursus remarks are devoted to the phrase *i ntr šd(i)t s3ḥw 3w*. The article is concluded by an epigraphical study of the texts. *L.Z.*

77064 BARGUET, Paul, Le cycle lunaire d' après deux textes d'Edfou, *RdE* 29 (1977), 14-20.

L'auteur traduit et commente deux textes symétriques d'Edfou (3,207,8 sq. et 211,2 sq. = pl. 69), qui décrivent le mouvement de la lune. Il les considère comme extrait du livre de "Connaître les mouvements des deux luminaires" dont le titre est conservé par le catalogue du temple (3,351,9). *Ph. Derchain*

BARNS, John W.B., see our number 77646.

77065 BARRACO, Robin A., Theodore A. REYMAN and T. Aiden COCKBURN, Paleobiochemical Analysis of an Egyptian Mummy, *Journal of Human Evolution*, London — New York — San Francisco 6 (1977), 533-546, with 3 pl.

After some remarks on methods and materials used by the ancient Egyptians in mummification, the authors analyse and discuss the results of the analysis of protein and lipid material in the tissues of a mummy from the Ptolemaic Period in the Philadelphia Art Museum.
L.Z.

77066 BARRELET, Marie-Thérèse, Un inventaire de Kar-Tukulti-Ninurta: Textiles décorés assyriens et autres, *Revue d' Assyriologie et d' Archéologie Orientale*, Paris 71 (1977), 51-92, with 27 ill. and 2 fig.

On account of a cloth inventory from the Middle Assyrian palace at Kar-Tukulti-Ninurta the author discusses in the second section of the article the various techniques shown in polychrome decorated tissues in Egypt. She devotes ample attention to the woven gobelin-like tapestry produced on the vertical weaving loom and embroidery from the tombs of Tuthmosis IV and Tutankhamon, the tucking and button (*point noué*) techniques, and that producing geometric patterns on galoons and ribbons. The specialism probably originates from the Syrian region.
L.Z.

77067   BAR-YOSEF, Ofer, Anna BELFER, Avner GOREN and Patricia SMITH, The Nawamis near ᶜEin Ḥuderah (Eastern Sinai), *Israel Exploration Journal*, Jerusalem 27 (1977), 65-88, with 1 map, 4 fig., 5 tables and 4 plates.
Of the circular structures in Southern Sinai, known to the Bedawîn as *nawamis* and most probably being tombs, 24 of the 42 of the ᶜEin Ḥuderah group are investigated as to construction, contents and human skeletal remains. Also a short inventory of the 42 *nawamis* is given.
They may have belonged to the original local population of Southern Sinai and their society had more ties with the Egyptian world than with Palestine.
L.Z.

77068   BASCH, Lucien, Trières grecques, phéniciennes et égyptiennes, *The Journal of Hellenic Studies*, London 97 (1977), 1-10, with 2 pl.
The author reexamines Lloyd's arguments on the trireme expressed in our numbers 72447 and particularly 75459, and stresses the Phoenician naval skill.
L.Z.

77069   BASILE, Corrado, Metodo usato dagli antichi Egizi per la fabbricazione et la preservazione della carta-papiro, *Aegyptus* 57 (1977), 190-199, with 7 ill. on 4 pl.
Dans la fabrication ancienne du papyrus, la nature de l'adhésif et la diversité de colorisation demeuraient pour nous problématiques. Černý notait que la pression des deux couches végétables croisées avait parfois suffi à l'adhérence. La plante, étudiée in vivo près de Syracuse, est riche en mucilage. Au moment de son plein développement, la tige fournit elle-même un matériau très lié. Au delà, elle se dessèche et l'altération des enzymes l'assombrit. L'auteur a obtenu par pression une adhérence excellente, après trempage dans une solution pareille à celle que mentionne Pline, Hist. Nat. 35, 52, pour le tannage des peaux. Des analyses chimiques faites en Italie et en Allemagne sur des papyrus du Nouvel Empire et de l'époque romaine étayent l'idée d'un trempage dans l'"eau et limon" de Basse Égypte (sulfate d'alun et nitrate de soude). Elles décèlent une présence d'alun de 4% contre 1% dans le végétal frais. Après choix de la tige puis sélection de la partie immergée, il devait y avoir trempage, pression et séchage, pression nouvelle pour pousser les nervures au verso, enfin usage de colle pour réunir les feuillets du rouleau.
J. Custers

77070   BASTA, Lotfy L., Sorcery and Scientific Medicine in Ancient Egypt, *Journal. Oklahoma State Medical Association*, Oklahoma City 69,

No. 5 (May 1976), 173-180, with 2 fig. and 3 ill.
General article for the interested reader, dealing with subjects such as gods connected with medicine, diseases, surgery, sorcerers, gynaecology and obstetrics, and scientific method. *L.Z.*

77071 BAUMEISTER, Th., Die Mentalität des frühen ägyptischen Mönchtums, *Zeitschrift für Kirchengeschichte*, Stuttgart 2/3 (1977), 145-160.
Discussing the mentality of the early Egyptian monasticism, the author briefly touches upon the influences exerted by the ancient Egyptian mentality as expressed in the wisdom literature. *L.Z.*

77072 BAYER, Gerhard and Hans-Georg WIEDEMANN, Ägyptisch Blau, ein synthetisches Farbpigment des Altertums, wissenschaftlich betrachtet, *Sandoz Bulletin*, Basel Nr. 40 (1976), 19-39, with 30 fig. and ill. (mostly in colour) and 6 tables.
After an introduction on the distribution of so-called "Egyptian blue" on ancient Egyptian objects, the authors present a technical analysis.
L.Z.

77073 BEINLICH, Horst, Noch einmal zu Horus-Mati im 10. o.äg.Gau, *GM* Heft 24 (1977), 15-21.
Es wird daraus verwiesen, daß Mati als provisorischer Name (Arbeitsausdruck) aufzufassen sei. Die Belege für einen Kult des Horus-Schu im 10.o.äg.Gau sind nicht stichhaltig, dagegen ist der Kult des Horus-Mati ausreichend bezeugt. Auch der Kult des Ruti wird negiert zugunsten des Horus-Mati. Bezüglich des Miysis wird gesagt, daß nicht jeder *m3j-ḥz3* mit Miysis identisch und damit an Leontopolis gebunden ist. Damit wird ein Filialkult des Miysis von Leontopolis im 10.o.äg.Gau abgelehnt. Im Namen des "Horus-Mati" ist jedoch nur die Lesung der Konsonantengruppe *m3* sicher. Eine Lesung bzw. Übersetzung des Namens ist zur Zeit nicht möglich. Vgl. auch unsere Nummern 77192 und 77299. *Inge Hofmann*

77074 BELÇAGUI, Horacio, El grupo-X: grupo etnico o fase cultural?, *Aegyptus Antiquus* 2 (1977), 32-66, with 1 plan, 3 fig. and 2 maps.
After introductory remarks on the X-group and the history of Nubia between the 3rd and 6th centuries A.D. the author surveys the arguments of Emery and Kirwan for the attribution of the nationality of the X-group to a particular people. In a last section he discusses the actual state of the problem, particularly the aspects of the origin of the

X-group culture, of the Ballâna-Qustul kingdom and the racial determination of the X-group. *L.Z.*

BELFER, Anna, see our number 77067.

77075 BELL, Lanny David, Interpreters and Egyptianized Nubians in Ancient Egyptian Foreign Policy: Aspects of the History of Egypt and Nubia, *Dissertation Abstracts International,* Ann Arbor, Mich. 37, No. 11 (May 1977), 7111/2-A.

Abstract of a thesis University of Pennsylvania, 1976 (Order No. 77-10,136; 287 p.).

A philological investigation of the Egyptian word *ї͑3w* (Late Egyptian *3ᶜᶜ),* literally meaning "babbler", but extended to "interpreter". *L.Z.*

77076 BELL, Martha R. and Angela MILWARD, Mycenaean Pottery and Amarna, *Newsletter ARCE* Nos. 99/100 (Winter/Spring 1977), 10.

Abstract of a paper.

77077 BELOVA, G.A., Пятая мероитская конференция (июнь 1976 г.), ВДИ No. 4 (142), 1977, 224-228.

"The Vth Conference on Meroitics (June 1976)".

BEN-ARIEH, Sara, see our number 77266.

77078 BEN-TOR, Amnon, Cult-scenes on Early Bronze Age Cylinder Seal Impressions from Palestine, *Levant,* London 9 (1977), 90-100, with 28 fig.

The author attempts to show that an Early Bronze Age cylinder seal from Gezer bears Egyptian signs and motifs and depicts a cultic scene, possibly referring to the cult of Neith or Anubis. *L.Z.*

BERGER, Catherine, see our number 77452.

77079 BERGER, Jacques-Édouard, L' oeil & l'éternité. Portraits romains d' Égypte. Recherches iconographiques René Creux, [Paudex], Fontainemore-Flammarion, [1977] (23.5 × 33 cm; 224 p., 2 maps, 3 fig., 224 ill., 24 colour ill., colour ill. on cover).

This volume on mummy portraits is of importance because of its numerous and very fine photographs, many of them in colour. The text deals with the history of the Faiyûm, from Narmer to Hypatia, the daughter of the philosopher Theon of Alexandria. In chapter 2 a survey is given of early travellers and historians, down to the early 19th century A.D., while in chapter 3 the discovery of the Graeco-Roman cemeteries is discussed and in chapter 4 the tombs from the

first centuries A.D. with their contents.
Chapter 5 is devoted to the function of the portraits, leading to the conclusion that they were made for the houses and eventually adapted to be used for the dead. Chapter 6 deals with the psychology of the portraits and their interpreters; chapter 7 with remarks about portraits by classical authors; chapter 8 with painting techniques of the mummy portraits. There follows a catalogue of the mummy portraits in the various museums, with 117 small-scale photographs. An index on p. 221-222.

77080 BERLANDINI, Jocelyne, Varia Memphitica II (II-III), *BIFAO* 77 (1977), 29-44, with 11 pl.

Sequel to our number 76072.
The first part of the article deals with the tomb of the overseer of the harim Pay, presenting some additions to our number 75512. They are: part of a wall relief (Musée Rodin NI 235 and 104 = Louvre E. 15562) and a pyramidion (Louvre N 362 = D 21). The pieces are described, their texts given in hieroglyphs and translation, their style, date and the place of the tomb being discussed. The tomb will have been sited at Saqqâra S. of the Unas-causeway and may date from the very end of the XVIIIth Dynasty.
The second part is devoted to the tomb of the general of the army Kasa, which is to be sought in the same area and may date from the first reigns of the XIXth Dynasty. Four stelae from it are preserved in the Musée Borely, Marseille (see our number 72525, nos. 280-283, with colour photographs). The author here discusses another stela (Kestner Museum 1935, 200-196) and five shawabtis, as well as the prosopography of their owner, and style, date and place of the tomb.

77081 BERLEV, O.D., Статуэтка царицы эпохи позднего среднего царства из Кавы, *in:* Мероэ, 60-63, with a French summary on p. 292-293.

"Die Statuette einer Königin aus der Zeit des späten Mittelreichs von Kawa."
Die Inschrift auf der Statuette 0715 aus Kawa kann nicht zu (ḥmt njswt) wrt ergänzt werden, sondern sie beinhaltet den Namen der Königin *Nbw-m-ḥ3t,* der Frau des Königs *Sḫm-rᶜw w3ḏ-ḫᶜj(w) Sbk-m-z3f.* Die Statuette ist das älteste datierte Monument, das im Kawa gefunden wurde. *Inge Hofmann*

BERLEV, Oleg D., see also our numbers 77355 and 77356.

77082 BERNAND, André, Pan du désert, Leiden, E.J. Brill, 1977 (21.7 × 27.5 cm; XXIV + 308 p., 71 pl.); rev. *Acta Archaeologica Academiae*

Scientiarum Hungaricae 30 (1978), 473-474 (L. Castiglione); *Aegyptus* 58 (1978), 304-310 (Giovanni Geraci); *CdE* LII, No. 104 (1977), 375-377 (P.J. Sijpesteijn). Pr. fl.290

With this volume the author concludes his publication of the Greek and Latin inscriptions from the Eastern Desert related to Pan (for the preceding volumes, see our numbers 72072 and 72073).
After an introduction sketching the importance of the Eastern Desert in the Graeco-Roman Period the volume deals with 87 texts, divided into six groups: the Wâdi Bîr el-Ain and its area; from Qena to Myos Hormos (Mons Porphyrites and Mons Claudianus); from Qena to Philoteras (Safâga); from Coptos to Berenice; the inscriptions from the Nile Valley referring to Pan or the Eastern Desert, and those of unknown provenance. In some chapters, apart from text, translation and comments on the inscriptions, the author presents extracts from travel-stories of scholars visiting the area under discussion.
In his conclusion (p. 269-278) Bernand presents a survey of his ideas about Pan, his sanctuaries and his worshippers, on account of the material discussed in the three volumes. There follow tables of concordances and extensive indexes.
The plates bear maps and plans, and photographs and/or drawings of almost all inscriptions of the volume.

77083   BERNHARDT, Karl-Heinz, Der alte Libanon, Wien und München, Verlag Anton Schroll & Co, [1977] (18.7 × 22.2 cm; 240 p., 5 colour ill. [1 on cover], 90 ill., 33 fig., 10 maps [1 folding], 4 plans).
Pr. DM 42

By its very nature this book on the ancient Lebanon often refers to ancient Egypt in all its chapters, although the presence of only a small index of personal and geographical names does not permit to locate them easily. Particularly the chapter on the cedar forests (p. 22-51) deals with subjects as the tree species used as timber, the importance of wood and its products from the Lebanon for Egypt, how and where the timber was acquired, the ups and downs of the commerce for the Egyptians. In the chapter on the connections of Egypt with the Lebanon (p. 64-89) the author mainly discusses the Egyptian vicissitudes in the various historical periods, paying ample attention to the special position of Byblos. The last chapter in which Egypt is frequently mentioned is that on the struggle between Egypt and Assyria in the Late Period (p. 130-155). *L.Z.*

77084   BERZINA, S. Ya., "Эфиопика" Гелиодора как источник по истории Мероэ, *in:* Мероэ, 146-190, with a French summary on p. 295.

"Die 'Aithiopika' des Heliodor, Quelle zur Geschichte von Meroe."
Die Aithiopika des Heliodor ist nicht nur ein Liebesroman mit mystischen und sozialutopischen Elementen, sondern enthält Angaben über das meroitische Reich des 3. nachchristlichen Jahrhunderts: über die geographische Lage, die Natur, die Zusammensetzung der Bevölkerung, Wirtschaft, Ortschaften, Verwaltungswesen, Kulte und Glaubensformen, Bewaffnung und Militärwesen, politische Situation. Heliodor hat seine Informationen bei seinem Aufenthalt im Niltal, wenigstens in der Region des 1. Kataraktes, bezogen.   *Inge Hofmann*

77085   BERZINA, S. Ya., Мероэ и Китай в I-VIII вв.н.э., *in:* Мероэ, 214-240, with 1 fig. and 6 ill. on 3 pl. and a French summary on p. 297.

"Meroe und China, 1. bis 8. Jahrhundert der christlichen Ära."
Die chinesischen Bronzegefäße in den meroitischen und nobatischen Nekropolen sowie die Darstellungen afrikanischer Tiere auf Monumenten der Han- und T'ang-Dynastie werfen die Frage der Beziehungen zwischen dem meroitischen Reich und China auf. Als Luxusgüter und überseeische Kuriositäten gelangten chinesische Waren ins Niltal und in die europäischen Provinzen Roms, während die afrikanische Tierwelt im chinesischen Kaiserkult eine Rolle spielte. Beziehungen zwischen Meroe und China gibt es wenigstens seit dem 2. Jahrhundert n.Chr., wie wir griechischen und chinesischen Berichten entnehmen können.   *Inge Hofmann*

77086   [BERZINA] BERSINA, S. J., and E. E. MINKOWSKAJA, Die Namen der Könige von Kusch, *Studia aegyptiaca* 3 (1977), 1-16.

The authors study the components occurring in the names of the Kushite royal family from a semantic point of view. They discuss first the element *amani* (from *'Imn*), which in some instances may mean "hidden" (e.g. in Amanirenas = "Her name is hidden" and Natakamani = "Thou art hidden"), but also, as later in the Congo and Bantu languages, "Lord" (e.g. Amaniastabork = "Lord of the Astabor river").
Other elements discussed are *qo* or *qore*, "ruler"; Horus or Ara; toponyms (e.g. Napatadakhete); *yeshbohe;* "incarnation"; *irki*, "prince"; *tertekes*, "priest".

77087   BIANCHI, R.S., The Striding Draped Male Figure of Ptolemaic Egypt (Volumes 1-III), *Dissertation Abstracts International,* Ann Arbor, Mich., 37, No. 9 (March 1977), 5408-A.

Abstract of a thesis New York University, 1976 (Order No. 77-5364; 701 p.).

The author studies the Graeco-Roman striding male figure draped in a costume which reveals the form of the body underneath. Chapter 1 identifies the various garments of the costume, chapter 2 deals with their history. Chapter 3 studies the Egyptian conception and execution of this statuary, to the attributes of which, mostly floral, chapter 4 is devoted. In chapter 5 the Egyptian character of these sculptures is further explored.

Volumes II and III contain the catalogue of 125 examples, each with ample description, discussion and data. *L.Z.*

BIEDENKOPF-ZIEHNER, Anne, see our number 77633.

BIETAK, Manfred, see our numbers 77056 and 77381.

77088   BIGA, Maria Giovanna, Matrimoni dinastici nel Vicino Oriente Antico, *Rivista* 51 (1977), 1-5.

The author adds remarks to W. Röllig's lemma on marriage in the Reallexikon der Assyriologie, one of which, nr. 22, is concerned with Tuthmosis III. Compare also our number 74619. *L.Z.*

BIGGS, Robert D., see our numbers 77386 and 77810.

77089   BILLIGMEIER, J.-Chr., Origin of the Greek Word *Phoinix, Talanta,* Leiden 8/9 (1977), 1-4.

The author derives the Greek work phoenix, basically meaning i.a. "guitarlike instrument", "date palm (Phoenix dactylifera)" and "phoenix-bird" from the Egyptian words *bīnt,* Coptic ⲂⲞⲒⲚⲈ "harp"; *bīnt,* originally *bīnr,* Coptic ⲂⲚ̄, "date palm"; and *byn* (Coptic ⲂⲎⲚⲈ, "swallow"?), "a bird". He argues that the terms were borrowed at an early date by the Greeks from the Egyptians and melted into one Greek word. *L.Z.*

77090   BILLY, G., Population Changes in Egypt and Nubia, *Journal of Human Evolution,* London — New York — San Francisco 6 (1977), 697-704, with 1 map, 2 tables and 3 fig.

The two marginal elements in a basic population type stretching from the Faiyûm (broad skull) to the South (Nubians with negroid traits) are differentiated by a series of infiltrations in opposing directions during the long history of population changes in Nubia and Egypt.
L.Z.

77091   BINGEN, Jean, Rapport des directeurs pour l'année 1976, *CdE* LII, No. 103 (1977), 5-9.

77092   BINGEN, Jean, avec la collaboration de Marianne LAWUILLON-BLUME et Jan QUAEGEBEUR, Au temps où on lisait le grec en Égypte. Catalogue de l'exposition de papyrus et d'ostraca, Bruxelles, Fondation Égyptologique Reine Élisabeth, 1977 (15.5 × 23.7 cm; 39 p.); at head of title: Musées Royaux d'Art et d'Histoire.

The booklet contains the catalogue of an exhibition of documents of interest for papyrologists from the Musée du Cinquantenaire, organized by its Egyptian Department on the occasion of the 15th International Congress of Papyrologists in Brussels, 1977.
The sections nos. 13-15, concerned with the Demotic papyri (juridical-administrative documents), no. 16, concerned with Demotic ostraca and wooden mummy labels, and no. 17 containing the Coptic documents were described by Jan Quaegebeur.   L.Z.

77093   BLAND, Louise & Jaromír MÁLEK, Nemtywer, the Beholder of the Beauty of his Lord (Ashmolean Museum 1885.504), *Orientalia Lovaniensia Periodica,* Leuven 8 (1977), 119-123, with 1 fig. and 1 pl.

The authors draw the attention to the considerable number of persons whose names are formed with the name of the god *Nmty* that are known from the Memphite area during the late O.K. They present a list of 10 such names, adding an eleventh by their publication of the false-door Ashmolean Museum 1885.504. The owner was the *ỉmy-r sr(w)*, Beholder of the Beauty of his Lord *Nmty-wr* (abbreviated *Wrỉ*). The piece is dated to the VIth Dynasty.

77094   BLANKENBERG-van DELDEN, C., Once Again Some More Commemorative Scarabs of Amenophis III, *JEA* 63 (1977), 83-87, with 2 pl.

Lists 9 scarabs of the 'marriage' & 'lion-hunt' type located in Great Britain, Israel and U.S.A.   *E. Uphill*

77095   BLUMENTHAL, Elke, Darstellung und Selbstdarstellung des ägyptischen Königtums. Untersuchungen zur schriftlichen Überlieferung des Mittleren Reiches. Dissertation zur Promotion B, Leipzig, 1977 (quarto; VI + 247 p. in typescript).

Die Promotionsschrift enthält vier Aufsätze. Der erste, umfangreichste, "Die Selbstdarstellung des Königtums in der Literatur des Mittleren Reiches" (S.1-157) ist Teil einer Monographie über das Bild des Königs in den Textgattungen des M.R., die sich in Arbeit befindet und unmittelbar an die phraseologischen Untersuchungen der Verfasserin (cfr unsere Nummer 70068) anschließt. Die drei kleineren

Aufsätze sind bereits publiziert in unseren Nummern 74079, 76085 und 77097.
Methodische Gemeinsamkeit der Beiträge ist die Erkenntnis, daß die ägyptische Königsideologie nur auf Grund der Textgattungen ermittelt und verstanden werden kann, in denen sie überliefert ist. In dem Hauptteil der Arbeit werden drei Literaturwerke über das Königtum mit den Mitteln der Form- oder Gattungskritik analysiert: die Lehre für Merikare, die Prophezeiung des Neferti und die Lehre Amenemhets. Dabei zeigt sich, daß den Texten Gattungen zugrundeliegen, die in der Beamtenschaft beheimatet sind (Weisheitslehre, Autobiographie, Unterhaltungserzählung, Prophezeiung), und daß mit den Formvorbildern auch die Ideale der Gattungen auf den König übertragen, allerdings dabei auch modifiziert worden sind. Daraus ergibt sich, daß die hohe Beamtenschaft der Adressat der drei Texte gewesen ist. Da sie jeweils einen jungen Herrscher begünstigen, könnten ihre Autoren im Auftrag dieser Herrscher gearbeitet haben. So darf man sie als Selbstdarstellung des Königtums verstehen und in ihnen eine Huldigung an die einflußreiche Gesellschaftsschicht der gehobenen Beamtenschaft erkennen, aus der die Könige des M.R. ursprünglich selbst hervorgegangen sind.
In den anderen Aufsätzen wird die Kenntnis der Gattungszugehörigkeit der Quellen für die Beantwortung einer terminologischen Frage, die Rekonstruktion eines fragmentarischen Textes und die Datierung einer Textgruppe nutzbar gemacht.

E. Blumenthal

77096 BLUMENTHAL, Elke, Hundert Jahre Ägyptisches Museum in Leipzig. Neueröffnung und Symposium, Leipzig 1976, *Ethnographisch-archäologische Zeitschrift,* Berlin 18 (1977), 160-163.
Short note on the occasion of the reopening of the Egyptian Museum in Leipzig in 1976. There is also some information on a symposion on actual questions of Egyptian archaeology, held in Leipzig at the same time. *L.Z.*

77097 BLUMENTHAL, Elke, Die Koptosstele des Königs Rahotep (London U.C. 14327), in: *Ägypten und Kusch,* 63-80, with 3 pl.
Die Stele des Königs $S\underline{h}m-R^c-w3\underline{h}-\underline{h}^cw$ Rahotep wurde 1893/94 von Petrie in den Fundamenten des ptolemäischen Tempels von Koptos gefunden und in das University College London gebracht. Sie ist ein Kronzeuge für die Existenz dieses Königs der 2. Zwischenzeit. Die Stele wird unter einem bisher nicht beachteten Gesichtspunkt

untersucht, der zum besseren Verständnis der lückenhaften Inschrift beiträgt. Trotz einiger Unklarheiten und vieler Textlücken geht aus der Gliederung und den phraseologischen Einzelheiten hervor, daß die Inschrift nach dem Schema der Königsnovelle gestaltet war. Parallelen anderer Königsnovellen erlauben nun nicht nur, den Ausgang der Inschrift in großen Zügen zu rekonstruieren, sondern ermöglichen auch die Ergänzung einzelner Textlücken. *Inge Hofmann*

77098 BLUMENTHAL, Elke, Die Textgattung Expeditionsbericht in Ägypten, *in: Fragen an die altägyptische Literatur*, 85-118.

The article, studying the expedition report (mainly from areas as the Wâdi Hammâmât, the Sinai, Wâdi el-Hûdi and Hatnub) as a genre in order to extract its characteristics and to distinguish it from expedition inscriptions in a wider sense, is divided into two parts.

The first part discusses the following groups of inscriptions: the conspicuous and careful royal texts; the great number of those by officials stressing their good qualifications; royal and private representations; and autobiographies in Hatnub.

The second part deals with the expedition report as such, which shows particularities in form and contents. The author discusses the main elements such as sending, departure, return, success, products and fulfilment of the assignment, apart from other themes as the uniqueness of the achievement, the relation king-official, the success as gift of the god, and the servitude of nature. Not immediately to the realm of the expedition report belong the recording of wonders in the Wâdi Hammâmât and influences of the royal novel in the N.K. Then the author discusses the *wpt-nswt*, the O.K. precursor of the expedition report proper, the relation and differences between the expedition report and autobiography, and the relative unity of the genre, although with local peculiarities, as well as problems of other inscriptions in not exclusively mining areas, expecially Nubia. The last section of the article is devoted to expedition reports as parts of autobiographies in tombs and on stelae, a tendency which starts with Weni and Harkhuf and grows stronger in the M. K. and of which the place of conception is hard to determine. *L.Z.*

77099 BOARDMAN, John and Diana SCARISBRICK, The Ralph Harari Collection of Finger Rings, [London], Thames and Hudson, [1977] (18.3 × 25.6 cm; 149 p., 2 colour pl., colour ill. on cover, 216 ill. on 52 pl.).

After a preface on the person of the collector, the catalogue of his collection of finger rings is presented. The Egyptian items bear the

catalogue numbers 92-98 (p. 43-44) and two Phoenician ones in Egyptianizing style nos. 90-91. There are only short descriptions and data (those of nos. 92-96 are by J. Málek). All objects are illustrated.
L.Z.

77100 BÖHLIG, Alexander, Zu N̄- im Koptischen, *GM* Heft 23 (1977), 11-23.

Das N mit supraliniearem Strich im Koptischen hat sehr verschiedene Bedeutungen und ist auf jeweils verschiedenen Ursprung zurückzuführen. Untersucht wird das Problem des koptischen N̄ hinsichtlich seiner Bedeutung als Präposition und als Partikel zur Anknüpfung des direkten Objekts einerseits und als Partikel zur Anknüpfung des Attributs und des Genetivs andererseits. Besonders verwiesen wird auf den Parallelismus zwischen dem Ägyptischen und dem Semitischen. *Inge Hofmann*

77101 BOESSNECK, Joachim, Eine kleine Aufsammlung von Tierknochen aus Elephantine, *MDAIK* 33 (1977), 27-29, with 1 pl.

Description of the animal bones found during the excavations on Elephantine. They belong to an adult cat, a kitten, and a spoonbill. The find dates from the XVIIIth Dynasty.

77102 BOGOSLOWSKI, Evgeni S., Die "Auf-den-Ruf-Hörenden" in der Privatwirtschaft unter der 18. Dynastie, *in: Ägypten und Kusch,* 81-95.

In den Wandmalereien und Inschriften der 18. Dynastie begegnen wir oft mit den unterschiedlichsten Arbeiten beschäftigte Leute, die von den Ägyptern *sḏmw* ꜥš "Auf-den-Ruf-Hörende" genannt wurden. Damit ist ein Dienstverhältnis ausgedrückt, das mit dem eigentlichen Amt nichts zu tun hat. Alle Arbeiter eines Gutshofes waren, unabhängig von ihrer sozialökonomischen Lage, von ihrem Amt in der Wirtschaft in erster Linie "Auf-den-Ruf-Hörende" in bezug auf den Wirtschaftsbesitzer. Die Herren waren beliebige Beamte, von den höchsten Würdenträgern bis zu gewöhnlichen Angestellten, deren "Auf-den-Ruf-Hörende" wohl hauptsächlich Sklaven waren. Unter den Sklaven in den Wirtschaften von Amtspersonen sind sowohl äthiopische als auch syrische Sklaven anzutreffen. Zur Zeit des Neuen Reiches hatte das Wort *nḥsj* selbst oft die Bedeutung "äthiopischer Sklave". *Inge Hofmann*

BOLTIN, Lee, see our number 77130.
BONHÊME, Marie-Ange, see our number 77453.

77103 BOSSE-GRIFFITHS, Kate, A Beset Amulet from the Amarna Period, *JEA* 63 (1977), 98-106, with 2 pl. and 4 fig.

Three bead-collars with pendant amulets exist in the Wellcome Collection at University College Swansea, the pendants being described here as 'Fan-collar', 'Heart-collar' and 'Bes-collar'. On comparison with other figures of the deity it became clear that this was the female form Beset. *E. Uphill*

77104 BOSWORTH, C. E., Al-Jabartī and the Frankish Archaeologists, *International Journal of Middle East Studies*, Cambridge, Mass. 8 (1977), 229-236.

After an introduction on the Arab attitude towards ancient Egypt, the author presents a translation and a commentary on the passages of the historical chronicle of al-Jabartī relating to activities of Salt, Burckhardt, Belzoni and Caviglia. *L.Z.*

77105 BOURRIAU, Janine, Museum Acquisitions, 1975. Egyptian Antiquities Acquired in 1975 by Museums in the United Kingdom, *JEA* 63 (1977), 171-174, with 2 pl.

Sequel to our number 76099. Lists 133 objects with some details.

BOURRIAU, Janine, see also our number 77134.

77106 BRACK, Annelies und Artur, Das Grab des Tjanuni. Theben Nr. 74, Mainz am Rhein, Verlag Philipp von Zabern, [1977] (27 × 36 cm; 112 p., 53 fig., 66 pl. [16 in colour]) = Archäologische Veröffentlichungen. Deutsches Archäologisches Institut, Abteilung Kairo, 19.
Pr. DM 180

For a preliminary report on the tomb and its recent clearing, see our number 75090.

After an introduction dealing i.a. with position (high up on the Sheikh ᶜAbd el-Qurna hill), present state and history of the tomb, the main part is devoted to its architecture, its decoration and the objects found in it. The description of the decoration begins with general remarks on technique and present state, elements of the decoration and the themes, either cultic or biographical. Among the latter particularly scenes in which the king is represented, scenes with Tjanuni in his function of officer, and the inscriptions. This part terminates with discussion of the distribution of the scenes.

There follows a minute description of each separate scene, with copies, transliterations and translations of the texts. The part on the finds includes discussion of the door-frame and a stela now in Turin

(Nos 1643-1645), and a fragment of a double statue. Among the small finds from the excavations in 1973-75 are pots (some decorated), funerary cones and ostraca.

The last part of the book (p. 82-96) presents the conclusions, discussing the tomb as a historical, a religious and an artistic monument. Tjanuni, an army general, functioned under Tuthmosis III, Amenophis II and Tuthmosis IV, as appears from his autobiography (pl. 41 and p. 46-47). His titles, career, family, and relations with the court are studied.

There follow a number of lists, indicating i.a. the frequency of mentions of the various titles, the gods and their epithets, the colours of the hieroglyphs, the minerological-chemical composition of the colours, and the main elements of the scenes.

Sixteen colour plates represent elements of the decoration and some of the decorated pots recently found in the tomb. The other plates in black-and-white and in drawing show the position of the tomb, its decoration, the finds, the plan, etc.

BRADLEY, Rebecca J., see our number 77700.

BRAUNSTEIN-SILVESTRE, Florence, see our number 77532.

77107   BRENTJES, Burchard, Der Aufstand gegen Enlil. Volksbewegungen im Alten Orient, *Das Altertum,* Berlin 23 (1977), 206-212, with 1 ill. and 1 fig.

Although mainly concerned with revolutionary forces in ancient Mesopotamia, the author also devotes some remarks to the F.I.P. Compare our no. 77306.   *L.Z.*

77108   BRENTJES, Burchard, Eine Glaspaste-Statuette aus der ehemaligen Golenischeff-Sammlung, *in: Ägypten und Kusch,* 97, with 1 pl.

Das Staatliche Museum der Schönen Künste "A.S. Puschkin" bewahrt unter der Nr. I, 1a, 3447 eine kleine ägyptische Figur auf, die aus der ehemaligen V.S. Golenischeff-Sammlung stammt; dort trug sie die Inventarnummer 2804. Die Glaspaste-Statuette stellt einen langschwänzigen Haarschaf-Widder dar, der als weißes Tier mit schwarzem Kopf wiedergegeben ist. Der Verfasser sucht das Vorbild dieses Schwarzkopfschafes im Sudan, das der Hersteller mit bemerkenswertem Geschick nachbildete und damit die älteste (?) Darstellung eines Schwarzkopfschafes ist.   *Inge Hofmann*

77109   BRESCIANI, Edda, Ancora sulla dea-cobra che allatta il coccodrilo. Una stele dal sacello del VII km della Via Appia a Roma, *Aegyptus* 57 (1977), 11-13, with 1 pl.

The author adds to our number 75094 another example of the goddess Isis having the body of a cobra and surmounted by the bovine horns and solar disk, who is nursing the crocodile Sobek-Horus, found on a stela on the Via Appia Antica at Rome (now Roma, Museo Nazionale Inv. Nr. 121190). L.Z.

77110 BRESCIANI, [Edda], [Michel] MUSZYNSKI and [Sergio] PERNIGOTTI, Ostraka demotici da Ossirinco, *Studi classici e orientali*, Pisa 27 (1977), 13-78, with 26 pl.

Sequel to our number 76107.

This time 96 ostraca are published, namely: an account of cereals and water, three letters and a school-exercise by Bresciani; sixty short memoranda (with facsimiles) by the late Muszynski; thirty-one accounts and fragments of various nature by Pernigotti. Each text is presented in photograph, transliteration and translation with comments. On p. 73-78 an index to the names.

77111 BRESCIANI, E., S. PERNIGOTTI, M. P. GIANGERI SILVIS, La tomba di Ciennehebu, capo della flotta del re, Pisa, Giardini Editori e Stampatori, [1977] (21.5 × 29.5 cm; 102 p., 63 pl. [4 folding, 23 in colour]) = Biblioteca degli studi classici e orientali, 7 = Serie egittologia. Tombe d'età saitica a Saqqara, 1; rev. *Oriens Antiquus* 17 (1978), 243-244 (Sergio Donadoni). Pr. L.15,000

The series of publications of work by the university of Pisa on tombs of Saqqâra from the Saite Period starts with the tomb of the *ỉmy-r ḥꜥw nswt* Tjanenhebu, situated S. of the Unas Pyramid (see Porter-Moss III.2², 648).

After a preface by Mme Bresciani the first chapter, by the same author, discusses what is known about Tjanenhebu and describes the substructure of the tomb (the superstructure is destroyed) and its reliefs, with translations of the inscriptions (some of them spells from the P.T.).

The second chapter, by Sergio Pernigotti, deals with the sarcophagus, shawabtis and canopic vessels of Tjanenhebu. Of the former the lid is now lost (but its texts are known from a copy by Barsanti), the body in the Cairo Museum (JdE 35136). They too bear P.T. which are here translated, as are the texts on the canopic vessel (now Cairo JdE 34330). All texts dealt with in both chapter 1 and 2 are presented in handcopies on the plates.

The third chapter, by Maria Paola Giangeri Silvis, is devoted to the remains of the funerary equipment, particularly wooden objects and jewellery, that has been found on three different places in the tomb.

The plates bear plans, photographs of the tomb, and photographs and a few drawings of the objects, of which some also are given in colour photograph. Indexes on p. 101-102.

77112   BRIEND, Jacques and Marie-Joseph SEUX, Textes du Proche-Orient ancien et histoire d' Israel, Paris, Les Éditions du Cerf, 1977 (13.6 × 18.1 cm; 188 p.). Pr. F.F.38

The authors offer translations with short introductions and discussions of texts relating to the history of Canaan (Israel in the second and first millenia B.C.).
The Egyptian texts are in the first part of the book. We mention the longer ones: Sinuhe, The Kamose Stelae, The Amarna Letters, and Wenamon. *L.Z.*

77113   BRIER, Bob, Ancient Egyptian Philosophy: A Re-evaluation, *Newsletter ARCE* Nos. 99/100 (Winter/Spring), 16.

Abstract of a paper.

77114   BRINKS, Jürgen und Wolfhart WESTENDORF, *gmḥ.wj* "Doppelter Teil der Tür", *GM* Heft 23 (1977), 25-29, with 3 fig.

Die "Architektur" des Körperbaues ermöglicht es, Begriffe aus der Architektur bei der Beschreibung von Körperteilen zu verwenden. Dazu gehört auch das *Urk.* I, 99, 17 auftretende *gmḥ.wj*, das von *WB* V 171, 13 mit "doppelter Teil an der Tür" umschrieben wird. Orthographie und Bedeutung werden untersucht; die Verfasser kommen zu dem Ergebnis der Deutung "Einrahmung", ausgehend vom *gmḥ* "sehen" über "Augenpartie, Schläfe" und von dort übertragen auf das architektonische Element der beiderseitigen Einrahmung der Tür. Das Determinativ wird erklärt als die Grundriß-Gestalt eines Formsteins für die Konstruktion der beidseitigen vertikalen Laibung (Wange) einer Tür, eines Durchgangs oder der Rahmung einer Kultnische. *Inge Hofmann*

77115   BROVARSKI, Edward, An Allegory of Death, *JEA* 63 (1977), 178.

Theban tombs sometimes show an empty chair piled with funerary bouquets and a funerary priest performing rituals before it, which is here linked with an allegory for the deceased. *E. Uphill*

77116   BROVARSKI, Edward, The Doors of Heaven, *Orientalia* 46 (1977), 107-115, with 4 fig.

L'expression *wn ꜥ3.wy pt* "shrine opener" était connue à Basse Epoque. L'auteur relève *ꜥ3.wy pt* dès l'Ancien Empire, notamment chez Mererouka, et ensuite à Médinet Habou. Dans les premiers exemples, la construction entière est l'*ỉbw n wʿb*: "Tente de purification". L'*ỉbw* royal équivaudrait au temple de la vallée des pyramides. L'*ỉbw* des particuliers, pavillon temporaire, aurait été dressé sur le quai de l'*ỉbw* royal. Le mot *3bw*, dans l'inscription de Débéhen, rapproché par des modernes, devrait en fait se traduire "achèvement".

Il fut encore distinguer la *wʿbt nt wt* : atelier d'embaumement privé, bien attesté à l'Ancien Empire. La *wʿbt du Sud,* proche de la mention des artisans, signifierait l'atelier du mobilier funéraire; elle est aussi dite de Sokaris. Le Sud n'y marquerait pas un emplacement relatif des deux ateliers, mais le rapport géographique avec Memphis ou Gîza. La *wʿbt* royale semble désigner l'atelier d'embaumement du souverain; elle pourrait néanmoins correspondre à la *wʿbt* du Sud. A l'Ancien Empire, *wʿbt* n'aurait pas encore pris le sens de tombeau; celui de cuisine dériverait de celui d'atelier "du Sud". J. Custers

77117 BRUCKHEIMER, M. and Y. SALOMON, Some Comments on R.J. Gillings' Analysis of the 2/n Table in the Rhind Papyrus, *Historia Mathematica,* New York and London 4 (1977), 445-452.

The article contains an extensive review of our number 72249, consisting of considerations on general historical comments, on mathematical and computational issues, and of two appendices illustrating the comments. L.Z.

77118 BRUNNER, Hellmut, Eberhard Otto (26. Februar 1913 bis 11. Oktober 1974), *AfO* 25 (1974/77), 349-350, with portrait.

Obituary notice. Compare our number 74845.

77119 BRUNNER, Hellmut, Serge Sauneron (3. Januar 1927 bis 3. Juni 1976), *AfO* 25 (1974/77), 351.

Obituary notice. Compare our number 76869.

77120 BRUNNER, Hellmut, Die südlichen Räume des Tempels von Luxor. Unter Mitarbeit von Johanna Dittmar, Lucie Lamy, Frank Teichmann und mit einem Abschnitt von Emma Brunner-Traut, Mainz am Rhein, Verlag Philipp von Zabern, [1977] (27 × 36 cm; 92 p., 42 fig. including 3 plans, 196 pl. containing fig., ill. and plans) = Archäologische Veröffentlichungen. Deutsches Archäologisches Institut. Abteilung Kairo, 18; rev. *BiOr* 35 (1978), 94-95 (Philippe Derchain); *Mundus* 15 (1979), 268-270 (Wolfgang Schenkel).

Pr. DM 190

Die Reliefs und Inschriften der Räume XV - XXII des bekannten Tempels sind hier erstmals zusammenhängend durch Nachzeichnungen publiziert. Die Veröffentlichung beschränkt sich auf die Bestandsaufnahme des heutigen Zustandes, von Übersetzungen, Ergänzungen und Interpretationen wurde abgesehen. Ein Überblick über die Gestalten und Beiworte des Amun und der anderen Götter schließt den beschreibenden Teil ab. In der Einleitung und im Schlußkapitel wird zur Zweckbestimmung der Räume Stellung genommen. Entgegen der üblichen Deutung des Tempels von Luxor als "südlicher Harîm" des Amun, der nur zur heiligen Hochzeit besucht wurde, vertritt Verfasser die Auffassung, daß der Tempel das Heiligtum eines "Amun von Luxor" mit ortsfestem Kultbild gewesen sei, der am Opetfest vom Amun von Karnak mit seinem Gefolge besucht wurde. Der vor dem Allerheiligsten liegende Säulensaal XVII, dessen Längsachse quer zur Tempelachse in Ost-West-Richtung verläuft, wird neben seiner kultischen Funktion als Durchgangs- und Speisetischraum als 'Saal der Sonnenbahn" erklärt. Ein Exkurs von E. Brunner-Traut spricht die Frage der Künstlerhandschriften an. Ein Sachregister. *E. M. Wolf-Brinkmann*

77121 BR[UNNER], H[ellmut], Jeanne Vandier d'Abbadie (26. Sept. 1899 bis 25. April 1977), *AfO* 25 (1974/77), 357.

Obituary notice. Compare our number 77849.

77122 BRUNNER, Hellmut, Verkündigung an Tiere, *in: Fragen an die altägyptische Literatur,* 119-124.

The author discusses five votive hymns in which the dedicant proclaims the divine power not only to human beings but also to animals, namely fishes and birds, the territories of which complement that of man. Animals took part in the relation god-man by their being created and nourished, for which they thank god by gestures, dancing and singing, but here they also hear of the proclamation of god's powerful actions. *L.Z.*

77123 BRUNNER, Hellmut, Vogelschau in Ägypten, *GM* Heft 25 (1977), 45-46.

Es handelt sich um eine Stelle in dem Amarnabrief EA 35, einem Schreiben des Königs von Alašia an den ägyptischen König, in dem um einen "Adlerdeuter" gebeten wird. Wenn in Ägypten Adler auch kaum vorkommen, so zeigt der Text doch, daß es eigene Vogelflugdeuter gab. Ägyptische Texte sagen darüber nichts, und die Vorstellungswelt der Zeichendeutung paßt nicht recht zur ägyptischen Weltanschauung. *Inge Hofmann*

BRUNNER, Hellmut, see also our number 77450.

77124   BRUNNER-TRAUT, Emma, Die altägyptische Grabkammer Seschemnofers III. aus Gîsa. Eine Stiftung des Geheimen Hofrats Dr. h.c. Ernst von Sieglin an die Tübinger Universität, Mainz am Rhein, Verlag Philipp von Zabern, [1977] (21 × 27.2 cm; 34 p., 1 map, 1 plan, 28 pl., 4 loose folding pl. [with fig.], 5 colour pl., colour frontispiece = colour ill. on cover); rev. *Mundus* 15 (1979), 188-189 (Birgit Schlick-Nolte). Pr. DM 25

Publication of the reliefs from the tomb chapel of Seschemnefer III preserved in Tübingen (Inv. no. 3), which came from the West Field of the Gîza necropolis (G 5170, cfr. Junker, Gîza III, Wien [1938], 192-215).

The first chapter begins with a section on the donator, Ernst von Sieglin, and his importance for the egyptology. Then the publication of the tomb by Junker is discussed: it was based on the water-colours of the Sieglin expedition, which are here reproduced. The mastaba in general and the funerary cult are briefly dealt with.

The second chapter is devoted to the tomb of Seschemnefer III itself and its owner. There follows in chapter 3 a detailed description of the chapel as a whole and of the reliefs on all four walls, with translations of the texts.

On the plates all the reliefs in black-and-white photographs. The loose sheets give the representations of entire walls in line drawings.

77125   BRUNNER-TRAUT, Emma, Der Katzmäusekrieg — Folge von Rauschgift, *GM* Heft 25 (1977), 47-51.

In der Geschichte des Krieges der Katzen und Mäuse, die sich, wahrscheinlich von Ägypten aus, weltweit verbreitet hat, kommt es zu einer Phase, in der die Mäuse angreifen und die Katzen fliehen. Aus Tierversuchen erfährt man, daß Katzen bei mäßigen Gaben von LSD Angst vor Mäusen haben, da sich die Raum- und Körperdimensionen verändern: schart fixierte Objekte nehmen eine unwahrscheinliche Größe an. LSD ist zwar ein Kunstprodukt aus den Lysergsäure-Alkaloiden, die im Mutterkornpilz vorkommen. Dieser aber war im Alten Ägypten ein verbreiteter Parasit der dort angebauten Getreidearten. Die Mäuse fraßen in den Silos mit dem Korn auch Mutterkorn; das Lysergsäureamid wird spätestens einen Tag später wieder ausgeschieden. Während nur eine Maus wegen ihrer relativ geringen Reaktion auf die Droge "normal" bleibt, berauscht sich die Katze, wenn sie diese Maus frißt, an dem in der Maus gesammelten Giftstoff und flüchtet nun in panikartiger Angst vor Mäusen, bis das

Gift abgebaut ist.
Mehr noch als bei einer Katze muß das Mutterkorn auf den Menschen als Rauschgift gewirkt haben. Darauf sollten vor allem die medizinischen Texte untersucht werden. *Inge Hofmann*

77126 BRUNNER-TRAUT, Emma, Der Sehgott und der Hörgott in Literatur und Theologie, *in: Fragen an die altägyptische Literatur*, 125-145, with 8 fig. on 3 pl.

Proceeding from the Demotic fable of Seeing-bird and Hearing-bird, which are literary compositions from the conception of the gods Seeing and Hearing, the author discusses these gods, which are attested first in the history of "The Sporting King" and, in representation, in the early XVIIIth Dynasty at Karnak as well as in the temples of Sethi I and Ramses II at Abydos, where they are related to Thoth and Sheshat. After having argued that the name of Seeing derives from an old verb *irỉ*, "to see", just as *irt*, "eye", the author deals with evidence from the Ramesseum, Medinet Habu, Hibis, Edfu, Dendera, Armant and Philae, from which an increasing importance in late texts is apparent. Two manifestations of Khons-Thoth, namely Khons-*wn-nḫỉ* and Khons-*p3-ỉr-sḫr*, represented as baboons on the gate of Ptolemy III Euergetes and considered to be hypostases of the eye and ear of the sun god, have a link with both gods, and also with Seeing-bird and Hearing-bird. *L.Z.*

77127 BRUNNER-TRAUT, Emma, Tiergeschichten aus dem Pharaonenland. Erzählt und mit altägyptischen Bildern ausgestattet, Mainz am Rhein, Verlag Philipp von Zabern, [1977] (22 × 20 cm; 71 p., numerous fig.). Pr. DM 24

A book for young children in which the author tells seven fables. The tales are based on (in some instances slightly adapted) Egyptian drawings, mainly those on ostraca and in the fairy-tale papyri in London, Turin and Cairo. These are so combined that they illustrate the fables which the author aptly composed from Egyptian motifs, later fables, and her own phantasy.

BRUNNER-TRAUT, Emma, see also our number 77120.

77128 BRUNSCH, Wolfgang, Noch einmal zu ⲂⲞⲐⲞⲠ, *Enchoria* 7 (1977), 191-192.

The equation ⲂⲞⲐⲞⲠ *Wḏ3-ḥr* (Οτευρις) of the name of the Egyptian sage in the Coptic story of Cambyses as proposed by H. J. Thissen in *Enchoria* 2 (1977), 137-139 (compare our number 72705), cannot be maintained any longer. Perhaps the name is not Egyptian at all.
W. Brunsch

BRUNSCH, Wolfgang, see also our number 77633.

77129 BRUWIER, Marie-Cécile, L'usage du siège en Égypte, à la XVIIIe dynastie, *Revue des archéologues et historiens d'art de Louvain,* Louvain 9 (1976), 267.
Abstract of a small thesis.

77130 BUCKLEY, Tom, Harry BURTON, and Lee BOLTIN, Suche und Entdeckung des Grabes von Tutenchamun [und] Der Grabschatz König Tutanchamuns, *Du,* Zürich 37, No. 432 (Februar 1977), 24-65, with 1 map, 1 plan, 1 fig., 47 ill. (13 in colour, 1 on cover) and an English summary on an unnumbered front page.

In this article written on the occasion of the Tutankhamon exhibition travelling through the U.S.A. Tom Buckley relates on p. 24-39 the story of the search and the discovery of the tomb of Tutankhamon, while the rest of the article is devoted to splendid photographs of the treasures from the tomb. See also the editorial by Dominik Keller on p. 22-23. L.Z.

77131 BUDISCHOVSKY, Marie-Christine, La diffusion des cultes isiaques autour de la mer adriatique. I. Inscriptions et monuments, Leiden, E.J. Brill, 1977 (15.5 × 24 cm; XX + 248 p., frontispiece, 106 pl., 1 folding map) = Études préliminaires aux religions orientales dans l'empire romain publiés par M.J. Vermaseren, 61; rev. *Comptes rendus de l'Académie des Inscriptions et Belles-Lettres,* 1978, 360-361 (Jean Leclant). Pr. fl. 180

This first volume contains, apart from a preface, a bibliography and an introduction explaining the organization of the catalogue, only the catalogue itself, while volume II will contain the synthesis of the material.

The documents are arranged after the Roman provinces in which they are found, going from Apulia along the Italian coast to Aquileia and then S. through modern Yugoslavia (= Histria, Dalmatia and Salonae). The categories of objects listed are: inscriptions, statues and statuettes, jewels and gems, vessels and glasses, coins, and some other categories of documents. Each object is minutely described, with technical data and bibliographical references.
Indexes on p. 223-240.

77132 BÜLL, Reinhard, Das grosse Buch vom Wachs. Geschichte, Kultur, Technik, [Band] I [und] 2, München, Verlag Georg D.W. Callwey, 1977 (21.2 × 29.7 cm; 1089 p., numerous maps, fig. and ill. [partly in colour]).

In this enormous book dealing with all aspects of apiculture and wax, there are spread references to ancient and Graeco-Roman Egypt; see particularly p. 325 and p. 1060, s.v. Ägypten.   *L.Z.*

77133   BUHL, Marie-Louise, Some Western-Asiatic Bronze Figurines and a Few Remarks on Julius Løytved as an Antiquarian, *Acta Archaeologica,* København 48 (1977), 139-154, with 19 ill.

The author identifies a bronze statuette in the Egyptian Museum, West Berlin (Inv. No. 20613), found at Beni Hasan in M.K. tomb no. 294 by J. Garstang as being an import from Byblos.   *L.Z.*

77134   Bulletin de liaison du Groupe Internationale d'Étude de la Céramique égyptienne. II, [Le Caire, Institut français d'Archéologie orientale], 1977 (16 × 24 cm; II + 21 p.).

Sequel to our number 75114.

The second number of the Bulletin, prefaced by Jean Vercoutter, again consists of two parts. In the first (p. 1-15), brief informations on pottery from 26 sites in Egypt and the Sudan, in a geographical order from Tanis to Meroe, each by an other scholar. In the second (17-21), short communications of a general character, beginning with a progress report on the "Introductory Guide to Ancient Egyptian Pottery" by Janine Bourriau.

77135   BURKARD, Günter, Textkrititsche Untersuchungen zu ägyptischen Weisheitslehren des Alten und Mittleren Reiches, Wiesbaden, Otto Harrassowitz, 1977 (17.4 × 24.9 cm; XIII + 340 p., 1 pl.) = Ägyptologische Abhandlungen. Herausgegeben von Wolfgang Helck, 34; rev. *BiOr* 35 (1978), 47 (Hans Goedicke); *ZDMG* 129 (1979), 406 (J[ürgen] v. B[eckerath]).   Pr. DM 68

In the introduction the author deals with the aims of a critical analysis of text variants; they are: to try to reconstruct the original texts, and if that is out of the question, to locate the deviation as precisely as possible, and to make a distinction between accidental and conscious text changes. Most literary texts having come to us as copies, it is necessary to know how these texts were copied: from dictation, by copying from a model, and by writing down from the memory. So three types of errors correspond to these: reading, hearing and thought errors. Since wisdom literature texts are written on papyrus, writing boards and ostraca, and offer a great number of sources from various periods, the author has chosen for his investigation the texts of Ptahhotep, Merikare, Amenemhat I, Duakheti and the Instruction of a Man for his Son (Kagemni as being incomplete and only known from one text, and Djedefhor as being too fragmentary are left out of consideration), of which he gives the pertinent references.

These five texts form the basis of subdivision in some of the chapters, as in the very long chapter 1 in which the author deals with the various types of errors. He first discusses reading errors due to similarity of hieratic signs, omissions due to skipping caused by identical or homonymous words occurring at the beginning or end of phrases (homoiarchon or homoioteleuton) and changes in the texts caused by haplo- or dittography; then thought errors consisting of omission of verses without recognizable mechanical or redactional reason, of changes in the verse order, of contamination of verses or maxims and of the use of synonymous words; and, lastly, with hearing errors, errors of carelessness, and specific divergences of Late Egyptian (only in Amenemhat and Duakheti). The second chapter is devoted to redactional text changes, those maintaining the original extent as well as those leading to enlargement (only in Ptahhotep). The first two chapters offer summaries at the end of the sections or the chapter. In chapter 3 the author discusses unexplained places and text corruptions, and adds an excursus on the 9th maxim of Ptahhotep and the problem of ambiguity.

The chapters 4 and 5 are short, devoted respectively to the formal structure of 37 maxims of the Wisdom of Ptahhotep, and propositions for corrections in the publications and miscellaneous problems.

The last chapter offers a summary consisting of short sections on each of the texts discussed.

At the end of the book an index of text quotations, a very short one on Egyptian words, a few pages of latest additions, and a photograph and transcription of P. Berlin 23045 containing a few lines of Amenemhat and dating from the XXVIth to XXXth Dynasties. *L.Z.*

BURKARD, Günter, see also our number 77633.

77136 BURKERT, Walter, Das hunderttorige Theben und die Datierung der Ilias, *Wiener Studien,* Wien — Köln — Graz 10 (1976), 5-21.

After stating that the reason why the Greeks called *W3st* Θῆβαι is unknown the author deals with two references to the city, in the Iliad (I 381 ff.) and the Odyssey (δ 127). Against the general opinion he argues that the latter is an interpolation, the former belonging to the original text. Certainly it dates from the post-bronze-age period. It then reflects the flourishing of Thebes under the Kushite Dynasty which was well known through the booty Assurbanipal carried off in 663 B.C. A date for the Iliad about 660 is not impossible.

77137 BURKHARDT, Adelheid, Bemerkungen zu den demotischen Graffiti von Meroiten im Dodekaschoinos, in: *Ägypten und Kusch,* 99-106.

Eine kleine Anzahl der 508 demotischen Graffiti aus dem Dodekaschoinos stammt von Meroiten. Sie heben sich innerhalb der Gruppe der recht gleichförmigen ägyptischen Anbetungsinschriften durch ungewöhnliche Lebendigkeit und Ausführlichkeit ab. Besondere Beachtung verdienen die für die Meroiten als typisch anzusehenden persönlichen Gebete, die bei den Ägyptern praktisch fehlen. Die meroitischen Inschriften, als deren Kriterium die Personennamen und Aufbau und Inhalt der Inschriften dienten, ließen sich in vier Typen einteilen; nur 14 Graffiti ließen sich ihnen nicht zuordnen, ohne dabei eigene Typen zu bilden. Am Beispiel Ph. 417 wird der syntaktische Aufbau aufgezeigt; Bericht und Gebet lösen sich ab. Die meroitischen Inschriften des Dodekaschoinos zeigen wohl nur eine Transponierung der meroitischen Redeweise ins Demotische, so daß von daher eine Untersuchung vergleichbarer meroitischer Inschriften neu belebt werden könnte. *Inge Hofmann*

77138 BURKHARDT, Adelheid, Das Dodekaschoinos und die Meroiten. Ein Beitrag zur Untersuchung der demotischen Graffiti des Dodekaschoinos und zur Geschichte des ägyptisch-meroitischen Grenzgebietes, *Ethnographisch-archäologische Zeitschrift,* Berlin 18 (1977), 85-89.

Der vorliegende Artikel ist die Kurzfassung einer Dissertation, die in der Reihe *Meroitica* publiziert werden woll. Sie befaßt sich mit dem Dodekaschoinos, das der Isis von Philae unterstand, dessen Geschichte vom Neolithikum bis zur christlichen Epoche dargestellt wird. Untersucht wurden vor allem die von Griffith publizierten demotischen Inschriften, die von Ägyptern und Meroiten verfaßt wurden und die miteinander verglichen werden. Dabei fällt auf, daß die Meroiten im Gegensatz zu den Ägyptern persönliche Gebete an die Gottheit bevorzugen. Die Inschriften können in vier Typen gegliedert werden, von denen die des Typs 4 im 1. nachchristlichen Jahrhundert angebracht wurden. Anscheinend lag zu dieser Zeit das höchste Amt eines "Strategen", das hier stets mit dem eines "Verwalters der Isis" verbunden war, in den Händen von Meroiten. Ein großer Teil der von Meroiten verfaßten demotischen Inschriften aus dem 2. und 3. Jahrhundert n. Chr. gehören der Familie des Wayekiye. Möglicherweise unterstand das Dodekaschoinos in der Mitte des 3. Jahrhunderts überhaupt den Meroiten. *Inge Hofmann*

77139   [BURRI, Carla M.], Bolletino d'Informazioni. Sezione archeologica. Istituto Italiano di Cultura per la R.A.E., No. 42 (Dicembre 1976 — Febbraio 1977), 23 p.

Sequel to our number 76130, containing reports on several excavation activities, e.g. by the Italians in Qurna, Mrs. Schiff Giorgini at Soleb, the Austrians at Tell ed-Dab{c}a, the Poles at Kadero, the Germans at Dashur, etc.

77140   [BURRI, Carla M.], Bolletino d'Informazioni. Sezione archeologica. Istituto Italiano di Cultura per la R.A.E., No. 43 (Marzo — Maggio 1977), 25 p.

Sequel to our preceding number.
The major reports in the number deal with excavations at Kôm Mâdi, in the area of Gebel Barkal, in the Oasis el-Dâkhla, in Karnak, Thebes West and Saqqâra.

77141   [BURRI, Carla M.], Bolletino d'Informazioni. Sezione archeologica. Istituto Italiano di Cultura per la R.A.E., No. 44 (Luglio — Ottobre 1977), 20 p.

Sequel to our preceding number, containing reports on activities on Philae, in Asâsîf, Naqâda, Gîza, Abydos, Malqata and other sites.

BURTON, Harry, see our number 77130.

77142   BUTLER, T., The Face of Egypt: Permanence and Change in Egyptian Art, *The Connoisseur,* London Vol. 195, No. 784 (June 1977), 148.

Short notice on an exhibition in the Katonah Gallery (Newchester County, New York).   *L.Z.*

77143   BUTTERFIELD, William C., Medicine Depicted in Ancient Egyptian Art, *Connecticut Medicine,* New Haven 40, No. 7 (July 1976), 459-466, with 18 ill.

The author presents a sketch of ancient Egyptian medicine, stressing that specialization has to be understood in the sense of limitation to a narrow spectrum of disease.   *L.Z.*

77144   CALDERINI, Aristide, Dizionario dei nomi geografici e topografici dell'Egitto greco-romano. A cura di Sergio Daris. Volume secondo. Fascicolo quarto. Θεαδελφεια–Θωψις, [Milano], Cisalpino-Goliardica, [1977] (21.5 × 31 cm; [IV +] 76 p. [= p. 241-302]).

Sequel to our number 76134.

77145 The Cambridge Ancient History. Plates to Volumes I and II. New Edition. Edited by I.E.S. Edwards, the late C.J. Gadd, N.G.L. Hammond [and] E. Sollberger, Cambridge, Cambridge University Press, [1977] (15.7 × 23 cm; XLII p., 181 pl.); rev. *BiOr* 35 (1978), 177-178 (Josef Klíma); *Boletin de la Asociacion Española de Orientalistas* 14 (1978), 284-285 (F.M. Pareja). Pr. £7.50

Plate volume to our numbers 70104, 71109, 73133 and 75126.
The text consists of a preface and the table of contents, indicating the chapters to which the plates belong.
To ancient Egypt pertain pl. 9-12 (Predynastic Period), 25-29 (Early Dynastic Period), 31-33 (O.K.), 43b-45 (M.K.), 69-71 (S.I.P.), 86-97 (early N.K.), 134-135 (late XVIIIth Dynasty), 153-155a (second half N.K.), 163 (late N.K.). The illustrations represent some less well known objects, e.g. the stela of Tjetji (Brit. Mus. 614), and the wooden board with the names of early kings (Cairo JE 37734).
Some more illustrations from ancient Egypt occur among those to the chapters on Syria and Palestine, e.g. 38c (the Cheops boat) and 101 (the Mekal stela from Beth-Shan).

77146 CAMINOS, Ricardo A., The Moscow Literary Letter, *in: Fragen an die altägyptische Literatur,* 147-153.

Account of the contents of the Moscow Literary Letter Pap. Pushkin Museum 127, without philological commentary and critical notes. The story is divided into four sections: the formal preamble, the tale proper of the wandering outcast, the report of his hard times and the end expressing some hope. See our next number. *L.Z.*

77147 CAMINOS, Ricardo A., A Tale of Woe. From a Hieratic Papyrus in the A.S. Pushkin Museum of Fine Arts in Moscow, Oxford, Griffith Institute. Ashmolean Museum, 1977 (25 × 34.3 cm; XII + 99 p., 13 pl. [6 folding]). Pr. £12

The Papyrus Pushkin 127, published in an editio princeps by Korostovtsev in 1961 (our number 61413), is a narrative work of fiction told within the framework of a letter. A certain Wermai, formerly a father-of-the-god priest in the temple of Re-Atum at Heliopolis, tells his friend Usima're'nakhte about his misfortunes; how he roamed the country and came to the Great Oasis where he found a poverty-stricken locality dominated by an unscrupulous 'omdeh. However, he still kept faith in an unnamed benefactor, probably the Hero-King.
In the introduction Caminos deals with the provenance of the papyrus

(it was found near el-Hîba in a vessel, together with the Golenishev Onomasticon of Amenemope and the Report of Wenamun), its recent history, outer appearance, palaeographic features, language and (very bad) spelling. He also presents a survey of its contents.

The text itself is divided into four sections, each translated and fully commented upon in a separate chapter: preliminaries (the epistolary preamble); the wandering outcast; hard times; a glimmer of hope. In chapter 6 a consecutive translation is given. Chapter 7 is devoted to the three jottings on the verso.

Chapter 8 contains a paraphrase of the tale, remarks on its date (composed not earlier c. 1300 B.C., the present copy from about 1000 B.C.) and its literary value.

Full indexes on p. 81-99. On the plates a map of Egypt, diagrams of the papyrus, clear photographs and the transcription, the latter on folding plates so that it can be used side-by-side with the photographs.

77148 CAMPAGNANO, Antonella, Antonella MARESCA, Tito ORLANDI, Quattro Omilie Copte. Vita di Giovanni Chrisostomo, Encomi dei 24 Vegliardi (Ps. Proclo e Anonimo), Encomio di Michele Arcangelo, di Eustazio di Tracia. Edizione, traduzione e commento, [Milano], Cisalpino — Goliardica, 1977 (17 × 24 cm; 189 p., 8 pl.) = Testi e documenti per lo studio dell' antichità. Serie copto, 60; rev. *CdE* LIV, No. 107 (1979), 177-179 (L.S.B. MacCoull).

Publication of four Coptic homilies from several manuscripts (some fragmentary) preserved in various collections.

The first part, by Orlandi, deals with the homily on the life of Johannes Chrisostomus; the second, by Mme Maresca, with two homilies on the 24 Elders of the Apocalyps (one by Proclus, one anonymous); the third, by Mme Campagnano, with the homily on the Archangel Michael by Eustatius of Thrace.

Each part contains the Coptic text with a few notes and the translation on opposite pages, preceded by an introduction in which the manuscripts and matters such as authorship and position of the homily in the Coptic liturgy are discussed.

Indexes on p. 175-189.

77149 CARLTON, Eric, Ideology and Social Order, London, Routledge & Kegan Paul, [1977] (14 × 21.5 cm; [VI +] 320 p.); series: International Library of Sociology.

In this study on the influence of ideology on social structure and value-orientation the author uses the contrasts between ancient Egypt and classical Athens in order to evaluate the relationship between a belief-system and social forms or patterns of behaviour. In his concept Egypt is a model for the Archaic type of society, Athens for the so-called Seminal type (see p. 60-62).

A sketch of the Egyptian historical development is given on p. 64-70, while in each of the following chapters a special section is devoted to Egypt, as another one to Athens. So Egypt is dealt with on p. 80-85 (family and kinship), 92-94 (education), 103-110 (systems of social differentiation), 131-140 (basis of economic organization), 158-165 (political and legal organization), 182-191 (military organization and expansionism), and 209-220 (systems of ideation). The conclusions are presented on p. 232-243.

The bibliography on Egypt (307-309) combines popular and scientific works and omits important recent studies. Indexes on p. 313-320.

77150 CASTIGLIONE, L., Eine neuere Darstellung des Pharos und die Kultstatue des alexandrinischen Paneions, *Acta Archaeologica Academiae Scientiarum Hungaricae,* Budapest 29 (1977), 351-362, with 6 ill. and 1 fig.

The author discusses the common features of the ancient Egyptian god Min and his Greek counterpart, in this case a Pan figure from the Alexandrian Paneion.
L.Z.

77151 CASTIGLIONE, László, Ujabb régészeti adatok a Sarapis-kultusz kialakulásához, *Archaeologiai Értesitő,* Budapest 104 (1977), 176-188, with 13 ill. and an English summary on p. 188.

"New Data to the Development of the Serapis Cult".

The author, who has earlier argued that the form of the Serapis representations has gradually developed (see our number 58122), adduces further arguments for his thesis. The early representations show the god not only as Zeus, but (by the *atef*-crown and the horns of Amon) as Zeus-Amon-Osiris.

77152 CASTILLOS, Juan Jose, An Analysis of the Tombs in Cemeteries 1300 and 1400-1500 at Armant, *Newsletter SSEA* 7, No. 2 (March 1977), 4-23.

Sequel to our number 76141.

The approach of this study is basically the same as in the preceding one. The author analyses the contents of 144 tombs from the Predynastic and Early Dynastic Periods found by Mond and Myers near Armant. Although several tombs have been robbed only the precious materials (copper, gold, ivory, etc.) were removed.

After tabulating the data the main conclusions are (p. 21-23): the more recent tombs were larger and wealthier; bodies lying on their right side or with the head facing south (local east) occur extensively in small tombs; a few tombs disregard the orientations according to the course of the Nile and follow the orientation to the points of the compass; women are better equipped than men and men better than children.

77153 CASTIONI, Christiane — Dominique DÉROBERT — Robert HARI — Jocelyne MULLER-AUBERT — Bérengère STAHL-GUINAUD, Égypte, [no place, no publisher, 1977] (17 × 24 cm; 32 p., 16 pl. [= p. 9-24], 2 fig., colour ill. on cover).

In this booklet, written by former and actual students of Charles Maystre, on the occasion of his seventieth birthday, eighteen objects in the Egyptian collection of the Museum in Geneva are discussed.
On p. 1 a "Hommage à Charles Maystre", on p. 2-3 an introduction with i.a. some remarks to the collection. The objects described range from a prehistoric granite vessel to a sistrum, a mirror and an Ibis statuette from the Ptolemaic Period and include stelae, statues, reliefs, etc. All are represented by a fine photograph, while to their description the relevant data such as date, provenance and bibliography are added.

CAUVILLE, Sylvie, see our number 77028.

77154 CAZELLES, H., La localisation de Goshen: problème de méthode, in: La Toponymie Antique. Actes du Colloque de Strasbourg 12-14 Juin 1975, Leiden, E.J. Brill, 1977 (= Université des Sciences Humaines de Strasbourg. Travaux du Centre de Recherche sur le Proche-Orient et la Grèce Antiques, 4), 143-150.

The author investigates the problem of the O.T. land of Goshen. He presents a survey of various scholarly opinions and argues that Goshen might have been situated in the South of Judea submitted to Egypt, near Sigeleg in the Simeonite region. The tradition about Pi-Ramesse (Raamses) and that about Goshen should then have got mixed up in the early tradition of the O.T. L.Z.

ČEJKA, Jiři, see our number 77733.

77155 de CENIVAL, Françoise, Deux papyrus inédits de Lille avec une révision du P. dém. Lille 31, Enchoria 7 (1977), 1-49, with 8 pl. (4 folding).

Publication of P. dém. Lille 97 recto (register of male persons: Ghoran — 3rd century B.C.), P. dém. Lille 97 verso (register of female members of a religious association: Ghoran — 4th or 3rd

century B.C.), P. dém. Lille 98 (account of a mixed religious association (?): Ghoran — 245 B.C.) and a re-publication of P. dém. Lille 31 (register of priestesses of a religious association: Ghoran — 3rd century B.C.).
Finally all these texts are dealt with in a general commentary.
W. Brunsch

77156   de CENIVAL, J.L., Les écritures du verbe *m33* «voir» dans les Textes des Sarcophages. Leurs conséquences théoriques, *RdE* 29 (1977), 21-37.

L'auteur a réuni tous les exemples de l'emploi du verbe *m33* dans les C.T. en vue d'établir les règles de l'emploi des différentes formes (*m3*, *m33*, et *m3n*), d'où il ressort que la distribution entre *m3* (dont *m3n* semble n'être qu'une variante) et *m33* correspond à celle que Gardiner (Grammar, p. 94-95, 111 et 262) avait établie.   *Ph. Derchain*

ČERNÝ, Jaroslav, see our number 77754.

77157   CHERPION, Nadine, Index et errata du volume 15 de la Propyläen Kunstgeschichte: C. Vandersleyen, Das alte Ägypten, Berlin, 1975, *GM* Heft 26 (1977), 69-87.

Zu dem genannten Werk (vgl. unsere Nr. 75751) werden zwei Indices gegeben: 1. Liste der Inventarnummern der Werke in der Reihenfolge ihrer Abbildungen. 2. Liste der Werke, geordnet nach den Museen als ihrem Verwahrort. Eine dritte Liste der Errata beansprucht keine Vollständigkeit. *Inge Hofmann*

77158   CHERPION, Nadine, Mode et société à l'époque amarnienne, *Revue des archéologues et historiens d'art de Louvain,* Louvain 10 (1977), 18-25, with 9 fig.

The author describes the various ways in which Mahou (Amarna tomb No. 9) wears his tunic on representations in his tomb, and further devotes attention to the various crowns worn by Akhenaten and Nefertiti. *L.Z.*

77159   CHERPION, Nadine, Les usages vestimentaires de la société amarnienne d'après les tombes privées, *Revue des archéologues et historiens d'art de Louvain,* Louvain 9 (1976), 266-267.

Abstract of a small thesis.

77160   CHESHIRE, Wendy, A New Demotic Loan from Gebelen, *Enchoria* 7 (1977), 51-54, with 1 pl.

Publication of P. Philadelphia 16744, University Museum, University of Pennsylvania (loan of wheat: Gebelein — 96 B.C.). Contracting party A is the well known Peteharsemteus, son of Panebchoumis and Kobahetesis, studied recently by P.W. Pestman in Pap. Lugd. Bat. XIV (1965), 47-105 (our number 65373). *W. Brunsch*

CHEVRIER, Henri, see our number 77453.

77161 CHRISTOPHE, Louis-A., Campagne internationale de l'UNESCO pour la sauvegarde des sites et monuments de Nubie. Bibliographie préparée, [Paris], Unesco, [1977] (15.2 × 24.3 cm; 123 p., colour ill. on cover, frontispiece, 3 ill., 1 map).

After a preface by the director general of UNESCO, the bibliography proper follows. First one listing books and articles in alphabetical arrangement after the authors, in total comprising 718 entries.

The second bibliography, containing slightly more entries (721), is divided into two parts: the first offers the systematical arrangement after subjects, such as historical periods, ceramics, architecture and general archaeology, although without cross-references. The second part deals with the sites in a geographical order, from Philae to the deep South, only separated by more general subject headings both for Egyptian and Sudanese Nubia.

At the end of the book an authors' index to the second, systematic-geographical bibliography. *L.Z.*

77162 Chronique d'Égypte. Bulletin périodique de la Fondation Égyptologique Reine Élisabeth. Publié avec l'aide financière du Ministère de l'Éducation Nationale et de la Culture Française, du Ministère de l'Éducation Nationale et de la Culture Néerlandaise et de la Fondation Universitaire de Belgique. Tables des Tomes XXXVI — L. 1961-1975 (Numéros 71-100), Bruxelles, Fondation Égyptologique Reine Élisabeth, 1977 (16.4 × 25 cm; 63 p.).

The index is arranged after periods: Pharaonic, Greco-Roman and Christian Egypt, and subdivided into articles including chronicles and book-reviews. Necrologies at the end. *L.Z.*

77163 CLAMER, Christa, A Burial Cave Near Nablus (Tell Balata), *Israel Exploration Journal,* Jerusalem 27 (1977), 48.

The find of various Egyptian objects in a burial cave near Nablûs shows that ancient Shechem enjoyed strong contacts with XVIIIth Dynasty Egypt. *L.Z.*

CLARK, J. Desmond, see our number 77318.

77164 CLARYSSE, W. et M. MUSZYNSKI, P. IFAO III 19, *BIFAO* 77 (1977), 193-196, with 2 facsimiles and 1 pl.

Discussion of a fragmentary papyrus with a Greek text and three lines in Demotic on the verso. The text is given in photograph, facsimile and translation.

77165 CLÈRE, J.J., Sur l'existence d'un temple du Nouvel Empire à Dêbôd en Basse-Nubie, in: *Ägypten und Kusch,* 107-113, with 1 pl.

Von Dâbôd ist ein Tempel bekannt, der unter dem nubischen König Adikhalamani begonnen und von Ptolemaios VI., Augustus und Tiberius vollendet wurde. Die Ortschaft war bekannt als *T3-ḥwt,* "der Tempel". Der Name von Dâbôd findet sich auch noch in Kalâbsha, Dendûr und Dakka, verbunden mit dem Namen Amuns, d.h. der Amun von Dâbôd besaß ein Sanktuar in den Tempeln der drei genannten Ortschaften. Seit 1969 ist nun ein Amun von Dâbôd aus dem Neuen Reich bekannt; aus dem Kunsthandel stammt ein Sandsteinblock mit einer Inschrift, in der die Triade Amun-Re von Dâbôd, Mut und Chons angerufen wird. Somit gab es bereits im Neuen Reich einen Tempel in Dâbôd. *Inge Hofmann*

COCKBURN, T. Aiden, see our number 77065.

77166 COONEY, John D., Egyptian Treasures, *Architectural Digest,* Los Angeles 34, No. 2 (March 1977), 136-137 and 172, with 12 ill.

The author deals with privately collecting in general. *L.Z.*

77167 COQUIN, R.G., A propos des rouleaux coptes-arabes de l'évêque Timothée, *BiOr* 34 (1977), 142-147.

Review article of our number 75590.

77168 COQUIN, René-Georges, Apollon de Titkooḥ ou/et Apollon de Bawīt?, *Orientalia* 46 (1977), 435-446, with 1 pl.

Orlandi, dans son édition de la Vie copte de Phib (notre No. 75571), identifie l'un à l'autre les moines Apollon de Titkooḥ et de Baoûît. Ce ne serait pas une raison de confondre les deux localités. L'anachorète, après avoir voyagé, s'établit à Titkooḥ, sépulture de son ami Phib, et y instaure un curieux rite annuel de "metanoïa", fixé au 25 Paophi. Ce récit se retrouve dans le Synaxaire et la fête figure au calendrier du Monastère Blanc.

La Vie de Phib serait traduite du grec, ce qui expliquerait la double signification donnée au mot copte ⲛⲁϩⲧ⸗(ⲥ̄): prostration/pénitence. Ce dernier terme ajoute au dictionnaire de Crum une référence précieuse. La Vie éclairerait aussi une peinture copte de Saqqârah, où un moine s'incline en même temps devant Apollon et devant un prêtre dont le nom est effacé. Comme on célébrait Phib le même jour que son ami, le prêtre représenterait Phib et préciserait sa fonction. *J. Custers*

77169 Corpus antiquitatum aegyptiacarum. Lose-Blatt-Katalog ägyptischer Altertümer. Pelizaeus-Museum. Hildesheim. Lieferung 1 = Eva MARTIN-PARDEY, Plastik des Alten Reiches. Teil 1, Mainz/Rhein, Verlag Philipp von Zabern, 1977 (21 × 30 cm; portefolio containing [I +] 80 loose p., 102 loose pl.). Pr. DM 68

This first fascicile, composed along the lines described in *GM* 21 (our number 76164), is devoted to the O.K. statuary in the Pelizaeus-Museum, Hildesheim. All together 29 pieces are dealt with, 13 statues, 4 group-statues, 4 heads and 8 smaller or larger fragments. All pieces came from Gîza, partly from Steindorff's excavations and partly from those of Junker.

Apart from technical data (inventory number, material, measurements, date and provenance) a description is presented discussing the state of preservation and the representation, with the texts given in transliteration, and the technical details. Added are references to the occurrence of photographs. Each statue is presented from its four sides, in some instances with a fifth picture of a detail, e.g. the inscription. For smaller pieces, e.g. heads, two photographs are printed on one sheet.

Some of the persons represented by the statues are tomb-owners; others are servants, for instance a brewer (No. 18), two milling women (Nos. 19 and 20), a baker (No. 2140) and the torso of a brewer's assistant (No. 2142). Together these 29 pieces are roughly half of the O.K. statuary present in the museum.

77170 Le CORSU, France, Isis. Mythe et mystères, Paris, Société d'Édition "Les Belles Lettres", 1977 (15.5 × 24.5 cm; X + 318 p., 81 ill., 18 fig., 3 plans); series: Collection d'études mythologiques publiée sous le patronage du Centre de Recherches Mythologiques de l'Université de Paris; rev. *CdE* LIII, No. 106 (1978), 385-390 (Michel Malaise); *Comptes rendus de l'Académie des Inscriptions et Belles-Lettres*, 1978, 359-360 (Jean Leclant); *Revue Archéologique*, 1979, 351-353 (Gisèle Clerc).

After a preface by J. Leclant the author presents her study in five parts.

The first part is concerned with the Pharaonic period and deals in six chapters with Osiris and Re, the Osiris myth, the iconography and roles of Isis, particularly as goddess of magic and healing, the temple at Philae and her cult there, mysteries and initiations, and the Sed-festival. Then follows the second part on the Hellenistic period with subjects such as Serapis, Alexandria, Isis-Demeter and Osiris-Dionysos, Isis and the Ptolemaic queens, her clergy and her mysteries. Also the wider context is studied: the Ptolemaic iconography of Isis, Harpocrates, Serapis and Bes; the evolution of the moral attitude; and the Isis aretologies and their Egyptian origin.

In the third part, on Isis in Italy during the Empire, the author studies, after having described the Iseum of Pompei and her clergy and cult, the initiation into the Isiac mysteries in some detail on account of Apuleius' "Golden Ass". Other subjects dealt with in this part are traces of Isiaca in Campania and Latium, Isis in Rome, Isis and the classical authors, the magical and astrological evolution of the cults, and other oriental gods.

The fourth and fifth parts of the book are devoted to the spread of the Isis cults all over the Roman Empire, beginning with Egypt, and its aftermath up to free-masonry. After the conclusion follows the bibliography to the chapters and the index. *L.Z.*

77171 COSTAS, Alvimar, Preparação ao estudo da língua Egípcia, *Studia. Departemento de letras. Faculdade de Filosofia de Passos* (1) (1976), 143-265.

Brief introduction to the Egyptian script and language in Portuguese. Part 1 contains a survey of the bibliography of the subject and an introduction to the history of the language, part 2 a sketch of the grammar, part 3 a bibliography of works used for this introduction.

77172 COUROYER, B., Alternances de pronoms personnels en égyptien et en sémitique, *Revue Biblique,* Paris 84 (1977), 365-374.

Proceeding from the curious formulae in letters: (nṯrw) îmî ꜥnḫ.k (XIXth Dynasty) and (nṯrw) îmî n.k. ꜥnḫ (XXth-XXIst Dynasties), a mixture of oratio recta and oratio obliqua, the author discusses other instances of this use of pronouns, i.a. in oaths in legal documents and in the Instruction of Amenemope. He explains it from the idea that letters constitute for the writer a direct contact, in which he himself is "I", the adressee "you" and every other person "he". In the other instances the pronoun also refers to the interested person, e.g. the accused.

In the second section a similar use of pronouns in Semitic languages is dealt with.

77173 COUROYER, B., Le «glaive» de Béhémoth, *Revue Biblique,* Paris 84 (1977), 59-79.

Studying the exact meaning of the word ḥereb in Job 60, 19-20, which is normally translated with "sword", the author discusses in this connection the Egyptian loanword ḥrp mentioned together with sft and ḥpš, the word ḫ3b, "hippopotamus, (animal with) curved teeth", and the word ḫ3b, "sickle". L.Z.

77174 COX, J. Stevens, The Construction of an Ancient Egyptian Wig (c. 1400 B.C.) in the British Museum, *JEA* 63 (1977), 67-70, with 1 pl. and 3 fig.

The method of anchoring the hair to the foundation was found to be unlike any other published method. The hair was human, impregnated with a mixture of beeswax and resin, being composed of three hundred strands of about four hundred hairs. E. Uphill

CREUX, René, see our number 77079.

CROWFOOT, Elizabeth, see our number 77601.

77175 CROWFOOT PAYNE, J., A. KACZMARCZYK, and S.J. FLEMING, Forged Decoration on Predynastic Pots, *JEA* 63 (1977), 5-12, with 6 fig.

Adds a number of new examples to those forgeries recognized by Brunton. These are in the Ashmolean, Gulbenkian and University College collections and all were purchased. Results of tests on paint pigment and thermoluminescence dates of the fabrics are included, the latter giving dates of around 5000 B.P. with fairly high + − factors.
E. Uphill

77176 CRUZ-URIBE, Eugene, On the Wife of Merneptah, *GM* Heft 24 (1977), 23-31.

Nach ausführlicher Diskussion kommt Verfasser zu dem Ergebnis, daß in der Zeit Ramses II./Merneptah vier Frauen königlichen Blutes zu unterscheiden sind, die alle den Namen Isisnofret tragen:
1. Isisnofret — Gemahlin Ramses' II. und Mutter von Khaemwast und Merneptah.
2. Isisnofret — Tochter Ramses' II.
3. Isisnofret — Tochter des Khaemwast und Gemahlin des Merneptah.
4. Isisnofret — Tochter des Merneptah.

In einem Anhang wird auf zwei Statuen des Merneptah aus Luksor aufmerksam gemacht. Auf der Seite einer Statue ist das Relief einer

Isisnofret mit dem Titel einer großen königlichen Gemahlin, auf der anderen das Relief der Bantanat mit den Titel: Königstochter, Königsschwester, große königliche Gemahlin angebracht. Es wird vermutet, daß die Statuen Ramses II. gehörten und von Merneptah usurpiert wurden. Damit kann diese Isisnofret nicht die Gemahlin des Merneptah gewesen sein. *Inge Hofmann*

77177 CULICAN, W., Seals in Bronze Mounts, *Rivista di Studi Fenici*, Roma 5 (1977), 1-4, with 3 pl.

The author discusses seals in bronze mounts, some of which show Egyptian motifs or even are of Egyptian origin. *L.Z.*

77178 DĄBROWSKA-SMEKTAŁA, Elżbieta, New Parallels to the Spell 398 of the Coffin Texts, *in: Ägypten und Kusch*, 115-120, with 4 fig. and 1 pl.

Die Sammlung des Nationalmuseums von Warschau enthält zwei vollständige Holzsärge und einige Fragmente von Särgen, die zusammen mit anderen Objekten 1939 von Michałowski nach Polen gebracht worden waren. Der Katalog dieser Objekte wird nun fertiggestellt. Unter den Inschriften gibt es zwei Parallelen aus Meir zu Spruch 398, beide sind allerdings unvollständig und zeigen Lücken.
Inge Hofmann

77179 DANELIUS, Eva, The Identification of the Biblical "Queen of Sheba" with Hatshepsut, "Queen of Egypt and Ethiopia" — as Proclaimed by Immanuel Velikovsky — In the Light of New Archaeological Discoveries, *Kronos*, Glassboro, N.J. 1, No. 3 (Fall 1976), 3-18 and No. 4 (Winter 1976), 9-24, with 2 ill. and 1 map.

The author seriously defends the plausibility of Velikovsky's thesis of the identity of the Biblical Queen of Sheba with Hatshepsut. In order to achieve this she first presents a survey of scholarly opinion on the chronology and Velikovsky's method of attacking the problem. Then she devotes a lengthy discussion to the different opinions on the dating of Negev settlements on account of archaeological material. The low chronology of Glueck and Albright (as against the high one of Rothenberg and Aharoni) would perfectly fit Velikovsky's theory. In the third part she discusses the name of the Queen of Sheba as given by Josephus: Nikaule (= Makare?), the route of the queen via Qosseir and the Red Sea to Jerusalem, the extensive evidence from the Punt reliefs, which may point as well to the Gulf of Aqâba, and from the copper mining centre of Timna.

At the end the author states correctly that there remains, however, a slight difficulty concerning the dating of Ramses III and Ramses IV. Therefore certain conclusions should be postponed until after Velikovsky's final datings for these pharaohs (which in view of the death of the author will probably be a hopeless wish).

It is to be feared that not in all cases Velikovsky's revised chronology provides such an acceptable interpretation for events hitherto unexplained by the archaeologists as in the above case. *L.Z.*

77180 DARBY, William J., Paul GHALIOUNGUI [and] Louis GRIVETTI, Food: the Gift of Osiris, 2 volumes, London-New York-San Francisco, Academic Press, 1977 (17.5 × 22.5 cm; [Vol.I:] XXXIV + 452 + XLII p., colour frontispiece, numerous ill. and fig., 5 colour pl'., 4 ill. on endpapers; [Vol. II:] XXXIV + 425 + XLII p., colour frontispiece, 13 maps, numerous ill. and fig., 2 colour pl., 4 ill. on endpapers); rev. *BiOr* 35 (1978), 68-70 (Jac. J. Janssen).

Pr. set $25/£12.50

The two volumes contain the same introduction and the same indexes, only the table of contents, the lists of illustrations and the text itself (in total 877 p.) being different.

The lavishly illustrated volumes together consist of 19 chapters, dealing, apart from an introduction and a chapter on the nutritional state of the ancient Egyptians, with various kinds of food: meat (beef, pork, and various mammals); fowl and eggs; fish, reptiles, shell fish, molluscs and arthropods; sweeting agents (mainly honey); and salt, all in vol. I. Grains, bread, beer, wine (chapters 14 and 15), aquatic marsh plants, vegetables and legumes, fruit, fats and dairy products, and spices and herbs are discussed in vol. II. Each chapter is followed by some notes.

A large number of aspects are discussed, of philological and literary, religious and magical, botanical and zoological, medical and medicinal nature, while the evidence quoted reaches from the Prehistoric Period to the Roman Age and even to our own times. Numerous scholars of all fields are quoted while the illustration also covers all ages and subjects.

DARIS, Sergio, see our number 77144.

77181 DAUMAS, François, Le problème de la monnaie dans l'Égypte avant Alexandre, *Mélanges de l'École française de Rome. Antiquité,* Roma 89 (1977), 425-442, with 1 ill. and 1 pl.

The first part of the article deals with the š˘t and the *dbn* from the O. to the N.K. and is based on older literature (no reference is made to the fairly large evidence from Deir el-Medîna; see our numbers 3245 and

75361). The author then discusses the first Egyptian coins with the inscription *nbw nfr,* which date from the XXXth Dynasty. The problem why this happened so late the author attempts to solve by pointing out the metaphysical qualities ascribed to gold by the Egyptians.

77182   DAUMAS, François, Vers les vois mystiques en Égypte ancienne, *Nouvelles. Institut Catholique de Paris,* Paris, 1976-1977, No. 1 (Février 1977), 128-144.

After introductory remarks on the scantiness of knowledge of mysticism in ancient Egypt, the author first deals with the more regular visions and auditions of gods in royal inscriptions and those of the Hermetic tradition in the Graeco-Roman Period. Then he discusses the ancient Egyptians' attitude towards purity, ascetism (and drunkenness), personal piety, and silence (as opposed to the "hot man") as means of contact with the god. He then looks for testimonies concerning the hidden, interior aspects of life, for which he adduces evidence from the great Cairo hymn to Amon (the accent on the hidden nature of Amon seems witness of mystical extasy), from a prayer to Toth in P. Sallier VIII, 2-6 stressing the interior life, from the Lebensmüde, and from the biography of Petosiris at Tûna el-Gebel which testifies to his contact with the god at night.   *L.Z.*

77183   DAVEY, C.J., The Structure of the Meidum Pyramid, *JEA* 63 (1977), 174.

An answer to two points raised by Professor K. Mendelssohn in our number 76542.   *E. Uphill*

77184   DAVIES, W.V., Tut'ankhamūn's Razor-Box: a Problem in Lexicography, *JEA* 63 (1977), 107-111, with 2 pl.

Discusses the word *dg3* found in the label text on casket no. 68 and shows that it was one of two types of razor used in the New Kingdom. The word is also equated with Demotic *tk*.
See now also Guillemette Andreu, *JEA* 65 (1979), 166-167.   *E. Uphill*
DAVIES, W. Vivian, see also our number 77302.
DAVIS, Virginia Lee, see our number 77221.

77185   DAVIS, Whitney M., The Ascension-Myth in the Pyramid Texts, *JNES* 36 (1977), 161-179.

A new assessment of this important religious belief in the light of new discoveries since Breasted's pioneer work and using the Faulkner translation as a basis. The article is divided into nine sections making up a kind of 'Pilgrim's Progress' as the dead king ascended to the hereafter. These involve ritual cleansing, vindication, help from various deities, the deceased taking his place as a star, ritual transmission of his life force, arrival at the Celestial Gate, and the crossing of the Celestial River to arrive at the Fields of Rushes, leading to his final recognition by the sun-god. *E. Uphill*

77186 DEBIESME, Anne-Marie, Recherches sur l'apiculture en Asie Antérieure ancienne: Étude iconographique de l'abeille et essai de reconstitution des anciennes techniques apicoles, *Revue des archéologues et historiens d'art de Louvain,* Louvain 9 (1976), 264-265.

Abstract of a small thesis, in which i.a. Egyptian sources are used.
L.Z.

77187 DECKER, Wolfgang, Sportliche Elemente im altägyptischen Krönungsritual. Überlegungen zur Sphinx-Stele Amenophis' II., *SAK* 5 (1977), 1-20, with 1 plan.

In this study on the Sphinx Stela of Amenophis II the author first stresses its paramount importance for our knowledge about sport in ancient Egypt. He presents a new translation of the relevant passages of the text and argues that they reflect the "chivalrous" spirit of the XVIIIth Dynasty. However, of the four "sports" the text mentions, three (running, keeping the helm and shooting, riding being the exception) are connected with the old coronation and *heb-sed* rituals, as some details clearly demonstrate; e.g., the shooting of four arrows and the resemblance between the word *stỉ*, "shooting" and *Sṯtyw*, "Asiatics". The author concludes that there are close relations between the sportive performances of Amenophis II and the beginning of his reign.

77188 DECKER, Wolfgang, Zur Bogenprobe des Odysseus, *Kölner Beiträge zur Sportwissenschaft.* Jahrbuch der Deutschen Sporthochschule, Köln 6 (1977), 149-153, with 1 fig.

Some additional material to Burkert's article, our number 73124.

77189 Deir el-Bahari (Habitat préhistorique) fasc. II. Travaux de la mission archéologique de l'Université Jagellone en Égypte. Redacteur: Janusz K. Kozłowski, [Kraków], Nakładem Uniwersytetu Jagiellońskiego. Państowe Wydawnictwo Naukowe, [1977] (17 × 24 cm; 59 p., 1 plan, 21 fig. [2 folding], 3 ill., 4 tables [3 folding], 28 pl. with drawings) =

Zeszyty Naukowe Uniwersytetu Jagiellońskiego, 472 = Prace archeologiczne, zeszyt 25. Pr. Zł 20

Sequel to our number 76183.

The publication contains two chapters. The first one, by Wiesław Heflik and Janusz K. Kozłowski, deals with the geological, mineralogical and petrographical characteristics of the sediments in the circus of Deir el-Bahari. The second, by Barbara Drobniewicz, Bolesław Ginter and Janusz K. Kozłowski, discusses the site No. 16/74 and presents an analysis of the palaeolithic utensils found here, which can be arranged in four series, from Middle to Late Palaeolithic. For a summary, see *Recherches Archéologiques de 1976*, Kraków, L'institut d'archéologie de l'Université de Cracovie, 1977, 44-45.

77190   DEMBSKA, Albertyna i Krystyna ŁYCZKOWSKA, Wystawa w Muzeum Narodowym "Starożytne kultury Egiptu i Mezopotamii", *Przegląd Orientalistyczny*, Warszawa No. 4 (104), 1977, 342-344, with 4 pl.

Short note on an exhibition "The Ancient Cultures of Egypt and Mesopotamia", held in 1977 at the National Museum in Warsaw. For the catalogue compare our number 77726.   *L.Z.*

77191   DEMISCH, Heinz, Die Sphinx. Geschichte ihrer Darstellung von den Anfängen bis zur Gegenwart, [Stuttgart], Urachhaus, [1977] (20.5 × 29 cm; 300 p., 630 fig. and ill.). Pr. DM 88

Chapter 1 of this history of the sphinx, its role and representations is devoted to ancient Egypt (p. 16-39; notes p. 239-243). The author deals with the following subjects: the Sphinx of Gîza and the question whether it represents the Sun-god (his conclusion is that it actually represents the king adoring the Sun-god); various types of sphinxes, particularly lying figures, but also in a sitting, standing, and walking position; the sphinx treading down the enemies; the sphinx with parts of a bull's body (a type not occurring in Egypt); the composite figure of Tutu; the Sphinx in the Graeco-Roman Period. The chapter is, like the entire book, very well illustrated.

Other chapters that may be of importance to Egyptologists are: the Introduction about the sphinx in general and the Conclusions (chapter 13) discussing aspects of sphinx representations in various civilizations, particularly section 7: the sphinx and the sun; section 8: the Egyptian double sphinx (*aker*).

77192	DERCHAIN, Philippe, Geburt und Tod eines Gottes, *GM* Heft 24 (1977), 33-34.

Vgl. unsere Nummer 77298.

Hinsichtlich der Mythologie des 10. o. äg. Gaus wird der Frage nachgegangen, ob neben einem Gott, der nach Verfasser weiterhin *Ḥr m3ᶜty* gelesen werden muß, ein Gott *Ḥr m3ᶜ ḫrw* existierte; sie wird verneint und nur ein Horus mit dem Beinamen "der Beiden Gerechtigkeiten" angenommen. *Inge Hofmann*

77193	DERCHAIN-URTEL, Maria Theresia, Eine 'einfache' Szene im Mammisi von Dendera, *GM* Heft 25 (1977), 53-58.

Auf der Nordseite des Sanktuars des römischen Mammisis in Dendera wird in einer Szene die Geburt des Harsiese dargestellt: die vierzehn Mitglieder der "Thebanischen Neunheit" bringen dem Neugeborenen Gaben. Die Reihe beschließt Thot, der auf das Einfangen des Mondauges hinweist, das in seinen 15 Bestandteilen wieder hergestellt werden muß. Es werden Parallelen angeführt, in denen diese "Arbeit" beschrieben werden; jeweils 14 Götter bringen Produkte, und Thot folgt als fünfzehnter.

Die auf dem Mammisi dargestellte Szene, in der Harsiese in der Mitte auf einem Sockel steht und von Isis und Osiris mit jeweils nach oben und unten ausgestreckten Händen gehalten wird, wird als Hieroglyphe für den Aufgang der Sonne gedeutet. *Inge Hofmann*

DÉROBERT, Dominique, see our number 77153.

DERRIDA, Jacques, see our number 77782.

77194	DESANGES, Jehan, Philologica quaedam necnon Aethiopica, *in: Mélanges offerts à Léopold Sédar Senghor,* Langues, Littérature — Histoire anciennes. Les Nouvelles Éditions Africaines, 107-120.

Die Untersuchung befaßt sich mit folgenden Stellen antiker Schriftsteller: 1. Plinius d. Ältere, H.N., VI, 190: im Süden von Meroe wohnen die Hipsodoren, die sich ihren Körper rot bemalen. Die Erklärung, wonach diese sich ihrer schwarzen Hautfarbe schämten (hi pudore), wird abgelehnt. II. Plinius d. Ältere, H.N., XXI, 29: Zimt als Produkt der "barbarischen" Küste, deren Lage und ihr Bekanntsein seit der hellenistischen Zeit werden dargelegt. III. Expositio totius mundi et gentium, 35: untersucht wird eine Stelle dieser Schrift aus der Zeit Konstantins, die sich mit Aromata und der "barbarischen" Küste befaßt. IV. Synesius, epist. 122: Priester der Axumiten sollen in der libyschen Wüste kurz nach 400 n. Chr. kriegerisch gegen Stämme der Kyrenaika vorgegangen sein. Es dürfte sich dabei wohl um Priester von Ausigda gehandelt haben. V. Hieronymus, epist. 125, 3: statt "ad urbem maximam" muß "ad urbem Auxumam" gelesen werden; dann war es Axum, das auf dem Weg zum Paradies lag. *Inge Hofmann*

DESROCHES NOBLECOURT, Christiane, see our numbers 77029, 77211 and 77295.

77195   DINKLER, Erich, König Ezana von Aksum und das Christentum. Ein Randproblem der Geschichte Nubiens, *in: Ägypten und Kusch*, 121-132, with 1 pl.

Es wird der Frage nachgegangen, ob der im zweiten Drittel des 4. Jahrhunderts lebende König Ezana das Christentum zur Staatsreligion seines aksumitischen Reiches erhoben und auf dieser Basis seine glänzenden Siege erfochten hat und ob das Christentum Nubien bereits im 4. Jahrhundert vom Atbara her erreichte. *Inge Hofmann*

DITTMAR, Johanna, see our number 77120.

77196   DOETSCH-AMBERGER, Ellen, Zwei Gemmenamulette aus Kölner Privatbesitz, *GM* Heft 26 (1977), 7-12 with 4 ill.

Es werden zwei Gemmenamulette mit ägyptischen Motiven vorgestellt: 1. Gemme mit Sonnensymbolik. Im Zentrum der Bildseite sitzt ein Kind mit Sonnenscheibe auf dem Kopf auf einem Lotoskelch, umgeben von einem Löwen, einem Krokodil, einer Mumie mit Sonnenscheibe auf dem Kopf, einem Skarabäus, einem Falken, einem Bock, einem sitzenden Hund, einem Ibis, einer sitzenden menschlichen Gestalt; auf der Rückseite befindet sich eine siebenzeilige Inschrift. 2. Gemme mit kompletter XABPAX-Formel. Auf der Bildseite ist Thot auf einem Sockel stehend in Menschengestalt mit Ibiskopf und Atefkrone, in den Händen *w3s*-Zepter und *s3*-Zeichen dargestellt, umgeben von der Inschrift BAINXWWWX. Auf der Rückseite steht ein ithyphallischer Affe mit Schlangenkopf und langem Schwanz im Zentrum, umgeben von einem Uroboros und der Inschrift ABPAXWBPAWWWEPBHΘ. Vor der Affen stehen die Buchstaben XOC, hinter ihm POX, in den Händen hält er ein H. *Inge Hofmann*

77197   DOLLFUS, Marc-Adrien, La mission de L. Méhédin en Égypte (1861), *BSFE* No. 80 (octobre 1977), 7-20, with 2 ill.

Léon Eugène Méhédin (Laigle, Orne, 1828 — Bonsecours, près de Rouen, 1905) eut une carrière assez mouvementée, et parfois un rôle de précurseur. Après des études d'architecture à Paris, il prend parti pour le futur Napoléon III, qui sera son protecteur. Attaché photographique aux Armées, il dresse panoramas et plans. Dès 1854, il manifeste de l'intérêt pour l'Égypte, peut-être sous l'influence de Lottin de Laval. (Sur ce dernier, on trouvera pp. 11-12 des compléments au *Who was who,* notamment quelques mots de son procédé de moulage, utilisé en Égypte déjà par lui en 1844 et 1850, ensuite par Méhédin; documents au musée de Bernay). Méhédin, en mission longtemps préparée, photographie Abou Simbel, extérieur et intérieur (!) ainsi que Philae, et moule seul en quatre mois l'obélisque oriental de Louqsor. Le khédive Ismaîl le décore, et favorise le transport des moulages à Paris. La Légion d'honneur, longuement sollicitée, viendra finalement, après une mission d'archéologie au Mexique. Méhédin projeta pendant plus de vingt ans un musée de plein air. Il laissa un énorme album photographique, "Souvenirs de ma vie", et divers documents, conservés au Louvre et aux Archives Nationales.   *J. Custers*

DOLPHIN, Lambert T., see our number 77543.

77198   DOMNING, Daryl P., Some Examples of Ancient Egyptian Ropework, *CdE* LII, No. 103 (1977), 49-61, with 4 fig.

L'auteur étudie en technicien la fabrication de quelques cables et noeuds égyptiens d'après des exemplaires conservés au Lowie Museum of Anthropology, University of California, Berkeley et met en lumière les différences technologiques qui les séparent des méthodes européennes.   *Ph. Derchain*

77199   DONADONI, S., [Jebel Barkal], *Nyame Akuma,* Calgary No. 11 (November 1977), 50-52, with 1 fig.

In der letzten Grabungskampagne wurden am Jebel Barkal die Komplexe B 1300 und B 1400 freigelegt; B 1300 besteht in der Hauptsache aus Ziegelsteinen und ist nach Norden orientiert, B 1400 besteht aus Stein und ist nach Nordwesten orientiert. Zwischen beiden Komplexen liegen Sandsteinblöcke. Westlich von B 1300 und nördlich von B 1400 liegt ein großes Gebäude aus Ziegeln, das fast viereckig ist und im Augenblick als "Palast" bezeichnet wird. Das Programm des Aufsuchens älterer, vormeroitischer Komplexe wurde weitergeführt.
   Inge Hofmann

77200   DONADONI, Sergio, Sulla situazione giuridica della Nubia nell' impero egiziano, *in: Ägypten und Kusch,* 133-137.

Es wird die rechtliche und verwaltungsmäßige Situation untersucht, die zwischen den kolonisatorischen Ägyptern auf der einen und den unterworfenen Nubiern auf der anderen Seite seit der 12. Dynastie bestand. Während der 18. Dynastie kam es zu einer wirklichen Zusammenarbeit; in der Verwaltung der ägyptischen Provinz läßt sich oft nicht feststellen, ob es sich um einen ägyptischen Beamten oder um einen einheimischen Herrscher handelt. Das Verhältnis zwischen den ägyptischen Beamten und den Stammeshäuptlingen scheint nicht wesentlich anders als in Syrien gewesen zu sein; eine Ausnahme bildet allerdings die Institution des *s3 nswt*. *Inge Hofmann*

77201 DONDELINGER, Edmund, Der Obelisk. Ein Steinmal ägyptischer Weltanschauung, Graz, Akademische Druck- u. Verlagsanstalt, 1977 (22.5 × 28 cm; 103 p., 2 maps, 1 plan, 124 fig., 24 pl.); rev. *Antike Welt* 9, No. 3 (1978), 62-63 (anonymous).

The book contains more than the title suggests, several chapters discussing specific religious concepts or the development of Egyptian religion the connection of which with obelisks is rather loose. A large number of scientific views of various scholars are quoted, including the most recent ones (e.g. our number 77513), but the author does not defend a theory of his own, the study being intended for the modern Egypt traveller.

The first chapter deals with erected stones, masseben, menhirs, hermes, etc. Chapter 2 is devoted to the words for obelisk, Arab. *misalla,* Eg. *tḫn* and *mnw*. Proceeding from the determinative of *tḫnwy* in *P.T.* §1178a, a bull's head, the author discusses in chapter 3 the *iwn*-pillar as a symbol of fertility. In chapter 4 *bnbn* and *bnw* are dealt with, in chapter 5 primeval water and primeval hill, while chapter 6, in which all these concepts are connected with the obelisk, presents a theological explanation of the pyramidion.

Chapter 7 gives a survey of the Egyptian cosmogonies. Chapter 8 discusses the Pyramid Age, chapter 9 the Sun-religion and its history during the O.K., with a reconstruction of the religious "parties" of Horus, Re (of Heliopolis and Letopolis) and Atum.

Chapter 10 is devoted to the Sun-sanctuaries of the O.K. and the growing influence of the Osiris cult; chapter 11 to obelisks as a pair, the obelisks of the M. and N.K. Chapter 12 presents a description of the making and transport of the obelisks, while the last chapter, beginning with the Lateran obelisk, its history and scenes, also deals with representations of obelisks on scarabs and the history of the obelisk in the Amarna Period and afterwards.

77202 DONDELINGER, Edmund, Die Treibtafel des Herodot am Bug des ägyptischen Nilschiffes, *Almogaren,* Graz 7 (1976), 1977, 234-237, with 1 fig.

Abstract of our number 76205.

77203 DONOHUE, V.A., A Bibliography of Elise Jenny Baumgartel, *JEA* 63 (1977), 48-51.

Contains an appreciation of this prehistorian and lists 35 items of her publications including her five main books and studies.   *E. Uphill*

DRENKHAHN, Rosemarie, see our numbers 77477 and 77478.

DREYER, Günter, see our number 77389.

DROBNIEWICZ, Barbara, see our number 77189.

77204 DUNAND, Maurice, Les rois de Sidon au temps des Perses, *Mélanges de l'Université Saint-Joseph,* Beyrouth 49 (1975-76), 489-499.

In this article on the kings of Sidon in the Achaemenid Period there are some references to the role of the king of Sidon in Cambyses' campaign to Egypt.   *L.Z.*

77205 DZIERŻYKRAY-ROGALSKI, Tadeusz, Fosse commune dans l'Allée de Sphinx conduisant au temple d'Amon à Karnak, *Africana-Bulletin,* Warszawa 25 (1976), 37-49, with 6 pl., 1 plan and 1 fig.

The author analyses the skeletal remains of several persons, found at three spots behind the avenue of the sphinxes near the entrance of the Amon temple at Karnak.   *L.Z.*

77206 EATON, E.R. and Hugh McKERRELL, Near Eastern Alloying and Some Textual Evidence for the Early Use of Arsenical Copper, *World Archaeology,* London 8 (1976-1977), 169-191, with 3 maps, 11 tables and 1 fig.

In this article on the evidence for arsenic copper in the ancient Near East the authors argue that the word $\underline{d}^cm$ may be better identified as a word for arsenical or arsenic-coated copper, and that later, as the use of this material became less common, it was also used of precious metals in general.   *L.Z.*

77207 EATON-KRAUß, Marianne, The *khat* Headdress to the End of the Amarna period, *SAK* 5 (1977), 21-39.

The author discusses the *khat (ḫ3t)* headdress which resembles the *nemes* but differs from it in that it shows no lappets; it is a bag-like kerchief. The general term for it is ^cfnt, the word *khat* indicating a

royal headdress, a pendant of the *nemes*. It occurs already in the O.K., but particularly during the XVIIIth Dynasty. It is also worn by goddesses, and that Tiyi and Nefertiti are wearing it may indicate that they were venerated as female deities.
On p. 33-39 a catalogue (37 numbers) of royal statues wearing the *khat*.

77208 EDEL, Elmar, Die keilschriftliche Wiedergabe von ♀🕮𓏺 in den Ramsesbriefen, *GM* Heft 25 (1977), 59-62.

Der keilschriftkundige ägyptische Briefschreiber stellt die typisch ägyptische Phrase '*nḫ wḏ3 snb* im Akkadischen um zu *snb wḏ3 'nḫ*. Die wahrscheinlichste Erklärung dafür ist die, daß '*nḫ wḏ3 snb* als hieroglyphische Schreibung zwar völlig unveränderlich in seiner Stellung war, daß man aber in der freien Rede an keine feste Wortstellung bei dieser Formel gebunden war, denn es gibt auch in ägyptischen Briefen Umstellungen.   *Inge Hofmann*

EDELSTEIN, Gershon, see our number 77266.

EDWARDS, I.E.S., see our number 77145.

77209 EGLOFF, Michel, Kellia. La poterie copte. Quatre siècles d'artisanat et d'échanges en Basse-Égypte, Genève, Georg. Librairie de l'Université, [1977] (26.6 × 36.6 cm; Tome 1 [Texte]: 233 p., colour frontispiece, 3 fig., 3 tables; Tome 2 [Planches]: [IV p.] + 121 pl. [4 in colour] containing fig., ill., 3 plans and 3 maps, 9 tables [5 folding]) = Recherches suisses d'archéologie copte dirigées par Rodolphe Kasser, 3.

Sequel to our number 72369.
This volume is concerned with Coptic pottery. On p. 191-195, on the origins of pottery, there is a short survey tracing back to ancient Egyptian technique and traditions.
At the end of the book summaries in French, German and English.
                                                                                               L.Z.

77210 L'Égypte ancienne au Musée de Grenoble, [no place, no publisher, no date] (19 × 21 cm; 32 p., 1 map, 39 ill., 8 colour ill., colour ill. on cover).

This is a guide to the Egyptian collection in the Musée de Peinture et Sculpture at Grenoble, intended for the general public.
From the collection, which largely consists of the objects collected by the Comte Louis de Saint Ferriol, only some choice pieces are mentioned and these within a continuous description. They are

represented by photographs. From the most famous ones we mention: the Qubân stela of Ramses II (No. 5); reliefs from the Montu-temple at Armant, among which a very fine one of the kneeling Tuthmosis III (No. 16); a stela of the vizier User (No. 2); the mummy cases of the Amon priest Nehemes-Montu (XXIst Dynasty; No. 48) and of a Psamtik (No. 22). Several minor objects (shabtis, amulets, bronzes, etc.) are of a high quality.

A complete, up-to-date guide to the collection has been published by Gabrielle Kueny and Jean Yoyotte in 1979 ("Grenoble, musée des Beaux-Arts. Collection égyptienne, Paris, Editions de la Réunion des musées nationaux, 1979.)

77211 L'Égypte des Pharaons, Marcq-en-Baroeul, Fondation Anne et Albert Prouvost Septentrion, Octobre 1977-Janvier 1978 (21 × 21 cm; 45 [unnumbered] p., 1 map, 28 ill., 2 colour ill. on cover).

Catalogue of an exhibition of objects from the Louvre Museum in Marcq-en-Baroeul (N. France), with a preface and an introduction by Mme Ch. Desroches Noblecourt. The captions to the 103 numbers have been written by members of the staff of the Louvre Museum. The objects illustrate as well art and social life as the world of the dead, and are briefly described. Among them was the photographic reconstruction of the tomb of Nofertari. On the last pages an introduction to Egyptomania in France and five objects pertaining to that subject.

77212 ELANSKAYA, A.I., Нубийская стела X в. с. греческой надписью, *in:* Мероэ, 273-277, with 1 ill. on a pl. and a French summary on p. 300.

"Die Nubische Stele mit griechischer Inschrift vom 10. Jahrundert." Der Artikel befaßt sich mit der Analyse und Wiederherstellung der griechischen Inschrift auf einer Stele, die 1970 in Amantago im Süden von Alt-Dongola gefunden wurde. Der Text enthält wahrscheinlich den Namen Taya, einer Frau, die am 26. Mai 939 gestorben ist. Dank des genauen Datums bietet die Stele eine wichtige Hilfe in der Epigraphie und gibt zusätzliches Material für die Regeln der Datierung. Diese Regeln waren in Nubien an der Wende vom 1. zum 2. Jahrtausend in Gebrauch.   *Inge Hofmann*

77213 ELANSKAYA, A. I., Zum Gedenken an P. V. Jernstedt (1890-1966), *Wissenschaftliche Zeitschrift der Martin-Luther Universität Halle-Wittenberg,* Gesellschafts-und sprachwissenschaftliche Reihe, Halle-Wittenberg 26 (1977), 93-99.

German translation (by Peter Nagel) of our number 67289, followed by a bibliography. A list of obituaries has been added.

77214 ELANSKAYA, Alla I., ⲬⲈ en tant qu' indice d' irréalité en copte, in: *Ägypten und Kusch,* 139-142.

Die irreale Funktion von ⲬⲈ wird wohl dadurch bestimmt, daß es eine direkte oder indirekte Rede einleitet. Anders als bei einem beobachteten Ereignis, richtet sich die Beschreibung eines solchen, indem die Rede einer anderen Person mitgeteilt wird, an deren Imagination, d.h. Irrealität. *Inge Hofmann*

77215 van ELDEREN, Bastiaan and James M. ROBINSON, The Second Season of the Nag Hammadi Excavation. 22 November — 29 December 1976, *Newsletter ARCE* Nos. 99/100 (Winter/Spring 1977), 36-54, with 2 maps and 4 ill.

Sequel to our numbers 76671 and 76672.
The authors first give background information on the Pachomian monastery at Faw Qibli and then present a report of the 1976 excavations on the site as well as a summary. Among the ancillary projects of the 1976 season was the continuation of the work on the VIth Dynasty tomb of Thauti (Tomb 73) at Gebel el-Târif. The same article has also been published (without the ill.) in *GM* Heft 24 (1977), 57-73. *L.Z.*

77216 EMANUELE, P. Daniel, Ancient Square Rigging, With and Without Lifts, *The International Journal of Nautical Archaeology and Underwater Exploration,* London 6 (1977), 181-185, with 3 ill.

In this article on ancient ship's rigging with or without lifts some attention is paid to Egyptian ships, as depicted in the Punt reliefs of the Deir el-Bahri temple. *L.Z.*

77217 ENDESFELDER, Erika, Sklaven (ḥmw) in der Nekropole von Deir el Medine, *Altorientalische Forschungen,* Berlin 5 (1977), 17-24.

Proceeding from the assumption that the word ḥm means "slave" in the XIXth and XXth Dynasties, the author lists and discusses the evidence for female slaves in Deir el-Medîna, as well in the service of the community as also in private possession. She concludes that persons designated as ḥm, ḥmt, ḥmw or b3kw were slaves in the juridical sense of the word.
Compare also our number 77727. *L.Z.*

77218 ENDESFELDER, Erika, Über die ökonomischen und sozialen Verhältnisse der Reiche von Napata und Meroe, *in: Ägypten und Kusch,* 143-164.

Es wird versucht, allgemeine historische Gesetzmäßigkeiten, die bei frühen Staatenbildungen eine Rolle spielen, auf die Reiche von Napata und Meroe anzuwenden, und die ökonomischen und sozialen Prozesse darzustellen, die im Raum von Kusch vor sich gegangen sein, zur Herausbildung des napatanisch-meroitischen Staates geführt und schließlich auch dessen Untergang bestimmt haben könnten. Nach einem kurzen historischen Abriß wird die ökonomische Basis der Reiche von Napata und Meroe hinsichtlich folgender Punkte untersucht: Landwirtschaft, Viehzucht, Handwerk mit besonderer Beachtung der Einführung der Eisengewinnung und -bearbeitung, Handel. Abschließend werden die gesellschaftlichen und politischen Verhältnisse in den Reichen von Napata und Meroe dargestellt; der Staat, die Verwendung von Sklaven und die Priesterschaft werden genauer untersucht. Die Verfasserin kommt zu dem Ergebnis, daß auf Grund des jahrhundertelangen ägyptischen Einflusses bei der Herausbildung des eigenen Staates weitgehend ägyptische Formen gewählt wurden. Auf kulturellem Gebiet wird immer stärker eine eigenständige Entwicklung sichtbar.. Während zu Beginn des 1. nachchristlichen Jahrtausends die Zentralgewalt im Kernland verfiel, nahm die Entwicklung in Unternubien einen ungeheuren Aufschwung. Das Privateigentum setzte sich durch, ganz im Gegensatz zu Meroe, das dieses Stadium nicht erreicht hatte und so zwangsläufig zugrunde gehen mußte. Die Eroberung durch Ezana war nur ein Schlußstrich, nicht aber die eigentliche Ursache des Unterganges. *Inge Hofmann*

77219 ENGELS, Hermann, Quadrature of the Circle in Ancient Egypt, *Historia Mathematica,* New York and London 4 (1977), 137-140.

The author attempts to find a simple explanation for the fact that the area of circle was approximated by a square with great precision by the ancient Egyptian mathematicians. *L.Z.*

77220 ERTMAN, Earl L., A Talatat Scene of Foreign Female Prisoners, *Newsletter ARCE* Nos. 99/100 (Winter/Spring), 17.

Abstract of a paper.

77221 𓁹 for Eye. Egyptian Images & Inscriptions. April 2, 1977 through February, 1978, New Orleans Museum of Art, Wisner Education Wing, [1977] (22.8 × 15.3 cm; 34 unnumbered pages, ill. on covers, fig. on endpapers, 2 maps, 8 fig., 18 colour ill.).

Catalogue of an exhibition in the New Orleans Museum of Art, consisting mainly of objects from the Museum of Fine Arts, Boston, to which have been added two objects from private collections (nos. 16 and 36, not illustrated) and five from the museum itself (four shawabtis, nos. 68-71).

After a foreword by Virginia Lee Davis and an introduction by Annabelle Herbert and Margaret Ann Henderson the booklet is divided into short sections, partly consisting of quotations from Egyptian texts in translation by various scholars, illustrated by small colour photographs of objects here exhibited. Only a few of them are described. We mention among them a wooden pectoral with glass and stone inlay representing Isis and Nephthys, from the XIXth Dynasty (no. 17; from the museum's own collection).

At the end the catalogue itself (86 numbers), with technical details, and a short bibliography.

77222   The Facsimile Edition of the Nag Hammadi Codices. Codex I. Published under the Auspices of the Department of Antiquities of the Arab Republic of Egypt in Conjunction with the United Nations Educational, Scientific and Cultural Organization, Leiden, E.J. Brill, 1977 (24 × 33 cm; XXXI p., 144 pl.); rev. *Biblical Archaeologist* 42 (1979), 249-250 (George W. MacRae); *Rivista* 52 (1978), 268-272 (Tito Orlandi).   Pr. cloth fl.280

Sequel to our number 76242.

In the preface, in Arabic and English, James M. Robinson describes the recent history of the codex and enumerates the publications of its texts. The plates bear photographs of the 138 p., while the last two are devoted to the 68 unidentified inscribed fragments.   *L.Z.*

77223   The Facsimile Edition of the Nag Hammadi Codices. Codices IX and X. Published under the Auspices of the Department of Antiquities of the Arab Republic of Egypt in Conjunction with the United Nations Educational, Scientific and Cultural Organization, Leiden, E.J. Brill, 1977 (24 × 33 cm; XXVII p., 144 pl.); rev. *Biblica* 59 (1978), 572-574 (H. Quecke); *Biblical Archaeologist* 42 (1979), 249-250 (George W. MacRae); *Rivista* 52 (1978), 268-272 (Tito Orlandi).   Pr. fl.280

Sequel to our preceding number.

The preface, by James M. Robinson and, as usually, in Arabic and English, presents the technical details of the two codices. It relates their finding and the history of their study, and gives a minute description of their covers and outer appearances.

Both texts are fragmentary, codex X even to an extreme degree, and, since it lacks parallel texts, the reconstruction of its pagination and the placing of the fragments have been very difficult.

The plates bear photographs of the cover, the 74 pages and numerous tiny fragments of codex IX (pls. 1-78), and of the cover and the remains of the pages of codex X (pls. 81-144). From this text there are at least some more or less connected words of the first 42 pages; of p. 43-68 only very little has been preserved.

77224 FAGAN, Brian M., Augusta Mariette and Verdi's *Aïda*, *Antiquity* 51 (1977), 55.

The author argues, on the authority of Professor Charles Carrol, that although the inspiration for Verdi's "Aïda" came from Mariette, he never set eyes on the drafts of the libretto.
See, however, our number 76388.
A reply to the present article by Meltzer in *Antiquity* 52 (1978), 50-51.

FALES, F. Mario, see our numbers 77013 and 77014.

77225 FARAG, Sami, Gamal WAHBA and Adel FARID, Reused Blocks from a Temple of Amasis at Philae. A Preliminary Report (Notizie da File, I), *Oriens Antiquus* 16 (1977), 315-324, with 4 fig. and 18 pl.

The authors reconstitute two scenes pertaining to Isis and Hathor from reused blocks of a temple of Amasis at Philae, the existence of which pushes forward the history of the Isis worship at Philae at least two centuries.   L.Z.

FARID, Adel, see our preceding number.

77226 FAULKNER, R. O., The Ancient Egyptian Coffin Texts. Volume II. Spells 355-787, Warminster, Aris & Phillips Ltd, [1977] (16.7 × 24 cm; X + 308 p.); rev. *CdE* LIV, No. 107 (1979), 74-76 (Ph. Derchain).   Pr. £10

Sequel to our number 73226.
Apart from a preface, a list of abbreviations and some addenda and corrigenda to vol. I, the volume contains translations of spells 355-787 (= De Buck's edition, vol. V and VI), each spell followed by a few notes. References to de Buck's edition are placed in the margin.
Since vol. II would have been inconveniently bulky if it had also contained the spells of de Buck's volume VII and the indexes, these are dealt with in a third volume that has appeared in 1978.

FAULKNER, Raymond O., see also our number 77710.

77227 FAZZINI, Richard and James MANNING, Archaeological Work at Thebes by the Brooklyn Museum under the Auspices of the American Research Center in Egypt, 1975-1977, *Newsletter ARCE* Nos. 101/102 (Summer/Fall 1977), 12-27, with 4 ill., 1 map and 1 plan.

The first part of the article is concerned with work in the precinct of the Mut temple at Karnak, carried out by the Brooklyn Museum. After a preliminary survey in the first season (Jan.-Febr. 1976), the Mut expedition started its second season in December 1976 with work on the Khonsu-pa-chered temple in the N.E. corner of the precinct of which the history is discussed. In the first court of the Mut temple a headless torso of a Divine Consort of Amun from the XXVth or XXVIth Dynasty was discovered. Considerable attention was paid to the study of the Sakhmet statues of which the colossal one in the second court of the Mut temple may be attributed to Sheshonq I. The main discovery was that of a gateway of Taharqa, in the vicinity of which also a Ptolemaic chapel was cleared.

The rest of the article is devoted to clearing, recording and conserving activities in the tomb of Ramses II in the Valley of the Kings. *L.Z.*

77228 FEDDEN, Robin, Egypt. Land of the Valley, [London], John Murray, [1977] (13.5 × 22 cm; 158 p., 1 map, 32 pl.). Pr. £5.50

In this general book on modern Egypt there are several references to ancient Egypt, for which see the index.

There is also a German edition: Ägypten. Fünftausend Jahre Niltal, München, Prestel Verlag, 1978. *L.Z.*

FEUCHT, Erika, see our number 77054.

FILLIOL, René, see our numbers 77768, 77769, 77770 and 77771.

77229 FISCHER, Henry G., Encore *Sh3.śn (RdE* 24, 64-71), *RdE* 29 (1977), 226.

Complément bibliographique à l'article mentionné dans le titre (notre No. 72232). *Ph. Derchain*

77230 FISCHER, Henry G., The Evolution of Composite Hieroglyphs in Ancient Egypt, *Metropolitan Museum Journal,* New York 12 (1977), 5-19, with 10 fig.

Deals with two types of composites — one in which the elements impinge, the second in which one element traverses the other. The second type was scarcely used before the Heracleopolitan Period; it became progressively more frequent thereafter, with increasing lack of concern for the compatibility of the elements thus combined. This evolution parallels other developments in Egyptian art, which similarly violated the classical propriety of the O.K. The hieroglyphic examples are dated as closely as possible, with particular attention to the older periods down to the late N.K. *H.G. Fischer*

77231 FISCHER, Henry G., *Ḥrw* 'Bottom' and *t3ḥt* 'Dregs' (Brooklyn 57.140), *JEA* 63 (1977), 176.

Suggests the reading 'you should give the bottom of your bowls and the dregs of your jars' for this passage (see our number 74356, p. 59).
E. Uphill

77232 FISCHER, Henry G., More Ancient Egyptian Names of Dogs and Other Animals, *Metropolitan Museum Journal*, New York 12 (1977), 173-178, with 1 fig. and 4 ill.

Ten additions to our numbers 58333 and 61239, extending the evidence down through the Late Period. Also an incomplete name, attributed to a N.K. cat. *H.G. Fischer*

77233 FISCHER, Henry George, The Orientation of Hieroglyphs. Part I. Reversals, New York, The Metropolitan Museum of Art, 1977 (23.5 × 31 cm; XXIV + 147 p., frontispiece, 126 fig. including plans) = Egyptian Studies 2.

This volume of the series is devoted to those situations which call for a change in the usual rightward facing of the hieroglyphic signs and the right to left direction of their reading. The author illustrates his argument by referring to a large number of actual objects of various kinds (stelae, statues, temple walls, etc.), all presented in drawing. Moreover, the notes contain a wealth of additional information.
The first chapter begins with a discussion of the unity of Egyptian art and writing and of the dominant rightward orientation of the signs. Three factors are responsible for the reversal of a figure, in art as well as in writing: confrontation (e.g., the elements of a royal pectoral), symmetry (e.g., on portals and offering slabs), and concordance between scene and writing. The concordant reversal may be due to factors beyond the immediate vicinity of the scene or inscription. Several categories are discussed: backs and fronts of portable objects (knife handles, daggers, etc.), stelae (reversals resulting from their original position), the sides and backs of statues, pendants and pectorals, coffins, and temples.
Chapter 2, called "Vocative Reversals", deals with statements proceeding from the mouth of a person and, therefore, orientated away from him. Special cases are the reversal of *ḏd.f* preceding a

statement and of *wḏ-nswt* preceding the adressee.

In chapter 3 Fischer discusses concordant reversals within a single line: reversal of subject (offerings and their bearers), of object (e.g., the singing "to" musical accompaniment), reversals relating to divinities (e.g. of divine names and of the terminal phrase in ritual captions), and some other special instances.

In chapter 4 reversal of individual hieroglyphs is studied, particularly of the signs 𓊽 and 𓊨, in which the sail is blown backwards (actually this is seldom the case in the inscriptions); the writings of *šmt iwt*, "going and coming" and of *ᶜk prt*, "entering and going forth", with the legs-sign reversed; the sign ᐱ or ᐳ, 𓃭 and ⎮.

Chapter 5 presents a chronological synopsis, discussing the development from the Archaic to the Ramesside Period.

In the Appendix four groups of texts are translated and commented upon: those on the wooden statue from Deir el-Medîna, MMA 65.114; on a fragment in Lepsius, *Denkmäler, Text* I, p. 127; on Cairo C.G. 1431 (see *Urk. IV,* 118) and on Cairo C.G. 20513 (a F.I.P. stela).

Egyptian Studies 3 will deal with retrograde orientation and will include an index to both volumes.

77234 FISCHER, Henry G., The Provenance of a Fragment Attributed to *Ḥnw* at Saqqâra, *JEA* 63 (1977), 175.

The writer suggests that this fragment mentioned by Edel is probably contemporary with Unis of the Fifth Dynasty, while the tomb at the causeway is at the end of the Sixth Dynasty.   E. Uphill

77235 FISCHER, Henry G., Some Iconographic and Literary Comparisons, in: *Fragen an die altägyptische Literatur,* 155-170, with 11 fig.

Stressing the importance of comparing iconographic and textual evidence the author deals with four subjects: 1. The serpent of the Shipwrecked Sailor 62-66 is presumably rather to be attributed to the teratological hybrids, monstruously looking apotropaic demons, than to the other category of hybrids, the syncretistic representations. 2. The concept of the son as his father's "staff of old age", first attested in the M.K., is expressed in puns in the Eloquent Peasant B1, 22 where *Nmty-nḫt,* son of *'Isry* uses a stick of green tamarisk (*îsr*) to beat the peasant, and in B1, 278, when the peasant, in appealing to *Rnsy* son of *Mrw,* says "I have plied my sounding pole (*mry*)". 3. The servants of Djedi (Pap. Westcar 7, 15-16) possibly just rub and massage his feet and head, no oil or unguent being used, for which the author adduces some pictorial evidence. 4. Pap. Westcar 5,15 is illustrated by fish pendants, actual and depicted, representing the catfish (Synodontis) with its dangerous fins, which are characteristic of the M.K.

For the courtly diversions of females dressed as males (Pap. Westcar 5, 1ff.) there is also pictorial evidence in M.K. tombs, which may be explained by the assumption of royal manners and prerogatives by the provincial governors of the XIIth Dynasty.

These connections stress the M.K. setting of the stories of the O.K. Pharaohs.
L.Z.

FISCHER, Henry G., see also our number 77024.

FLEMING, S.J. see our number 77175.

77236 FLINDER, Alexander, The Island of Jezirat Fara'un. Its Ancient Harbour, Anchorage and Marine Defence Installations, *The International Journal of Nautical Archaeology and Underwater Exploration,* London 6 (1977), 127-139, with 4 plans, 1 map and 8 ill.

The author notes that Rothenberg's argument that the island of Jezirat Fara'un, some 10 km south of Eilat and 250 m offshore the Sinai mainland, was a Pharaonic mining harbour is convincing. *L.Z.*

77237 FOSTER, John L., The "Hymn to Osiris" as a Literary Monument, *Newsletter ARCE* Nos. 99/100 (Winter/Spring 1977), 13.

Abstract of a paper.

77238 FOSTER, John L., Thought Couplets and Clause Sequences in a Literary Text: The Maxims of Ptah-Hotep, Toronto, Canada, The Society for the Study of Egyptian Antiquities, 1977 (14.6 × 20.6 cm; [V +] 45 p., 26 p. of hieroglyphic transcriptions, 4 charts) = The Society for the Study of Egyptian Antiquities Publications, 5; rev. *Newsletter SSEA* 7, No. 4 (August 1977), 23-24 (David Lorton).

After an introduction on couplet patterning in the preface and a definition of the so-called thought couplet in the introduction, the author points out, in part I of the Discussion the importance of Pap. Prisse, supported by the B.M. Papyri, to establish the verse point structure. However, of the 37 maxims he has only taken into consideration the maxims 1-3, 5-9, 11-14, 16-20, 22, 24 and 26. Part II compares the maxims with the Hymn to the Nile. After a clarification of the 4 distribution charts containing sentence constructions in Part III, conclusions are drawn in Part IV as to the occurrence of sentence patterns in the first or second line of the thought couplet, or in one of the two elements in such lines, if present. Part V is concerned with the principles governing the sequence of independent and dependent clauses, while Part VI deals with the various indicators, such as $ỉw$, nn, pw, vetitive m and particles, and Part VII with problems of co- and subordination, negation and emphasis. In the last part (VIII) the author applies the rules of positions and sequence derived from verse-pointed maxims to those without, and draws conclusions as to the importance of the concept of the thought couplet in Egyptian literary style and the dependency of the relationship of grammatical forms upon their position within the thought couplet.

Notes on p. 30-34, translations of maxims, p. 35-41, and hieroglyphic transcriptions on pl. 1-26. *L.Z.*

77239 FÓTI, L., Hermes Trismegistos im "Zauberberg", *Studia aegyptiaca* 3 (1977), 17-28.

The author studies the Hermes Trismegistos motif as it is applied in Thomas Mann's "Der Zauberberg".

FOUQUET, Alain, see our numbers 77768, 77769, 77770 and 77771.

77240 FOX, Michael V., A Study of Antef, *Orientalia* 46 (1977), 393-423.

Introduction, commentaire et analyse littéraire du "chant qui se trouve dans le tombeau du roi Antef, devant le harpiste". Ce texte figure au papyrus Harris 500. La tombe de Paatenemheb présente le poème moins complet, dépourvu de titre mais plus ancien. Dans le genre de composition préexistant, les ensevelis étaient proclamés "heureux". Cependant l'introduction déjà jette une note de scepticisme sur l'efficacité du matériel funéraire. La première moitié (constatations objectives) aboutira à la conclusion que personne ne revient nous dire ce qu'il en est. La seconde (conseils directs) conclut avec mélancolie que dans la mort nul n'emporte ses biens. Les classiques "béatitudes" magiques et informatives se retourneraient donc en destruction et en protestation d'ignorance. Non par philosophie logique mais dans une dramatique tension, qui mène à préconiser aux yeux des vivants les divertissements, source pour eux d'oubli "salutaire". Les expressions liées aux anciennes recettes de durée heureuse ($wḏ3$) sont appliquées à la vie présente. Le tout s'achève par un soupir. Le terme technique $m3wt$ désignerait soit le refrain, soit le mode ou la mélodie. L'usage des négations bn et bw, l'intervention fréquente du présent pseudo-verbal, les tournures typiques de la XVIIIe dynastie exprimant l'idée du *Lebensmüde*, sans compter une cause nouvelle de désespoir: les déprédations amarniennes, permettraient de dater le morceau de cette dernière période. Néferhotep viendrait bientôt le contredire. Le titre du papyrus, probablement factice, placerait la composition sous un

ancien roi au nom significatif: Emporté (He has been taken). La postérité littéraire cherchera surtout à exorciser le chant "d'Antef" et fondera l'apaisement temporel sur les promesses d'éternité, les garantissant par le culte et la morale.
Voir aussi nos numéros 77050 et 77270. *J. Custers*

FRONZAROLI, Pelio, see our number 77015.

77241 FUNK, Wolf-Peter, Zur Syntax des koptischen Qualitativs, ZÄS 104 (1977), 25-39.

Verfasser erörtert problematische Beispiele des Qualitativgebrauchs. Er legt dar dass es sich in einigen Fällen in Wirklichkeit nicht um ein Qualitativ handelt. In anderen gibt es eine textgeschichtliche (fremder Dialekteinfluss) oder orthographische (Schreibfehler) Erklärung.
Teil II in ZÄS 105 (1978), 94-114. *M. Heerma van Voss*

77242 FUSCALDO, Perla, El culto oficial de las divinidades asiaticas en Egipto durante el Imperio Nuevo, *Revista del Instituto de Historia Antiqua Oriental,* Buenos Aires 3 (1976), 127-144.

Der Vortrag wurde unter dem Titel "The Official Cult of the Canaanite Deities in Egypt during the New Kingdom" auf dem 39 Congreso Internacional de Ciencias Humanas en Asia y Africa del Norte 1976 in Mexiko gehalten.
Im Zuge der ägyptischen Expansionspolitik während des Neuen Reiches dringen asiatische Gottheiten in die ägyptische Religion ein, allen voran Reshef, Baal, Anat, Astarte und Hauron, Kriegs- und Schutzgottheiten, deren Wohlwollen man sich auch im Niltal sichern wollte. Sie behalten teils ihren ursprünglichen Charakter bei, nehmen teils neue Eigenschaften an, teils wird ihr Kult in die bestehenden Tempel übernommen, teils erhalten sie neue, eigene, mit einheimischer oder fremder Priesterschaft. Ein Phänomen kultureller Auslandskontakte, wie es sich in Ägypten nie mehr wiederholen sollte.
I. Gamer-Wallert

77243 GAÁL, E., Tuthmōsis III as Storm-God?, *Studia aegyptiaca* 3 (1977), 29-37, with 3 fig.

The author first deals with line 15 of the 'poetical' stela of Tuthmosis III, where he finds an allusion to the Ugaritic Ba^{c}al, interpreted as Seth. In this connection he recognizes in line 18 the god Hadat in "the Protector who appears on the back of a wild bull" (against Faulkner, in: Simpson, The Literature of Ancient Egypt = our number 72668, 287 note 6).

77244 GABALLA, G.A. The Chief Worker in Fine Gold, Ptahmay — An Inquest, *GM* Heft 26 (1977), 13-16, with 2 fig. and 2 ill.

1892 verwies Lieblein auf Namen und Titel eines Ptahmay und seiner Familie, die er auf Mauerfragmenten im alten Boulaq-Museum gesehen hatte. Eines der wohl noch nicht veröffentlichten Fragmenten steht jetzt im Raum 19 im Parterre des Kairener Museums unter der nummer *TR* No. 11.1.25.12. Es ist aus Kalkstein und stammt vermutlich aus Saqqara wo es sich wohl im Gang der Grabkapelle befand. Ptahmay trägt den seltenen Titel ḥry îrw nbw p3ḳt. Sein Sohn Kuku, der ihm das Opfer bringt, nennt die Hausfrau Tiy und einen gewissen Mahy, dessen Zugehörigkeit zur Familie des Ptahmay unklar ist. Das Fragment stammt aus der Amarna-Zeit.   *Inge Hofmann*

77245 GABALLA, G.A., The Memphite Tomb-Chapel of Mose, Warminster, Aris & Phillips Ltd, [1977] (21 × 29.6 cm; VI + 40 p., 63 pl.).   Pr. £12.50

The N.K. tomb-chapel of Mose at Saqqâra has long been famous on account of its unique legal text (Gardiner, The Inscription of Mes, Leipzig, 1905 = Untersuchungen zur Geschichte und Altertumskunde Aegyptens IV, 3). The entire chapel is here studied for the first time. In chapter I the history of the tomb is discussed. Originally situated above the mortuary temple of Queen Iput and the mastaba of queen Khuit, N. of the Teti complex, it has insufficiently been described by Loret. At present its blocks are scattered all over the globe, many of them being preserved in the Cairo Museum, others in Hannover and Sydney, still others perhaps somewhere in Saqqâra but now lost.

Chapter 2 contains an attempt at reconstructing the chapel (see plan, pl.1), which consisted of an open court and four rooms at its W. side. The author indicates the place of the blocks that are preserved; those of doubtful location are listed on p. 6. In the Cairo Museum are, among other fragments, large parts of the back walls of rooms II and III, with a sitting statue of Mose in the former (see pl. 2a and 18a).

Chapter 3 is devoted to a description of the scenes, with a translation of the texts. Chapter 4 deals with the legal text, which covered the N. and S. walls of the court. The blocks of the N. wall are now almost all in the Cairo Museum (*TR* 17.5.25.8; see pl. 50-57, and a handwritten copy on pl. 58-60), the blocks of the S. wall are lost. The text is translated, with comments, so far as necessary, in addition to those of Gardiner.

In chapter 5 the author discusses the history of Mose's family and presents a survey of the lawsuit. There follow genealogies of the family which descended from a Neshi who occurs on the Kamose stela.

Notes on p. 33-36; index p. 37-39. On the plates i.a. photographs and drawings of the scenes, in some instances accompanied by a copy of the texts. For the present place of the blocks, see the list to the plates, p. 40.

77246 GABALLA, G.A., Three Acephalous Stelae, *JEA* 63 (1977), 122-126, with 4 pl.

These damaged stelae are all in Room 19 Cairo Museum and have received little if any previous treatment. The first is a private poetical one honouring the king and sun-god, the second a royal one, of Theban origin probably, and the third that of Aniy, overseer of goldsmiths. Translations and commentaries are given in each case.

E. Uphill

77247 GABALLA, G.A. and KITCHEN, K.A., A Vocabulary-Index to Urkunden IV, *GM* Heft 23 (1977), 9.

Die Verfasser sind mit der Anfertigung eines Wörterbuches zu *Urk. IV* beschäftigt; dazu kommt noch der Supplementband von Helck (Historisch-Biographische Texte der 2. Zwischenzeit und neue Texte der 18. Dynastie, Wiesbaden, 1975; unsere Nummer 75321). Eingeschlossen sollen auch alle Korrigenda zu *Urk. IV* werden. Deshalb wenden sich die Unterzeichneten (Adressen sind angegeben) mit einer dringenden Bitte an alle diejenigen, denen diesbezügliche Korrekturen bekannt sind, sie ihnen zu übermitteln. *Inge Hofmann*

77248 GABRA, Gawdat, The Site of Hager Edfu as the New Kingdom Cemetery of Edfu, *CdE* LII, No. 104 (1977), 207-222, with 4 ill. and 3 fig.

A 4 km d'Edfou, à l'ouest, se trouve le site d'une nécropole du Nouvel Empire dont l'auteur a exploré une partie. Il livre ici une description sommaire, un plan, une copie de quelques inscriptions et deux photographies peu lisibles des reliefs d'une tombe ayant appartenu à un certain Satem qui vivait sous le règne d'Ahmosis I.

Ph. Derchain

GADD †, Cyril J., see our number 77145.

77249 GAMER-WALLERT, Ingrid, Un fragmento de estatua del antiguo Egipto, en Badajoz, *Trabajos de Prehistoria*, Madrid 34 (1977), 417-421, with 8 pl.

Publication of a fragmentary diorite statue in the Provincial Archaeological Museum at Badajoz (Inv. No. 4036). It is the torso of a squatting or kneeling figure with a (now headless) baboon on its head. After discussing some similar statues, i.a. the block-statue of the later king Siptah (Louvre E. 25413; cfr. our number 71586) the author concludes that it has probably been placed in the temple of Thebes or in that of Hermopolis, and dates from the Ramesside Period. How it came to Spain is uncertain.

77250 GAMER-WALLERT, Ingrid, Ein neuer Skarabäus vom Jardín bei Torre del Mar, *Madrider Mitteilungen,* Heidelberg 18 (1977), 98-100, with 1 fig.

Description of another scarab in a silver setting found in a tomb in the Finca del Jardín near Torre del Mar (for the first one, see our number 75243). It dates from the Late Period. *L.Z.*

77251 GAMER-WALLERT, Ingrid, Zur Frage der "Laufzeit" ägyptischer Funde aus Hispanischen Nekropolen und ihrer ursprünglichen Bestimmung, *in: XIX. Deutscher Orientalistentag,* 16-21, with 4 pl.

Abstract of a lecture.
The author discusses the problem of the transport term of some of the more than 500 Egyptian objects found on the Iberian peninsula. Most of the smaller pieces such as amulets and small vessels were destined for export and have a short transport term, but the other pieces taken by theft from necropoleis and temples in the Delta may have gone quite different ways during a long transporting term. Therefore, these pieces cannot be used for dating purposes of necropoleis on the Iberian peninsula. *L.Z.*

GAMER-WALLERT, Ingrid, see also our number 77450.

GARBINI, Giovanni, see our number 77015.

GEMPELER, Robert, see our number 77389.

77252 GENAILLE, Nicole, Le sistre Strozzi (à propos des objets cultuels isiaques en Italie), *BSFE* Nos. 77-78 (octobre 1976 et mars 1977), 55-67, with 5 ill. and 1 plan.

L'auteur s'intéresse aux instruments de musique antiques trouvés en Italie et qui témoignent des cultes égyptiens dans le monde gréco-romain. Le sistre est souvent figuré mais assez rares en sont les exemplaires venus de fouilles; la plupart ont été découverts depuis longtemps et la trace de leur provenance est perdue. Le Musée de Florence possède deux sistres d'époque romaine, dont le plus simple, no. 5641, présente de fortes analogies avec des instruments du British Museum et du musée de Bologne. L'opuscule "De Sistris" (1691) du bénédictin Bacchini pourrait représenter et commenter le sistre de Florence, ou du moins un exemplaire du même type. Mis au jour dans une nécropole de la Via Aurelia, dans une propriété des Corsini, il fut offert par eux à Leon Strozzi. Le sistre était donc déposé dans une tombe. Bacchini pensait qu'il s'agissait d'un travail romain, se fondant sur l'aspect de pomme de pin d'un ornement, auquel il attribuait une valeur syncrétiste. Pour Genaille il s'agit en réalité d'un *atef* déformé, mais les 4 ou 6 exemplaires connus de ce modèle, trouvés en Italie, conduisent à y reconnaître des imitations romaines.

J. Custers

77253 GEORGE, Beate, Eine löwenköpfige Nilpferdgöttin in Stockholm, *Medelhavsmuseet Bulletin*, Stockholm 12 (1977), 38-44, with 20 ill.

Publication of a faience lion-headed statuette (8 cm high) of the hippopotamus goddess in the Medelhavsmuseet (MME 1969:584). The piece is minutely described and dated to the Late Period. The author presents on account of it a survey of the role of the hippopotamus goddess and her representation.

In an appendix 17 small statuettes of the goddess in the collection, all with a hippopotamus head, are briefly described.

77254 GEORGE, Beate, Ein Mumienporträt im Medelhavsmuseet, *Medelhavsmuseet Bulletin*, Stockholm 12 (1977), 45-47, with 3 ill.

The author publishes a mummy portrait representing a young man, recently acquired by the Medelhavsmuseet (MME 1977:5), and makes some remarks regarding this type of portrait. The present example may date from the 2nd century A.D.

77255 Van GERVEN, Dennis P., George J. ARMELAGOS, Arthur ROHR, Continuity and Change in Cranial Morphology of Three Nubian Archaeological Populations, *Man*, London 12 (1977), 270-277, with 1 fig. and 5 tables.

Report on an analysis of 174 crania from the Meroitic, X-group and Christian Periods from Wâdi Halfa. The authors conclude to a general pattern of morphological continuity, confirming the results of other recent studies (see, e.g., our numbers 66243 and 67070).

77256 GEUS, Francis, Découvertes récentes au Soudan. La fouille d'el Kadada, *BSFE* No. 79 (juin 1977), 7-21, with 2 maps, 1 plan, 1 fig. and 10 ill.

Bericht über die Ausgrabungen des Sudan Antiquities Service in el Kadada, nördlich von Shendi. Fünf Grabstätten wurden entdeckt, deren Inhalt darauf schließen läßt, daß die Kultur der neolithischen Epoche angehört. Auch die Grabungsarbeiten an einem Kôm brachten neolithische Gräber zutage; an Beigaben enthielten sie u.a. Angelhaken aus Muschelsubstanz, Knochenharpunen, Perlen aus Straußeneierschalen, Amazonit, Karneol. Die Skelette, bei denen sich besonders zerbrochene Vasen befanden, hatten die Beine unterschiedlich stark angezogen. Große halbrunde Gefäße enthielten die Beisetzungen von Kindern mit den gleichen Grabbeigaben, wie sie die Erwachsenen hatten. Die Gefäße, meist schwarz, sind häufig dekoriert.

Darüberhinaus wurden meroitische Gräber eruiert, die wahrscheinlich der Napata-Zeit angehören. Die Skelette sind entweder ausgestreckt oder mehr oder weniger zusammengezogen. Tongefäße und Bronzegegenstände (Ringe, Armbänder, Vasen, Löffel) fanden sich; in einem großen Grab wurde ein Depot von Eisenpfeilspitzen entdeckt. *Inge Hofmann*

GEUS, Francis, see also our number 77768.

77257 GHALIOUNGUI, P., The Persistence and Spread of Some Obstetric Concepts Held in Ancient Egypt, *ASAE* 62 (1977), 141-154.

The author discusses some passages from the medical papyri dealing with gynaecology, embryology and obstetrics (amenorrhoea, uterus and placenta, the formation of the foetus, confinement), and argues that the Egyptian concepts still occur with the classical scholars.

GHALIOUNGUI, Paul, see also our number 77180.

77258 GHISLAIN, Jean-Claude, Bruxelles. Égypte éternelle, *Archeologia*, Paris No. 102 (janvier 1977), 79, with 1 ill.

Note on the exhibition of pieces from Brooklyn in Brussels, 1976-1977. Compare our number 76225.

77259 GHONEIM, Wafik, Die ökonomische Bedeutung des Rindes im alten Ägypten, Bonn, Rudolf Habelt Verlag GmbH, 1977 (14.7 × 21 cm; [VII +] 270 p., 32 fig.) = Habelts Dissertationsdrucke. Reihe Ägyptologie, 3. Pr. DM 36

After an introduction the author deals in the first chapter with the sources. They appear to be mainly representations in relief and painting; objects of daily use (palettes, knife handles, etc.), and particularly written documents are treated as minor sources.

Chapter 2 discusses the domestication of cattle. It is uncertain whether the Egyptian cattle is the descendant of the N. African Bos primigenius opisthonomus, or whether it has been imported from elsewhere. The first traces of oxen date from Naqâda I.

In chapter 3 breeding and races (classified after the shape of the horns) are discussed, with sections on the representations of cattle, the cowherd, and the names of cattle (*ỉw3, ng, ḥr-ḏbc*, and a few lines on *wnḏw*, p. 80). Ghoneim argues that *ỉw3* indicates slaughtering animals and *ng* draught-animals, while *ḥr-ḏbc* is used for the hornless ox.

Chapter 4 is devoted to the spread in space and time of the races, with sections on trade in general, the foreign trade with northern and southern countries, the question whether the available cattle was sufficient for the needs of the population, and (once more) the origin of Egyptian cattle.

Chapter 5 (p. 101-240), called "Bedeutung im ökonomischen Bereich", consists of three parts: the ox as draught-animal and beast-of-burden (drawing carriages, sledges, and plows; the harness; threshing, a section actually containing remarks on the system of agriculture); cattle as provider of meat (slaughtering, the slaughter-house, the meat-offerings); cattle as provider of milk (the technical side of milking, milk products, milk-offerings).

In the last chapter two subjects are dealt with: the management of the herds, and the prices of cattle.

The book is a compilation of recent and older, in some cases antiquated literature to the subject, while the important study of Fernande Hartmann, "L'agriculture dans l'ancienne Égypte" (Paris, Librairies-Imprimeries Réunies, 1923) is mentioned in the bibliography (p. 262) with a German title and as a work of Robert Hartmann. Some parts of the book contain digressions which hardly seem to have any connection with the main subject, e.g., the sections on foundations for the dead, the daily offerings and the "Umlauf" (p. 197-204).

Bibliography on p. 256-270; no index.

GIANGERI SILVIS, Maria Paola, see our number 77111.

GIBSON, McGuire, see our numbers 77368 and 77810.

GIJSELINGS, G., see our number 77763.

77260   GILBERT, Pierre, Le temple de Thoutmosis III à Deir-el-Bahari, *CdE* LII, No. 104 (1977), 252-259.

Article de compte rendu de la publication du temple de Thoutmosis III à Deir-el Bahari par Jadwiga Lipińska (notre No. 77480).

Ph. Derchain

77261 GILULA, Mordechai, Egyptian *nḥt* = Coptic *naḥte* "to believe", *JNES* 36 (1977), 295-296.

The author presents a new translation of lines 4-5 of the Armant stela of Tuthmosis III, translating *r rdīt nḥt īmyw-ḥt* as "in order that posterity believe". The same *nḥt* (Copt. ⲚⲀϨⲦⲈ) occurs in the Piankhy stela, 1.30 (*n nḥty.n.f wr(r)yt.f*, "for he did not trust his chariot") and in Kawa stela VI, 23 (*nḥd*), and probably elsewhere.

77262 GILULA, Mordechai, The Smiting of the First-Born — An Egyptian Myth?, *Tel Aviv*, Tel Aviv 4, Nos 1-2 (1977), 94-95.

The worst of the ten plagues (*Ex.* 7-11; 12, 29-31) is brought into connection with P.T. 399a-b ("Cannibal Hymn") and C.T. II, 163b-c; C.T. VI, 178, where a day or night of the slaying of the first-born is mentioned. This mythical element may very well play a role in the Biblical account. L.Z.

77263 GILULA, Mordechai, The Stative Form of the Verb *sḏm* 'to hear', *JARCE* 14 (1977), 37-40.

Combating the current opinion that the verb *sḏm* 'to hear' is unable to form a stative, the author produces Middle Egyptian counterexamples and re-analyzes a phrase in Pap. Brooklyn 35.1446 (our number 3943), insertion C, 7 (pl. V; perhaps *mk sḏm(w) īrī(w)*). He next studies independent statives of several verbs following the particles *mk* and *īw* in C.T. passages (II, 166, h; 167, b; 175, b; f) and concludes that *īw* marks an adverbial predication. This is illustrated by *īw īsš.t* 'how are things?' and *īsš.t pw* 'what is this?' in C.T. VI (*not* V), 52, e.
J.F. Borghouts

GINTER, Bolesław, see our number 77189.

77264 GITTON, Michel, Nefertary II, *Orientalia Lovaniensia Periodica*, Leuven 8 (1977), 125-127.

The author defends against Harris (see our number 75312) his thesis that one of the queens of Tuthmosis IV was called Nefertari, adducing some new documents.

GITTON, Michel, see also our number 77453.

77265 GIVEON, Raphael, Egyptian Finger Rings and Seals from South of Gaza, *Tel Aviv*, Tel Aviv 4 (1977), 66-70, with 2 pl.

The author describes some finger rings and seals originating from a Late Bronze Age cemetery near Deir el-Balah (see our number 73205), at present in a private collection. L.Z.

77266 GIVEON, Raphael, The Egyptian Objects, *in:* Sara Ben-Arieh and Gershon Edelstein, Akko. Tombs near the Persian Garden = *ᶜAtiqot,* Jerusalem, English series 12 (1977), 70-71, with 2 fig. and 1 pl.

The author describes three finger rings, a bead, a silver seal and a bronze arrowhead, found in Late Bronze Age tombs near Akko. *L.Z.*

77267 GIVEON, Raphael, Egyptology in Israel, *GM* Heft 2 (1977), 7-12.

Die Hebrew University in Jerusalem hat ein Department of Egyptology, das in drei Sektionen eingeteilt ist: Literatur, Religion, Sprachen. Die Tel Aviv Universität hat in ihrem Department of Archaeology and Ancient Near Eastern Studies auch eine Sektion für Ägyptologie. An der Universität von Haifa und der Ben Gurion Universität des Negev in Beer Sheba wird zwar Ägyptisch gelehrt, doch haben sie noch keine Institute oder Abteilungen für Ägyptologie. Sodann werden die ägyptologischen Sammlungen aufgeführt; alle archäologischen Sammlungen enthalten ägyptisches Material, das durch jede Grabung vermehrt wird. Doch wirkt sich die politische Isolation Israels von Ägypten und seine geographische Isolation von den Wissenschaftszentren in Europa und den USA negativ auf das Studium der Ägyptologie aus. Abschließend wird die Bedeutung der ägyptischen Kultur für die Kultur des alten Israel unterstrichen.

Inge Hofmann

77268 GIVEON, Raphael, Inscriptions of Sahurēᶜ and Sesostris I from Wadi Khariğ (Sinai), *BASOR* No. 226 (April, 1977), 61-63, with 2 fig. and 2 ill.

The author publishes an Egyptian rock inscription of Sahure at Wadi Khariğ, who was so far only attested at Maghara, and a much eroded stela of Sesostris I, this being his first monument outside the Serabit el-Khadim.

For corrections concerning the inscriptions, see now Giveon and Edel, *BASOR* No. 232 (Fall, 1978), 76-78. *L.Z.*

77269 GIVEON, Raphael, Remarks on the Transmission of Egyptian Lists of Asiatic Toponyms, *in: Fragen an die altägyptische Literatur,* 171-183.

The author, dealing with the problem of toponym lists as a contribution to the history of Egypt and its relations with its Asiatic neighbours, takes as examples a statue of Tuthmosis III (Cairo C.G. No. 42192; JdE No. 37005), reinscribed by Scheshonk I for Psusennes II, and column bases from the Soleb temple of Amenophis III. He reconstructs the history of the transmission of the Asiatic list on the statue with the help of copies from the same list from the time of Ramses II, and traces the origin of the African list. As regards the list on the Soleb column bases, the author assumes that names from Soleb were copied at Aksha and Amara-West, and argues that the Soleb material cannot exclusively come from the great lists of Tuthmosis III, but may have been transmitted from an other model not being a monumental inscription.   L.Z.

77270   GOEDICKE, Hans, The Date of the "Antef-Song", *in: Fragen an die altägyptische Literatur,* 185-196.

The author completely reinterprets the opening lines of the Antef harper's song in Pap. Harris 500 (Pap. BM 10060, 6, 2 ff) in between groups of love songs. By taking *in.tw.f* as epitheton for the deceased instead of the name Antef, the cartouche for *rn,* "name", the following *m3ᶜ-ḫrw* as the first word of the song proper and *ḥsw m bînt* as "the singer in misery" on account of the weak-bird determinative, apart from other small suggestions, the following result is obtained: "A praising which is in the home of 'one who is carried away' (= name)/the blessed one, who is before (Osiris), while the singer is in misery/the bequest of this old man is this: Oh good man, the good fate has passed".

By this rendering the Antef song would be no longer an anachronism in the carpe diem lyrics originating from the New Kingdom after the Amarna Period. Compare also our numbers 77050 and 77240.   L.Z.

77271   GOEDICKE, Hans, A New Hyksos Inscription, *Newsletter SSEA* 7, No. 4 (August 1977), 10-12.

The author discusses the inscription on a headless sphinx recently offered in a sale, which bears a cartouche of Sesostris III. The inscription mentions "...Apopis, beloved of Wadjyt, Mistress of *'Imt"* and an official whose name is read as *'Iḥwyr.* The piece may originally have come from Nabêsha.

77272   GOEDICKE, Hans, An Old Kingdom Weight, *Newsletter SSEA* 7, No. 3 (May 1977), 6-8.

On account of an O.K. weight of 2 *deben* belonging to an overseer of works *K3-tp* the author argues that the O.K. *deben* weighed 14.1 grams and suggests that the value unit *šᶜt* may correspond to 28.2 grams of copper.

77273   GOEDICKE, Hans, The Protocol of Neferyt (The Prophecy of Neferti), [Baltimore, Maryland, The Johns Hopkins University Press,

1977] (17.2 × 26.1 cm; VII + 206 p.). Series: The Johns Hopkins Near Eastern Studies.

In the introduction the author presents his general discussion of the text. After a bibliographical survey the first section deals with the nature of the text. The author attacks the interpretations of a political or a prophetic character of the text and then begins to set forth his own views. He argues in favour of the historicity of the speaker, whose name he proposes to read Neferyt and to be identical with Nefery mentioned as one of the great writers in P. Ch. Beatty IV. He points out that Neferyt wrote the work without a royal commission from Amenemhat I and why he chose the setting of Snefru's court. Neferyt was brought before the King as an informant about the bad situation in the East Delta and his pronouncements were rather an initiative, a petition to challenge Amenemhat I, so far only King of the South, to come into action to assume the double crown, and thus to improve the situation in the Delta. The setting of the court of Snefru was chosen as a safeguard, since he could not be sure of the king's reaction. So the lacking completion of the frame-story becomes understandable. Neferyt's ingenuity might have led him to choose the names of Snefru or Imeny instead of Amenemhat because they mean "he who makes proper" ("he who puts things in order" referring to the things to be done in the Delta) and Imeny "the hiding one", since the King had not so far come into action. On account of the above "The Protocol of Neferyt" is suggested as the new designation.

In the second section, concerned with the literary form, first remarks are made on two literary devices, namely the introduction in the form of the royal novel and the transcription of Neferyt's verbal statements by the king. The author states that the problem of the Asiatics in the Delta is the sole concern of the text. This problem aggravated the situation there resulting from an extreme drought. Against this background Neferyt utters his prospects, foreseeable and predictable, but not from prophetic visions. The rest of the section is devoted to the discussion of the stylistic devices used in these statements, often in comparison with the "Instruction for Merikare".

In the last section, on the historical aspects, the author amply discusses the experience on which Neferyt's anticipations must have been based, although stressing first that the historical information contained in it serves the aims of a literary composition. He collects references to famine before the XIIth Dynasty in order to bring them into a chronological scheme and reaches the thesis that a severe famine caused by drought occurred in the reign of Antef II Wakh-ankh, and another lesser one in that of Antef III Nakht-neb-tep-nefer or possibly even as late as the early years of Montuhotep II. A minor drought occurring at the time of Neferyt's protocol, inspired the comparison with the previous severe experience. Because of these calamities of such an extent that they must as well have been felt in the neighbouring countries the Asiatic infiltration into the Delta must have increased so strongly that the fortifications called "Wall of the Ruler" turned out to be necessary.

The second chapter is divided into 22 coherent sections, all labelled with a heading summarizing the contents. They contain the translation and an extensive commentary provided with over 400 notes. The third chapter contains the running translation, only divided by the same summarizing headings as in the commentary.

At the end of the book an index of Egyptian words and one to text passages cited. *L.Z.*

77274 GOEDICKE, Hans, A Reply, *Catholic Biblical Quarterly,* Washington 39 (1977), 270-271.

A reply to Hughes' review of our number 75268 in the same periodical.

77275 GOEDICKE, Hans, 727 vor Christus, *WZKM* 69 (1977), 1-19.

After a sketch of the political history of the T.I.P. from 1050 to 750 B.C. and proceeding from the question why the politically skilled Hosea tried to shake off the Assyrian supremacy and why he tried to secure an alliance with So, King of Egypt (2 Kings 17,4) in 727 B.C., the author reexamines the various identifications, particularly that of Kitchen in favour of Osorkon IV from Tanis, made in our number 73405, which are all rejected. His earlier proposal to identify this name with Sais, the capital of the unnamed king Tefnakhte, is defended. The author then attempts to demonstrate the shift of the supremacy from Tanis to Sais from the first and political part of the Shabaka Stone (Memphite Theology), which deals with the division of the land between Horus and Seth and its rearrangement upon a proposal by Geb, which may reflect the political fact of a shift of power. The author argues that this may very well be the rise to power of Tefnakhte in 726/5 B.C., and that also the raid by Piye (Pianchi), as a fanatical Amun-worshipper, a confederate of the threatened Theban theocracy, may be explained from this. *L.Z.*

77276 GÖRG, Manfred, Die Bildsprache in Jes 28,1, *Biblische Notizen,* Bamberg Heft 3 (1977), 17-23, with 2 fig.

A reaction to our number 74225. The author attempts to explain the presence of the gazelle head in the headdress of the god Reshef through the shift from a warlike to an erotic character, which last trait may have connected him with the fertility god Min in whose cult the gazelle plays a role. *L.Z.*

77277 GÖRG, Manfred, Der Ekstatiker von Byblos, *GM* Heft 23 (1977), 31-33.

Anmerkung zu unserer Nr. 76217. Es wird nach einem semitischen Äquivalent gesucht, dessen Transkription sich formal nicht von der Schreibung des Konsonantenbestandes des ägyptischen ᶜ*dd* unterscheidet und im Semitischen *ḥzj* gefunden.
Vgl. Aelred Cody's Aufsatz in *JEA* 65 (1979), 99-106. *Inge Hofmann*

77278 GÖRG, Manfred, Ein Fachausdruck israelitischer Architektur, *Biblische Notizen,* Bamberg Heft 3 (1977), 14-16.

The author proposes to consider the word *ḏrᶜt*, "wooden plank" as a loanword from the Hebrew *ṣlᶜ*, which word is a term in Israelite architecture. *L.Z.*

77279 GÖRG, Manfred, Die "Heimat Bileams", *Biblische Notizen,* Bamberg Heft 1 (1976), 24-28.

The author makes several remarks on some Asiatic toponyms as present in various Egyptian sources. *L.Z.*

77280 GÖRG, Manfred, Jahwe — ein Toponym ?, *Biblische Notizen,* Bamberg Heft 1 (1976), 7-14.

The author discusses several toponyms from Egyptian M.K.-N.K. sources resembling the Hebrew tetragram for the name of God, and concludes that the younger spellings can be connected with the tetragram. They designate then probably a toponym from Southern Palestine, which may have given its name to or borrowed it from the local god. *L.Z.*

77281 GÖRG, Manfred, Komparatistische Untersuchungen an ägyptischer und israelitischer Literatur, in: *Fragen an die altägyptische Literatur,* 197-215.

On the basis of W. Richter's book "Exegese als Literaturwissenschaft", Göttingen, 1971, the author discusses methodological aspects of comparative literature with respect to the O.T. and Egyptian literature. The discussion is exemplified by comparing 1 Kings 3,3-15 with the Sphinx-stela of Tuthmosis IV, and Nathan's prophecy in 2 Sam. 7,1-29 with the Prophecy of Neferty. His considerations result in the thesis that a literary verification for both literatures is needed to prove commonly shared ideas. *L.Z.*

77282 GÖRG, Manfred, Die Kopfbedeckung des Hohenpriesters, *Biblische Notizen*, Bamberg Heft 3 (1977), 24-26.

The author discusses three terms for the head-dress of the Israelite high priest: Hebrew *mṣnpt/ṣnyp*, "turban", of which the connection with the Egyptian word *tnfyt* is uncertain; Hebrew *ṣyṣ*, from which the Egyptian loan word *ḏḏ*, "flowers" (?) derives; Hebrew *nzr*, "diadem", possibly connected with the Egyptian word for the snake goddess *nṯrt* (see also our number 77286). *L.Z.*

77283 GÖRG, Manfred, Die Lade als Thronsockel, *Biblische Notizen*, Bamberg Heft 1 (1976), 29-30, with 1 fig.

Additional remarks to our numbers 76296 and 77285. *L.Z.*

77284 GÖRG, Manfred, Der Mensch als Königliches Kind nach Ps 8,3, *Biblische Notizen*, Bamberg Heft 3 (1977), 7-13, with 1 fig.

Discussing the meaning of Psalms 8,3 the author points to Egyptian evidence, particularly Ramses II, in order to elucidate the conception of the power of small (royal) children. *L.Z.*

77285 GÖRG, Manfred, Eine neue Deutung für *kăpporaet*, *ZAW* 89 (1977), 115-118.

The technical term *kăpporaet* in the cultic language of Israel probably derives, in a contracted form, from Egyptian *kp n rdwy* "sole of the foot". See also M. Görg, *Biblische Notizen* 5 (1978), 12. *L.Z.*

77286 GÖRG, Manfred, Weiteres zu *nzr* ("Diadem"), *Biblische Notizen*, Bamberg Heft 4 (1977), 7-8.

Addition to our number 77282.

77287 GÖRG, Manfred, "Wo lag das Paradies?". Einige Beobachtungen zu einer alten Frage, *Biblische Notizen*, Bamberg Heft 2 (1977), 23-32.

Discussing the river of paradise called Pishon (Hebr. *pjšwn*), the author points to a possible Egyptian origin of the name (*p3 ḥnw*). *L.Z.*

77288 GÖRG, Manfred, *zimiu* und *lamassu*, *GM* Heft 23 (1977), 35-36.

Die keilschriftlichen Umschreibungen ägyptischer Wörter in der Geschenkliste Amenophis' IV. enthält u.a. die ungeklärte Form *zi-mi-u* (EA 14 I 68), die als Äquivalent des akkadischen *lamassu* "Statuette" interpretiert wurde. Zum Vergleich in graphischer wie semantischer Beziehung wird das ägyptische *tm3* herangezogen, das als "Eigenschaftswort in Verbindung mit Körperteilen" seit dem A.R. belegt ist; *tm3* [c] kann in der Bedeutung "mit kräftigem Arm" u.a. als Götterattribut und als "Name eines göttlichen Wesens" Verwendung finden. Verfasser interpretiert *zimiu* als Wiedergabe des hieroglyphischen Ausdruckes *tm3* [c]; dazu kommt eine enge Verwandtschaft von *lamassu* und *tm3* [c], da beide Formen eine schützende Gottheit meinen können. *Inge Hofmann*

77289 GÖRG, M., Zum Wechsel k/q in ägyptischen Transkriptionen, *JEA* 63 (1977), 178-180.

The author discusses the changes between the writing of k and q in such foreign names as the town of Carcemish between the reigns of Tuthmosis III and Ramses III as shown in their name lists. *E. Uphill*

77290 *Göttinger Miszellen.* Beiträge zur ägyptologischen Diskussion. Gesamtinhaltsverzeichnis und Indizes zu den Heften 1-20, Göttingen, 1977.

Index volume to the first twenty numbers of *GM*. It contains a list of their articles alphabetically arranged after the author's names; a list of author's names after the categories of the publications; indexes of catchwords, museums and collections, references to texts, Egyptian words and hieroglyphs, Coptic words, and words in other languages.

77291 GOMAÀ, Farouk, Probleme der Lokalisierung von ägyptischen Ortsnamen, *in: XIX. Deutscher Orientalistentag*, 22-29, with 2 maps.

After discussing the problem of the identification of Egyptian place names from Greek, Coptic and Arabic toponyms, which is also hampered by climatological and political causes the author draws attention to the source of Arabic cadastral names, which was extensively used by Mohammed Ramzi's "Geographical Dictionary of Egyptian towns and villages from Pharaonic times to 1945" (5 vols, in Arabic). He then presents 13 examples from this book. *L.Z.*

77292 GOMEZ BISTUER, Alcides O., Nota sobre los succesores de Ramses II y el fin de la dinastia XIX, *Aegyptus Antiquus* 2 (1977), 67-79.

The author discusses the following subjects: Merenptah in Asia, the nebulous end of the XIXth dynasty, Siptah and Bay, and Queen Twosre. *L.Z.*

77293 GONZALES, Père Antonius, Voyage en Égypte. 1665-1666. Traduit du néerlandais, presenté et annoté par Charles Libois, [2 vols], [Le

Caire, Institut français d'Archéologie orientale du Caire, 1977] (16.5 × 19.5 cm; [vol.I:] LX + 392 p., double frontispiece, 14 pl., ill. on cover; [vol. II:] XIV + 478 p. [= p. 393-870], 6 pl., folding map, ill. on cover) = Collection des voyageurs occidentaux en Égypte, 19.

P. Gonzales, born in 1604 at Mechelen as the son of a Spaniard, lived during three years in the Near East, among which for some time as priest of the French consul and the French merchants at Cairo. Returned to Europe he published his "Jerusalem Travels" in six books in 1673.

In the introduction the editor presents information about the publication and its author, listing, for instance, the few extant copies of the original edition and sketching life and character of its author, the language of the book (a simple Dutch), its value, sources, and influence.

The main part of the volumes consists of a French translation of those parts which deal with Egypt, mainly books IV and VI. The former (in vol.I), on his life in Cairo, contains original information about manners and customs, population and government as Gonzales saw them; the latter (in vol. II) contains a compilation of remarks on biological and mineralogical matters, although original observations and religious explications are not absent.

Very extensive indexes on p. 705-868.

GOREN, Avner, see our number 77067.

77294 GOSTYNSKI (†), Tadeusz, Sur l'histoire ancienne des Lébou du Cap-Vert, *Bulletin de l'Institut Fondamental d'Afrique Noire,* Dakar 38 (1976), 223-233.

The author argues that the Lebu tribe at present at Capo Verde are the descendants of the ancient Libu known from the Egyptian sources. Also the *Temehu,* the *Tjehenu* and the *Meshwesh* are discussed in a short historical survey. At the end there is a comparison between the Lebu and the Wolof languages. *L.Z.*

77295 GOYON, Georges, Le secret des bâtisseurs des grandes pyramides. Khéops, Paris, Éditions Pygmalion, [1977] (18 × 25 cm; 318 p., frontispiece [fig.], 103 fig., 16 pl.).

After a preface by Mme Chr. Desroches Noblecourt and a foreword by the author in which he i.a. refutes wild theories of the "pyramidiots", but also the ideas of architects who do not know sufficiently about ancient Egypt, the author deals in six chapters with all various aspects of the construction of pyramids, particularly that of Cheops.

In chapter 1, on the meaning of a pyramid complex, Goyon presents a survey of the development of the royal tomb from the beginning of the Egyptian civilization onwards. He also discusses the organization of the workmen whose total number he calculates to be about 20,000 (see the appendix, p. 291-292). In chapter 2 the major theories about the construction technique pass the review, e.g. those of Lepsius, Petrie, Borchardt, and Hölscher. They are all rejected, while that of Wheeler — an enveloping ramp — is accepted as the most probable, although with slight alterations. Chapter 3 deals with the preparations of the work: the task of the astronomers, the calculations, the plan, the state of the site before the work started, the quarries, tools, transport of blocks, the causeway, etc.

In chapter 4 and 5 the building proper is discussed in detail; the preparation of the site, the types of masonry used, the construction of the enveloping ramp, the gradual progress of the work, the housing of the workmen, etc.; and, in chapter 5, the rooms in the interior of the pyramid, the last stages of the work, the placing of the pyramidion and the removal of scaffolding. A short chapter 6 is devoted to the connected monuments: the funerary temple, the barks, the causeway and the satellite pyramids.

Added are still two chapters. The subject of chapter 7 are the funerary ceremonies at the burial of the king, the daily ritual in the funerary temple, and the closing of the galleries, while chapter 8 is devoted to the violation of the pyramid in later ages.

After a concluding chapter (p. 283-287) follow the appendix, the notes, and an index to names.

77296   GOYON, Jean-Claude, Un phylactère tardif: le Papyrus 3233 a et b du Musée du Louvre, *BIFAO* 77 (1977), 45-54, with 2 fig. and 1 pl.

Publication of two strips of papyrus (Pap. Louvre 3233 a and b), which belong together and constitute a talisman. The first part bears the representation of a row of animals and divinities in human shape, the other a hieratic text and the figure of a monster. Goyon describes the pieces, and presents a translation of the text, with several references to other magical texts. He dates them to the Saito-Persian Period and suggests that they were a new-year's present for a child providing protection against dangers and fear of them.

77297   GRAEFE, Erhart, Der Falkengott des 10.o.äg. Gaus in der Ptolemäerzeit, *GM* Heft 26 (1977), 17-22.

Vgl. unsere Nummern 77073 und 77192.

Verfasser trennt die Gottesnamen jetzt in zwei Gruppen, und zwar

Ḥr-m3ᶜtj und ᶜ*rkw-jnsw* für Miysis. Ein gemeinsamer Gottesbegriff hinter den drei verschiedenen Schreibungen wird nicht vermutet, sondern *Ḥr-(p3)-m3ᶜtj* für eine tatsächlich existierende Kultform des Gaugottes des 10. Gaus gehalten, der, in der Ptolemäerzeit auftauchend, vorläufig noch keine Vorgeschichte hat.
Für eine Erwiderung, siehe jetzt H. Beinlich, *GM* Heft 29 (1978). 11.

Inge Hofmann

77298 GRAEFE, Erhart, Horus-der-Gerechte, Miysis, der Doppellöwe und Horus-Triumphator im 10. oäg. Gau, *GM* Heft 23 (1977), 37-43.

Es wird Bezug genommen auf die Dissertation von Beinlich (vgl. unsere Nr. 76066), in der eine Sonderform des Horus im 10. Gau als "Horus-Mati" herausgestellt wurde. Verfasser stellt fest, daß es sich bei diesem *Ḥr -(p3)- m3ᶜtj* um vier verschiedene Götter handelt: 1. *Ḥr-p3-m3ᶜtj*, 2. Miysis, 3. einen Doppellöwen *rwtj* (?), 4. *Ḥr-m3ᶜ-ḫrw*.

Inge Hofmann

77299 GRAEFE, Erhart, "*jn mnḫ*..." (Ti, Taf. 133), *GM* Heft 26 (1977), 23-25.

Vgl. unsere Nummer 76210. Es geht um einen Deutungsversuch einer Beischrift zu einer Handwerkerszene des A.R. bei Ti, die über einem Mann steht, der mit Schlegel und "Meißel" ein nicht genau bestimmbares (Holz)stück bearbeitet. Statt der Lesung bei Drenkhahn "Oh Meißel, laß dick (*wmt*) sein deine Löcher" schlägt Verfasser vor "Der Lochbeitel läßt seine Löcher (Aussparungen?) dick (breit?, weit?) sein".

Inge Hofmann

77300 GRAEFE, Erhart, Ein Wiederaufgetauchtes Relieffragment aus dem Grabe des Maya in Saqqara, *MDAIK* 33 (1977), 31-33, with 1 pl.

In addition to his study of the tomb of Maya in Saqqâra S. in *MDAIK* 31 (our number 75283) the author publishes a relief at present in the Memorial Art Gallery of the University of Rochester (Inv. no. 42.55). It represents the standing Maya (the adjoining block with his wife Meret is still lost; both have been seen by Lepsius). Remarks concerning the court of the tomb at the end.

77301 GRENIER, Jean-Claude, Anubis alexandrin et romain, Leiden, E. J. Brill, 1977 (15.5 × 24 cm; XXIV + 212 p., frontispiece, 44 pl., 2 folding maps) = Études préliminaires aux religions orientales dans l'empire romain publiés par M. J. Vermaseren, 57; rev. *CdE* LIV, No. 107 (1979), 171-174 (Michel Malaise). Pr. fl. 160

In the introduction the author discusses first the characteristics of Anubis in pharaonic times, about which no monograph has yet been written. He deals i.a. with canine deities, the name *'Inpw*, the epithets of the god, his rôle as god of cemeteries and of the XVIIIth Upper Egyptian nome (Pap. Jumilhac), and particularly with his function as god of mummification and psychopompus. He suggests that originally he did not belong to the Osirian circles but was a funerary divinity of his own merits, and discusses the uncertainty about his mother (Isis, Nephthys, the cow-goddess Ḥesat, Bastet?).

From p. 22 onwards Anubis' rôle in the Graeco-Roman Period and his place in the pantheon is studied. He was no longer exclusively a funerary deity, although he kept his functions as psychopompus and guard of the tomb.

Then follows a catalogue of 283 Graeco-Roman sources (two in the Addendum on p. 187): mythographic and literary texts, inscriptions, iconographic documents (statues, statuettes, reliefs, paintings, lamps, etc.). In the conclusion (p. 168-186) the author discusses the meaning of Anubis in the Alexandrian and Roman religion.

The plates represent many of the objects mentioned, 1-7 from the Pharaonic Period.

Indexes on p. 188-205.

GRIESHAMMER, Reinhard, see our number 77054.

77302 [GRIFFITHS, J. Gwyn], Editorial Foreword, *JEA* 63 (1977), 1-4.

In this editorial foreword there are sections on North Saqqâra, by H. S. Smith; work in the Saqqâra tomb of Horemheb, by G. T. Martin; on unpublished tombs of the Old Kingdom at Saqqâra, by W. V. Davies; El-ᶜAmarna, by Barry J. Kemp; and an obituary notice of John A. Wilson, by Edward F. Wente. *L.Z.*

77303 GRIFFITHS, J. Gwyn, Hermes and the Marrow in a Love-Charm, *Zeitschrift für Papyrologie und Epigrafik,* Bonn 26 (1977), 287-288.

The author elucidates the passage of a short love-spell from Roman Oxyrhynchus in which Hermes has to do with marrow, by connecting Hermes with Thoth, powerful in magic, and the marrow with procreative powers, which connection is already present in ancient Egyptian belief. *L.Z.*

77304 GRILLETO, Renato R., Carie et usure dentaire chez les Égyptiens prédynastiques et dynastiques de la collection de Turin (Italie), *L'Anthropologie,* Paris 81 (1977), 459-472, with 8 tables, 4 fig., 3 ill. and summaries in French, Italian and English on p. 470-471.

The author compares the teeth of Predynastic and Dynastic Egyptians in the G. Marro osteological collection in Turin and concludes that the

Predynastic Egyptians were more and to a higher degree affected by caries and dental attrition.   *L.Z.*

GRIVETTI, Louis, see our number 77180.

77305   GROSSMANN, Peter, Abu Mena. Achter vorläufiger Bericht. Kampagnen 1975 und 1976, *MDAIK* 33 (1977), 35-45, with 1 fig., 3 plans and 4 pl.

Sequel to our number 70232.
Continued excavation in 1975 and 1976 have led to more extensive knowledge about the churches that are here described.

GROSSMANN, Peter, see also our number 77389.

77306   GRUNERT, Stefan, Die ägyptische Revolution im 3. Jahrtausend v.u.Z., *Das Altertum,* Berlin 23 (1977), 213-218, with 3 ill. and 1 fig.

Proceeding from the text of the Admonitions of Ipuwer, the author deals with the problems of the Egyptian society during the periods of decline.
Compare our number 77107.   *L.Z.*

77307   GUILMOT, Max, Les initiés et les rites initiatiques en Égypte ancienne, Paris, Éditions Robert Laffont, 1977 (13.6 × 21.4 cm; 266 p., 1 plan, 1 map, 5 fig., 8 pl.); series: Les portes de l'étrange.

After the first chapter discussing initiation in general and dealing with the initiation process during life, the types of initiation, archaic as well as classical, and the initiation in the wisdom of a high spiritual order, the author devotes his attention to the initiates, the places of initiation, and its significance in Egypt in the following chapters.

In the second chapter, in which the scarcity and reticence of the Egyptian sources is stressed, the initiates are dealt with. Chapter 3, the most extensive one, discusses respectively the initiation rites at Abydos, Busiris and Karnak for which the author uses as a vital source the hieratic papyrus Leiden T 32 of the priest Harsiesis, dating from the beginning of the first century A.D., of which the relevant parts are translated. Much attention is paid to Abydos as the burial place of Osiris, and the Osireion of Sethi I. The chapter ends with an appendix on Apuleius of Madauros dealing with his initiation in the Greek Isiac mysteries.

After a short chapter (4) on the absence of a relation between the individual initiation process and the festival of the Osiris mysteries, the author discusses in chapter 5 the significance of initiation in Egypt and presents in his last chapter a synthesis of the initiation procedure

in Egypt.
Index at the end of the book. *L.Z.*

77308 GUNDEL, Hans Georg, Katalog der literarischen Papyri in der Giessener Universitätsbibliothek. Zweite durchgesehene und erweiterte Auflage des Kurzberichtes 12, 1962 = *Kurzberichte aus den Giessener Papyrussammlungen* No. 39 (1977), 1-52, with 16 pl.

A list of the Coptic texts and the hieratic and Demotic texts on p. 37-40. The hieratic texts consist of fragments of late B.D. copies and an invocation to gods. The Demotic document is of a juridical character. Relevant data such as date, provenance and bibliography are given. *L.Z.*

77309 GUNDLACH, Rolf, Der Denkstein des Königs Ahmose. Zur Inhaltsstruktur der Königsnovelle, *in: Fragen an die altägyptische Literatur,* 217-239, with 1 pl.

The author first explains his method of analyzing the structure of the content of a text, which is concerned with the classification of the relations between the text elements of a content, and his distinction between relations of significant overlapping or identity such as pronomina, temporal relations (past, present, future) and combinatory relations. This description system forms the basis for a source and a historical interpretation of the royal novel on the stela of king Ahmose in Abydos (Urk. IV, 26,12-29,4), which reports about a conversation between Ahmose and Ahmes-Nefertari in which the king tells why he decided to build a pyramid chapel for his grandmother in Abydos. Using his own numbering of text elements, he then presents his analysis of the source elements and his historical interpretation.

On the basis of the above analysis he reaches the conclusion that the meaning of Ahmose's royal novel is to render the activity of the king, both in its general aspect and as concrete example, as a magical creation of reality. The text with reference numbers at the end of the article. *L.Z.*

77310 GURALNICK, Eleanor, The Egyptian Canons, *Newsletter ARCE* Nos. 99/100 (Winter/Spring 1977), 14-15.

Abstract of a paper.

GUTBUB, Adolphe, see our number 77403.

77311 GUZMÁN, Solano Pena, The Numerals, *ASAE* 62 (1977), 185-199.

The article deals with concordances in the grammatical use of the numerals in a large number of languages, particularly of the Hamite family. Sections are devoted to the vigesimal system and the dual in Egyptian.

77312   HABACHI, Labib, Mentuhotp, the Vizier and Son-in-law of Taharqa, in: *Ägypten und Kusch,* 165-170, with 7 pl.

Es wird Bezug genommen auf den Skarabäus der Golenischeff-Sammlung, der jetzt im Puschkin-Museum unter der Inventarnummer I, Ia 2398 aufbewahrt wird (vgl. unsere Nummer 67268). Der bisher unbekannte Vizier Mentuhotep kommt nun auch auf einer Quarzitstele vor, die kürzlich vom Kairener Museum erworben wurde. Aus der dort erhaltenen Inschrift und Darstellung geht hervor, daß er mit Amenardis der Jüngeren, der Tochter des Taharqa verheiratet war. Die Stele stammt vermutlich aus Heliopolis. Außerdem gibt es ein Statuenpaar aus schwarzem Granit, vom dem der eine Teil im Louvre (A 49), der andere im Ägyptischen Museum in Berlin (Nr. 8803) steht. Eine der beiden dargestellten Personen ist unbekannt, die andere ist der Prophet und Hohepriester von Athribis, Mentuhotep.
Inge Hofmann

77313   HABACHI, Labib, New Light on Objects of Unknown Provenance (I). A Strange Monument of Amenemhet IV and a Similar Uninscribed One, *GM* Heft 26 (1977), 27-36, with 5 fig. and 2 ill.

Zu einem von G. Brunton in *ASAE* 39 (1939) veröffentlichten Podest, der 1910 an das Kairener Museum gelangte und unter der J. E. No. 42906 registriert wurde, fand der Verfasser im Koptischen Museum von Alt-Kairo ein ähnliches Exemplar. Es ist allerdings unbeschrieben, hat aber fast die gleichen Dimensionen wie das Podest aus dem Kairener Museum und kann deshalb ebenfalls Amenemhet IV. zugeschrieben werden. Beide Stücke scheinen von Kher-Aha oder Per-Pedjet zu stammen, wo wahrscheinlich ein pharaonischer Tempel stand.
Inge Hofmann

77314   HABACHI, Labib, Tavole d'offerta, are e bacili da libagione n. 22001-22067, Torino, Edizioni d'Arte Fratelli Pozzo, [1977] (24 × 32 cm; 171 p., numerous fig., 45 pl., 2 folding pl. [= p. 93-96]; series: Catalogo del Museo Egizio di Torino. Serie seconda-Collezioni. Volume 2; rev. *Oriens Antiquus* 18 (1979), 83-84 (Tiziana Baldacci).
Pr. L.25,000

This catalogue of the offering tables, altars and libation basins preserved in the Egyptian collection at Turin begins with a preface by the author in Arabic and Italian, a bibliography, and an introduction in which the objects in general are discussed.

The catalogue itself contains 67 numbers: 41 tables, 21 basins including 2 supports, and 5 altars or parts of them. Some objects are only fragmentarily preserved. They are chronologically arranged, from the IVth Dynasty to the Roman Period. For each the old number, the name of its original owner, provenance, material, date, present state of conservation and bibliography, if existing, are noted. The objects are also briefly described, the texts translated, and, when possible, a comment concerning the owner and his family is added. Drawings, some in margine, illustrate the objects, while important texts are given in facsimile. The objects come from various sites, while of a few the provenance is unknown. Groups came from Gîza, Asyût, Deir el-Medîna and Gebelein.

Three objects required more space than normal: N. 22053, the base of an altar from Memphis, probably from Sethi II and inscribed with the name of Pepy I and a list of 50 cult sites (summary p. 76-77); N. 22054, a round offering table from the late XXVth or early XXVIth Dynasty, with scenes on its side (summary p. 90-92); N. 22055, an altar of Nectanebo with scenes and a list of cult sites (summary on p. 104-105).

Concordances p. 117; indexes p. 118-121. Photographs of all pieces and of some details on p. 125-169.

77315   HABACHI, Labib and Pierre ANUS, Le tombeau de Naÿ à Gournet Mar^{c}eï (No. 271), [Le Caire], Publications de l'Institut français d'Archéologie orientale, [1977] (27.3 × 35.5 cm; [VIII +] 32 p., colour frontispiece, 17 fig. including plans [5 folding], 2 maps, 7 pl.) = Mémoires publiés par les membres de l'Institut français d'Archéologie orientale du Caire, 97.

Although it is nowhere stated it seems that the text of this volume is due to the first author (translated by Serge Sauneron), the drawings to the second.

Theban tomb no. 271, situated on the top of Qurnet Mura^{c}i and dated to the reign of Eye, belongs to a royal official of that king called Nay. It is here published for the first time (cfr. Porter-Moss, I, 1,2nd ed., 350).

Proceeding from the observation that the tomb is directed to the funerary temple of Eye the author discusses in the first chapter the relations between the tombs of high officials in the Theban necropolis and the temples of their masters. He concludes that only in a few instances the officials succeeded in building their tombs in the neighbourhood of the funerary temple.

Chapter 2 is devoted to the architecture of tomb 271. It consists of a cave with a large transversal pillar hall and a small axial room, and was one of the largest in the necropolis. It bears not a single trace of decoration, probably because of the condition of the rock of Qurnet Muraᶜi. 12 m. above the cave there is the chapel, originally built in a pyramid as i.a. an inscription proves. The decorations here preserved are studied in chapter 3.

Each scene is minutely described, the texts given in transliteration and translation with comments. Moreover, they are presented in line drawings. Added are some fragments found on the floor and parts of the limestone door.

The last chapter is devoted to the owner of the tomb. Although obviously a favourite of king Eye little is known about him. His titles are listed and studied, the most important being *wr swnw, it-ntr, imy-r k3t* and *sš nfrw*.

Index on p. 31-32. The plates bear views of the tomb and photographs of the decorations of the chapel, including details.

77316 HAINSWORTH, M. et J. LECLANT, Préliminaires à un Répertoire d'Epigraphie Méroitique (REM), (suite 1), *MNL* No. 18 (Octobre 1977), 15-18.

Die Arbeiten von S. Wenig am Tempel von Amara brachten weitere 7 Inschriften zutage, die bei Griffith nicht enthalten sind und die Nummern REM 0144-0150 erhalten. Die Inschriften REM 1148, 1151 (vgl unsere Nr. 77794), 1152 A und B werden beschrieben und auf den Ort ihrer Publikation hingewiesen. In einem Annex folgt ein Index der Fundorte der Inschriften nach dem Répertoire Descriptif.
Inge Hofmann

HAINSWORTH, Michael, see also our number 77019.

77317 el HAKEM, Ahmed, [Field-Work], *Nyame Akuma,* Calgary No. 11 (November 1977), 48-49.

Beim Dorf Nofalab, 8 km südlich von Sarurab, wurden neolithische Fundstätten entdeckt; ein Friedhof gehört zum Bauda-Typ, der andere zu einem neuen Typ. Es konnten am Skelettmaterial interessante paläopathologische Beobachtungen gemacht werden. Auf der Islang-Insel wurden weitere Bauda-Typen entdeckt, außerdem wurden Funde getätigt, die ähnlich denen der nubischen A-Gruppe und Arkells Omdurman Bridge Culture sind. *Inge Hofmann*

77318 HÅLAND, Randi, Archaeological Classification and Ethnic Groups: a Case Study from Sudanese Nubia; J. Desmond CLARK, Bruce G. TRIGGER, Fred WENDORF, Anthony E. MARKS & Joel L.

SHINER, Comments on Archaeological Classification and Ethnic Groups, *Norwegian Archaeological Review,* Oslo-Bergen-Tromsø 10 (1977), 1-31, with 1 map, 4 fig. and 1 table.

Discussion, with comments and reply, of the attempt of archaeologists to reconstruct cultural history in terms of migration, diffusion or invention on the basis of the classification of artifacts, exemplified here by the case of Sudanese Nubia. *L.Z.*

77319   HALL, Alice J., Dazzling Legacy of an Ancient Quest, *National Geographic,* Washington D.C. 151, No. 3 (March 1977), 292-311, with 32 colour ill. (1 on cover).

A series of fine photographs relating to ancient Egypt, with explanatory captions. *L.Z.*

77320   HALL, Emma Swan, Harpocrates and Other Child Deities in Ancient Egyptian Sculpture, *JARCE* 14 (1977), 55-58, with 6 pl.

The iconography of Harpocrates is studied (with remarks on that of Khonsu, Harsomthus and Ihy) as well as similar representations of the king as a child. Horus as a falcon is considered the adult aspect (as Haroeris) of Horus the Child. Hellenistic and Roman sculpture is likewise taken into account. *J.F. Borghouts*

77321   HAMILTON, Alice and K. Corey KEEBLE, Scenes from Egyptian Life. Three Stained Glass Windows by Henry Holiday, *Rotunda,* Toronto 10, No. 1 (Spring 1977), 16-19, with 3 ill. (2 in colour).

On three fine stained glass windows in the University of Toronto showing scenes from ancient Egyptian life. The work was designed and executed about 1915 by Henry Holiday. *L.Z.*

HAMMOND, N. G. L., see our number 77145.

77322   HANI, Jean, La religion égyptienne dans la pensée de Plutarque, Paris, Société d'Édition "Les Belles-Lettres", 1976 (15.5 × 24.5 cm; [VI +] 492 p., frontispiece); series: Collection d'études mythologiques publiée sous le patronage du Centre de Recherches Mythologiques de l'Université de Paris.

After an introduction on Plutarch's interest in Egyptian religion and his sources of information the author presents his book in three parts. He deals first with the myth of Osiris (*de Iside* 12,355 — 19,358) following in the chapters the order of Plutarch's book, and summarizes his investigations in a conclusion.

In the second part, on the Osirian theology, the author discusses the essential elements of Plutarch's theology: the allegorical interpretation of the myth and the metaphysical one based on Platonic dualism and the demonological doctrine. Two chapters are devoted to Plutarch's refutation of the historical interpretation of the myth on account of the theory of Euhemer and the Stoical explanation of elements of the myth as natural phenomena. The rest of this part of the book is concerned with Plutarch's treatment of the identification Osiris-Dionysos and of the Orphian mysteries; that of Osiris in his funerary aspect and Serapis; and of Osiris, Isis and Seth in their astral aspects.

In the third part the author studies Plutarch's attitude towards the cult of Osiris: priests, temple and cult, ritual prescriptions, the Osiris mysteries and festivals, the cult of Osirian and Typhonian animals.

In the general conclusion the author evaluates Plutarch's *de Iside* as regards its importance for the history of religions, and as a philosophical and religious testament. There follow at the end i.a. an index on cited passages, a general one, and a chronology after periods with mention of the main documents.
L.Z.

77323 HANKOFF, Leon D., Why the Healing Gods Are Twins, *The Yale Journal of Biology and Medicine,* New York 50 (1977), 307-319.

In this article on the association of twins with health-giving powers Egypt is also dealt with. First the author discusses the umbilical cord and the placenta of Pharaoh, concepts and customs about which are compared with other African cultures. Then the author turns to the placenta and discusses its connection with the *ka,* Khonsu and the moon (healing abilities), and the mythology of sun and moon as eyes of the sky.
L.Z.

77324 HANZÁK, Jan, Egyptian Mummies of Animals in Czechoslovak Collections (= Eugen STROUHAL, Multidisciplinary Research on Egyptian Mummies in Czechoslovakia, VI), *ZÄS* 104 (1977), 86-88, with 6 ill. on 2 pl.

A radiographic examination of vertebrates. 14 fish species were identified, 9 cats and 2 dogs. Birds were represented by 12 species. There were 18 crocodile mummies and one snake.
M. Heerma van Voss

77325 HARI, Robert, À propos d'un scarabée royal inédit: le thème de Thot en cynocéphale, *Aegyptus* 57 (1977), 3-10, with 3 pl.

Figurative scarabs depicting Thoth with a baboon's head with on top the lunar disk and crescent occur rather frequently from Amenhotep

II to Ramses II. The scarab here discussed is distinguished in the series by its high quality of manufacture and detail. It represents a kneeling king offering to a baboon on a socle, wearing the lunar crescent and disk. The author lists the series of scarabs showing a king offering a conical loaf, two vases or an image of Maat to, or adoring the cynocephalous Thoth. Since the scarabs, so far as bearing legends, mention Ramses II, the author thinks of a systematical emission comparable to that of Amenophis III, may be at the occasion of some important ceremony of the Thoth temple of Ramses II at Hermopolis. Then the author lists 48 scarabs showing Thoth as lord of Hermopolis (*nb Ḥmnw*), as cynocephalous plus royal cartouche or royal name without cartouche, belonging to six kings, in particular Tuthmosis III and especially Ramses II. In the case of Tuthmosis III the element Thoth is a satisfactory explanation, but Ramses II, strong supporter of Amon, or rather strong opponent against Atonism, may have stressed the traditional cults in Hermopolis, just opposite Amarna, where he removed the remnants of buildings to Aton. Although it was hardly possible to construct an Amon temple at the sacred place of Thoth, he stressed the return to tradition by venerating the local god.

L.Z.

77326 HARI, Robert, La figuration du lion dans les scarabées royaux égyptiens, *SAK* 5 (1977), 41-46, with 1 pl.

The author studies and classifies 268 scarabs, dating from Mykerinos to Apries and bearing representations of lions and sphinxes, either sitting, lying or walking. He discusses the various features and attributes. In this connection he publishes two instances, acquired at Luxor and probably from Deir el-Medîna, with representations of a lying lion crowned with the "Amon plumes", but with different other elements. They are to be dated to the time of Ramses II.

HARI, Robert, see also our numbers 77153 and 77653.

HARRIS, James E., see our number 77376.

77327 HARRIS, J. R., Akhenaten or Nefertiti?, *Acta Orientalia*, Copenhagen 38 (1977), 5-10.

Studying the allegedly sexless colossal statue of Akhnaton from Karnak (Cairo JE 55938) the author suggests it to be an image of Nefertiti and adduces some noteworthy points in favour of this opinion. The importance of Nefertiti at Karnak and her eventual kingly status justifies her appearance in parallel with Akhnaton. As for the significance of the colossi, they may represent, parallel to

Akhnaton assimilated to Shu, the queen as Tefnut (eventually equated with Hathor). Moreover, this solution discards the problem of an emasculated Akhnaton posing as cosmic creator. *L.Z.*

77328 HARRIS, J. R., A Fine Piece of Egyptian Faience, *Burlington Magazine,* London 119, No. 890 (May 1977), 340-343, with 5 ill.

Publication of a faience knob from the Amarna Period in a private collection in Copenhagen. The representations on the piece emphasize the similar formal status of the royal couple, and allude to their solar nature. *L.Z.*

77329 HARTE, Ben, Treasures of Tutankhamun, *The Lamp,* New York 59, No. 2 (Summer 1977), 28-33, with 15 colour ill. (1 on cover).

Short note to the Tutankhamun exhibition travelling through the U.S.A. *L.Z.*

HAYES, John H., see our numbers 77534 and 77745.

77330 HAYNES, [University of Arizona Reports], *Nyame Akuma,* Calgary No. 10 (1977), 27.

Erforschung neolithischer Stätten in der Nubischen Wüste und, in Zusammenarbeit mit dem Egyptian Geological Survey, Auffindung und Registrierung von holozänen Playa-Lagerungen in der westlichen Wüste. *Inge Hofmann*

77331 HEERMA VAN VOSS, M., Aegyptologie in den Niederlanden, *GM* Heft 24 (1977), 13-14.

Aufgezählt werden die Forschungsprojekte, die an den Universitäten in Leiden, Utrecht und Amsterdam laufen; weitere Zentren sind die Universität von Groningen, das Rijksmuseum van Oudheden in Leiden, das Allard Pierson Museum in Amsterdam. Sie sind, wie auch die "Oosters Genootschap in Nederland" vor allem auf wissenschaftlicher Ebene tätig. Weite Kreise erreicht "Ex Oriente Lux" durch Vorträge und Veröffentlichungen. Hochschulpolitisch muß gesagt werden, daß die beteiligten Fachgruppen z.Z. beschlagnahmt sind von der Aufgabe, die Ausbildung der Studenten aufs neue zu strukturieren und programmieren (Studienverkürzung) und ihre Dozier- und Forschungstätigkeiten weitgehend zu planen. *Inge Hofmann*

77332 HEERMA VAN VOSS, M., De Egyptische dodenliteratuur aan het einde van Nieuwe Rijk, *Het Profiel,* Amsterdam, 1977-'78, No. 1, 4.

A sketch of the funerary literature during Dynasty XXI. Compare our number 76352.

77333 HEERMA VAN VOSS, M., Emery, *De Grote Oosthoek*⁷, Utrecht 6, [1977], 639.

Biography and bibliography; cfr. our number 71651.

77334 HEERMA VAN VOSS, M., Over het dateren van Dodenboeken, *Phoenix*, Leiden 23 (1977), 84-89, with 2 ill.

The author discusses some criteria for the dating of B.D. mss, such as historical relations, representations of the owner, drawing and painting techniques of the illustrations, writing and orthography, choice, redaction and disposition of spells, selection and themes of the vignettes and other elements. The dating of B.D. mss. is illustrated by two examples.   L.Z.

77335 HEERMA VAN VOSS, M.S.H.G., Religionswissenschaft, in: *Antworten*, [Zürich-Köln-Lahr], Benziger Verlag — Verlag Ernst Kaüfmann, [1977], 204-205; rev. *Theologische Rundschau* 43 (1978), 312 (Günter Lanczkowski).

In dieser Forschungsgeschichte ist die ägyptische Religion besonders berücksichtigt worden.

HEFLIK, Wiesław, see our number 77189.

77336 HELCK, Wolfgang, *'Ink wʿ jm.ṯn*, "Ich bin ja einer von euch", *ZÄS* 104 (1977), 89-93.

Herausgabe einer Inschrift aus dem Mastaba des Isi in Saqqâra, auf die Fischer verweist in unserer Nummer 65176, 51. Isi gehörte in der VI. Dynastie einer festgefügten Gruppe von Totendienern an, die als Kultgemeinschaft zusammenlebten.

Neubearbeitung von Edel in *ZÄS* 106 (1979), 105-116.

    M. Heerma van Voss

77337 HELCK, Wolfgang, Die Lehre für König Merikare, Wiesbaden, Otto Harrassowitz, 1977 (17. × 24 cm; [III +] 95 p.); series: Kleine ägyptische Texte; rev. *Mundus* 15 (1979), 281-282 (Hellmut Brunner).   Pr. DM 24.80

On p. 1 the author lists the three mss. of the text which have been preserved and its major translations and discussions, followed by a note on the date of the mss. On p. 2 a plan of the fragments of Pap. Moscow 4658 which have been preserved. The rest of the volume contains a handwritten copy of the text after Pap. Leningrad 1116 A (P), followed by the variants where available. The text is divided into sections, each followed by textual notes, a translation, and in some instances notes to it. On p. 93 the text of the colophon in P, without a translation. On p. 94-95 remarks concerning the differences between the mss. and scribal errors.

77338 HELCK, Wolfgang, Der Verfasser einer Königsinschrift, in: Fragen an die altägyptische Literatur, 241-256.
Refuting the thesis of locally composed royal inscriptions the author first mentions some examples from the Urk. IV and the KRI of which the versions have largely the same text, and discusses their divergences either caused by the copying from the model text, or made on purpose for locally important reasons or due to lack of space. Next he devotes his attention to the Karnak and Memphis versions of Amenhotep II's Asiatic campaign, where can be noticed that the identical passages occurring at regular intervals are not important for the course of events and, thus, must be explained from the coincidental imperfect condition of the hieratic model of the Memphite version, while he adds some other particularities.
Since evidently historical texts are based on a model, composed centrally and sent from there, he raises the question of their mixture of factual truth based on campaign diaries and ideological fiction added in the centre. The problem of the booty lists can be explained from their being sent separately.
At the end the hieroglyphic versions of the Karnak and Memphis parallel texts.
L.Z.

77339 HELCK, Wolfgang, Die "Weihinschrift" aus dem Taltempel des Sonnenheiligtums des Königs Neuserre bei Abu Gurob, SAK 5 (1977), 47-77, with 2 fig. and 2 folding pl.
The fragments of an offering list from the Valley Temple of Neuserre's Sun Temple in Abû Ghûrab (published by Kees in von Bissing, Re-Heiligtum III, 28-32 = Nos. 427-528) are here studied. Helck attempts to combine them to a more or less coherent text, proceeding from the assumptions that they form two inscriptions and that the text follows a chronological order. At the end he gives a list of the festivals mentioned, stating that they are the same as occur in the formal offering text list of the O.K., augmented by those mentioned in the Kahun papyrus concerning the payment of dancers and by some not known from elsewhere. Helck also discusses the ist rations and other deliveries occurring in the text. For a reconstruction of the inscriptions, see p. 2 and 3.

77340 HELCK, Wolfgang, Zum thebanischen Grab Nr. 353, *GM* Heft 24 (1977), 35-40, with 2 plans.

Es handelt sich um das sog. "geheime Grab" des Obersten Domänenverwalters des Amuntempels Senmut, das in einem Steinbruch nördlich des Aufwegs zum Tempel von Deir el-Bahri seinen Eingang hat und sich unter den Vorhof des Totentempels der Hatschepsut erstreckt. Die obersten Kulträume fehlen, drei kleine Räume folgen einander an dem immer tiefer in die Erde hinabgehenden Korridor, von denen nur der oberste Raum ausgeschmückt ist. Seine Reliefs zeigen eindeutig, daß die Kammer für Senmut bestimmt war. Eine Anlage gleicher Art haben wir in dem sog. Bâb el-Hosân, der unterirdischen Anlage vor dem Totentempel Menthuhoteps, die unter die Pyramide am Anfang des Bauwerkes führt. In dieser Anlage war die Statue des Königs beigesetzt, und zwar im Sedfestgewand, so daß es sich um jenes Ritual des Begrabens des "alten Königs" am Vorabend des Erneuerungsfestes, an dem er verjüngt wiedererscheint, handelt. Es wird die Frage gestellt, ob nicht auch Grab 353 als Statuengrab für den Vorabend des Sedfestes der Hatschepsut gedacht war. Dafür käme die zweite, unvollendete Kammer in Frage, in der ihre Statue beigesetzt werden sollte. Sie hat allerdings kein Sedfest gefeiert. Wahrscheinlich sollte in der obersten Kammer eine Statue des Senmut "begraben" werden. Vielleicht waren auch die Nebenpyramiden und das Südgrab des Djoserbezirks Grabmäler für die Statuen der Könige, die am Vorabend des Sedfestes begraben wurden.   *Inge Hofmann*

HELCK, Wolfgang, see also our numbers 77009, 77477 and 77478.

HENDERSON, Margaret Ann, see our number 77221.

77341 HEPPER, F. Nigel, On the Transference of Ancient Plant Names, *Palestine Exploration Quarterly,* London 109 (1977), 129-130, with 1 fig.

The author stresses the confusion caused by the transference of ancient plant names to more or less analogous modern kinds. The problem is exemplified by "ebony" which word is derived from Egyptian *hbny,* but does not indicate the tree Dalbergia melanoxylon, used by the ancient Egyptians.   *L.Z.*

HERBERT, Annabelle, see our number 77221.

HERRMANN, Joachim, see our number 77346.

77342 HERRMANN, Siegfried, Die Auseinandersetzung mit dem Schöpfergott, *in: Fragen an die altägyptische Literatur,* 257-273.

Proceeding from Otto's conception of the reproach to god (our number 1972), further developed by Fecht in our number 72227, and defending his definition of the Admonitions in our number 57246, the author discusses the composition of the Eloquent Peasant and points out its resemblance to the Admonitions, where, as Fecht states, the reproach takes a central position around which the other pertaining sections are grouped. He argues that the text is essentially concerned with justice, that the qualities and epitheta of the addressed go beyond the human factor and that it is the creator god himself who is addressed. This is evident from several discourses mentioning Re, who is strongly invited to guarantee Ma^{c}at. In this respect the discourses of the Eloquent Peasant belong to the dispute literature, and are in a way comparable to the O.T. story of Job as a just person in conflict with God.

At the end the author presents in translation the section of the text relating to the address to and the dispute with the demiurge.   *L.Z.*

77343   HERZOG, Rolf, Die Fundumstände einer meroitischen Statuengruppe, *in: Ägypten und Kusch,* 171-174, with 1 pl.

Es handelt sich um die meroitische Statuengruppe CG 684 des Museums in Kairo, die bereits 1882 in das Museum für Ägyptische Altertümer gelangte. Sie wurde 1881 von dem deutschen Fotografen Carl Berghoff bei den Pyramiden von Meroe ausgegraben und dem kurzfristig amtierenden Generalgouverneur des Sudan, Karl Giegler Pascha zugesandt. Seine Leute lehnten die Statue als Darstellung böser Geister jedoch ab, und so sandte Giegler sie, dem Wunsche Masperos entsprechend, auf dem Wasserwege von Khartûm nach Kairo.
Inge Hofmann

77344   HILLER, Stefan, Kretisch-orientalische Kulturbeziehungen, *AfO* 25 (1974/77), 301-305.

Bibliographical survey of recent literature on the cultural relations between Crete and Ancient Near Eastern cultures.   *L.Z.*

77345   HINKEL, Friedrich W., The Archaeological Map of the Sudan, *Nyame Akuma,* Calgary No. 10 (1977), 57-58.

Introduction to our following number.

77346   HINKEL, Friedrich W., The Archaeological Map of the Sudan. A Guide to its Use and Explanation of its Principles. With the Co-operation of Anthony J. Mills. Forewords by Joachim Herrmann and Nigm ed Din Mohammed Sherif and with a Contribution by William

Y. Adams, Berlin, Akademie Verlag, 1977 (20.5 × 29 cm; VIII + 32 p., 5 maps, 3 fig.); at head of title: Akademie der Wissenschaften der DDR. Zentralinstitut für Alte Geschichte und Archäologie.

Nach einer kurzen Einführung in die Geschichte Nubiens und des Sudan von William Y. Adams wird die archäologische Karte des Sudan (A.M.S.) vorgestellt. Einer ihrer wichtigsten Zwecke ist es, alle archäologischen Fundstätten des Sudan zusammenzustellen und aller Interessierten zugänglich zu machen: die Lokalisierung, eine kurze Beschreibung der Fundstätte, Illustrationen, veröffentlichte Hinweise, Hinweise auf unpubliziertes Material in Archiven und Sammlungen beinhaltet die Information. Es wird erwartet, daß die Gesamtveröffentlichung der A.M.S. zehn Haupthefte umfaßt, wobei das erste Heft Informationen bieten und ein Führer sein will zur Handhabung der A.M.S. Hefte II-X umfassen jeweils ein Gebiet des Sudan, zu dem eine "unit map" gehört. Supplementhefte werden alle Informationen über eine "unit map" auf den neuesten Forschungsstand bringen.

Der erste Band (Band II) ist erschienen in 1979.   *Inge Hofmann*

77347   HINKEL, Friedrich W., Ein neues Triumphalbild des meroitischen Löwen, *in: Ägypten und Kusch,* 175-182, with 1 plan, 2 fig. and 5 ill on 4 pl.

Von den 9 in Basa gefundenen Löwenskulpturen wurden 6 in die Anlagen des Nationalmuseums von Khartûm transportiert. Von der zurückgelassenen Statuen L 7, L 8 und L 9 wird die letztere einer genaueren Prüfung unterzogen. Die in zwei Teile zerfallene Figur fand sich etwa 23 m südlich des den ehemaligen Hafir markierenden Zentralkreises. Das Material ist der übliche schwarz-braune eisenhaltige Sandstein. Das obere Teilstück stellt einen aufrecht sitzenden Löwen in ungefährer Lebensgröße dar; das untere Teilstück besteht aus einer Basisplatte mit einem davon abgesetzten darüber liegendem Sockel, der bei keinem der anderen Basa-Löwen vorkommt. An der rechten Seitenfläche des Sockels ist im erhabenen Relief die Gestalt eines ausgestreckt und auf seinem Bauch liegender Menschen zu sehen; auf der linken Seite sind nur noch Spuren vorhanden. Doch kann es als gewiß gelten, daß der Löwe auf zwei ausgestreckten Menschen hockte, die man in der vorgefundenen Haltung als Gefangene oder Feinde bezeichnen muß. Eine Darstellung des Löwentriumphes findet sich mehrfach in der meroitischen Kunst; die Statue L 9 von Basa mit dem aufgerichteten Oberkörper und auf nebeneinanderliegenden Opfern sitzend ist eine uns bis jetzt nicht bekannte Variation dieses Themas.   *Inge Hofmann*

77348 HINKEL, F. W., Reconstruction and Restoration Work at the Northern Group of Pyramids at Begrawiya (Meroe) and the Historical Buildings of Suakin (Red Sea Province), *Nyame Akuma,* Calgary No. 11 (November 1977), 53-55.

Die Arbeiten auf dem Nordfriedhof von Begrawîya zeitigten folgende Ergebnisse: 1. Pyramide Beg. N 19 wurde vorsichtig abgebrochen; die 800 Blöcke sollen in der nächsten Saison wiedererrichtet werden. 2. Pyramide N. 27 wurde auf neuen Fundamenten aufgerichtet. Unter Mitverwendung herumliegender Blöcke konnten einige Reliefszenen auf den Kapellenwänden rekonstruiert werden. 3. Während der Arbeiten konnten Beobachtungen zu den Pyramidenstrukturen gemacht werden. 4. Ungefähr 250 herumliegende Relief- und Architekturblöcke verschiedener Pyramiden wurden sichergestellt und bei ihren ursprünglichen Kapellen aufgestellt. *Inge Hofmann*

77349 HINTZE, Fritz, Beobachtungen zur altnubischen Grammatik V. Das Futurum, *Altorientalische Forschungen,* Berlin 5 (1977), 37-43.

Die verschiedenen Formen der Futurbildung im Altnubischen werden voneinander getrennt: Futurum II wird mit dem Morphem *-d-*, Futurum I mit dem Morphem *-arr-* gebildet, wobei dem ersteren die Bedeutung eines beabsichtigten Geschehens in der Zukunft zugrundeliegt, dem letzteren die eines notwendigen Geschehens. Beide Arten des Futurums treten in drei Stufen auf. *Inge Hofmann*

77350 HINTZE, Fritz, Berliner koptische Ostraka aus Elefantine, *ZÄS* 104 (1977), 97-112, with 19 ill.

Hintze veröffentlicht dreizehn Ostraka aus der Berliner Papyrussammlung, alle von Rubensohn in 1906-1907 gefunden. Es handelt sich um elf Schuldurkunden, einen Schuldschein und eine Empfangsbestätigung. *M. Heerma van Voss*

77351 HINTZE, Fritz, Genetivkonstruktion. Artikel und Nominalsatz im Meroitischen, *in:* Мероэ, 22-36.

Es werden drei eng miteinander verflochtene Fragenkomplexe behandelt: die Genetivkonstruktion in der Nominalgruppe, die Bedeutung des "Artikels" *-l(i)* und die Verwendung dieses "Artikels" in den Deskriptionssätzen. Die Genetivkonstruktion in der Nominalgruppe geschieht durch Anfügung von Suffixen an das dem Regens unmittelbar folgende Rektum, und zwar das Suffix *-s* an Götternamen sowie an die Wörter "König" und "Kandake" und *-lis* an alle übrigen Wörter. Eine seltene Nebenform des Genetivs auf *-s* scheint mit *-o* gebildet zu sein; sie ist mit einiger Sicherheit bisher nur bei dem Gottesnamen *Mš* belegt.

Die zweite Frage gilt der syntaktischen Verwendung und der Bedeutung des Formativs *-li,* das mit einiger Zurückhaltung als "Artikel" angesprochen werden kann. In gewissen Fällen hat es die Funktion der Nominalisierung, die auch bei den Deskriptionssätzen eine Rolle spielt. Mit seiner Hilfe werden die verbalen Ausdrücke der Deskriptionssätze zu "Verbalnomina" umgebildet. *Inge Hofmann*

77352 HINTZE, Fritz, Ein koptischer Lehrvertrag, *ZÄS* 104 (1977), 93-96, with 1 ill.

Veröffentlichung des Ostrakons Berlin P. 14790 unbekannter Herkunft. Es enthält einen Lehrvertrag, wie Zambon sie als Urkunden in griechischer Sprache in *Aegyptus* 15 (1935), 3-66 zusammengestellt hat. *M. Heerma van Voss*

77353 HINTZE, Ursula, Verzeichnis der Schriften von Fritz Hintze, *in: Ägypten und Kusch,* 507-512, with portrait = frontispiece.

Es handelt sich um die Zusammenstellung der Arbeiten des Jubilars von 1943 bis zu den noch in Druck befindlichen Schriften.

Inge Hofmann

77354 HOCHFIELD, Sylvia, "Wonderful Things...", *Art News,* New York 76, No. 1 (January 1977), 54-57, with 6 ill. (3 in colour).

Short note on the Tutankhamun exhibition travelling through the U.S.A. *L.Z.*

77355 HODJACHE, Svetlana et Oleg BERLEV, Objets royaux du Musée des Beaux-Arts Pouchkine à Moscou, *CdE* LII, No. 103 (1977), 22-39, with 2 fig. and 3 ill.

Les auteurs publient une pointe de lance portant les cartouches d'Amosis Ier et la mention de la prise d'Avaris. Se fondant sur l'orthographe du nom d'Amosis, ils voudraient dater la victoire d'après l'an 17 du règne, et non plus de l'an 11. Ils discutent longuement l'orthographe du nom d'Avaris et la situation de la ville, sans toutefois mentionner l'étude de Bietak, parue dans Tell ed Dab°a II en 1975, dont ils n'ont probablement pas pu prendre connaissance (notre No. 75065). En même temps, ils publient un scarabée de Ramsès II mentionnant la fondation de Silé.

Dans une seconde notule, ils publient un sceau et une empreinte de sceau de Cambyse.

Les quatre objets proviennent de la collection Golénicheff (Inv. I.1.a.1762 = Gol.859; I.1.a.2416 = Gol.416; I.1.a.4431 = Gol.992 et I.1.a.4006 = Gol.993 respectivement). *Ph. Derchain*

77356　HODJACHE, Svetlana I. [et] Oleg D. BERLEV, Le père du fondateur de la dynastie des princes de *Tjḥḫtj* en Nubie, in: *Ägypten und Kusch*, 183-188, with 4 pl.

Es werden zwei Stelen aus der Sammlung Golenischeff vorgestellt, die Licht werfen auf das nubische Fürstentum *Tjḥḫtj* des Neuen Reiches und die heute im Musée des Beaux-Arts Pouchkine in Moskau aufbewahrt werden: GMII I.1.a. 5628 = Golenischeff, 4122 und GMII I. 1. a. 5629 = Golenischeff, 4089. Die erste ist die Grabstele eines *Ttj*, genannt *Ḏ3j-wj-ᶜ*, der im Distrikt oder im Ort Elephantine unter den letzten Königen der 17. Dynastie und vielleicht unter Amenophis I. lebte. Die zweite Stele wurde wahrscheinlich lange nach dem Tod dieses Mannes errichtet, nachdem sein Sohn Fürst von *Tjḥḫtj* geworden war.　　　　　　　　　　　　　　*Inge Hofmann*

HOFFMANN, Herbert, see our number 77529.

77357　HOFFMEIER, James K., Tents in Egypt and the Ancient Near East, *Newsletter SSEA* 7, No. 3 (May 1977), 13-28, with 2 pl. and 1 fig.

Proceeding from a remark by van Seters that references to Abraham's tent reflect a mid-first millenium milieu the author studies the evidence for tents in Egyptian texts and representations. He first lists 21 instances from texts, arranged in a retrograde chronological sequence, and then discusses each of them, making several original remarks.

The word for "tent" was *ỉm*, while *ỉhy/ỉhw* indicates a "camp" and *ᶜᶜny*, "enclosure", that is "the king's quarters". The O.K. word for "tent", reoccurring in the XIXth Dynasty, was *ḥn*, perhaps "leather tent", while in two instances one finds *ỉ3hrw*, derived from אֹהֶל. From the representations it appears that the tents were shaped like the hieroglyph *sḥ*. This word may indicate their ritualistic function.

The author concludes that the Egyptians used tents on foreign expeditions, but that they were also known as the dwellings of bedouin tribes (see, e.g. *Admon.* 10, 1-2 and *Sin.* B. 145-146).

77358　HOFMANN, Inge, Bemerkungen zum Gott Sabomakal, *BiOr* 34 (1977), 139-142.

Proceeding from two representations of *Sbwjmkr* (Sabomakal) on the walls of the Lion Temple in Musawwarât es-Sufra the author argues against Wenig (our number 74799) that this is not an original Meroitic divinity. His name, which may mean "*sbo* is the god", does not occur elsewhere; possibly it was merely popular etymology. Iconographically the god is much alike Atum. If *sbo* would appear to mean "creator" the identification would be fairly certain. Anyhow, our material does not prove that it was an indigenous god.

77359 HOFMANN, I., Chronologische Probleme zur Bauperiode 6 der Großen Anlage von Musawwarat es Sufra, *MNL* No. 18 (Octobre 1977), 19-27.

Die vermutete Bauzeit von 200 Jahren für die Periode 6 der Großen Anlage von Musawwarât es Sufra stimmt mit dem bisher vorliegenden archäologischen Material nicht überein: zu Beginn der Etappe 6 a werden Uräenfriese begraben, die knapp vor 200 v. Chr. geschaffen wurden; die jüngsten Werte der C-14-Datierung aus dem Aufschüttungsmaterial ergaben 250/228 v. Chr., und aus dem gleichen Zeitraum stammt die Bronzemünze des Ptolemaios III. aus dem Fußboden des Zentraltempels. Für die Bauetappe 6 b gibt es keine Daten, doch aus der Etappe 6 c stammen Kartuschenfragmente, die mit einiger Wahrscheinlichkeit Arnekhamani, etwa 240-220 v. Chr., zugeschrieben werden können. Aus der gleichen Periode stammt die C-14-Datierung 270 ± 80 v. Chr. Die gesamte Etappe 6 umfaßt also nach dem Material einen Zeitraum von vielleicht 3 Jahrzehnten.
Inge Hofmann

77360 HOFMANN, Inge, Der Feldzug des C. Petronius nach Nubien und seine Bedeutung für die meroitische Chronologie, in: *Ägypten und Kusch*, 189-205.

Kritisch untersucht wird der von vier antiken Schriftstellern erwähnte Feldzug des römischen Statthalters von Ägypten, C. Petronius im Jahre 24 v. Chr., der ihn bis nach Napata am 4. Katarakt geführt haben soll. Verfasser kommt zu dem Ergebnis, daß der Zug nur bis zum 2. Katarakt erfolgte; das von Petronius militärisch gesicherte Dreißigmeilenland wurde von Augustus auf das alte Gebiet des Dodekaschoinos zurückgenommen. Eine Beteiligung des meroitischen Herrscherhauses an dem Aufstand im Dreißigmeilenland konnte nicht nachgewiesen werden.
Inge Hofmann

77361 HOFMANN, Inge, Die Große Göttin des Ostmittelmeerraumes im meroitischen Reich, *SAK* 5 (1977), 79-121, with 35 fig.

Es wird dem Vorkommen der kleinen nackten Frauenfiguren im Sudan seit der A-Kultur nachgegangen (zu ihrer Existenz im Ostmittelmeerraum vgl. unsere Nr. 71262). Sie lassen sich bis in die christliche Zeit hinein verfolgen; jedoch nur für die meroitische Zeit kann festgestellt werden, daß die im Ostmittelmeerraum ursprünglich erotisch-aggressive Göttin vonseiten der meroitischen Theologie in

eine Göttin mit betont fraulichem Charakter und in eine mit betont kriegerischem Charakter entwickelt wird. Letztgenannte wird dem kriegerischen Löwengott Apedemak zugeordnet. (Zu einem Nachtrag vgl. unsere nächste Nr.).
Inge Hofmann

77362 HOFMANN, Inge, Miszellen zu einigen meroitischen Götterdarstellungen, *GM* Heft 24 (1977), 41-49, with 3 fig.

1. Zum Krokodilskult im meroitischen Reich: es gibt einige Beispiele von Krokodilsdarstellungen, gelegentlich in der besonderen Form des Suchos mit dem Falkenkopf, die sich bis in die X-Kultur hielt. Aus meroitischen Texten ist ein Gott Suchos wahrscheinlich nicht bekannt.
2. Mandulis in meroitischer Darstellung? Es handelt sich um die Darstellung eines anthropomorphen Gottes mit kurzem Schurz, langer Perücke und *hmhm*-Krone auf einer Säule des Amuntempels von Amara; mit großer Wahrscheinlichkeit handelt es sich dabei aber um Chons, nicht um Mandulis.
2. "Herakles" im meroitischen Pantheon: Diodor und Strabo berichten, daß im meroitischen Reich u.a. Herakles verehrt würde. Gemeint ist wahrscheinlich Schu als Himmelträger, wie er sich z.B. als Fayence-Figur in Beg. N. 6 findet.
4. Eine weitere Darstellung der Göttin mit dem Falkenemblem: Abbildung auf einem Ring aus Beg.N. 6, auf der die Göttin mit dem Falken auf dem Kopf einem kleinen Kind die Brust reicht. Vgl. unsere Nummer 77361.
5. Eine Königin als Trägerin der *hmhm*-Krone: entgegen der Ansicht, daß nicht einmal weibliche Gottheiten eine *hmhm*-Krone tragen (vgl. unsere Nummern 74799 und 77364) konnte eine solche sogar bei einer Königin nachgewiesen werden, nämlich bei Amanitore auf Darstellungen des Amuntempels von Naqa.
Inge Hofmann

77363 HOFMANN, Inge, Zu den meroitischen Titeln *ktke* und *pqr*, in: *XIX. Deutscher Orientalistentag*, 1400-1409.

Die Untersuchung zeitigt als Ergebnis, daß eine Kandake (*ktke*) möglicherweise als "Titularschwester" aufzufassen ist, d.h. eine Frau der gleichen Generation wie der König, die den Titel (-*ke*) eines Schwester (*kdi*-) erhält. Ob König und Kandake leibliche oder Halbgeschwister sind ober ob das Verhältnis noch weiter gefaßt werden muß (Kandake als weibliche Verwandte der gleichen Generation) ist ungewiß. Die Funktion eines *pqr* dürfte in der Hauptsache militärisch gewesen sein; möglicherweise haben wir in ihm einen Vizier zu sehen, der nach dem König der zweite Mann im Staat war.
Inge Hofmann

77364 HOFMANN, Inge, Zur Darstellung von Schu und Tefnut im meroitischen Reich, *GM* Heft 23 (1977), 45-47, with 1 fig.

Der Interpretation der dreiköpfigen Tierplastiken aus dem Löwentempel von Musawwârat es Sufra als Amun, flankiert von den löwenköpfigen Göttern Sebiumeker und Arensnuphis, durch Wenig (vgl. unsere Nr. 74799) muß widersprochen werden: die Löwen repräsentieren sicher Schu und Tefnut, da das Argument, weibliche Gottheiten trügen nie die *hmhm*-Krone durch ein Beispiel aus dem Tempel des Month und der Rait-tàui in Hermonthis, in dem sich eine Darstellung der säugenden Sobk-Neith mit *hmhm*-Krone befindet, widerlegt werden konnte.
Inge Hofmann

77365 HOFMANN, Inge, Zur Sozialstruktur einer spätmeroitischen Stadt in Unternubien, *Anthropos,* Freiburg 72 (1977), 193-224, with 1 map and 10 fig.

Es wurde der Versuch unternommen, die Sozialstruktur der unternubischen Stadt Karanog im 3. Jahrhundert n. Chr. darzulegen, wie sie aus den Totentexten herauszuarbeiten wär. Soweit aus den Texten abzulesen ist, waren die Männer entweder am Tempel eines Gottes (der Haupttempel war der des Amanap, des "Amun von Luksor", an dem aber auch andere Götter Kulte hatten) oder in der zivilen Verwaltung beschäftigt. Es fällt auf, daß oft mehrere Mitglieder einer Familie im Tempel oder Heiligtum desselben Gottes tätig sind. Möglicherweise versuchten sich die Familienmitglieder gegenseitig an ihrem Arbeitsplatz unterzubringen, ohne daß wir daraus eine rechtliche Institution nachweisen könnten. Trotz der Fülle des Materials gerade aus Karanog mußte immer wieder festgestellt werden, daß wir über Spekulationen nicht hinauskommen und es für die Aufstellung verbindlicher Thesen noch zu früh ist. *Inge Hofmann*

77366 HOLM-RASMUSSEN, Torben, Nektanebos II and Temple M at Karnak (North), *GM* Heft 26 (1977), 37-41, with 2 fig.

Es wird ein großer Sandsteinblock beim sog. Tempel M von Karnak vorgestellt, der außerhalb des Temenos des Amun an der Nordecke der Mauer lag. Auf der Langseite ist ein Relief angebracht das eine Sphinx mit Königskopf vor Amun und dem falkenköpfigen Khonsu-Thoth zeigt. Aufgrund eines ähnlichen Reliefs kann geschlossen werden, daß bereits Nektanebos II. mit der Dekorierung des Tempels M von Karnak begann, die dann unter den Ptolemäern fortgeführt wurde. In diesem Tempel wurde auch Thoth verehrt und dem Vornamen des Nektanebos II. wurde ein "geliebt von Thoth" beigefügt.
Inge Hofmann

77367 HOLTHOER, Rostislav, New Kingdom Pharaonic Sites. The Pottery. With a Contribution by Hans-Åke Nordström, Stockholm, Esselte Studium, 1977 (24.5 × 31 cm; XX + 190 p., 72 fig., 74 pl., 11 tables) = The Scandinavian Joint Expedition to Sudanese Nubia Publications, 5:1.

Die Studie beschäftigt sich mit der auf der Töpferscheibe hergestellten Keramik von Friedhöfen und Siedlungen der mittelnubischen und pharaonischen Epoche, die in den Jahren 1961-64 in dem Konzessionsgebiet der Scandinavian Joint Expedition gefunden wurde. Das Material besteht aus ungefähr 3000 vollständigen oder fast vollständigen Gefäßen und einer großen Anzahl von Scherben. Nach einer allgemeinen Einführung (Material; Keramologie; Studien zur ägyptischen und nubischen Töpferei) folgt als Teil I ein Überblick über die Gefäßherstellung im alten Ägypten (Quellen; Quellen zum Alten Reich; Quellen zur 1. Zwischenzeit, Quellen zum Mittleren Reich; Quellen zum Neuen Reich; Quellen zur Spätzeit), die keramische Technologie im alten Ägypten und die ägyptische Terminologie. Teil II untersucht die "Classification of Properties", der eine Untersuchung von Nordström über die Klassifikation der auf der Töpferscheibe hergestellten Keramik beigefügt ist, Teil III die Typologie und Typenbeschreibung. Es folgt eine ausführliche Bibliographie.
Inge Hofmann

77368 HOPE, Colin, Two Examples of Egyptian Blue-painted Pottery in the Medelhavsmuseet, *Medelhavsmuseet Bulletin,* Stockholm 12 (1977), 7-11, with 3 ill.

Publication of two blue-painted vessels in the collection of the Medelhavsmuseet, one a funnel necked storage jar with an ovoid body and a pointed neck (MM 18600), the other a small jar with a wide mouth and a piriform body (MM 11119). Both bear a decoration of floral and linear motifs. The author describes the vessels, comments upon the pigments (cobalt) and their application, and upon the motifs of the decoration. As regards their date, the author suggests the reigns of either Amenophis III or Akhnaton, since exact parallels came from Malkata.

HORNBOSTEL, Wilhelm, see our number 77449.

HOVING, Thomas, see our number 77751.

77369 HUARD, Paul et Léone ALLARD, Les chasseurs anciens du Nil et leurs témoignages gravés à Uweinat, au Sahara tchadien et au Fezzan oriental, *Bulletin de la Société Préhistorique Française,* Paris 74 (1977), 642-660, with 1 map and 10 fig.

The authors study the rock-drawings from the Hunters civilization that occur as well in the Sahara as in the Nile Valley. It appears that the earliest instances in both areas date from the same phase, the development in the Sahara and the Nile Valley being different.

77370 HUFSCHMIDT, Hans-Joachim, Körperproportionen in Plastik und Malerei. Ein anthropometrischer und kulturhistorischer Versuch, *Archiv für Psychiatrie und Nervenkrankheiten,* Berlin-Heidelberg-New York 224 (1977), 187-202, with 7 ill., 1 fig., 4 tables and summaries in English and German on p. 187.

In this study of body proportions in sculpture and painting Egypt is also dealt with. The author states that the Egyptian proportions of the New Kingdom resemble those of the East-African negroes, for which the influx of negroid elements in that period was responsible.   *L.Z.*

77371 HUSSON, Constance, L'offrande du miroir dans les temples égyptiens de l'époque gréco-romaine. Publiée avec le concours du Centre National de la Recherche Scientifique, Lyon, Institut V. Loret — Université Lyon II, 1977 (16 × 24 cm; 311 p., 21 fig., 10 ill. and 18 pl. containing 7 plans, 35 ill. and 5 fig.).

The book, being concerned with the mirror in Graeco-Roman temple rituals, starts in the first chapter with a historical survey of the mirror in Pharaonic Egypt and deals with the mirror as object, its name and its symbolism in the various periods. In the second and by far the longest chapter the author has collected and translated the texts accompanying the scene in 14 Graeco-Roman temples (mainly Dendera, Edfu, Philae, and Kôm Ombo), after having described the scene of the king offering a mirror to a goddess and having depicted their various headdresses and crowns, as well as the mirrors.

In the third chapter, containing the commentary of the offering texts, the author first classifies the documents and then lists the goddesses and their company and the kings involved. The offering of the mirror was meant to appease the goddess. Certain texts, showing only slight variations, permit to establish some important themes of the offering, elements of which have to do with the ideology of kingship, the procession of the image of the goddess, the Isis myth, the unification of the goddess with the sun disk, and astral aspects. Chapter 4 discusses the place of the ritual in the liturgy and the temple, with special attention to the Hathor temple at Dendera.

Indexes on names and epithets of the deities, on the epithets of the king and the queen, on toponyms, on names of metals and thrones, and a list of texts sources at the end of the book.   *L.Z.*

77372 IBRAHIM, Mohiy E. A., Some names of the Temple of Edfu, *ASAE* 62 (1977), 207-217.

A list of names and epithets of the town and the temple of Edfu occurring in its inscriptions. The pertinent sentences are presented in hieroglyphs and translation. The list is preceded by a short introduction.

77373 IMAMOVIĆ, Enver, Antički kultni i votivni spomenici na području Bosne i Hercegovine, Sarajevo, Veselin Masleša, 1977 (17.4 × 24.2 cm; 518 p., fig., ill. and maps in text, French summary on p. 481-493); series: Biblioteka kulturno nasledje.

"Cultic and Votive Antique Monuments on the Territory of Bosnia and Herzegovina".

A brief chapter is devoted to Isis (p. 257-260), and one to Serapis (261-263), with exhaustive bibliography. Their traces are noted in the entire Roman Dalmatia and several in adjoining provinces. A lost Isis statuette and a bust of Serapis (cf. our number 71108) are presented in the catalogue (438-439, ill. 213).

Cf. Ljubica Zotović, Старинар, Београд 28-29 (1977-1978), 293-294.

S.P. Tutundžić

77374 *Información Arqueologica*. Boletín Informativo del Instituto de Prehistoria y Arqueología de la Diputación Provincial de Barcelona, Barcelona No. 22. Extraordinario (1976), 83-122, with 1 fig. and 19 ill.

Special issue entirely devoted to the exhibition of Pharaonic art in Madrid and Zaragoza, April-May 1976.

The issue is intended for non-Egyptologists and contains i.a. a general survey of Egyptian art by Josep Padró i Parcerisa (p. 88-99) and short communications on special subjects.

77375 INSLEY, C. D., Inventory of the late Dr. B. G. Haycock's papers, *MNL* No. 18 (Octobre 1977), 35.

Das vollständige Inventar mit den Papieren befindet sich in der Sudan Library, University of Khartoum. Der bereits publizierten Bibliographie (vgl. unsere Nr. 74844) muß noch hinzugefügt werden: Studies in Ancient Languages of the Sudan, Khartoum, 1970, und: Language in the Sudan (im Druck).   *Inge Hofmann*

IRVIN, Dorothy, see our number 77745.

77376 ISKANDER, Zaky and James E. HARRIS, A Skull with Silver Bridge to Replace a Central Incisor, *ASAE* 62 (1977), 85-90, with 4 pl.

In a tomb excavated at Tura el-Asmant in 1952 a skeleton (probably from the Ptolemaic Period) was found, of which a tooth, the right central incisor of the upper jaw, was fixed with a silver wire. It was done by drilling a hole through it, very probably outside the mouth, so that it is an instance of an actual bridge. A second instance, from the IVth Dynasty, was found by Junker at Gîza, but here gold was used.

ISSAWI, Bahai, see our number 77681.

JACOB-ROST, Liane, see our number 77726.

77377 JACQ, Christian, Akhenaton et Néfertiti. Le couple solaire, Paris, Éditions Robert Laffont, [1976] (13.2 × 19.9 cm; 252 p., 8 pl.); series: Les énigmes de l'univers.

Popular account of the story of Akhenaton and Nefertiti, without notes. Concise bibliography at the end. *L.Z.*

77378 JACQUET, Joël, Une civilization méconnue, Méroé, *Sciences et Avenir*, Paris No. 358 (décembre 1976), 1194-1199, with 7 ill., 1 map and 1 fig.

A rapid survey for the general reader of the Meroitic civilization. *L.Z.*

77379 JANKUHN, Dieter, Der Spruch: *"Die Häuser im Wasser zu bauen"* [*CT* VI, Sp.571] (Zur Frage der Lokalisierung der Nekropole von Buto-Sais), *RdE* 29 (1977), 38-42.

Le thème du chapitre 571 des *C.T.* traduit et commenté dans cet article concerne les dangers de submersion qui menacent par des périodes de très hautes eaux des nécropoles du delta installées sur des dunes.

Ph. Derchain

77380 JANSSEN, Jac. J., Kha^{c}emtōre, a Well-to-do Workman, *OMRO* 58 (1977), 221-232, with 3 pl.

Proceeding from the peculiar standard-bearing statue of the necropolis workman Kha^{c}emtōre in the Leiden Museum of Antiquities (Inv. No. D 18) the author draws up a prosopography of the owner and his family from the scattered information known. Then the author clarifies the well-to-do status of him and his fellow-workmen, so often underestimated by Egyptologists, demonstrating from numerous documents on rations, strikes, financial state, etc., how they were able to attain such a status and stressing the appreciation of their technical abilities by private persons during their frequent days-off.

L.Z.

77381 JARITZ, Horst und Manfred BIETAK, Zweierlei Pegeleichungen zum Messen der Nilfluthöhen im Alten Ägypten. Untersuchung zum neuentdeckten Nilometer des Chnum-Tempels von Elephantine (Strabon, XVII.1.48), *MDAIK* 33 (1977), 47-62, with 2 folding fig., 1 plan and 3 pl.

Study on account of the recently discovered Nilometer connected with a basin at the S.E. corner of the late Khnum temple.
The construction is described and dated to the Post-Saite Period. Two different, overlapping gouge systems occur, one of which the usual system, the other (B) with a higher zero level. There occur also two systems in the inscriptions of the kiosk of Sesostris I, of which the second indicates the average height of the inundation above the fields in Upper Egypt. The authors argue that this second system agrees with system B of Elephantine, and that this is probable meant in the text of the Palermo stone. Comparison of the O.K. with the M.K. data shows a lower inundation in the later period.
The Demotic inscription in the Nilometer is given in transliteration and translation. The basin may have been intended to measure the water level according to system B. This Nilometer is argued to be that described by Strabo.

JARITZ, Horst, see also our numbers 77056 and 77389.

77382 JAROŠ, Karl, unter Mitarbeit von Marianne LEIMLEHNER und Grete SWEDIK, Ägypten und Vorderasien. Eine kleine Chronographie bis zum Auftreten Alexander des Grossen, Linz-Wien-Passau, Veritas-Verlag/Stuttgart, KBW Verlag, [1977] (12.2 × 19 cm; 206 p., 5 plans, 20 maps, 1 ill., 20 fig., fig. on cover); rev. *Anthropos* 72 (1977), 621 (Joseph Henninger); *ZAW* 89 (1976), 305-306 ([G. Fohrer]). Pr. DM 14.50

This chronological survey of the history of ancient Egypt and the ancient Near East is intended for students and the general public. It consists of four chapters, each beginning with sections on Egypt. As regards Egyptian history, most facts related are in accordance with the compendium of von Beckerath (our No. 71057). The room each period occupies is small; for instance, the XIth Dynasty is dealt with on half a page (p. 26), the XIXth on just over 2 pages (57-59).

77383 JARRETT, J.C., The Song of Lament: An Artistic Women's Heritage (A Study of the Modern Greek Lamenting Tradition and its Ancient Western Asiatic and Mediterranean Prototypes), *Dissertation Abstracts International,* Ann Arbor, Mich. 38, No. 4 (October 1977), 1727-A.

Abstract of a thesis Wesleyan University, 1977 (Order No. 77-21,720; 294 p.). Part 1 examines the ancient prototypes for the lament and the lamenter in the ancient Near East and the Mediterranean. *L.Z.*

JEFFREYS, D.G., see our number 77717.

JOHANNES, Dieter, see our number 77051.

77384 JOHNSON, Janet H., Avoid Hard Work, Taxes, and Bosses: Be a Scribe!, *Newsletter ARCE* Nos. 99/100 (Winter/Spring 1977), 17.

Abstract of a paper.

77385 JOHNSON, Janet H., Louvre E 3229: A Demotic Magical Text, *Enchoria* 7 (1977), 55-102, with 8 pl.

Publication of P. Louvre E 3229 (collection of magical spells: 3rd century A.D.). The commentary includes a comparison with the Magical Papyrus London-Leiden and Leiden I 384. *W. Brunsch*

77386 JOHNSON, Janet H., Private Name Seals of the Middle Kingdom, *in: Seals and Sealing in the Ancient Near East.* Edited by McGuire Gibson and Robert D. Biggs, Malibu, Undena Publications, 1977 (= Bibliotheca Mesopotamica. Primary sources and interpretative analyses for the study of Mesopotamian civilization and its influences from late prehistory to the end of the cuneiform tradition. Edited by Giorgio Buccellati, 6), 141-145.

The introduction of name and title(s) on private late M.K. seals probably reflects two historical changes, namely the rise of the individual's expectations in the afterlife and the conscious development of a highly organized, hierarchical central government bureaucracy.

Compare our number 77810. *L.Z.*

77387 JUNGE, Friedrich, Die Welt der Klagen, *in: Fragen an die altägyptische Literatur,* 275-284.

Although M.K. literary texts such as the Admonitions, Khakheperreseneb, the Dispute of a Man with his Ba, the Eloquent Peasant and Neferti support the data about the chaos in the F.I.P., the complaints they contain place them in a literary tradition. The recurring principle of the complaints, so far not determined form-critically and attributed to a genre, is the opposition pair, the theme of which is the death-like condition of the world, while the complaints do not form a literary genre, but a speech usage resulting from an interhuman situation. The complaints being topoi reversing what the royal dogma should guarantee, they have no value as sources for the political history.

The cosmic order as opposed to the chaos and abstracted as $m3^ct$ versus $isft$, should maintain the situation of the poor, according to the conception of the world by the high officials responsible for this type of literature. Therefore there is no place for the parvenu, since he is a representative of the chaos, and possesses knowledge only to be acquired through the normal hierarchical way of pupils and mentors. That the upstart causes fear for that reason, is a situation still largely applicable to the present world. L.Z.

JUNGWIRTH, Johann, see our number 77733.

KACZMARCZYK, A., see our number 77175.

77388 KACZMAREK, Hieronim, Bemerkungen zu den neuesten Sedfeststudien, *Folia Orientalia*, Kraków 18 (1977), 283-289.

A review article of our number 74348.

77389 KAISER, Werner, Günter DREYER, Robert GEMPELER, Peter GROSSMANN und Horst JARITZ, Stadt und Tempel von Elephantine. Siebter Grabungsbericht, *MDAIK* 33 (1977), 63-100, with 2 fig., 10 plans and 14 pl.

Sequel to our number 76409.

The main object of the campaigns of 1976 has been the older and oldest levels of the Satet temple. In section 1 a survey of the history of this temple is given, followed in section 2 by more detailed discussion of the M. and O.K. levels and the objects there found.

Section 3 deals with the researches in the area of the Khnum temple; section 4 with those in the settled area S. of it, particularly with the W. side of the entrance of the O.K. temple. In the fifth section the quay N. of the temple area is discussed. The last section mentions further results of the study of the Coptic pottery, with a catalogue of types and discussion of the chronology.

77390 KÁKOSY, L., Bark and Chariot, *Studia aegyptiaca* 3 (1977), 57-65, with 1 ill. and 2 fig.

Although the Sun-god, covering immense distances along the heaven, had to move at the highest possible speed it seems that his course was not connected with the chariot. However, the author suggests that the falcon figure bearing a sun-disk on its head, fitted on the pole of one of Tutankhamon's chariots, may mean that it was conceived as the vehicle of the sun-god. An inscription on a whip from the same tomb

77391 KÁKOSY, László, Ein literarisch-mythologisches Motiv: Osiris als Gott des Kampfes und der Rache, *in: Fragen an die altägyptische Literatur,* 285-288.

The author draws attention to the marginal aspect of Osiris as god of war and revenge, although then functioning as restorer of justice and normally not by personal intervention. L.Z.

77392 KÁKOSY, L., The Primordial Birth of the King, *Studia aegyptiaca* 3 (1977), 67-73.

Proceeding from a passage in the stela behind the Memnon colossi in which Amon states to have created Amenophis III before all other gods, the author seeks the underlying idea of the concept of primordial birth in the myth of the Golden Age. It was placed back into this time of innocence following the creation. The argument is illustrated by quotations from P.T., C.T. and B.D.

KAMIR, Sid Ahmed Abd el Magid, see our numbers 77768, 77769, 77770 and 77771.

KAMIR, Yussef, see our number 77768.

77393 KANAWATI, Naguib, The Egyptian Administration in the Old Kingdom. Evidence on its Economic Decline, Warminster, Aris & Phillips Ltd., [1977] (21 × 29.5 cm; IV + 165 p., 15 fig.). Pr. £10.50

The aim of this study (a thesis at the Macquarie University, Australia, 1972) is to examine statistically the trend in the wealth of the O.K. officials by means of a study of the costliness of their tombs and to discuss the possible rôle of the administration in the economic decline which is believed to be the major factor in the fall of the O.K.

In the introduction the author sets forth the method of this research. He argues that a man paid for the construction of his tomb out of his own income, although some pieces may have been given by the king. Hence size and elaboration of the tomb reflect his wealth. Kanawati first has studied the trend in the costliness of the tombs of the viziers (see our number 75377). He then established that the officials can be divided into three groups: higher, middle and lower. It appeared that data for 23 higher and 13 middle officials from the capital produced similar trends as that of the viziers, as also did the data for the remaining lower officials. As regard rock tombs, their area appears to be one tenth of that of a freestanding tomb belonging to an official of an equal category in the same period.

In Part II the material on which the study is based is presented, a list of 397 tombs arranged alphabetically after the names of the owners. For a key to these tables, see p. 5-8.

The second chapter of Part I is devoted to the officials in the capital, the third to those in the provinces of Upper Egypt. Each chapter first deals with the date of the tombs and their sequence, and then it presents an outline of the basic results as regards the trends of wealth (vizualized in 15 graphs). In the last chapter the historical results and the general conclusions are presented.

Apart from numerous minor observations and suggestions the conclusions are: the resources of the lower and middle rank officials declined during the O.K., the latter group being unable to build a tomb from the reign of Unas onwards, the former from that of Pepi I. The same trend is found for the higher officials, including the viziers, but interrupted by temporary rises, and again it is the trend for the provincial officials during the VIth Dynasty, evidence for the preceding period being minimal. The reason for the decline is not, as has been suggested, decentralization, for the provincial tombs show the same trend. Moreover, the biography of *K3r* and other evidence suggest a still strong influence of the king over provincial officials during the reign of Pepi II. The actual reason for the decline is an increase in the number of officials, which in a relatively static economy means a decrease in individual income, and, hence, in efficiency of the administration.

As regards the cause of the fluctuations in the resources of the higher officials and the nomarchs, the author suggests that after every interruption in the proper succession the new ruler attempted to "buy" the cooperation of these officials.

In appendix 1 the date of each of the 397 tombs here used as material is indicated; in appendix 2 the author deals with the two middle officials *K̲3r* and *'Idw* whose tombs are recently published by Simpson (our number 76724).

Bibliography on p. 157-160; indices p. 161-165.

77394 KANAWATI, Naguib, The Identification of $D̲^cw/Šm3î$ and $D̲^cw$ in the Decoration of Their Tomb at Deir el-Gebrawi, *JEA* 63 (1977), 59-62.

This unique Old Kingdom tomb contained a father and son buried in the same structure and thus poses a problem as to which one the scenes refer. The article shows that the artist used three methods to distinguish them. *E. Uphill*

77395 KANAWATI, Naguib, Was *Ibj* of Deir el-Gebrawi a Polygamist ?, *SAK* 5 (1977), 123-129.

Studying the family relations of *'Ibî*, the owner of tomb No. 8 in Deir el-Gebrâwi, the author argues that he had children by two wives within the same period. One of them is not depicted in the tomb, perhaps because she was dead or divorced when it was built.

77396 KAPLONY, Peter, Die Definition der schönen Literatur im alten Ägypten, *in: Fragen an die altägyptische Literatur,* 289-314.

First the author presents some examples of abstraction in the fields of writing, religion, representational art and the funerary cult, where referential shift in the negative sense can be noticed in its profanation, and discusses next the word *ḥmww*, "artist" and related words, as well as other problems of literature and authorship. The last part of the article investigates the main genres of literature and their original functional models: wisdom literature from general and specific royal decrees and service regulations; characteristics from those in service regulations and scientific literature; individual autobiographies from ideal autobiographies; discourses such as disputes and monologues from the juridical sphere; letters from private letters; royal stories and general prophecies from annals and the institutional royal oracle; marvel stories from birth legends, dream reading, letters to the dead, etc.; stories on gods from the field of religion, and lastly profane songs from cult songs for the king and the gods. *L.Z.*

77397 KAPLONY, Peter, Die Rollsiegel des Alten Reichs. I. Allgemeiner Teil mit Studien zum Königtum des Alten Reichs, Bruxelles, Fondation Égyptologique Reine Élisabeth, 1977 (22 × 28.5 cm; XII + 380 p.) = Monumenta Aegyptiaca, 2. Pr. Fr.b.1900

After an introduction about the major problems of the study of cylinder seals in general the first chapter is devoted to the meaning and chronology of the seals from the O.K. Various kinds, e.g. the office seals and seals of officials, and important points such as the personal character of the office seal and its use in private matters pass the review.

Chapter 2 presents a classification of the seals after inscriptions. Chapter 3 is devoted to the royal titulary occurring on seals, i.a. the criteria for presence or omission of the ring-name and other royal titles on Horus-name seals. Chapter 4 deals with the heraldry of the

representations: the *srḫ* with a falcon or a sphinx above it, groups of figures of the king with Re and Hathor, or with Nekhbet and Wadjet, and many more. An excursus on the pictogram *Wnjs 23* is added.
In chapter 5 the author discusses the more important historical data on the seals: the kings of the mid Vth Dynasty and their order, coregencies, Sun-cults and royal cults, the management of Sun-temples, *mrt*-sanctuaries and pyramids, etc. In chapter 6 the important sites where (unpublished) cylinder seals have been found are discussed, e.g. Abûsîr, the Valley Temple of the Bent Pyramid and Buhen.
In the last chapter technical indications to the catalogue which will be published in volume 2.

77398   KARIG, Joachim Selim, Corpus Antiquitatum Aegyptiacarum, *ZÄS* 104 (1977), 39-46.

Verfasser drückt die Vorläufige Fassung der Richtlinien zur Veröffentlichung ägyptischer Altertümer als Lose-Blatt-Katalog ab. Als Einführung erzählt er die bisherige Geschichte des internationalen Unternehmens.

Vgl. unsere Nummer 76164.   *M. Heerma van Voss*

77399   KARIG, Joachim S., Göttinger Miszellen. Beiträge zur ägyptologischen Diskussion. Herausgegeben von Mitarbeitern des Ägyptologischen Seminars der Universität Göttingen, Göttingen, 1972 ff., *ZDMG* 127 (1977), 83-86.

The author evaluates the first nine issues of the *GM*.

77400   KATER-SIBBES, G.J.F. and M.J. VERMASEREN, Apis, III. Inscriptions, Coins and Addenda, Leiden, E.J. Brill, 1977 (16 × 24 cm; XII + 53 p., 2 folding maps, 28 pl., coloured frontispiece) = Études préliminaires aux religions orientales dans l'Empire romain publiées par M.J. Vermaseren, 48; rev. *Acta Archaeologica Academiae Scientiarum Hungaricae* 30 (1978), 473-474 (L. Castiglione); *BiOr* 35 (1978), 105-106 (Ladislav Vidman); *CdE* LIV, No. 107 (1979), 93-94 (Michel Malaise).   Pr. fl.72

Sequel to our numbers 75385 and 75386.
The present volume deals with a few inscriptions related to the Apis cult, and for the major part with coins issued in various cities bearing a representation of Apis, testifying to either the worship of the bull in the city or the reverence to a specific emperor, e.g. Hadrianus or Julianus. The catalogue of the coins comprises 149 numbers, each with a brief description and bibliographical references.

There follow addenda to vols I (p. 38-40) and II (41-47), and indexes to the present volume. Many of the objects listed are represented on the pl.

77401 KATZNELSON, I. S., Тутанхамон и сокравища его гробницы, Москва, Издательство "Наука". Главная редакция восточной литературы, 1976 (12.4 x 20.1 cm; 152 p., 31 ill., 1 fig., 1 plan); at head of title: Академия наук СССР. Институт востоковедения.

'Tutankhamun and the Treasures of his Tomb'.
An initial chapter on 'Tutankhamon and his time' (p. 7-18) is followed by one on 'tombs and robbers' (19-41). After a brief survey of earlier exploration of the Theban necropolis (42-46), the search and actual discovery by Carter are described (47-52 and 53-63). The rest of the book is mainly concerned with details on the four rooms and their contents (64-135); concluding chapters on the gradual oblivion of the king and his tomb (136-143) and the artistic importance of the finds (144-150). *J.F. Borghouts*

KEEBLE, K. Corey, see our number 77321.

77402 KEEL, Othmar, Der Bogen als Herrschaftssymbol. Einige unveröffentlichte Skarabäen aus Ägypten und Israel zum Thema "Jagd und Krieg", *Zeitschrift des Deutschen Palästina-Vereins*, Wiesbaden 93 (1977), 141-177, with 36 fig. and 4 pl.

The author first discusses scenes in which the hunt of dangerous animals and the victory over Egypt's enemies are parallel and even interchangeable themes. For this equality evidenced by the compository symmetry the author presents examples from various periods beginning with the M.K. Even more clear in this respect are those scenes in which hunt and war motifs are fused in one representation. Evidence for human beings and animals being the subject of royal archery comes exclusively from small objects of art, on which there is more liberty for motifs than on monumental reliefs. The next theme discussed is Pharaoh who, while sitting on a throne, shoots with a bow at animals and/or human beings, the oldest evidence for which dates back to Tutankhamun. The author pays particular attention to two scenes on objects from Tutankhamun's tomb, one showing the king sitting on a folding chair and shooting at a papyrus-thicket with birds, and the other showing the king sitting on a chair with back and bow-shooting at fowl and fish. The fourth section of the article is devoted to scenes representing the king who sits on a throne and shoots at animals and human beings, for which he gives 8 examples from scarabs. The figure of the king can even be replaced by his cartouche. Then the author describes various compositions in the Egyptian iconography in which the bow is present as the symbol of power and sovereignty over defeated enemies, although the bow can also symbolize, as in the Nine Bows, the resistance and defensive power of other peoples. The last part of the amply illustrated article is devoted to the bow as symbol in the O.T. *L.Z.*

77403 KEEL, Othmar, Jahwe-Visionen und Siegelkunst. Eine neue Deutung der Majestätsschilderungen in Jes. 6, Ez 1 und 10 und Sach 4. Mit einem Beitrag von A. Gutbub über die vier Winde in Ägypten, Stuttgart, Verlag Katholisches Bibelwerk, [1977] (13.2 × 20.6 cm; 410 p., 257 fig., 5 pl.) = Stuttgarter Bibelstudien, 84/85; rev. *ZAW* 90 (1978), 309-310 ([G. Fohrer]).

The author examines the backgrounds of the elements occurring in O.T. visions concerning Jahwe, comparing them with material from oriental art. Although particularly material from the Near East is adduced that from ancient Egypt is by no means absent.

We mention, for example, the following subjects: the throne (p. 33-36), snakes with human bodies (76-77), the uraeus (83-103), the ram with four heads (222-223) and the lettuce and the fan of Min (282-284); in other sections Egypt is also frequently mentioned.

The appendix, by Alphonse Gutbub (328-353), is devoted to texts and representations of the Four Winds in Egypt. It first presents a list of 18 representations in temple reliefs and on coffins from the Graeco-Roman Period (either with animal or human bodies). After briefly mentioning two earlier texts to the subject (P.T. 497b and C.T. 162) the author studies the "Theban system" of the Late Period in which the Four Winds are represented either as animals with ram's heads or as genii, and compares it with two scenes of the Kôm Ombo temple. The book is very well illustrated by numerous drawings which constitute an essential part of the argument. An extensive bibliography on p. 361-383; indexes on p. 393-410.

77404 KEEL, Othmar, Vögel als Boten. Studien zu Ps 68, 12-14, Gen 8, 6-12, Koh 10,20 und zu dem Aussenden von Botenvögeln in Ägypten. Mit einem Beitrag von Urs Winter zu Ps 56, 1 und zur Ikonographie der Göttin mit der Taube, Freiburg/Schweiz, Universitätsverlag — Göttingen, Vandenhoeck & Ruprecht, 1977 (15.5 × 23 cm; 164 p., 7 ill., 38 fig.); series: Orbis biblicus et orientalis, 14; rev. *BiOr* 35 (1978), 67-68 (E. Lipiński); *Journal of Biblical Literature* 98 (1979), 433-434 (Ronald J. Williams); *ZAW* 89 (1977), 456 ([G. Fohrer]). Pr. DM 32

The author continues his iconographic studies of passages from the O.T. and their relation to Egyptian rituals (see our numbers 74386 and 74387) with this book on birds as messengers. The Egyptian evidence, presented in chapter V (p. 103-142) and illustrated by drawings and photographs of reliefs, once more constitutes an important original contribution to Egyptology.

In the first section of the chapter birds as navigation aids in Egypt are discussed, for which the author particularly points out the occurrence of pintail ducks in representations of Syrian ships in the tombs of Kenamon and Khaemhet. The other section, on birds as messengers of coronation and victory, contains a catalogue of texts and representations of the ritual of setting birds free at festivals (eleven instances), with an extensive discussion of each. The author also deals with the types of birds (in some instances *swrw*, not the *sr*-goose, in others the roller); reminiscences to the rite in Greek texts and representations on a cylinder seal and a Megiddo ivory; and the meaning of the rite (summary on p. 141-142).

77405   KEEL, Othmar, Die Welt der altorientalischen Bildsymbolik und das Alte Testament. Am Beispiel der Psalmen, [Zürich, Einsiedeln, Köln], Benzinger Verlag/[Neukirchen-Vluyn], Neukirchener Verlag, [1977] (17.8 × 25.7 cm; 391 p., 1 map, 500 + 41 fig. [including numerous plans], 24 pl.); rev. *ZAW* 80 (1978), 310 ([G. Fohrer]).

Second, revised and enlarged edition of our number 72370.
On p. 330-348 one finds corrigenda and addenda to the first edition and to the bibliography.

77406   KELLER, C. A., Two Painters of the Tomb of Ramesses IV, *Newsletter ARCE* Nos. 99/100 (Winter/Spring 1977), 16.

Abstract of a paper.

KELLER, Dominik, see our number 77130.

77407   KEMP, Barry J., A Building of Amenophis III at Kôm El-ᶜAbd, *JEA* 63 (1977), 71-82, with 2 pl., 2 fig., 1 map and 1 plan.

An unusual set of buildings lies 3.5 km S.W. of Amenophis III's palace at Malkata, and 200 m W. of the fertile ground of the valley, briefly reported on by Myers in *JEA* 23 (1937), 118. One part is composed of a platform 45m × 40m and 3.75 m high, the other of a group of 7 houses four of which are in one block. Surface finds of pottery fall into later periods. It is suggested that these form a palace pavilion for occasional use, comparable with some of the Amarna buildings, and that it was a 'rest-house' comparable with some of the Amarna buildings, even perhaps used at chariot races held on the adjoining desert as postulated by Myers. *E. Uphill*

77408 KEMP, Barry J., The Early Development of Towns in Egypt, *Antiquity* 51 (1977), 185-200, with 1 map, 3 plans, 3 fig. and 3 pl.

After criticizing the views of Helck and Wilson as regards the absence of urbanism in Egypt, a view exclusively based on textual evidence, the author reports on his survey carried out on some town sites: Abydos, Tell Edfu and Memphis, and a few other centres in Upper Egypt. One of his conclusions is that several of them were resited in the N.K., from off the old mounds and presumably in favour of the flood plain.

The last section deals with the character and origin of towns, suggesting that they may have been mainly agricultural towns; that Upper Egypt never experienced the classic city-state phase; that in the late prehistory Negada and Hieraconpolis may have been primate towns, centres of a larger area in which the population was settled in small dispersed villages, and that during the O.K. from this stage developed a fairly full range of settlement sites (size-rank distribution). His main conclusions are: ancient Egypt was an urbanized society of a relatively normal type, and this aspect of society finds little reflection in the surviving inscriptions.

77409 KEMP, Barry J., An Incised Sherd from Kahun, Egypt, *JNES* 36 (1977), 289-292, with 1 fig. and 1 ill.

A sherd of a hand-made bowl decorated with two sets of lines crossing each other at an angle, at present in the British Museum (No. 55289), has been found by Petrie at Kahûn. It is of a type characteristic for the pan-grave culture. The single item does not mean, however, that there was a pan-grave settlement phase at Kahûn.

77410 KEMP, Barry J., The Palace of Apries at Memphis, *MDAIK* 33 (1977), 101-108, with 2 fig. (one folding), 1 folding plan and 3 pl.

The author examined the palace of Apries at Memphis in order to verify some details mentioned by Petrie. He concludes that there is no reason to assume that it was built on top of earlier palaces. The constructional methods used for building the platform on which the palace stood are discussed. On its South a great sloping avenue appears to have led up to this platform.

KEMP, Barry J., see also our number 77302.

77411   KENDALL, Timothy, The Rock-Cut Statue Niche as Decoration in Old Kingdom Tombs, *Newsletter ARCE* Nos. 99/100 (Winter/Spring 1977), 17.

Abstract of a paper.

77412   KESSLER, Dieter, Neue Funde in Mittelägypten (Vorbericht über einen Survey in den Region von al-Minia), *in: XIX. Deutscher Orientalistentag*, 31-35, with 1 pl.

During a survey in 1974-1975 in the region of el-Minya several pharaonic objects were found. The author describes 8 documents from sites in the fertile area West of the Nile and some others from the East side.
                                                                                                                                    L.Z.

77413   KHOURY, René, Quelques notes additionnelles au *"Voyage en Égypte"* de Pierre Belon (1547). (Édition de l'IFAO, 1970), *BIFAO* 77 (1977), 261-270.

Some notices, mostly on biological matters, to our number 70053.

77414   KING, Charles, Hieroglyphs to Alphabets, London, Frederick Muller Limited, [1977] (13.5 × 21.8 cm; 133 p., 5 fig., 7 ill.); rev. *BiOr* 34 (1977), 305 (anonymous).   Pr. £3.95

The author gives a sketch of the development of writing for the general reader, including a lot of information about historical background, religion and magic, the rediscovery of Egyptian hieroglyphic writing, etc. The facts here mentioned are not always quite accurate and some of the hieroglyphic texts given in a written copy contain small slips, the author evidently not being a professional Egyptologist.

The last chapters (p. 93-129) deal with cuneiform and other scripts.

77415   KIRCHHEIMER, Franz, Ein fossiler *Nautilus* und die aus ihm in ägyptisierender Manier gestaltete Skulptur, *Der Aufschluss. Zeitschrift für die Freunde der Mineralogie und Geologie,* Heidelberg 28 (Dezember 1977), 509-524, with 5 ill.

The author publishes a sculpture of a head formed from the stone core of the hull of a large nautilus. First he extensively describes the fossil and then the sculpture. The piece is hardly datable and is generally felt by the experts to be certainly not ancient Egyptian.   *L.Z.*

77416   KISCHKEWITZ, Hannelore, Zur temporären Einwohnung des Gottes im König, *in: Ägypten und Kusch*, 207-212.

In der Phraseologie der Könige des Neuen Reiches wird sehr häufig der König als Bild des Gottes bezeichnet, doch wurde diese Formel nicht Bestandteil der kanonischen fünffältigen Titulatur. Die Identität König-Gott hat sich seit dem Alten Reich zu einer Konsubstantialität gewandelt; die Definition des Königs als Bild Gottes hatte einen eindeutig physischen Aspekt. Zu Beginn des Neuen Reiches wurde auf einer Stele des Königs Amosis (*Urk.* IV, 18, 15-16) versucht, die Neubewertung des Königs im ideologischen Gefüge auch in einer möglichen Deutung als Kultbild zu überprüfen, in dem der Gott gerade seine Einwohnung vollzogen hat. Diese Deutung konnte sich jedoch nicht durchsetzen, was letztlich auch die Singularität des Beleges beweist. *Inge Hofmann*

77417 KISS, Zsolt, Les fouilles polonaises en Égypte et au Soudan, en 1975, *Africana-Bulletin,* Warszawa 25 (1976), 129-132.

Short note on the work of the Polish mission at Alexandria, Deir el-Bahri and Kadero. *L.Z.*

77418 KITCHEN, Kenneth A., Historical Observations on Ramesside Nubia, *in: Ägypten und Kusch,* 213-225, with 1 map.

In dem Artikel werden die militärischen Aktionen der Ramessidenzeit in Nubien untersucht: Ramses I. hat in Nubien keine Aktionen durchgeführt; Sethos I. mußte wahrscheinlich in seinem 8. Jahr eine Revolte in Irem niederschlagen, das bei Kerma vermutet wird. 20 Jahre später kam es unter Ramses II. zu einem neuen Zusammenstoß mit Irem; in seinem 44. Jahr unternimmt der Vizekönig Setau eine Razzia in die südlichen Oasen Unternubiens. Unter Merenptah kam es im Zusammenhang mit dem Libyerkrieg zu einer Revolte in Wawat. Ramses III. rühmt sich, einen Aufstand in Tirawayu und Irem niedergeschlagen zu haben; da Tirawayu von der üblichen Orthographie abweicht, mag diese Notiz historisch sein. *Inge Hofmann*

77419 KITCHEN, K.A., On the Princedoms of Late-Libyan Egypt, *CdE* LII, No. 103 (1977), 40-48.

Article de recension des problèmes de chronologie étudiés par Farouk Gomaà, Die libyschen Fürstentümer des Deltas (notre No. 74251), qui s'est servi essentiellement du cadre proposé par von Beckerath (notre No. 71057), mais que l'auteur a lui-même modifié dans The Third Intermediate Period in Egypt, (notre No. 72379 = 73405). Un certain nombre de problèmes d'attribution de monuments sont également discutés. *Ph. Derchain*

77420 KITCHEN, K.A., Ramesside Inscriptions. Historical and Biographical. II. Fascicle 8, Oxford, B.H. Blackwell Ltd, [1977] (20.5 × 28.5 cm; 32 p. [= II, 417-448]); rev. *BiOr* 35 (1978), 49-50 (W. Helck); *RdE* 30 (1978), 185-188 (France Le Corsu).

A sequel to our number 76446.
The Royal Monuments — Geographical Series is continued with the inscriptions from Tanis, all originally from Pi-Ramesse. We mention: those from the major and lesser obelisks, granite columns, single statues of the king, dyads (king and deity), triads (king and flanking deities). L.Z.

77421 KITCHEN, K.A., Ramesside Inscriptions. Historical and Biographical. II. Fascicle 9, Oxford, B.H. Blackwell Ltd, [1977] (20.5 × 28.5 cm; 32 p. [= II, 449-480]); rev. *BiOr* 35 (1978), 49-50 (W. Helck); *RdE* 30 (1978), 185-188 (France Le Corsu).

Sequel to our preceding number.
The inscriptions from Tanis — Pi-Ramesse are continued with other statuary. Then follow two series of cults for the royal statues from Pi-Ramesse. The Tanis — Pi-Ramesse inscriptions end with offering tables, architectural parts from the temples and various elements from the vineyards and palace at Pi-Ramesse.
The third part of the Geographical Series of Royal Monuments in the East Delta is devoted to other sites such as Mendes, Bubastis, Athribis, and Tell el-Yahûdîya. The Geographical Series is continued by the inscriptions from the Central and West Delta, and the Libyan Marshes.
The fascicle ends with the obelisks originating from Heliopolis, but now in Rome, London and New York. L.Z.

77422 KITCHEN, K.A., Ramesside Inscriptions. Historical and Biographical. V, Fascicle 4, Oxford, B.H. Blackwell Ltd, [1977] (20 × 28.5 cm; 32 p. [= V, 193-224]); rev. *BiOr* 35 (1978), 49-50 (W. Helck); *RdE* 30 (1978), 185-188 (France Le Corsu).

Sequel to our number 72378.
The Festivals of the Gods are continued with the Festivals of Sokar and Amon, both from Medînet Habu, those of the Festivals of Min and Amon, from the Amon-temple of Ramses III at Karnak, and the Festival of Min from Medînet Habu and the Ramesseum. L.Z.

77423 KITCHEN, K.A., Ramesside Inscriptions. Historical and Biographical. V. Fascicle 5, Oxford, B.H. Blackwell Ltd, [1977] (20 × 28.5 cm; 32 p. [= V, 225-256]); rev. *BiOr* 35 (1978), 49-50 (W.

Helck); *RdE* 30 (1978), 185-188 (France Le Corsu).
Continuation of our preceding number.
After the Festivals of the Gods are concluded with that of Amon in the Amon-temple of Ramses III at Karnak and that of the Valley from Medînet Habu, the fascicle is continued by the Dated Series of the Royal and Related Monuments. They range from i.a. a donation stela from Madâmûd of year 2, through inscriptions from W. Silsila of the years 5 and 6, an inscription of year 12 of vizier To and texts of Penpato from the year 15 to the great double stela from Karnak of the year 20. The series ends with a stela from Koptos of the year 29.
On the last pages a Geographical Series of Royal and Related Monuments from Western Asia, comprising i.a. monuments from Beth-Shan. *L.Z.*

KITCHEN, Kenneth A., see also our number 77247.

77424 KLASENS, A., Rijksmuseum van Oudheden, *Nederlandse Rijksmusea*, 's Gravenhage 97 (1975), 1977, 249-260, with 5 ill.
Various objects from the animal necropolis at Saqqâra were donated by the Egypt Exploration Society, among which a phallophory, and bronze and faience statuettes of gods.
The main acquisition was a tomb stela from the 3rd century A.D. and probably originating from el-Bahnassa (Oxyrhynchus), bearing on one side the representation of a man and on the other, but upside down, that of a woman. At the end a short report on the Dutch-English excavations carried out in the tomb of Horemheb. *L.Z.*

77425 KLENGEL, Horst, Das Land Kusch in den Keilschrifttexten von Amarna, in: *Ägypten und Kusch*, 227-232.
In den Amarnatexten kommt der Ländername Kaši (geschrieben Ka-ši, Ka-si, Ka-a-ša) vor, der mit Kusch gleichgesetzt werden kann. Die Belege finden sich durchweg in Briefen aus den frühen Regierungsjahren Amenophis' IV. Kaši kann durch einen Schrägstrich mit dem Ländernamen Meluḫḫa gleichgesetzt werden, ein Gebiet, das südlich und süd-östlich von Ägypten zu suchen ist. Damit haben wir allerdings noch kein sicheres Zeugnis für eine tatsächliche Übereinstimmung dessen, was man in der Amarnazeit im Vorderen Orient unter Meluḫḫa bzw. Kaši verstand. Während Rib-Adda Soldaten aus dieser Gegend erbittet, handelt es sich in anderen Briefen um Diener, die wegen ihrer Dunkelhäutigkeit wohl das Prestige der vorderorientalischen Könige erhöhen sollten. In einem Amarna-Brief aus Kumidi handelt es sich um eine Umsiedlung von Ḫapiru-Leuten

nach Kāša. Kaši-Leute befanden sich zur Zeit der Amarna-Briefe auch in Palästina, u.a. Teile der besonders geschätzen Bogentruppen von Kusch.
Inge Hofmann

77426 KOELBING, Huldrych M., Arzt und Patient in der antiken Welt, Zürich und München, Artemis Verlag, [1977] (13 × 21 cm; 240 p.); series: Die Bibliothek der Alten Welt, Reihe Forschung und Deutung; rev. *Journal of the History of Medicine and Allied Sciences* 33 (1978), 564 (Wolf D. Seufert). Pr. S.F.48

The first part (p. 27-41) of the second chapter is completely devoted to ancient Egypt. The author deals with aspects such as medicine originating in the priestly sphere, specialisms, the Papyrus Edwin Smith, pharmacopoeia, surgery and payment. *L.Z.*

77427 KOERNER, Reinhard, Zu den griechischen Inschriften vom Gebel Abu Dirwa, *in: Ägypten und Kusch*, 233-234, with 4 fig. on 2 pl.

Aus den griechischen Inschriften vom Gebel Abû Dirwa südwestlich von Dakka ergibt sich, daß die Soldaten der römischen Garnison von Dakka im 2. nachchristlichen Jahrhundert dort eine Gottheit Pauthnuphis = Thot von Pnubs, verehrten. Die 1908 von Maspero untersuchten und publizierten Texte wurden erst 1959 wieder aufgenommen, wodurch Masperos Lesungen teils ein wenig verbessert, teils etwas vermehrt werden konnten. *Inge Hofmann*

77428 KOROSTOVTSEV, Michail A., A propos du genre "historique" dans la littérature de l'ancienne Égypte, *in: Fragen an die altägyptische Literatur*, 315-324.

The author draws attention to the almost unknown work by V.V. Struve on Manetho and his time, published in Russian in 1928. He resumes the book in which Struve argues that in Manetho's time the standard of historiography was higher than commonly assumed by Egyptologists and that his sources must have been many and reliable, since the Egyptians held their history in high esteem, this even resulting in a "historical genre" in literature. *L.Z.*

77429 KOROSTOVTSEV, Michail A., Le verbe auxiliaire ỉw en néo-égyptien, *in: Ägypten und Kusch*, 235-241.

Es wird die Funktion des Hilfsverbs ỉw im Neuägyptischen untersucht und seine Bedeutung zur Bildung des 3. Futurums dargelegt; die unterschiedlichen Meinungen der Ägyptologen werden einander gegenübergestellt. *Inge Hofmann*

77430 von KORVIN-KRASINSKI, Cyrill, Vorchristliche matriarchalische Einflüsse in der Gestaltung ältester koptischer und armenischer Kreuze, *Symbolon*. Jahrbuch für Symbolforschung, Köln Neue Folge 3 (1977), 37-73, with 9 fig. and 14 ill.

The author deals with the Christian cross in various shapes, in which he recognizes a "symbol-survival". He i.a. deals with the Coptic "crux ansata" derived from the ʿnḫ-sign, but perhaps also influenced by stylized representations of the Punic goddess Tamit with outstretched arms. In the ʿnḫ-sign of the Amarna Period some authors have recognized also solar influence.

KOZIŃSKI, Wiesław, see our number 77483.

77431 KOZLOFF, Arielle P., Ancient Art, *The Bulletin of the Cleveland Museum of Art*, Cleveland 64, No. 7 (June 1977), 159, with 1 ill.

Among the acquisitions of the Museum are a painted relief fragment from Amenophis III's funerary temple joining another relief fragment also in Cleveland, and an Amarna relief with the head of Nefertiti (see our numbers 77432 and 77471).   *L.Z.*

77432 KOZLOFF, Arielle P., Nefertiti, Beloved of the Living Disk, *The Bulletin of the Cleveland Museum of Art*, Cleveland 64, No. 9 (November 1977), 287-298, with 13 ill. and 1 colour ill. on cover.

The author publishes some talatat recently acquired by the Cleveland Museum of Art (CMA 76.4; 59.188; 59.186), the first two bearing portraits of Queen Nefertiti with the Nubian wig. The first one is still fully coloured, in the last one she wears the long curled wig with feathers which is always shown when she was in the presence of the king.
A fourth relief (CMA 59.187) bears the scene of men hoeing the earth, carved in slightly raised relief. It was probably a representation of builders at work.

77433 KOZLOFF, Arielle P., A New Interpretation of an Old Amarna Enigma, *AJA* 81 (1977), 101-103, with 4 ill.

The author presents a new interpretation for an Amarna relief in the Norbert Schimmel Collection, New York, showing the heads of four foreigners, four arms holding a pole and four strands beneath the chins of the heads: four foreign fan-bearers and horses before a chariot, of which only the four reins are visible.   *L.Z.*

77434 KOZŁOWSKI, Janusz K. and Joachim ŚLIWA, Deir el-Bahari (Badania misji archeologicznej Uniwersytetu Jagiellońskiego w roku

1974), *Sprawozdania archeologiczne,* Wrocław-Warszawa-Kraków-Gdańsk 28 (1976), 37-51, with 3 ill., 5 fig. and an English summary on p. 50-51.

"Deir el-Bahari (Investigations of the Archaeological Mission of the Jagiellonian University in 1974)."

The investigations of a prehistoric settlement in the Deir el-Bahri region in 1974 centred around three problems: the exploitation of flint from the Theban limestone, the study of the prehistoric rock engravings and their chronological classification, and the stratigraphy of the quaternary deposits in the valley. *L.Z.*

KOZŁOWSKI, Janusz K., see also our number 77189.

77435 KRAUSE, M., Das Internationale Kolloquium über die Zukunft der Koptischen Studien und die Gründung der International Association for Coptic Studies, Kairo, Dezember 1976, *Oriens Christianus,* Wiesbaden 61 (1977), 128-130.

Report of the Coptological Congress held in Cairo, December 1976. Compare now The Future of Coptic Studies, edited by R. McL. Wilson, Leiden, E.J. Brill, 1978. *L.Z.*

77436 KRAUSE, Martin, Nubien und Ägypten in christlicher Zeit. Übereinstimmungen auf dem Gebiet der Archäologie, *in: Ägypten und Kusch,* 243-256.

Als Folge der gemeinsamen Religion und des regen Austausches von Menschen zwischen Nubien und Ägypten werden folgende Gemeinsamkeiten in beiden Ländern festgestellt: Bischofsporträts, übereinstimmende Ikonographie von Wandmalereien, übereinstimmende Klostergrundrisse. *Inge Hofmann*

77437 KRAUSPE, Renate, Zwei Rundplastiken im Ägyptischen Museum der Staatlichen Museen zu Berlin, *in: Ägypten und Kusch,* 257-264, with 4 pl.

Es handelt sich dabei: 1. um das Oberteil einer Statuette (Berlin 24190) aus der 18. Dynastie, über deren Herkunft nichts bekannt war. Durch Vergleich mit anderen Plastiken ergibt sich, daß es sich um eine Statuette Amenophis II. handelt und damit identisch ist mit dem Stück Berlin 2057, das seit dem 2. Weltkrieg als verschollen gilt. Berlin 2057 wurde zusammen mit Berlin 2056 von Lepsius aus Ben Naga mitgebracht. Beide Statuetten sind der 1906 in Semna-Ost-Tempel (Kumma) gefundenen Khartoumer Statuette 30 verwandt und sind mit großer Wahrscheinlichkeit während der meroitischen Epoche von dort nach Ben Naga verschleppt worden. 2. Kopf einer Statuette (Berlin 24186), über deren Herkunft nichts bekannt ist und die wohl den Königsplastiken Amenophis II. zuzurechnen ist. *Inge Hofmann*

77438 KRAUß, Rolf, Untersuchungen zu König Amenmesse (2. Teil), *SAK* 5 (1977), 131-174.

Sequel to our number 76467.
The author first lists and discusses the evidence for the viceroy of Kush Messuy who occupied the office under Merenptah and Sethi II, arguing that he was the later king Amenmesse. Then he deals with Amenmesse's mother Takhat, probably the wife of Sethi II and a daughter of Ramses II. A summary of the revolt and reign of Amenmesse on p. 141-145, followed by a discussion of the chronology of the late XIXth Dynasty and the transition to the XXth Dynasty.
A next section presents a list of the texts referring to Amenmesse and those incorrectly ascribed to him. The last section deals with the necropolis workmen from this period (a list on p. 163-167).
Two excursuses discuss *B3kt-wr-nr*, very probably Amenmesse's wife, and Siptah's reign and origin. An addendum to the stelae LD III, 204d (see our number 76467, p. 170 and 183) on p. 172-174.

77439 KRAVTCHENKO, S.L., Некоторые замечания в связи с вновь найденной греческой надписью Эзаны, царя Аксума, *in:* Мероэ, 282-286, with a French summary on p. 301.

"Einige Überlegungen zur griechischen Inschrift auf der Stele des Ezana, Königs von Axum".
Der Artikel beschäftigt sich mit der griechischen Inschrift des Ezana, die 1969 in Enda Kaleb gefunden wurde und die den Feldzug des Ezana nach Nubien behandelt. Sie bekräftigt die bekannten Tatsachen und bietet weitere Information bezüglich dieser Epoche der aksumitischen Geschichte. *Inge Hofmann*

77440 KRAVTCHENKO, S.L., О торговых связях Аксума в первые века нашей эры, *in:* Мероэ, 241-251, with a French summary on p. 298.

"Die Handelsbeziehungen von Axum am Anfang der christlichen Ära".
Anhand von Monumenten der materiellen Kultur, von schriftlichen Berichten und anderen Zeugnissen werden die Beziehungen zwischen Meroe und Axum untersucht. Kusch war das Zentrum des Transithandels, selbst als Axum das wirtschaftliche Übergewicht durch den Handel an der Rotmeerküste erhielt. Es werden zahlreiche Funde besprochen, die auf einen umfangreichen Wirtschaftsaustausch zwischen Meroe und Axum hinweisen. *Inge Hofmann*

77441 KREBS, Walter, Die neolithischen Rinderhirten der Sahara und die Masai, *in: Ägypten und Kusch,* 265-277, with 3 maps and 4 fig. on 4 pl.

Es wird versucht eine Verbindung herzustellen zwischen den hauptsächlich in Kenya lebenden Masai und den Rinderhirten der Sahara im Neolithikum. Verfasser nimmt an, daß sie während der Austrocknung der Arabischen Halbinsel nach Nordafrika vordrangen, und zwar vor Beginn der ägyptischen Reichseinigung. Von dort wurden sie nach Süden abgedrängt. Auch Beziehungen zwischen den Masai und der Bevölkerung von Punt wurden vermutet. Die alte Merkersche These von einem gemeinsamen Ursprung der jüdischen, babylonischen und Masai-Mythen mit einer gemeinsamen Urheimat auf der Arabischen Halbinsel wird verteidigt. *Inge Hofmann*

77442 KREMLEV, N.T., Население Мероэ во время похода Эзаны, *in:* Мероэ, 264-272, with a French summary on p. 299-300.

"Das Volk von Meroe während der Kampagne des Ezana."

Es werden die ethnischen Verhältnisse in der 1. Hälfte des 1. nachchristlichen Jahrtausends im meroitischen Reich untersucht. Am Ende des 3. Jahrhunderts n.Chr. werden zum erstenmal die "Noubae" im Norden von Meroe erwähnt. Die Inschrift des Ezana zeigt, daß Kasu ein geographischer Begriff ist, während die Noba eine Bevölkerung sind. Die "schwarzen Nobas", die die Insel von Meroe bewohnen, sind negroide Nubier, die "roten Nobas" sind eine Übergangsrasse zwischen der europäischen und negroiden Rasse und korrespondieren mit der X-Gruppe und den Nobaten. Die Nobaten sind wohl aus dem Norden von Napata gekommen. König Silko soll die "schwarzen Nobas" oder die Bevölkerung der Region von Napata bekämpft haben.
Inge Hofmann

KRÓLIK, H., see our number 77681.

77443 KRZYŻANIAK, Lech, Early Farming Cultures on the Lower Nile. The Predynastic Period in Egypt, Varsovie, Éditions Scientifiques de Pologne, 1977 (19.5 × 25 cm; 171 p., 2 maps, 2 plans, 43 fig., 7 tables, 4 loose folding maps) = Travaux du Centre d'Archéologie méditerranéenne de l'Académie polonaise des Sciences sous la direction de K. Michałowski, Tome 21; rev. *BiOr* 35 (1978), 73-74 (Fekri A. Hassan).

In the introduction to this study of the Predynastic Period the author states that it is an attempt at reconstructing the main trends and stages of cultural development of the communities along the Lower Nile during the 4th millenium B.C. which lead up to and resulted in the

formation of the early class system of the Egyptian society; this as against earlier studies which were "confined to the registration of data of a purely archaeological nature".
The author presents a chronological survey of earlier studies to the subject and sketches his own methods of investigatory procedures. To him the production of material goods is the major creative force in the development of the social and political structure and the ideology, that is, chiefly, the religious beliefs, although the three spheres are interdependent.
The first chapter contains a description of the main features of the natural environment along the Nile and a survey of the plant cultivation in this region as known from later sources. Chapter 2 summarizes the development of the communities on the Lower Nile in the time prior to the introduction of the food producing economy, with sections comparing the situation in Egypt with those in SW Asia and NE Africa.
Chapter 3 is devoted to the period of the natural irrigation, divided into an early and a later stage. To the former belong the Faiyûm A and the Badari units, to the latter the Merimde, the problematic Omari A, and the Amra (= Naqada I) units. Preceding to the discussion of these "units" there is a section on the natural environment and two on the general characteristics of each of the phases, while in a last section the main trends in the adjacent areas are discussed.
Chapter 4, called "The Period of the Beginning of Controlled Irrigation", follows the same scheme: natural environment, general characteristics, a section on the problematical Omari B unit and a long one (p. 138-164) on the Gerzean (= Naqada II) unit, and a last one on adjacent areas.
It strikes the reader that for the actual historicity of the main criterium in his classification, the beginning of controlled irrigation, the author does not bring forward any proof; on p. 139-140 he even states it to be "probable" that people at that time "began to construct the first basin irrigation system". Numerous other statements, e.g. that "a real money system and a universal form of exchange emerged" (p. 129) remain also without actual proofs.
A summary on p. 168-169. No indexes.

77444 KRZYŻANIAK, Lech, New archaeozoological studies on animal remains from the Neolithic Kadero, *Nyame Akuma,* Calgary No. 11 (November 1977), 56.

Die vorherrschenden Tiere in Kadero waren domestizierte Rinder mit schweren Hörnern; Schafe, Ziegen und Hunde sind weniger zahlreich

vertreten. Unter den Wildtieren wurden Wildkatze, Stachelschwein, Gazelle, Nilpferd und Warzenschwein eruiert. Mollusken waren reichlich vertreten.
Inge Hofmann

77445 KRZYŻANIAK, L., Polish Excavations at Kadero, *Nyame Akuma*, Calgary No. 10 (1977), 45-46.

Fortsetzung unserer Nummern 75423 und 76471.
Die Ausgrabung war auf die neolithische Siedlung konzentriert. Weiteres "Khartoum Neolithic"-Material kam zum Vorschein. Außerdem wurde weiteres Skelettmaterial domestizierter Tiere gefunden. Zwei Radiocarbon-Daten ergaben für das neolithische Kadero die Periode 4100 bzw. 3800 v. Chr.
Inge Hofmann

77446 KUCHMAN, Lisa, Clay Anthropoid Coffins in Egypt, *Newsletter ARCE* Nos. 99/100 (Winter/Spring 1977), 9.

Abstract of a paper.

77447 KUCHMAN, Lisa, The Titles of Queenship: Part I, The Evidence from the Old Kingdom, *Newsletter SSEA* 7, No. 3 (May 1977), 9-12, with 1 table.

In this first part of the series the author lists (chart) and briefly discusses the queen's titles in the O.K. (for the translations, see Appendix 1), dividing them into titles of relationship, of religious function and of royal position. Appendix 2 lists the monuments supplying queens' tables.

77448 KUHLMANN, Klaus P., Der Thron im alten Ägypten. Untersuchungen zu Semantik, Ikonographie und Symbolik eines Herrschaftszeichens, Glückstadt, Verlag J.J. Augustin, 1977 (21 × 29.7 cm; XVI + 114 p., 20 fig., 5 pl.) = Abhandlungen des Deutschen Archäologischen Instituts Kairo. Ägyptologische Reihe. Band 10.; rev. *Anthropos* 73 (1978), 615-617 (Inge Hofmann).
Pr. DM 102

In the introduction to this thesis (Tübingen, 1970) the author explains the scheme of the study and presents remarks regarding his system of transcription. He also discusses the fundamental function of ruler's thrones in general and that in ancient Egypt in particular, stressing that with a squatting people such as the Egyptian a sitting position indicates a high status (cfr 𓀁 as against 𓀀). Throne and dais are hence inseparable and constitute a unit among the regalia.
In the second chapter several words for "throne" are discussed, e.g. *ḫndw, wṯs, tpy-rdww, mn-bdt* and *isbt*. Chapter 3 is devoted to the

word-family *st, st wrt* and *nst*. The following subjects are dealt with: the palaeography of the sign 𓊨 and variants; its phonetic value; semantics of the conception *st*, e.g. the range of its use; meaning and range of use of *st wrt;* the double aspect of raising; the palaeography of the sign 𓊧 ; semantics, range and meaning of *nst*.

Chapter 4 studies the occurrences of the throne in texts. Chapter 5 deals with representations of thrones, the block-throne and the lion-throne, each with various types, and the appurtenances, e.g. footstool, mat, kiosk, canopy and dais. The symbolic meaning of these objects is the subject of chapter 6.

In the last two chapters connected points are dealt with: in chapter 7 the problem whether Isis is the personification of the throne, which the author denies, and in chapter 8 eleven functions the names of which are composed with the word for "throne".

Indexes on p. 109-114.

77449 Kunst der Antike. Schätze aus norddeutschem Privatbesitz. [Von] Wilhelm Hornbostel und Mitarbeiter, Mainz/Rhein, Verlag Philipp von Zabern, [1977] (19.1 × 23.6 cm; XVI + 556 p., 6 colour pl. [2 on covers], 709 ill.). At head of title: Museum für Kunst und Gewerbe Hamburg.

The catalogue is divided after material. The Egyptian part has been taken care of by Hartwig Altenmüller. Since the Egyptian material is much spread in this catalogue we mention all pieces.

In the section of stone objects: Nos. 1 and 2, two Protodynastic vases; nos. 3-5, resp. a relief, a false door and an offering table from the O.K.; an inscribed block from the M.K. (No. 8); No. 9, an Amarna relief; No. 10, a Late Period canopic vessel; No. 22, a votive stela from the Graeco-Roman Period. In the section of bronzes: No. 40, Ptah, XXVIth Dynasty; No. 41, standing mummy figure, Late Period; No. 46, Isis and Osiris, XXVIth Dynasty; No. 47, a lion goddess, Late Period; Nos. 48-49, Neith, XXVIth Dynasty; No. 62, enthroned Amon, Late Period. In the ceramics section: No. 162, a decorated Naqâda vessel; No. 163, an Amarna vessel. And lastly: No. 440, a faience shawabti, from the XXIst and a stuccoed wooden piece from a coffin from the XXIInd Dynasty (No. 443).   *L.Z.*

77450 Kunst und Altertum. Aus den Sammlungen der Universität. 500 Jahre Eberhard-Karls-Universität Tübingen 1477-1977, Tübingen, Universitätsbibliothek, 1977 (14.8 × 20.9 cm; 215 p., 6 maps, 10 fig., 117 ill., 10 colour ill. on 8 pl., colour ill. on cover) = Ausstellungskataloge der Universität Tübingen Nr. 7.

In this catalogue of various collections belonging to the University of Tübingen, prefaced by Hellmut Brunner, the collection of the Egyptological Institute is dealt with on p. 175-204.

After a brief introduction about the history of the collection (many objects came from the Landesmuseum and the Lindenmuseum in Stuttgart) by Ingrid Gamer-Wallert she and five collaborators deal with ninety-four objects in all. For several of them only the essential data are listed, groups of the same nature being preceded by general remarks, while the more important pieces are briefly described and in some instances presented by photographs. We mention: the mastaba of Seshemnofer III (see our number 77124), a wooden statuette of Amenophis I, a fragmentary stelophorous statue of Khawi (owner of Theban tomb no. 214), a small votive stela of the scribe of the necropolis Ramose, a lintel of the scribe Butehamon, etc. Apart from stelae and pieces of sculpture there are bronzes, objects of daily life, tomb equipment, a late sarcophagus, and amulets.

77451 KURTH, Dieter, Götter determinieren Götter, *SAK* 5 (1977), 175-181.

The author discusses the phenomenon occurring in the texts of the late temples that the name of a god is followed, either directly or after a title appended to the first name, by the name of one or more other gods. These name or names act as a "determinative". Shu, e.g., determines the preceding god as a sky-bearer, Re as a sun-god, etc. The analogy with determinatives in the writing is elaborated and the importance of the phenomenon for the study of syncretism indicated.

LABRE†, Yves, see our numbers 77768, 77769 and 77771.

77452 LABROUSSE, A., J.-Ph. LAUER et J. LECLANT, avec collaboration de C. BERGER et I. PIERRE, Mission archéologique de Saqqara. II. Le temple haut du complexe funéraire du roi Ounas, [Le Caire], Publication de l'Institut français d'Archéologie Orientale du Caire, 1977 (20.3 × 27.5 cm; VIII + 150 p., 1 map, 10 plans [5 folding], 143 fig. [some on folding sheets], 41 pl. [including 1 folding plan]) = Bibliothèque d'étude, 73; rev. *Comptes rendus de l'Académie des Inscriptions et Belles-Lettres*, 1978, 151-152 (Jean Leclant).

Sequel to our number 72403.

The first chapter briefly summarizes the results of earlier researches and excavations in the mortuary temple of Unas: those of Barsanti (1899-1901 and 1903), Firth (1929-1930), Lauer (1936-1937 and 1939), the Service des Antiquités (1937 to 1949), as well as mentioning the

study by the authors (1974-1976) on which the present publication is based.
Chapter 2 contains a minute description of the architecture of the building, divided into three sections: the foremost part, the inner temple, and the annexes (the satellite pyramid, the enclosure wall, the court around pyramid and inner temple, the chapel at the N. side of the pyramid). All rooms and building elements are studied, some of them bearing reliefs (Documents 1-18). The chapter is lavishly illustrated by plans and drawings.
The third chapter is devoted to those decoration fragments of which the original position is uncertain (the 18 architectonic elements are included in chapter 2). There are 101 fragments of wall scenes: royal titularies and scenes in which the king appears (e.g., scenes of the Sed-festival and of prisoners), divinities, processions of offering bearers, parts of inscriptions, etc. Then follow Doc. 120-128, elements which belong to the building of Djedkare-Isesi, and Doc. 129-132, elements of statuary and material of uncertain origin. These documents are all carefully described, the majority also represented in photograph and drawing.
A bibliography on p. 133-136.

77453 LACAU, Pierre et Henri CHEVRIER, avec la collaboration de M.-A. BONHÊME et M. GITTON, Une chapelle d'Hatshepsout à Karnak. I, [Le Caire], Le Service des Antiquités de l'Égypte avec la collaboration de l'Institut français d'Archéologie orientale du Caire, 1977 (27 × 34 cm; XXVIII + 465 p., 3 plans, 29 fig.).
This is the text volume of the long expected publication of Hatshepsut's "Red Chapel", for which, as Vercoutter states in his preface and Yoyotte in the introduction, apart from the main authors, Chevrier and Lacau, several others have been responsible, until it was finally seen through the press by Mm. Bonhême and l'Abbé Gitton. The plate volume was published in 1979.
In the introductory part, beside the foreword and bibliography, there is presented a list of published blocks, by Gitton and Yoyotte, and a chronological survey of their discovery, by Gitton.
The study itself begins with a chapter (p. 1-19) on the history of the discovery of the blocks and the unique construction methods used in building the monument, by Chevrier. The rest of the book, by Lacau, contains a minute description and an extensive discussion of the building and each of its walls.
First a general description of the monument, which was a bark-station originally set up in the centre of Hatshepsut's older construction in

front of the M.K. temple at Karnak. Afterwards it has been demolished by Tuthmosis III. Of its more than 470 blocks actually 319 have been rediscovered, enough to enable a reliable reconstruction. In special chapters the author deals with the measurements and the substructure of the monument.

Then follows the discussion of the outer and inner walls, their reliefs and texts (given in hieroglyphs and translation, with commentary). First the W. and E. façades (45-68), then the geographical procession which is depicted in the first register of all four outer walls (69-92). On the N. and S. façades in the second register one finds a historical text, parallel to that in Deir el-Bahri, of which only small fragments have been preserved (92-153). The more complete third register has on the S. side the procession of Amon's bark from Karnak to Luxor, on the N. side its visit to Deir el-Bahri (153-173), while the fifth register shows the return travels (173-204); from the fourth only a few parts have been found (204-212). The sixth register bears offering scenes (213-228); the seventh the presentation of monuments (consecration of gold and of two obelisks) and the coronation of the queen (228-256). The eighth (upper) register bears a decoration by Tuthmosis III.

The next chapter is devoted to the decoration of the inner walls of the vestibule and the sanctuary (306-390), and is followed by a discussion of the doors and of some blocks which could not be placed. The last chapter briefly deals with the history of the buildings on the site: the sanctuary of Tuthmosis III, and that of Philippus Arrhidaeus which replaced it.

Extensive indexes on p. 419-447; a table of concordances between the numbers of the blocks and the pages of their discussion in this study on p. 449-456.

77454   LANDA, N. [and] I. LAPIS, Скульптура столиц и провинций древнего Египта, путеводитель по выставке из фона музея. Под редакцией Б. Б. Пиотровского, Ленинград, Издательство "Аврора", 1977 (11 x 14 cm; 32 p., 1 map, 18 ill., 2 ill. on covers); at head of title: Государственный ордена Ленина Эрмитаж.

'Sculpture from capitals and provinces of Ancient Egypt'.
A concise history of sculpture as far as illustrated by pieces from the Ermitage collection at the occasion of an exhibition.
See our number 74181.
J.F. Borghouts

LANDY, David, see our number 77044.

77455 LAPERRUQUE, Marcel, De l'Égypte ancienne à la Bible. Symbole, symbolismes, Paris, Lauzeray International, 1977 (13.8 × 21 cm; 154 p., 15 pl., ill. on cover).
Study on the parallels between the Hebrew tradition as related in the Bible and the Egyptian civilization.
After an introduction briefly mentioning some subjects, i.a. the offering of the first-born child, circumcision, solar cult, the author deals in separate chapters with: the cult of trees and high places; the funerary cult; dreams; the Hebrews in Egypt; language and literature; the first men (Adam, Eve, Cain, Abel, Seth); the Flood and the Tower of Babel; the name; the temple; God; the Creation.
In his conclusion (p. 133) the author stresses that there appear to exist strong resemblances between Hebrew and Egyptian traditions as well as, where the origins of religious concepts is apparently quite different, a similarity of thinking and traces of mutual influence.

LAPIS, Irma Alexandrovna, see our number 77454.

77456 LAUER, Jean-Philippe, Les pyramides de Sakkarah, Cinquième Édition, revue et augmentée, Le Caire, Imprimerie de l'Institut français d'Archéologie orientale, 1977 (13.5 × 19.5 cm; 2 × 32 + 1 p., 58 pl., 2 ill. on cover) = Bibliothèque générale, 3.
This is the fifth, revised and augmented edition of a guide to Saqqâra for the general reader. The text is in English and French on opposite pages. The author deals more extensively with the Djoser complex (p. 2-15), while shorter chapters are devoted to the pyramid of Sekhemkhet, that of Unas and that of Userkaf. In the last chapter not only the Teti pyramid is described, but also three major mastabas in its neighbourhood as well as the Serapeum and the mastabas of Ti and Ptahhotep.
The booklet is lavishly illustrated with 78 photographs and plans on the plates.

77457 LAUER, Jean-Philippe, Rapport sur les travaux à Saqqarah (26 Novembre 1969-25 Mars 1970), *ASAE* 62 (1977), 201-205, with 6 pl.
Brief report on the author's work in Saqqâra in 1969-1970. For a more extensive version, see our number 70335.

77458 LAUER, Jean-Philippe, Le triangle sacré dans les plans des monuments de l'Ancien Empire, *BIFAO* 77 (1977), 55-78, with 14 plans.
The author discusses the application of the sacred triangle with sides

3-4-5 to the plans of buildings during the O.K., early tombs, pyramid complexes and Sun-temples, all together eleven instances, which demonstrate the rôle of the geometry of the triangles in Egyptian architecture.

LAUER, Jean-Philippe, see also our number 77452.

LAUFFRAY, Jean, see our number 77056.

LAWUILLON-BLUME, Marianne, see our number 77092.

77459 LEAHY, Anthony, Egyptian Geography and Settlement Patterns, in: *Mycenaean Geography*. Proceedings of the Cambridge Colloquium, September 1976. Edited by John Bintliff, Cambridge, The British Association for Mycenaean Studies, 1977, 94-97.

In the section of comparative studies of geographical and textual-geographical research in Old and New World civilizations, of a colloquium on Mycenaean geography, held in September 1976 at Cambridge, the author presents a survey of the ways in which the Nile has influenced population distribution in Egypt. The survey owes particularly to our number 76132.
L.Z.

77460 LEAHY, Anthony, The Osiris "Bed" Reconsidered, *Orientalia* 46 (1977), 424-434, with 8 ill. on 4 pl.

Le "lit" d'Osiris en basalte noir catalogué J.E. 32090 au Musée du Caire (Abydos, tombe de Djer, fouilles Amélineau) montre la momie étendue sur une couche funéraire en forme de lions, accompagnée des faucons Horus et Isis. Ni le style ni les cartouches effacés de la bande inscrite n'ont pu fournir d'élément précis de datation. Le seul nom reconnaissable: Horus *Ḏd Ḫprw,* amène à exclure l'hypothèse d'une inscription archaïsante de la XXVe ou XXVIe dynastie. On ne voit guère comment compléter les lectures de Daressy, mais l'épigraphie, jusqu'ici négligée, s'avère instructive. Considerées dans leur ensemble, la mention d'Oupouaout, la graphie de Khentimen*tiou* et surtout celle d'Osiris (le signe de l'oeil sous celui du lit) amènent l'auteur à proposer comme date la Seconde Période Intermédiaire. Malgré l'éventualité d'une finale en $-\ell$, le nom du souverain consécrateur pourrait être Khendjer.
J. Custers

77461 LEAHY, Anthony, A Scribe of Abydos in the Ninth Century B.C., *GM* Heft 23 (1977), 49-54, with 1 pl.

In der ägyptischen Sammlung des Fitzwilliam-Museums, Cambridge, befindet sich der untere Teil einer Türlaibung aus Kalkstein (Nr. E.SS.47), deren Herkunft und Ankauf nicht bekannt ist. Ein Teil der

Opferformeln sowie Name und Titel des Verstorbenen sind erhalten. Es handelt sich um den Schreiber des göttlichen Buches namens Pediese, dessen übrige Denkmäler ebenfalls herangezogen werden. So läßt sich eruieren, daß Pediese um 800 v. Chr. gestorben ist, zwei Generationen vor Takeloth III.
Inge Hofmann

77462 LEBEL, M., Расчистка росписи стелы Ипи, Сообщения государственного ордена Ленина Эрмитажа, Ленинград 41 (1976), 54-57, with 2 ill.
"The Cleaning of the Inscription of the Stela of Ipy."

77463 Leben im ägyptischen Altertum. Literatur — Urkunden — Briefe — aus vier Jahrtausenden, [Berlin], Herausgegeben von den Staatliche Museen zu Berlin, Papyrussammlung, 1977 (14 × 20 cm; 139 p., 7 fig., 12 colour pl.).
This booklet contains translations for the general reader of a large number of texts from Egypt, from various periods and in various languages. Translations and introductory remarks are from the hand of Ulrich Luft and Günter Poetke. All texts are preserved in the Papyrus-Sammlung, Berlin.
After a preface and short chapters on writing materials and the Egyptian languages and scripts various kinds of documents (literary texts, letters, juridical documents, etc.) in hieratic, hieroglyphic and demotic writing are translated and discussed on p. 10-45. Coptic texts on p. 98-110. The translations present short bits of longer texts or complete shorter ones (e.g. letters), while their museum number, date, material, and provenance are noted.
The rest of the volume contains translations from Aramaic, Latin, Greek and Arabic sources, and on p. 119-124 short discussions of objects connected with writing.

LECH, J., see our number 77681.

77464 LECLANT, Jean, Fouilles et travaux en Égypte en au Soudan, 1975-1976, *Orientalia* 46 (1977), 233-299, with 30 ill. on 24 pl.
Sequel to our number 76485.
The yearly survey of archaeological discoveries and studies is this time divided into 64 numbers for Egypt, 20 for the Sudan, and 15 for other countries. Larger notes in the chapter on Egypt deal with Tell ed-Dab[c]a, Abûsîr, Memphis, Saqqâra, Dashûr, Heracleopolis, the region of el-Minya, Antinoupolis, Nag[c] Hammadi, Karnak and the Theban West Bank, el-Kâb, Aswân, the Oases of Sîwa and Khârga, the coast of the Red Sea, and Philae. In the Sudan chapter the longer entries

deal with a survey S. of the Dal cataract and excavations at Kerma, Old Dongola, Gebel Barkal, Meroe, Kadada, Geili and Kadero as well as surveys in S. and W. Sudan. Outside Egypt several excavations in Israel, Syria and Greece are mentioned. Indexes on p. 295-299.

77465 LECLANT, Jean, Histoire de la diffusion des cultes égyptiennes, *Annuaire. École Pratique des Hautes Études.* V[e] section — sciences religieuses, Paris 85 (1976-1977), fasc. 3, 203-207.

Sequel to our number 76486.

The survey deals with researches on the diffusion of the Isis cults, meroitic studies, campaigns and conferences, and publications. *L.Z.*

77466 LECLANT, Jean, Recherches à la pyramide de Pépi Ier à Saqqarah (1972-1976), *BSFE* Nos. 77-78 (octobre 1976 et mars 1977), 26-38, with 4 ill. and 1 plan.

Dans l'appartement funéraire, les déblaiements et restaurations progressent. L'auteur énumère les principales reconstitutions de textes gravés. On signalera une paroi intacte, une autre presque intégralement remontée, qui qualifie d'Osiris le défunt triomphant; certains textes de conjuration trouvent leur parallèle chez Mérenrê. Les nouveaux chapitres, compléments et groupements éclairent notre connaissance de la disposition générale des textes. L'interdit proscrivant les signes d'hommes s'étendait à plusieurs animaux.

Au temple haut, la fouille atteint la chaussée d'accès. Les éléments dégagés sont remis en place à mesure de leur découverte. Bien des dimensions correspondent à des nombres ronds de coudées. La rigole d'écoulement dans l'axe allait du sanctuaire à l'entrée du temple. L'existence d'un serdab est exclue. Parmi les nombreux petits fragments de décoration se reconnaissent le triomphe sur les Libyens et une scène d'allaitement. Un corpus des fragments de poterie est en préparation. Plusieurs réaménagements sont apparus; ils témoignent surtout de la place du culte de Pépi Ier au Moyen Empire. Près de la double porte a été dégagée une tombe ayant appartenu à un certain Hemi.

J. Custers

77467 LECLANT, Jean, Recherches sur la toponyme méroïtique, *in: La Toponymie Antique,* Actes du Colloque de Strasbourg 12-14 juin 1975, Leiden, E.J. Brill, 1977 (= Université des Sciences Humaines de Strasbourg. Travaux du Centre de Recherche sur le Proche-Orient et la Grèce Antiques, 4), 151-162.

Unsere Kenntnis meroitischer Toponyme stammt aus den Berichten der griechischen und römischen Schriftsteller sowie aus dem

meroitischen Textmaterial selbst. Hier ergibt sich aber die Schwierigkeit, daß das als Lokativsuffix erkannte "t^e" auch bei der Bildung topophorer Anthroponyme verwendet wird. Es werden eine Anzahl von vermuteten Ortsnamen und die mit ihnen verbundene Problematik dargelegt. Ihre Lokalisierung ist dann gesichert, wenn sich das meroitische Toponym in einem heutigen nubischen oder arabischen Ortsnamen erkennen läßt.
Inge Hofmann

77468   LECLANT, J., Soleb — Sedeinga, *Nyame Akuma,* Calgary No. 10 (1977), 46.
Kurzer Bericht über die Veröffentlichungen der Ausgrabungsergebnisse von Soleb durch M. Schiff Giorgini und die Weiterarbeit an der großen meroitischen Nekropole von Sedeinga durch J. Leclant.
Inge Hofmann

77469   LECLANT, Jean, Les textes de la pyramide de Pépi Ier (Saqqara): Reconstitution de la paroi est de l'antichambre, *Comptes rendus de l'Académie des Inscriptions et Belles-Lettres,* Paris, 1977, 269-288, with 1 plan, 8 ill., 1 table and 1 folding pl.
In this report about the reconstruction of the walls inscribed with P.T. in the pyramid of Pepy I the author deals particularly with the E. wall of the antechamber, of which large parts were not seen by Maspero and hence not included in Sethe's publication. The author and his collaborators were able to place about 1100 new squares of the text as against the 650 copied by Maspero, so that 62% of the inscription is now known. The texts are discussed, some "new" sentences translated, and the conclusions for the meaning briefly stated. The first 22 cols. deal with food for the deceased, cols. 23-42 contain spells against obnoxious forces such as snakes, bulls and lions. At the end a discussion of striking spellings and shapes of signs.
On the folding plate a drawing of the entire inscription as now reconstructed. On p. 284-287 a table of concordances between the spells on this wall and their places in editions and in other pyramids.

77470   LECLANT, Jean, Third International Meroitic Conference. Toronto, 11-15 Octobre 1977, *Orientalia* 46 (1977), 478-479.
Short report on the Third International Meroitic Conference, held in Toronto, October 1977.

LECLANT, Jean, see also our numbers 77170, 77316 and 77452.

LEE, Sandra L., see our number 77728.

77471 LEE, Sherman E., The Year in Review for 1976, *The Bulletin of the Cleveland Museum of Art*, Cleveland Ohio 64, No. 2 (February 1977), 39-79, with 75 ill. (1 in colour).

Among the acquisitions were a relief from the lost funerary temple of Amenophis III (acc. no. 76.51) and a head of Nefertiti on a relief (acc. no. 76.4), both joining pieces already in the collection. Both pieces are illustrated.
L.Z.

77472 LEEK, F. Filce, How Old was Tut'ankhamūn ?, *JEA* 63 (1977), 112-115, with 1 pl.

The writer disagrees with Derry's estimate of the age of this Pharaoh and points out that he made no use of the dental evidence, but confined his calculations to ossification of the epiphyseal joints. As a result he would lower the age to sixteen or at most seventeen years instead of eighteen.
E. Uphill

LEIMLEHNER, Marianne, see our number 77382.

77473 LESKO, Leonard H., King Tut's Wine Cellar, [Berkeley, California, B.C. Scribe Publications, 1977] (21.5 × 27.8 cm; 49 p., colour ill. on cover, 2 maps, frontispiece, 10 fig., 1 plan, 34 ill. including 4 in colour).

This nicely illustrated booklet, although intended for the general public, contains several remarks of scientific importance. The author first deals with the origin of Egyptian wines and their mentions by classical authors, after which a survey of Egyptian viticulture is presented. There follow chapters on the wine cellar of Tutankhamon (see also the list on p. 49) and on the wine labels from el-ʿAmarna and Malkata. The next chapter contains quotations from Egyptian sources concerning the wisdom of moderation. After discussing the wine of the Ramesside Period the author devotes the last chapter to tableware. A postscript is concerned with modern Egyptian wines.

77474 LESKO, Leonard H., Dieter Mueller. 1935-1977, *Newsletter ARCE* Nos. 101/102 (Summer/Fall 1977), 1-2.

Obituary notice. Compare our number 77848.

77475 LETELLIER, Bernadette, Un souhait de bonne année en faveur d'une reine kouchite, *RdE* 29 (1977), 43-52, with 1 pl.

L'auteur publie un sceau de faïence conservé au Louvre (Inv. E.10302) au nom d'une reine Maletarata que l'on peut identifier avec une des deux Maletaral déjà connues et plus probablement avec celle de la pyramide méroitique Nu. 25 de Reisner. La date pourrait être le 6e siècle a.C. *Ph. Derchain*

LETELLIER, Bernadette, see also our number 77029.

77476 LEWIN, Peter K., Mummies That I Have Known. A Pediatrician's Venture in the Field of Paleopathology, *American Journal of Diseases of Children*, Chicago 131 (March 1977), 349-350, with 3 ill.

Short description of the activities of a pediatrician in the field of medical archaeology. For his investigation with others of a mummy, see our numbers 74443 and 76495.

77477 Lexikon der Ägyptologie. Begründet von Wolfgang Helck und Eberhard Otto. Lieferung 15 [and] 16 (Band II, Lieferung 7-8). Herausgegeben von Wolfgang Helck und Wolfhart Westendorf unter Mitwirkung von Rosemarie Drenkhahn, Wiesbaden, Otto Harrassowitz, 1977 (20 × 28 cm; 316 col. [= col. 961-1276], 4 fig., 7 plans, 3 charts); rev. *Mundus* 15 (1979), 20-21 (Hellmut Brunner).

Sequel to our number 76496.

With these two fascicles vol. II (Erntefest — Hordjedef) is completed. A loose leaf introduction is added listing the names of the authors, abbreviations, some additions and corrections, etc.

The fascicles contain as usual several longer lemmata on more important subjects as well as a wealth of shorter ones. We mention, e.g., those on harps and Harper's songs, harim, Haroeris and other forms of Horus, Hathor, Hatshepsut, houses, Heracleopolis and Hermopolis, heart, hieroglyphs, high priests of various temples.

77478 Lexikon der Ägyptologie. Begründet von Wolfgang Helck und Eberhard Otto. Lieferung 17 (Band III, Lieferung 1). Herausgegeben von Wolfgang Helck und Wolfhart Westendorf unter Mitwirkung von Rosemarie Drenkhahn, Wiesbaden, Otto Harrassowitz, 1977 (20 × 28 cm; 160 col., 2 fig., 1 map).

Sequel to our preceding number, covering the lemmata Horhekenu-Inkarnation (to be continued).

The fascicle contains i.a. lemmata on Horus and compositions with Horus (Horus und Seth, Horus-Chentechai, Horus von Edfu, Horusauge, Horusmythe, etc.), Huy (I and II), Hunger and Hungersnotstele, Hurriten, Hyksos, Hymnus, Ichneumon, Ikonographie, and many more.

LIBOIS, Charles, see our number 77293.

77479   LINKE, Max, Georg Schweinfurth und sein Wirken als Geograph, *Petermanns Geographische Mitteilungen,* Gotha/Leipzig 121, Heft 4 (1977), 247-251.

Biographical article about George Schweinfurth and his significance as a geographer. Much attention is paid to his interest in Egypt.   L.Z.

77480   LIPIŃSKA, Jadwiga, Deir el-Bahari. II. The Temple of Tuthmosis III. Architecture, Varsovie, PWN — Éditions scientifiques de Pologne, 1977 (20.3 × 29.1 cm; 100 p., 53 fig. [2 folding], including plans, 67 ill. on 32 pl. [= p. 69-100], 6 loose plans and 1 loose fig.); at head of title: Centre d'archéologie méditerranéenne de l'académie polonaise des sciences et centre polonaise d'archéologie méditerranéenne dans la République Arabe d'Égypte au Caire sous la direction de Kazimierz Michałowski; rev. *AJA* 82 (1978), 405-406 (Anthony Spalinger); *BiOr* 35 (1978), 94 (Geneviève Sée); *CdE* LII, No. 104 (1977), 252-259 (Pierre Gilbert); *Przegląd Orientalistyczny* No. 2 (106), 1978, 181-182 (Elżbieta Dąbrowska-Smektała).

This is the final report on the temple of Tuthmosis III in Deir el-Bahari discovered by the Polish excavators between and behind the temples of Hatshepsut and Mentuhotep I. For the hieratic graffiti on the columns see our number 74475; publication of other inscriptional material will follow. The temple, called Djeser-Akhet, built during the last decade of Tuthmosis' reign, has been destroyed, probably by a rock-slip, at the end of the XXth Dynasty. Subsequently it was used as a quarry, as many tools found during the excavations attest. After the XXVIth Dynasty and again in the Coptic Period the site was used as a cemetery.

In chapter 1 the author presents a survey of the excavations in the years 1962-1967 and a general description. Chapter 2 is devoted to a detailed description of the various parts of the temple, discussing its location and building materials, the platform and pavement, walls, columns, the granite doorway closing the great hall from the W., and the stairs, with a long excursus on the quarry or transportation marks. In chapter 3 the reconstruction of the various elements of the temple is dealt with: the hypostyle hall, the central and side chapels, the Hathor shrine (discovered by Naville; its speos now in the Cairo Museum), the forepart of the temple with the ramps and porticos, the causeway with the kiosk in the middle of it (found by the German excavators of the Montuhotep temple), and the valley temple (not yet located). Many clear drawings illustrate the text, while the photographs (p. 69-100) represent general views, details of the construction as they are found, and reliefs and statues discovered in the remains.

In the last chapter the author makes remarks as to the history and meaning of the temple. She i.a. mentions ostraca recording its construction and connects its date with the effacing of name and portraits of Hatshepsut. Whether the Djeser-Akhet was a mortuary temple of the king is uncertain.

7481 LIPIŃSKA, Jadwiga, An Example of Ancient Egyptian Restoration of Sculpture, *in: Ägypten und Kusch*, 279-281, with 8 ill. on 4 pl.

Im Tempel Tutmosis III. in Deir el-Bahri wurden unter den Fußbodenplatten Stücke einer dunkelgrauen Granitstatue gefunden, die dort "begraben" waren. Sie gehörten zu einer Statue des Amun, die während der Amarna-Zeit zerschlagen und später in frommer Gesinnung beigesetzt wurde. Neun Kalksteinstücke einer sitzenden männlichen Statue stammen aus demselben Tempel; auch diese Statue war zerschlagen, danach aber wieder restauriert worden. Auch sie stellte den Gott dar. Die Restauration erfolgte wahrscheinlich in der Zeit Ramses II. *Inge Hofmann*

7482 LIPIŃSKA, Jadwiga, Historia architektury starożytnego Egiptu, [Warszawa], Wydawnictwa Uniwersytetu Warszawskiego, 1977 (17 × 24 cm; 258 p., 2 folding maps, 165 ill., fig. and plans [2 folding],ill. on cover); at head of title: Uniwersytet Warszawski. Instytut Historyczny; rev. *Przegląd Orientalistyczny* No. 1 (105), 1978, 75 (Irena Pomorska). Pr. zł.24

"History of the Architecture of Ancient Egypt".
This university handbook deals with Egyptian architecture in a chronological order. After a preface and an introductory chapter on building materials and transport there are chapters on the Prehistoric and Archaic Periods, on the O.K., the M.K. and the N.K., the Late and the Ptolemaic-Roman Periods. Each of these discusses separately the religious (royal and private tombs and temples) and the domestic architecture, those of the Archaic Period, the M.K. and the N.K. also the military architecture. Conclusions on p. 233-236, followed by a short bibliography, indexes and a chronological table.

7483 LIPIŃSKA, Jadwiga, Wiesław KOZIŃSKI, Cywilizacja miedzi i kamienia. Technika starożytnego Egiptu, Warszawa, Państwowe Wydawnictwo Naukowe, 1977 (16.5 × 24 cm; VIII + 584 p., 343 ill. [including plans, sections, drawings and photographs], 73 fig., fig. on cover, ill. on endpapers; rev. *Przegląd Orientalistyczny* No. 2 (106), 1978, 180-181 (Elżbieta Dąbrowska-Smektała). Pr. zł.120

"A Civilization of Copper and Stone. Technics in Ancient Egypt".

This study of ancient Egyptian technology was begun by both authors and, after the death of Mr. Koziński, completed by Mrs. Lipińska alone. It is important in that it not only gives the usual data about materials and techniques, but also a description of engineering in agriculture and irrigation, of transport, military architecture and building crafts.

After a preface by Prof. Michałowski and a foreword about the two authors the book contains 13 chapters, divided into a more practical and a more theoretical part.

Chapter 1 deals with masonry and sculpture; chapter 2 with painting, including painting on vessels and on papyrus; chapter 3 with joinery and wood-carving: furniture, building elements, tomb furniture, boats, chariots, bows, etc.; chapter 4 with mining and metals; chapter 5 with goldsmithery and jewellery; chapter 6 with ceramics and glazes; chapter 7 with basketry and leather work; chapter 8 with mummification and tomb equipment.

The second part discusses the following subjects: chapter 9: mathematics and astronomy, including calendars; chapter 10: engineering in agriculture, with sections on irrigation, surveying, etc.; chapter 11: transport and communications; chapter 12 (the longest chapter, p. 348-506): architecture, including sections on organization of the building process, town-planning, and military architecture; chapter 13: artists and artisans.

Conclusions on p. 522-525. A chronological table (527-529). Notes on metrology (530-531); a glossary of tools (with 73 drawings): p. 532-540. Bibliography, including bibliographies to the separate chapters (541-549) and extensive indexes (550-570).

77484   LIPIŃSKA, Jadwiga [and] Marek MARCINIAK, Mitologia starożytnego Egiptu, Warszawa, Wydawnictwa Artystyczne i Filmowe, 1977 (12 × 16 cm; 230 p., 77 ill. and fig., 8 colour ill.); series: Mitologie świata.

"Ancient Egyptian Mythology".

Apart from an introduction the book contains chapters on: creation of the world and man; the Osiris mystery; the rule of the world; myth and magic. A glossary to gods and demons on p. 195-217. Translations of texts by Marciniak.

77485   LIPIŃSKI, E., An Ugaritic Letter to Amenophis III Concerning Trade with Alašiya, *Iraq,* London 39 (1977), 213-217.

The author translates and studies an Ugaritic letter which may be a draft, a copy or an archive translation of a message sent to Amenophis

III by an Egyptian official, probably an *ỉmy-r ḫtm,* on his return from Alašiya. It appears that the king of Alašiya wanted the Pharaoh's consent to sell him ships from Egypt.

77486 LISE, Giorgio, La civica raccolta egizia. Castello Sforzesco. Seconda edizione ampliata, Milano, Ripartizione Cultura e Spettacolo, 1976 (17 × 24 cm; LX + 95 p., 1 map, 17 fig., 89 + 40 ill. [1 in colour]); at head of title: Comune di Milano.

The preface to the first edition (not seen by us) contains the story of the installation of objects from ancient Egypt in Milan for exhibition in the subterranean rooms of the Castello Sforzesco in Milan, which were formerly in the Museo Archeologico of the city.

After a general introduction on ancient Egypt follows the catalogue proper. The first room contains objects relating to the funerary cult: various sarcophagi from the T.I.P. and the Saite Period and funerary papyri. In the second room the other objects are exhibited: shawabtis, scarabs and other amulets, bronze statuettes of gods from the Late Period, stelae, Ptolemaic sculpture models, and particularly a statue of Amenemhat III.

The more important objects are illustrated by black-and-white photographs. The guide is concluded by a bibliography and a general index. L.Z.

77487 LISE, Giorgio, Medicina dell' antico Egitto, Milano, Cordani Editore, [no date] (21.7 × 23.8 cm; 123 p., colour frontispiece, 54 ill. [3 in colour], 6 fig.).

After introductory remarks on Egyptian medicine in general the author deals with religion and medicine, the documents, doctors with their names arranged after dynasties with their hieroglyphic equivalents, the terminology of parts of the body (also in a table), medical knowledge, connections between magic and medicine, pharmacopoeia and cosmetics, and mummification. After a chapter containing more general information on the ancient Egyptians, the book ends with a bibliography. L.Z.

LIVERANI, Mario, see our numbers 77013, 77014 and 77015.

LIZANA SALAFRANCA, Joaquín G., see our number 77669.

77488 LLOYD, Alan B., Necho and the Red Sea: Some Considerations, *JEA* 63 (1977), 142-155, with 1 fig.

This article discusses the validity of the two stories concerning the immense maritime achievements of this reign. It is accepted that the digging of a Nile-Red Sea canal is likely to have been inaugurated if not completed at this time, but that the story in Herodotus relating to the circumnavigation of Africa should be given less credence. The two points as to the sowing and reaping of crops by the navigators, and the sun's position are both explained away, at least to the author's satisfaction.   *E. Uphill*

77489   LOPRIENO, Antonio, A proposito delle consonanti dentali e velari in egiziano ed in semitico, *Annali. Istituto Orientale di Napoli,* Napoli 37 (1977), 125-142.

The author studies the development of the pronunciation of velar and dental consonants in L. Eg., basing his argument on transcriptions of Semitic words in Egyptian, and indicates the differences in development between Semitic languages and Egyptian.

77490   LORENZEN, Eivind, Canon and 'Thumbs' in Egyptian Art, *JAOS* 97 (1977), 531-539, with 4 fig.

A review article of our number 75358 in which the author states that the lack of technical proof of basic units is the main failure in Erik Iversen's attempts to analyze the grids.   *L.Z.*

77491   LORTON, David, The Title "Book of Knowing the Creations of Re and of Felling Apophis": a Grammatical Note on the Titles and Headings of Egyptian Religious Compositions, *GM* Heft 23 (1977), 55-63.

Papyrus Bremner-Rhind enthält zwei Versionen der im Titel genannten Komposition; das Problem liegt in der unterschiedlichen Schreibung des zweiten Wortes, nämlich ⲟ̄ⲱ und ⲟ̄ , dessen Verwendung untersucht wird. Verfasser kommt zu dem Ergebnis, daß der Schreiber, dessen Sprache demotisch war, das Nomen *mḏ3t* als indefinit kennzeichnen wollte und deshalb ein *nty* nachsetzte.

Inge Hofmann

77492   LORTON, David, The Treatment of Criminals in Ancient Egypt through the New Kingdom, *Journal of the Economic and Social History of the Orient,* Leiden 20 (1977), 2-64.

This article appears in the setting of a series of articles on the treatment of criminals in the Ancient Near East, four of which were read as papers at the 185th Annual Meeting of the American Oriental Society in Columbus, Ohio, April 22-24, 1975.

Lorton extensively analyzes the available data on the punishment of criminals in Egypt. Many documents from various periods are partly translated and commented upon, particularly a number of texts from Deir el-Medîna. Among the punishments mentioned in the material the author points out the denial of burial rights and "debaptism". In his concluding remarks (p. 50-53) he i.a. states that there may have been a difference between the law during the N.K. and that of earlier periods, although N.K. law cannot be called more harsh from the Egyptian point of view.

In an appendix on codified law in Egypt the Demotic Code of Hermopolis is compared as regards its formulations with older decrees, and the meaning of the word *hp* is studied. Some addenda to the article on p. 62-64.

The article has also appeared in a separately published offprint: The Treatment of Criminals in the Ancient Near East. Edited by Jack M. Sasson, Leiden, E.J. Brill, 1977.

77493 LORTON, David, The "Triumphal Poem" of the Creator in Papyrus Bremner-Rhind, *Newsletter SSEA* 7, No. 4 (August 1977), 17-23.

Translation with commentary of the creation story of Pap. Bremner-Rhind. Applying Foster's basic concepts (see our number 77238) the author was able to cast the poem into twenty-two lines and to demonstrate its quatrain structure.

77494 LOYRETTE, Anne-Marie, L'Égypte des Pharaons, *Archeologia*, Paris No. 113 (décembre 1977), 58-66, with 11 ill. (3 in colour) and 1 colour ill. on cover.

Short description of an exhibition at the Galerie Septentrion at Marcq-en-Baroeul near Lille, where objects from the Louvre and the Musée de Limoges were on display end 1977 — beginning 1978.

The richly illustrated catalogue of the exhibition called "L'Égypte des Pharaons" is due to Christiane Ziegler (our number 77211). *L.Z.*

77495 LÜDDECKENS, Erich, *nḥsj* und *kš* in ägyptischen Personennamen, in: *Ägypten und Kusch*, 283-291.

Das als Bevölkerungsbezeichnung bereits im A.R. vorkommende *nḥsj* begegnet als Personenname *Nḥsj* "Südländer" o.ä. seit dem M.R. und bleibt als solcher in dieser kurzen Form bis in die Spätzeit gebräuchlich, auch als dann Namen wie *P3-nḥsj* "der Südländer" und *T3-nḥsj.t* "die Südländerin" danebentreten. Erst seit dem M.R. ist *k3š* als Landname belegt; Personennamen wie *P3(-n)-k3š* kommen erst spät vor. Die entsprechende Bildung ist demotisch als Pa-igš in Theben für das 3. vorchristliche Jahrhundert und als *P3-gš* im Fajum für die Kaiserzeit belegt. Die unterschiedlichen Schreibweisen im

Griechischen und Koptischen werden dargelegt. Es werden zwei Ergebnisse gewonnen: 1. Namensformen, die als Zeugen einer der großen, aus dem Koptischen bekannten Mundarten erkannt wurden, lassen keineswegs mit Sicherheit darauf schließen, daß die Träger solcher Namen auch in den Gebieten bzw. Landesteilen dieser Mundarten zuhause waren. 2. Im Verlaufe der geschichtlichen Entwicklung im Ptolemäerreich und dann unter der Römerherrschaft wurden ägyptische Namen oft auch im Lande geborenen Nichtägyptern gegeben, Namen, die von vornherein nur griechisch geschrieben wurden, deren ursprüngliche Bedeutung bald verloren ging und deren Schreibweise sich änderte. *Inge Hofmann*

77496 LÜDDECKENS, Erich, Zum demotischen Gedicht vom Harfner, *in: Fragen an die altägyptische Literatur,* 325-348.

After sketching the history of the interpretation of a Demotic Harper's song in the Kunsthistorisches Museum, Vienna (Inv. No. 3877), which describes the life of a relegated, possibly professional singer and harper, called Hr-$wd3$, the author publishes lines 3, 11 (51) — 4, 16 (76) with transliteration, translation and commentary. *L.Z.*

77497 LUFT, Ulrich, Bemerkungen zu zwei Liebesgedichten auf Papyrus Chester Beatty I, *in: Ägypten und Kusch,* 293-302.

Es handelt sich um die beiden Gedichte, die auf Pap. Chester Beatty I ro. XVI, 9 — XVII, 1 überliefert sind. Der Text ist nicht frei von Korrekturen und Fehlern, aber sonst in der üblichen Art der späten Ramessidenzeit geschrieben, gut lesbar und mit Verspunkten versehen. Die Verspunkte wurden beibehalten; in dieser Ordnung sind die Verse verständlich und kommen der von Fecht vertretenen These relativer Sinneinheiten entgegen. Beide Lieder werden in Transkription und Übersetzung mit einem Kommentar wiedergegeben. Abschließend wird das Ergebnis gewonnen, daß die ägyptische Liebesdichtung auf ausländische Wörter verzichten konnte; sie hatte in Ägypten selbst genug Nährboden, um aus sich heraus Gedichte zu schaffen, die ohne Peinlichkeit Liebeserlebnisse beschrieben. *Inge Hofmann*

77498 LUFT, U., Das Totenbuch des Neferrenpet (Grab 336), *Studia aegyptiaca* 3 (1977), 81-87.

The author discusses the owner of the copy of the B.D. in the University Museum, Philadelphia, published by Ranke in 1950 (our number 1496). He is called Neferronpet, his wife Ḥuynefert. Luft argues that he is a stone-mason from Deir el-Medîna, the owner of

Theban tomb No. 336. He studies his family and dates the copy of the B.D. to the years sixty or seventy of the 13th century B.C.

77499 LUFT, Ulrich, Das Totenbuch des Ptahmose. Papyrus Kraków MNK IX — 752/1-4, *ZÄS* 104 (1977), 46-75, with 3 pl.

Herausgabe eines Papyrus im Nationalmuseum Krakau (Sammlung des Czartoryski-Museums), nach 1944 aus unbekannten polnischen Besitz erworben. Es handelt sich um Fragmente vom Totenbuch eines Ptahmose, der "Meister der Lapislazuli-Hersteller des Herrn der beiden Länder" war, wohl in der XIX. Dynastie.

Verfasser beschäftigt sich mit Beschreibung (Länge 2.75 m), Schrift, 20 Texten, Filiation, Titel, 5 Vignetten, graphischen Besonderheiten, Datierung und philologischen Kommentar (einschlieslich der Rückenleiste).

Luft fügt eine Liste bei der ihm bekannten (102) Totenbücher aus der XVIII bis XX. Dynastie. In dieser Aufstellung und im Aufsatz fehlt unter mehreren Exemplaren das aus dem Grabe des Cha, Turin Supplemento 8438, Ed. Schiaparelli. *M. Heerma van Voss*

LUFT, Ulrich, see also our number 77463.

77500 ŁUKASZEWICZ, Adam, Papirusy z Sakkary, *Meander,* Warszawa 32 (1977), 245-260, with 1 ill.

"Papyri from Sakkara".
On the papyri found at Sakkara by W.B. Emery in 1966-7 and by G.T. Martin in 1971-3.
Compare our number 75651.

LUKONIN, W., see our number 77011.

77501 LYMAN, John, Thera Ship Parallels with Burma and Egypt, *The Mariner's Mirror,* Cambridge 63 (1977), 96.

Short note on parallels between ships from Thera and Egypt. See also a query on the same subject in the same periodical by M. Scott on p. 295. *L.Z.*

ŁYCZKOWSKA, Krystyna, see our number 77190.

McKERRELL, Hugh, see our number 77206.

77502 MADDIN, Robert, Tamara Stech WHEELER, James D. MUHLY, Tin in the Ancient Near East: Old Questions and New Finds, *Expedition,* Philadelphia, Penn. 19, No. 2 (Winter 1977), 35-47, with 23 ill., 2 maps, 2 fig. and 1 table.

The authors discuss the occurrence of tin in the ancient Near East the origin of which is still a mystery. They present a survey of the geology and metallurgy of tin, its occurrence in texts, and the (rare) actual finds antedating 1200 B.C. (2 from Egypt). Then they describe two ingots in the Haifa Museum of Ancient Art inscribed with Cypro-Minoan markings, which may help us to solve the riddle.

77503 MAHER, Ragi, Preliminary Report on an Excavation at Nagᶜ El-Hagg Zeidan, *CdE* LII, No. 104 (1977), 203-206, with 1 fig. and 2 ill.

Deux pages de texte et six croquis de potterie constituent le rapport préliminaire d'une fouille de quinze jours qui avait pour but de sauver une nécropole prédynastique située à peu de distance de Hassaya dans les environs d'Edfou. *Ph. Derchain*

77504 MALAISE, Michel, La position de la femme sur les stèles du Moyen Empire, *SAK* 5 (1977), 183-198.

The author investigates on account of 68 dated stelae from the M.K. whether the position of women represented on them reflects their position in society. Although there appears to be a definite change in the reign of Amenemhat II, the attitude of lovingly touching the husband or son in several instances being replaced by a neutral attitude or a position opposite the man or elsewhere on the stelae, there are other explanations for the change than a development in the juridical status of the women.

77505 MÁLEK, Jaromír, A Graffito of Year 17 of Amenemḥēt II at el-Ḥôsh, *GM* Heft 24 (1977), 51-52.

Die zwei von Sir John Gardner Wilkinson gemachten Kopien eines Graffito bei el-Ḥôsh, die sich im Griffith-Institut in Oxford befinden, werden vorgestellt: die Inschrift wurde von dem Schreiber Dedutjeni angefertigt und in das 17. Jahr des Amenemhet II. datiert.

Inge Hofmann

77506 MÁLEK, Jaromír, New Ushebtis of the Third Intermediate Period in the Ashmolean Museum, *JEA* 63 (1977), 180-181.

These are nos. 1975.238-1975.241 and 1975.328, and are mostly of God's Fathers, being in three cases from Abydos. Details of material, size and inscriptions are given. *E. Uphill*

77507 MÁLEK, Jaromír, Shabtis of Pedamenope (Theb. Tb.33) in the Ashmolean and Fitzwilliam Museums, *JEA* 63 (1977), 137-141, with 1 pl. and 3 fig.

Six examples of serpentine, glazed stone and faience are briefly described and texts given. *E. Uphill*

MÁLEK, Jaromír, see also our numbers 77093 and 77099.

77508 MALENKO, Vlado, A Statuette of Isis from Ohrid, *Archaeologia Iugoslavica,* Beograd 15 (1974), 1977, 33-34, with 3 ill.

For the first of the two statuettes studied in the article, see our no. 76520. *S.P. Tutundžić*

des MALPEINES, Léonard, see our number 77782.

77509 MANNICHE, Lise, Some Aspects of Ancient Egyptian Sexual Life, *Acta Orientalia,* Copenhagen 38 (1977), 11-23, with 4 fig. and 2 pl.

The author presents a survey of some aspects of ancient Egyptian sexual life, as yet treated with utmost discretion, stressing the scantiness of Egyptian evidence in this respect. First she discusses the attitude of the ancient Egyptians towards sex, particularly its prohibition in holy places and extra-marital intercourse and adultery. In the next section, on homosexuality, she deals with the equally negative opinion of the Egyptians on homosexuality as an act of agression, with pederasty, and with the absence of evidence for artificial means to fulfill homosexual acts. Then she cites some examples of sodomy existing in imagination, and necrophilia with reference to embalmers. The last section is concerned with the positions of intercourse, face-to-face variants being considered as normal, although the *coitus a tergo* also seems to have been rather popular in Egypt. *L.Z.*

MANNING, James, see our number 77227.

77510 MARAGIOGLIO, V. [e] C. RINALDI, L'architettura delle Piramidi Menfite. Parte VIII. La Piramide de Neuserrâ, la "Small Pyramid" di Abu Sir, la "Piramide distrutta" di Saqqara ed il Complesso di Zedkarâ Isesi e della sua Regina. Con un Excursus di Alessandro Roccati. English Translation by A.E. Howell, Rapallo, Officine Grafiche Canessa, 1977 (24.5 × 34.5 cm; Testo: 125 p.; Tavole: 19 loose folded sheets with plans and drawings in portefolio); rev. *BiOr* 35 (1978), 84-85 (Alexander Badawy).

Sequel to our number 70372.

This volume dealing with the pyramids of the last three rulers of the Vth Dynasty completes the description of the architecture of the royal funerary complexes from that period; at least, if King Unas is reckoned to the next dynasty, as the authors argue in the preface.

The first chapter is devoted to the funerary complex of Neuserre at Abûsîr. After an introduction the pyramid itself is described, the mortuary temple, the satellite pyramid, the causeway and the Valley Temple. From p. 40-53 there follow 30 observations to details, i.a. dealing with construction techniques, many of them stating differences from Borchardt's study of the monument.

In the two following chapters buildings of a more uncertain nature are discussed: the "Small Pyramid" at Abûsîr, excavated by Perring but at present unidentified, of which the owner and the exact nature are obscure; and the "Destroyed Pyramid" situated E. of the Teti pyramid at Saqqâra, ascribed to Menkauhor.

The next chapter is concerned with the funerary complex of Djedkare Isesi in the centre of Saqqâra, formerly called Haram esh-Shawâf. After detailed description of its now largely destroyed superstructure, the funerary chambers, the mortuary temple, the satellite pyramid and the causeway, 20 observations to details are noted.

The last chapter deals with the adjoining complex of Isesi's Queen. Its superstructure is now reduced to a small mound, but the mortuary temple can be discussed in detail. Eight observations are added.

In an excursus Roccati publishes graffiti found in the temple of the Isesi Pyramid referring to its personnel; facsimiles of the texts on the loose sheet no. 17 in the portefolio.

Notes to the tables on p. 119-120; bibliography p. 121-122.

As usual in the series the text in English and that in Italian is printed on opposite pages.

MARCINIAK, Marek, see our number 77484.

MARESCA, Antonella, see our number 77148.

MARKS, Anthony E., see our number 77318.

77511 MARTIN, Geoffrey T., Excavations at the Memphite Tomb of Ḥoremḥeb, 1976: Preliminary Report, *JEA* 63 (1977), 13-19, with 3 pl. and 1 plan.

Describes the excavation of Chapels A and B, west of the first court, the excavation of the western part of the tomb and the clearance of the forecourt. Interesting blocks of the Ramesside period and small finds were discovered, while blocks in the east face of the pylon were found to be usurped from the Djoser pyramid complex. Others may come from the Unas causeway. The chapels appear to have been used later as anchorites' dwellings and produced a possible seated statue of Horemheb and his wife, as well as a stela showing him seated with a funerary-priest. The original titles have been chiselled out and a uraeus added to his headdress. Among the interesting scenes are those showing foreign captives from Asia and Africa.   *E. Uphill*

77512 MARTIN, Geoffrey T., Le tombeau d'Horemheb à Saqqarah, *BSFE* Nos. 77-78 (octobre 1976 et mars 1977), 11-25, with 8 ill. and 1 plan.

L'expédition E.E.S. — Musée de Leiden a trouvé, au sud de la chaussée d'Ounas, le tombeau memphite d'Horemheb, construit quand il n'était que Régent de Toutankhamon. Au delà d'une avant-cour et d'un pylône s'étend une grande cour à portique; un relief y représentait le Régent décorant un anonyme. Deux chapelles flanquent la salle aux statues, où fut découvert un papyrus portant les *maximes d'Ani*. La Seconde cour conserve une colonne entière et des reliefs nombreux, souvent d'exceptionnelle qualité; l'épouse du futur roi y est mentionnée. Plusieurs raccords s'imposent avec des reliefs connus, conservés notamment à Bologne et au British Museum. C'était ici le Général en chef qui au mur Est recevait des étrangers: un bloc s'ajuste au "fragment Zizinia". La figuration d'intérieur, dans le coin N-E, rappelle Amarna. Au mur Nord prenaient place des rites funéraires memphites et au mur Sud la présentation des captifs, que complète le groupe de blocs conservés à Leiden. A l'Ouest s'ouvrent trois chapelles, qui énumèrent les titres du propriétaire et abritaient la stèle cintrée maintenant à Leningrad. *J. Custers*

MARTIN, Geoffrey T., see also our number 77302.

77513 MARTIN, Karl, Ein Garantsymbol des Lebens. Untersuchungen zu Ursprung und Geschichte des altägyptischen Obelisken bis zum Ende des Neuen Reiches, Hildesheim, Gerstenberg Verlag, 1977 (17 × 24 cm; XVIII + 253 p., 5 folding tables [= p. 223-227], 23 pl. [= p. 231-253], colour frontispiece) = Hildesheimer Ägyptologische Beiträge. Herausgegeben von Arne Eggebrecht, 3; rev. *BiOr* 35 (1978), 98-101 (Bengt Birkstam); *CdE* LIV, No. 107 (1979), 82-85 (Agnes Rammant-Peeters); *Rivista* 52 (1978), 107-108 (S. Donadoni); *WZKM* 70 (1978), 110-113 (Günther Hölbl). Pr. DM 35

This study on obelisks, a dissertation (Münster, 1975), consists, apart from an introduction and a chapter on the aetiology of the obelisk, of chapters on the sources from the O., M. and N.K. On various pages the author stresses the necessity to keep in mind that Egyptian conceptions differed from one period to the other, so that it is incorrect to use late sources for the explanation of early phenomena. In the first chapter Martin argues, i.a. from some P.T., that Atum and his *benben* did not have behind them a long prehistory when he was connected with Re who was largely to replace him during the IVth Dynasty. Originally there were no relations between the *benben* and the *iwn* and *ḏd* pillars. In discussing the Sun-temples from the Vth

Dynasty the author argues that it is quite uncertain that they have been built after the model of the Heliopolis temple. Originally they seem to have contained no obelisk but merely a truncated pyramid (the "hill of sand"), on which later on an obelisk was erected. It symbolizes the mutual relations of earth/king and heaven/Re, which guaranteed the welfare of the country.

Discussion of the evidence from the O.K. begins with the written sources. The word for "obelisk", *tḫn,* usually *tḫnwy,* is connected with the verb *ḫn,* "to alight", which may also mean "to bring offerings". Hence the *tḫn* — the *t*-prefix has habitative meaning — expresses both directions of the relation King-Sungod. In the section on actual temple obelisks the author deals with the recently found fragment from Heliopolis (Teti), the only certain one from the period. Tomb obelisks, however, occur frequently (see tables, p. 223-227), mainly in the area of Memphis but also in Qubbet el-Hâwa where officials of the central government were buried. They are all of limestone (Memphis) or sandstone (Aswân), the colour of which may point at rebirth, while apart from that of Teti all royal obelisks in Egypt are made of red granite, pointing at the sun and life.

In the chapter on the M.K. the author discusses the Heliopolis obelisk of Sesostris I, symbol of his *sed*-festival; the "obelisk" of Abgîg, a unique type of monolith, some fragments from Heliopolis found at Tanis (probably late XIIth Dynasty) and some later monuments. He i.a. concludes that the Theban tomb pyramidion was derived from the Memphite obelisk. Private obelisks do not anymore occur with the tombs, only as votive offerings.

The last and largest chapter, on the M.K., first deals with obelisks from the private sphere, occurring in representations of funerals — probably due to the influence of the *hebsed*-ritual, which does not mean that the rite depicted was enacted during the funeral — and as actual objects, small wooden obelisks probably used as amulets.

A long section is devoted to the royal obelisks from Heliopolis and Thebes, where they still functioned in the old way since these were the political, economic and religious centres. Smaller obelisks came from a number of other temples (Elephantine, Tôd, Abydos, etc.). There were also "secondary obelisks", votive donations and temple utensils. The last section, on the Amarna Period, argues that then a new "obelisk" was created, the anepigraph *Benben,* revivified from an almost forgotten ancient idea which was in no way connected with Amon. It was a cult object, the seat of a god, and not connected with the king either, hence quite different in conception and sometimes in material from the genuine obelisks. The Ramessides never returned to

the old conceptions.
A summary on p. 201-203, a few documents about Sun-Temples on p. 204-207 (i.a. seal impressions from the E. Berlin museum in drawing); indexes p. 209-219.

77514 MARTIN, Richard A., Mummies. New edition revised and edited by David P. Silverman, [Chicago], Field Museum of Natural History, 1976 (14 × 21.5 cm; 18 p., colour ill. on cover, 18 fig., 11 pl.) = Popular Series. Anthropology, 36.

The author presents a popular account on mummies for the interested museum-visitor. The plates have their captions on the opposite pages.
L.Z.

MARTIN-PARDEY, Eva, see our number 77169.

77515 MASSON, Olivier, Quelques bronzes égyptiens à inscription grecque, *RdE* 29 (1977), 53-67, with 3 pl.

Publication de quatre objets datables entre 550 et 325 a.C. Ce sont: une plaquette pour Amon (New York Metropolitan Museum Inv. 21.2.65); une statuette d'Isis allaitant Horus (Caire JE 36571); une statuette d'Apis "Panepi" (Londres, British Museum, Inv. 97.2-25.1); statuette d'Osiris Lune (Berlin, Staatlichen Museen der Stiftung Preussischer Kulturbesitz, 2458). *Ph. Derchain*

77516 MATOUK, Fouad S., Corpus du scarabée égyptien. Tome deux. Analyse thématique. Ouvrage couronné par l'Académie Libanaise, [no place, no publisher, 1977] (22 × 28 cm; 416 p., numerous fig. [on p. 319-370] and ill. [on p. 373-413]); rev. *Antiquaries Journal* 58 (1978), 176-177 (Peter A. Clayton).

Sequel to our number 71393.
In the present volume the author studies the representations occurring on the undersides of scarab-seals and their elements. Once more the study is based on the collection Matouk-Blanchard, although throughout referring to other collections so far as published (that in Basel, see our number 76387, could of course not yet be consulted).
In the preface the author presents an outline of the book, while the introduction gives general information concerning various subjects, such as: the first researches into the subject, the way in which scarab representations reflect Egyptian religion, forms, dimensions, use and materials of scarabs, the history of the scarab, its possibilities as source of information, etc.
The 24 chapters each deal with a particular type or element of representation. They are arranged as a catalogue, similar to that in

vol. I. The chapters i.a. deal with: divinities; mammals, birds, reptiles and other animals; human attitudes, women, royal attitudes; parts of the human body; plants; geometrical and hieroglyphic decorations; crowns, collars, sceptres; etc.

Indexes on p. 253-288.

There follows a repertory of hieroglyphic signs cited in vols. I and II, arranged after the order of the catalogue of the IFAO, but with the numbers of Gardiner's sign-list added.

The hundreds of small drawings of all types of representations are an essential element of the study, while all representations on scarabs of the collection Matouk-Blanchard are given in small photographs.

This volume is distributed by Brill, London (Pr. £37.50).

MATTHIAE, Paolo, see our number 77013.

77517 MAYSTRE, Charles, Le grand-prêtre memphite du relief Berlin 12411, in: Ägypten und Kusch, 303-307, with 1 pl.

Es handelt sich um das sogenannte Berliner "Trauerrelief" aus dem Grab eines Hohenpriesters von Memphis, dessen Name von Erman Neferronpet gelesen wurde. Verfasser zieht jedoch die Stele des Brit. Mus. No. 972 heran, da auf beiden Objekten dieselben Personen genannt werden. Der Hohepriester hieß Ty, der auch auf anderen Monumenten belegt ist. Seine hohe Funktion erhielt er zu einer Zeit, als Horemheb bereits sehr mächtig, aber noch nicht König war.

Inge Hofmann

77518 MEEKS, Dimitri, Notes de lexicographie (§ 5-8), *BIFAO* 77 (1977), 79-88.

Sequel to our numbers 74482 and 76534.

The author deals with the following words not mentioned in the *W.B.*: *strt*, "upper eyelid" (occurring i.a. in *B.D.*, ch. 172); *ḏʿ-m-pt*, "squall"; *kḥss*, "bed", "bier" and *ntntt*, "bladder", "membrane".

77519 MEGALLY, Mounir, Notions de comptabilité. A propos du Papyrus E. 3226 du Musée du Louvre, [Le Caire], Institut français d'Archéologie orientale du Caire, 1977 (20 × 27.5 cm; XIV + 145 p., 6 pl.) = Bibliothèque d'étude, 72.

This is the second part of vol. II of the author's thesis. Compare our number 69408.

77520 MEGALLY, Mounir, Recherches sur l'économie, l'administration et la comptabilité égyptiennes à la XVIIIe Dynastie d'après le Papyrus E. 3226 du Louvre, [Le Caire], Institut français d'Archéologie orientale du Caire, 1977 (20 × 27.5 cm; XXXII + 295 p., 8 pl.) = Bibliothèque d'étude, 71.

This is the first part of Vol. II of the author's thesis. Compare our number 69408.

77521 MELTZER, Edmund S., "Heart", ib or *inb in Egyptian?, *JNES* 36 (1977), 149-151.

Following the plea of Carleton T. Hodge for a more critical approach to Egypto-Semitic sound correspondences and his suggestion that the Egyptian word "heart" should be read ilb thus giving a better equation with Semitic *libbu,* the writer cites evidence to suggest that this may not be so, but allows the validity of its value at the proto-stage of Egyptian.

Cfr our number 77651. *E. Uphill*

77522 MELTZER, Edmund S., '*Iw wn/nn wn* + Indefinite Noun in Middle Egyptian, *Newsletter ARCE* Nos. 99/100 (Winter/Spring 1977), 11.

Abstract of a paper.

77523 MÉNARD, Jacques É., L'Authentikos Logos. Texte établi et présenté, Québec, Les Presses de l'Université Laval, 1977 (15.7 × 24 cm; VIII + 79 p.) = Bibliothèque copte de Nag Hammadi. Section: Textes, 2; rev. *Biblica* 60 (1979), 122-127 (H. Quecke); *BiOr* 35 (1978), 3-21 (J. Zandee); *Revue d'Histoire et de Philosophie Réligieuses* 58 (1978), 315-316 (D.A. Bertrand). Pr. Can.$12

The author presents the text of the *Authentikos Logos* (Nag Hammadi VI, 3, p. 22,1-35,24.) with the translation on the opposite pages, notes to the transcription and a commentary. In the introduction he discusses the literary genre and the doctrine of the text, and he sketches its contents. The book is concluded by indexes to Greek and Coptic words. *L.Z.*

77524 MÉNARD, Jacques É., La lettre de Pierre à Philippe. Texte établi et présenté, Québec, Les Presses de l'Université Laval, 1977 (15.5 × 24 cm; XIV + 61 p.) = Bibliothèque Copte de Nag Hammadi. Section: Textes , 1; rev. *Biblica* 60 (1979), 122-127 (H. Quecke); *WZKM* 70 (1978), 101-103 (Robert Haardt).

This first volume of the series is devoted to the Letter of St. Peter to St. Philip that occurs in Nag Hammadi Codex VIII. The author presents the Coptic text and the translation on opposite pages, followed by notes to the transcription and translation, a commentary, and an index of Greek and Coptic words. In the preceding chapters the letter is described and remarks are made on the literary genre and on the doctrine of the letter.

77525 MENU, Bernadette, Les rapports de dépendance en Égypte à l'époque saïte et perse, *Revue historique de droit français et étranger,* Paris 55 (1977), 391-401.

The author investigates the problem whether there existed actual slavery during the Late Period, studying fifteen contracts written in Demotic and "abnormal hieratic" (some unpublished). She first states that the difference between $ḥm$ and $b3k$ had disappeared in that time, although even during the N.K. these people possessed at least some rights. Two categories of contracts are studied: the sales of a person by himself, and so-called "sales of slaves". Mme Menu reaches the conclusion that they actually dealt with the hire of services, although their form was that of a sales contract. Slavery did not exist in the Late Period.

77526 MENU, Bernadette, La "stèle" d'Ahmès Nefertary dans son contexte historique et juridique. À propos de: M. Gitton, "La résiliation d'une fonction réligieuse: nouvelle interprétation de la stéle de donation d'Ahmès Nefertary", *BIFAO* 77 (1977), 89-100.

The author, once more discussing the donation text of Ahmose-Nofretari (see our number 71403), argues that M. Gitton (see our number 76284) misinterpreted her statements. Questioning the correctness of Helck's restorations (see our number 75321) she stresses that an $îmyt-pr$ is an "acte lié originellement à la constitution ou à la protection d'ensembles économiques immuables et autonomes", translating it as "acte à titre universel". She presents a translation of the text different from that of M. Gitton and draws the following conclusions: it is the king who sells the function of second prophet, and he also provides the price on behalf of his wife in order to assure her rights and to constitute a capital for executing the function; the queen declares to be satisfied about the price (which her husband paid for her); she receives (temporarily) the function, which in time will go to her son Ahmose and thus be separated from her own function of Divine Consort.

77527 du MESNIL du BUISSON, R., [Le cylindre archaïque de Byblos], *Syria,* Paris 54 (1977), 294-295, with 1 fig.

Letter-to-the-Editor, being an answer to our number 76292.

77528 METZGER, Bruce M., The Early Versions of the New Testament. Their Origin, Transmission, and Limitations, Oxford, Clarendon Press, 1977 (14 × 20.6 cm; XX + 498 p.).

In this study on the early versions of the N.T. in various languages (Syriac, Armenian, Latin, Gothic, etc.) a chapter (p. 99-152) is devoted to the Coptic versions. It deals successively with: the introduction of Christianity into Egypt (a still rather obscure matter) and the translation of the N.T.; early manuscripts of the Coptic N.T. in the various dialects; date and mutual relationships of these translations (with a lengthy quotation from Kasser's article on the dialects, our number 65274); textual affinities of the Coptic versions. In a fifth section J. Martin Plumley discusses the limitations of Coptic in representing Greek. He lists the main points on which Coptic, particularly its grammar, differs from Greek, quoting in several instances the Greek and the Coptic text with a literal translation of the latter.

77529 METZLER, Dieter and Herbert HOFFMANN, Zur Theorie und Methode der Erforschung von Rassismus in der Antike, *Kritische Berichte,* Giessen 5 (1977), 5-20, with 2 ill.

Discussing the Greek attitude towards negroes i.a. on account of a vessel in the form of a negro-and-crocodile, the author suggests that an Egyptian faience object from the 6th century B.C. representing a crocodile devouring a negro has only a ritual meaning, and is not meant as a burlesque. *L.Z.*

77530 de MEULENAERE, Herman, Derechef Arensnouphis, *CdE* LII, No. 104 (1977), 245-251.

L'auteur reprend le problème des origines du dieu nommé dans le titre de son article et se fondant sur l'analyse de noms propres suggère qu'à l'origine il se serait appelé *irt-mš'-nfr* et n'aurait été qu'une hypostase de Khnoum d'Eléphantine, devenue peu à peu indépendante, adoptée ensuite par les Méroïtiques; il rejette ainsi les opinions récentes de plusieurs égyptologues, notamment Hofmann (notre No. 76379), Winter (Lexikon der Ägyptologie s.v., et notre No. 73804) et Wenig (nos Nos. 73780 et 74799). *Ph. Derchain*

de MEULENAERE, Herman, see also our number 77024.

77531 MICHAŁOWSKI, Kazimierz, Das christliche Nubien 1158-1272, *in: Ägypten und Kusch,* 309-313.

In dem Beitrag werden die Endetappen der Entwicklung des

unabhängigen christlichen Königreiches Nubiens dargelegt. Wahrscheinlich wurden während der Kämpfe bei Adindan 1175 die Kathedrale von Faras zerstört. Nubien geriet in wirtschaftliche und politische Abhängigkeit vom islamischen Ägypten, was zur Zerrüttung des Staatssystems und zum Zusammenbruch des Königsmacht in Nubien führte. Zwar konnte 1272 der nubische König David noch erfolgreich gegen die Araber kämpfen, aber im Zuge seiner Verfolgung drang die arabische Armee bis Dongola vor. Davids Nachfolger waren nur noch Marionetten des arabischen Ägypten.

Inge Hofmann

MICHAŁOWSKI, Kazimierz, see also our number 77726.

77532 MIDANT-REYNES, Béatrix et Florence BRAUNSTEIN-SILVESTRE, Le chameau en Égypte, *Orientalia* 46 (1977), 337-362, with 1 pl.

Aucun mot égyptien antérieur au copte ne désigne le chameau. Celui que Chabas comprenait *kamaa(l)*, doit se lire *kîkî* et désigne le cynocéphale. Le chameau ne figure pas davantage sur les monuments pharaoniques. La bibliographie énumère pourtant 150 titres, prouvant ou contestant, avec autant de conviction, que le camelus était domestiqué de bonne heure. Parmi les 18 documents archéologiques où l'on avait cru déceler l'animal, il n'en est que deux qui répondraient aux exigences d'une identification sérieuse. La côte de camélidé (dromadaire, Moyen Empire) de Sayala (mission Bietak, 1966) pose un problème par son isolement, et la statuette en céramique de Rifeh (fouilles Petrie, 1907), pièce ramesside importée, est postérieure à l'introduction en Asie du "bactrianus" à deux bosses. Ni les récits de la Genèse, ch. 12 et 37, ni les gravures rupestres, d'une datation incertaine, ne peuvent être pris en considération. Avant le XIIe siècle, on ne peut prouver que le chameau ait apparu en Égypte, même d'une manière sporadique. Il n'y fut employé couramment comme bête de somme qu'à partir de l'époque ptolémaïque, soit plus d'un demi-millénaire après son apparition en Asie occidentale.

J. Custers

MILGRAM, James W., see our number 77728.

77533 MILLARD, Anne, Meryet-Amūn on a Limestone Fragment in Cambridge, *JEA* 63 (1977), 127-130, with 1 pl.

This fragment from the Gayer-Anderson collection measures 10 × 9 cm and shows a woman of the Ramesside period, with five columns of hieroglyphic text naming her King's Great Wife Meryet-Amūn. There is also a reference to Amenophis I, despite which it seems likely that this queen is really the daughter wife of Ramesses II, only paying homage to the deified king. *E. Uphill*

77534 MILLER, J. Maxwell, The Israelite Occupation of Canaan, *in: Israelite and Judaean History.* Edited by John H. Hayes and J. Maxwell Miller, London, SCM Press Ltd, [1977] (series: the Old Testament Library), 213-284.

The above title is that of the fourth chapter in this book on Israelite history. The chapter, by J.M. Miller, contains a section (§2) on Egyptian sources concerning the Israelite occupation of Canaan and has subsections called: The Canaanite city-states: the ethnic and social composition of the population of L.B. Palestine; the earliest references to Edom, Moab, and Israel; and the Sea-Peoples. As everywhere in the book the section is preceded by a basic bibliography on the subject.
Compare our number 77745. *L.Z.*

MILLER, J. Maxwell, see also our number 77745.

77535 MILLET, N.B., Egyptian Department, *Annual Report. Royal Ontario Museum,* Toronto 27 (1976-1977), 16-17.

Report on the activities of the department, at home as well as abroad. *L.Z.*

77536 MILLET, Nicholas B., Some Meroitic Ostraka, *in: Ägypten und Kusch,* 315-324, with 1 pl.

Eines der Probleme bei der Entzifferung des Meroitischen ist unsere Unkenntnis der Verbalstruktur; wir kennen keine Pronomina und können keine Personenkennzeichner isolieren. Eine Kategorie von Texten könnte allerdings dazu verhelfen, die pronominalen oder verbalen Kennzeichnungen der 1. und 2. Person ausfindig zu machen, nämlich die Kategorie der Korrespondenz. Unter den zahlreichen meroitischen Ostraka scheinen einige Texte diesen Typ zu bilden; der Verfasser stellt fünf "Briefe" vor. Mehr als eine Pseudoübersetzung wird jedoch nicht erreicht. *Inge Hofmann*

77537 MILLET, N.B., et alii, Autopsy of an Egyptian Mummy (Nakht-ROM 1), *Canadian Medical Association Journal/Journal de l'Association Médicale Canadienne,* Ottawa Vol. 117, No. 5 (September 3, 1977), 461-476, with 1 colour ill. on cover, 11 ill., 2 fig. and 1 table.

This report on the autopsy of the mummy of the weaver Nakht in th Royal Ontario Museum, Toronto (see our number 74443) consists o several sections written by various authors, each dealing with thei specialisms: the archaeological background by N.B. Millet; the radio logical examination by D.F. Rideout; gross anatomic an miscellaneous studies, by John W. Scott, Patrick D. Horne, Gerald D Hart and Howard Savage; examination of ears, by George E. Lyn and Jaime T. Benitez; histopathologic investigation, by Theodore A Reyman, Michael R. Zimmermann and Peter K. Lewin; *Tricinell spiralis cyst,* by V. de Boni, M.M. Lenczner, and John W. Scott analysis of protein extract, by Robin A. Barracq; blood-group testing by Gerald D. Hart, Inge Kvas, and Marja L. Soots. *L.Z*

MILLS, Anthony J., see our number 77346.

MILWARD, Angela, see our number 77076.

77538 MINKOVSKAYA, E.E., Львиноголовый бог Апедемак, *in:* Мероэ 67-133, with a French summary on p. 293-294.

"Der Löwengott Apedemak".

Die Gestalt des Gottes wird unter allen ihren Aspekten untersucht. E soll der höchste Gott des meroitischen Reiches sein, ein kriegerische Löwengott und ein Gott der Fruchtbarkeit. Herausgestellt wird sein enge Beziehung zum König. Es gibt keinen indischen Einfluß auf di Ikonographie des Gottes. *Inge Hofmann*

MINKOVSKAYA, E.E., see also our number 77086.

77539 MOHAMMED, Abbas, [Report], *Nyame Akuma,* Calgary No. 1((1977), 44-45.

Zwei vorgeschichtliche Fundstätten im Sudan wurden untersucht: 1 das Gebiet zwischen Wadi Sayidna und Sorourab nördlich vo Omdurman. Dort wurde Early Khartoum- und Shaheinab-Materia festgestellt. Keramik mit "incised wavy line" - und "dotted wav line" - Verzierung wurde entdeckt, außerdem Tierknochen un Fischgräten. 2. Upper Wadi Hawar Basin in Nord-Darfur: ein Anzahl von Fundstätten, zeitlich von der "neolithischen" bis zu "Eisenzeit" - Periode reichend, konnten lokalisiert werden.

Inge Hofmann

MOKHTAR, Gamal E., see our number 77543.

77540 MOORE, Albert C., Iconography of Religions. An Introduction Philadelphia, Fortress Press, [1977] (22 × 24.5 cm; [VI +] 337 p., 24 ill. and fig.).

The introduction to the iconography of religions presents a systematic approach to the types and meaning of images used in a representative range of religions. Among them are two examples of polytheism in the ancient world, one of which is found in Egypt (p. 66-76). Three points are discussed: the use of symbolism, the place of animal form, and the cultic significance of the images of divinities. On each of these points the author makes important remarks. Some of the drawings show odd details, e.g. the beard of Akhnaton on fig. 40.

MOSCATI, Sabatino, see our numbers 77013, 77014 and 77015.

77541 MOUCHACCA, Jean, Les champignons de Ramsès II, *La Recherche*, Paris 8, No. 84 (décembre 1977), 1108-1109, with 2 ill.

Note on the treatment of the mummy of Ramses II in France.   L.Z.

77542 MOUSSA, Ahmed M. und Hartwig ALTENMÜLLER, Das Grab des Nianchchnum und Chnumhotep. Photographien von D. Johannes. Zeichnungen von W. Ruhm, Mainz am Rhein, Verlag Philipp von Zabern, [1977] (27 × 36 cm; 179 p., plan, colour frontispiece, 92 pl., 26 fig. [10 folding] including a plan on unnumbered pl.) = Old Kingdom Tombs at the Causeway of King Unas at Saqqara Excavated by the Department of Antiquities, 3 = Archäologische Veröffentlichungen. Deutsches Archäologisches Institut Abteilung Kairo, 21.   Pr. DM 198

In einem alten Steinbruch des Djoser entstand ca. 2360/50 das Grab der Brüder Nianchchnum und Chnumhotep, "Aufseher der Nagelpfleger des Palastes" unter Neuserre. Die beim Bau des Unasaufweges abgerissenen und verschütteten Teile, zwei Felskammern, die Fundamente einer Vorhalle und zahlreiche dekorierte Blöcke wurden seit 1964 bei den Ausgrabungsarbeiten im Süden des Aufweges entdeckt und ermöglichten bis 1972 einen Wiederaufbau. In seinem jetzigen Zustand besteht das Grab aus 7 Räumen mit ca. 62,72 m² und entspricht in Raumordnung und Dekoration den Gräbern des Ti und Ptahhotep I. in Saqqâra.

Die vorliegende Publikation enthält zunächst eine Beschreibung der Anlage und Ausstattung des Grabes, der Kleinfunde und Nebenbestattungen. Die beiden Grabherren, ihre Stellung und Familie, behandelt der zweite Abschnitt. Nach einer Übersicht über die Verteilung der Szenen an den Wänden werden diese im dritten Abschnitt ausführlich beschrieben und kommentiert. Inschriften sind in Umschrift und Übersetzung angegeben. Die Szenen zeigen ungewöhnlich ausführliche Darstellungen aus dem täglichen Leben, von der Bestattung und dem Opferritual; sie sind in den Fototafeln vollständig erfaßt. Eine Liste führt bemerkenswerte polychrome Hieroglyphen auf. Drei Indices (Personennamen, Titel und Berufsbezeichnungen, ägyptische Wörter) erleichtern das Nachschlagen. *E.M. Wolf-Brinkmann*

77543 MOUSSA, Ali Helmi, Lambert T. DOLPHIN and Gamal MOKHTAR, Applications of Modern Sensing Techniques to Egyptology. A Report of the 1977 Field Experiments by a Joint Team Prepared for National Science Foundation. Office of International Programs, Washington, Menlo Park, Calif., SRI International Radio Physics Laboratory, 1977 (20.1 × 27.3 cm; XVIII + 173 p., colour frontispiece, 13 plans, 7 maps, 56 ill. [2 in colour], 51 fig., 2 tables).

A joint research team of SRI International, California, the Ain Shams University and the Antiquities Department in Cairo, working together since 1974 to apply new and traditional geophysical techniques in Egypt, presents here the report of their field work in 1977.

After the introduction on the problems of radar techniques, which became manifest in 1974, and the introduction of new techniques, they deal with the scope of research and give brief site descriptions of Alexandria, Tanis, Saqqâra, Gîza and Luxor. The main chapter is concerned with field measurements: aerial photography of the areas, magnetometry, resistivity and acoustic sounder measurements resp. at Gîza and the Sphinx; Gîza, particularly the Sphinx and Saqqâra; and Gîza, particularly the Cheops pyramid, Saqqâra and the King's Valley at Thebes. The report ends with conclusions and recommendations, two technical appendices and a list of references. *L.Z.*

77544 MÜLLER, C. Detlef G., Was lehrt uns die ägyptische Literatur über die Eheethik im Nillande, *in: Fragen an die altägyptische Literatur,* 349-360.

The author demonstrates from Coptic literature that the ancient Egyptian values concerning love and marriage, the positive aspect of a harmonious marital life as well as the negative of warnings against women and unfaithfulness, as they appear in ancient Egyptian wisdom literature, were so fundamental to the civilization that they were still very alive in the Christian Period. *L.Z.*

77545 MÜLLER, Ingeborg, Der Vizekönig Merimose, *in: Ägypten und Kusch,* 325-329, with 1 pl.

Im 5. Jahr Amenophis' III. kommt es in Nubien zu Kampfhandlungen, über die der Vizekönig Merimose auf einer Stele aus Semna ausführlich berichtet. Es handelte sich um das Eindringen von Nomaden aus Gebieten östlich des Nil, mit denen auch der Nachfolger des Merimose unter Amenophis IV. kämpfen muß. Merimose ist von 27 Stelen, Statuen, Grabbeigaben, Architekturteilen und Felsinschriften aus Ägypten und Nubien bekannt, so daß seine Laufbahn rekonstruiert werden kann. Er starb vermutlich noch vor dem 30. Jahr Amenophis' III. und wurde in Theben-West bestattet. Der mittlere und innere anthropomorphe Sarg aus grauem Granit befinden sich im Britischen Museum. Der Deckel und das Unterteil eines dritten, des äußeren, ebenfalls anthropomorphen Sarges wurde 1940 in einem Grabgewölbe in Theben-West gefunden. Er ist aus Rosengranit hergestellt. Die Unterteile des mittleren und inneren sowie der Deckel des mittleren Sarges im Britischen Museum bestehen aus mehreren Bruchstücken; zwei Fragmente von diesen beiden Särgen befinden sich im Louvre bzw. im Prager Museum. Ein drittes in der Nationalgalerie in Oslo wurde bisher nicht als Teil dieser Särge identifiziert. Dieses Fragment wird hier in Transkription und Übersetzung publiziert.   *Inge Hofmann*

MÜLLER, Ingeborg, see our number 77726.

77546   MÜLLER, Wolfgang, Ägyptisches Museum und Papyrus-Sammlung, *Forschungen und Berichte* 18 (1977), 210-212.

Sequel to our number 68422.
Report on the activities of the Staatliche Museen, followed by a list of exhibitions of museum pieces elsewhere, and of publications of museum materials.   *L.Z.*

MÜLLER, Wolfgang, see also our number 77726.

MUHLY, James D., see our number 77502.

MULLER-AUBERT, Jocelyne, see our number 77153.

77547   MUNRO, John M., The French Description. They came, they saw, they measured, *Aramco World Magazine,* New York 27, No. 2 (March-April 1976), 14-25, with 36 ill. (2 on front and back cover).

The author shortly relates the history of the "Description de l'Égypte".
Some of the small-scale reproductions from the original are concerned with ancient Egypt.   *L.Z.*

77548   MUNRO, Peter, Aman-em-hat, (Sohn) des Qen-Atum, *GM* Heft 26 (1977), 43-52, with 2 fig. and 2 ill.

Vorgestellt wird ein kürzlich vom Kestner-Museum erworbener Torso einer Sitzfigur aus der 18. Dynastie, der trotz seines fragmentarischen Zustandes ästhetisch eindrucksvoll und mit einigen Besonderheiten seiner Inschrift auch für den Historiker und den Philologen beachtenswert ist (Inv. Nr. K.M.1976.76). Gemäß der Schriftzeichen gehört die Figur in die Zeit Thutmosis' III./Amenophis' II.; gemäß der Inschrift auf der linken Seite des Sitzes stellt sie dar den "Königsschreiber, Vorstehers der Stätte, Wedelträger und Gefolgsmann seines Herrn bei dessen Schritten auf dem südlichen und nördlichen Fremdland '*Imn-m-ḥ3t*, den *Qn-'Itm* (gezeugt) hat".

Inge Hofmann

77549 MURNANE, William J., Ancient Egyptian Coregencies, Chicago, Illinois, The Oriental Institute, [1977] (17.2 × 24.2 cm; XVIII + 272 p., 8 plans) = The Oriental Institute of the University of Chicago. Studies in Ancient Oriental Civilization, 40.

The study is devoted to the phenomenon of coregency in the entire Egyptian history down to the Roman Period, dealing with all certain and hypothetical instances.

Chapter 1, on the M.K., begins with a discussion of the dating system, after which all coregencies that are reasonably certain pass the review. Three appendices deal with particular problems, among which the chronological framework for coregencies of the XIIth Dynasty.

In chapter 2 four sections are successively devoted to the N.K., the T.I.P., the Ptolemaic and the Roman Periods. Each of them begins with general remarks after which the certain instances are discussed. Particularly the coregency between Sethi I and Ramses II takes much room (p. 57-87), while those later than the N.K. are only briefly dealt with.

Chapter 3 presents the evidence of all hypothetical coregencies: two from the O.K. (Pepi I - Merenre and Merenre-Pepi II); almost every ruler of the XVIIIth Dynasty not yet discussed in chapter 2 (the problem of a coregency between Amenophis III and Akhnaton on p. 123-169); from the later N.K. Horemheb-Ramses I, Ramses I-Sethi I and Sethnakht-Ramses III; some pharaohs from the XXIInd and several from the XXVth Dynasties, and from the Late Period Nectanebo I-Teos. Only in a few fairly certain instances an opinion is expressed. The others are reserved for chapter 4 which presents a comparative analysis of the evidence, evaluating the indications, e.g. juxtaposed materials in an architectural context, juxtaposition of names on objects and papyri with dates of two kings. The results of this analysis are applied to the evidence of chapter 3. It appears that there is no general principle according to which doubtful instances can find a clear solution.

In chapter 5 the author presents his ideas concerning the dynamics of the coregency in Egyptian history, dealing i.a. with the relations between the partners and the reason why a coregency came into being. He concludes that it was used as a safeguard against factionalism and civil war and that it was mostly a reaction against a specific challenge, hence the variability in the junior partner's real status (particularly discussed for Sesostris I and Ramses II).

An appendix (267-272) deals with the question whether the epithets $dỉ$-$^cnḫ$ and $m3^c$-$ḫrw$ can be used as an indication whether the person was alive or dead; it appears not to be the case.

No indexes.

77550 MUßGNUG, Reinhard, Wem gehört Nofretete?, Anmerkungen zu dem deutsch-deutschen Streit um den ehemals preußischen Kulturbesitz. Vortrag gehalten vor der Berliner Juristischen Gesellschaft am 1. Dezember 1976, Berlin-New York, de Gruyter, 1977 (14.7 × 22.5 cm; 40 p.) = Schriftenreihe der juristischen Gesellschaft e.V. Berlin, 52.

Juridical treatise on the rightfulness of the West German ownership of the famous head of Nefertiti, which is disputed by the DDR.   *L.Z.*

77551 MUSZYNSKI†, Michel, Les "associations religieuses" en Égypte d'après les sources hiéroglyphiques, démotiques et grecques, *Orientalia Lovaniensia Periodica,* Leuven 8 (1977), 145-174.

In this posthumous article the late Muszynski presents a survey of our knowledge about the *snt,* the religious association known in Egypt from the Saite Period onwards. On account of the 72 sources he collected (see p. 163-174) he discusses the terminology of the articles of the association, their customs and their membership. He argues i.a. that they are religious rather than cult associations, mutual aid being an important feature for their members. Their origin may be due to the wish to preserve the Egyptian identity against the influx of foreigners.

77552 MUSZYNSKI†, Michel, P. Turin Cat. 2070/154, *Oriens Antiquus* 16 (1977), 183-200, with 4 pl. (2 folding).

The late author studies in this posthumous article Pap. Turin 2070/154 recently published by Allam, "Hieratische Ostraka und Papyri" (our number 73020), pls. 120-121. He describes the outer appearance of the sheet which belongs to the "Journal of the

Necropolis" and bears one column of text both on the recto and the verso. The text is given in facsimile and transcription, with a translation and an extensive commentary.

The author dates the text to the reign of Ramses VII and discusses the division of the properties of workman Nekhmin recorded on the verso, particularly the family relations and the reasons for the mentioned division of the inheritance.

MUSZYNSKI, Michel, see also our numbers 77110 and 77164.

77553 MYŚLIWIEC, K., Zur Ikonographie des Gottes 'Ηρων, *Studia aegyptiaca* 3 (1977), 89-97, with 2 ill. and 1 fig.

The author studies the iconography of the god 'Ηρων, identified with Atum. The former is usually represented as a horseman, but both are connected with a snake.

77554 NAGY, Étienne, Fragments de sistres au Musée des Beaux Arts, *Bulletin du Musée Hongrois des Beaux Arts,* Budapest 48-49 (1977), 49-70, with 17 ill.

The author first describes the two types of sistra, the sššt with a building resembling a monumental gateway (incorrectly called a naos) on the Hathor capital, and the simpler sḫm, the arched sistrum. There follows a discussion of the meaning of sistra, symbols of renewal and appeasement, and of their occurrences in cult, at festivals and in funerary ceremonies.

Then three fragments of sistra from the Late Period, preserved in the collection at Budapest, are described. One of them, handle plus capital, bears parts of a figure which may be a sitting cat. A fourth, arched sistrum from the Roman Period is complete.

A Hungarian version of the same article (Szisztrum töredékek a Szépművészeti Múzeumban), without ill., on p. 201-208.

77555 NAGY, I., Remarques sur quelques formules stellaires des textes religieux d'époque saïte, *Studia aegyptiaca* 3 (1977), 99-117, with 3 fig.

The author collects the texts on Saite coffins which refer to stars, presenting some in hieroglyphs and all in translation with some commentary. The importance of this genre in the Saite Period is due to a tendency to situate once more the netherworld in the celestial spheres, a tendency already beginning from the XXIst-XXIInd Dynasties onwards.

77556 NEL, Philip, The Concept "Father" in the Wisdom Literature of the Ancient Near East, *Journal of Northwest Semitic Languages,* Stellenbosch 5 (1977), 53-66.

Dealing with the concept "father" in the ancient Near Eastern context, the author also discusses the Egyptian word *it* as kinship terminology and in the educational sphere as a word for the wisdom teacher. He adds some remarks on the title *it-ntr,* "father of God".
L.Z.

77557 NĚMEČKOVÁ, Alena, Histology of Egyptian Mummified Tissues from Czechoslovak Collections (= Eugen STROUHAL, Multidisciplinary Research on Egyptian Mummies in Czechoslovakia, VII), *ZÄS* 104 (1977), 142-144, with 3 ill. on 1 pl.

Examination of a selection of human tissues.
Samples of skin, sinews and cerebral tissues were studied. The epidermis and hair follicles could be identified.
Note also the supplement to our number 76108. *M. Heerma van Voss*

77558 NEUBERT, Otto, Tutankhamon. Kralj u zlatnim kovčezima, Zagreb, Stvarnost, 1977 (13.5 × 20.5 cm; 216 p., 54 ill. [25 in colours], colour ill. on cover).

"Tut-ankh-Amon. The King in the Gold Coffins."
An abbreviated Serbo-Croatian version, in parts translated freely, of our number 4775.

77559 NIBBI, Alessandra, Ancient Egyptians in the Sinai, *Palestine Exploration Quarterly,* London 109 (1977), 125-128, with 1 map.

The author makes some remarks on the Sinai in relation to ancient Egypt: the absence of Egyptian burials and transportation of the dead back to Egypt; the presence of silver, gold, turquoise and lapis-lazuli in the Sinai, according to the Egyptian inscriptions; copper working in the Sinai and the recording of an expedition looking for ore in the region of Atika (present Gebel Atāqah?) and travelling along the Wadî Tumilât — Bitter Lakes route.
L.Z.

77560 NIBBI, Alessandra, The Shipwrecked Sailor Again, *GM* Heft 24 (1977), 53-55.

Vgl. unsere Nummer 76540.
Es geht um das Problem einer Übersetzung von *w3ḏ-wr* als Meer, die nicht erwiesen ist, die Bedeutung von "Norden" in Dokumenten aus dem Süden, die Fruchtbarkeit des Sinai-Gebietes in frühdynastischer

Zeit, die größer war, als man bisher angenommen hat (es fand sich dort die Darstellung einer Giraffe). Es wird angenommen, daß nahezu aller Weihrauch aus dem Norden kam; die Insel des Schiffbrüchigen wird weiterhin im Roten Meer vermutet.

Inge Hofmann

77561 NIBBI, Alessandra, Some Remarks on *Copper*, *JARCE* 14 (1977), 59-66, with 8 fig.

1. The term *bỉ3* originally refers to copper, not to iron. The affiliation of *bỉ3* with two basic meanings, viz. 'to separate' and 'wonder' as worked out in our number 71219 may very well be taken to refer to the melting process, resp. to the brilliancy of the product. These meanings hardly fit in with the more complicated technological process of winning iron from its ore. 2. The material for early iron beads when not of meteoritic origin was perhaps obtained as a by-product of copper melting. It is known that droplets of iron are expelled when copper is being melted from its ore. 3. On mining and smelting areas (Sinai and Eastern Dessert). 4. On crucibles with their typical pointed form (cf. our number 62120), often incorrectly identified as ingots, and the ways to keep them upright during the heating. Pairs were kept together by dowels and holes. 5. The reading of ⌂ ̊ . *bỉ3* is possible (*bỉ3 rwḏ* discussed), but *ḥmt* (not *ḥmty*) as well. This term, connected with 'three', might for instance refer to a three-stage production process.

J.F. Borghouts

77562 NIBLEY, Hugh, The Message of the Joseph Smith Papyri. An Egyptian Endowment, Salt Lake City, Utah, Deseret Book Company, 1976 (21.1 × 28.4 cm; XIII + 305 p., 2 plans, 15 ill., 107 fig.).

After the preambulatory explanation containing an apology for Joseph Smith, the founder of the Church of the Latter-Day Saints, the author describes in the first chapter the nature of the Book of Breathings, its importance as a source concerned with initiation and mysteries, and the classification of the various Breathing Texts. He makes clear that the Pap. Joseph Smith XI and X containing the Book of Breathings were wrongly identified by others with Joseph Smith's Book of Abraham.

The second chapter presents the Pap. Joseph Smith XI and X in photograph, complete as well as line by line, with a transcription from right to left and vice-versa, a somewhat adapted transliteration and a translation with explanatory notes, while chapter 3 is devoted to the problem of understanding and translating, especially as regards the way their prophet did it. Chapter 4 deals with a more complete text of the Book of Breathings (Pap. Louvre No. 3284) given in de Horrack's

facsimile (Bibliothèque Égyptologique 17, 1878, 110-137, pl. 7-13), the translation of which is divided by subject headings designating the six main topics, they being the main themes of mysteries everywhere. Then follows the translation of another Book of Breathings (Pap. Louvre No. 3279), a discussion of the inscriptions of the tomb of Petosiris, and some vignettes of the XXIst Dynasty mythological Papyrus of Herweben with captions.
The main part of the book is concerned with the extensive commentary of the complete version of the Book of Breathings (ms. Pap. Louvre No. 3284) divided after the main topics: nature and purpose of the book; purification rites and entering the temple; the creation of man; the garden story; the long road back; the fearful passage; and culmination and conclusion.
At the end there follow excerpts from various Jewish and Christian texts, exemplifying the close connection between the Book of Breathings and their world of thought.
It is to be noted that although this book shows clear traces of Mormon viewpoints, its author has made a serious scientific attempt to make full use of Egyptological literature. *L.Z.*

77563 NICCACCI, Alviero, Il messaggio di Tefnakht (Stele di Piankhi, lin. 126-140), *Liber Annuus Studii Biblici Francescani,* Jerusalem 27 (1977), 213-228, with 2 pl.

The author studes lines 126-140 of the Piankhi stela, the message sent by Tefnakht. He gives a translation with comments, particularly about grammatical points, while he presents a photograph and a facsimile of this part of the text on the plates. On p. 127-128 his conclusions as regards orthography, grammar and meaning of the passage.

77564 NOBERASCO, Giorgio, Analisi statistica di alcuni documenti di carattere religioso provenienti da Deir el Medina, Torino, G. Giappichelli Editore, [1977] (23.5 × 31.8 cm; 24 p., 6 tables) = Catalogo del Museo Egizio di Torino. Serie Seconda-Collezioni, Volume 1 — Appendice.

In this statistical study on the attitude of the necropolis workmen of Deir el-Medîna towards the gods the author deals in the first section with the methodological problems. He then lists first the museums and collections in which the 509 traced Deir el-Medîna stelae are present, with the relevant bibliography, and then analyzes the distribution of the stelae and the divinities recorded on them, dividing them after dynasties, after which he elaborates the data statistically. The last sections are devoted to other considerations concerning the divinities and to a short conclusion.

Obviously the statistical study is not yet exhausted, since there is added on 40 loosely added pages in typescript a fifth section on the characteristics of the various divinities recorded in Deir el-Medîna, which will possibly appear later in a more fashionable form. *L.Z.*

NOLTE, Birgit, see our number 77024.

NORDSTRÖM, Hans-Åke, see our number 77367.

77565 NORTH, Robert, Akhenaten Secularized?, *Biblica,* Roma 58 (1977), 246-258.

A critical evaluation without notes of Aldred's ideas on Akhenaten as expressed in our number 71008. At the end of the article the author draws up a balance of agreement and disagreement, and presents his views in short in a conclusion. *L.Z.*

77566 NUNN, J.F. and Carol A.R. ANDREWS, Egyptian Antiquities at the Royal College of Surgeons of England, *Annals of the Royal College of Surgeons of England,* London 59 (1977), 342-347, with 7 ill.

A brief description of the Egyptian antiquities in the collection of the Royal College of Surgeons, formed by the former president Sir John Bland-Sutton: a bronze Osiris (69 cm), two calcite canopic jars from the XIXth or XXVIth Dynasty, a XXVIth Dynasty shawabti and five amulets. Also in the possession of the college are some fine brass copies of aegyptiaca, the originals of which are as yet unknown. *L.Z.*

77567 el-NUR, Osama, Проблема "Группы-С" в истории культуры Древнего Судана, *in:* Мероэ, 252-263, with a French summary on p. 298-299.

"Das Problem der 'C-Gruppe' in der Kulturgeschichte des alten Sudan".

Die Ausgrabungen haben den Erweis gebracht, daß die C-Gruppe die direkte Fortführung der A-Gruppe ist und sich aus ihr entwickelt hat. Wegen der ägyptischen Raubzüge sahen sich die Repräsentanten der A-Kultur veranlaßt, sich in die Gegend südlich des 2. Kataraktes zurückzuziehen, was sich auch durch die Gemeinsamkeiten der C- und der Kerma-Kultur wahrscheinlich machen läßt. Die Gemeinsamkeiten zeigen sich im Bestattungsritual, in der ethnischen Verwandtschaft, in Kunstgegenständen und in den verschiedenen Motiven der Keramik. Die Theorien von Adams werden bestätigt (vgl. unsere Nr. 64004).

Inge Hofmann

*7568 el-NUR, Osama, О древнеегипетском названии ḫnt - ḥn - nfr, in: Мероэ, 64-66, with a French summary on p. 293.

"Zur Bezeichnung ḫnt-ḥn-nfr im Altägyptischen."
In griechischen Texten findet sich das Toponym ḫnt-ḥn-nfr zuerst in der Zeit des Amasis. Da sich im Grab des Huy ḫnt-ḥn-nfr von el-Kab bis Napata erstreckt, soll das Toponym mit "Südtal des Nil" übersetzt werden; die wörtliche Übersetzung sei "forme sud magnifique".
Inge Hofmann

*7569 OGDON, Jorge Roberto, The Celestial Ferryman in the Pyramid Texts, [Buenos Aires], Instituto de Egiptologia de la Argentina, [1977] (22 × 33.9 cm; 12 p. in offset).

The purpose of the paper is to study the origin, the personality and the role of the celestial ferryman in the funerary literature. The first section, on the mythological origin of the celestial ferryman (P.T. 594 a — 601c), deals with his role in the Horus and Seth configuration according to Heliopolitan thought. The following sections discuss his personality on account of his names and the gods by whom he can be replaced, the Winding Waterway and the conditions for its crossing on the part of the king in the P.T. After a survey of the myth of the Celestial Ferryman and the Winding Waterway in the C.T. and the B.D. follows a last section in which the author presents his conclusions. *L.Z.*

*7570 OGDON, Jorge Roberto, Un ex-voto ramesida procedente de Mit Rahine-Menfis, *Aegyptus Antiquus* 2 (1977), 80-82, with 1 fig.

Note concerning a Ramesside ex-voto originating from Mit Rahîna, which mentions Ptah and Sakhmet. *L.Z.*

*7571 OGDON, Jorge Roberto, Observaciones sobre los entes llamados Tekenu, [Buenos Aires], Instituto de Egiptologia de la Argentina, 1977 (22 × 27.9 cm; 12 p. in offset, 8 fig.).

The author presents a survey of the problem of the Tekenu and discusses particularly possible pre- and protodynastic evidence. *L.Z.*

OGDON, Jorge Roberto, see also our number 77063.

*7572 OGDON, Ricardo Edgard, Reflexiones sobre la religion Atoniana, *Aegyptus Antiquus* 2 (1977), 83-86.

The author shortly surveys some opinions concerning the Amarna religious reform. *L.Z.*

77573 ONASCH, Christian, Kusch in der Sicht von Ägyptern und Griechen *in: Ägypten und Kusch,* 331-336.

Ausgangspunkt der Untersuchung ist die Erwähnung des Landes *Kns* am Löwentempel von Musawwarât es Sufra. Dem ägyptozentrischer Weltbild entspricht die feindselige und verächtliche Einstellung der Ägypter gegenüber den Kuschiten, während diese für die Griechen ein den Göttern besonders nahestehendes mythisches Urvolk am Rande der Erde waren. Ihr Land wurde zum Wunschbild einer besseren Welt und geriet in den Bereich utopischer Spekulationen (vgl. Aithiopika des Heliodor). *Inge Hofmann*

ORLANDI, Tito, see our number 77148.

77574 OSING, Jürgen, Die Patenschaft der Götter für die Königir Hatschepsut, *in: Fragen an die altägyptische Literatur,* 361-383.

The author discusses the scene in the upper register of the divine birth legend of Hatshepsut in her temple at Deir el-Bahâri, in which Amon introduces the queen as a young child to the gods of Upper and Lower Egypt. The text of the introduction by Amon and the answer of the gods (*Urk.* IV, 244, 3-245, 6) is given in metrical transliteration and translation, and is amply commented upon. On the basis of an analysis of its formal structure, the train of thought and the contents characterized as a sponsorship of the gods, the author reconstructs the lacuna in verse lines 13-14 as *dỉ.n n.s (13) n[.k ḫꜥy(t?) ḥr s.t Ḥrw (14, sm3.n] n.s t3wy m ḥtpw*. Since the proposed reconstruction shows a similarity in rhythm and vocalic assonance of both verses, they are presented in verse rhythm and full pronunciation as they will have sounded in official XVIIIth Dynasty language. *L.Z*

77575 OSING, Jürgen, Der Tempel Sethos' I. in Gurna. Die Reliefs und Inschriften. Band 1. Photographien von Peter Grunwald und Dieter Johannes, Mainz am Rhein, Verlag Philipp von Zabern, [1977] (27 × 36 cm; 69 p., 44 pl.) = Archäologische Veröffentlichungen Deutsches Archäologisches Institut Abteilung Kairo, 20. Pr. DM 105

Dieser erste Band einer Publikation des gesamten Tempels, welche die Reliefs, die Inschriften, die Grabungsergebnisse und die Architektur umfassen soll, enthält die Reliefs und Inschriften der nördlichen und südlichen Außenwand, des Sonnenhofes und der Räume XXI bis XXVII, XXXII und XXXIII (nach Nelson, Key Plans).

Die Dekoration der in diesem Band erfaßten Teile des Tempels erfolgte unter Ramses II. Die Szenen, in waagerechten Registern angeordnet, zeigen den König bei der Ausführung wechselnder

Kulthandlungen aus dem Opferritual vor jeweils einem Gott oder einer Göttin. Die Einleitung gibt eine Übersicht über die Gemeinsamkeiten der einzelnen Reliefszenen in Bezug auf Haltung, Kleidung und Attribute des Königs und der Götter, die Anordnung von Sonnenscheibe und Uräen, die formelhaften Inschriften und Farbspuren, und weist hin auf Abweichungen vom Schema, z.B. die Darstellung von Ahmes-Nefertari und Amenophis I. anstelle des Königs. Anschließend folgt eine detaillierte Beschreibung der Szenen mit Angabe der Texte in Hieroglyphen bzw. in Umschrift. Die Analyse der Szenenfolgen jeweils am Ende eines Kapitels liefert einen Überblick über die Verteilung der Gottheiten und ihrer Gaben auf der Wandfläche. Hierbei ist Amon-Re immer alternierend mit anderen Gottheiten dargestellt. Der Exkurs "Repräsentative Ausschnitte aus dem Opferritual in der Dekoration von Tempelwänden" bringt eine Zusammenstellung des Vorkommens bestimmter Szenen, vor allem in den thebanischen Tempeln des Neuen Reiches, und zwar für die Gruppe A:Wein — Milch — Weihräuchern und Libation und die Gruppe B:Maat — Wein — Weihräuchern und Libation — Speisen. Photographien sämtlicher Szenen finden sich auf Tafeln 1 bis 44.

E.M. Wolf-Brinkmann

7576 OSING, Jürgen, Vier Ostraka aus Giza, *MDAIK* 33 (1977), 109-111, with 1 pl.

Publication with photograph, transliteration, translation and comments of four ostraca found at Gîza. The larger two have already been published by Goedicke and Wente (our number 62228). One of them bears a passage of the Instruction of a Man for his Son.

7577 OSING, Jürgen, Zur Korregenz Amenophis III. — Amenophis IV., *GM* Heft 26 (1977), 53.

Ein fragmentarisch erhaltenes Relief im Luxor-Tempel wurde als nun vermeintlich definitiven Beleg für eine Korregenz Amenophis' IV. mit Amenophis III. in Anspruch genommen (vgl. unsere Nr. 76333); interpretiert man aber die kleinere Figur hinter Amenophis III. als den königlichen Ka, dann verliert die Darstellung ihre historische Relevanz.
Vgl. unsere Nummer 77549. *Inge Hofmann*

7578 OSING, Jürgen, Zur Syntax der Biographie des *Wnj, Orientalia* 46 (1977), 165-182.

Entre les IVe et VIe dynasties, l'ancien égyptien a dû évoluer. L'étude synchronique de textes développés permettra sans doute un jour d[e] percevoir les transformations progressives. La biographie d'Oun[i] permet déjà des conclusions au sujet de la syntaxe, car elle conjugu[e] au passé des phrases nombreuses. L'auteur répartit ces dernières e[n] catégories connues, notamment en imparfait et plus-que-parfait. Dan[s] les propositions affirmatives, il constate à l'actif imparfait une flexio[n] verbale différente, tant en indépendante qu'en subordonnée, d'aprè[s] la nature du sujet, substantif ou pronom. Une pareille distinctio[n] s'observe dans les subordonnées, au passif plus-que-parfait. Mai[s] cette différence ne peut se vérifier pour aucun intransitif. Du passi[f] imparfait, seule apparaît la subordonnée à sujet nominal. Un schém[a] groupe les 16 types attestés d'affirmation. Sont analysées d'autre part le̱s propositions négatives (toutes au p-q-parfait: "jamais... avan[t] moi"); puis les substantivées; les cinq cas de forme relative; le[s] fréquentes circonstancielles, toujours introduites par *st̲* l'Existentialsatz ("il y avait là") et le sujet mis en évidence par *ỉn* Tout cela conduit l'auteur à discuter la traduction et les restitution[s] qu'il convient d'admettre pour plusieurs passages.   J. Custer[s].

77579   OSMAN, Ali, New Lights On Medieval Nubia, *Nyame Akuma* Calgary No. 10 (1977), 47-50.

Untersucht wurden eine Reihe von mittelalterlichen nubische[n] Dokumenten, die von J.M. Plumley in Qasr Ibrim gefunden worde[n] waren. Besonders interessant sind einige Landschenkungsurkunden Kornverteilungsregister und zwei Geschäftsbriefe. Eine Liste vo[n] Amtstiteln, die in den Dokumenten vorkamen, wurd[e] zusammengestellt und mit modernen nubischen Titeln in Verbindun[g] gebracht.   *Inge Hofmann*

77580   OTTO, Eberhard, Zur Komposition von Coffin Texts Spell 1130, *in Fragen an die altägyptische Literatur,* 1-18.

After a general discussion of the sources and the redaction criticism o[f] the C.T. and their genres the author discusses C.T. VII, Spell 1130 which forms the end of the Book of Two Ways. The text which i[s] given in translation with short comments is divided into: 461c-e title o[f] the spell and introduction of the speaker, the Lord-of-All; 462a-468[b] his great aretology as creator and sun god; 468c-469f second discours[e] of the Lord-of-All, but spoken by the deceased identified with him 469g-471b identification; 471c-471f profitable position for the deceased; 471g epilogue. Then the author discusses the conceptua[l] oppositions in the great aretology: air-water; human beings-gods[;]

light-darkness; sun god — god of the hereafter, who merge in the end, while other questions such as the "Sitz im Leben" and date must remain open. L.Z.

OTTO, Eberhard, see also our numbers 77477 and 77478.

77581 PADRÓ I PARCERISA, Josep, Los decretos trilingues ptolemaicos y su importancia para la comparación de las estructuras políticas y sociales de Egipto faraonico y helenístico, *Memorias de Historia Antigua,* Orviedo 1 (1977), 55-63.

Comparing royal titulary, indications for the army, the clergy, the administration, the people and the calendar in the Greek and the Egyptian texts of the Ptolemaic trilingual decrees, the author discusses in how far the Greek government meant a continuation of or a break with the preceding situation. He i.a. concludes that the position of the clergy was much improved.

77582 PADRÓ I PARCERISA, Josep, L'Egipte Antic i Catalunya, Lleida, Artis Estudis Grafics, 1976 (17.2 × 24.5 cm; 30 p., 1 map, 4 ill.); at head of title: Catedra de Cultura Catalana "Samuel Gili i Gaya".

Text of a lecture in the Catalan language concerning the relations between Catalonia and ancient Egypt. The author points out that the Egyptian objects discovered in that region (see map on p. 10) came there by the Phoenicians in the first millennium B.C., and discusses some of them.

PADRÓ I PARCERISA, Josep, see also our number 77374.

7583 PANIĆ, Miroslava, Egyptian Stele from the Town Museum in Varaždin, Зборник Филозофског Факултета, Beograd 13,1 (1976), [1977], 1-8, with 1 ill. and 1 fig. on 2 pl.

Analysis, transliteration and translation with commentary of the stela of *Mry-Mry,* surnamed *Ḥy.* He was probably a high official during the reign of Amenhotep III. S.P. Tutundžić

7584 PANIĆ-LJUBISAVLJEVIĆ, Miroslava, O jednom muškom ličnom imenu iz vremena novoga carstva, *Živa antika.* Antiquité vivante, Skoplje 27 (1977), 191-192.

"About a Masculine Proper Name from the Time of the New Kingdom."

On the stela in Varaždin (see our preceding number) the name of the deceased is written in two variations: 𓏶𓏤𓂀𓀀 and 𓏶𓏤𓀀𓏤𓀀 to which the author does not find an identical example. The author assumes that the reason for the two variations is the popularity of the name with the root "to love", whereby orthographic mistakes might have occurred. *S.P. Tutundžić*

77585 PARLASCA, Klaus, Ägyptisierende Bauglieder und Reliefs aus Rom im Ägyptischen Museum, *Forschungen und Berichte* 18 (1977), 59-65, with 2 ill. and 5 pl.

The author describes and discusses some Egyptianizing architectural parts and reliefs from Rome in the Staatliche Museen zu Berlin. *L.Z.*

77586 PARLASCA, Klaus, Ritratti di mummie. Tavole 61-120 — Numeri 247-496, Roma, "L'Erma" di Bretschneider, [1977] (24.5 × 35 cm; 97 p., 1 colour pl., 60 pl., 1 ill. on cover) = Repertorio d'arte dell' Egitto greco-romano a cura di A. Adriani. Serie B-Volume, 2.

Sequel to our number 69007.
The author describes mummy portraits, mainly originating from Hawara and particularly er-Rubayat. The indexes are to be found before the description proper. *L.Z.*

77587 PARLEBAS, Jacques, Die Herkunft der Achtheit von Hermopolis, in: *XIX. Deutscher Orientalistentag*, 36-38.

The members of the Hermopolitan Ogdoad have almost the same name as the four poles of heaven, the determinative for which in the C.T. has been changed into that for mammals (Sign F 27). Hence their representation in the form of baboons in the XVIIIth Dynasty. *L.Z*

77588 PAVLOVA, O.I., Античные авторы о культе Амона в Куше, *in:* Мероэ, 134-145, with a French summary on p. 294.

"Die klassischen Schriftsteller über den Kult des Amun in Kusch."
Bemerkungen über den Amun-Kult von Kusch sind hauptsächlich in den Werken von Herodot, Diodor, Strabon und Plinius d. Älteren erhalten. Insbesondere wird auf die Funktion des Orakels hingewiesen sowie auf die Rolle der Priester im täglichen Leben, besonders bei der Königswahl. Über das Aussehen des Gottes haben wir nur ägyptische und meroitische Zeugnisse; sie zeigen, daß der thebanische Amun der Prototyp des Amun von Kusch ist. *Inge Hofmann*

PAULISSEN, E., see our number 77763.

77589 PECK, William H., A Newly Discovered Example of Decorated Pre Dynastic Pottery in the Detroit Institute of Arts, *Bulletin of the Detroit Institute of Arts,* Detroit 55 (1977), 216-218, with 1 ill. and fig.

Publication of a predynastic vase bearing the representation of a giraffe.

7590 PERC, Bernarda, Stanje in perspektive jugoslovanske egiptologije, in: Simpozij Orientalistika in neuvrščeni svet. Stanje in perspektive jugoslovanske orientalistike. Ljubljana 4 in 5 dec. 1975, Ljubljana, Slovensko orientalistično društvo, 1977 (= Orientalistika 1), 63-64, with an English summary on p.64.

"Position and Perspectives of Yugoslav Egyptology."
The author mentions aspects of the activities and contributors in the field of Egyptology in the broadest sense besides suggestions on joint actions. *S.P. Tutundžić*

7591 PERDU, Olivier, Khenemet-nefer-hedjet: une princesse et deux reines du Moyen Empire, *RdE* 29 (1977), 68-85.

Vingt-cinq documents portent le nom repris dans le titre de l'article, que l'on peut repartir entre trois personnes: 1. une princesse qui vivait au temps d'Amenemhat II, dont on ne peut savoir toutefois les relations avec le roi; 2. une reine (Kh. *wrt*) épouse principale de Sésostris II; 3. une reine (Kh. *ḥrd*) épouse principale de Sésostris III. *Ph. Derchain*

7592 PERDUE, Leo G., Wisdom and Cult. A Critical Analysis of the Views of Cult in the Wisdom Literatures of Israel and the Ancient Near East, [Missoula, Montana], Scholars Press, [1977] (13.7 × 21.2 cm; XIII + 390 p.) = Society of Biblical Literature. Dissertation Series, 30; rev. *Journal of Biblical Literature* 97 (1978), 583-584 (Roland E. Murphy). Pr. $6

In this book on the views of cult by the wise in the Wisdom Literatures of Israel and the Ancient Near East, the introductory chapter mainly deals with former opinions on the relation between wisdom and cult in the Near East. Only the second chapter is exclusively devoted to Egypt. In the first and general part the author discusses the world view of the Egyptian wise concerning the concept of Ma^{c}at in its cosmic, social and anthropological contexts: Ma^{c}at and the demiurge and the other gods, Ma^{c}at and the Pharaoh and his administration, and Ma^{c}at and mankind in general, and he concludes that the principle of retribution played an important role in assuring reward for the wise.

In the second part he turns to the more specific problem whether cult played any part in the world view of the sage and for that reason he scrutinizes the relevant wisdom literature in chronological order with respect to precepts on the subject, and he discusses them. For the

F.I.P. he discusses the Lebensmüde, the Song of the Harper (negative view on cult) and the Admonitions and Merikare (positive). After the positive, loyalistic literature of the M.K. (Amenemhat; Instructions o a Man for his Son; Sehetepibre) he continues with the negative Praise of Learned Scribes from P. Chester Beatty IV, and Ani and Amenemope (positive). From the later period ᶜOnchsheshonqy is critical, contrary to P. Insinger.

The author concludes that the sphere of cult was of considerable concern to the wise in ancient Egypt. In chapter 6, containing the general conclusions, there are spread remarks on the ancient Egyptian Wisdom Literature and there is given a list of references to elements o cult in Egyptian and Mesopotamian wisdom sources.

Notes at the end of each chapter. The book is concluded by an extensive bibliography. *L.Z*

77593 PÉREZ DIE, Maria del Carmen, Notas sobre cuatro vasos egipcios de alabastro procedentes de Torre del Mar (Málaga), conservados en el Museo Arqueológico Nacional de Madrid, *Revista de Archivos Bibliotecas y Museos,* Madrid 79 (1976), 903-918, with 1 map, 5 fig and 4 pl.

Publication of four Egyptian alabaster vessels, preserved since 1876 in the National Archaeological Museum in Madrid (Inv. Nos 16801-'804). They came from Torre del Mar and may be dated to the T.I.P. The author discusses the modern history of the vessels describes each of them carefully, and deals with Egyptian alabaste vessels found in Spain in general.

77594 PERNIGOTTI, Sergio, Un frammento di papiro copto, *Aegyptus* 5ʹ (1977), 96-100, with 1 pl.

The Coptic papyrus fragment of the Institute of Papyrology, Milan (P. med. 43), dealing with an administrative matter, is presented with photograph, transcription, and translation with commentary. *L.Z*

77595 PERNIGOTTI, Sergio, Un frammento di statua saitica nel Museo Civico di Bologna, *Studi classici e orientali,* Pisa 26 (1977), 271-276 with 2 ill. and 1 fig. on a pl.

The author deals with a fragment of a basalt block statuette (19 × 1: cm) preserved in Bologna (No. 1812) and representing the *îmy-îs* of Nebet-Ḥetepet Aat (ᶜ3t). In the inscription are mentioned the temples of Hathor-Nebet-Ḥetepet and Atum of the Sycamore as well as Psammetichus I.

77596 PERNIGOTTI, Sergio, Un mattone con iscrizione magica nel Museo Civico di Bologna, *Oriens Antiquus* 16 (1977), 35-40, with 1 fig. and 1 pl.

Publication of a 'magical brick' from the collection of the Museo Civico in Bologna (possibly no. 3321). It was placed at the West side of a tomb and served as pedestal of a *ḏd* amulet, as the inscription proves. The text is given in facsimile and translation, with comments. It contains the name of the god Ha, which proves its Memphite origin, and that of the *imy-r isty* Padipep, a man from the XXVIth Dynasty of whom several monuments are known. His tomb at Saqqâra seems to have been found by clandestine digging before 1847, when his sarcophagus came to Vienna.

PERNIGOTTI, Sergio, see also our numbers 77110 and 77111.

77597 PESTMAN, P.W., avec la collaboration de J. QUAEGEBEUR et R.L. VOS, Recueil de textes démotiques et bilingues. I: Transcriptions. II: Traductions. III: Index et planches, Leiden, E.J. Brill, 1977 (21.5 × 29 cm; [I:] XIV + 161 p., [II:] 135 p., 3 folding tables; [III:] VI + 124 p., 21 pl. [7 folding]); rev. *CdE* LIII, No. 105 (1978), 187-188 (Jean Bingen). Pr. fl.180

Publication of 23 texts, partly Demotic and partly bilingual Greek-Demotic, of which some have been published before in a not quite satisfactory way or incompletely, while others appear here in print for the first time. The original aim was to compose an equivalent to the "Sammelbuch griechischer Urkunden aus Ägypten", but that appeared still impossible.

The photographs of each of the 23 documents are to be found in vol. III, the description of its outer appearance with bibliographical references and transliteration with notes and examples of the writing in facsimile in vol. I, while vol. II contains translations with commentary to the contents of the texts. The very extensive indexes in vol. III (124 p.) include i.a. lists of words and grammatical forms, palaeographical tables to some sign-groups and a list of Greek-Demotic equivalents.

Vol. I begins with an introduction and remarks concerning the scheme of the study and the transcription system. The texts here presented are divided into two groups: 12 from the Ptolemaic and 11 from the Roman Period. To the former belong three Demotic documents from the archive of Horos, son of Petosiris (Pap. Brooklyn 37.1781, 37.1839 A and B), and three from that of the merchant *Ḥr-m-ḥj*, son of Herienupis (P. Brooklyn 37.1802 and .1803, and 37.1796), all six from the Memphite region. The latter group has recently been published by Pierce (see our number 72560) and was included because of the different point of view of the present authors.

Then follow the Demotic P. BM 10.394, two papyri from Dublin (1659 and 1660), and one from Warsaw (148.288), all from Thebes; an Egyptian graffito from Abydos written in Greek letters, and a Greek inscription (Alexandria 26.050) containing some Egyptian words in Greek script.

The second group consists of two Greek papyri with a Demotic subscription (P. Geneva inv. 123 and P. Strasbourg inv. 1105), both from the Faiyûm, and nine mummy labels from the region of Panopolis/Akhmîm (8 in Amsterdam, 1 in Leiden), one in Demotic, the others bilingual; of each a facsimile is given of the Demotic text. In appendices the supervisors of the notaries at Djeme, four families of that place, and the countersigns of the documents are discussed.

Vol. II contains apart from a translation and detailed study of each of the documents introductions to the archives (nos 1-3; 4-6; 8-9), with genealogical tables on folding pages.

77598   PETERSON, Bengt, Gesicht und Kunststil. Ein Repertorium der ägyptischen Kunstentwicklung der Spätzeit anhand von Grabfiguren, *Medelhavsmuseet Bulletin,* Stockholm 12 (1977), 12-37, with 32 ill.

Study of the geographical differences and historical development of the Egyptian sculptural style from the XXVIth Dynasty onwards on account of the faces of 32 shawabtis preserved in the Medelhavsmuseet and representing 21 different persons. Each piece is represented by three photographs, while technical data and many parallels in other collections are mentioned.

The shawabtis here studied are arranged in a geographical order, since from the names and titles of their owners their homes could be identified. They came from various places in the Delta, from Saqqâra, Herakleopolis and Thebes, while from a few the provenance is unknown. They illustrate not only local characteristics, e.g. realistic tendencies in the Delta, classicism at Saqqâra, and a particular style at Herakleopolis, but also a gradual decline. Except for some fine instances from the XXVIth Dynasty most were mass products.

77599   PHILIPS, Allan K., Horemheb, Founder of the XIXth Dynasty? O. Cairo 25646 Reconsidered, *Orientalia* 46 (1977), 116-121.

Once more discussing the occurrences of royal names on O. Cairo 25646 (cfr i.a. our number 2018), particularly those of Mentuhotep and Horemheb on the "verso" (actually the recto), the author argues that they suggest that Horemheb was conceived to be the inaugurator of a new era. He adduces more arguments from monuments from Deir el-Medîna for Horemheb's position as first king of the XIXth Dynasty.

PIERRE, Isabelle, see our number 77452.

77600 PIHART, Anne-Marie, Les Stèles funéraires privées, rectangulaires à gorge, du Nouvel Empire Égyptien, *Revue des archéologues et historiens d'art de Louvain*, Louvain 9 (1976), 265-266.

Abstract of a small thesis.

PINTORE, Franco, see our number 77013.

77601 PLUMLEY, J. Martin, W.Y. ADAMS, and Elizabeth CROWFOOT, Qaṣr Ibrim, 1976, *JEA* 63 (1977), 29-47, with 3 plans, 2 fig. and 4 pl.

The main areas excavated lay at the S.W. sector of the site. The X-Group houses were examined and the Taharqa temple reexamined. The six houses proved to have been two stories high and a group of papyrus letters was found on the floor of the largest. The fortification walls proved to be mainly Bosnian but were found to go back to the Meroitic period. More than 160 complete pottery vessels were found, mostly X-Group refuse deposit material, the total of sherds now found exceeding 100,000. Most interesting among the finds was the lower part of a standing black granite statue of Ramesses III. Textile finds covered the whole period from 250 B.C. — A.D. 1811.
E. Uphill

PLUMLEY, J. Martin, see also our number 77528.

POETKE, Günter, see our number 77463.

77602 *Polja*, Novi Sad, 22nd Year, No. 217, March 1977 (24.2 × 33.8 cm; 36 p., 2 fig., 20 ill.).

"Fields".

This number of review for "culture, art and social questions" is devoted to Ancient Egypt. It mostly contains translated passages from egyptological monographs. Of the articles, we mention: Peter Selem, *Slika i simbol* (p. 5-7): "Picture and Symbol (the science of visual communication in predynastic Egypt)". Ljubinka Radovanović, *Ko je Anubis?* (20-26): "Who is Anubis?" A religious-philosophical approach.
S.P. Tutundžić

POMERANZEWA, N.A., see our number 77011.

77603 POSENER, Georges, Catalogue des ostraca hiératiques littéraires de Deir el-Médineh. Tome III (fasc. 1) — Nos. 1267-1409, [Le Caire], Institut français d'Archéologie orientale, 1977 (25 × 32 cm; 32 p., 32 pl. [=pl. 1-23]) = Documents de fouilles, 20.

Sequel to our number 72565.

The first fascicle of Vol. III mainly contains ostraca with some lines from the *Instruction of Amenemhat* (nos. 1267-1395). Only the verso of no. 1365 bears a fragment of a L.Eg. text. This series is given on the plates in transcription only, while of the other numbers there is also a facsimile. Their subjects are lines from: the *Instruction of Hardjedef* (1396); the Wisdom Text of O. Michaelides 16 (1397-1402); the satirical letter from P. Anastasi I (1403-1405); a prayer to Amon (1406); the *Prophecy of Neferti* (1407); a mythological text (1408) and a prayer and hymn to Amon (1409).

On the pl. one finds also facsimiles and transcriptions of the nos. 1410-1436 which are not yet described in the present fascicle.

The descriptions (p. 1-32) follow the pattern usual for this publication series. For the lines from the *Instruction of Amenemhet* the corresponding lines of P. Millingen are indicated; for the other texts there are similar references to standard texts or publications, if possible.

77604 POSENER, Georges, La complainte de l'échanson Bay, *in: Fragen an die altägyptische Literatur,* 385-397.

After an introductory survey of representations of and texts on the person of the royal scribe and cup-bearer of Sethi II Bay, who rose to the highest ranks in the time of Siptah, the author discusses O. Cairo 25766, which is a prayer of Bay to Amon, in order to see Thebes, and more specifically its women. The author argues that it consists of well-known literary topoi and that it is not an autograph but was composed in his name by some local scribe with satirical intentions. *L.Z.*

77605 POSENER, Georges, [Fouilles dirigées par M. Vercoutter dans l'oasis de Dakhleh], *Comptes rendues d l'Académie des Inscriptions et Belles-Lettres,* Paris, 1977, 267-268.

Short note on the investigations carried out by the IFAO under the directorship of J. Vercoutter in the Dâkhla Oasis. *L.Z.*

77606 POSENER, Georges, L'or de Pount, *in: Ägypten und Kusch,* 337-342.

Punt wird meist im Zusammenhang mit Myrrhe genannt, deren Verbreitungsgebiet zu ausgedehnt ist, als daß man von daher schließen könnte, wo Punt lag. Nun kam aber auch eine große Quantität Gold aus Punt, das an einer Stelle "grünes Gold von Amu" genannt wird. Von dorther kam auch "weißes Gold" und Elektrum. Amu kann nicht am Roten Meer gelegen haben, sondern es muß ein großes Bergwerksgebiet umfaßt haben, das sein Gold einerseits nach Punt, andererseits bis zum 3. Nilkatarakt lieferte. Punt selbst lag im Küstenbereich des Roten Meeres, wahrscheinlich in der Höhe des heutigen Port Sudan. *Inge Hofmann*

7607 POSENER, Georges, Philologie et archéologie égyptiennes, *Annuaire du Collège de France,* Paris 77 (1976-1977), 503-512.

Sequel to our number 76638.
(1) The study of unedited execration texts of the early 12th Dynasty on alabaster plaques in Cairo (cf. G. Posener, *Mélanges Dussaud* [1939], 313-317) is continued and the toponymic material exploited. Starting with Nubian rulers whose names are followed by short depreciatory phrases (reminding one of similar customs in magic ritual) these are followed by parts of Egypt, then again by Nubian countries. Certain terms, like *W3w3.t,* occur in both sections. A short Libyan paragraph mentions the countries inhabited by the *Ṯmḥw,* like *Hbks* (cf. C.T. VI, 213.d) and *Hbḳs.* Concluding with Egyptian names, there is mention of one Antef-oker, probably the vizier's son. (2) Similar documents from Mirgissa, Saqqara and Lisht have been studied.

J.F. Borghouts

7608 POSENER, Georges, Les quarante rouleaux de lois, *GM* Heft 25 (1977), 63-66.

Gegenstand der Untersuchung ist das Wort *šśm,* das nach WB. IV, 545, 10 gebraucht wird "von den (ledernen) Gesetzbüchern, die vor dem Wesir ausgebreitet liegen". Doch gibt es mehrere Beispiele des Wortes, die das WB. nicht kennt. Diese zeigen, daß *šśm* einen wichtigen Gegenstand verkörperte, der als Beiwort zur Kennzeichnung großer Richter diente. Auch in der medizinischen Literatur finden sich Wörter der Wurzel *šśm,* die alle auf eine Rötung der Augen hinweisen in der Bedeutung, daß ein Blutandrang verursacht wird, der eine Spannung und Konzentration bewirkt. Die Grundbedeutung der Wurzel *šśm* beinhaltet die Funktionen der Sehnen und Muskeln wie sie sich auch bei Faserstoffen finden. *Inge Hofmann*

POSENER, Georges, see also our number 77754.

77609 POSENER-KRIÉGER, Paule, A propos du *bš3*, *GM* Heft 25 (1977), 67-71.

Es werden die Belege untersucht, in denen die Körnerfrucht *bš* genannt wird. Aus den Papyri von Gebelein kann erschlossen werden daß es sich bei *bš3* um ein Korn handelt, das mehr oder weniger fein zerkleinert ist und das zur Bierbereitung benötigt wurde. Deswegen findet es sich auch in den Dokumenten, die sich auf Ernten und Steuerabgaben beziehen. *Inge Hofmann*

77610 POSENER-KRIÉGER, P., Les mesures des étoffes à l'Ancien Empire, *RdE* 29 (1977), 86-96, with 4 fig.

L'auteur définit les valeurs des signes ⊥, ⊥⊥ et ⊥⊥⊥ dans les listes d'étoffes de l'Ancien Empire comme l'expression des multiples de l'unité de surface (10 coudées) des étoffes. Elle tente de rétablir le système alors en vigueur, qui fut également utilisé dans des documents de Gébélein. Il semble qu'il ait existé deux références fondamentales, l'une de multiples décimaux, l'autre de division binaire de l'unité de base. *Ph. Derchain*

77611 POWELL, Berry B., The Significance of The So-called "Horns of Consecration", *Kadmos,* Berlin-New York 16 (1977), 70-82, with 1 fig.

The author draws attention to the resemblance of the Minoan Horns of Consecration to the Egyptian depiction of the horizon, as an alternative for the generally accepted significance as bull horns. Then he describes six Egyptian representations of the horizon mountains.
L.Z

77612 PRICE WILLIAMS, D., The Tombs of the Middle Bronze Age II Period from the '500' Cemetery at Tell Fara (South), London, Institute of Archaeology, 1977 (21 × 30 cm; X + 154 p., 1 map, 11 fig. including plans) = Institute of Archaeology. Occasional Publication No. 1.

In 1928 Petrie and his staff excavated a cemetery N.W. of Tell Fara (South) to which he gave the number 500. Apart from a few tombs from other periods (here ignored) it contained 43 tombs from M.B. II. The contents being at present distributed over several collections those of eight tombs could not be retraced. Those of the remaining 35 are here published.

After an introduction the author discusses the evidence from the field records for reconstruction of tomb groups and the objects here found (pottery, scarabs, bronze tools and weapons, etc.) in general. Then follows the catalogue proper (p. 14-145) listing all objects and discussing each tomb in detail, with plans and drawings of some objects.

A discussion and interpretation of the cemetery on p. 146-152. The tombs are classified according to five distinct styles, which represent in many ways a progression of size. Their distribution and chronology on account of scarabs and pottery is discussed. One scarab (fig. 10,2) is of importance since it bears the name of Pharaoh *Ma-ib-re*.

No indication regarding the size of the population of Fara in that period can be deducted from the tombs.

On p. 153 the results of a chemical analysis of some bronze objects.

77613 PRIESE, Karl-Heinz, Notizen zu den meroitischen Totentexten, *in:* Мероэ, 37-59.

Es handelt sich um den zweiten Teil der "Notizen zu den meroitischen Totentexten"; zum 1. Teil vgl. unsere Nr. 71469. Der 2. Teil befaßt sich mit der Invokation; es handelt sich dabei um Ausdrücke, die aus dem Namen einer Gottheit oder einem entsprechenden Appellativum bestehen und eine Endung *-i* aufweisen, die wohl vokativische Funktion hat. Nach einer Untersuchung der verschiedenen Schreibarten der Götternamen und einer Deutung der Appellative, werden die Ausdrücke der erweiterten Invokation behandelt. Für das Epitheton *wet+tr+r* wird die Bedeutung "der, der Leben gibt", "Lebensspender" vermutet, für *wetñ/qetñ* dagegen "der, welchem Leben/Sein zugehört" oder "der, welcher Leben /Sein *tn* macht".

Inge Hofmann

77614 PRIESE, Karl-Heinz, Eine verschollene Bauinschrift des frühmeroitischen Königs Aktisanes (?) vom Gebel Barkal, *in: Ägypten und Kusch,* 343-367, with 2 pl.

Im Notizbuch von M. Weidenbach findet sich auf S. 113 unter der Überschrift "Nuri, d. 31. Mai 44" die Zeichnung eines Inschriftenbruchstückes, das wahrscheinlich identisch ist mit dem, das Lepsius in Nuri bemerkt hat und das nach seiner Beschreibung in der Nähe von Nu. 6, dem Grab des Anlamani, gelegen haben müßte. Das Bruchstück wurde von einer breiteren Platte abgesät und auf den Fundplatz verschleppt, denn weder gehörten Darstellung und Inschrift zur Dekoration einer der Pyramidenkapellen in Nuri, noch ist der Stein in einer von ihnen verbaut gewesen. Die Inschrift ist eine offizielle Widmungsinschrift zu einem Tempelbau für den thebanischen Amun als Gastgott am Gebel Barkal. Der Thronname des Königs lautet Mn-$m3^ct$-R^c stp-n-$'Imn$, der bereits von zwei weiteren Denkmälern vom

Gebel Barkal bekannt ist (Kh. 5225, Kh. 5227). Durch Kombination der verschiedenen Denkmäler ergibt sich als Eigenname des Königs *Ktsn* oder *Gtsn* mit unbekannter Vokalisation. Diodor I, 60 erwähnt einen äthiopischen König Aktisanes; wenn dieser identisch ist mit *Ktsn*, dann kann er spätestens zur Zeit Ptolemaios' I. regiert haben.

Inge Hofmann

77615 PURDY, Strother, Sinuhe and the Question of Literary Types, *ZÄS* 104 (1977), 112-127.

A discussion and a review of opinions on the literary type of *Sinuhe*. The author notes a dominating position of religion and death as its most striking characteristic.

Two stories are involved in the composition: there is an inner ending at B 156. The complicated work offers both adventure and promise of life after death.

M. Heerma van Voss

77616 de PURY, Albert, Sagesse et révélation dans l'Ancien Testament, *Revue de Théologie et de Philosophie,* Lausanne 27 (1977), 1-50.

In order to work out a clear distinction between the specificity of the O.T. religion compared with others in the Ancient Near East as regards revelation the author makes use of the non-specific phenomenon of wisdom. Proceeding from the concept of *hokmāh* in the section on Ancient Near Eastern Wisdom (p. 3-23) he argues that the sages were well aware of the causality between behaviour according to the cosmic order and fate: senseless behaviour means unbalancing Ma^{c}at, but Ma^{c}at puts the balance in equilibrium again by itself. He then quotes examples from the Near Eastern context in order to illustrate the positive virtues of life: hard work, indulgence, discretion, lack of interest in wealth, temperance, particularly with respect to drinking and women, optimism and serenity, in short selfconsciousness leading to success in life. But on the other hand, the wise should act also in the interest of others (autobiographies!), even an enemy, for which he quotes some examples. The basic criterion of these ethics is experience, which paradoxically contrasts with the authoritarian way of education.

After remarks on the relation between cosmic order and demiurge and on pessimistic Hebrew literature still showing the fundamental characteristics of wisdom since they only reject the arrogant, rigid, dogmatic type of wisdom, he enumerates these four characteristics: empiricism, humbleness, curiousness, and knowledge of the unpredictability of the cosmic order and God.

L.Z.

77617   PUSCH, Edgar B., Eine unbeachtete Brettspielart, *SAK* 5 (1977), 199-212, with 3 fig.

The author describes a variant of the board-game of 20 fields that has two blocks of 3 × 4 fields each, connected by a row of 7 fields. Three instances are known: Pap.Turin No. 1.775, Cairo JdE 88006 and Brit. Mus. 38429, all three to be dated to the first half of the XXth Dynasty. From the Turin Papyrus it appears that the game was called *n sm3 20 2*, which is to be rendered as "(game) of the united two twenty (fields)". The origin may be connected with the wish written on the Turin Papyrus to be the thirty-first among "the thirty gods".

77618   QUAEGEBEUR, J., Anubis, fils d'Osiris, le vacher, *Studia aegyptiaca* 3 (1977), 119-130.

On account of a passage in the Old-Coptic letter recently published by Satzinger (our number 75652), which reads: "Anubis, son of Osiris, the cowherd" (πελοις = *p3 mr ỉḥ*), the author discusses who are Anubis' parents and whether he is elsewhere also called "cowherd". The position as son of Osiris is frequently mentioned, although explained in several ways, while he is said to be the son of Nephthys, Isis and other goddesses, but particularly of the cow-goddess Hesat. The author adduces evidence that he is frequently called "cowherd".

77619   QUAEGEBEUR, Jan, De Griekse weergave van korte Egyptische dodenteksten, *Phoenix*, Leiden 22 (1976), 1977, 49-59, with 2 ill. and 4 fig.

After sketching the cultural position of the Greeks living in Ptolemaic Egypt the author discusses a few Greek adaptations in mummy labels of Egyptian funerary texts, particularly paying attention to the way in which the concept *ba* has been rendered.

77620   QUAEGEBEUR, Jan, Note sur L'Heresieion d'Antinoe, *Zeitschrift für Papyrologie und Epigraphik*, Bonn 24 (1977), 246-250.

The author argues that the Heresieion at Antinoe is a temple of Hariesis, Horus-*ḥsy*, that is Horus glorified after or by his immersion into the water, and that it is dedicated to the cult of a drowned person.

L.Z.

77621   QUAEGEBEUR, Jan, Les "Saints" égyptiens préchrétiens, *Orientalia Lovaniensia Periodica*, Leuven 8 (1977), 129-143.

Discussing the precursors of the Coptic saints, that is, persons who received public veneration in ancient Egypt, the author first argues that there is no Egyptian equivalent for "saint". Apart from Imhotep and Amenhotep son of Hapu (see our number 77809) several other persons, royal as well as non-royal, have been venerated. Quaegebeur then discusses the word *ḥsy,* said to be used for those who were drowned, but actually indicating a glorified status that could be reached in other ways too. Similar terms used in the Late Period are *ḥry,* "superior", and *rmṯ-ꜥ3,* which both also are used as a honorific funerary title.

77622 QUAEGEBEUR, Jan, Tithoes, dieu oraculaire?, *Enchoria* 7 (1977), 103-108.

New examples for the type of personal names *Ḏd-ḥr* — "The face of NN said — (may he/she live)", namely:
Ḏd-ḥr-p3-trš ("The face of the flamingo said"); *Ḏd-ḥr-p3-ỉmy* ("The face of the cat said"); *Ḏd-ḥr-p3-ỉšwr ("The face of the Syrian said");* **Ḏd-ḥr-p3-nm* — Τεαπναμις ("The face of the dwarf said"), and **Twtw-m-ḏd-ḥr* — Τιθοεντεως ("Toutou is the speaking face").

W. Brunsch

QUAEGEBEUR, Jan, see also our numbers 77092 and 77597.

77623 QUECKE, Hans, Eine Handvoll Pachomianischer Texte, *in: XIX. Deutscher Orientalistentag,* 221-229.

The author describes some texts of Pachomius in the Chester Beatty Library in Dublin, which are still unpublished. L.Z.

77624 QUECKE, Hans, Ich habe nichts hinzugefügt und nichts weggenommen. Zur Wahrheitsbeteuerung koptischer Martyrien, *in: Fragen an die altägyptische Literatur,* 399-416.

The author discusses the declaration of the truth formula "I have not added anything, I have not taken out anything", which expression, typical of the Coptic martyrdoms, the author argues not to have any connection with a passage in the Wisdom of Ptahhotep (line 608), contrary to the opinion expressed in our number 2953. L.Z.

77625 QUECKE, Hans, Das Lukasevangelium saïdisch. Text der Handschrift PPalau Rib. Inv.-Nr. 181 mit den Varianten der Handschrift M 569, Barcelona, 1977 (16 × 22 cm; 279 p., 1 fig., 2 pl., frontispiece) = Papyrologica Castroctaviana. Studia et textus, 6; rev. *Biblica* 59 (1978), 439-442 (Yvonne Janssens).

Sequel to our number 72575.

This time the Gospel according to St. Luke in the Pap. Palau-Ribes 181 is published, once more particularly compared in the notes with the Ms. M 569 of the Pierpont Morgan Library.

The edition of the text with the notes (p. 95-275) is preceded by an introduction dealing with the outer appearance and the writing of the ms., scribal errors, language and orthography, variants with regard to other mss., the age of the ms. and its writers.

77626 QUECKE, Hans, Eine neue koptische Bibelhandschrift II (P. Palau Rib. Inv.-Nr. 181), *Orientalia* 46 (1977), 300-303.

Announcement of our preceding number.

77627 RABBAN, Abner, ספנות וספינות נציורי-הקיר של תרה *Qadmoniot,* Jerusalem 10, No. 1 (= 37) (1977), 18-21, with 8 fig., 1 ill., and 1 colour folding pl.

"Ships and Shipping in the Wall Paintings of Thera".
The author refers to Egyptian evidence as regards ships. *L.Z.*

77628 el-RABIᶜI, Abdel-Méguid, Familles abydéniennes du Moyen Empire, *CdE* LII, No. 103 (1977), 13-21.

Cet article apporte une série de compléments aux groupes de documents abydéniens reconstitués par W.K. Simpson, The Terrace of the Great God at Abydos (notre No. 74688). Douze familles nouvelles ont été ainsi retrouvées par l'auteur, qui en signale d'autre part dix-sept autres mentionnées dans la littérature mais que Simpson ne signale pas. *Ph. Derchain*

77629 RABINO MASSA, E., Presence of Thalassemia in Egyptian Mummies, *Journal of Human Evolution,* London-New York-San Francisco 6 (1977), 225.

Short note on the presence of thalassemia in Egyptian mummies.

RADOVANOVIĆ, Ljubinka, see our number 77602.

77630 RALSTON, Bruce Lawrence, I Swear by Imhotep the Physician, *New York State Journal of Medicine,* New York 77, No. 13 (November 1977), 2148-2152, with 2 ill.

The author presents a brief survey of our knowledge about Imhotep, mainly as a physician, and shortly discusses possible Egyptian influence on Greek medicine. *L.Z.*

77631 RALSTON, Bruce Lawrence, Medical Reinterpretation of Case Four of the Edwin Smith Surgical Papyrus, *JEA* 63 (1977), 116-121, with 2 pl.

Identifies this with a type of skull fracture compound-elevated resulting from a blow by a weapon. In 1930 it was not possible for

Breasted to connect *pšn* with this due to its disappearance from medical literature, owing to the vanishing use of such weapons in warfare.

E. Uphill

77632 RAMOND, Pierre, Les stèles égyptiennes du Musée G. Labit à Toulouse, [Le Caire], Institut français d'Archéologie orientale, 1977 (20 × 27.5 cm; X + 87 p., 17 fig., 15 pl.) = Bibliothèque d'étude, 62.

Publication of fifteen stelae preserved in the Musée Georges Labit in Toulouse (for a catalogue of the museum, see our number 71231). One other stela in the collection (No. 1175) has been omitted since it was published by Varille in *Kêmi* 3(1935), 39-43.

In his introduction the author mentions earlier publications of the pieces. There follow concordances between their numbers in the various publications. The catalogue itself consists of 15 sections, each devoted to one piece. It is extensively described, with all data such as measurements, date and provenance (if known), while the texts are given in printed hieroglyphs and translation with comments, with a bibliography. Moreover, there is of each of them a drawing and a photograph.

Numbers 1-4 date from the M.K., 5 (probably) and 6 from the end of the S.I.P., 7-11 from the N.K., 12 and 13 from the late dynasties, 14 from the Ptolemaic and 15 possibly from the Persian Period. In most instances the provenance is unknown, but the nos. 1-3 are from Abydos. Most stelae are well preserved, no. 7 being an exception. Of the persons mentioned in the texts no one is of outstanding importance, although a few are known from elsewhere.

This model publication has indexes (p. 69-78) and a bibliography at the end.

77633 RANKE, Hermann, Die ägyptischen Personennamen. Band III. Verzeichnis der Bestandteile. Zusammengestellt von A. Biedenkopf-Ziehner, W. Brunsch, G. Burkard, H.-J. Thissen, K.-Th. Zauzich, Glückstadt, Verlag J.J. Augustin, [1977] (23 × 31 cm; 142 p.).

Pr. DM 170

Sequel to our number 2534.

In this third volume of "Ranke PN" the names presented in his volumes I and II are listed alphabetically after their second and following elements. Frequent elements such as *ỉb* or *mś* constitute a separate entry with the pertinent heading, less frequent ones are combined to one entry (e.g. *ỉś*..., comprising *ỉś/ỉsy/ỉśw/ỉśr/ỉssr/ỉsd*). Corrections to Ranke's material are rare. The publication is intended as a means to restore half destroyed or to recognize badly legible names.

RAUMSCHÜSSEL, Martin, see our number 77010.

77634 RAWSON, Jessica, Animals in Art, London, British Museum Publications Limited, 1977 (18.5 × 25.2 cm; X + 150 p., 189 + 5 ill., frontispiece, 1 map, 2 colour ill. on cover, 8 colour pl., ill. on endpaper).

The book has been inspired by the British Museum exhibition "Animals in Art", end 1977 — beginning 1978. Most references to ancient Egypt can be found in the sections on animals in the service of man and animals in thought and religion.
See also the index, s.v. Egypt. *L.Z.*

77635 RAY, J.D., The Complaint of Herieu, *RdE* 29 (1977), 97-116, with 2 pl.

Edition des Pap.Louvre E.3333 et 3334, datés par l'auteur de 199/198 (Epiphane), relatifs aux misères qu'on a faites à un hermopolitain embaumeur d'ibis dans un lieu qu'il n'est pas possible de définir. La situation est comparable à celle décrite dans le P.Ryland IX.
On a donné des photographies, transcriptions phonétiques, traductions et commentaires des deux documents. *Ph. Derchain*

77636 REDFORD, Donald B., The Excavations of the University Museum Akhenaten Temple Project at Karnak, *Expedition,* Philadelphia 19, No. 4 (Summer 1977), 33-38, with 1 map, 1 plan and 6 ill.

In this article for the general reader on the Akhenaten Temple Project the author deals primarily with the architecture and lay-out of the buildings erected by Akhenaten at East Karnak. *L.Z.*

77637 REDFORD, Donald B., The Latest Phase in the History of East Karnak, *Newsletter ARCE* Nos. 99/100 (Winter/Spring), 11.
Abstract of a paper.

77638 REDFORD, Donald B., The Oases in Egyptian History to Classical Times. Part II. c. 2100 B.C.[—] c. 1650 B.C., *Newsletter SSEA* 7, No. 2 (March 1977), 2-4, with 3 ill.
Sequel to our number 76665.
In this part the history of the oases from the XIth Dynasty to the end of the Middle Kingdom is sketched.

77639 REDFORD, Donald B., The Oases in Egyptian History to Classical Times. Part III. c. 1650 B.C.-1000 B.C., *Newsletter SSEA* 7, No. 3 (May 1977), 2-6, with 1 pl.

Sequel to our preceding number.
Continuing his discussion of the history of the oases the author deals with the S.I.P. and the N.K. He mentions their strategic importance in the time of Kamose, their administration and prosperity, their role as places of refuge and exile, and the influx of Libyan elements since the end of the 13th century B.C.

77640 REDFORD, Donald B., The Oases in Egyptian History to Classical Times. Part IV. c. 1000 B.C.-630 B.C., *Newsletter SSEA* 7, No. 4 (August 1977), 7-10.

Sequel to our preceding number.
During the T.I.P. the oases may have become virtually independent. Under the Saite kings, however, the foundation was laid for their later prosperity. In Bahrîya a local authority was appointed, while the southern oases were connected with the Abydos temple. Khârga became a key point in the oasis route to the Sudan. The northern oases, Sîwa included, were the field for military activities against Libya.

77641 REDFORD, Donald B., Preliminary Report of the First Season of Excavation in East Karnak, 1975-76, *JARCE* 14 (1977), 9-32, with 1 map, 2 plans and 5 fig. on 8 unnumbered pl. and 21 pl. containing ill.

(1) Re-analysis of dumps remaining from Chevrier's 1925 digging to the east of the Nectanebo Gate which at the time yielded i.a. the well-known 'sexless' statues of Akhenaten as the remains of an Aten temple (*ASAE* 26 [1926], 121 sqq and later reports). Two trial squares in the older dumps and trenches produced a 'reversed' stratigraphy deeper digging, below the 1925 surface, a Saite-Persian settlement as well as bricks mentioning the XXIst Dynasty highpriest $Mn\text{-}ḫpr\text{-}r^c$. (2) Constructional features of this Aten temple, identification of some scenes from talatats, comments on statues aforesaid and identification of the name as $Gm(.t)\text{-}p3\text{-}ïtn$. J.F. Borghout.

77642 REDFORD, Donald B., Some Observations on Egyptian Chronology of the Eighth and Seventh Centuries B.C. (Chronologies in Old World Archaeology, 1976), *AJA* 81 (1977), 82-83.

The author discusses the problems of chronology between the close of the N.K. and the beginning of the XXVth Dynasty 712-711 B.C. At the end he draws some broad conclusions as to the XXIInd-XXIVth Dynasties. L.Z

77643 REINEKE, Walter-Friedrich, Ein Nubienfeldzug unter Königin Hatschepsut, *in: Ägypten und Kusch,* 369-376, with 1 pl.

Vorgestellt wird die Inschrift Nr. 562 (21-D-1/2) aus dem 12. Jahr der Königin Hatschepsut in Tangur, in der das "Niederschlagen des elenden Kusch" berichtet wird. Damit sind 4 Nubienfeldzüge unter Hatschepsut bekannt (unter der Voraussetzung, daß der Feldzug, an dem Ti teilnahm, nicht mit dem der Tangur-Inschrift identisch ist). Die Tangur-Inschrift stellt das früheste Beispiel einer Doppeldatierung mit den Namen der Hatschepsut und Thutmosis' III. dar; der Feldzug wird eine der ersten militärischen Handlungen des Oberbefehlshabers der Armee, des noch jugendlichen Thutmosis, gewesen sein, die er auf Befehl der Hatschepsut durchzuführen hatte.   *Inge Hofmann*

REINOLD, Jacques, see our number 77768.

77644   REKUCKI, Jerzy, Egipskie stoły ofiarne, *Rocznik Muzeum Narodowego w Warszawie,* Warszawa 21 (1977), 19-74, with 42 fig., 12 ill. and summaries in Russian and French on p. 72-74.
"Egyptian Offering Tables".
The author traces back the origin of the offering table to the $ḥtp$-mat destined for the offerings, which together with the loaf has become its essential decoration element. The offering table, serving purification and nourishment purposes, was placed in front of the false door in such a way that the loaf of the $ḥtp$-sign and the libation were directed towards the tomb. Next the author discusses the development from the O.K. with its three types up to the Ptolemaic Period, the usage gradually disappearing in the Roman Period.
In the last part follows the catalogue of 12 offering tables in the National Museum in Warsaw, eight of which from the Franco-Polish excavations at Edfu.   *L.Z.*

REYMAN, Theodore A., see our number 77065.

77645   REYMOND, E.A.E., From the Contents of the Libraries of the Suchos Temples in the Fayyum. Part II. From Ancient Egyptian Hermetic Writings, Wien, In Kommission bei Verlag Brüder Hollinek, 1977 (21 × 29.7 cm; 221 p., 6 folding pl.) = Mitteilungen aus der Papyrussammlung der Österreichischen Nationalbibliothek (Papyrus Erzherzog Rainer). Neue Serie, XI. Folge; at head of title: Österreichische Nationalbibliothek.
Sequel to our number 76668, also dealing with documents from the libraries of Sobk temples in the Faiyûm.
In part 1 the author attributes the papyri (except for Pap. Vindob. D 6330) to the papyrus finds on the Kom el-Chariana and Kom el-Dîme, points out that the texts are probably copies of texts much earlier in

date rather than original compositions of the Roman Period, and makes some remarks on their importance as learned temple documents. In a long excursus she discusses first the contents and significance of the most important papyrus, Pap. Vindob. D 6319, relating to the history of Egyptian temples, which should be a relic of a scientifically and systematically arranged collection of records describing the successive stages in the historical developments of temples in general; then she deals with the other texts.

In part 2 she presents the texts in handwritten transliteration and translation on opposite pages, provided with data such as provenance, condition, date and palaeography, and a commentary. The part is divided into four sections, each concerned with a particular papyrus. The first, Pap. D 6319, comes from the Suchos temple at Crocodilopolis, as does also Pap. D 6330, published here by the author since it deals with the management of temples. Next come Pap. D 6321, from Crocodilopolis, concerned with the sacred scripts (*itnw*) of Ptah on protection, and Pap. D 6336 and D 6343, respectively from Dîme and Crocodilopolis, concerned with the Sacred Writings of Thoth, namely the *mre-rḥw*, "Pursuing Wisdom" (resp. for Pap. D 6336, "The Book on the Dynamis" and for Pap. D 6343, "Thoth's Book on Natural History"). They all contain parts of a collection of Hermetic writings. The last text, Pap. Vindob. D 6614, contains Hermetika from the temple of Neith.

Part 3 consists of separate indexes on the Egyptian words in the various groups of papyri, short general ones on deities and localities, and an integrated list of words, referring to the separate indexes. L.Z.

77646 REYMOND, E.A.E. and the late J.W.B. BARNS, Alexandria and Memphis. Some Historical Observations, *Orientalia* 46 (1977), 1-33.

The article consists of two papers. Part I, by the first author, deals with the dynasty of 12 Hereditary Princes (*rpˁt*) and High Priests of Memphis who together cover the entire Ptolemaic Period. Their stelae present important evidence for the history of that time, particularly about the close relations between this Egyptian family and the rulers (one of the High Priests married a royal princess), for whom they acted as viceroys of Memphis, while Harmakhis seems to have claimed the title of King.

In part II (edited by Mrs. Reymond) the late Professor Barns presents observations on some problems of the Ptolemaic history, confronting accounts of Greek and Latin authors with the evidence presented in Part I.

RINALDI, Celeste, see our number 77510.

77647 RITCHIE, J.M., The Roots of Chaos: An Egyptian Source for the Caucasian Chalk Circle, *German Life & Letters*, Oxford 31 (1977-1978), 89-96.

The author demonstrates that in his "Essay on Writing the Truth" Bertolt Brecht used parts from the "Admonitions of an Egyptian Sage", taken and sometimes slightly adapted from Erman's translation in his "Literatur". But by means of a transformation the lines can also be found in a much hidden way in the "Song of Chaos" in his play "The Caucasian Chalk Circle". *L.Z.*

ROBINSON, James M., see our numbers 77215, 77222 and 77223.

77648 ROCCATI, A., L'iscrizione sulla *kotyle* di Pontecagnano, *in:* Bruno d'Agostino, Tombe "principesche" dell'orientalizante antico da Pontecagnano, Roma, Accademia Nazionale dei Lincei, 1977 (= Monumenti antichi. Serie Miscellanea-volume II-I (XLIX della Serie Generale)), 35-36.

The author shortly discusses some pseudohieroglyphs from tombs at Pontecagnano. *L.Z.*

ROCCATI, Alessandro, see also our number 77510.

RODRIGUEZ, François, see our numbers 77768, 77769, 77770 and 77771.

ROHR, Arthur, see our number 77255.

77649 ROQUET, Gérard, Une épitaphe copte de Nag^c ad-Dayr, *RdE* 29 (1977), 117-124, with 1 pl.

L'auteur publie et commente la photographie d'une épitaphe copte qu'il à prise dans l'église de Nag^c ed-Deir, nécropole de Girga. La date proposée est le 8/9e siècle.
Le commentaire est essentiellement philologique. *Ph. Derchain*

77650 ROQUET, Gérard, Inscriptions bohaïriques de Dayr Abū Maqār, *BIFAO* 77 (1977), 163-179, with 1 pl.

Publication of three Bohairic inscriptions from the monastery of Deir Abû Maqâr.

77651 ROQUET, Gérard, Le nom du "lynx", *j(n)b* comme anthroponyme (3e dynastie), *BIFAO* 77 (1977), 113-117.

Proceeding from Edel's suggestion that the writing *ỉbt* has to be read as *ỉ(n)bt* (see our number 75196, 28-30), the author draws up a list of words occurring in scriptio defectiva, med. def. He states that the defective writing shows a tendency to disappear. As for the translation of $\hat{i}(n)b$, the author agrees with Edel that it means "lynx".

77652 ROQUET, Gérard, šmt(=j) "ma belle-mère" (6ᵉ dynastie), *BIFAO* 77 (1977), 119-127, with 1 fig.

Proceeding from a false door in the Ny Carlsberg Glyptothek (AEIN 20) the author discusses the word šmt, "mother-in-law" (see also Fischer, *Varia* = our number 76255, 19-21). Translating the central text of the false door he also points out the inversed writing of $\underline{d}d.f$ and the way in which family relations between donator and donated are indicated in general.

77653 ROSELLINI, Hippolito, Monumenti dell' Egitto e della Nubia. Vol. I: Monumenti storici. Vol. II: Monumenti civili. Vol. III: Monumenti del culto. (Reprographie de l'édition originale), Genève, Éditions de Belles-Lettres, 1977 (21 × 29.7 cm; [vol. I:] VI + 6 p., 169 pl.; [vol. II:] 6 p., 135 pl.; [vol. III:] 6 p., 86 pl.); at head of title: Collection des classiques égyptologiques; rev. *CdE* LIV, No. 107 (1979), 73-74 (Paul-André Faes); *Oriens Antiquus* 17 (1978), 323 (Sergio Pernigotti).

Pr. set S.F.110

After having reedited Champollion's Monuments (our number 70119) with his Notices Descriptives (our number 73145) and Lepsius' Denkmäler (our number 71362) with the Text volumes (our number 75448) the same publisher here brings the reedition on a reduced scale of the plates of Rosellini's Monuments, which have originally been published in Pisa between 1832 and 1844.

In a short preface Robert Hari sketches the unhappy history of the relations between Champollion and Rosellini and their publications; for a more complete study of the subject, see Hari, *Genava* 18 (our number 70244).

77654 ROSENVASSER, Abraham, Aksha: Arqueología de la Nubia. Exposición del material proveniente de las capillas de Seti I y del templo de Ramses II (Aksha, Nubia Sudanesa). (Palabras pronunciadas en el acto de la inauguración de la Sala, en el Museo de Ciencias Naturales de la Plata, el 20 de diciembre de 1977), [Buenos Aires], Universidad de Buenos Aires. Facultad de Filosofía y Letras. Instituto de Historia Antigua Oriental, 1977 (15.6 × 22.6 cm; II + 18 p., 1 folding pl.) = [Publicaciones del Instituto de Historia Antigua Oriental]. Colleccion Estudios, 7.

Dieser Vortrag wurde zur Eröffnung einer Ausstellung im Naturkundlichen Museum von La Plata im Dezember 1977 gehalten, wo erstmalig die Fundobjekte gezeigt wurden, die eine argentinische Mission in den Jahren 1962 und 1963 bei der Freilegung des Tempelbezirks Ramses'II. in Akshah machte, aber auch im Bereich einer nahegelegenen christlichen Kirche und von A- und C-Gruppen-Friedhöfen. Verfasser stellt sie in ihren historischen Rahmen.

I. Gamer-Wallert

77655 ROSENVASSER, Abraham, Introducción a la literatura egipcia. Las formas literarias (con un Apéndice), *Revista del Instituto de Historia Antigua Oriental,* Buenos Aires 3 (1976), 7-105, with 1 folding fig.

Einleitend gibt Verfasser eine Zusammenfassung von Fechts Untersuchungen zur altägyptischen Metrik. Anschließend werden die literarischen Formen und stilistischen Mittel vorgestellt, die dem altägyptischen Schriftsteller zur Verfügung standen, wie Wiederholung, Wortspiele, Alliteration, Parallelismus membrorum, Ellipse, Steigerung, Vergleich und Metapher.

In einem Appendix (S.47-105) werden Auszüge von Werken der altägyptischen Literatur in spanischer Übersetzung abgedruckt, u.a. des sog. Kannibalen-Spruches, des Lebensmüden, des Schabaka-Steines, der Geschichte von der Zerstörung des Menschengeschlechts, der List der Isis, des Horus-Mythos, des Apophis-Buches, aus den Märchen des Pap. Westcar, dem Zweibrüdermärchen.

I. Gamer-Wallert

77656 ROSENVASSER, A., Pharaonic Egypt and Israel in the Light of Isaiah's Oracles against Egypt, *Revista del Instituto de Historia Antigua Oriental,* Buenos Aires 3 (1976), 107-125.

The author presents a survey of the, normally rather friendly relations between Israel and Egypt, and studies in this connection the oracles of Isaiah, first warning against relying on the alliance with Egypt, but later on changing the point of view.

77657 ROTH, Ann Mary, Ahhotep II and Amenhotep I, *Newsletter ARCE* Nos. 99/100 (Winter/Spring 1977), 10.

Abstract of a paper.

77658 RTVELADZE, Ye. V., Несколько древнеегипетских предметов из северной Бактрии, Советская Археология, Москва No. 2, 1977, 235-238, with 1 fig.

"Quelques objets de l'ancien Égypte trouvés en Bactriane du Nord."

77659 RÜHLMANN, Gerhard, Der Götterthron mit dem Türornament, *in:* *Ägypten und Kusch*, 377-389, with 13 fig.

Seit der 18. Dynastie treten in gewissen Darstellungen Thronstühle auf, deren Seiten als Ganzes in der Art von Prunkscheintüren oder Gebäudefassaden gestaltet sind. Ursprünglich von der Residenzfassade abgeleitet, ist das der Prunkscheintür zugrunde liegende Sinnbild schon frühzeitig in den Horustitel eingegangen und als hieroglyphisches Zeichen "serech" verwendet worden. Der Serech als Gebäude hat sich in seiner Bedeutung zum Begriff "Thron" hin entwickelt, der sich im Bereich der Jenseitswelt besonders seit dem Neuen Reich oft an Götterpodesten findet. Unter den inthronisierten Göttern oder vergöttlichten Menschen steht Osiris als Beherrscher und Richter des Totenreiches im Mittelpunkt. Throne mit einer seitlich angebrachten Nische sind auch in der Akkadzeit im mesopotamischen Bereich bekannt; sie dienen vor allem dem Sonnengott als oberstem Gesetzgeber und Richter, der nachts die Unterwelt durchfährt, als Sitz. In Ägypten wie in Vorderasien handelt es sich also übereinstimmend um richtende Gottheiten mit ausgeprägten Beziehungen zur Jenseitswelt; in beiden Fällen wurden alte Königsvorstellungen in den Gottesbegriff hineingetragen und auf das Jenseits, die Toten- und Unterwelt, ausgedehnt. *Inge Hofmann*

77660 RUFFLE, John, Heritage of the Pharaohs. An Introduction to Egyptian Architecture, Oxford, Phaidon, [1977] (21 × 24.5 cm; 224 p., frontispiece, 135 ill., 32 colour ill., 13 fig., 5 maps and 6 plans, ill on cover). Pr. £5.95

An introduction to Egyptian history and archaeology intended for the general reader and traveller to Egypt.

After a first chapter on the history of Egyptology, the geography of the country and the history in general, the author deals in 7 chapters with Egyptian history from Predynastic to Roman times. Each chapter, apart from the political history, discusses the art and architecture of a period.

Chapters 9 to 13 are devoted to general subjects: the structure of the state (with sections on royal titulary and regalia, seals, palaces, weights and measures, and travel and transport); farming and domestic life (i.a. food and drink, houses and furniture, containers and equipment, dress, pastimes); cultural life (language, writing, and literature; the scribe's equipment, arts and artists, doctors and medicine); crafts and industries (metal-, stone-, and woodworking, etc.); religious life (i.a. purpose and design of the temple, and

personal belief); and the world of the dead (funerary belief and rituals, tomb equipment).
The well chosen figures to each chapter, photographs, plans and drawings, illustrate the argument. The colour illustrations are somewhat arbitrarily strewn over the entire book.
Bibliography for further reading (entirely English) on p. 212-215; index p. 220-224. There has also appeared an American edition: The Egyptians: An Introduction to Egyptian Archaeology, Ithaca, New York, Cornell University Press, 1977 (Pr. $12.50).

77661 RUPP, Alfred, Vergehen und Bleiben. Religionsgeschichtliche Studien zum Personsverständnis in Ägypten und im Alten Testament, Saarbrücken, Homo et Religio. Verlag der Forschungsgruppe für Anthropologie und Religionsgeschichte, 1976 (14.1 × 20.6 cm; X + 329 p.) = Forschungen zur Anthropologie und Religionsgeschichte, 2; rev. *Ugarit-Forschungen* 10 (1978), 488 (O. Loretz).   Pr. DM 39

This study, which is the second part of the author's Habilitationsschrift, contains the application of the methods explained in its first part on the problem of the personality in the critical situation between perishing and lasting. It consists of three parts: one devoted to Ancient Egypt (p. 13-163), one to the O.T., and one comparing the results of the two preceding parts.

As regards the Egyptian concepts, the author mainly bases his arguments on the N.K. funerary literature: the Amduat, the Book of the Gates, the Book of the Caverns and the B.D. He begins with an exposé of the concept of the universe of Egypt, its limits, nature, origin and end, followed by a chapter on the critical situation of perishing and lasting as part of the expectations concerning the netherworld. Then the author deals with the possibilities of a transition from this world to the other. Since each funerary text contains an independent and arbitrary choice from the ideas occurring in a civilization the author then deals with each of his sources, discussing their motifs and structure, i.a. the formulae used. In the next chapter the heuristic points of the critical situation and the phase that follows it pass the review: place and time, the (friendly or hostile) divine partners in the crisis, the process itself, and the physical and spiritual elements involved: *3ḫ, ỉwf, ỉrw, b3,* etc. The last chapters of the Egyptian part are devoted to "norm and crisis" and the identity of the personality during the critical situation.
Indexes and bibliography on p. 262-329.

77662 [hieroglyph] RUSSELL, Jeffrey Burton, The Devil. Perception of Evil from Antiquity to Primitive Christianity, Ithaca and London, Cornell University Press, [1977] (15.4 × 22.8 cm; 276 p., 50 fig. and ill.).

This is a historical study of the concept "Devil", the personification of Evil. On p. 76-84 the author deals with Egypt, paying particularly attention to Seth as the antagonist of Horus. He discusses several aspects of their opposition, while mentioning at the end also Apopis and Sakhmet.

77663 RUSSMANN, Edna R., A Rediscovered Monument of the Eighth Century B.C., *Newsletter ARCE* Nos. 99/100 (Winter/Spring 1977), 8.

Abstract of a paper.

RUSSMANN, Edna R., see also our number 77024.

77664 RUSZCZYC, Barbara, Taharqa à Tell Atrib, in: *Ägypten und Kusch,* 391-395, with 1 fig., 6 ill. and 2 plans on 6 pl.

Unter der römischen Wasserleitung von Tell Atrîb wurden zwei Blöcke ausgegraben, die sich nicht an ihrem ursprünglichen Ort befanden. Die Inschrift enthielt die ausgekratzte Kartusche Taharqas; die Blöcke waren von Psammetich II. usurpiert worden, dessen Frau Tahout in Tell Atrîb bestattet war. Die Blöcke stammen von einem Gebäude, das Taharqa in Tell Atrîb erbaut hatte und das wohl noch erhalten war, als Psammetich II. die Kartuschen des Äthiopenkönigs auskratzte. *Inge Hofmann*

RYAN, T.M., see our number 77681.

RYCHTEROVÁ, Vlasta, see our number 77733.

72665 RYHINER, Marie-Louise, A propos de trigrammes panthéistes, *RdE* 29 (1977), 125-137.

L'auteur étudie les groupes [hieroglyphs] et [hieroglyphs] attestés entre autre dans le chapitre 162 du Livre des Morts, et propose de reconnaître une graphie "mystique" du nom d'Atoum sous le premier groupe, dont elle a réuni 34 exemples. Elle passe ensuite en revue les diverses possibilités d'interprétation des deux groupes de signes. *Ph. Derchain*

77666 SAFFIRIO, Luigi, Razioni e salari in natura nell' antico Egitto. Considerazioni dietetiche e socio-economiche, *Aegyptus* 57 (1977), 14-78.

This study deals with the rations recorded to have been delivered to individuals during the various periods of the Egyptian history. Fifteen documents are discussed, one from the O.K., seven from the M.K. and also seven from the N.K. That from the O.K. (Abu Sir Papyri, pl. 40) does not present much evidence (Saffirio's numbers on p. 16 are partly incorrect). From the M.K. the author deals with two Wâdi Hammâmât inscriptions, one papyrus of Hekanakhte, an ostracon of Meketre, Pap. Reisner I and II, and Pap. Berlin 10005.

In the section on the N.K. the author first discusses how much flour can be won from 1 *khar* of grain. The main documents for this period are the stela of Sethi I at Gebel el-Silsila, Pap. Leiden I 350, one Kahun papyrus, two Wâdi Hammâmât inscriptions, and particularly the abundant material from Deir el-Medîna (p. 38-60), from which it appears possible to calculate the quantities and nutritional value of the rations of the workmen. Conclusions on p. 61-70.

In appendix 1 the quantities of grain used for a particular quantity of beer are discussed. Appendix 2 is a list of the quantities of fish delivered to the workmen of Deir el-Medîna (after Botti-Peet, Giornale, pl. 47 ff.).

77667 SAGRAMOSO, Guido, La fonografia delle prime scritture e la scrittura alfabetica, *Acme,* Milano 30 (1977), 459-484.

The author poses the question how the Egyptian script was able to conserve the semantic value of the words, though only writing a combination of radical consonants. He first studies origin and nature of the Sumerian, then of the Egyptian script, summarizing the ideas of several scholars (e.g. Sethe and Schott) and stressing that evidently the Egyptian system of combining phonograms with ideograms and determinatives was fairly unequivocal. He argues that the writing came into existence by processes of segmentation and simplification, "neglecting" the vowels in various ways: dropping the endings, suppressing weak consonants (*3, ỉ* and *w*) and straightforward dropping of vocals (in Sumerian the system was different).

In the last section he deals with the invention of the Semitic alphabet.

77668 de SAINT-BLANQUAT, Henri, Les maladies des momies [égyptiennes], *Sciences et Avenir,* Paris No. 353 (Juillet 1976), 674-679, with 8 ill. (5 in colour).

The author describes the deteriorated state of some of the mummies of Egyptian pharaohs. *L.Z.*

77669 SALAFRANCA, Joaquín G. Lizana, Un escarabeo con texto menfita, *Boletin de la Asociacion Española de Orientalistas,* Madrid 13 (1977), 257-259, with 2 fig.

Note on a scarab from the Museo Arqueológico Nacional (Inv. No. 2.331) bearing one of the so-called Memphite maxims (see our number 57158).   *L.Z.*

77670 SALEH, Mohamed, Three Old-Kingdom Tombs at Thebes. I. The Tomb of Unas-Ankh no. 413. II. The Tomb of Khenty no. 405. III. The Tomb of Ihy no. 186, Mainz am Rhein, Verlag Philipp von Zabern, [1977] (27 × 35.3 cm; 28 p., 2 colour pl., 65 ill. on 16 pl., 19 pl. [6 folding] containing 1 map, 2 plans and 16 fig.) = Deutsches Archäologisches Institut, Abteilung Kairo. Archäologische Veröffentlichungen, 14.

In the introduction the author sets forth what is known about the Theban necropolis previous to the M.K., dealing especially with the five known O.K. tombs which have escaped later destruction. More tombs may still be discovered.

Three of the five are the subject of the present publication: those of Unas-Ankh (late Vth or early VIth Dynasty), of Khenty (VIth Dynasty) and of Ihy (probably VIth Dynasty). To each of them a chapter is devoted in which are discussed titles and family of the tomb-owner, the architecture and the painted decoration of the tomb, the finds (only in the tomb of Unas-ankh), and the date of the tomb. The texts are presented in hieroglyphs, in some instances restored after older publications. At the end (p. 27), remarks on the chronology of the O.K. tombs at Thebes.

The colour plates represent some of the best preserved scenes, those in black-and-white and the drawings the entire wall decoration.

SALOMON, Y., see our number 77117.

77671 SAMOYAULT, Jean-Pierre, Chefs-d'oeuvre en tôle vernie de l'époque consulaire et impériale (1801-1806), *La Revue du Louvre et des Musées de France,* Paris 27 (1977), 322-334, with 15 ill.

Among the objects discussed is an Egyptianizing metal vase.   *L.Z.*

77672 SAMSON, Julia, Nefertiti's Regality, *JEA* 63 (1977), 88-97, with 3 fig.

The writer cites the at present larger number of Karnak reliefs that show Nefertiti rather than the king, and presents further scenes from the Amarna tombs to support the idea that the queen is enthroned with the king, performs an equal part in acts of worship, and wears crowns not just suitable for a consort. The problem of the Smenkhkare names is also discussed and it is suggested that the queen was accorded that 'divinity' usually attributed to kings.   *E. Uphill*

77673 SAUNERON, Serge, Une statue-cube de l'époque bubastite, *BIFAO* 77 (1977), 23-27, with 3 pl.

Publication of a fragmentary block statue of a certain Djedptahiufᶜankh, at present in a private collection in Cairo. It bears an inscription of five lines, and some more on the socle. The latter contains an allusion to the triple use of offerings: before the god himself, on the offering table of a deceased or a secondary divinity, and at the end as food for the temple personnel.

SAUNERON, Serge, see also our number 77315.

77674 el-SĀWI, Ahmed, Preliminary Report of the Excavations at Kom Abu Bello. Seasons 1971, 1972, 1973, 1974, 1975, *ZÄS* 104 (1977), 75-78, with 4 ill.

The Egyptian Antiquities Department team explored part of the Roman cemetery in the southern sector of the site. Most tombs belong to the 3rd or the 4th century A.D. One of the stelae, Exc. Nr. 1604, shows a jackal and a falcon on shelves (? Fig. 3). *M. Heerma van Voss*

77675 el-SĀWI, Ahmed, Preliminary Report on Tell Basta Excavations. Seasons 1969, 1970, 1971, *ZÄS* 104 (1977), 127-131, with 1 plan and 7 ill.

Sequel to our number 64142. Another part of the newly found cat cemetery was discovered and explored.
The author publishes three objects representing the goddess Bastet:
1. in her boat; late stela, Reg. Nr. 1800, fig. 4;
2. with Ptah, a king and the winged sun-disk; N. K. or late stela, Nr. 2007, fig. 5-6;
3. holding an aegis (?); late faience statuette, Nr. 2006, fig. 7-8.

M. Heerma van Voss

77676 SAYED, Abdel Monem A. H., Discovery of the Site of the 12th Dynasty Port at Wadi Gawasis on the Red Sea Shore. (Preliminary Report on the Excavations of the Faculty of Arts, University of Alexandria, in the Eastern Desert of Egypt — March 1976), *RdE* 29 (1977), 138-178, with 3 maps, 1 plan, 2 fig, 3 ill. and 9 pl.

Les fouilles en question ont mis au jour les vestiges d'un port égyptien du Moyen Empire à quelques km au sud de Wady Gâsus. A côté d'un certain nombre d'objets tardifs et d'ostraca grecs et démotiques, on peut signaler la découverte d'une stèle et d'une petite chapelle faite d'ancres remployées remontant à la 12e dynastie. L'auteur s'est également préoccupé de reconnaître les routes antiques menant au site. *Ph. Derchain*

77677 el-SAYED, Ramadan, Au sujet de la statue Caire CG. 662, *BIFAO* 77 (1977), 101-111, with 2 pl.

Publication of the remaining lower part of a naophorous statue preserved in the Cairo Museum (numbered 3/10/1928 and 6/6/1956), representing a certain Padeg-akhet who is also known from other monuments. The statue may have been placed in the temple of Neith at Sais and dates from the XXVIth Dynasty. The author describes the piece, presents the texts in hieroglyphs and translation, and discusses the career and family of its owner, a member of a well-known Saite family.

SCARISBRICK, Diana, see our number 77099.

77678 SCHADEN, Otto J., A Third Intermediate Period Mummy in the Minneapolis Institute of Art, *Newsletter ARCE* Nos. 99/100 (Winter/Spring 1977), 18.

Abstract of a paper.

SCHAMP, Heinz, see our number 77009.

77679 SCHENKEL, Wolfgang, Kultmythos und Märtyrerlegende. Zur Kontinuität des ägyptischen Denkens, Wiesbaden, Otto Harrassowitz, 1977 (17 × 24 cm; 135 p., 15 fig.) = Göttinger Orientforschungen. Veröffentlichungen des Sonderforschungsbereiches Orientalistik an der Georg-August-Universität Göttingen. IV. Reihe: Ägypten, 5; rev. *ZDMG* 129 (1979), 406 (J[ürgen] v. B[eckerath]). Pr. DM 18

After a foreword explaining the author's attitude towards the material dealt with in this book, the author states in his introduction to recognize the basic motifs of the Coptic Martyr Legend as investigated in our number 72060 in the Myth of the Winged Sun-Disk in the Horus temple at Edfu. The second chapter, by far the longest, is divided into 5 sections. In the first the myth is presented in drawing and description of the eight tableaus and translation, of the legenda as well as of the story and its episodes. In the second section, on the decoration scheme of the myth, he concludes that the text is skilfully adapted on account of the requirements of the space division. Then he discusses in the third section the 15 episodes, all arranged according to almost the same scheme: presentation of the actors, victory and its celebration. In general the scenes illustrate one of the episodes in the tableau. Attention is paid to correspondences of the spots where the action of the myth takes place with the building inscription underneath the three registers of the wall the middle one of which is occupied by the myth. The fourth section is devoted to the basic Myth of the Double Victory (at Edfu and in Nubia) in the broader context of the Myth of the Winged Sun Disk. A later and abbreviated parallel at Edfu and versions from Kom Ombo and Esna are translated. The sense of the myth is the twofold destruction of the enemy. The last section discusses the various units in the amplified full version originating from the redactor's wish to include the Egyptian world as a whole and to bring other cults of Horus under the supremacy of that of Horus of Edfu.

In the last chapter the author explains the transformation of the cult myth into the Martyr Legend of which the two main motifs are to legitimate the cult (cult etiology) and the care for the physical soundness of the martyr. The first is clearly visible in the Myth: the action is directed towards the legitimation of Horus as heir of Re, of his installation at Edfu against the enemies of Re, and consequently of the dominant position of Edfu among the Horus cults. The paradox of the repeated deaths of the martyr and the multiple destruction of the enemies in the myth is solved by the position of the dead. On the one hand, death is negatively valued in ancient Egypt, but means victory in the case of destruction of the enemy; on the other hand, however, positively by the Christian since it means redemption from the worldly misery and the victory of the good party. For the pagan Egyptian the king guarantees the order, but for the Christian the power and suppression of the state represent the inimical element, which is conquered by death. Since the myth formed part of a public festival of the Edfu temple, knowledge of the myth could be spread among the population. Index at the end of the book. *L.Z.*

77680 SCHENKEL, Wolfgang, Zur Frage der Vorlagen spätzeitlicher "Kopien", *in: Fragen an die altägyptische Literatur,* 417-441, with 2 tables and 1 fig.

The author investigates the question to what kind of model the normally two-dimensional copies of the Late Period can be traced back. A text-critical investigation of scenes from the Southern Hall of Offerings at Hatshepsut's temple at Deir el-Bahri, of which copies exist in the tombs of Aba (Theban Tomb 36) and of Pabasa (Theban Tomb 279) demonstrates that in this case it is certain that they were not copied from the nearby original, but most probably from a model in a temple archive, where two-dimensional models could easily be stored.

77681 SCHILD, Romuald and Fred WENDORF, The Prehistory of Dakhla Oasis and the Adjacent Desert. With a Chapter on Geology by Bahai

Issawi and Contributions by F.A. Servello, H. Królik, J. Lech, and T.M. Ryan, Wrocław-Warszawa-Kraków-Gdańsk, Zakład Narodowy Imienia Ossolińskich. Wydawnictwo Polskiej Adakemii Nauk, 1977 (17 × 24.6 cm; 259 p., 18 tables, 5 folding maps, 13 ill., 23 fig. [1 folding], 93 pl. [=p.167-259]); at head of title: Polska Akademia Nauk. Instytut Historii Kultury Materialnej.

After the first two chapters on the geomorphology and the geology of the Dâkhla area (by B. Issawi) follows the chapter on the Late Acheulian near Balât, in which most room is devoted to two site reports. The same procedure is followed for the Dyke area, while discussions conclude the two parts. The book ends with a bibliography, an appendix on the climate in the Western Desert, and a summary in Polish. *L.Z.*

77682 SCHLÖGL, Hermann, Der Sonnengott auf der Blüte. Eine ägyptische Kosmogonie des Neuen Reiches, Genève, Éditions de Belles-Lettres, 1977 (21 × 30 cm; 72 p., 5 ill.) = Aegyptiaca Helvetica. Herausgegeben von/publiée par Ägyptologisches Seminar der Universität Basel et Centre d'études orientales de l'Université de Genève, 5; rev. *CdE* LIII, No. 106 (1978), 265-267 (Bengt Birkstam).

The author proceeds from Morenz' study "Der Gott auf der Blume" (our number 3470), using the German word "Blüte" as a botanical term instead of colloquial "Blume"; actually the flower is always the blue lotus (Nymphaea caerulea). It is the aim of the present work to establish the time in which the cosmogonic conception did arise.

Chapter 1 deals with P.T. and C.T., where the idea of a god on a plant frequently occurs, not, however, as an early form of the later concept, since the connection between god and flower is merely attributive and no relation with cosmogony is demonstrable.

In chapter 2 the author attempts to arrange texts and representations in a chronological order, dealing with royal names and figures on a flower, the development of cosmogonic conception, and the Horus children on the flower. In one excursus he discusses Morenz' theory that the god was Herishef and refutes it, in a second the connection between Nefertem and the flower is studied. The god is never depicted on the flower, as is frequently suggested.

In a summary (p. 33-34), the author presents his main conclusions. The conception did not occur before the N.K.; even the famous head of Tutankhamon on a flower is not yet a prototype as regards the idea. The concept only came into being in the early XIXth Dynasty or slightly earlier, when also representations of the Horus children on the flower are first found. More frequent than those of the young sun-god are representations of the sun-god in his nightly form, until the XXIth Dynasty when those of Harpocrates begin to preponderate.

The third chapter contains short descriptions of 58 monuments, mainly from the N.K. and the T.I.P., divided into four groups: the nightly sun-god (in four types), the king, the royal child and the scarab on the flower, and one single instance of the falcon-headed sun-god from the Late Period. Five ill. represent as yet unpublished instances. Notes and bibliography on p. 55-69.

77683 SCHLÖGL, Hermann, Michel SGUAITAMATTI, Arbeiter des Jenseits. Ägyptische Totenfiguren (Uschebtis), [Zürich], Archäologische Sammlung der Universität Zürich, 1977 (14 × 21.5 cm; 40 p., 26 ill., ill. on cover) = Zürcher Archäologische Hefte, 2.

Publication of eight major shawabti figures from the archaeological collection of the University of Zürich. After a brief introduction to the subject in general the pieces are each minutely described, while all necessary data (texts in hieroglyphs on p. 38-39) as well as two or more photographs are added. They represent various types, e.g. a figure of Akhnaton (Inv. L 44) and one clad in daily dress (Inv. L 45). The last piece (Inv. F. 988), which fairly frequently occurs in the literature and is said to date from the Amarna Period, is here argued to be a fake, together with its parallels in Toulouse (Musée Labit, Inv. Nr. 49.29; see Ramond, our number 71231, 35), in Cairo (JdE 39590) and in Chicago (Or. Inst. Nr. 10754). They are probably made by the sculptor J.J. Rifaud.

77684 SCHMITZ, Bettina, Bemerkungen zu einigen königlichen Geschenken, *SAK* 5 (1977), 213-219.

Apart from the "gold of valour" various staffs and weapons are mentioned in texts as royal presents. The author studies three actual objects of this kind, characterized by the mention of the royal name and that of the receiver: a staff recently published by Berlev (see our number 74067), a throw-stick presented by a king Taᶜo to a royal son *Twiw* (Mariette, Mon. Div., pl. 51), and the bow also published by Berlev (our number 76073). The latter was not presented to Ameny but to a *šmsw* called *Mnw-m-ḥb.f-nb*.

77685 SCHNEIDER, Hans D., Shabtis. An Introduction to the History of Ancient Egyptian Funerary Statuettes with a Catalogue of the Collection of Shabtis in the National Museum of Antiquities at Leiden, [3 parts], Leiden, Rijksmuseum van Oudheden, 1977 (Part I: 15.5 ×

23.6 cm; XXVI + 367 p., 1 map, ill. on cover; Part II: 15.5 × 23.6 cm; V + 276 p., 1 map, 56 pl. with texts [= pl. 80-135], ill. on cover; Part III: 21.6 × 29.7 cm; 80 pl. with ill., 36 pl. with fig. [3 folding], ill. on cover) = Collections of the National Museum of Antiquities at Leiden, 2; rev. *CdE* LIV, No. 107 (1979), 57-72 (Jacques F. Aubert).
Pr. fl.90

Part 1 of this thesis contains a thorough study of the shabti throughout the Egyptian history.

In chapter 1 the background is sketched: the irrigation, the relations between masters and servants, the prerequisites of eternal life, etc. The last section deals with O.K. and early M.K. funerary statues as procurers of food.

Chapter 2 is devoted to the shabti in the M.K. and contains i.a. sections on the concept of the shabti, a translation with comments of the biographical text of Neḥa (el-Qatta, tomb no. 2), of the various C.T. spells "for giving a man's family back to him in the god's land" (Sp. 131 ff.), and of the two versions of the Shabti Spell (472) from that corpus. On p. 67-68 a summary of the conclusions, concerning the concept of the shabti in the M.K., followed by a discussion of the application of "substitute figures" in magic and the shabti.

In chapter 3 the development of the shabti spell from the M.K. to the Ptolemaic Period is discussed. The author lists criteria for a division into 7 versions, with several variants. For text-examples of the versions see fig. 3-10 of the plate volume. Conclusions of this chapter on p. 152-155.

Chapter 4 deals with the iconography of the statuettes, which are divided according to their principal forms and elements (wigs, implements, text position) into 12 classes. References are given to many examples. The author discusses also materials and manufacture, surface treatment, the meaning of colour and varnish, the shabti makers and the ateliers, and the relationship between shabtis and anthropoid mummy cases.

In chapters 5 to 7 the development of the shabti during the N.K., its concept during the T.I.P. and the Late Period (e.g. the appearance of shabti gangs), and its decline during the Ptolemaic Period are studied. The last section, on Pancrates, deals with an echo of the shabti in the Hellenistic literature.

A chronological table with the sigla used for the classes and the versions of the spell on p. 355-357; an index of subjects on p. 358-367. Part 2 contains the catalogue of the 972 shabti figures in the Leiden collection, preceded by an introduction in which the author deals with the old tradition of collecting these statuettes and with the growth of the collection in the Leiden Museum. He also presents information about museographical problems (various kinds of inventory numbers, catalogues and publications) and about the arrangement of the catalogue.

The catalogue itself (p. 25-223) presents full information about each single object (the characteristics indicated by the sigla explained in part 1) and translations of the texts. These texts themselves are given in a handwritten copy on the pages numbered 80-135 at the end of the volume. Photographs of all statuettes (from 3 or 4 sides), exact duplicates excepted, on the plates of part 3. Indexes to names and titles and concordances between various inventory numbers and the present catalogue on p. 224-275.

77686 SCHOTT, Erika, Die Biographie des Ka-em-tenenet, *in: Fragen an die altägyptische Literatur,* 443-461c, with 5 fig. on 2 loose pl.

The author publishes the biography of *K3-m-ṯnnt* from Saqqâra (Urk.I, 181-186), preserved on 4 blocks, which are here rearranged in a new order: block E (185,12-186,7); B (181,7-182,7); D (184,11-185,7) and C (182,11-184,7). She sketches the development of the autobiography in the O.K., the principal elements of which are name (and titles), dedicatory inscriptions by the son and passages from the ideal biography, and argues that it was more concerned with the endurance of tomb and funerary cult than of the owner.

Later on autobiographies were embellished and enlarged with i.a. royal decrees, probably originally present on separate stelae.

From Isesi onwards the personal relationship between king and tomb owner is expressed, and from the Fifth Dynasty onwards the autobiography is modelled as a life story.

Due to an error of the publisher, the discussed text is added separately on a loose leaf. *L.Z.*

77687 SCHOTT, Erika, Bücher und Bibliotheken im alten Ägypten, *GM* Heft 25 (1977), 73-80.

Bericht über den Fortgang des Werkes über "Bücher und Bibliotheken im alten Ägypten" (vgl. unsere Nr. 72646) aus dem Nachlaß von Siegfried Schott. Begonnen wurde mit dem zweiten Band, dem Register der Buch- und Spruchtitel und der Termini technici. Die Arbeit ist bis zum Stichwort *r3* "Spruch" gelangt. Zu den Spruchtiteln werden einige Beobachtungen mitgeteilt: bereits Pyramidensprüche besaßen Titel, die aber nicht auf die Wand übertragen wurden, weil sie nicht mitgelesen wurden, sondern nur dem Zweck dienten, zusammengerollten Papyrusblättern ihren Inhalt von außen anzusehen. Man verwendet auch Titel um Sprüche zu zitieren, wobei sogar ein Spruch mit zwei Titeln bezeichnet werden kann. Es gibt auch Titel, die zusätzliche Informationen enthalten und vielleicht mitrezitiert wurden. Da von den Pyramidensprüchen Abschriften aus der späteren Zeit fehlen, wissen wir nicht, was die Zitate von Spruchtiteln in den Pyramidentexten bedeuten. Die angelegte Spruchtitel-Sammlung soll dazu verhelfen, anhand von Varianten der Bedeutung von Spruchtiteln nachzugehen und Anhaltspunkte für die Beantwortung der Frage zu finden, aus welchen Gründen und in welcher Form Sprüche mit Titeln versehen werden. *Inge Hofmann*

77688 SCHULMAN, Alan R., Nofretity, ᶜAnkhesenamūn, and the Amka Affair, *Newsletter ARCE* Nos. 99/100 (Winter/Spring 1977), 17.
Abstract of a paper.

77689 SCHULMAN, Alan R., Reshep on Horseback?, *Newsletter SSEA* 7, No. 4 (August 1977), 13-17.
Although several texts connect the god Reshep with riding and horsemanship there is no unequivocal evidence, either textual or pictorial, that he actually rode on a horseback. Some texts, however, seem to suggest that he was chariot-borne.

77690 SCHULZE, Peter H., Herrin beider Länder. Hatschepsut, [Bergisch Gladbach], Gustav Lübbe Verlag, [1976] (18.3 × 25 cm; 255 p., 49 ill., 7 colour pl., 3 maps, 1 plan); rev. *BiOr* 34 (1977), 176-178 (William J. Murnane). Pr. DM 52
Although not written by an Egyptologist, the book presents a well-informed general survey of the reign and the personality of Hatshepsut. In order to elucidate the story of queen Hatshepsut for the interested reader, the author deals with other, more general Egyptological subjects as well. *L.Z.*

77691 SCHWAB, D.E., Some Issues of Identification Raised by Textual Material Relating to the 23rd to 26th Egyptian Dynasties, *ZÄS* 104 (1977), 131-141.
The author is utilizing biblical, hieroglyphic and cuneiform historical sources, as well as the chronologies dressed by Tadmor for Assyria, and by Kitchen for Egypt.
Schwab's deductions may be illustrated by the results regarding Dynasty XXIV. For Tefnakht a reign is suggested from c. 726-718 (at least), for Bocchoris one from c. 718-713/2.
No specific king is meant in *2 Kings* 17: 4 ("So, king of Egypt").
M. Heerma van Voss

77692 SCUPAK, N., לשון משותפות לספרות ולספרוה התכמה המצרית, למקרא ולהקר המזרה הקרום. שנתון, על כמה מטבעות, Jerusalem — Tel Aviv 2 (1977), 233-237, with an English summary on p. XX.

"Some Common Idioms in the Biblical and the Egyptian Wisdom Literatures."

The author investigates four word pairs from the O.T. and Egyptian Wisdom Literature, two of which are the titles מוסר /sb3yt and תורה מצות /tp rd, having the meanings of instruction, discipline, corporal punishment resp. God's or a man's command and a teacher's instruction.

The word פתי נתך /ḥm denotes the positive type of fool, while כסיל אויל לץ /wḫ3 denotes the negative type. *L.Z.*

77693 SEARIGHT, Rodney, Early Explorers at Abu Simbel, *The Illustrated London News,* London, Vol. 265, No. 6953 (December 1977), 81-83, with 4 ill. (2 in colour).

On account of a watercolour recently acquired by him the author describes the expeditions of Henry Salt and his company to Abu Simbel from 1817-1819. *L.Z.*

SELEM, Petar, see our number 77602.

SERVELLO, F.A., see our number 77681.

SEUX, Marie-Joseph, see our number 77112.

77694 SEYFRIED, Karl-J., Zur Deutung der Bezeichnung ⟨✝⟩ u.ä., *GM* Heft 23 (1977), 65-70, with 3 fig. and 1 table.

In einer Handwerkerszene der 6. Dynastie aus Deshasheh wird das Bearbeiten von Stäben dargestellt, wobei in einer Beischrift die Tätigkeit der Arbeiter erklärt wird. Aufgrund anderer herangezogener Beispiele möchte Verfasser das Verbum "sᶜk3" = gerade machen, vorschlagen. In dem Bestandteil "imyt-r" scheint die Bezeichnung einer Stabart vorzuliegen, für die Verfasser mit einiger Sicherheit mindestens sieben weitere Belege beibringt.

Vgl. jetzt auch: Henry G. Fischer, Notes on Sticks and Staves in Ancient Egypt, *Metropolitan Museum Journal,* New York 13 (1978), 5-7. *Inge Hofmann*

SGUAITAMATTI, Michel, see our number 77683.

77695 SHAW-EAGLE, Joanna, King Tut Tours America, *Aramco World Magazine,* New York 28, No. 3 (May-June 1977), 22-33, with 24 colour ill. (1 on cover) and 8 ill.

Short note to the Tutankhamon exhibition travelling through the U.S.A. The second part called "To dazzle the mind and the eye... Treasures of Tutankhamen" consists of photographs by Katrina Thomas, Harry Burton and Lee Boltin. *L.Z.*

77696 SHEA, William H., A Date for the Recently Discovered Eastern Canal of Egypt, *BASOR* No. 226 (April, 1977), 31-38, with 4 ill., 3 maps and 1 fig.

Proceeding from the evidence for the ancient, so called Eastern Canal (see our number 75701) extending across the Northern Half of the Isthmus of Suez, the Southernmost section of which extends between Lake Timsah (Ismailia) and Lake Ballah, the author tries to identify the canal. He discusses the well-known relief of Sethi I before the waterway (called there *dnỉt*) in the Karnak temple. The identification with the Pelusiac Branch of the Nile is rejected. Since the canal's purpose was probably defence against the Asiatics and since such a defensive work is unlikely to have been undertaken by the aggressive XVIIIth Dynasty Pharaohs, the author dates back its construction to the F.I.P. or early M.K. in which period there was much trouble with the Asiatics. He discusses possible references to it or its planning in the *Instruction for Merikare*, the *Prophecy of Neferty* and *Sinuhe* (called there the Wall of the Ruler). He proposes that the canal projected for Merikare was dug by Amenemhat I and lined by his Wall of the Ruler, that it is depicted on Sethi's relief, and that it is the canal discussed in our number 75701. *L.Z.*

77697 SHEA, William Henry, Famines in the Early History of Egypt and Syro-Palestine, *Dissertation Abstracts International,* Ann Arbor, Mich. 37, No. 10 (April 1977), 6664-A.

Abstract of a thesis University of Michigan, 1976 (Order No. 77-8035; 268 p.).

The author studies 26 Egyptian famine texts from the Vth to the XIIIth Dynasties; five (and probably six more) relate to famines caused by inadequate Nile inundations, while six others (and probably nine more) are connected with socio-political conditions. *L.Z.*

77698 SHEIKHOLESLAMI, Cynthia May, Thebes as a Necropolis in the Libyan Period, *Newsletter ARCE* Nos. 99/100 (Winter/Spring 1977), 8.

Abstract of a paper.

77699 SHENNUM, David, English-Egyptian Index of Faulkner's Concise Dictionary of Middle Egyptian, Malibu, Undena Publications, 1977 (21.7 × 28 cm; [VI +] 178 p.) = Aids and Research Tools in Ancient Near Eastern Studies, 1; rev. *ZAW* 90 (1978), 456 ([G. Fohrer])

This is an English-Egyptian index to Faulkner's Concise Dictionary (our number 62176). Each English word is followed by the Egyptian translation, in many instances with an indication such as n. (= noun), vb. 3inf., or the preposition used after the verb, and the number of the page. A short introduction and a list of abbreviations precede.

SHERIF, Nigm ed Din Mohammed, see our number 77346.

SHINER, Joel L., see our number 77318.

77700 SHINNIE, P.L. and R.J. BRADLEY, A New Meroitic Royal Name, *MNL* No. 18 (Octobre 1977), 29-31, with 1 ill.

In einem kleinen meroitischen Tempel in Meshra al-Hassan südlich von Meroe wurde ein Sandsteinwidder gefunden, der sehr große Ähnlichkeit mit dem Widder von Soba aufweist. Auch er trägt in einer Kartusche in meroitischen Hieroglyphen einen Königsnamen, der bisher noch nicht belegt war: Amankheremy... (REM 1151). Der König könnte der 58. Generation mit der Begräbnisstätte Beg. N. 37 zugewiesen werden, doch sind die Generationen 52 bis 59 überhaupt spekulativ, so daß Amankheremy einer der Herrscher jenes Zeitraumes gewesen sein mag.   *Inge Hofmann*

77701 SHIRUN, Irene, Parallelismus Membrorum und Vers, *in: Fragen an die altägyptische Literatur,* 463-492.

Proceeding from a choice of examples of the parallelismus membrorum taken mainly from the Story of Sinuhe, but also from the first Hymn to Sesostris III and the Shipwrecked Sailor, the author investigates the relation to its verse members, and of the verse with respect to its length and syntactical elements. For this purpose she introduces the term "value" which is to be distinguished from the cola of Fecht's metric rules and presents a list of the values of the various grammatical-syntactical elements, which only partly coincide with the list given by Fecht. She discusses first the complete parallelism having a complete clause in the second verse member, consisting of two lines and four or six values. The incomplete parallelism with complete second verse member is subdivided according to variations of the three element scheme with or without compensation (four to seven values) and of the five element scheme (three lines; seven to nine, or twelve values). The incomplete parallelism having an incomplete second member can show an extra (?), a partial, a normal or no compensation. The alternating parallelism consists of four lines with incomplete clauses in the second and fourth half-member. In her conclusion the author makes remarks on the strophe forms, the motifs and the prosody of the examples. *L.Z.*

77702 SHISHA-HALEVY, Ariel, Bohairic ⲦⲰⲞⲨⲚ (ⲦⲰⲚ⸗): A Case of Lexemic Grammaticalisation, *Enchoria* 7 (1977), 109-113.

The author examines the distribution of the alternants ⲦⲰⲞⲨⲚ⸗ and ⲦⲰⲚ⸗ (presuffixal allomorphs of the lexeme), ⲦⲰⲞⲨⲚ (absolute allomorph) and ⲦⲰⲞⲨⲚⲞⲨ (by-form of the absolute allomorph) in Bohairic. *W. Brunsch*

77703 SHISHA-HALEVY, Ariel, Protatic ⲈϤϢⲰⲦⲘ̄: Some Additional Material, *Orientalia* 46 (1977), 127-128.

Some additions to our number 74676.

77704 SHISHA-HALEVY, Ariel, ⲦⲰ ⲈⲦⲰ: A Shenoutean Coptic Idiom and a Suggestion for its Analysis, *WZKM* 69 (1976), 33-39.

The author discusses the almost exclusively Shenoutean argumentative-idiomatic expression ⲦⲰ ⲈⲦⲰ Ⲛ̄-X (ⲘⲚ̄-Y), which means approximately "how different is X" resp. "what a difference there is between X and Y; You cannot compare X and Y", as well as some irregular instances. He suggests that, if ⲦⲰ is an Akhmimic spelling of ⲦⲰⲚ, Eg. *tn*, "where", for which colloquial use of the adverb he adduces some examples from several modern languages, then ⲦⲰ ⲈⲦⲰ might mean "where and whither" and that Ⲛ̄-(X ⲘⲚ̄-Y) is the logical subject in which Ⲛ̄-is the mark of the mediate direct object governed by a not expressed verb, such as "to take" or "to put", the resulting tentative explanation being "(take) X and Y, where and whither?" *L.Z.*

77705 SIJPESTEIJN, P.J., Geneeskunst in het oude Egypte, *Spiegel Historiael*, Haarlem 12 (1977), 38-44, with 8 ill.

Survey of Egyptian medicine and medical papyri for the general reader.

77706 SILVERMAN, David, An Eighteenth Dynasty Wall Painting in the Collection of the Oriental Institute Museum, *Newsletter ARCE* Nos. 99/100 (Winter/Spring 1977), 10.

Abstract of a paper.

SILVERMAN, David P., see also our number 77514.

77707 SIMPSON, William Kelly, An Additional Dog's Name from a Giza Mastaba, *JEA* 63 (1977), 175, with 1 fig.

Gives an additional name *'Inhb* from a block in G2042a to the list of J.M.A. Janssen and H.G. Fischer (our numbers 58333 and 61239).
E. Uphill

77708 SIMPSON, William Kelly, Amor Dei: *ntr mrr rmt m t3 w3* (Sh. Sai. 147-148) and the Embrace, *in: Fragen an die altägyptische Literatur,* 493-498.

Proceeding from the passage in the Sh. Sailor 147-148 the author discusses the concept amor dei, expressed in the verb *mrî,* which is generally directed from a superior giver to an inferior recipient, the reverse occurring only from the Ramesside Period onwards in the personal piety. The embrace, being its parallel in representations, shows the reverse in the husband and wife pair statues. *L.Z.*

77709 SIMPSON, William Kelly, The Face of Egypt: Permanence and Change in Egyptian Art, [Katonah, The Katonah Art Gallery, 1977] (21.6 × 30.3 cm; 72 p., 1 map, 82 ill., 2 ill. on cover).

Catalogue of an exhibition of Egyptian art, first held in the Katonah Gallery (March 13-May 15, 1977), and afterwards in the Dallas Museum of Fine Arts (June 14-August 28, 1977).

After a preface and an introduction about permanence and change in Egyptian art (by Simpson), there follows the catalogue itself, describing the 71 objects: stelae, statues, reliefs, bronzes, and a few other objects. They are divided into three groups: rulers and officials (1-48), gods and goddesses (49-59), and animals (60-71). Each object is described and represented in photograph, in several instances with views from various sides. The technical data are given on p. 67-70.

The objects came from several museums and private collections, and some have never been published before. We mention e.g., the seated statuette of an official of the XIIth Dynasty from the collection of Mrs. John D. Rockefeller 3rd (no. 11) or the playing monkeys from the Ptolemaic Period, from a private collection (no. 68).

77710 SIMPSON, William Kelly, The Literature of Ancient Egypt. An Anthology of Stories, Instructions and Poetry. New Edition. With Translations by R.O. Faulkner, E.F. Wente, Jr., and W.K. Simpson, New Haven and London, Yale University Press, [1977] (13 × 20.5 cm; VIII + 350 p., 4 pl., fig. on cover).

This is the third slightly revised edition as a paperback of our number 72668. No essential alterations have been made. As regards the

Loyalist Instruction, for instance, the author states (p. 198) that the recent edition by Posener (our number 76636) could not yet be utilized.

77711 SKEAT, T.C., A Letter from the King of the Blemmyes to the King of the Noubades, *JEA* 63 (1977), 159-170, with 1 pl. and 1 folding p.

Es handelt sich um den in Qasr Ibrîm gefundenen Brief des Blemmyerkönigs Phonen an den König der Noubades namens Abourni. Die Interpretation ist wegen des "chaotischen" Griechisch nicht einfach. Der Brief ist eine Antwort auf ein Schreiben des Abourni. Silko, der durch seine Triumphalinschrift von Kalâbsha seit langem bekannt ist (die Inschrift wird am Ende des Artikels wiedergegeben), hat offensichtlich gegen Phonen gekämpft, dessen Bruder Eienei aber wohl mit ihm konspirierte, woraufhin die Blemmyer von Abourni bekämpft wurden. In den Auseinandersetzungen mit den Kleinkönigen scheint Silko aber doch schließlich Sieger geblieben zu sein, so daß der Brief vor der Kalâbsha-Inschrift angefertigt worden sein muß. Im weiteren geht es um Territorialansprüche der Blemmyer.

In einem Appendix werden Anmerkungen von E.G. Turner angeführt.
Inge Hofmann

77712 ŚLIWA, Joachim, Łukasz Dobrzański and His Excavations in Egypt, 1895, *in: Ägypten und Kusch,* 397-400.

Die polnischen Verdienste um die Erforschung der Ägyptologie auf dem Gebiet der Archäologie werden gewürdigt. Außer Tadeusz Smoleński (1884-1909) wird Łukasz Dobrzański (1864-1909) genannt, dessen archäologische Tätigkeit fast vollständig in Vergessenheit geraten ist. Von seinen Ausgrabungen 1895 bei Koptos brachte er lediglich ein Alabastergefäß mit, das er 1896 dem Kunsthistorischen Museum in Wien verkaufte (Inv. Nr. 6296). Über das Leben des Archäologen und Fotografen werden einige Daten gegeben.
Inge Hofmann

77713 ŚLIWA, Joachim, Egyptian and Nubian Pottery in the Collection of the Archåeology Museum in Cracow. I. Arminna E and Toshka W, *in: Recherches archéologiques de 1975,* Kraków, L'Institut d'Archéologie de l'Université de Cracovie, 1976, 68-71.

The pottery material from Arminna and Toshka in the collection of the Archaeology Museum in Cracow originates from Junker's Nubian excavations in 1911-12.
L.Z.

77714   ŚLIWA, Joachim, Egyptian and Nubian Pottery in the Collection of the Archaeology Museum in Cracow. II. El-Kubanieh North and South, *in: Recherches Archéologiques de 1976,* Kraków, L'Institut d'Archéologie de l'Université de Cracovie, 1977, 57-60, with 1 fig.

Sequel to our preceding number.
The collection of Egyptian and Nubian Pottery in the Archaeology Museum in Cracow came from Junker's excavations in 1910-1914. The author here mentions vessels from the A- and C-group cemeteries in el-Kûbânîya (S. of Aswân), and some other objects from the same sites.

77715   ŚLIWA, Joachim, Egyptian Bronze Statuettes in the Cracow Collections, *in: Recherches Archéologiques de 1976,* Kraków, L'Institut d'Archéologie de l'Université de Cracovie, 1977, 61-62.

Short summary of the author's earlier studies of the subject. Compare our numbers 70511 and 71582.

77716   ŚLIWA, Joachim, Egyptian Sculpture in the Collection of the Archaeology Museum in Cracow, *in: Recherches Archéologiques de 1975,* Kraków, L'Institut d'Archéologie de l'Université de Cracovie, 1976, 71-75, with 6 ill.

The author shortly describes six pieces of sculpture in the collection of the Archaeology Museum in Cracow.
Compare our number 76732.   *L.Z.*

ŚLIWA, Joachim, see also our number 77434.

77717   SMITH, H.S. and D.G. JEFFREYS, The Sacred Animal Necropolis, North Saqqâra: 1975/76, *JEA* 63 (1977), 20-28, with 1 plan and 1 pl.

Mastabas and rock-cut tombs of the Early Dynastic and O.K. necropolis were excavated, as well as a 'pillared wall' and Late Period rock tomb. Along the outside of the Temple Enclosure several caches of bronze figurines and situlae were found. The archaeological evidence suggests robbery and destruction of existing structures preceding the Christian occupation, and perhaps pottery contemporary with it.   *E. Uphill*

SMITH, Harry S., see also our number 77302.

77718   SMITH, Mark, A New Version of a Well-known Egyptian Hymn, *Enchoria* 7 (1977), 115-149, with 1 pl.

Publication of the Ostracon Hess without number, the photo of which was found in the files of W. Spiegelberg in the Research Archives of the Oriental Institute at the University of Chicago. The ostracon dates from Late Ptolemaic or early Roman time and bears a portion of a hymn to the god Amon-Re. The text is compared with the hieroglyphic version of this hymn on the walls of the temple of Darius I at Hibis. *W. Brunsch*

SMITH, Patricia, see our number 77067.

77719 SMITH, R.W., The Akhenaten Temple Project, *in: Research Reports. National Geographic Society*. Abstracts and reviews of research and exploration authorized under grants from the National Geographic Society during the year 1968, Washington D.C., National Geographic Society, [1976], 379-388, with 3 ill.

Report on the Akhenaten Temple Project. Compare our numbers 70514, 70515, 72682 and 76737. *L.Z.*

SOLLBERGER, E., see our number 77145.

77720 SOLOV'EVA, S.S., Война 663 г. до н.э. между Ассирией и Кушем за господство над Египтом *in:* Мероэ, 191-213, with 3 ill. on 2 pl. and a French summary on p. 296-297.

"Der Krieg von 663 v. Chr. zwischen Assyrien und Kusch um die Herrschaft über Ägypten."

Unter Zuhilfenahme der assyrischen, ägyptischen und kuschitischen Dokumente, des archäologischen Materials und der Berichte der antiken Schriftsteller, lassen sich die Ereignisse und militärischen Aktionen von 663 v.Chr. rekonstruieren. Das Augenmerk wird besonders auf die Ereignisse im Delta gerichtet. Bald nach dem Krieg von 663 konnte sich Ägypten von der assyrischen und kuschitischen Herrschaft befreien und sich unter der 26. saitischen Dynastie unabhängig entwickeln. *Inge Hofmann*

77721 SOYEZ, Brigitte, Byblos et la fête des Adonies, Leiden, E. J. Brill, 1977 (15.5 × 24 cm; X + 92 p., 6 maps, 5 plans, 1 fig., 15 pl.) = Études préliminaires aux réligions orientales dans l'empire romain publiées par M.J. Vermaseren, 60.

Although this study is mainly outside the scope of the AEB, the last chapter in which Isis and Hathor are mentioned in their relationship to the Lady of Byblos may be of importance for the history of the Egyptian religion in the Graeco-Roman world.

77722 SPALINGER, Anthony, The Concept of Kingship in Dynasty XXVI, *Newsletter ARCE* Nos. 99/100 (Winter/Spring 1977), 9.

Abstract of a paper.

77723 SPALINGER, Anthony, A Critical Analysis of the "Annals" of Thutmose III (*Stücke* V-VI), *JARCE* 14 (1977), 41-54, with 1 pl.

A stylistic and structural analysis of this part of the Annals (= Urk. IV, 684-734; cf. our number 882) which also exemplifies the use of certain terms (like *w3ỉ r*, 'to fall into [a state]') and to which the hitherto unpublished fragment British Museum 1684 is added (p. 50 and pl. 23). Referring to a selection of campaigns, these reports were drawn up on the base of original war reports and booty lists, but a consecutive narration is missing; they were meant to glorify the king's heroic exploits. *J.F. Borghouts*

77724 SPALINGER, Anthony, Egypt and Babylonia: A Survey (c. 620 B.C. - 550 B.C.), *SAK* 5 (1977), 221-244.

The author presents a survey of Egypt's policy in the Levant during the years 620 - 550 B.C., characterizing it as "commercial in intent, benevolent in application, laissez-faire in nature, and short in duration". He subsequently deals with the relations between Egypt, Babylonia and Judea under Psammetichus I, the naval power of Necho and his successors, the suggested invasion of Egypt by Nebuchadnezzar in the reign of Apries, the revolt of Amasis, etc.

77725 STADELMANN, Rainer, Der Tempel Sethos' I. in Gurna. Dritter Grabungsbericht, *MDAIK* 33 (1977), 125-131, with 1 plan and 5 pl.

Sequel to our number 75703.

Report on the 5th and 6th campaigns. Investigation of the storehouses N. of the temple, still seen by Lepsius, showed that they were used as dwellings in the XXth-XXVIth Dynasties and, as the brick-stamps demonstrate, had been built by Sethi I himself. Their plan corresponds with that of the storehouses of Sethi's temple in Abydos.

Sondages under the temple proper brought to light foundation deposits of Sethi and of Ramses I, both at the S.W. corner. In the court S. of the temple only houses of the Ptolemaic Period were found. The plan of the destroyed N.W. corner of the temple actually differs from the usual reconstruction.

STADELMANN, Rainer, see also our numbers 77046 and 77056.

STAHL-GUINAUD, Bérengère, see our number 77153.

77726 Starożytne Kultury Egiptu i Mezopotamii, Warszawa, Museum Narodowe w Warszawie, 1977 (17 × 24 cm; 66 p., 30 pl., 2 maps, 2 ill on cover).

Catalogue of an exhibition of Egyptian and Mesopotamian antiquities from the East Berlin collections, held at Warsaw.

After a preface (by Kazimierz Michałowski) and an introduction (by Wolfgang Müller and Liane Jacob-Rost) there follow a map of Egypt, a chronological table, and a general introduction to the Egyptian objects by Ingeborg Müller. She deals with: the cult of the deceased, deities and priests, the power of the king and state, daily life, and literature and writing, the same categories in which the objects themselves are divided. Their very brief description, mostly no more than two to four lines, is printed on p. 31-44. All together 283 Egyptian objects were exhibited, seventeen of which are depicted on the plates.

The second part of the description and the plates are devoted to Mesopotamia.

77727 STEINMANN, Frank, Gab es im alten Ägypten Sklavenarbeit in der Sphäre der handwerklich-künstlerischen Produktion?, *Altorientalische Forschungen,* Berlin 5 (1977), 25-31.

The author discusses whether in Egypt slaves were used as artisans and artists. He reaches the conclusion that there is no evidence for it, although a few were engaged in the households of artisans. For transport and work in the quarries direct producers ("unmittelbare Produzenten") were used as well as prisoners of war; when the latter went to the workshops they got the status of *mrt*.

Compare also our number 77217.

77728 STENN, Frederick F., James W. MILGRAM, Sandra L. LEE, Raymond J. WEIGAND, Arthur VEIS, Biochemical Identification of Homogentisic Acid Pigment in an Ochronotic Egyptian Mummy, *Science,* New York 197, No. 4303 (5 August 1977), 566-568, with 2 ill. and 3 figs.

An investigation of the mummy of the custodian of the granary Harwa in the Field Museum of Natural History, Chicago, made evident that the man suffered from ochronosis, an autosomal recessive disorder. *L.Z.*

77729 STERN, E. Marianne, A Glass Bowl of Isings' Form 2 from the Tomb of an Ethiopian Candace, *OMRO* 58 (1977), 63-72, with 5 fig. on a pl.

Zur Diskussion steht ein Gefäß aus opakem rotem Glas, das der Form 2 bei Isings entspricht und aus der Pyramide Barkal 4 stammt. Diese wird der Königin Amanirenas zugesprochen und diese mit der berühmten Kandake identifiziert, gegen die Petronius zu Felde gezogen sein soll. Es wird vermutet, daß das Glasgefäß aus der Beute stammt, die die Meroiten bei ihrem Überfall auf Syene erbeuteten.

Inge Hofmann

77730 STÖRK, Lothar, Die Nashörner. Verbreitungs- und kulturgeschichtliche Materialen unter besonderer Berücksichtigung der afrikanischen Arten und des altägyptischen Kulturbereiches, [Hamburg, Verlag Born GmbH], 1977 (14 × 20.5 cm; VIII + 583 p., 15 maps, 284 ill. and fig.); rev. *ZDMG* 129 (1979), 407 H[enning] W[iesner]).

Pr. DM 50

Das vorliegende umfangreiche Werk stellte sich zur Aufgabe, Materialien für künftig zu leistende umfassende Darstellungen der altägyptischen Fauna und ihres Wandels im Gefolge menschlicher und klimatischer Einflüsse bereitzustellen sowie auch Nachbardisziplinen und zoographisch und zoohistorisch Interessierten Informationen zu liefern. Die Untersuchung ist chronologisch aufgebaut. Sie beginnt mit einer Auseinandersetzung mit den von Butzer vorgetragenen Thesen zur Entwicklung der altägyptischen Fauna. In diesem vornehmlich methodischen Erörterungen dienenden Abschnitt ist nicht nur von Nashörnern, sondern auch von einer Reihe weiterer signifikanter Vertreter der ägyptischen Tierwelt die Rede. Das folgende Kapitel behandelt die Zoologie der Nashörner; darauf folgt ein Überblick über die fossilen Rhinocerotiden mit der Absicht, die spezifische Entwicklung dieser Tierformen auf dem afrikanischen Kontinent darzustellen.

Mit den Felsbildern liegen die ersten ausführlichen ägyptischen Zeugnisse vor. Kernstück der aus dynastischer Zeit stammenden Belege bildet die Nashorndarstellung auf dem Pylon des Tempels zu Erment sowie der Bericht über eine Nashornjagd Thutmosis' III. auf einem in demselben Tempel gefundenen Stele. Dieser Komplex wirft Datierungsfragen und Lokalisierungsprobleme von Südvölkertoponymen auf. Ein kurzer Ausblick auf die meroitische Kultur leitet zum griechisch-römischen Altertum über, in dem die Tiere in Schrift und Bild gut bezeugt sind. In der koptischen Kultur spielte das Nashorn keine Rolle; erst die Araber berichten wieder ausführlich davon, wie die Zusammenstellung der Berichte und Darstellungen lehrt. Die Nashörner in China und Hinterindien sowie das Kapitel über europäische Reiseberichte und Darstellungen schließen das Werk ab, nicht ohne die Einhörner und andere kulturhistorisch interessante Kuriosa zu behandeln. Es folgt ein ausführliches Literatur - und Abbildungsverzeichnis (S. 529-583). *Inge Hofmann*

77731   STRICKER, B.H., Het oude verbond, *OMRO* 58 (1977), 235-236.

In this short note on the Old Covenant, it being a marriage between God and nation, there are some references to ancient Egypt.   *L.Z.*

77732   STROUHAL, E., [Report], *Nyame Akuma,* Calgary No. 10 (1977), 28.

In der kürzlich entdeckten Mastaba der Prinzessin Khekeretnebti wurden in der Hauptgrabkammer die Überreste ihrer Mumie gefunden, die einer 25-35 Jahre alten Frau gehörten. In einer zweiten Grabkammer fanden sich verstreute Überreste der 17-18 Jahre alten Frau Tisethor. Außer Zahnpathologie konnen keine weiteren pathologischen Veränderungen festgestellt werden.
Des weiteren wurde das spätzeitliche anthropologische Material untersucht, das im Grab des Königs Horemhab gefunden wurde. Es handelte sich um Massenbegräbnisse; etwa 200 Einzelpersonen waren in dem Material repräsentiert. Es konnten zwei Fälle von osteolytischen Metastasen entdeckt werden.   *Inge Hofmann*

77733   STROUHAL, Eugen und Johann JUNGWIRTH, unter Mitwirkung von Jiři ČEJKA, Vlasta RYCHTEROVÁ, Karel TOBOLA und Zdeněk URBANEC, Ein verkalktes Myoma uteri aus der späten Römerzeit in Ägypisch-Nubien, *Mitteilungen der anthropologischen Gesellschaft in Wien,* Horn-Wien 107 (1977), 215-221, with 10 ill. on 7 pl. and 1 table.

Im Grab Nr. 75 des Grabhügels C III in Sayala, der in das 3. — 4. nachchristliche Jahrhundert zu datieren ist (vgl. unsere Nummern 66056 und 71550), wurde im Becken einer 35-45jährigen Frau ein 123 mm langes, kegelförmiges Gebilde mit nodöser Struktur gefunden. Nach der makroskopischen, röntgenologischen und mikroskopischen Untersuchung und nach der chemischen Analyse handelt es sich höchstwahrscheinlich um einen kalzifizierten Uterus-Tumor. Für diesen Befund eines verkalten Myoms aus einer archäologisch ausgegrabenen Bestattung gibt es in der laufenden anthropologischen oder paläopathologischen Literatur keine Analogie.   *Inge Hofmann*

STROUHAL, Eugen, see also our numbers 77324, 77557 and 77746.

77734   SUGI, Isamu, [Sekai no rekishi, 1, Tokyo, Kodai Oriento, 1977] (12 × 18 cm; XIV + 439 p., 4 colour pl., maps, fig. and ill.).
"World History, Part 1".
Part of this book on the history of the Ancient Near East is devoted to ancient Egypt.   *L.Z.*

SWEDIK, Grete, see our number 77382.

7735 TADEMA, Auke A. and Bob TADEMA SPORRY, Operatie Farao's. Egypte's tempéls gered!, Haarlem, Fibula-Van Dishoeck, [1977] (20.5 × 25.5 cm; 168 p., frontispiece, 2 maps, 27 plans, 6 fig., 184 ill. [34 in colour], 4 colour ill. on cover).

This is a survey for the general public of the Nubian salvage campaign and its results, with descriptions of all more important Nubian monuments and their history. Particularly important is the abundant illustration.

After a short introduction about the High Dam and the UNESCO appeal for the salvage of Nubian antiquities the authors give a survey of Nubian history ("Land of the Spirits"). The next chapter deals with the prehistory, rock drawings and stone implements.

There follow 25 chapters, each devoted to a single monument or a group of monuments in Nubia, in a geographical order from S. to N., beginning with the fortresses of Semna to the temple of Debôd. Apart from the fortresses and all the main temples there are discussions of the Faras cathedral, city and church of Abdallah Nîrqi, the tombs of Hekanefer (Tôshka) and Pennut (ᶜAniba), the rock of Qasr Ibrîm, etc. A description and survey of the history of the monuments is given, with a plan and a chart with data about their building, removal and, eventually, rebuilding.

The last chapter deals with Philae and the preparations for removal of its monuments to Agilkia.

There has appeared also a German edition: Unternehmen Pharao. Die Rettung der ägyptischen Tempel, Bergisch-Gladbach, 1978 (Pr. DM 34).

7736 TAIT, W.J., Papyri from Tebtunis in Egyptian and Greek (P. Tebt. Tait), London, Egypt Exploration Society, 1977 (25 × 31 cm; XVI + 118 p., 12 pl.) = Texts from Excavations edited by T.G.H. James. Third Memoir; rev. *Orientalia* 48 (1979), 285-286 (J. O'Callaghan).

The fragmentary texts here published have been selected from among about 500 small bits of papyrus in a box, probably purchased by Grenfell and Hunt after their excavations 1898-1900 at Tebtunis. From inner evidence the provenance from that place is probable for some of them. The lot here published consists of 23 Demotic, 11 hieratic, 3 hieroglyphic and 16 Greek texts.

In the introduction the author i.a. deals with the date of the texts, dividing the Demotic ones after their palaeography into five groups, and with the system of transliterating Demotic.

Each of the 53 documents is minutely described; the Demotic ones are given in transliteration, the hieratic in transcription in hieroglyphs, the hieroglyphic and Greek fragments in facsimile; and of each of them there is a translation with extensive comments, while at the end mostly a discussion of the contents is added. All are also given in photograph on the plates.

The Demotic fragments are, among others: four (or five) Inaros fragments; a *Kufi* fragment; a text featuring Hor-udja and a small piece mentioning Hordedef; two parts of a dream book; medical-magical and herbal texts; a word-list; a letter, etc.

The hieratic fragments bear: a part of the Faiyûm Geographica Papyrus (cfr Botti's edition = our number 59081, text A, 8.15 - 9,1) praises of Sobk, and several rituals. The hieroglyphic fragments are very small and contain: a few words of the Faiyûm Geographica Papyrus, a piece with titles of gods, and four bits of a ritual. The Greek texts too are of varied nature.

77737 [TAWFIK] TAWFICK, Sayed, Abdel Moneim Abu Bakr, 1907-1976, *Newsletter ARCE* Nos. 99/100 (Winter/Spring 1977), 2.

Obituary notice. See our number 77847.

77738 TAWFIK, Sayed, Amarna Kalkstein — Talatat aus Karnak, *GM* Heft 26 (1977), 55-62 with 3 ill.

Vorgestellt wird einer der beiden Kalkstein-Talatat, die unter den 35000 Sandstein-Talatat in Theben gefunden wurden und vermutlich irgendwann von Amarna nach Theben transportiert worden sind. (Zur Veröffentlichung des 1. Blockes vgl. unsere Nr. 76737). Der zweite Block zeigt auf zwei Seiten Dekorationen aus der Amarna-Zeit, wurde aber wahrscheinlich in der Ramessiden-Zeit noch einmal benutzt. Die eine Seite mit der Code-Nummer 017404306 zeigt oben rechts die Sonnenscheibe mit Uräus, von dem ein ꜥnḫ-Zeichen herabhängt und von der Sonnenstrahlen ausgehen. Links oben ist in neun verschieden langen Kolumnen ein Text eingraviert. Die andere Seite mit der Code-Nummer 017704306 zeigt ebenfalls eine Szene, in deren Zentrum die Sonnenscheibe steht, die von dem Namen und den Epitheta des Aton flankiert ist. Der Text erscheint in fünf Kolumnen. Die Texte auf beiden Seiten sind fast identisch; eine Übersetzungsversion wird vorgeschlagen. *Inge Hofmann*

77739 TAWFIK, Sayed, Eine Ritualszene aus Nefertitis "pillared courtyard" in Karnak, *GM* Heft 25 (1977), 81-88, with 2 ill. and 2 fig. on 3 pl.

Im Rahmen des "Akhenaten Temple Project" ist es gelungen, 11 Pfeiler von Nefertitis sog. "pillared courtyard" zusammenzusetzen. Sämtliche Blöcke zeigen ausnahmslos nur Abbildungen von Nefertiti hauptsächlich mit ihrer ältesten Tochter Meret-Aton. Jeder der Pfeiler hat vier dekorierte Seiten; jeweils drei davon zeigen Nefertiti in einer Einzelszene in Großformat unter der Sonnenscheibe, während sie auf der vierten in vier verschiedenen Ritualszenen erscheint. Verfasser bespricht die obere Hälfte einer solchen Opferszene aus einer der vierteiligen Darstellungsfolgen, in denen das Opferritual nur von Nefertiti vollzogen wird. *Inge Hofmann*

77740   THÉODORIDÈS, Aristide, L'art de trouver une fonction après la vieillesse, *Annuaire de l'Institut de Philologie et d'Histoire Orientales et Slaves*, Bruxelles 21 (1977), 67-81.

The author studies the meaning of the puzzling expression *m-ḫt i3wt* in the phrase *ir n.k t3y i3t sr(t) (k3) gm.k sw m-ḫt i3wt* in P. Anastasi III, 3,11 (= P. Anastasi V, 8,3-4), which text belongs to the genre of the Satire of Professions. First he argues that the ultimate purpose of a scribal career is to become a *sr,* a high official who is appointed by the king, and that such a position is necessary to obtain a burial in the necropolis of the officials on state expenses. This explains the expression "after old age" as meaning "in death". If *n.k.* is taken not as dativus ethicus, but as one of advantage, the phrase can best be translated: "Make favourable this task of high official, in order that you find its effects even after old age (= in death)." *L.Z.*

77741   THÉODORIDÈS, Aristide, La propriété et ses démembrements en droit pharaonique, *Revue internationale des droits de l'antiquité*, Bruxelles, 3e série, 24 (1977), 21-64.

In this article the author argues that in ancient Egyp there has existed the concept propriety with its attributes "usus", "fructus" and "abusus". He pays particular attention to the dissolution of proprieties, studying a large number of juridical texts from various periods, i.a the arrangements of Kaemnefert (Urk. I, 11-15) and Nikaᶜankh (Urk. I, 162), Pap. Kahun I.1, the contracts of Hapidjefa, and especially Pap. Berlin 9010, to which the second part of the article is devoted. For this text he refutes some of the conclusions drawn by Karin Gödecken in our number 76291.

77742   THÉODORIDÈS, Aristide, La XXXIe Session de la Société internationale Fernand De Visscher pour l'histoire des droits de l'antiquité. Trieste, 22-25 septembre 1976, *Revue internationale des droits de l'antiquité,* Bruxelles, 3e série, 24 (1977), 489-511.

Pour une résumée de la communication d'A. Théodoridès, Les droit réels dans l'Égypte pharaonique, voir p. 506-507. Voir aussi notre no précédent. *L.Z*

77743 THISSEN, H.-J., Zur Familie des Strategen Monkores, *Zeitschri für Papyrologie und Epigraphik,* Bonn 27 (1977), 181-191.

The author discusses 18 documents concerning a family of nom governors ($p3$-$srtyqws$ = mr $mš^c$/wr $^c3$ n $mš^c$) in the 1st century B.C among the members of which the most prominent names are Pamonthes ($P3$-$mnty$), Plenis ($P3$-lyn), Monkores (Mn-$k\hat{\imath}$-r^c) an Kalasiris (Gl-$šr$). *L.Z*

THISSEN, Heinz-Josef, see also our number 77633.

THOMAS, Nicholas, see our number 77025.

77744 THOMPSON, Thomas L., The Historicity of the Patriarcha Narratives: The Quest for the Historical Abraham, *Dissertatio Abstracts International,* Ann Arbor, Mich. 37, No. 9 (March 1977 5897/8-A.

Abstract of a thesis Temple University, 1976. Compare our numbe 74735.

77745 THOMPSON, Thomas L., and Dorothy IRVIN, The Joseph an Moses Narratives, *in: Israelite and Judaean History.* Edited by Joh H. Hayes and J. Maxwell Miller, London, SCM Press Ltd, [1977 (series: The Old Testament Library), 159-212.

The above title is that of the third chapter in this book on Israelit history. From §1, on the historical reconstruction of the Joseph an Moses narratives, written by T.L. Thompson, we mention the titles o the sections relevant to our field: the dating of the sojourn and th Exodus; the Egyptian background of the narratives; Semites in Egyp the Shashu and the Aramàean migration. In §3, on the narratives i the broader context of ancient Near Eastern narrative, by D. Irvir there are some references to literary motifs also occurring in Egyptia literature.

As everywhere in the book the paragraphs are preceded by a basi bibliography on the subject.

Compare our number 77534. *L.Z*

77746 TITLBACHOVÁ, Svatava and Zdeněk TITLBACH, Hair o Egyptian Mummies (= Eugen STROUHAL, Multidisciplinar

Research on Egyptian Mummies in Czechoslovakia, V), *ZÄS* 104 (1977), 79-85, with 6 ill. and 1 table.

A microscopic and macroscopic examination of fourteen samples. A negroid admixture was observed in three cases. *M. Heerma van Voss*

TOBOLA, Karel, see our number 77733.

77747 TÖRÖK, László, Inquiries into the Administration of Meroitic Nubia: I-II, *Orientalia* 46 (1977), 34-50.

Die vorliegende Untersuchung beschäftigt sich mit den Informationen, die wir hinsichtlich der Amtsfunktionen eines *pešto, rpʿi* und *pelmoš* haben. Amtssitz des *pešto*, des Vizekönigs für Nubien, war Faras. In einem zweiten Abschnitt wird die Reorganisation am Ende des 3. nachchristlichen Jahrhunderts dargestellt und die Gestalt des Königs Yesboḫeamani hervorgehoben, da er die meroitische Hegemonie bis Philae ausgedehnt habe.

Inge Hofmann

77748 TÖRÖK, László, Some Comments on the Social Position and Hierarchy of the Priests on Karanog Inscriptions, *in: Ägypten und Kusch*, 401-420, with 7 tables.

Anhand der Karanog-Inschriften wird versucht, die soziale Stellung und Hierarchie der Priester aufzuzeigen. Dazu bieten drei Quellen das Material: 1. die Familien der *pešto*-Prinzen, die Priester unter ihren Mitgliedern haben, 2. Priesterfamilien, die auch Laien-Mitglieder haben, 3. Familien mit ausschließlich priesterlichem Charakter. Abschließend wird ein *cursus honorum* der Priesterhierarchie bei den drei Hauptkulten in Karanog (bei Mash, Amanap und Amon) aufgestellt.

Inge Hofmann

TORT, Patrick, see our number 77782.

77749 TÓTH, I., Die ägyptischen theophoren Personennamen in Pannonien, *Studia aegyptiaca* 3 (1977), 149-159, with 3 tables.

Discussion of Egyptian theophorous personal names occurring in inscriptions from Pannonia.

77750 TÓTH, I., Ein "Viergötterstein" mit ägyptischen Göttern aus Savaria (ad CIL III 10908 = SIRIS 662), *Studia aegyptiaca* 3 (1977), 131-148, with 3 ill. and 1 fig.

On a marble basis found in Savaria an inscription mentions two Isis priests, while on the sides the figures of Osiris (-Serapis?), Horus and Anubis are represented; the Isis figure on the top is broken off. The author discusses the original dimensions of the monument and mentions another inscription of two Isis priests, this time a father and a son. In this context he studies the occurrence of family relations among the Isis priests.

TRAUTMANN, Jürgen, see our number 77009.

77751 [Treasures of Tutankhamon] = *Bulletin of the Metropolitan Museum of Art*, New York 34, No. 3 (Winter 1976/1977), with 20 colour ill. and 52 ill.

In the preface the director of the Metropolitan Museum of Art Thomas Hoving explains that this issue of the bulletin is completely devoted to the exhiibition Treasures of Tutankhamun and is drawn from the exhibition catalogue and I.E.S. Edwards, Tutankhamun: His Tomb and Its Treasures (our number 76223), from which also the interpretative captions were taken. *L.Z.*

77752 TRIGGER, Bruce G., The Classification of Meroitic: Geographical Considerations, *in: Ägypten und Kusch,* 421-435, with 1 fig. and 2 maps.

Nach einem kurzen Abriß über den Stand der Forschungsgeschichte folgt der Versuch einer Klassifizierung des Meroitischen, der davon ausgeht, welche Informationen hinsichtlich der Stellung dieser Sprache nur aufgrund geographischer Angaben erhältlich sind. In absteigender Ordnung der Wahrscheinlichkeit bietet sich folgendes Bild: 1. ostsudanisch — dann wäre das Meroitische oder eine nubische Sprache der nördlichste Vertreter dieser Gruppe; 2. nilo-saharanisch als allgemeinere Alternative zu ostsudanisch — dann wäre das Meroitische am nächsten verwandt mit Berta, Kunama oder Koman; 3. afro-asiatisch, am wahrscheinlichsten kuschitisch oder Omoto — aus geographischen Gründen kann diese Möglichkeit nicht ausgeschieden werden; 4. Kordofan-Sprachen — sie werden in der Nachbarschaft des meroitichen Kernlandes gesprochen und können früher weiter verbreitet gewesen sein; 5. eine Sprache, die keiner der jetzt in diesem Gebiet gesprochenen Sprachen verwandt ist. Danach würde das Meroitische in dieselbe Kategorie der rätselhaften alten Sprachen fallen, zu der das Sumerische, Etruskische und Baskische zählt. *Inge Hofmann*

TRIGGER, Bruce G., see also our number 77318.

TURNER, E.G., see our number 77711.

77753 TUTUNDŽIĆ, Sava P., Ein Beitrag zur Typologie der von den Beziehungen mit Palästina abhängigen Tongefässe aus Maadi, Зборник Филозофског Факултета, Београд 13,1 (1976), 1977, 9-15, with 2 pl.

Dealing with a particular type of late prehistoric vessels found at Ma^{c}âdi the author points out that they are of a type that belongs to the Ghassul IV period. Similar vessels occur in the Shephelah and the N. Negev. They demonstrate connections between this area and Ma^{c}âdi in the proto-urban period.

URBANEC, Zdeněk, see our number 77733.

77754 VALBELLE, Dominique, Catalogue des poids à inscriptions hiératiques de Deir el-Médineh. Nos 5001-5423. Incluant un manuscrit de Jaroslav Černy. Préface de G. Posener, [Le Caire], Publications de l'Institut français d'Archéologie orientale, [1977] (24.7 × 32 cm; [X +]138 p., frontispiece, 2 fig., 6 tables, 47 + 43 pl.) = Documents de fouilles, 16.

In the preface Posener describes how the publication of weights from Deir el-Medîna has grown out of a manuscript of Černy. While this ms. contained only 137 transcriptions and facsimiles (here printed with Černy's initials), the material has been enlarged by Mme Valbelle to 424 numbers.

The weights are mostly preserved in the French Institute in Cairo, but some are now in other collections (see p. 133). They consist of rough pieces of stone of various kinds, even including bits of pottery, some retouched in order to give them a fixed weight, and inscribed with a short text. From these texts it appears that they were used either as a substitute for a tool issued to a workman (then the stone was approximately of the same weight as the tool), or as receipts or mementos (in that case there is not necessarily any connection with the weight of the stone). In both instances they are only used once, unless adapted and re-inscribed for a second use. The weights for weighing fish, also inscribed, are not included in this volume.

In the introduction the author discusses in detail the use of the objects and their texts, dealing with various words indicating i.a. tools, vessels, fish, etc.; their dates (the entire Ramesside Period), and their writing. At the end descriptions and hieroglyphic transcriptions of 14 weights which had already been published elsewhere.

In the catalogue itself the objects are arranged according to a keyword in the texts. Each of them is briefly but carefully described, with mention of all data, according to the system usual in the series. Of all texts is given a transcription and (except for some which contain only the word *dbn* plus a number) a facsimile.

On p. 127 - 133 indexes and a concordance between the numbers of the present volume and those given by Černý, followed by a list of numbers of objects not preserved in the French Institute.

77755 VALBELLE, Dominique, Remarques sur les textes néo-égyptiens non littéraires (§6 - 10), *BIFAO* 77 (1977), 129 - 136.

Sequel to our number 76790.

The author discusses the formulae *nty m h3y r-^{c}* X and *nty (m) ts r-^{c}* X, of which the use of *r-^{c}* X alone is an abbreviation. They occur on weights and ostraca. The translation may be "ce qui revient à X", "ce qui a été attribué à X", *r-^{c}* alone meaning "destiné à".

The second subject of the article is the diacritical mark 𓏞 , occurring frequently in working-lists and indicating inactivity. The author concludes that in other texts it does not mean "corrected", as Gardiner has suggested, but rather "cancelled".

The last section deals with the substitution of the sign 𓇑 by 𓆛 in the word *wh^c*, "fisherman", occurring in four ostraca, which according to Mme Valbelle may be an error of the same scribe.

77756 VALLOGGIA, Michel, Un groupe inédit du Moyen Empire, *BIFAO* 77 (1977), 137 - 144, with 2 pl.

Publication of a granite group statuette (height 14.5 cm) of two standing men, at present in a private collection in Geneva. The author describes the piece, presents a facsimile of the texts with translation and comments, and discusses its style, date and provenance.

The piece is damaged, the faces and the lower left hand corner being lost. The men represented are called *Mgg* and *ʿw-n-ỉb*. On account of its style and the formulae in the texts the statuette is dated to the reign of Sesostris I. It may originally have come from Abydos.

77757 VANDERSLEYEN, C., Une stèle de l'an 18 d'Amosis à Hanovre, *CdE* LII, No. 104 (1977), 223-244, with 1 ill.

L'auteur édite et commente une stèle sur laquelle sont représentés Amosis et la princesse Satamon, datée de l'an 18 de ce roi. Après une série de considérations tendant à prouver l'authenticité du document, il concentre son attention sur la personne de la princesse nommée derrière le roi et résume son argumentation dans un tableau généalogique de la famille royale issue de la XVIIe dynastie.

Ph.Derchain

VEIS, Arthur, see our number 77728.

77758 te VELDE, H., Seth, God of Confusion. A Study of his Role in Egyptian Mythology and Religion. Reprint with some corrections, Leiden, E.J. Brill, 1977 (15.8 × 24.4 cm; XIII + 168 p., frontispiece, 12 pl.) = Probleme der Ägyptologie herausgegeben von Wolfgang Helck, 6.

Reprint with some corrections of our number 67575.
The author has added a preface to the second edition, in which he lists reviews and two review articles, as well as other works of importance for the present book and the study of the god Seth. *L.Z.*

77759 te VELDE, H., The Theme of the Separation of Heaven and Earth in Egyptian Mythology, *Studia aegyptiaca* 3 (1977), 161 - 170, with 1 fig.

The theme of the separation of heaven and earth occurs i.a. in solar hymns and magical texts. The separation is usually conceived to be a blessing, but there is also evidence of a negative view. The author discusses in this context the Geb and Nut representations, pointing out that Geb (the earth) in Egypt is male because there it is not the rain that causes fertility. He mentions variants of this representation with Shu lifting the sky; they all appear to date from the XXIst Dynasty or later and to occur in a funerary context, that is, connected with human rebirth.
The author prepares a monograph to the subject.

77760 VERCOUTTER, Jean, Les poids de Mirgissa et le "standard-cuivre" au Moyen Empire, *in: Ägypten und Kusch,* 437-445, with 3 tables and 2 pl.

Im Verlauf der Ausgrabungen im Innern des oberen Forts von Mirgissa wurden drei beschriebene ägyptische Gewichtsteine gefunden: die Standardeinheit für Gold beträgt 12,2 g. Das entspricht der üblichen Goldeinheit, die mehr oder weniger genau 13 g entspricht. Die Standardeinheit für Kupfer beträgt dagegen 27,5 g, also das Doppelte der Goldeinheit. Diese Standardeinheit entspricht auch den Funden aus Ägypten sowie den Einheiten, die in Werkzeugen angegeben sind. *Inge Hofmann*

77761 VERCOUTTER, Jean, Les travaux de l'Institut français d'Archéologie orientale en 1976-1977, *BIFAO* 77 (1977), 271 - 286, with 8 pl.

Sequel to our number 76687 by the new director of the French Institute.
After a sketch of the work of Serge Sauneron for the Institute the author presents the usual survey of the activities. Four pages (275 - 278)

are devoted to the first campaign in Balât (el-Dakhleh Oasis) in 1977, one to the continued work in Karnak N. There is a list of recent publications of the Institute and another of its members. On p. 285 one finds mentioned the tragic death of Michel Muszynski.

VERCOUTTER, Jean, see also our numbers 77134 and 77453.

77762   VERGOTE, J., La vocalisation des formes verbales en égyptien. Des matériaux nouveaux?, *BiOr* 34 (1977), 135 - 139.

A review article of our number 76612.

VERMASEREN, Maarten J., see our number 77400.

77763   VERMEERSCH, P.M., E. PAULISSEN, G. GIJSELINGS, Prospection préhistorique entre Asyut et Nag' Hammadi (Egypte), *Bulletin de la Société Royale Belge d'Anthropologie et de Préhistoire,* Bruxelles 88 (1977), 117 - 124, with 1 map and 2 fig.

Brief report on a survey of Prehistorical sites on the left bank between Asyût and Nagᶜ Hammadi. One site from the Predynastic Period was found; none from the Final and Upper Palaeolithic Age, but several from the Middle and Lower Palaeolithic Age.

77764   VERNER, Miroslav, Abusir '76, *Nový Orient,* Praha 32, No. 5, (1977), 152 - 154, with 2 pl. and 1 ill.

"Abusir, 1976".

77765   VERNUS, Pascal, L'écriture de l'Égypte ancienne, *in: L'espace et la lettre.* Écritures. Typographies, Paris, Union générale d'éditions, 1977 (= Cahiers Jussieu, No. 3), 61 - 77, with 1 ill. and 10 fig.

Description of the Egyptian script, dealing i.a. with the function of the signs, their direction, the system of writing, playful writings, etc.

77766   VERNUS, Pascal, Les Hurrites dans les sources égyptiennes, *in: Problèmes concernant les Hurrites,* Paris, Centre National de la Recherche Scientifique, 1977 (= Publications de l'URA, 8), 41 - 49.

Rejecting the arguments of Helck for an equalisation of the Hyksos and the Hurrites the author states that the latter ($\underline{H}3rw$ or $\underline{H}uru$) occur in Egyptian sources from Tuthmosis III to the Amarna Period, when the word became used as a designation for the Syro-Palestinian region in general, instead of the older $R\underline{t}nw$. The mention of $\underline{H}uru$ and Maryannu in several places in Palestine during the first half of the XVIIIth Dynasty prove that their area reached fairly wide to the south. Except for some names (cfr *ZÄS* 38 [1900], 16-18) they may have brought to Egypt the composite bow and the cuirass (*tryn*) but these may also have come like the chariot through the medium of the Semites. Whether the representations of the princes of Mitanni, Tunip and Kadesh show the true physical type of the Hurrites is uncertain.

77767   VERNUS, Pascal, Le mot "*št3w*", "branchages, bosquets, bois", *RdE* 29 (1977), 179-193.

Le mot *št3w* (*Wb*.4,555,12) apparaît dans plus de 20 contextes répartis du Moyen Empire à l'époque byzantine, desquels l'auteur à induit les sens indiqués dans le titre de l'article.   *Ph. Derchain*

77768   VILA, André, avec la collaboration de Francis GEUS, Yves LABRE†, Jacques REINOLD, Yussef et Sid Ahmed Abd el Magid KAMIR, Alain FOUQUET, René FILLIOL et François RODRIGUEZ, La prospection archéologique de la Vallée du Nil, au sud de la Cataracte de Dal (Nubie Soudanaise). Fascicule 5. Les districts de Ginis, Est et Ouest, Paris, Centre National de la Recherche Scientifique, 1977 (21 × 27 cm; 166 p., 6 maps, 83 fig., ill. and plans); at head of title: Section française de Recherches Archéologiques/Sudan Antiquities Service. Khartoum National Museum; rev. *Comptes rendus de l'Académie des Inscriptions et Belles-Lettres,* 1978, 177 - 178 (Jean Leclant); *Oriens Antiquus* 18 (1979), 82-83 (Sergio Donadoni).

Sequel to our number 76808.

Following the same scheme as the preceding volumes the present fascicle deals with a large number of sites in the District of Ginis, on both riverbanks. They cover all cultural phases, from the Palaeolithic to the post-Christian (see the index on p. 17-19). To most of them one to three or four pages are devoted, but the N.K. cave at Kashasha with its many finds (scarabs, amulets, shawabtis, vessels) take p. 149 - 160. The fascicle is again well illustrated by plans, drawings and photographs. For photographs of a choice of the pottery from Ginis, see p. 164 - 166.

77769   VILA, André, avec la collaboration de Yves LABRE† et Sid Ahmed Abd el Magid KAMIR, Alain FOUQUET, René FILLIOL et François RODRIGUEZ, La prospection archéologique de la Vallée du Nil, au sud de la Cataracte de Dal (Nubie Soudanaise). Fascicule 6. Le district d'Attab, Est et Ouest, Paris, Centre National de la Recherche Scientifique, 1977 (21 × 27 cm; 97 p., 5 maps, 52 fig., ill. and plans); at head of title: Section française de Recherches Archéologiques/Sudan Antiquities Service. Khartoum National Museum; rev.

Comptes rendus de l'Académie des Inscriptions et Belles Lettres, 1978, 177-178 (Jean Leclant); *Oriens Antiquus* 18 (1979), 82-83 (Sergio Donadoni).

Sequel to our preceding number.

Of the many sites in Attab West and East and on the Island of Gergetti here described no one is dated to the Meroitic or X-Group Period, but several to the Kerma culture and the Pharaonic and Christian Periods. From the N.K. date a rectangular building (p. 88-89) and a complex of basins and canals (93-96), both on the W. bank near Foshu.

77770 VILA, André, avec la collaboration de Alain FOUQUET, René FILLIOL, François RODRIGUEZ et Sid Ahmed Abd el Magid KAMIR, La prospection archéologique de la Vallée du Nil, au sud de la Cataracte de Dal (Nubie Soudanaise). Fascicule 7. Le district de Amara Ouest, Paris, Centre National de la Recherche Scientifique, 1977 (21 × 27 cm; 129 p., 5 maps [1 folding], 64 ill., fig. and plans); at head of title: Section française de Recherches Archéologiques/Sudan Antiquities Service. Khartoum National Museum; rev. *Comptes rendus de l'Académie des Inscriptions et Belles-Lettres,* 1978, 177-178 (Jean Leclant); *Oriens Antiquus* 18 (1979), 82-83 (Sergio Donadoni).

Sequel to our preceding number.

Once more among the sites of the area here studied several date from the Kerma and the N.K. Periods, while the temple from the latter is already known for a long time (see *Porter-Moss* VII, 157 - 164). A lintel with a text mentioning Hekanakht has been found (p. 27). Several other sites, cemeteries and villages, have been mentioned in the literature (see, e.g., Fairman, *JEA* 24 [1938], 151 - 156; *JEA* 25 [1939], 139 - 144).

77771 VILA, André, avec la collaboration de Yves LABRE †, Sid Ahmed Abd el Magid KAMIR, Alain FOUQUET, René FILLIOL et François RODRIGUEZ, La prospection archéologique de la Vallée du Nil, au sud de la Cataracte de Dal (Nubie Soudanaise). Fascicule 8. Le district d'Amara Est, Paris, Centre National de la Recherche Scientifique, 1977 (21 × 27 cm; 130 p., 5 maps, 65 ill., fig. and plans); at head of title: Section française de Recherches Archéologiques/Sudan Antiquities Service. Khartoum National Museum; rev. *Comptes rendus de l'Académie des Inscriptions et Belles-Lettres,* 1978, 177-178 (Jean Leclant); *Oriens Antiquus* 18 (1979), 82-83 (Sergio Donadoni).

Sequel to our preceding number.

The fascicle describes and depicts some inscriptions in hieroglyphs and in Meroitic writing, found in the neighbourhood of the Meroitic temple complex known for a long time (described on p. 28-49). The area contained important cemeteries and single tombs from Pharaonic and Meroitic times, but also traces from all other periods.

77772 VILÍMKOVÁ, M., Starověký Egypt, [Praha], Mladá Fronta, [1977] (15.7 × 24.3 cm; 341 p., 1 map, 293 ill. and fig., 41 colour ill.); series: Velké Epochy Kultury.

"Das alte Ägypten".

Eine allgemeinverständliche, übersichtliche Publikation, die den Leser mit der altägyptischen Zivilisation und Kultur bekanntmacht. Die einzelnen Kapitel lauten: Die Geburt einer Kultur; Die drei Reiche; Ägyptischer Staat und Gesellschaft; Der Alltag; Das Privatleben; Religion; Das Reich der Toten; Sprache, Schrift und Literatur; Die Anfänge von Wissenschaft und Technik; Bie bildende Kunst. Im Anhang des Buches finden sich eine Zeittafel, ein Literaturverzeichnis, ein Verzeichnis der Gottheiten, und besonders 334 Schwarzweiss- und Farbfotos, Zeichnungen und Rekonstruktionen. *Břetislav Vachala*

77773 VITTMANN, G., [Bibliographie]. Ägypten, *AfO* 25 (1974/77), 507-538.

A systematically arranged bibliography on Egyptological literature from the years 1973-1976, subdivided into the following headings: bibliographies; history of science, reports, methods; lexicon; field research, topography; museums and related subjects; history and chronology; religion; law and society; language and writing, subdivided into 1. grammar, writings and linguistics, 2. philology 3. Demotic; and lastly general works, cultural influence and legacy, and cultural history. *L.Z.*

77774 VITTMANN, Günther, Neues zu Pabasa, Obermajordomus der Nitokris, *SAK* 5 (1977), 245-264.

The author discusses the genealogy and the titles and functions of Pbasa on account of the evidence from his tomb, comparing them with those of other similar functionaries. He particularly deals with Pbasa's function of mayor of Thebes. At the end a revised list of these officials during the XXVth and XXVIth Dynasties (cfr Assmann, Das Grab der Basa = our number 73049).

77775 VITTMANN, Günther, Zu den "Schönen Namen" in der Spätzeit, *GM* Heft 23 (1977), 71-73.

Zu den von de Meulenaere (vgl. unsere Nummer 66418) zusammengestellten Trägern eines "Schönen Namens" aus der Spätzeit kommen inzwischen drei weitere Belege: 1. Uschebti Zagreb 671, gehörig dem *jmj-r št-škb P3-n-Pth-mn*(?) mit "Schönem Namen" *W3h-jb-R^c-s3-Nt*; 2. Statuette Kairo JE 37885, gehörig dem *Hrj* mit "Schönem Namen" *Hr-s3-3st*; 3. kleines Schistfragment im Louvre, ohne Nummer (ex-Guimet 16956), das den *Ibj* nennt, mit "Schönem Namen" (*W3h-jb-R^c*)-*s3-Nt*. Abschließend werden einige Korrekturen und Ergänzungen zu der erwähten Arbeit gebracht.

Inge Hofmann

77776   VITTMANN, Günther, Zum Verständnis der Weihformel *irjnf m mnwf*, *WZKM* 69 (1977), 21-32.

The author reexamines the various opinions on the dedicatory formula *ir.n.f m mnw.f n it.f* X — *irt* (and variants) *n.f* Y. He argues that *ir.n.f* normally has the intransitive meaning "to act", but has in some cases to be translated transitively, and he produces evidence that the word *mnw(w)* refers not to the actual object, but rather to the action of its erection, or even to an enduring action by which the king fulfils his royal duty for the god.   *L.Z.*

VOS, René L., see our number 77597.

77777   VYCICHL, Werner, Heliodors *Aithiopika* und die Volksstämme des Reiches Meroë, *in: Ägypten und Kusch*, 447-458.

Die Aithiopika des Heliodor wird als Fundgrube von Nachrichten über die religiösen Verhältnisse des meroitischen Reiches betrachtet, deren Zuverlässigkeit jedoch nicht nachgeprüft werden kann. Die Onomastik förderte keinen einzigen wirklich meroitischen Namen zutage. Bei den Angaben über die Volksstämme Meroes und ihre Geschenke zeigte es sich, daß keine Nachricht aus einer primären Quelle stammt. Es empfiehlt sich, die Angaben Heliodors über die meroitische Religion mit gebührender Vorsicht zu benützen und den Romanschriftsteller nicht als Autorität für meroitische Sitten und Gebräuche zu zitieren.   *Inge Hofmann*

77778   VYCICHL, Werner, Das Kollektivum des ägyptischen Nomens, *Altorientalische Forschungen*, Berlin 5 (1977), 33-35.

The author discusses the type of collective substantive with feminine ending, such as *rmtt*, "people" and *hrdt*, "children", the ending of which, unlike the simple feminine, is -*y.t*, either with or without stress.

L.Z.

77779 VYCICHL, Werner, Nisba-Formen des Typs *hatre, kame, sabe* im Ägyptisch-Koptischen, *Le Muséon*, Louvain 90 (1977), 435-438.

The author argues that, apart from the nisbe-formations having an unstressed -*īy*-ending in Egyptian, there existed also two other formations with stressed ending, which resulted in Coptic in an ending on -ⲁⲓ resp. -ⲉ and which were a general, and not a dialectical phenomenon in ancient Egyptian. *L.Z.*

WAHBA, Gamal, see our number 77225.

77780 van de WALLE, B., Deux monuments memphites au nom de Hordjedef Iteti, *JNES* 36 (1977), 17-24, with 2 ill.

The writer discusses two monuments belonging to this prince, the first a false foor found by Reisner near the tomb of Khufu's son at Gîza (G 7240), and now in the Boston Museum (No. 29-2-37). The inscription on this unusually invokes Anubis and Osiris. The other is a limestone offering table in the Rosicrucian Museum, San Jose, California (RC. 1684), giving some titles of the deceased. *E. Uphill*

77781 WÅNGSTEDT, Sten V., Demotische Ostraka: Varia I, *Orientalia Suecana*, Stockholm 25-26 (1976-1977), 5-41, with 12 ill. and 10 fig.

Publication of 20 Demotic ostraca preserved in various collections, about half of them from Thebes, the others from various sites. They date from the 3rd century B.C. to A.D. 122 and bear accounts and lists, the last one the drawing of a soldier accompanied by a few hardly legible words.
Each is given in transliteration and translation with comments, to which is added a photograph or a facsimile, in two instances both.

77782 WARBURTON, William, Essai sur les hiéroglyphes des égyptiens. Où l'on voit l'origine et le progrès du langage et de l'écriture, l'antiquité des sciences en Égypte, et l'origine du culte des animaux. Traduit par Léonard des Malpeines. Édition et notes par Patrick Tort précédé de Scribble (pouvoir/écrire) par Jacques Derrida et de transfigurations (archéologie du symbolique) par Patrick Tort, [Paris], Aubier Flammarion, [1977] (13.7 × 22.2 cm; 411 p., 13 fig.) = Collection Palimpseste dirigée par Charles Porset.

The main part of the book consists of Warburton's book "Essai sur les hiéroglyphes des égyptiens", translated in 1744 into French. *L.Z.*

77783 WARD, William A., Lexicographical Miscellanies, *SAK* 5 (1977), 265-292.

These lexicographical notes deal with the following words and phrases: *b3 ỉt(y) rpyt*, an epithet of Osiris in which *rpyt* means "She of the palanquin"; *wdḥ(?) nb*, "caster of gold"; *b3t/b3yt*, "pit, hiding place, treasure chest"; *bʿbʿ*, "bathe in liquid"; *br n ỉnr*, "field of stone = necropolis"; *pns*, "turn around" the head of an animal, and *pnś*, "turn up" earth, and related nouns; the etymology of *mhwt*, "words, speech"; the origin of *rwh*, "evening"; an additional note to *rḥb*, "flagon, jar" (see our number 61724, p. 40); another example of *šnʿ*, "underworld, tomb" (cfr our number 64423); *št*, "axe- or knife-handle".

77784 WARD, William A., Neferḥotep and his Friends. A Glimpse at the Lives of Ordinary Men, *JEA* 63 (1977), 63-66, with 1 pl.

The stela Leiden Museum V95 was first published by Steindorff who dismissed the last line of text as incomprehensible. The writer points out that this is in fact the most important part of the inscription, 'Alas! Have mercy on him!' being the touching plea of an old friend Nebsumenu, a simple carrier of bricks. *E. Uphill*

77785 WARD, William A., Scarabs of "Nubkheperra". A Note on the Interpretation of Design, *Berytus*, Beirut 25 (1977), 163-172, with 3 fig.

Proceeding from the principle that scarab designs consist of horizontal groups of signs rather than vertical columns, the author illustrates the principle by 44 examples of those scarabs thought to bear the name Nub-kheper-ra, the prenomen of Inyotef V of the XVIIth Dynasty. The author demonstrates that very few of the scarab designs can be said to include the royal name Nub-kheper-ra (the kheper-nub spellings can hardly be abbreviations!) and that most of the rest consists of horizontally grouped design scarabs, the central column of which happens by chance to contain the three hieroglyphs which make up the name Nub-kheper-ra. *L.Z.*

77786 WARTKE, Ralf, Zum Alabaster-Altar des Königs Sahu-Rē, *ZÄS* 104 (1977), 145-156, with 5 fig. and 3 pl. (2 folding).

Neuveröffentlichung-Rekonstruktion des Altares aus dem Säulenhof des Totentempels.

Borchardt bildete in 1910 56 Fragmente ab. Neulich sind 42 neue Splitter aus dem Magazinbeständen dazu gekommen; die Inventarnummer aller Stücke ist (Berlin) 24299. Von den 98 Teilen gehören 12

zum Alabasteraltar aus dem "Allerheiligsten": Abb. 5.
Dank der Neuanordnung sind für alle vier Seiten einige Darstellungen und das Bewegungsschema der Opferzüge gesichert. Die Gabenbringer der Ost- und der Westseite schreiten auf die "Vereinigung der Beiden Länder", in der Mitte der Seite abgebildet, zu. Unter den Opferträgern trifft man "Nilgötter" und Gauen an. Die grösste erhaltene Höhe des Altares beträgt 44 cm, die Seitenlänge circa 105 cm.
M. Heerma van Voss

77787 WAUGH, Daniel Clarke, *Azbuka znakami lits:* Egyptian Hieroglyphs in the Privy Chancellery Archive, *Oxford Slavonic Papers,* Oxford NS 10 (1977), 46-50, with 4 pl.

The author traces the hieroglyphic signs in a manuscript from the private archive of Tsar Alexis Michailovich (reign from 1645-1676) as originating from the Theodosian obelisk at Istanbul and as closely resembling its depiction in A. Kircher's Oedipus Aegyptiacus. At the end the author discusses how they came to Moscow and how they were understood there. *L.Z.*

WEIGAND, Raymond J., see our number 77728.

77788 WEINBERG, Saul S., World Archaeology in Mid-Missouri, *Archaeology* 30 (1977), 54-55, with 5 ill.

Amongst others the author shortly describes the Egyptian pieces in the Museum of Art and Archaeology, University of Missouri — Columbia. Apart from four pieces of sculpture presented by Petrie and a few small pots and pot-sherds, the collection has an O.K. statue of the count and overseer of priests Idi, an inscribed wooden sarcophagus of the F.I.P., a bronze Saite soul boat, a Late Period agate bowl, and a well-preserved mummy shroud of about A.D. 150.
L.Z.

77789 WEINFELD, Moshe, Ancient Near Eastern Patterns in Prophetic Literature, *Vetus Testamentum,* Leiden 27 (1977), 178-195.

Studying the problem of morality versus cult in Hebrew prophetic literature, the author also deals with the problem in Egyptian literature, particularly wisdom literature: in the "Instruction for Merikare" the issue is righteousness versus sacrifice, whereas in the "Shipwrecked Sailor" it is praise versus sacrifice. *L.Z.*

77790 WEINFELD, Moshe, Judge and Officer in Ancient Israel and in the Ancient Near East, *Israel Oriental Studies,* Tel-Aviv 7 (1977), 65-68.

In this discussion of the role of judges and officers in the entire ancient Near East, Egypt is also referred to in section 5 on instructions for the judges. The author quotes from the Restauration Stela of Horemheb and the Installation of the Vizier, which documents bear similarities to Biblical passages. Section 7 on the assistants of the judges refers to Egyptian pictorial material and Deir el-Medîna. *L.Z.*

77791 WEIPPERT, Manfred, Kanaanäische "Gravidenflaschen". Zur Geschichte einer ägyptischen Gefässgattung in der asiatischen Provinz, *Zeitschrift des Deutschen Palästina-Vereins,* Wiesbaden 93 (1977), 268-282, with 3 fig. and 2 pl.

The so-called provincial pregnancy bottle from Beth-Shan (see the catalogue in our number 70098), is most probably not of Egyptian origin, but has rather to be connected with gynaikomorphic pottery vessels in Canaan, of which the author draws up a list. He tries to determine the relation with the Egyptian pregnancy bottles and amply discusses their possible meaning in the Asiatic context. *L.Z.*

WENDORF, Fred, see our numbers 77318 and 77681.

77792 WENIG, Steffen, Meisterwerke der Amarnakunst, Leipzig, Insel-Verlag, 1977 (11.7 × 18.4 cm; 64 p., 40 pl. [5 in colour]) = Insel-Bücherei Nr. 990.

In this booklet on masterpieces of the Amarna art, mainly from the Berlin collections, the plates are presented first, after which the author gives a general introduction to the subject and short descriptions and data of the objects. *L.Z.*

77793 WENIG, Steffen, Die meroitische Königin Amanitore. Barkenuntersatz aus Wad Ban Naqa (Sudan), um 20 u. Z., Berlin 7261, *Neue Museumskunde,* Berlin 20 (1977), 82-83, with 1 pl. and summaries in German, Russian, English and French.

Anhand des Barkenuntersatzes Berlin 7261, der aus dem Isis-Tempel von Wad ban Naga' stammt und 1845 durch Richard Lepsius an das Berliner Ägyptische Museum gelangte und der zu den Hauptwerken der an meroitischen Altertümern reichen Berliner Sammlung gerechnet wird, gibt Verfasser einen kurzen Abriß der meroitischen Geschichte und Kunstentwicklung. Besonders verwiesen wird darauf, daß der Barkenuntersatz den Namen des Königs Natakamani und der Königin Amanitore in ägyptischen und meroitischen Hieroglyphen enthält und daß diese "Bilingue" den Ausgangspunkt für die Entzifferung der meroitischen Schrift bildete. *Inge Hofmann*

77794 WENIG, Steffen, Der meroitische Tempel von Amara, *in: Ägypten und Kusch*, 459-475, with 6 fig. and 9 ill. on 10 pl., 4 plans and 6 fig.

Bei dem auf dem Ostufer des Nil gelegenen Tempel von Amâra handelt es sich um ein Heiligtum, das von Natakamani erbaut wurde und von dem sich bis in das 19. Jahrhundert sechs Säulen sowie ein Raum mit mindestens zwei Säulen erhalten hatten. Nach einer Darlegung des Quellenmaterials folgt anhand der Berichte und erhaltenen Zeichnungen eine Baubeschreibung und ein Aufstellungs- und Dekorationsschema der Säulen. Auf allen Säulen findet sich die Einteilung der Darstellungen in vier Register, die durch vier von oben nach unten verlaufende Inschriftzeilen in jeweils vier Felder eingeteilt werden. Im untersten Register sind Nilgötter dargestellt, in den drei darüberliegenden Feldern ist jeweils eine königliche Person beim Opfer vor einer Gottheit erfaßt. Die Darstellungen des opfernden Königspaares sind von der Raummitte aus zu sehen, während die Darstellungen des Prinzen und der königlichen Familie auf der abgewandten Säulenseite liegen. Es wird angenommen, daß sich in der Säulenhalle bestimmte Riten abspielten, bei denen es wichtig war, daß die Darstellungen des Königspaares der Raummitte zugewandt waren.

Inge Hofmann

WENIG, Steffen, see also our number 77010.

WENTE, Edward F., see our numbers 77302 and 77710.

77795 WERNER, Edward K., The Amarna Period of Eighteenth Dynasty Egypt. Bibliography Supplement 1976, *Newsletter ARCE* Nos. 101/102 (Summer/Fall 1977), 41-65.

A supplementary article to the Amarna bibliography published in our numbers 76831 and 76832, aiming at updating the bibliography and its first supplement with books and articles from 1976 and at completing that of the 1965-1975 period. At the end an index on persons and titles of books and articles.

L.Z.

77796 WESSETZKY, Vilmos, Ägyptische Ewigkeits- und Lebenssymbole am Ornat des meroitischen Königs Arnekhamani, *in: Ägypten und Kusch*, 477-479, with 2 pl.

Untersucht werden die Symbole am Brust- und Oberarmschmuck des Königs Arnekhamani auf den Darstellungen des Apedemaktempels von Musawwarât es Sufra: Herz, Skarabäus mit Froschfüßen, vier Widderköpfen und *hmhm*-Krone. So lebten uralte ägyptische Kultsymbole in den Gebieten südlich von Ägypten weiter.

Inge Hofmann

77797 WESSETZKY, Vilmos, An der Grenze von Literatur und Geschichte, in: *Fragen an die altägyptische Literatur*, 499-502.

On account of the Story of Peteêse in the Demotic Rylands Papyri, which the talent of the scribe may have turned from a family document into a lively story, the author stresses the care that should be taken when distinguishing literature from other texts. *L.Z.*

77798 WESSETZKY, Vilmos, Gedanken über die Bearbeitung der altägyptischen Bibliothek, *GM* Heft 25 (1977), 89-93.

Es wird der Frage nachgegangen, ob es im vorhellenistischen Ägypten ein Bibliothekswesen gab; es scheint möglich, von Bibliotheken und Büchern zu sprechen, wenn man dabei auch beachten muß, daß sich diese Begriffe nicht mit den unseren decken können. Nur dort, wo es sich ausschließlich um spezielle Aktensammlungen handelt, können wir von Archiven sprechen, wo wir aber vermuten können, daß planmäßig auch Bücherrollen gesammelt wurden, von Bibliotheken. Die Mehrzahl der Bücher war in Tempeln untergebracht. Verfasser ist der Überzeugung, daß die künftigen archäologischen Untersuchungen der ägyptischen Heiligtümer und der dazugehörenden Bauten mehr als bisher über das Vorhandensein der gesuchten Aufbewahrungsorte der Buchrollen enthüllen werden. *Inge Hofmann*

77799 WESSETZKY, Vilmos, Reliefs aus dem Tempel Ptolemaios I. in Kom el-Ahmar-Sharuna in der Budapester und Wiener Ägyptischen Sammlung, *MDAIK* 33 (1977), 133-141, with 1 fig. and 4 pl.

In 1907 an expedition organized by Fülöp Back and headed by Smoleński brought back relief blocks from an at present disappeared temple at Shârûna built by Ptolemaios I. Of the 18 blocks 7 are now in Budapest, 5 in Vienna, one went to Cracow but is at present untraceable, while the whereabouts of five are unknown.
After an introduction about the importance of Ptolemaios' building activities and about Shârûna (*Ḥwt nswt*), the capital of the later 18th Upper Egyptian nome, the author publishes the blocks, translating the inscriptions and discussing the representations. At the end he deals with the toponyms and divine names and epithets in the texts as well as the artistic value of the reliefs.

77800 WESTENDORF, Wolfhart, Koptisches Handwörterbuch. Bearbeitet auf Grund des Koptischen Handwörterbuchs Wilhelm Spiegelbergs. Lieferung 7 [and] 8,, Heidelberg, Carl Winter — Universitätsverlag, 1977 (17.8 × 25 cm; 160 p., [= p. 481-640]); rev. *Mundus* 16 (1980), 46-47 (Alexander Böhlig). Pr. each fascicle DM 80

Sequel to our number 76835.
Apart from the last two pages of the list of place names (p. 481-482) the present fascicle consists of additions and corrections; many after Černý's "Coptic Etymological Dictionary" (our number 76144) and Osing's "Die Nominalbildung" (our number 76611). On p. 576-631 the index to German words; from 631 onwards to Egyptian words. To be continued in the next fascicle.

77801 WESTENDORF, Wolfhart, Koptisches Handwörterbuch. Bearbeitet auf Grund des Koptischen Handwörterbuchs Wilhelm Spiegelbergs. Lieferung 9, Heidelberg, Carl Winter — Universitätsverlag, 1977 (17.8 × 25 cm; XXIV + 39 p., [= p. 641-679]); rev. *Mundus* 16 (1980), 46-47 (Alexander Böhlig). Pr. DM 80

Sequel to our preceding number.
With this fascicle the entire work is complete. It contains the second part of the index to Egyptian words (p. 641-651), and the indexes to Demotic, Greek, Arabic, Hebrew, etc. words.
Moreover, the fascicle contains the preface, a "Nachwort" and the list of abbreviations.

77802 WESTENDORF, Wolfhart, Noch einmal: Die "Wiedergeburt" des heimgekehrten Sinuhe, *SAK* 5 (1977), 293-304, with 1 fig.

Continuing his studies about the *mnyt* and the rebirth ritual in *Sinuhe* (see our number 67614) the author first points out that his name means "Son of the Sycamore", that is, of Hathor, represented on earth by the queen. Sinuhe was her former servant. Westendorf then presents a new translation of the cultic hymn that follows the scene of Sinuhe's entrance, arguing that for him the queen, in her role as Hathor, is his "mother" who rejuvenates him, that is, makes him again an Egyptian.

77803 WESTENDORF, Wolfhart, Schießen und Zeugen. Eine Gemeinsamkeit afrikanischer und ägyptischer Vorstellungen, *in: Ägypten und Kusch*, 481-486, with 3 fig. and 3 ill. on 4 pl.

Mit Hilfe eines Motivs, das von Nordafrika bis Ägypten verbreitet ist, soll auf eine Ideenverwandtschaft zwischen Ägypten und seinem afrikanischen Nachbarn aufmerksam gemacht werden: es handelt sich um das Motiv des Mannes, der mit Pfeil und Bogen schießt und zugleich im Geschlechtsakt mit einer Frau verbunden ist. Zeremonialjagden, bei denen sich eine Verbindung von Schießen zu Zeugen herstellen läßt, gibt es nicht nur im heutigen Afrika, sondern findet sich auch in Ägypten im Bereich des Totenkultes. Auch hier dient dieses Motiv nicht der Darstellung des rein hedonistischen Jagd- oder Paarungsvergnügens, sondern es steht wie fast alle Belange des Totenkultes im Dienst der Erhaltung des Lebens, hier insbesondere der Zeugungskraft. *Inge Hofmann*

77804 WESTENDORF, Wolfhart, Die Sonne, der Weinstock und das Unkraut. Bemerkungen zu Nag Hammadi Codex II 144, *GM* Heft 23 (1977), 75-76.

Es handelt sich um Übersetzungsverbesserungen zu Codex II 144: statt "Bäume" muß "Sonne" gelesen werden, statt "Weinstock" besser "Sträucher" und statt 'Pflanzen' "Unkraut". *Inge Hofmann*

77805 WESTENDORF, Wolfhart, Das strandende Schiff. Zur Lesung und Übersetzung von Bauer B 1,58 = R 101, *in: Fragen an die altägyptische Literatur,* 503-509.

Discussing the passage on the foundering ship in Eloquent Peasant B 1,58: *nn shm.k h3^{cc}.k hr t3* = R 101: *nn sdw.k h3g.k hr t3,* the author considers the verb *shm* to be a variant of *shm* (*WB* IV, 269), Coptic ϭⲱϪⲘ, which bears the notion of a strong movement, and he adduces evidence for the change of *h* to *ḥ*, while he proposes to read *sdw* as *shm*. When dealing wit the verbs *h3^{cc}* and *h3g,* he proposes to read the second arm in **h3^{cc}* as the striking arm determinative and points to the equation of Semitic ^{c} = Egyptian *ḥ*, which can alternate with Eg. *g*. Since the word *h3^c* can mean "to deviate", he proposes to translate: "You must not navigate without control, so that you, getting off course, touch land". *L.Z.*

77806 WESTENDORF, Wolfhart, Zu Frühformen von Osiris und Isis, *GM* Heft 25 (1977), 95-113, with 4 fig.

Durch die enge Verbindung des Königtums mit der kosmischen Gottheit Osiris entstanden drei Aspekte dieser Mischgestalt: Osiris$_1$ = die kosmische Gottheit; Osiris$_2$ = der sterbende und auferstehende Gott; Osiris$_3$ = die Mischgestalt Osiris$_{1+2}$ (d.h. der tote König im Leibe der Gottheit). Osiris und Isis sind als Mitglieder der Neunheit von Heliopolis im Kosmos für den Ablauf des Sonnenzyklus zuständig; sie dienten der Sonne als "weibliches Komplement". Verfasser setzt sich mit den Namen von Isis und Osiris auseinander, die beide mit dem "Sitz" geschrieben werden. Sie sind also Varianten einer Grundidee, ihr gemeinsames Grundwort ist zudem ein Femininum. Der männliche Charakter wurde vom toten König übernommen, so daß uns als Partner der Isis in historischer Zeit nicht mehr die kosmische Gottheit Osiris$_1$ begegnet, sondern der im Kosmos inkorporierte tote König Osiris$_2$. Isis dagegen trägt als Göttin des Thrones im königlichen Kult den (toten) König, wie sie im Kosmos die Sonne getragen hat. Die ursprüngliche Gestalt der Göttin ist nicht der Thron, sondern die Raubkatze, und in den Raubkatzenbahren und -stühlen des Totenkults lebt die Löwin bis an das Ende der ägyptischen Geschichte weiter. Da der König im Totenkult die Rolle eingenommen hat, die im kosmischen Vorbild der Sonne zukommt, muß gesucht werden, ob sich eine die Sonne tragende Raubkatzengottheit finden läßt. Eine solche wird in dem Schlangenhalspanther der Narmerpalette gefunden. Das *w3s.t*-Tier, ein Panther mit Schlangenhals und Schakalkopf wird als Mischgestalt des Osiris gedeutet. Doch nach der Konzipierung der neuen Mischgestalt Osiris$_3$ hat sich der König so massiv durchgesetzt, daß er dieser Mischgestalt nicht nur ihr in der historischen Zeit gültiges Erscheinungsbild als König und das dazugehörige maskuline Genus aufgeprägt hat, sondern ihr auch seinen Namen *ntr* gegeben hat. Doch muß stets sorgfältig unterschieden werden, ob mit *ntr* der regierende König, der tote König oder eine "wirkliche" Gottheit gemeint ist. *Inge Hofmann*

WESTENDORF, Wolfhart, see also our numbers 77114, 77477 and 77478.

WHEELER, Tamara Stech, see our number 77502.

WIEDEMANN, Hans-Georg, see our number 77072.

77807 WIERCIŃSKI, Andrzej, Pyramids and Ziggurats as the Architectonic Representations of the Archetype of the Cosmic Mountain, *Almogaren*, Graz 7 (1976), 1977, 199-212.

Proceeding from the premise that pyramids and ziggurats represent the archetype of the cosmic mountain, which architectonic representation is realized qualitatively and numerically, the author interprets and analyses the data from Egypt.
Continued in the next issue of the same periodical 8 (1977), 1978. *L.Z.*

77808 WILDUNG, Dietrich, Egyptian Saints. Deification in Pharaonic Egypt, New York, New York University Press, 1977 (22.2 × 26.6 cm; XVI + 110 p., 19 fig., 45 ill.); series: Hagop Kevorkian Series on Near Eastern Art and Civilization; rev. *BiOr* 35 (1978), 63-64 (L. Kákosy); *WZKM* 70 (1978), 113-114 (Günther Vittmann); *ZDMG* 129 (1979), 159-160 (J[ürgen] v. B[eckerath]). Pr. $22.50

The study consists of three chapters. In the first, called "Sacred Kingship", the author stresses that divine kingship was limited to a king after he had died, and to him during the time of official performances when he was alive; he never was divine as a complete personality, although the pharaohs attempted by several means to persuade that they were true divinities. They assumed the ram's horn of Amon, for instance, erected colossi, portrayed themselves in close contact with the gods (particularly near the borders of the empire), provided themselves with a temple and a processional barge, etc. Still they never took over the shape or character of any great god, and were not venerated in more than one of their aspects.

Chapter 2 deals with Imhotep; chapter 3 with Amenhotep son of Hapu. They describe their earthly career and the history of their late veneration. See for these two saints the author's "Imhotep und Amenhotep", our following number.

The book is lavishly illustrated with fine photographs and drawings, but no indication is given as to the museum numbers and other technical details.

77809 WILDUNG, Dietrich, Imhotep und Amenhotep. Gottwerdung im alten Ägypten, München-Berlin, Deutscher Kunstverlag, 1977 (21 × 29.7 cm; VIII + 320 p., 39 fig., 67 pl.) = Münchner Ägyptologische Studien. Herausgegeben von Hans Wolfgang Müller, 36. Pr. DM 120

The author has assembled in this Habilitationsschrift (München, 1973) the evidence for the two non-royal persons who received in later ages divine veneration: Imhotep, and Amenhotep son of Hapu.

The first part (p. 5-188) is devoted to Imhotep. In 12 chapters the author deals with: contemporaneous sources (particularly the base of a royal statue Cairo JdE 49889); the sources from the O., M., and N. K. and the Late Period; the Memphite documents from the Ptolemaic and Roman Periods; the tradition concerning Imhotep in Greek and Latin literature; Arabic traditions; the Imhotep cult in various places of Lower Egypt and the Faiyûm, Upper Egypt outside Thebes, Nubia, Meroe and the oasis Bahrîya; and the Theban sources from the Ptolemaic and Roman Periods.

Each document is minutely discussed, with mention of its technical data and literature, in several instances illustrated by a drawing, while more important and some less well known representations occur in photograph on the plates. We mention as an example Wildung's reconstruction of col. III, 8-11 of the Turin Royal Canon (30-32), where he suggests to read the mention of Imhotep's death under King Hu[ni].

In an excursus (47) the author briefly discusses the numerous bronze statues of Imhotep, which require a separate study. Late documents of course call him Imhotep, while in the Arabic tradition his tomb near

Memphis is known as "the prison of Joseph". Among the monuments of his cult from the Greek Period are mentioned his temple on Philae built by Ptolemy V (152-162).

Part 2 (chapters 13-14) deal with the material for Imhotep and Amenhotep together, many times combined in one scene, from Karnak and Western Thebes, dating from the Graeco-Roman Period. In part 3 (chapters 15-18) the documents for Amenhotep alone are studied, in a chronologically retrograde order: Ptolemaic and Roman sources from Thebes, sources from the Late Period, from the T.I.P. and posthumous ones from the N.K., and contemporaneous documents (see for these, Varille, our number 68614). In an appendix about Amenhotep's tomb the author adduces evidence for seeing it in a rock tomb in the Vallée de l'Aigle (Wâdi en-Nisr) northwest of Deir el-Medîna. On p. 295-297 a biography of Amenhotep.

In the summary (298-302) the author explains how two architects, establishing during their lifetime Maat by conquering the chaos in their buildings, hence pre-eminently "sages", became afterwards "saints", mediators between man and the gods, at last even life-giving "Sondergötter" themselves, without ever completely losing their human dimensions. In his divine position Imhotep remained restricted to Memphis, Amenhotep to Thebes.

Indexes on p. 309-320.

77810 WILLIAMS, Bruce, Aspects of Sealing and Glyptic in Egypt before the New Kingdom, *in: Seals and Sealings in the Ancient Near East*. Edited by McGuire Gibson and Robert D. Biggs, Malibu, Undena Publications, 1977 (= Bibliotheca Mesopotamica. Primary sources and interpretative analyses for the study of Mesopotamian civilization and its influences from late prehistory to the end of the cuneiform tradition. Edited by Giorgio Buccellati, 6), 135-140.

The author presents a survey of seals and sealings before the N.K., stating at the end that sealing served as a certificate of intactness, and not for the authentication of documents or as signature.
Compare our number 77386. *L.Z.*

77811 WILSON, A.J., Timna. Cradle of the World's Copper Mining Industry, *Mining Magazine,* London 136 (1977), 262-271, with 7 ill., 2 fig. and 2 maps.

Report on the discoveries made by various expeditions to the copper mines at Timna, devoting much attention to the shafts-and-galleries system of the mines. *L.Z.*

77812 WILSON, Robert R., Genealogy and History in the Biblical World, New Haven and London, Yale University Press, 1977 (15.4 × 24. cm; XV + 222 p.) = Yale Near Eastern Researches, 7.

On p. 125-129 a short discussion of ancient Egyptian genealogies. Long genealogies do not appear before the XXIInd Dynasty and many of them exhibit the phenomenon of telescoping after the tracing back of the ancestral line into the XXIst Dynasty. There is evidence that the priests of the first millennium used an interesting combination of written and oral sources in order to maintain the dogma that their genealogies stretched accurately into antiquity. *L.Z*

77813 WINNICKI, Jan Krzysztof, Die Kalasirier der spätdynastischen und der Ptolemäischen Zeit. Zu einem Problem der ägyptischen Heeresgeschichte, *Historia,* Wiesbaden 26 (1977), 257-268.

The author collects evidence on and investigates the group among the machimoi called kalasirians (Demotic *gl-šr*). From the XXth Dynasty (*kr-šry*) to the first century B.C. the word *gl-šr* seems to have developed from an indication for a brave person to a technical expression for a group of soldiers in Herodotus' account, much, however, as to their exact role and origin remaining unsolved. Although they have lost in quantity and privileged position, they have partaken in the organizational structure of Egypt in connection with police work. *L.Z*

WINTER, Urs, see our number 77404.

77814 WISEMAN, D.J., Israel's literary neighbours in the 13th century B.C., *Journal of Northwest Semitic Languages,* Stellenbosch 5 (1977), 77-91.

Discussing the influence of Israel's neighbours in the 13th century B.C. in literature, the author questions the influence of the N.K. wisdom instruction on Israel. *L.Z*

77815 WOOD, Wendy Elisabeth, Early Wooden Tomb Sculpture in Ancient Egypt, *Dissertation Abstracts International,* Ann Arbor, Mich. 38, No. 13 (September 1977), 1079-A.

Abstract of a thesis Case Western Reserve University, 1977 (Order No. 77-18,854; 140 p.).

The author traces the origin and early development of wooden tomb statues in ancient Egypt, interprets their iconography, and evaluates their historical importance. *L.Z*

77816   WOOD, Wendy, A Reconstruction of the Reliefs of Hesy-Re, *Newsletter ARCE* Nos. 99/100 (Winter/Spring 1977), 15.

Abstract of a paper.

77817   WRIGHT, G.R.H., Ptolemaic Remains from Kalabsha Temple Reconstituted on Elephantine Island (1974-1975), *JEA* 63 (1977), 156-158, with 1 pl.

During the process of dismantling the large Mandulis temple remains of an earlier Ptolemaic temple were discovered, whose 250 blocks were reused in the latter. Work on rebuilding began in September 1974 and resulted in the reconstituting of its small sanctuary c. 7.5 × 5.5 m with an external height of 4.3 m. Of this about 20% of the original wall blocks survived. A gateway was also restored as 'scenic architecture' on Elephantine.   *E. Uphill*

77818   YOYOTTE, Jean, Contribution à l'histoire du chapitre 162 du Livre des Morts, *RdE* 29 (1977), 194-202.

L'auteur étudiant les traditions aux chap. 162-167 du Livre des Morts établit qu'ils ont dû être composés en milieu thébain à l'époque ramesside, vulgarisés sous forme de billets magiques au cours de la XXIe dyn. et par la suite annexés au "Livre de la sortie au jour" à la suite de la découverte d'un manuscrit contenant au moins une partie de ce texte dans le grand temple d'Amon de Tanis.

Dans une seconde note, il s'intéresse à la présence du chap. 162 sur une statue de vache provenant de Kôm Abû Yassin (CGC 676) et au rôle funéraire de la vache Ihet.   *Ph. Derchain*

77819   YOYOTTE, J., Une déesse nommée ʿAyt, *RdE* 29 (1977), 226-227.

Cette déesse rare est attestée par quelques monuments de Basse Époque et dans les noms propres Tariaios et Peteaios. Elle appartient à la mythologie héracléopolitaine.   *Ph. Derchain*

77820   YOYOTTE, Jean, Une notice biographique du roi Osiris, *BIFAO* 77 (1977), 145-149.

The author translates and comments upon a text from the temple of Dendera describing Osiris as a king, mentioning his titulary, his might, his place of birth and his parents, and his officials. With several classical authors Yoyotte finds allusions to this type of text.

77821   YOYOTTE, J., "Osorkon fils de Mehytouskhé", un pharaon oublié?, *BSFE* Nos. 77-78 (octobre 1976 et mars 1977), 39-54.

L'inscription généalogique d'Ankhefenkhons, personnage attaché au

culte de Khonsou thébain, figurait sur la terrasse surmontant le temple. L'ascendance paternelle comptait une "Tashaâkheper, la divine épouse du pharaon Osorkon, le fils de Mehytouskhé j.v." Divine épouse du pharaon, ce titre exceptionnel pourrait caractériser la femme d'un lointain souverain. Ce pharaon lui-même doit différer des quatre Osorkon répertoriés, le nom de leurs mères étant connu. Mais la stèle de Pasenhor (Serapeum) parle du père de Sheshonq Ier: Nimlot, "fils... de la mère du roi Mehytouskhé". Il en résulte qu'un pharaon de souche libyenne, Osorkon l'Ancien, frère de Nimlot et oncle de Sheshonq Ier, aurait régné de vingt à trente ans avant celui-ci, vers la fin de la XXIe dynastie "tanite". L'abrégé de Manéthon l'appelle Osochôr et lui assigne un règne de six ans. A cette date, une inscription de Karnak atteste pour un "an 2" le seul prénom, Aâkheperrê-l'élu-de-Rê. L'influence des colons militaires libyens avait laissé quelque trace dans la prosopographie thébaine même avant la fin de la XXe dynastie. Le mot dynastie, repris à Manéthon, recouvrirait l'hégémonie d'une ville ou de son dieu, non l'origine des souverains.
J. Custers

77822 YOYOTTE, Jean, Religion de l'Égypte ancienne, *Annuaire. École Pratique des Hautes Études.* V^e section — sciences réligieuses, Paris 85 [1976-1977], 193-201.

Report on the activities during the years 1971-1977, with particular attention for the geographical spreading of secondary cults of Thoth and the ritual of Mefky on a basalt block in Cairo (JdE. 45936). *L.Z.*

77823 YOYOTTE, Jean, Serge Sauneron (1927-1976), *BIFAO* 77 (1977), 1-21, with portrait = frontispiece.

Obituary article, followed by a bibliography of Serge Sauneron. Compare our number 76869.
See also our number 77761.

77824 YOYOTTE, J., Seshat maquilleuse, *RdE* 29 (1977), 227-228.

On sait depuis longtemps que le terme *sšt* porté par des femmes désigne des maquilleuses et non des scribes. Or il semble bien que ce rôle est également assumé par Séchat, depuis les Textes des Pyramides, même si cette déesse est souvent associée à l'écriture.
Ph. Derchain

77825 [YOYOTTE, Jean], Sujets de thèses I, *BSFE* No. 80 (Octobre 1977), 33-41.

List of theses in preparation on various French institutes and universities: Lille, Lyon, Montpellier, Paris (EPHE and Sorbonne) and Strasbourg, together 117 titles.

YOYOTTE, Jean, see also our number 77453.

77826 ŽABKAR, Louis V., Some Particular Features in the Representations of Apedemak, in: Ägypten und Kusch, 487-506, with 1 fig. and 3 ill. on 4 pl.

Als außergewöhnliche Darstellungen des Apedemak in der meroitischen Kunst werden ausführlich besprochen: Apedemak als Schlangenlöwe auf dem Pylon von Naqa, der Schlangenlöwe Apedemak von Semna-Süd, der dreiköpfige und vierarmige Apekemak von Naqa; die Möglichkeiten eines indischen Einflusses auf die meroitische Ikonographie werden abgestritten (vgl. auch unsere Nr. 75819). *Inge Hofmann*

ZACCAGNINI, Carlo, see our number 77014.

77827 ZADOK, Ran, On Some Egyptians in First-Millennium Mesopotamia, *GM* Heft 26 (1977), 63-68.

Ein neo-assyrisches Dokument aus dem Jahr 622 v. Chr., das zuerst in Transliteration 1914 veröffentlicht worden war und nun neu herausgegeben worden ist, enthält eine Reihe ägyptischer Namen, die meist für das Neue Reich und später belegt sind. Insgesamt können zwanzig Namen als ägyptisch verifiziert werden. *Inge Hofmann*

77828 ZANDEE, Jan, Bemerkungen zu einigen Kapiteln aus den Sargtexten, in: *Fragen an die altägyptische Literatur,* 511-529.

The author first translates and extensively comments upon Spell 355 = C.T. V, 1-7, dealing with the breathing of air the deceased needs in the hereafter. The spell belongs to those which provide the deceased with the normal necessities of life: air, food and drinks. To illustrate the importance of the provision of breathing air, the author discusses many passages from the P.T., C.T., and B.D. In the funerary offering the breathing of air is presented to the deceased in the form of the burning of myrrh or incense. C.T. Spell 297 is an important variant of Spell 355, the title of two variants of which is also met in B.D. 38 A-B (ꜥnḫ m ṯ3w m ḥrt-nṯr).

Dealing with C.T. V, 8-22 = Spell 356-362, translated and commented upon in our number 76855, the author only points out the relations of the spells with the Ritual of the Opening of the Mouth. *L.Z.*

77829 ZAUZICH, Karl-Theodor, Spätdemotische Papyrusurkunden IV, *Enchoria* 7 (1977), 151-180, with 7 pl. (3 folding).

The author continues his publication of late Demotic documents with P. Berlin P 8139 (Deed of cession of rights concerning the sale of a house: Dime — 2nd century A.D.), P. Berlin P. 15685 (Receipt of payment: Dime — Antoninus), P. Berlin P 15667 (Receipt of payment: Dime — 45./46 A.D.), P. Berlin P 8932 verso (Receipt of payment: Dime — 81/82 A.D.) and P. Berlin 23545 (Settlement of accounts in form of a list: Dime — 1st-2nd century A.D.). He adds an excursus on some equivalents in late Demotic and Greek tax-receipts and gives some corrections to earlier published documents.

W. Brunsch

77830 ZAUZICH, Karl-Theodor, Zwei neue demotische Ortsnamen, *Enchoria* 7 (1977), 195-197.

Two new demotic place-names: *P3-grg-Sbk* = Κερκεσοῦχα (Ὄρους) and *P3j-š3j* = Πισαι (Abshay).

W. Brunsch

77831 ZAUZICH, Karl-Theodor, Zwei übersehene Erwähnungen historischer Ereignisse der Ptolemaërzeit in demotischen Urkunden, *Enchoria* 7 (1977), 193.

The text on a stela found in 1969/70 at Saqqâra North (= our number 71176, pl. V, 4) mentions the expulsion of Ptolemy X Alexander respectively Ptolemy IX (89/88 B.C.).
P. Ox. Griffith L 1, 10 (see our number 75092, No. 14) bears a hint at Ptolemy VIth's journey to Phoenicia in his 32nd year of reign.

W. Brunsch

ZAUZICH, Karl-Theodor, see also our number 77633.

77832 ZAVADOVSKI, Yu. N., Анализ "Тураевской стелы" Эрмитажа, *in:* Мероэ, 15-21, with 1 ill. on a pl. and a French summary on p. 292.

"Eine Analyse der 'Stele Turaev' in der Ermitage".

Es werden Lesungsvorschläge für die Stele REM 1001 der Ermitage in Leningrad gemacht, da die Transkription anhand des Originals etwas anders ausfällt als nach den Fotos. Der veröffentlichte Teil läßt sich mehr oder weniger interpretieren.

Inge Hofmann

77833 ZAVADOVSKY, Yu. N., Андре Эйлер (1924-1971), *in:* Мероэ, 287-290.
Obituary notice of André Heyler, with a bibliography. Compare our number 72183.

77834 ZAVADOVSKI, Yu. N., Фонологическая система мероитского языка *in:* Мероэ, 4-14, with a French summary on p. 291-292.
"Das Phonologische System des Meroitischen".
Es wird vermutet, daß sich das meroitische Alphabet aus einem syllabischen Schriftsystem entwickelt hat, so daß jeder Konsonant den Wert K+V hat. In zwei Tabellen werden das Vokal- und das Konsonantensystem des Meroitischen aufgestellt. *Inge Hofmann*

77835 ZAYED, Abd el Hamid Ahmed, The Staircase of the God in Abydos, *ASAE* 62 (1977), 155-174, with 6 fig. and 2 pl.
The author discusses texts concerning and representations of the "Staircase of the Great God" (Spells from the P.T., archaic tablets, M.K. stelae, N.K. tomb scenes and the B.D.). Of the four staircases found by the excavators at Abydos none can be that of the Great God. Various opinions about its position are quoted, while the author mentions as a possibility that it was the slope of sand descending through "the Gap" (Pega).
For the subject, see now Simpson's study (our number 74688), 10-13.

77836 ZIBELIUS, Karola, Zur Mehrnamigkeit altägyptischer Orte, *in: XIX. Deutscher Orientalistentag,* 40-46.
The author discusses the phenomenon of Egyptian sites with more than one name, which can be due to several causes: nome capitals can also bear the name of the province; prevalence of administrative, territorial, or religious aspects; compound names with *pr* + local god besides the old name. The case of Memphis is particularly illustrated.
L.Z.

77837 ZIEGLER, Christiane, Le sistre d'Henouttaouy, *La Revue du Louvre et des Musées de France,* Paris 27 (1977), 1-4, with 6 ill. and 1 fig.
Publication of a very fine sistrum with gold inlay, preserved in the Louvre Museum (E. 11201). The piece with its Hathor head and other details and the engraved representations of divinities and inscriptions on the loop is carefully described. The texts contain dedications to the Theban triad and state that the object belonged to a chantress of Isis and Amon called Henuttawy, probably not the Divine Adoratrice of that name which would have been stated. The date of the piece is uncertain.

77838 ZIEGLER, Christiane, Tambours conservés au Musée du Louvre, *RdE* 29 (1977), 203-214, with 2 pl.

Publication de deux tambours du Louvre (N 1442 et N 1445) accompagnée d'un commentaire sur leur emploi appuyé sur l'étude des représentations figurées connues. *Ph. Derchain*

ZIEGLER, Christiane, see also our number 77029.

77839 ZIMMERMAN, M.R., Death at an Early Age: Tuberculosis in Ancient Egypt, *American Journal of Physical Anthropology*, Philadelphia 47, No. 1 (July 1977), 169.

Abstract of a paper read during the 46th Annual Meeting of the American Association of Physical Anthropologists. *L.Z.*

77840 ZIMMERMAN, Michael R., The Mummies of the Tomb of Nebwenenef: Paleopathology and Archeology, *JARCE* 14 (1977), 33-36, with 1 pl. including a map.

Analysis of mummified human material of various periods from the Theban tomb of *Nb-wnn.f* (No. 157) by rehydration technique reveals pathological features the more interesting when connected with living conditions (cfr especially our number 72372). Most interesting were the remains of a 5-year old child, died from tuberculosis whose lungs showed traces of anthracosis through inhalating smoke (from a household fire?). Tuberculosis would be contagious to a child when living in a close-cropped, multigenerational (including grandparents) household. Other well-documented cases were a (benign) tumor (not cancer), artherosclerosis and several of *spina bifida*. Though this causes serious invalidity, social conditions apparently permitted to keep such crippled persons in the community. All cases fit in with the rather marginal state of health in Ancient Egypt attested elsewhere.
J.F. Borghouts

77841 ZIVIE, Alain-Pierre, Un fragment de coudée de la XIe dynastie, *RdE* 29 (1977), 215-223, with 2 fig. and 1 ill.

Publication d'un fragment de coudée d'une collection privée parisienne. L'auteur annonce d'autres objets du même genre et fournit dans ses notes une bibliographie des coudées analogues déjà connues (voir notre No. 72808). *Ph. Derchain*

77842 ZIVIE, Alain-Pierre, L'ibis, Thot et la coudée, *BSFE* No. 79 (juin 1977), 22-41.

Selon Elien (De Natura Animalium, II 29) le pas de l'ibis vaut une coudée. La signification métrologique de l'oiseau ressort aussi d'un passage de Clément d'Alexandrie (Stromates V 7, 43,3). L'archétype de l'arpenteur est Thot; l'observation de son animal principal dut aller de pair avec l'interprétation mythique. Pour l'origine de *nỉ/nỉw* (Gardiner D 41), on songera à l'ibis ou à une confusion volontaire. Le mythe lunaire du "bras de Thot" perdu ou blessé paraît constituer, comme l'Oeil d'Horus, un parfait support pour des réinterprétations. Les coudées dites votives le concrétiseraient. Elles ont pu servir d'étalon métrique officiel, parfois d'inventaire symbolique du pays, d'aide-mémoire cultuel. Le Papyrus géographique de Tanis aussi bien que les passages de Clément et d'Apulée suggéreraient d'y voir des "digestes" de science sacerdotale. La palette du scribe peut illustrer la même idée et représenter la mesure ou l'arpentage. Elle constitue l'offrande spécifique à Thot; les formules évoquent la coudée ou son bras, garant de justice. *J. Custers*

77843 ZIVIE, Christiane M., En Égypte. Les temples de l'oasis méridionale. Témoins d'une intense vie réligieuse, *Archeologia,* Paris No. 110 (septembre 1977), 30-45, with 2 maps, 21 ill. (8 in colour) and 1 colour ill. on cover.

Describing the oases Khârga and Dâkhla the author deals for Khârga with the temple of Hibis at Khârga, built by Darius I, the Ptolemaic temple of Amon at Qasr es-Ghuieda, and the Roman temples at Dûsh dedicated to Osiris-Isis-Horus and at Nadûra dedicated to Amon-Mut-Khonsu, resp. for Dâkhla with the VIth Dynasty necropolis at Balât, the Roman village of Smint el-Kharâb, the Roman temple of Deir el-Hagar, and the 1st or 2nd century A.D. tombs at Muzauwaqa among which that of Petosiris. *L.Z.*

77844 ZIVIE, Christiane M., Entre Thèbes et Erment: le temple de Deir Chellouit, *BSFE* No. 80 (octobre 1977), 21-32, with 7 ill.

Ce temple modeste est situé au sud de Médinet Habou, sur la route d'Erment, et demeurait quasi ignoré. Une porte au cartouche d'Auguste le précédait jadis, dans une enceinte de briques crues à propylône s'ouvrant vers l'est. Ce portail, bâti à une époque allant de Galba à Domitien, est inégalement conservé mais garde des scènes en creux d'un style assez vigoureux, deux "hymnes de propagande" à Isis et une dédicace à Montou: ces inscriptions doivent se référer à un double culte local. Le temple est visiblement inachevé. A l'arrière s'ouvre une niche placée dans l'axe; toute autre décoration extérieure fait défaut. Un pronaos occupant toute la largeur mène à l'escalier des terrasses, à la cour *ouabet* et à des pièces anépigraphes. Le naos, construction à fruit, décoré à l'intérieur sous Hadrien, porte au fond

deux scènes dédiées à Isis, deux à Montou et deux hymnes à Isis. Parmi les offrandes figurent les bouquets montés dédiés à Amon "aniconique", l'obélisque se rapportant à Atoum et à Nebethétepet, et le tour du potier propre à Shou et Tefnout.
Voir aussi notre No. 77846.
J. Custers

77845   ZIVIE, Christiane M., Une nouvelle mention de Djedem, *RdE* 29 (1977), 229-230.

Ce toponyme, qui désigne vraisemblablement Tôd, étudié par Sauneron (notre No. 64428), est mentionné également dans les inscriptions de Deir Chellouit, qui confirment la localisation proposée.
Ph. Derchain

77846   ZIVIE, Christiane M., Trois campagnes épigraphiques au temple de Deir Chellouît, *BIFAO* 77 (1977), 151-161, with 7 pl., including 2 plans.

The small Isis and Montu temple of Deir el-Shelwît, dating from the Roman Period and situated c. 4 km South of Medînet Habu, has never been properly studied until today. In the years 1974-1976 the author has copied the texts from its propylon and the temple itself, the publication of which is now prepared. Reporting on her work the author stresses the extremely bad writing and the difficulties to decipher the texts. She describes the still standing parts of the building and their decoration, which dates from various periods between the reigns of Galba and Otho (A.D. 68) and Antoninus (see also our number 77844).

NECROLOGIES

77847   ABU BAKR, Abdel Moneim; *Newsletter ARCE* Nos. 99/100 (Winter/Spring 1977), 2 (Sayed Tawfick).

77848   MUELLER, Dieter: *Newsletter ARCE* Nos. 101/102 (Summer/Fall 1977), 1-2 (Leonard H. Lesko).

77849   VANDIER D'ABBADIE, Jeanne: *AfO* 25 (1974/77), 357 (H[ellmut] Br[unner]).

Migration, Diasporas and Citizenship

Series Editors: **Robin Cohen**, Director of the International Migration Institute and Professor of Development Studies, University of Oxford, UK and **Zig Layton-Henry**, Professor of Politics, University of Warwick, UK.

Editorial Board: **Rainer Baubock**, European University Institute, Italy; **James F. Hollifield**, Southern Methodist University, USA; **Jan Rath**, University of Amsterdam, The Netherlands.

The Migration, Diasporas and Citizenship series covers three important aspects of the migration progress. Firstly, the determinants, dynamics and characteristics of international migration. Secondly, the continuing attachment of many contemporary migrants to their places of origin, signified by the word 'diaspora', and thirdly the attempt, by contrast, to belong and gain acceptance in places of settlement, signified by the word 'citizenship'. The series publishes work that shows engagement with and a lively appreciation of the wider social and political issues that are influenced by international migration.

Also published in Migration Studies by Palgrave Macmillan

Rutvica Andrijasevic
MIGRATION, AGENCY AND CITIZENSHIP IN SEX TRAFFICKING

Claudine Attias-Donfut, Joanne Cook, Jaco Hoffman and Louise Waite (*editors*)
CITIZENSHIP, BELONGING AND INTERGENERATIONAL RELATIONS IN AFRICAN MIGRATION

Grete Brochmann, Anniken Hagelund (*authors*) with – Karin Borevi, Heidi Vad Jønsson, Klaus Petersen
IMMIGRATION POLICY AND THE SCANDINAVIAN WELFARE STATE 1945–2010

Gideon Calder, Phillip Cole and Jonathan Seglow
CITIZENSHIP ACQUISITION AND NATIONAL BELONGING: Migration, Membership and the Liberal Democratic State

Huub Dijstelbloem and Albert Meijer (*editors*)
MIGRATION AND THE NEW TECHNOLOGICAL BORDERS OF EUROPE

Thomas Faist and Andreas Ette (*editors*)
THE EUROPEANIZATION OF NATIONAL POLICIES AND POLITICS OF IMMIGRATION: Between Autonomy and the European Union

Thomas Faist and Peter Kivisto (*editors*)
DUAL CITIZENSHIP IN GLOBAL PERSPECTIVE: From Unitary to Multiple Citizenship

Katrine Fangen, Thomas Johansson and Nils Hammarén (*editors*)
YOUNG MIGRANTS: Exclusion and Belonging in Europe

Martin Geiger and Antoine Pécoud (*editors*)
THE POLITICS OF INTERNATIONAL MIGRATION MANAGEMENT

John R. Hinnells (*editor*)
RELIGIOUS RECONSTRUCTION IN THE SOUTH ASIAN DIASPORAS: From One Generation to Another

Ronit Lentin and Elena Moreo (*editors*)
MIGRANT ACTIVISM AND INTEGRATION FROM BELOW IN IRELAND

Ayhan Kaya
ISLAM, MIGRATION AND INTEGRATION: The Age of Securitization

Marie Macy and Alan H. Carling
ETHNIC, RACIAL AND RELIGIOUS INEQUALITIES: The Perils of Subjectivity

George Menz and Alexander Caviedes (*editors*)
LABOUR MIGRATION IN EUROPE

Laura Morales and Marco Giugni (*editors*)
SOCIAL CAPITAL, POLITICAL PARTICIPATION AND MIGRATION IN EUROPE: Making Multicultural Democracy Work?

Eric Morier-Genoud and Michel Cahen (*editors*)
IMPERIAL MIGRATIONS: Colonial Communities and Diaspora in the Portuguese World

Aspasia Papadopoulou-Kourkoula
TRANSIT MIGRATION: The Missing Link between Emigration and Settlement

Ludger Pries and Zeynep Sezgin (*editors*)
CROSS BORDER MIGRANT ORGANIZATIONS IN COMPARATIVE PERSPECTIVE

Prodromos Panayiotopoulos
ETHNICITY, MIGRATION AND ENTERPRISE

Vicky Squire
THE EXCLUSIONARY POLITICS OF ASYLUM

Anna Triandafyllidou and Thanos Maroukis (*editors*)
MIGRANT SMUGGLING: Irregular Migration from Asia and Africa to Europe

Vron Ware
MILITARY MIGRANTS: Fighting for YOUR Country

Lucy Williams
GLOBAL MARRIAGE: Cross-Border Marriage Migration in Global Context

Also by Eric Morier-Genoud

EMBROILED: Swiss Churches, South Africa and Apartheid
(*with C. Jeannerat and D. Péclard*)

SURE ROAD? Nationalisms in Angola, Guinea-Bissau and Mozambique

Also by Michel Cahen

LES BANDITS. Un historien au Mozambique, 1994

LA DIALECTIQUE DES SECRETS. Histoire et idéologie dans l'accouchement sous X et l'adoption plénière

ETHNICITE POLITIQUE. Pour une lecture réaliste de l'identité

MOZAMBIQUE, ANALYSE POLITIQUE DE CONJONCTURE 1990

MOZAMBIQUE, LA REVOLUTION IMPLOSEE.
Études sur douze années d'indépendance (1975–1987)

LA NATIONALISATION DU MONDE. Europe, Afrique, l'identité dans la démocratie

LE PORTUGAL BILINGUE. Histoire et droits politiques d'une minorité linguistique: la communauté mirandaise

---

Migration, Diasporas and Citizenship
**Series Standing Order ISBN 978–0-230–30078–1 (hardback) and
978–0-230–30079–8 (paperback)**
(*outside North America only*)

You can receive future titles in this series as they are published by placing a standing order. Please contact your bookseller or, in case of difficulty, write to us at the address below with your name and address, the title of the series and one of the ISBNs quoted above.

Customer Services Department, Macmillan Distribution Ltd, Houndmills, Basingstoke, Hampshire RG21 6XS, England

Imperial Migrations

Colonial Communities and Diaspora in the Portuguese World

Edited by

Eric Morier-Genoud
Queen's University Belfast, UK

and

Michel Cahen
Université de Bordeaux, CNRS, France

palgrave
macmillan

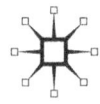

Selection and editorial matter © Eric Morier-Genoud and Michel Cahen 2012
Individual chapters © their respective authors 2012

All rights reserved. No reproduction, copy or transmission of this publication may be made without written permission.

No portion of this publication may be reproduced, copied or transmitted save with written permission or in accordance with the provisions of the Copyright, Designs and Patents Act 1988, or under the terms of any licence permitting limited copying issued by the Copyright Licensing Agency, Saffron House, 6–10 Kirby Street, London EC1N 8TS.

Any person who does any unauthorized act in relation to this publication may be liable to criminal prosecution and civil claims for damages.

The authors have asserted their rights to be identified as the authors of this work in accordance with the Copyright, Designs and Patents Act 1988.

First published 2012 by
PALGRAVE MACMILLAN

Palgrave Macmillan in the UK is an imprint of Macmillan Publishers Limited, registered in England, company number 785998, of Houndmills, Basingstoke, Hampshire RG21 6XS.

Palgrave Macmillan in the US is a division of St Martin's Press LLC, 175 Fifth Avenue, New York, NY 10010.

Palgrave Macmillan is the global academic imprint of the above companies and has companies and representatives throughout the world.

Palgrave® and Macmillan® are registered trademarks in the United States, the United Kingdom, Europe and other countries

ISBN 978-1-349-34604-2   ISBN 978-1-137-26500-5 (eBook)
DOI 10.1057/9781137265005

This book is printed on paper suitable for recycling and made from fully managed and sustained forest sources. Logging, pulping and manufacturing processes are expected to conform to the environmental regulations of the country of origin.

A catalogue record for this book is available from the British Library.

Library of Congress Cataloging-in-Publication Data

    Imperial migrations: colonial communities and diaspora in the Portuguese world/edited by Eric Morier-Genoud, Michel Cahen.
    p. cm.

    1. Portugal – Emigration and immigration – History. 2. Portugal – Colonies – History. I. Morier-Genoud, Eric. II. Cahen, Michel.

JV8261.I475 2012
304.809469—dc23   2012023559

10 9 8 7 6 5 4 3 2 1
21 20 19 18 17 16 15 14 13 12

Contents

List of Figures and Tables   vii

Acknowledgements   viii

Notes on Contributors   ix

1 Introduction: Portugal, Empire, and Migrations – Was There Ever an Autonomous Social Imperial Space?   1
Eric Morier-Genoud and Michel Cahen

Part I   Longue Durée Migrations in and around the Portuguese Empire

2 'Portuguese' Diasporas: A Survey of the Scholarly Literature   31
Edward A. Alpers with Molly Ball

3 Africans in Portuguese Society: Classification Ambiguities and Colonial Realities   72
Isabel Castro Henriques

Part II   Colonial Migrations in the Third Portuguese Empire

4 Colonial Migration to Angola and Mozambique: Constraints and Illusions   107
Cláudia Castelo

5 Imperial Actors? Cape Verdean Mentality in the Portuguese Empire under the *Estado Novo*, 1926–1974   129
Alexander Keese

6 Unlike the Other Whites? The Swiss in Mozambique under Colonialism   149
Sérgio Inácio Chichava

7 The Ismailis of Mozambique: History of a Twofold Migration (late 19th century–1975)   168
Nicole Khouri and Joana Pereira Leite

Part III Migrations at the Margins of the Third Empire

8 Representing the Portuguese Empire: Goan Consuls in British East Africa, c. 1910–1963 193
Margret Frenz

9 The Making of a Portuguese Community in South Africa, 1900–1994 213
Clive Glaser

10 From Mozambique to Brazil: The 'Good Portuguese' of the Chinese Athletic Club 239
Lorenzo Macagno

Part IV Ideology and Heritage

11 Luso-African Intimacies: Conceptions of National and Transnational Community 265
Rosa Williams

12 Mundo Pretuguês: Colonial and Postcolonial Diasporic Dis/articulations 286
AbdoolKarim Vakil

13 'Portugal Is in the Sky': Conceptual Considerations on Communities, Lusitanity, and Lusophony 297
Michel Cahen

14 Conclusion: Decolonisation and Diaspora 316
John Darwin

Index 327

though
List of Figures and Tables

Figures

3.1	'The mulatto women'	78
3.2	The Portuguese Empire at the turn of the century	82
3.3	'The little Negroes'	84
3.4	Advertising: 'color' and 'vice'	88
3.5	Anthropophagi	91
3.6	'The Negro of Casa Africana'	95
3.7	Evolution of the legally registered foreign population, 1960–1997	97

Tables

4.1	White population living in Angola and Mozambique, 1846–1973	113
4.2	Angola and Mozambique population by somatic groups, 1940–1970	115
4.3	Metropolitan passengers' arrivals and departures by steamer, 1943–1973	116
10.1	Census of the Chinese group individuals, 1928–1960 – Mozambique	244

Acknowledgements

This book has its origin in a workshop held at the University of Oxford between 24 and 27 September 2008, under the title 'Diaspora, Empire, and the Making of a Lusophone World'. The meeting was organised by Eric Morier-Genoud and Luisa Pinto Teixeira and held thanks to the support of the Instituto Camões, Oxford Research Network on Government in Africa (OReNGA), the Department of Politics and International Relations, St John's and St Cross Colleges, University of Oxford.

For the workshop (and to make its proceedings into a book), we have counted on the help of Robin Cohen, John Darwin, Gavin Williams, Shihan de Silva, Patricia Goldey, Oliver Bakewell, Jan-Georg Deutsch, Neil McFarlane, Wendy Urban-Mead, Victor Pereira, Sheila Pereira Khan, Jacinto Godinho, Patricia Ferraz de Matos, Thomas Earle, James Davis, and Kate Candy.

Institutional acknowledgment goes to Palgrave Macmillan (and its editor Philippa Grand), the Researchers' Association of the journal *Lusotopie*, the Centre for the Study of Africa and Development (CEsA) at the Instituto Superior de Economia e Gestão, Lisbon, Portugal, the Center Les Afriques dans le monde, University of Bordeaux, and Queen's University Belfast.

This book is published with the support of

- the Association des chercheurs de la revue *Lusotopie*, France,
- the Institut d'études politiques de Bordeaux,
- the Instituto Camões (through its Oxford's branch, UK),
- the Centro de Estudos sobre África e do Desenvolvimento (CEsA) of the Instituto Superior de Economia e Gestão da Universidade Técnica de Lisboa (Portugal).

Contributors

Edward A. Alpers is Professor of History at the University of California, Los Angeles. He has taught at the University of Dar es Salaam, Tanzania (1966–1968), and the Somali National University, Lafoole (1980) – at the latter as a Fulbright Senior Scholar. In 1994 he served as President of the African Studies Association. He has published widely on the history of East Africa and the Indian Ocean. His major publications include *Ivory and Slaves in East Central Africa* (1975); *Walter Rodney: Revolutionary and Scholar*, co-edited with Pierre-Michel Fontaine (1982); *Sidis and Scholars: Essays on African Indians*, co-edited with Amy Catlin-Jairazbhoy (2004); *Slave Routes and Oral Tradition in Southeastern Africa*, co-edited with Benigna Zimba and Allen F. Isaacman (2005); *Resisting Bondage in Indian Ocean Africa and Asia*, co-edited with Gwyn Campbell and Michael Salman (2007); *Cross-Currents and Community Networks: The History of the Indian Ocean World*, co-edited with Himanshu Prabha Ray (2007); and *East Africa and the Indian Ocean* (2009). His research focuses on slave trade and the dispersal of Africans in the Indian Ocean world.

Molly Ball is a graduate student at the University of California, Los Angeles, where she is completing her doctoral dissertation, entitled 'Inequality in São Paulo's Old Republic (1891–1930): A Wage Perspective'. Her research focuses on real wage determinants in the urban labour market, and she is particularly interested in questions of gender and immigrant discrimination as well as educational quality throughout Latin America. She received a Fulbright-Hays and NSEP Boren Fellowship to complete her dissertation fieldwork.

Michel Cahen is a political historian of modern colonial Portugal and contemporary Portuguese-speaking Africa. He is Senior Researcher at the Centre National de la Recherche Scientifique (CNRS) at the Institute of Political Studies of Bordeaux and Deputy Director of the Centre 'Les Afriques dans le monde.' From 1994 to 2009, he was Editor-in-Chief of *Lusotopie*, a journal devoted to the political analysis of spaces stemming from Portuguese colonisation and history. His main interests relate to Marxism and nationalism, identity and citizenship, political identity at the margins, coloniality, and globalisation. His most recent books are *Os outros. Um historiador em Moçambique, 1994* (2003) and *Le Portugal bilingue. Histoire et droits politiques d'une minorité linguistique: La communauté mirandaise* (2009).

Cláudia Castelo is a researcher at the Instituto de Investigação Científica Tropical [Tropical Research Institute], Lisbon. She received her PhD in 2005 from the Instituto de Ciências Sociais of the Universidade de Lisboa,

Portugal. She has written on colonial ideology, politics, and migration in the third Portuguese Empire, and she works presently on science, development, and empire, as well as colonial scientific heritage and memories. She is the author of *'O modo português de estar no mundo': O luso-tropicalismo e a ideologia colonial portuguesa (1933–1961)* (1999) and *Passagens para África: O povoamento de Angola e Moçambique com naturais da metrópole (1920–1974)* (2007).

Sérgio Inácio Chichava is a researcher at the Instituto de Estudos Sociais e Económicos (IESE), Mozambique, and Lecturer in Political Sociology and Political Studies at Eduardo Mondlane University. He obtained his PhD in 2007 from the Institute of Political Studies of Bordeaux, France. He works on Mozambique's relations with emerging economies. He is co-author, with Luís de Brito and others, of *Cidadania e Governação em Moçambique* (2009), *Desafios para Moçambique 2010* (2010), and *Desafios para Moçambique 2011* (2011).

John Darwin teaches Imperial and Global History at Oxford, where he is a Fellow of Nuffield College. His book *After Tamerlane: The Global History of Empire since 1405* (2007) won the Wolfson Prize in History in 2008. In 2009 he published *The Empire Project: The Rise and Fall of the British World System 1830–1970*. A short study of British imperialism over the *longue durée* will be published later in 2012.

Margret Frenz is Research Associate at the Centre for Global History, University of Oxford, and Visiting Fellow at St Cross College. She currently works on multiple migration movements across the Indian Ocean and beyond it. Her publications include *From Contact to Conquest: Transition to British Rule in Malabar, 1790–1805* (2003) and 'Migration, Identity, and Postcolonial Change in Uganda: A Goan Perspective', *Immigrants and Minorities* (forthcoming), and '*Swaraj* for Kenya, 1949–1965: The Ambiguities of Transnational Politics', *Past & Present* (forthcoming).

Clive Glaser lectures in history at the University of the Witwatersrand, in Johannesburg, South Africa. He gained his PhD at Cambridge in 1994 and is the author of *Bo-Tsotsi: The Youth Gangs of Soweto 1935–1976* (2000) and co-author (with Gail M. Gerhart) of *From Protest to Challenge*, volume 6: *Challenge and Victory, 1980–1990* (2010). He has written a number of articles on the history of youth, sexual practice, and crime in South Africa. In recent years he has turned his attention to immigrant history in South Africa, with particular focus on the Portuguese community. He edited the journal *African Studies* from 2001 to 2009 and is a member of the Wits History Workshop.

Isabel Castro Henriques is Professor of African and Colonial History at the University of Lisbon, Portugal and a founder of this university's African History Studies programme. She gained her PhD at Université Paris 1

Panthéon-Sorbonne in 1993. She works on two multi-disciplinary projects: 'Knowledge and Vision: Photography within the Portuguese Colonial Archive and Museum (1850–1950)' (ICS/UL), and 'The Making of a Slavery Museum in Lagos' (Algarve, Portugal). Her publications include *Commerce et changement en Angola au XIXe siècle* (1995; revised Portuguese edition, 1997); *A Rota dos Escravos: Angola e a rede do comércio negreiro* (1996); *São Tomé e Príncipe. A invenção de uma sociedade* (2000); *Os Pilares da Diferença. Relações Portugal-África, Séculos XV–XX* (2004); *Território e Identidade – a Construção da Angola Colonial* (2004); and *Os Africanos em Portugal: História e Memória (XV–XX)* (2009).

Alexander Keese is Research Group Director at Humboldt University, Berlin, financed by an ERC Starting Grant of the European Commission. He works on forced labour under colonial rule in West Central and South Central Africa from a comparative perspective. He is the author of *Living with Ambiguity: Integrating an African Elite in French and Portuguese Africa, 1930–61* (2007) and is editor of *Ethnicity and the Long-Term Perspective: The African Experience* (2010).

Nicole Khouri is Assistant Professor (Maître de conférences) at the Institut du développement économique et social (IEDES) at Université Paris 1 Panthéon-Sorbonne, and a researcher at the Centre d'études des mondes africains (CEMAf), CNRS/Université Paris 1. Her work focuses essentially on modernity and socio-religious movements in Egypt and the Middle East. She has also been doing research in the past ten years on the Indians in and from the Lusophone world, in particular the Ismailis from Mozambique. She has published in and directed special issues with Joana Pereira Leite in the journals *Lusotopie* (2008) and *Outre-Mers* (2008).

Lorenzo Macagno is Professor of Anthropology at the Federal University of Paraná, Brazil. He has been conducting fieldwork in Mozambique since 1996. His main research interests focus on the Portuguese colonial imaginary and its consequences, transnational identities, multiculturalism, and diasporas in the Lusophone world. He has been a visiting scholar at the Centre d'Étude d'Afrique Noire (now know as 'Les Afriques dans le monde') at the Institute of Political Studies of Bordeaux and in the Department of Anthropology at Columbia University, New York. He is the author of *Outros muçulmanos. Islão e narrativas coloniais* (2006) and co-editor, with Fernando Rosa Ribeiro and Patricia Santos Schermann, of *Histórias conectadas e dinâmicas pós-coloniais* (2008) and, with Silvia Montenegro and Verónica Giménez Béliveau, of *A Tríplice Fronteira. Espaços nacionais e dinâmicas locais* (2011).

Eric Morier-Genoud is Lecturer in African and Imperial History at Queen's University, Belfast, Northern Ireland. He has written extensively on religion and on politics in southern Africa. He works on missionaries and transnational sciences and politics, as well as war, memory, and memorial in contemporary Mozambique. He is co-editor of the journal *Social Sciences and Missions*; a co-author, with Caroline Jeannerat and Didier Péclard, of *Embroiled: Swiss Churches, South Africa and Apartheid* (2011); and the editor of *Sure Road? Nationalisms in Angola, Guinea-Bissau and Mozambique* (2012).

Joana Pereira Leite is Assistant Professor at the Instituto Superior de Economia e Gestão da Universidade Técnica de Lisboa (ISEG/UTL) and a researcher at the Centre of African and Development Studies (CEsA/ISEG) in Lisbon, Portugal. She trained as an economic historian and got her PhD from the École des Hautes Études en Sciences Sociales (EHESS) in Paris. She has published widely on topics such as the economics of the Portuguese Empire, colonialism, industrialisation, the social history of Mozambique, and the Indian diaspora in East and southern Africa.

AbdoolKarim Vakil is Lecturer in the Department of History and the Department of Spanish, Portuguese, and Latin American Studies at King's College, London. He is co-editor, with S. Sayyid, of *Thinking through Islamophobia: Global Perspectives* (2010) and co-author, with Fernando Amaro Monteiro and Mario Machaqueiro, of *Moçambique: Memória Falada do Islão e da Guerra* (2011).

Rosa Williams is a PhD candidate in History at the University of Chicago. She is writing her dissertation on the roles that biomedical ideas and practices played in processes of colonial state formation in Mozambique. She contributed a chapter titled 'Migration and Miscegenation: Maintaining Boundaries of Whiteness in the Narratives of the Portuguese Colonial State in Angola, 1875–1912' to Philip J. Havik and Malyn Newitt (eds), *Creole Societies in the Portuguese Colonial Empires* (2007).

1
Introduction: Portugal, Empire, and Migrations – Was There Ever an Autonomous Social Imperial Space?

Eric Morier-Genoud and Michel Cahen

It is a well-established understanding in historiography that empire building is closely linked to human migration, both as a cause and a consequence. The historiography on the subject is rich, with many articles and books about the movement of metropolitan people to the colonies as well as colonised individuals and groups moving within the empire and to the metropole (the mother country) during and after empire. As noted by many, the coincidence between empire and migration is not perfect since many people migrated during empire but outside the formal imperial space or within the imperial space but before or after formal subjugation. Still, the coincidence remains very important.[1]

What is less clear is whether empire building can – and historically did – result in the formation of *autonomous social spaces* of migration. By that, we mean spaces developed originally by metropolitan societies, but which became autonomous from the metropole and broader than the political space in which movement takes place at the demand of, above all, the state and large companies. Said differently, did empire create spaces which became quasi-natural for individuals and social groups within them and which had lasting significance, notably after the empire disintegrated?

It is our hypothesis that empires can create such autonomous social spaces of migration, though not necessarily during the formal period of subjugation. It is the aim of this book to investigate whether this process took place in the case of the Portuguese empire specifically. The Portuguese case is of particular value since Portugal was the first to engage in empire building in modern times and the last to decolonise (in 1975); hence it was the one with the most potential to create such an autonomous space of migration. In relation to the Portuguese-speaking historiography, this question is important because there is today much discussion about the heritage of empire, notably in relation to language and to an alleged natural connection between countries formerly colonised.

Before we push this discussion further and before we engage in case studies, we need to discuss some key concepts and historical dynamics in relation to migration, empire, and Portugal, to avoid misunderstandings. We need in particular to look at what kind of empire the Portuguese created and what the term *diaspora* means. The concepts of empire and diaspora have become so popular and prevalent that they are now polysemic and thus very problematic to use unless defined narrowly and precisely. Later in this introduction, we will examine the issue of imperial migrations, ideology, and heritage so as to be able to think critically about what happened after the Portuguese Empire ended, not least in relation to the alleged emergence of a lusophone identity.

Portugal, Empire, and imperialism

The concept of empire has today become so protean in the social sciences that it defies anyone from engaging in comparison. We will not enter here in a discussion about what an empire is generally speaking, but in relation to Portugal specifically. Our question is what kind of empire was the Portuguese Empire?

To start with, we need to distance ourselves from the generic concept of Michael Hardt and Antonio Negri in their book *Empire* (2001), which is based on the idea that capitalism has (almost) achieved its global expansion and that there is therefore no more imperialism (or only one single imperialism). Indeed, this is not a helpful point of departure, and it contradicts all the studies about capitalist expansion in the 19th and 20th centuries that led to the launch of colonial empires (not to mention the ancient and medieval empires). These studies do indicate a capitalist advance of course, but not one towards a teleological path to totality. On the contrary, they show many historical paths marked by indigenisation and the continuation of older modes of production, leading to what Marxist anthropologists and others have called an 'articulation of modes of production' (Rey 1971; Meillassoux 1960, 1964, 1975; Berman and Lonsdale 1992; Bayart 1994). These articulations had major consequences – for example, intercontinental migrations and major inter-African migrations (between countries as well as from the rural to the urban) – and this led to such articulations taking specific forms. In other words, there cannot be one Empire (except as a theoretical idealtype): historically there were and presumably will continue to be many empires that follow specific historical trajectories.

In the present book, we adopt the hypothesis that Portuguese imperialism was not of a special nature or exceptional; for example, that it would be uneconomic (Hammond 1966). We reckon instead that it belongs to the family of European imperialism and was driven by the same global factors

Introduction 3

driving capitalist economic expansion – a search for new markets and primary resources. This is not to say that there are no particular nuances or that we underestimate political or cultural aspects (Clarence-Smith 1985; Cahen 1987, 1995). It is rather an argument that the fundamental dynamics of imperialism were similar in the Portuguese case to those of other European metropoles. This is the premise from which our analysis needs to begin.

Of course the Portuguese Empire had particularities, but the main one is probably due simply to its historiography, which includes an influential thesis about the exceptionality of the Portuguese case. This thesis is quite old, emerging at first within Portuguese nationalism itself, and it was integrated in different ways and different places in the academic literature in Portugal as well as abroad: from within the most classic Lusotropicalism to a national-Christian ideology, and Third Worldism (see below). A more recent theoretical development (in the 1960s) even argues that Portuguese colonialism would have been a 'subaltern colonialism' since the metropole was itself a 'neo-colony' or an 'informal colony' of Great Britain. Portugal's colonies would therefore be territories held by procuration, second-degree colonies of other empires, to the point that its colonised people would not have clearly known who their master really was. Put forward by the historian Perry Anderson in 1961–2 (under the title 'ultracolonialism'; see more below), the argument was recently revived by the Portuguese sociologist Boaventura de Sousa Santos. He argues not only that Portugal was an informal British colony but that, since the 17th century, 'the dominance of discourses emanating from the British imperial space during the colonial period that sought to explain the nature of the current world order meant that it was difficult for those inhabiting the Lusophone space to voice experiences that did not match those of the British empire'.[2] From there he argues further:

> Could it be that the Portuguese colonized people have a double problem of self-representation: vis-à-vis the colonizer who colonized them, and vis-à-vis the colonizer who, not having colonized them, has nonetheless written the history of their colonial subjugation. Or, on the contrary, could it be that the problem of self-representation of the Portuguese colonizer creates a chaotic disjunction between the subject and the object of colonial representation which, in turn, creates a field apparently empty of representations (but in fact full of sub-codified representations) that gives the colonized enough leeway to attempt their self-subalternity? The question here is to determine whether those colonized by a subaltern colonialism are under-colonized or over-colonized. (Santos 2002, 11)

It is not our aim here to deny the relative dependence of Portugal in relation to the United Kingdom but rather to evaluate its importance. First, Sousa

Santos seems strangely to ignore other influences, notably the influence of Republican France on its imperial project and the capacity of Portugal itself to influence other empires.[3] And, since he goes back to the 17th century, how could he ignore the Dutch influence, so crucial in this period? More importantly, saying that Portugal was an informal British colony (until when?) and to deduce from this fact that its imperialism constructed only a subaltern colonialism can mean only that Portugal belonged to the periphery of the world, much like what was called later the Third World. The concept of 'semi-periphery',[4] often advanced to describe such a situation, does not resolve the contradiction in thinking, for it does not resolve the incompatibility between a Portugal which would have belonged to the *periphery of the center* and a country whose economic backwardness would have put it outside of the center, that is, in the *periphery of the world*. Unless we push the theorisation further and argue that, since the mid-19th century, there existed a stabilised category of intermediate countries. Such a hypothesis, hazy as it is (though it is common today to refer to emerging countries), is problematic though when we talk of the formation of imperial hegemony. It is true that countries in an America which still hesitated calling itself Latin (Bethel 2010) were not comparable to African states and African peoples that European powers were about to conquer; hence they could be called intermediate. But, as different as they may have been, they still belonged to the periphery of the capitalist world in expansion – part of a heterogeneous periphery, like the center itself, both produced by historical capitalism (Wallerstein 1996). In the case of Portugal, what we are talking about is an expanding metropole, part of a heterogeneous capitalist center.

To admit the heterogeneity of the capitalist center does not mean we question the latter's existence or nature. Instead it allows us to understand, in the *longue durée*, that, as cofounder with Genoa and Castile of the capitalist world system (Wallerstein 1996), Portugal remained at its historical heart. Had this not been the case, Portugal would not have remained independent; it would have lost its independence like Morocco. And even less would it have kept its empire; at best it would have lost its colonies to Western powers, like Turkey lost hers.

Paradoxically, the ideological notion that Portugal would have been a subaltern country has been reinforced by the Carnation Revolution, since a section of the April 1974 captains and the Portuguese Left theorised the quasi belonging of Portugal to the Third World – something which permitted it to claim a Lusitanian capacity to retain or build exceptional nonimperialist connections with Third World countries – in a kind of South-South relationship. Indeed, the Lusotropicalist myth (often referred to or discussed in this volume) about the innate quality of the Portuguese relation with the Tropics, even if it be painted red, continued after 1975.

William-Gervase Clarence-Smith (1985) has already dealt with some of these issues, countering, for example, Perry Anderson's thesis, which analysed Portugal as a case of ultracolonialism because of its alleged weakness (Anderson 1961–2). Anderson was not arguing that a European country maintained the link to its empire against a European integration. On the contrary, he showed that the Portuguese bourgeoisie wished to further integrate into Europe (in this sense, he disagreed with the future subalternist school), but its uncompetitive productive apparatus led it to keep its empire so as to be able to sell low-cost products in Europe. This hypothesis has been undermined by history, however; if the Portuguese Estado Novo regime could not survive decolonisation, Portuguese capitalism certainly did (Cahen 2008). It is worth quoting here extensively from the introduction of Clarence-Smith's book *The Third Portuguese Empire*:

> The origins of this book go back to the frustration which I felt when writing my doctoral thesis on southern Angola in the late nineteenth and early twentieth centuries. The emphasis of the thesis was on the African response to conquest, but I kept trying to find out why the Portuguese were there at all and what they were attempting to achieve. The standard answer[5] was that the Portuguese had no economic interest in empire and were motivated entirely by humiliated national pride.[6] If any region should have fitted this hypothesis it was southern Angola, an impoverished area on the edges of the Kalahari desert. And yet, the further I got into archives and libraries, the more uneasy I felt with the idea.
>
> There was an alternative explanation available, or rather a rider to the first one: Britain was using Portugal as a kind of 'front man' for its own imperial ambitions. This had the advantage of conciliating the idea that Portuguese colonialism was uneconomic with the Leninist theory of imperialism, according to which a country had to be bursting with surplus investment funds in order to expand. Portugal clearly did not fit the Leninist bill, whereas Britain equally clearly did. *The only hitch with this neat logical construction was that it did not mesh with the information which I was turning up, for Portugal was not a puppet of Britain and the interests of the two countries clashed constantly in the colonial field.* [our emphasis]
>
> The hypothesis with which I ended up is not original, but it is far more satisfactory. The driving force behind imperial expansion was the search for markets, to which I would add a constant preoccupation with the need for foreign exchange, in short a renewed mercantilism. Portugal, a developing but weak capitalist country, fitted perfectly with this explanation. [...]
>
> [Yet] I am no economic determinist, nor even 'in the last instance', and there is a place for understanding the autonomy of political and ideological motivations for Portuguese expansion. (Clarence-Smith 1985, vii)

Another very important aspect of Clarence-Smith's book is that it showed that Portuguese imperialism in the 19th and 20th centuries could not be understood merely within the political sphere controlled formally by Lisbon (that is to say, basically Portugal's African colonies); one has to include Brazil, even when one looks at the link between Portugal and Africa during the modern period (Alencastro 2000). Including Brazil in the equation causes the famous question of the lack of global profitability of Portuguese imperialism to collapse. Economic and financial links between Portugal and its former colony had developed dramatically since the latter's independence, and the same can be said about migration (leading to anti-Portuguese feelings in Brazil, which had a role in the collapse of the Brazilian Empire in 1889).[7]

In sum, it cannot be assumed that, because one country is in a situation of relative dependency to another, the former would become a colony, even an informal colony, of the latter and that the country would develop therefore a subaltern form of colonialism. All empirical research shows that the natives of the Portuguese colonies did not have much doubt about their identity as colonised and did not resent Britain behind Portugal. Conversely, when the Portuguese fought wars of conquest and, later, of counter insurrection – with many mass massacres (Pélissier 2004) – they battled with a clear and confident Portuguese nationalist conscience. And the latter was fully comparable to that of other imperialism and in no way subaltern, even if the Portuguese sometimes had to capitulate in the face of demands from Great Britain and even if these capitulations had considerable long-term political consequences. As to Africans, the coloniser they faced was definitely the Portuguese, to the point that some chose to side with the Germans during the First World War to try to get rid of the Portuguese (as illustrated in Sérgio Inácio Chichava's chapter). Of course there were instances of a state within the state, whether formalised (e.g. the charter companies in Mozambique) or not (e.g. Diamang in Angola), which express the weakness of Portugal. While, such companies also existed in other empires, the ones in the Portuguese colonies stopped operating late, only between 1929 and 1942. But Salazar's nationalism had a very concrete impact, notably at the economic level, and one should not underestimate it because of Portugal's alliance with Britain.

In the case of the charter companies, such as the Companhia de Moçambique (with mostly British, some French, and very little Portuguese capital), one can look at how the Governo do Território de Manica e Sofala strived to 'Portugalise' its administration (governor, administrators, police, money), including showing favoritism for the Roman Catholic Church at the expense of Protestant missions, to understand that the company took very seriously the fact that it was part of the Portuguese Empire. Determining 'whether the people colonised by a subaltern colonialism are under-colonized or over-colonized' (Santos 2002, 11) may sound tempting as a consequence of a purely theoretical thesis of subaltern colonialism, but it did not exist on the ground, historically speaking, for two reasons: (1) because it is simply historically impossible that a subaltern colonialism could independently exist from the end of the 17th century to 1974; (2) because the daily life of the native population in the Portuguese Empire (whether forced workers or the infinitesimal stratum of assimilated people) was not the life of a subcolonised people (either under- or overcolonised) but the life of colonised subjects *tout court*.

We have discussed the Portuguese Empire at such length for a good reason. The question under examination – whether the Portuguese Empire generated an autonomous social space of migration for the colonial population (this book will only marginally discuss the movement of colonised people; see below) – cannot be answered on the basis of the idea that the Portuguese Empire is somehow different. Essentially, the Portuguese Empire was not different from other empires. Hence, if the answer to our question is negative (i.e. the modern Portuguese Empire did not generate an autonomous social space of migration), it would not be because the Portuguese Empire was subaltern.

Again, it is true that the economic, financial, military, and political power of Lisbon was inferior to that of London and Paris. But it is a difference of degree, not of nature. Besides, it was not a difference to be noticed by the native people who were subjugated by the Portuguese. In other words, these differences between forms of imperialism do not remove the Portuguese from the family of modern European imperialism, springing from the expansion of the world system – on the contrary. Hence, the questions that we ask in this volume in relation to migration and colonies are exactly the same that one might want to ask about the other empires: (a) whether the migration that took place could form, in a major empire, a space politically circumscribed which would become not so much a natural as a social space of migration, (b) what was the impact of these migrations in the process of the formation of empire, and (c) what was the impact and legacy of such a space after empire. Needless to say, once this is agreed upon, we will be the first to recognise – and highlight in the present volume – the particularities of the Portuguese situation *between* and *within* the empires of this family of European imperialism. The fact that the Portuguese Empire was built on a long tradition of empires, that it had specific cultural traits (e.g. a singular national culture, a strong Catholicism, many vibrant imperial myths), and that it had unique social and demographic characters (e.g. strong petty-white milieus, old and highly heterogeneous Creole communities), leads us to the question of diaspora and colonial communities.

The Portuguese Empire, diaspora, and communities

The historical period covered in this volume is the short colonial 20th century, a period hardly comparable, in terms of migrations, to the previous centuries of merchant and slave trade. Emigration towards the first Asian and the second Brazilian Portuguese Empires was small in absolute numbers, but it constituted a very important and lengthy effort for a weakly populated motherland. The demographic effects of these movements of population were also very different, since they were migrations for life, with the few exceptions of those from high political or military rank. This definitive nature of migration explains why migrants were often persons who had been condemned to exile, convicted, as well as New Christians. Tellingly, two of the most well-known cases of 'return home' took place after the invention of the steamboat, namely the coming back of the Brasileiros (the Portuguese who migrated to Brazil) to the Beira region and northern Portugal, well known today because of the big and beautiful houses they built in Portugal, and the return of the Agudas (African slave traders established in Brazil) to the West African coast during the last period of the Brazilian slave trade (see Alpers and Ball's chapter). The formation of creolities was an outcome of the long distance between empire and colony and the difficulty of travel, as well as the product of an unbalanced sex ratio and slavery. This singular articulation occasionally produced Portuguese communities sui generis; for example, some Indian villages in Bengal still claim today to be Portuguese even though their inhabitants have probably never had any Portuguese blood in their veins – they might be the descendants to Asian mercenaries of Portuguese armies during the first Portuguese Empire (Caixeiro 2000).

In contrast, a majority of the Portuguese who went to Africa in the 20th century (whatever the politics of the New State, which was opposed to mass emigration to the colonies before World War II) left Portugal with the aim of coming back home (see Claudia Castelo's chapter). Often emigration was a way for them to leave the countryside in Portugal and enter the cities, be they in Africa (which the state claimed was part of Portugal itself). Of course, some migrants stayed in Africa and eventually died in the colonies where their children were born and grew up. Still, the majority of white people in Angola and Mozambique during the 20th century did not initially come to stay. And, tellingly, from about 1970 the balance between arrivals and departures began to change radically – there began to be more departures than arrivals in the colonies.

This book aims to show that the making of the third Portuguese Empire has not only been the work of heroes and satraps, of politicians, bishops, military, and rich businessmen, but also the work of communities and diasporas, including the ones of 'petty whites' and 'petty Asians'. These latter men and women had a role, whether we like it or not, in the making of the Portuguese Empire and in the formation of a possible Lusophone world today. If, as we have seen, some authors have argued that Portugal developed a relatively weak empire, it is also true that, because of this, Portugal relied heavily on diasporic/emigrated groups to create and maintain its empire.[8] Counterintuitively, the historiography has underestimated and understudied these communities. Their consideration in this volume should make a significant contribution to our understanding of the making, maintenance, and end of the Portuguese Empire.

Before we go any farther, we need to ask whether we can classify under the same concept of diaspora the communities that never were Portuguese (as in our Bengali example) and, say, the 20th-century white communities that did not have the time to stabilise in the long term (say over three generations). This remark does not mean to underrate the role of diasporas and immigrant communities in the making of the third Portuguese Empire and the making of a Lusophone world today. Rather, questioning the applicability of the term *diaspora* aims to specify (and avoid confusion over) social processes and historical trajectories. To start with, we need to enter the longstanding debate about what a diaspora is – not to resolve the debate nor define a *doxa* for this volume but to help us think critically and bring precision to our work and the topic at hand.

Diaspora is a term which has been widely criticised for its elastic if not elusive meaning. Christine Chivallon, a French geographer and anthropologist working on the black diaspora, concluded her latest book with the following words:

> In the event that the term 'diaspora' is still contested as an appropriate means of designating the innovative collective expressions derived from this trajectory of forced dispersion, we can at least concede that, as an analytical category, 'diaspora' remains a valid tool facilitating our approach to an astoundingly instructive cultural universe. (Chivallon 2011, 203)

Aside from the statement that the concept of diaspora is helpful, Chivallon's quote is important for the implicit and very important distinction she makes between the analytical category of diaspora and the identity of diaspora. Indeed, she says that while the concept of diaspora as a common identity may be contested and problematic, the analytical concept of diaspora has heuristic value to describe reality.

That distinction may remind the reader of the Marxist difference between 'class in itself' and 'class for itself.' Marxist theory says that one may consider a given proletariat milieu to exist as an analytical category (class *in* itself – as a social and economic classification) even if the proletarians in question have no class consciousness (class *for* itself). The same could be said for diaspora. But a problem emerges here in that we are dealing with a wholly subjective matter, not a social or economic categorisation. If we deal with an identity or an imagination, can we speak of a category 'in itself'?

To give a concrete example, can one speak of a diaspora in the case of the so-called Lusophone communities in the United States of America? Can there be a feeling of commonality, of brotherhood, between the Portuguese immigrants, the Portuguese Americans, the Cape Verdean immigrants, the Cape Verdean Americans, the Brazilian immigrants and the Brazilian Americans since they are all 'lusophone'? We believe not, unless these people think and believe that there is such a commonality. Is it meaningful therefore to speak of a Lusophone diaspora in the United States of America? One can build statistics about speakers of the Portuguese language, but can we talk seriously about a Lusophone diaspora if there is no feeling of belonging together, no common self-representation? A constructive answer may be to say that there cannot be diaspora *in* itself: there might be a diaspora only if it is *for* itself. And, from there, we can engage in a study of how a diaspora comes into being or is formed historically, rather than presume that a diaspora exists and impose a hypothesis onto reality and deduce facts from theory.

Robin Cohen's Weberian approach to diaspora is helpful here as it both defines and opens up the concept. The author creates an ideal type of diaspora against which one can compare and discuss concrete cases (Cohen 2008, 17). His ideal type of diaspora includes the following eight key characteristics: dispersal or expansion from homeland, collective memory and myth about the homeland, an idealisation of ancestral home, development of a return movement, a strong ethnic group consciousness, a troubled relationship with host societies, a sense of empathy and coresponsibility with one's coethnics, and finally, the possibility of a distinctive creative life (ibid.).

Building on this, Cohen goes on to construct a typology of subtypes of diasporas, three of which are particularly relevant for our discussion. First, there is the imperial (or quasi-imperial) diaspora; second, the trade diaspora; and third, the labour diaspora. To our mind, this corresponds to a class division between different diasporas, which is adequate and more useful than a mere distinction between elite and proletarian diasporas. These three subtypes also correspond to the majority of cases in the Portuguese Empire, especially if we allow for a combination of types. The point however is that there are many types of diasporas and that each type is usually diverse, with divisions along gender, generation, or caste lines (to mention only a few).

Considering all of Cohen's eight key characteristics, one finds a critical time factor. Indeed, it seems impossible to speak about diaspora as soon as migrants arrive somewhere. An immigrant community may have some characteristics of a diaspora (dreams about the motherland, for example), but if the children born in the arrival society integrate so deeply and quickly that such a community disappears after their parents' death, it is meaningless to speak of a diaspora. In other words, diasporas need historicity to exist – there is no immediate birth of a diaspora, no 'immediate history' (Soulet 2009)[9] of a diaspora. On the contrary, diasporas form only with time: after the first migrants pass away, their children and grandchildren need to maintain the community to be able to talk of a diaspora.

Seen and defined in this way, can we speak concretely of Portuguese diasporas? The answer varies, depending on the case studied and its context. In France, one can probably not speak of a Portuguese diaspora because, even in large Portuguese communities, the Portuguese identity has always disappeared after two or three generations. In contrast, in the United States in Bedford, Massachusetts, for example, a sense of community has remained after several generations, a community with its own organisation, specific cultural and religious events, and so on. In this case, we can speak of a Portuguese diaspora – which, needless to say, is different from a Lusophone diaspora.

Closer to our interest, can we speak of a diaspora in relation to the white Portuguese who went to Africa? The answer is difficult and politically loaded. We would argue that, in relation to the men and women who migrated at the end of the 1950s and the beginning of the 1960s, one may have seen (the beginnings of) a process of diaspora formation. Whether these settlers planned to return to Portugal or not, the majority of these men and women did not have time to develop into a diaspora, with historical depth, memory and mythification of the homeland, a troubled relationship with the host society, and so on. There probably were diasporic social formations among Portuguese whites, in particular, within the tiny white communities which had been in Africa for several generations – they were Portuguese (since their link to Africa was lived only through a colonial relationship), but their land was not Portugal anymore since Portugal was no longer a homeland to come back to even if it remained a founding reference (see Pimenta 2005, 2012). Similarly, one could refer to the Portuguese/Madeiran communities in South Africa, which were surprisingly more stable after the end of apartheid than the settler communities in Angola and Mozambique after decolonisation (see Clive Glaser's chapter). As Mozambique's historian Alexandre Lobato once wrote, 'I am perfectly Portuguese, but I am not a Portuguese from Portugal, I am a Portuguese from Lourenço Marques [today's Maputo], exactly as there are Portuguese from Lisbon or Porto, etc.' Such an utterance is typical of a diasporic man. But it is impossible to say that the whole Portuguese community in Africa was a diaspora.

Even if social sciences appeal for precision, the reality is that concepts are theoretically based, or ideal-types, which means in turn that concepts will never divide human groups and beings into 'chemically pure' categories. Hence, we may know what a community is in a broad sense and what a diaspora is in a more specific way – all diasporas are communities, but not all communities are diasporas. But it is impossible to locate the exact border between both types in real life. This said, the history of a diaspora will not be the same as the history of a mere community, as the cases of the Chinese, Goans, and Ismailis considered in the present book clearly show – see Lorenzo Macagno, Margret Frenz, Nicole Khouri, and Joana Leite's chapters.

If diaspora needs historicity to be characterised as diaspora, it does not mean that once a diaspora is formed, it is set in stone. As Clive Glaser points out in his chapter, a diaspora can actually disappear. In his case, it is clear that the Portuguese diaspora in South Africa (in its fourth or fifth generation) is diluting. In a very different case, Isabel Castro Henriques shows in her chapter that African slave communities in continental Portugal existed for a long time but did not survive the end of slavery in the European part of the empire. While they had been well organised before the 1773 decision of the Marquis of Pombal, notably in religious congregations of African/black Portuguese diasporas, they rapidly disappeared after that date. The disappearance of their social identity (slavery) seems to have been more powerful than the possible persistence of their ethnic one (blackness/African-ness), and both vanished progressively but quickly, leaving an important legacy for the Portuguese culture, toponymy, music, and the like (see Henriques' chapter and Henriques 2009a).

Of course, identities can always combine; hence, there may have been both Portuguese diasporas in South Africa and South African communities of Portuguese origin out of the same pot of people (so to speak). These may reveal different social and ideological trajectories: one of dilution and the other of genesis, both splitting apart at an unknown moment in history, the point being that the process is not only long-term, fractured, and internally diverse but also has multiple trajectories.

To conclude this section, it is worth highlighting the advantage of the problems of diaspora. The size of diasporas, their diversity, and their marginalisation might actually help us understand a bigger problem. Drawing on Partha Chatterjee (1993), we may argue indeed that diasporas have the potential of helping us understand the Portuguese Empire better because of their status. As subaltern and postcolonial studies have shown most effectively, the study of margins can reveal a lot about the core. Thereafter, following Partha Chatterjee, we could say that the study in the present volume of 'diasporic fragments' should help us better understand the 'imperial core'.

Diaspora, communities, and the formation of empire

A discussion of the terms *diaspora* and *community* is useful in itself, but we need to push the discussion further into the broader context – in our case, in relation to the empire. What we need to ask is not just whether there were diasporas in the Portuguese Empire and what kind of diasporas existed but also *which kind* of diaspora or community had *what kind* of relations with the Portuguese Empire. What kind of relation did a trade diaspora, say from Asia, have with the Portuguese Empire at different points in time? What kind of relation did the white Portuguese have with their (idealised) homeland? How did they contribute to the formation of empire, what function did they come to fulfil, what new connections did

Introduction 13

they provide, what kind of ideology did they have, and so on? Asking such questions should permit one to have a complex and subtle understanding of diaspora/community in the Portuguese Empire, and it should permit us to avoid falling into the trap of merely asking the political question which the Portuguese officials (and later on the African nationalists) asked – namely, were the diasporas in favour of or against empire, in favour of or against decolonisation?

Even at the political level, the issue is all but simple. To start with, the generations of white communities must be carefully distinguished. First, there were tiny but old Creole milieus, crucial for the founding myth of the Third Empire but considered with great distrust by Lisbon, which always feared the birth of 'new Brazils' (autonomism). Second, there were those we call 'old settlers' (*velhos colonos*), that is, white Portuguese who came from Portugal and Madeira before World War II and who were few, often poor, and sometimes socialist or anarchist (Capela 1983). During their days, white immigration was not important numerically, since Lisbon did not encourage it (in particular after the 1929 world crisis), and Brazil remained the main destination of all Portuguese emigration. Third, during the last period (since the end of the 1950s at the demographical level and with political signals after 1951–1954), white immigration to Africa became a priority for the government in Lisbon, not just because Portugal would have liked to 'create new Brazils', but also because it was a way for Portugal strategically to resist foreign capital and the 'winds of history' (decolonisation).

Moreover, with the constitutional reform of 1951,[10] the legal term 'colonies' was replaced by the words 'overseas provinces,' thus reviving the old concept of the liberal monarchy, which had been abandoned in 1930. This meant that the unity of the nation was politically reinforced; there was no longer one mother country and colonies belonging to the Empire, but only one Portugal with '*províncias*'. Everybody was therefore *directly* Portuguese, which implied the existence of different personal statuses within the same nation and political constitution. The Acto Colonial of 1930 was replaced by the Overseas Constitutional Law in July 1953[11]. This institutional engineering led to the use of political tools to prevent dangers from abroad – not yet the pressure from decolonisation but the growing influence of foreign capitalist companies. On 20 May 1954, the Portuguese government published a new Native Statute (the previous one dated from 1926)[12] in response to a rise in the number of 'detribalised natives.' The new statute's conditions for assimilation[13] made it more difficult for skilled black workers to compete with white settlers in the market of qualified labour (Cahen 1983–1984). At around the same time (1953), the government launched a series of development plans for the colonies (Pereira 2012). From then on, Lisbon strove to overcome a dangerous contradiction: it needed to encourage a massive immigration to Africa in order to protect the Empire against foreign capitalist penetration, but at the same time, it feared the transformation of the white working class into a wealthy Lusocolonial petit-bourgeoisie which would inevitably become 'brazilianist' and autonomist – as the electoral results of Humberto Delgado, the candidate of the Republican opposition in 1958 seemed to indicate.[14] It is not by chance that 1965 was the year of the publication of the new Foreign Investment Code and the year of the main immigration to Africa, just after the creation (in 1962) of the Juntas províncais de Povoamento (Provincial Settlement Council) (Penvenne 2005). Without going any further, the periodisation we have painted is sufficient to contest the tradition of arguing for a Portuguese specificity in having always developed a settlers' colonisation. The reality is that it depended on the periods and the contexts, and it varied in degrees.

The Portuguese white population was never a tool sufficient to keep, save, and develop the colonies – colonial population had to be larger, in spite of Salazarist nationalism. Mixed-race people and *assimilados* were tiny groups. Thus, we need to study what kind of contribution the other Europeans and other colonial subjects made to Portuguese imperialism at different points in time (occupation, colonialism, decolonisation). How did they relate to empire, how did they contribute to it (or not), and how did they develop an imperial culture themselves or contribute to the general imperial culture?[15] What specificities did these diasporas and communities or some of their elements bring to the Portuguese imperial system and culture? The chapter of Sérgio Chichava, Lorenzo Macagno, Margret Frenz and that of Nicole Khouri and Joana Pereira Leite bring us some very useful answers about the Swiss, the Chinese, and the Indian Ismailis in relation to Mozambique; but the same questions could be raised for all the Portuguese colonies in Africa about the Greeks, Italians, Lebanese (in Guinea), and the other Indians (in Mozambique), as well as for areas at the fringe of empire (see Margret Frenz's chapter on the Goans in East Africa). A special case is examined in this volume with the Cape Verdean diaspora, mostly present in Portuguese Guinea and São Tomé but also in Angola and Mozambique. In his chapter, Alexander Keese brings precious information about this long dynamic. It is the history of a huge political error on the part of the Portuguese administration in the last colonial period. Confronted during the 1960s with growing difficulties in recruiting skilled European colonial officers (when jobs in trade or industry were now flourishing and far more lucrative than being a civil servant) and realising the need to Africanise its imperial apparatus of state to refound its legitimacy, Lisbon expanded its use of Cape Verdeans. The result was not as expected because Angolans and Mozambicans perceived Cape Verdean officers just as they perceived white Portuguese officers. At the same time, this choice prevented Portugal from making the effort of Africanising its administration, and it induced yet more contradictions within the heterogeneous colonial population at a time when colonised people were developing liberation struggles.

A social area of migration?

It is necessary now to come back to our original question about whether the Portuguese Empire generated an autonomous social area of migration. As we saw, the answer cannot be simple, and it probably is a mostly negative one. Even if the Portuguese state did not board migrants onto ships and planes,[16] the migration of white people to the colonies was not stable, and it was highly sensitive to political contexts. If Brazil had not slowed down immigration in the mid-1950s, Portuguese society would have definitively continued to emigrate to this former colony rather than to Africa. And, at the beginning of the 1960s, it was emigration to western Europe and France which was willingly practiced by most Portuguese migrants. Emigration to Africa never succeeded in becoming the main trend in emigration, even if it must not be underestimated either: it concerned probably about 25 per cent of the whole, thanks to its politicised context. The same can be said about Cape Verdeans, who were not considered native and could migrate far more freely than the natives of the continental colonies. But it would be difficult to consider the Cape Verdean colonial officers appointed in Guinea, Angola, and Mozambique as a migration trend. The migration to São Tomé and Príncipe had been highly organised by the colonial government as a solution to the starvation of the 1940s; Cape Verdeans had always preferred migrating to the United States or Holland.

In contrast, one can find something of an imperial social area of migration on the side of non-Portuguese colonial subjects. The Portuguese government, for example, never did anything to attract the several Indian communities that established themselves in Mozambique, yet they travelled there nonetheless. Even more interesting is the case of the Ismailis, who, when they decided to leave Mozambique in 1972, did not leave the Empire but went to Portugal itself, which was still under a dictatorship. Many Madeirans also went to South Africa from the end of the 19th century onwards, sometime directly and sometimes through a preliminary stay in Mozambique; thus, they built their own social area of migration, combining two empires. Goans migrated to British East Africa but rarely migrated thereafter back to the Portuguese Empire, even if Portuguese Goa and, therefore, Portugal itself, remained a point of reference. Overall there seem to have existed separate and impermeable Goan trajectories – those who went to the British Empire seldom crossed with those who went to Mozambique; they were in different professions, more merchants in the first case and more bureaucratic jobs in the second. Last but not least, the Chinese from Mozambique migrated within the Empire but not in the Third Empire. They migrated in the late second Portuguese Empire, a majority of them choosing to go to Brazil instead of Portugal after decolonisation!

Such heterogeneity of situations shows how the Portuguese Empire only very modestly succeeded in becoming a social area of migration for its colonial populations. As we have noted above, another book would be necessary to study the migration of colonised people within the empire; the subject would demand that we deal with completely different trajectories, not just of those occupying the lands but also of those who escaped legally or illegally these same lands or disappeared within them. Alpers' chapter partly covers this problematic, but the rest of our book does not. For reasons of coherence and space, we have decided to focus on the colonial rather than the colonised people. This said we may still note that some migrations of the colonised population were 'managed' by the Portuguese (rather than repressed), as the historical trend of Mozambicans going to the more developed capitalism of South Africa and Southern Rhodesia shows (in particular to the mines of the Rand, which became an essential source of income for the Bank of Portugal; see First 1983, Leite 1990, Lachartre and Vidal 2001). Other colonised people's migrations were also essential for the political history of the colony, as in the case of the Bakongos' emigration to Kinshasa from the 1940s (Marcum 1969–1978; Pélissier 1978; Messiant 2006). The point, though, is that the migrations of colonised people were not about moving within the empire (with the exception of those who were not officially considered natives, i.e. the Cape Verdeans and Santomeans) but about going abroad (except when forced into migration, as in the case of Angolans and Mozambicans deported to São Tomé or the seasonal or annual migrations of *contratados* in the two African colonies – officially they were indentured labourers, but in practice they were forced labourers – up to 1962). Said differently, the Portuguese Empire was not a social area of migration for the colonised people but a social area of repulsion – right up to the 1960s,[17] and so the migration of the colonised people is only partly embraced in our book in two chapters: in the state of the art by E. Alpers (with M. Ball) and in Isabel Castro Henriques' contribution. In the latter, it is something of a false exception, since migrating Africans were legally no longer natives (*indígenas*) when they arrived in Portugal (in small numbers up to the 1970s), even if they fell under the Native Statute in Guinea, Angola, and Mozambique.[18]

Coming back to colonial people, one useful way to think at the theoretical level about their relation to the social area of migration is to reflect on what would have happened if decolonisation had not occurred or had occurred in a completely different way (e.g. independence without decolonisation). The case of Zimbabwe after 1979 (up to the antiwhite turn of Robert Mugabe) helps us think about such a hypothesis. Drawing from that example, we can advance that it is very probable that many more Portuguese colonial people would have stayed in Africa, perhaps half of them, as opposed to what happened – more than 99 per cent left.[19] Obviously there would not have been any 'Brazilian trend,' with hundreds of thousands of Portuguese going to Africa *after* independence (in spite of some appearances in this direction today, see below). Indeed, colonialism in Africa was very different from the case of Latin America, which includes Brazil. There the colonised people (the first Indian nations) were eliminated or greatly reduced in numbers (except in some Andean countries), and a new society was born thereafter, shaped and developed by the coloniser. Hence, the independent Latin American societies are not colonised societies but actually colonial societies – and the presence of black slaves (who could not reconstitute African societies there)[20] does not change this reality in any way. In such a colonial society, there are no structural difficulties in receiving more and more immigrants since the social formation is itself the fruit of colonialism. In contrast, in Africa, indigenous societies may have been conquered, humiliated, exploited, and acculturated, but they have never been eliminated or marginalised. They remained African societies, with their domestic mode of production, be they articulated to the global modes of production as we noted before. Therefore, every European individual immigrating to Africa had to conquer and carve out a social space out of or from the existing indigenous African society. Such a phenomenon was possible under the colonial minority rule as well as under apartheid, but it became impossible with independence under majority rule (even if a neocolonial independence). Significantly, some white minorities could have stayed for historical reasons, but there were no conditions for the development of a new 'Brazilian trend,' and these minorities would have slowly declined or become assimilated. Needless to say, the integration of Portugal into the European Union was another, additional, external reason for the nonexistence of whites going to the former imperial territories.

To conclude this section, we may connect our subject to today's new Portuguese migrations to Africa. Indeed, how does one relate to the other? Is there a continuation of an imperial social area of migration? To talk of Angola alone, there were 21,000 Portuguese immigrants in that country in 2003, and by 2011, there were no less than 97,616 nationals registered with the two Portuguese consulates in Angola – almost a fivefold increase in eight years.[21] The reality, however, is that the main reason for this new wave of emigration to Africa is the social and economic crisis in Portugal. Moreover, while colonial emigration to Africa concerned, historically speaking, Portuguese of higher social status (higher in Mozambique than Angola) while those going to France or Brazil were Portuguese of a lower level (Castelo 2007), the general characteristic of today's Portuguese emigration everywhere is of a middle-class nature – and the very latest trend in Angola confirms this. Portuguese go to Angola (and secondarily to Mozambique)[22] mainly in search of professional opportunities, and they leave Portugal with a plan to come back some years later. There is therefore no social continuity between this wave of migrants and the former colonial settler community, even if it is not by chance that very often the new migrants are sons or nephews of former white 'Angolans' or 'Mozambicans' – owing to the persistence of the myth of Africa and the

African memories of many Portuguese families. Which means, first, that this is a new (unconnected) wave of migration from Portugal and, second, that it is still too early to ascertain whether this new wave will be as significant and lasting as its predecessor, that is, whether it will develop a process of a diaspora building.

We need to discuss here an exception, even if it is perhaps an exception more formal than real. Indeed, there is one group of people for whom the Third Empire fully became a social area of migration, namely the Indian Ismailis of Mozambique who decided to leave Mozambique for Portugal in 1972, when Portugal was still the motherland of the Empire. Could it mean that, for this diaspora at least, the empire was really a social space of migration? The answer is both positive and negative. Aga Khan had understood that the empire was coming to an end, and so the decision to migrate from Mozambique to Portugal was taken in view of the ending of the Empire – in other words, the community was positioning itself already in the next period. Still, this non-Portuguese community went to Portugal because it had acquired cultural proximity with Portugal and its empire, for example, the ability to speak Portuguese. Of course the Portuguese *retornados* predominantly also returned to Portugal (though some went to South Africa, Brazil, Australia, and elsewhere), but this happened only because the Empire had ceased to exist, and they returned 'home.' Chinese also left the new African countries, but, for reasons explained in Lorenzo Macagno's chapter, a majority of them did not go to Portugal but to Brazil (Curitiba or São Paulo). Coming back to the Ismailis, they went to Portugal after 1972 but started to return to Mozambique in the mid-1990s. While this may seem to show that a social space of migration did exist for them and possibly other communities, there also seem to be elements which make them comparable to the Portuguese going to Angola today – they are migrating for short-term job opportunities more than with the idea of making their life there. This dynamic will need to be fully investigated (which Ismailis are going back, with what motivation, etc). For now, we may note that there is an exception in relation to the Portuguese imperial social area of migration, though it is still unclear whether it is a significant exception or just one that proves the rule (as the French saying goes).

All in all, if the Third Empire has predominantly not succeeded in becoming a social space of migration, it is not because it was not a relevant reality and imagined community for its colonial populations. John Darwin presents his view on this issue in the concluding chapter. For our part, we would like to advance the argument that Portugal is not a singular case in this respect but rather just another case, with its specificities and nuances. No settler colonisation has succeeded in the long term in the modern period in a place where colonised societies have managed to remain the majority. Latin and North America, Australia, and New Zealand are not exceptions precisely because their colonial societies exterminated or reduced to inconsequence the colonised populations. Has it ever been possible for another empire to become a social area of colonial migrations? Think of the pieds-noirs in Algeria only half of whom were French (the other half being Spanish, Italian, or Arab Jews) and who thus straddled empires. Think of the French in Ivory Coast, who were more numerous after independence, after Empire, than during colonialism, and the Caribbean people of the French 'old colonies' (Martinique, Guadeloupe, Réunion) who migrated to France in greater numbers after their complete integration into the republic than before (thus within the framework of a decolonisation without independence). The French Empire does not seem to have succeeded in becoming a social space of migration either, at least during the period of formal subjugation. Maybe the British Empire had more success in creating such a social space of migration, though if this is the case, it is probably more a matter of degree than of substance. Be that as it may, let us note finally that, whether they succeeded in creating a social space of migration or not, empires were also imagined entities. And this is particularly true in the Portuguese case, with a historically deep integration of Africa into the national imagining.

Ideology and heritage

We noted at the start of this introduction that, if political decolonisation may undo an empire, this might not translate into an automatic corresponding and concomitant undoing of all autonomous elements connected to it. In the last section, we mentioned cases of migration after empire which took place within the former imperial space. In this section, we want to discuss the ideological dynamics which were part of empire and lasted after empire. We are interested in the heritage of empire as well as the ideas and cultures which formed during empire and have continuities today in whole, in part, or in a new form. In some way it is a reflexive exercise, to look critically at how our societies think today about empire and how this heritage is managed and fought over. Just as importantly, the fact is that ideas and culture are an integral part of the dynamics of empire. Empire influenced and shaped profoundly everyone's ways of life and outlook in both the metropole and the colonies (Cooper and Stoler 1997). In turn, members of the empire, not least the imperial migrants, reappropriated the official script and developed their own set of ideas, contributing to cultures which continued in some form after the end of empire (Hall 2000; Blanchard and Lemaire 2003, 2004).

In the Portuguese case, the best example of a surviving, or rather reinvented, imperial structure and ideology comes with the Comunidade dos Paises de Língua Portuguesa (CPLP, the Community of Portuguese-speaking Countries). This is an interstate organisation which was launched in 1996 on the basis of the unification of a more informal state grouping entitled Cimeira dos Cinco (Summit of the Five) related to the five Paises Africanos de Língua Oficial Portuguesa (PALOP), and the old Comunidade Luso-Brasileira (Luso-Brazilian Community).[23] The aim of the new grouping is to gather all the Portuguese-speaking countries in the world, following on the example of the *Francophonie*, give them a formal body and tighten their social, cultural, and economic relations. Like its French counterpart, CPLP effectively groups countries which are Portugal's former colonies. Interestingly, however, the launch of CPLP did not refer to the colonial past but talked instead of an organisation which built on an existing community of people and countries which shared a language. Was this just a rhetorical trick? There were of course plenty of politics involved in the launching of the CPLP (see Rosa Williams' chapter and Cahen 2003). But the idea pushed forward by its non-African proponents (the governments of Portugal and Brazil), in spite of being unacceptable for its African members (Mozambique, Angola, Guinea-Bissau, and Cape Verde), not least in the title of the organisation, is that there exists a community of people, a Lusophone community, which shares a culture, developed on the basis of the Portuguese language. This raises two connected questions: Is there such a Lusophone community? And is the discourse around the CPLP, if not the organisation itself, not in reality an inheritance of an imperial past?

The question of the existence of a Lusophone community is complex. First, we need to ask whether the majority of people in the CPLP countries speak Portuguese. Drawing on studies by Michel Cahen and others, we can answer that the majority of citizens in former Portuguese colonial territories do not speak Portuguese fluently, if at all (Chapter 1; Cahen 1990, 2004). In Mozambique today, for example, only 6.5 per cent of the population claims Portuguese as its mother tongue, and only 39.6 per cent understands Portuguese (Cahen, Waniez, and Brustlein 2002). Hence, there is no objective basis for the existence of a community sharing the Portuguese language.[24] That is not to say that such a community cannot exist. What it means is that it does not exist on the basis of language, as claimed. In that sense, PALOP was a more accurate acronym since it implied that member states shared the same *official* language (rather than its population sharing the same language). Secondly, we need to note that a community can exist solely as a subjective reality, or as an 'imagined community.' In fact, we noted earlier that a community comes into being only if people believe it exists. If this is the case, then our question becomes whether a belief in a Lusophone community exists in the world today. While no systematic study has been carried out on the subject, circumstantial evidence suggests that this is not the case. In most of the CPLP countries, there is no sense of a Luso identity and often only a weak national identity (Cahen 1990; Morier-Genoud 2012). Thereafter, we may say that the Lusophone identity and community is at best the affair of *some* national elites and politicians who presumably share Portuguese as a native language, have connected cultural references, and travel within the former imperial space (for education, training, holidays, and so on).

If there is no Lusophone community *in* itself and little *for* itself, we need then to unpack the discourse around the CPLP and enquire how much of it is an imperial inheritance. Needless to say, there is little direct continuity between Portuguese imperialism and the new weltanschauung pushed for by the CPLP today. But the fact is that the discourse of today's politicians, be they Portuguese or from the former Portuguese colonies, draws heavily on a repertoire which revives, willingly or not, the imperial languages and several imperial myths. Among others, it builds on the colonial Lusotropical repertoire so as to claim a community of affection and therefore a community of action (see Rosa Williams' chapter). Such discourse seems to be little more than a discourse for the CPLP, these politicians, and their support base, and it operates on the basis of a 'working misunderstanding.' Brazilian politicians, for example, join in such a discourse, but they do not aim at rebuilding a community of language with Portugal at its center. Instead they join in the Lusophone discourse so as to be able to access markets and do politics with Portuguese-speaking countries without passing through Portugal. In other words, this neo-imperial discourse is a reinvention which suits, to a sufficient extent, the purpose of various political actors and governments. Does this mean it is an empty shell? Probably not, because it has consequences, and it has an impact on contemporary cultures – presumably fostering from above this very Lusophony which is imagined by so few. In addition, this discourse is not an empty shell because many people do not accept the official Lusophone discourse and politics (with its imperial and colonial undertones), but they engage it if only to subvert it. Between avoidance, resistance, and subversion, they reappropriate and reinvent the ideology and the heritage of empire and thus contribute to the formation of a new real, nonofficial, Lusophone identity, if not yet community (see AbdoolKarim Vakil's chapter).

How do imperial communities and diasporas relate to this question of Lusophony, ideology, and heritage? In terms of ideology, the question of the adherence of imperial communities and diasporas to imperialism has been well analysed, and studies have shown how the issue is far more complex and complicated than previously thought (see Castelo's chapter). In relation to diasporas more specifically, the issue remains largely underinvestigated. At first sight, it is far from obvious that diasporas in the Portuguese Empire would adhere to or assimilate the Portuguese imperial discourse (or fragments thereof) about civilisation, religion, and, later on, Lusotropicalism. Yet what Frenz and Macagno show in this volume is that some diasporas (Goans and Chinese in this case) did adhere to the imperial ethos and ideology.

Maybe they did so because they were a prime object of that ideology and because they benefited from the policy which went with it – they were the exemplary social groups which the Portuguese used to demonstrate that social mobility was possible for nonwhites and to show that Lusotropicalism was a reality. While adhered to by some diasporas, Macagno shows that this imperial ideology eventually crashed against a wall at independence, when postimperial Portugal decided to change the rules of the game and refused nationality to the majority of Chinese arriving from Mozambique. These Chinese thought they were already Portuguese, since they had been accepted and recognised by the colonial society of Mozambique, but this was suddenly not the case anymore; so they moved to Brazil. Interestingly and somewhat paradoxically, CPLP continues this exclusion of Lusophone diasporas and foreign communities since it builds on states and national communities (which often do not speak Portuguese, as we have seen) rather than on linguistic or cultural communities – of course, this is an interstate alliance, not a social one. Thus, CPLP seems, like so many, to be blind to how diasporas not only contributed to empire but were also sometimes made into Lusophone elements.

Conclusion

All in all, was there ever a social and autonomous Portuguese imperial space, distinct from the formal empire? The question cannot be definitively answered, but many elements of a complex answer will be provided in the coming pages. In many respects, we can say that there was no autonomous space of migration in the Portuguese Empire. As we have seen, most Portuguese men and women preferred going to Brazil, Europe, or South Africa rather than going to the colonies. That means that the state had to have a 'visible hand' to make people go to its imperial territories and become settlers. In some respects, one can also see that the second and third Portuguese Empires gave birth to a kind of path dependency which created autonomy for a social space of migration after the empires collapsed. Diasporas and communities moved in the postimperial space (Portuguese to Brazil up to the 1950s, Brazilians to Portugal after Portugal became a member of the European Union, Ismailis from Mozambique to Portugal mainly after 1974, Chinese from Mozambique to Brazil, *retornados* from Angola and Mozambique to Portugal and Brazil after 1974, and Cape Verdeans to Portugal, more after 1974 than ever before). Others tried to stay inside the imperial space after independence (Cape Verdeans in São Tomé and Angola, Indians in Mozambique). Last but not least, today some individuals come back to the former colonies (middle-class Portuguese to Angola, Ismailis to Mozambique). Ideological elements beyond decolonisation have also continued after independence, even among the diasporas, even if manipulated and reinvented. During the period of formal subjugation, the Third

Introduction 23

Empire was not uneconomic, but it was clearly 'undemographic.' Could we say that it inaugurated a new kind of victory – a postmortem one?

Notes

1. For a recent overview of migration and the British Empire, see Harper and Constantine 2010. For some recent work, see, among others, Watt 2009, Chilton 2007, and Constantine 1990.
2. Sousa Santos as quoted by Soares 2006, 11. It is worth noting that Anthony Soares, though in a finely shaded cautious way, sustains the view of Sousa Santos that we are criticising here.
3. Alexander Keese has convincingly demonstrated the Portuguese capacity to influence the French colonial model, at least during some specific periods (Keese 2007).
4. It is worth noting that 'informal colony' is a concept even more radical (and more questionable) than 'semi-colony': though 'informal', such a colony is *completely* a colony – not a 'semi' colony.
5. Clarence-Smith refers, in particular, to Hammond 1966.
6. Portugal's humiliation came on 11 January 1890, when the British gave the Portuguese government an ultimatum demanding the withdrawal of Portuguese military forces, led by Major Serpa Pinto, from the territory which lay between what became the colonies of Angola and Mozambique (present-day Zimbabwe and Zambia), an area which Portugal claimed as its own. The rapidity with which the Portuguese monarchy gave in to the British exigencies was experienced as a humiliation by a large part of the Portuguese population and elites, and it was to be one of the causes of the Republican revolution in 1910.
7. For a critical review of Clarence-Smith, see Cahen 1995.
8. The Indian diasporas, for example, were involved in financing some of the occupation and the business of the empire. Goans and Cape Verdeans staffed the colonial administration in Guinea Bissau, Angola, and Mozambique. And Italians, Swiss, and other foreign individuals were key to running the education and health system for Africans in the colonies, as well as many a capitalist company.
9. According to the French historian Jean-François Soulet, immediate history is the most contemporary phase of modern history; it is a history that is investigated with living witnesses. For example, in France it has become impossible to continue to do immediate history, and write first-person accounts, of the First World War, since the last poilus (the 'hairies', a popular nickname for trench soldiers) just died four years ago (2008).
10. Assembleia nacional (1952), *Constituição política da República portuguesa, actualizada de harmonia com a Lei n° 2.048 de 11 de Junho de 1951*, Lisbon.
11. *Lei Orgânica do Ultramar*, Law n° 2.066, 27 July 1953.
12. Ministério do Ultramar 1954, 'Decreto-Lei n° 39.666. Estatuto dos Indígenas Portugueses das Províncias da Guiné, Angola e Moçambique', *Diário do Governo* (Lisbon), I series, no. 110, 20 May, pp. 560–565.
13. Assimilation was the process by which a 'native' became a Portuguese citizen. Far from the ideology speaking highly of this 'tradition,' assimilation has remained always a very tiny phenomenon, in particular in Mozambique and Portuguese Guinea (it was a little bit more important in Angola), but always below

0.5 per cent of the whole population (Cape Verde Islands and São Tomé had no Native Statute). In 1950, mixed-race people represented, according to the official census, 0.60 per cent of the entire population of the African colonies (Cape Verde excluded; 1.57 per cent included).
14. Humberto Delgado officially won the elections in Beira (second city of Mozambique) and in Nova Lisboa (Huambo, second city of Angola). It is probable, if there had not been fraud, that he would have won the elections in the colonies and in Portugal itself.
15. Among the classics on the subject, see Catherine Hall 2000; in 2003 Patrick Harries organised a conference on 'Imperial Cultures in Countries without Colonies.' See the event's webpage at: http://pages.unibas.ch/afrika/nocolonies/.
16. The projects of direct colonisation, such as the *colonatos* (peasant settler schemes), were highly publicised but were extremely expensive for small groups or peasants going to the Tropics.
17. We are not speaking here of the exiles provoked by the colonial wars since 1961, and a remark must be made: Noting that the Portuguese Empire may have been a social area of repulsion does not mean that, in the long term, Portuguese colonisation was generally worse than other ones or more archaic. These features have to be cautiously analysed in terms of periodicity. But there is little doubt that, since the end of the 1940s, when compulsory labour disappeared in the other empires but spread massively in continental Portuguese Africa, at that period (from the Second World War up to 1958–61), Portuguese colonisation experienced an archaic twitching (Cahen 1987, 1995), exacerbated in southern and eastern Africa by the rapid development of British and South African colonial capitalism (Alpers 1984).
18. The situation of native Africans in Portugal was not clear. In the 1926 Native Statute, *indigenato* was a sociolegal status within the colony itself. In the 1954 statute, by force of the constitutional reform of 1951 unifying the nation, the quality of indigenousness or assimilation was made strictly individual in the entire area of the nation (§ unique of Article 1: 'The statute of the Portuguese indigenous people is personal and must be honoured in any part of the Portuguese territory where the individual who enjoys it is found.'). In principle, a native (*indígena*) coming to Portugal had henceforth to be considered there as a native too. But there was no forced labour, hut tax, paramount chiefs and distinct statistics to manage the natives in Portugal, so the distinction meant little in practice. Besides, the 1954 statute was never applied completely, up to its revocation in 1962. That is why the very small number of native Africans from Guinea, Angola, and Mozambique living in Portugal before 1962 were not considered native there (neither were they citizens). At the time, they could be included within the 'colonial migrations,' as Cape Verdeans and Santomeans, besides the white, Indian, and Chinese migrations. It is one more justification for the presence of a chapter about the Africans in Portugal in a book on colonial migrations.
19. Even if some individuals (or relatives) have come back to Angola and Mozambique since the middle of the 1990s, the number of Portuguese who, whether they became naturalised (white) Mozambicans/Angolans/Guineans or not, have permanently stayed is minute (see below).
20. Quilombos and Mocambos were not African societies reconstituted in Brazil, but black slave republics created at the margins of (but sociologically within) the colonial society, created sui generis by people violently integrated within the

colonial society. There are a few exceptions of deeply African rooted reconstitutions of societies, such as the Saramaka communities, who fled from Brazil to Suriname and later to French Guyana, where social relationships are typical of African societies (including matrilineal clans, etc.).
21. Mariana Correia Pinto, 'Angola: Reconstruir a vida num país em construção,' *Público* (Lisbon), 19 December 2011. In 2010, there were 91,900 Portuguese in Angola according to the statistics of *Direcção-Geral dos Assuntos Consulares e Comunidades Portuguesas*, Lisbon.
22. Migrants registered with the Portuguese consulate in Maputo have increased by 30 to 40 per cent in the last two year. See Nastasya Tay, 'Portugal's Migrants Hope for New Life in Old African Colony,' *The Guardian*, 22 December 2011.
23. CPLP includes Angola, Brazil, Cape Verde, Guinea-Bissau, Portugal, Mozambique, São Tomé, and Príncipe and Timor. Equatorial Guinea and Senegal are associated members. It is worth noting that Mozambique was a member of the Commonwealth, while Cape Verde, Guinea-Bissau, and São Tomé and Príncipe were members of the *Francophonie*, before joining the CPLP.
24. A disclaimer is in order here. When choosing the title of this book, we faced several possibilities, and a strong contender was 'Imperial Migrations in the Lusophone World.' We eventually chose not to use the term 'Lusophone World', because the term/concept Lusophone is very problematic as we have just seen. Can we speak of a Lusophone or Portuguese-speaking world? At best it is problematic. We decided therefore to use 'Portuguese World.' This is relevant because during the third Portuguese Empire (1885–1975), the empire constituted a 'Portuguese world,' at least politically. The term may sound a little outdated, but it is more precise and adequate – it is therefore better to talk of a Portuguese world during empire than to read back into the past a problematic Lusophone one.

References

Alencastro, Luíz Felipe de (2000), *O trato dos viventes: formação do Brasil no Atlântico Sul, séculos xvi e xvii*. Companhia das Letras, São Paulo.
Alpers, Edward A. (1984), '"To Seek a Better Life": The Implications of Migration from Mozambique to Tanganyika for Class Formation and Political Behavior', *Canadian Journal of African Studies/Revue canadienne des études africaines* 18, no. 2, pp. 367–388.
Anderson, Perry (1961–1962), 'Portugal and the End of Ultra-colonialism', *New Left Review* 1, nos 15–17.
Bayart, Jean-François (1994), 'Hors de la "vallée malheureuse" de l'africanisme', *Revue française de sciences politiques* (Paris) 44, no. 1, pp. 136–139.
Berman, Bruce, and Lonsdale, John (1992), *Unhappy Valley. Conflict in Kenya and Africa. 1. State and Class*. James Currey, London
Bethel, Leslie (2010), 'Brazil and "Latin America"', *Journal of Latin American Studies*, 42, pp. 457–485.
Bethencourt, Francisco, and Alencastro, Luiz Felipe de (2004), *L'Empire portugais face aux autres Empires, xvi-xixe siècles*. Maisonneuve & Larose/Centre Calouste Gulbenkian, Paris.
Blanchard, Pascal, and Lemaire, Sandrine (2003), *Culture coloniale. La France conquise par son Empire, 1871–1931*. Éditions Autrement, Paris.

Blanchard, Pascal, and Lemaire, Sandrine (2004), *Culture impériale. Les colonies au cœur de la République, 1931–1961*. Éditions Autrement, Paris.

Burbank, Jane, and Cooper, Frederick (2011), *Empires in World History: Power and the Politics of Difference*. Princeton University Press, Princeton (NJ).

Cahen, Michel (1983–1984), 'Corporatisme et colonialisme: Approche du cas mozambicain (1933–1979)', *Cahiers d'Études Africaines* (Paris) no. 92, pp. 383–417; no. 93, pp. 5–24.

Cahen, Michel (1987), 'Lénine, l'impérialisme portugais, Gervase Clarence-Smith', *Cahiers d'études Africaines* (Paris) nos 107–108, pp. 435–442.

Cahen, Michel (1990), 'Le Mozambique: Une Nation africaine de langue officielle portugaise? *Canadian Journal of African Studies* 24, no. 3, pp. 315–347.

Cahen, Michel (1995), 'Sur quelques mythes et réalités de la colonisation et de la décolonisation portugaise', in Charles-Robert Ageron and Marc Michel (eds), *Les décolonisations comparées. Actes du Colloque d'Aix-en-Provence*. Karthala, Paris, pp. 333–351.

Cahen, Michel (2003), 'What Good Is Portugal to an African', in Stewart Lloyd-Jones and António Costa Pinto (eds), *The Last Empire: Thirty Years of Portuguese Decolonization*. Intellect Books, Bristol and Portland, pp. 83–98.

Cahen, Michel (2004), 'Lusitanidade, "lusofonidade" e modernidade. Uma exploração nos conceitos de identidade e de nação', *Episteme. Revista interdisciplinar da Universitade técnica de Lisboa*. Lisbon, UTL, V (13–44): 123–139.

Cahen, Michel (2008), 'Salazarisme, fascisme et colonialisme. Problèmes d'interprétation en sciences sociales, ou le sébastianisme de l'exception,' *Portuguese Studies Review* (Trent University, Canada) 15, no. 1, pp. 87–113.

Cahen, Michel (2012), 'Indigenato before Race? Some Proposals on Portuguese Forced Labour Law in Mozambique and the African Empire (1926–1962)', in Francisco Bethencourt and Adrian Pearce (eds.), *Racism and Ethnic Relations in the Portuguese-Speaking World*, Oxford University Press, New York.

Cahen, Michel, Waniez, Philippe, and Brustlein, Violette (2002), 'Pour un atlas social et culturel du Mozambique', *Lusotopie* 1, pp. 305–362.

Caixeiro, Mariana Cândida (2000), 'True Christian or True Portuguese? Origin Assertion in a Christian Village in Bengal, India', *Lusotopie* 7, pp. 233–252.

Capela, José (1983), *O Movimento Operário em Lourenço Marques: 1898–1927*. Afrontamento, Porto.

Castelo, Claudia (2007), *Passagens para África: O povoamento de Angola e Moçambique com naturais da metrópole (1920–1974)*. Edições Afrontamento, Porto.

Chatterjee, Partha (1993), *The Nation and Its Fragments. Colonial and Postcolonial Histories*. Princeton University Press, Princeton (NJ).

Chilton, Lisa (2007), *Agents of Empire: British Female Migration to Canada and Australia, 1860s–1930*. University of Toronto Press, Toronto.

Chivallon, Christine (2011), *The Black Diaspora of the Americas: Experiences and Theories of the Caribbean*. Ian Randle, Kingston (Jamaica). 1st French edn, 2004.

Clarence-Smith, William-Gervase (1985), *The Third Portuguese Empire, 1825–1975: A Study in Economic Imperialism*. Manchester University Press, Manchester.

Cohen, Robin (2008 [1997]), *Global Diaspora: An Introduction*. Routledge, London.

Constantine, Stephen (ed.) (1990), *Emigrants and Empire: British Settlement in the Dominions between the Wars*. Manchester University Press, Manchester.

Cooper, Frederick, and Stoler, Ann Laura (eds) (1997), *Tensions of Empire: Colonial Cultures in a Bourgeois World*. University of California Press, Berkeley.

Derluguian, Georgi M. (2007), 'The Worlds Which the Portuguese, the Russians, and the Turks Created: Empires on Europe's Periphery', *Lusotopie* 15, no. 2, pp. 3–10.
First, Ruth (1983), *Black Gold: The Mozambican Miner, Proletarian and Peasant*. Palgrave Macmillan, Basingstoke.
Hall, Catherine (2000), *Cultures of Empire: A Reader. Colonizers in Britain and the Empire in the Nineteenth and Twentieth Centuries*. Manchester University Press, Manchester.
Hammond, Richard James (1966), *Portugal and Africa, 1815–1910: A Study in Uneconomic Imperialism*. Stanford University Press, Stanford.
Hardt, Michael, and Negri, Antonio (2001), *Empire*. Harvard University Press, Cambridge (MA).
Harper, Marjory, and Constantine, Stephen (eds) (2010), *Migration and Empire*. Oxford University Press, Oxford.
Keese, Alexander (2007), *Living with Ambiguity: Integrating an African Elite in French and Portuguese Africa, 1930–61*. Franz Steiner Verlag, Stuttgart.
Lachartre, Brigitte, and Vidal, Dominique (eds.) (2009), 'Afrique australe, Afrique lusophone. Mondes fragmentés, histoires liées' (dossier), *Lusotopie* 15, no. 1, pp. 47–155.
Leite, Joana Pereira (1990), 'La formation de l'économie coloniale au Mozambique, pacte colonial et industrialisation: Du colonialisme portugais aux réseaux informels de sujétion marchande, 1930–1974', PhD diss., École des hautes études en sciences sociales, Paris.
Marcum, John (1969), *The Angola Revolution*, vol. 1: *The Anatomy of an Explosion (1950–1962)*; (1978), vol. 2: *Exile Politics and Guerilla Warfare, 1962–1976*. MIT Press, Cambridge (MA).
Meillassoux, Claude (1960), 'Essai d'interprétation du phénomène économique dans les sociétés traditionnelles d'auto-subsistance', *Cahiers d'études africaines* (Paris, Ehess), December 4, pp. 38–77.
Meillassoux, Claude (1964), *Anthropologie économique des Gouro de la Côte d'Ivoire: De l'économie de subsistance à l'agriculture commerciale*. Mouton, Paris.
Meillassoux, Claude (1975), *Femmes, greniers et capitaux*. Maspéro, Paris.
Messiant, Christine (2006), *Angola 1961. Histoire et société, les prémisses du mouvement nationaliste*. Schlettwein, Basel.
Morier-Genoud, Eric (ed.) (2012), *Sure Road? Nationalisms in Angola, Guinea-Bissau and Mozambique*. Brill, Leiden.
Pélissier, René (1978), *La Colonie du Minotaure: 1926–1961*. Éditions Pélissier, Orgeval (France).
Pélissier, René (2004), *Les campagnes coloniales du Portugal*. Pygmalion, Paris.
Penvenne, Jeanne Marie (2005), 'Settling against the Tide: The Layered Contradiction of Twentieth Century Portuguese Settlement in Mozambique', in Caroline Elkins and Susan Pederson (eds.), *Settlers Colonialism in the Twentieth Century: Projects, Practice and Legacies*. Routledge, New York.
Pereira, Victor (2012), 'A economia do Império e os planos de fomento'. in Miguel Bandeira Jeronimo (ed), *O império colonial em questão*, Edições 70, Lisbon, 2012.
Pimenta, Fernando Tavares (2005), *Brancos de Angola. Autonomismo e Nacionalismo, 1900–1961*. Minerva, Coimbra.
Pimenta, Fernando Tavares (2012), 'Angola's Euro-African Nationalism: The United Angolan Front', in Eric Morier-Genoud (ed.), *Sure Road? Nationalisms in Angola, Guinea-Bissau and Mozambique*, Brill, Leiden.

Plant, George Frederick (1951), *Oversea Settlement: Migration from the United Kingdom to the Dominions*. Oxford University Press, Oxford.

Rey, Pierre-Philippe (1971), *Colonialisme, néo-colonialisme et transition au capitalisme*. Maspéro, Paris.

Santos, Boaventura de Sousa (2002), 'Between Prospero and Caliban: Colonialism, Postcolonialism and Inter-identity', *Luso-Brazilian Review* 39, no. 2, pp. 9–43.

Soares, Anthony (ed.) (2006), *Towards a Portuguese Postcolonialism*. Lusophone Studies, 4. University of Bristol, Bristol.

Soulet, Jean-François (2009), *L'histoire immédiate: Historiographie, sources et méthodes*. Armand Colin, Paris.

Wallerstein, Immanuel (1996 [1983]), *Historical Capitalism*. Verso, Brooklyn (NY) and London.

Watt, Lori (2009), *When Empire Comes Home: Repatriation and Reintegration in Postwar Japan*, Harvard University Asia Center, Cambridge (MA).

Part I

Longue-Durée Migrations in and around the Portuguese Empire

2
'Portuguese' Diasporas: A Survey of the Scholarly Literature

Edward A. Alpers with Molly Ball

The importance of the Portuguese diaspora cannot be overemphasized.[1]

The task we have set for ourselves is to provide an introduction to the range of historical and social science scholarly literature that addresses the global diasporas of Portuguese-speaking people and the formation of a Lusophone world.[2] Our chapter is organised chronologically to reflect the three principal phases of this long history, beginning with Portuguese expansion up to the end of the 18th century, continuing through the second and third Portuguese Empires, and concluding with the period following the end of the corporatist state in Portugal. Since we are historians, our approach to the subject matter is primarily historical and historiographical, although the most recent work tends to be sociological or anthropological. Since we are, however, well aware of the fact that not all subjects of the former Portuguese colonial empire speak Portuguese, our survey transcends Lusophonia to include such non-Lusophone diasporic communities. In general, however, while we include the Atlantic African islands in our analysis, except where noted in the text, we make no systematic attempt to discuss migrations by African colonial subjects of Portugal or African citizens of those postcolonial nation-states. Thus, although we use both Luspohone and Portuguese in the body of the text, the title of our chapter refers to Portuguese diasporas to indicate the range of migrations we discuss, rather than assuming there to be a monolithic Portuguese diaspora. Indeed, one of the principal themes that emerges from our survey focuses on issues of identity. Equally, it will become clear that differences among these diasporas and differentiation within them—including class, culture, gender, and religion—are perhaps

---

[1] Newitt, M. (2005), *A History of Portuguese Expansion, 1400–1668*, Routledge, London and New York, p. 255.
[2] The authors thank coeditor Michel Cahen for his close reading of our chapter and for his many valuable suggestions for additional materials.

more significant today than the similar, if not common, origins that they share.[3] In addition, we will point to work that remains to be done on the broadly defined topic; for despite a rich tradition of scholarship on the Portuguese Empire and an emerging body of work on modern emigration, there are clearly many lacunae in the literature and any number of research projects that might be taken up with profit.

Phase I: Portuguese expansion and Portuguese diasporas to 1800

The literature on Portuguese expansion is vast and we make no attempt here to review it comprehensively.[4] However, it is useful to remind ourselves that Portuguese expansion is not the same as the Lusophone diaspora, although initially the two were coterminous. For a very long time the story of Portuguese expansion and, even more so, that of Portuguese overseas settlement during this early period focused on official documentation and official schemes for populating the newly acquired Portuguese Empire with Portuguese settlers. An excellent example of this approach is António da Silva Rego's 1957 lectures at the University of the Witwatersrand, in South Africa, where he was Visiting Luis de Camões Professor of Portuguese Studies, published as *Portuguese Colonization in the Sixteenth Century: A Study of the Royal Ordinances (Regimentos)* (Johannesburg: Witwatersrand University Press, 1965). Silva Rego was a fine scholar, but he was also thoroughly imbued with the prevailing Eurocentric Portuguese ideology of empire, as his definition of colonisation makes evident: 'the historical event, by which the inhabitants of a country leave their own motherland and come into contact with other peoples of an inferior or different culture or civilization, and try to establish relations with them' (p. 1). This kind of approach to Portuguese colonisation, but especially its glorifying representation to the non-Portuguese world, is vividly reflected in Manuel Múrias' *Short History of Portuguese Colonization* (Lisbon, 1940).[5]

---

[3] Difference and differentiation were major themes of the international conference 'Le Portugal en relation avec l'Afrique: Récits, connexions, identités (XVe–XVIIIe siècle)', Université de Paris 1 Panthéon-Sorbonne, 22–23 October 2010.

[4] For a very good short critical review of Asia, see van Veen, E. (2000), *Decay or Defeat? An Inquiry into the Portuguese Decline in Asia 1580–1645*, Research School of Asian, African, and Amerindian Studies, Universiteit Leiden, Leiden, pp. 3–7; for an excellent bibliographical review that focuses on Portuguese settlement before the 19th century, see Russell-Wood, A. J. R. (2007), 'Patterns of Settlement in the Portuguese Empire, 1400–1800', in Bethencourt, F. and Curto, D. R. (eds.), *Portuguese Oceanic Expansion, 1400–1800*, Cambridge University Press, Cambridge, pp. 190–196.

[5] Although it is not indicated on the cover page, this short and badly translated book was produced by the Comissão Executiva dos Centenários, Secção de Propaganda e Recepção of the Agência Geral das Colónias. The year 1940 was, of course, the tercentenary of the restoration of the Portuguese monarchy after sixty years of the

'Portuguese' Diasporas: A Survey of the Scholarly Literature 33

In general, scholars of Portuguese expansion agree that there were both internal and external factors at work in the Portuguese diaspora. However, it is worth noting that both Malyn Newitt and John Russell-Wood emphasise the role played by internal, domestic forces in pushing prospective Portuguese settlers out of Portugal over the various attractions – both real and imagined – of external enticements.[6] While they certainly do not ignore the role of official settlement schemes during this period, especially noting its significance in the 15th-century settlement of the Atlantic islands,[7] scholars of Portuguese expansion and settlement place much greater emphasis on other factors in Portuguese settlement over the following three centuries. Frédéric Mauro's pioneering *Le Portugal et l'Atlantique au xviie siècle, 1570–1670: Étude économique* (Paris: Sevpen, 1960; revised second edition, Paris: Fondation Calouste Gulbenkian, Centre Culturel Portugais, 1983) provides an economic interpretation on the Portuguese diaspora during this critical period. Charles Boxer, whose still engaging *The Portuguese Seaborne Empire: 1415–1825* (New York: Knopf, 1969) remains a foundational contribution for the study of Portuguese expansion, says relatively little directly about the Lusophone diaspora in his wide-ranging overview, but his many illustrations of 'soldiers, settlers, and vagabonds' (see Chapter 13), for example, mark a move away from exclusive focus on official settlement schemes. Similarly, Vitorino Magalhães Godinho's pioneering essay on Portuguese emigration points the way for a less institutional approach to the subject.[8] Sanjay Subrahmanyam subsequently reevaluated Godinho's numbers and conclusions, distinguishing between settlement in the official realm of the *Estado da Índia* and its less well defined boundaries in the East, while also carefully exploring the various unofficial presences in the region.[9] Timothy Coates takes up the group of

---

dual monarchy of the Philippine dynasty (1580–1640). The date on the title page is somewhat misleading, as the printing of this short volume did not actually occur until July 1941.

[6] Newitt, *History of Portuguese Expansion*; Russell-Wood, 'Patterns of Settlement', p. 162.

[7] See, i.a., Santos, J. M. dos (1989), *Os Açores nos Séculos XV e XVI*, Secretaria Regional da Educação e Cultura, Direcção Regional dos Assuntos Culturais, Universidade dos Açores, Centro de Estudos Gaspar Frutuoso; Pinto, M. L. R., and Rodrigues, T. M. F. (1993), 'Aspectos do povoamento das ilhas da Madeira e Pôrto Santo nos séculos XV e XVI', in *Actas: III Colóquio Internacional de História da Madeira*, Funchal, pp. 403–471; Matos, A. T. de (ed.) (2005), *A colonização Atlântica*, vol. 3, tomes 1 and 2, in Serrão, J., and Marques, A. H. de Oliveira (eds.), *Nova História da Expansão Portuguesa*, Editorial Estampa, Lisbon.

[8] Godinho, V. M. (1978), 'L'émigration portugaise (xve–xxe siècles): Une constante structurelle et les réponses aux changements du monde', *Revista de História Económica e Social* 1, pp. 5–32.

[9] Subrahmanyam, S. (1993), *The Portuguese Empire in Asia, 1500–1700*, Longman, New York, for the early 16th century, see especially chapter 9. For an interesting collection of biographies that focus on individual officials without neglecting the

settlers characterised by Boxer as 'vagabonds' by examining official forced migration in his *Convicts and Orphans: Forced and State-Sponsored Colonizers in the Portuguese Empire, 1550–1755* (Stanford, CA: Stanford University Press, 2001), while Geraldo Pieroni has published several books on punishment and exiles in Brazil.[10] In his characteristically learned and accessible history of early Portuguese expansion, Newitt especially emphasises the significance of informal settlement during these centuries; he argues, 'Perhaps the biggest problem in understanding Portuguese overseas expansion arises from too great a focus on the formal empire – on the central narrative of officially organised expeditions, international treaties and military conquests.'[11] In a chapter titled 'The Great Portuguese Diaspora, 1515–1550,' Newitt draws the reader's attention to 'an "unofficial" empire made up of settlements founded by Portuguese traders, mercenaries, missionaries and adventurers.... The growth of these unofficial settlements clearly shows how Portuguese expansion acquired a dynamic of its own and ceased to depend on initiatives from Lisbon.'[12] In particular, Newitt contends, 'There were numerous informal Portuguese communities, large and small, scattered throughout the East which constituted a commercial, cultural and religious network far wider and more intricate in its pattern than that provided by the formal empire of fortresses and captaincies controlled from Goa.'[13] Although Russell-Wood does not say much in his overview about informal settlement, he does recognise the significance of 'settlements of Portuguese outside the administrative sphere of influence of royal government.'[14] In his recent comprehensive history of the Portuguese Empire, A. R. Disney also pays close attention to

---

complexities of the Portuguese presence, see McPherson, K., and Subrahmanyam, S. (eds.) (2005), *From Biography to History: Essays in the History of Portuguese Asia (1500–1800)*, Transbooks, New Delhi. See also, Cruz, M. A. L. (1986), 'Exiles and Renegades in Portuguese India', *Indian Economic and Social History Review* 23, no. 3, pp. 249–262.

[10] Pieroni, G. (2000), *Os excluídos do reino: A Inquisição portuguesa e o degredo para o Brasil colônia*, Editora Universidade de Brasília & Imprensa Oficial do Estado, Brasília & São Paulo; Pieroni, G. (2000), *Vadios e Ciganos, heréticos e bruxas: Os degregados no Brasil-colônia*, Bertrand Brasil, Rio de Janeiro; and Pieroni, G. (2003), *Banidos: A Inquisição e a lista dos cristãos-novos condenados a viver no Brasil*, Bertrand Brasil, Rio de Janeiro. Our thanks to James Sweet for bringing Pieroni's work to our attention.

[11] Newitt, *History of Portuguese Expansion*, p. 254.

[12] Ibid., pp. 98–99; for details see pp. 121–129, 144.

[13] Ibid., pp. 190–192, quoted at 190–191.

[14] Russell-Wood, 'Patterns of Settlement', p. 185. In fact, Russell-Wood highlights informal settlement in his chapter 'The Gold Cycle c. 1690–1750', in Bethell, L. (ed.) (1984), *The Cambridge History of Latin America*, vol. 1, Cambridge University Press, Cambridge, pp. 190–243, as does Silva, A. M.-D. (1984), who discusses Azorean immigration in the Amazon and southern regions in 'Imperial re-organization 1750–1808,' in ibid., pp. 244–283.

this phenomenon.[15] More important, we think, is Russell-Wood's emphasis on differentiation in patterns of settlement, arguing that 'Portuguese kings had no grand plan for overseas settlements nor...was there a coherent or sustained policy for settlement. Instead there was experimentation with different models, false starts, and even an ad hoc quality to settlement and colonization.'[16] It is worth noting, however, that informal Portuguese settlement also occurred closer to home on the Iberian peninsula.[17]

Several other broad themes have emerged in more recent work on Portuguese settlement before about 1800. Building on scattered references in Boxer's classic synthesis and then more explicitly a few years later in his *Mary and Misogyny*, modern scholars have paid increasing attention to the place of Portuguese women – or their absence – in the Portuguese diaspora.[18] Articles by Muriel Nazzani and Alida Metcalf on women in colonial Brazil appeared in a 1993 collection on families in European expansion, edited by the prolific Brazilian historian Maria Beatriz Nizza da Silva.[19] The following year witnessed 'O Rosto Feminino da Expansão Portuguesa', a major international congress that resulted in two hefty volumes of papers that discussed a wide range of specific topics, including those focusing on the role of women (both Portuguese and non-Portuguese) before 1800.[20] In his important book Coates has much of value to add about colonial women emigrants, while in 2002 Silva published an important general study on women and ordinary people in colonial society, and Sister Emma Maria, AC, published a study of women in Goa in the colonial era, with special emphasis on shelters and convents established for women, particularly the

---

[15] Disney, A. R. (2009), *History of Portugal and the Portuguese Empire*, vol. 2, Cambridge University Press, Cambridge, pp. 50–52, 172–200.
[16] Russell-Wood, 'Patterns of Settlement,' p. 165. A valuable collection of articles covering many of these themes is Coates, T. (2007), 'The Evolution of the Portuguese Atlantic' (a special thematic issue in honor of Ursula Lamb), *Portuguese Studies Review* 15, nos. 1–2.
[17] Alemán, I. R. (2007), *Emigrantes de Origen Extranjero en Málaga (1564–1700)*, Universidad de Málaga, Málaga, ch. 6, 'El desplazamiento Portugués hacia Málaga,' pp. 73–82.
[18] See Boxer, C. R. (1975), *Mary and Misogyny: Women in Iberian Expansion Overseas 1415–1825: Some Facts, Fancies and Personalities*, Duckworth, London. See also the more partisan approach of Sanceau, E. (1979), *Mulheres Portuguesas no Ultramar*, Livraria Civilização, Porto.
[19] Nazzani, M. (1998), 'Parents and Daughters: Change in the Practice of Dowry in São Paulo (1600–1770),' and Metcalf, A. (1998), 'Women and Means: Women and Family Property in Colonial Brazil,' both in Silva, M. B. Nizza da (ed.) (1998), *Families in the Expansion of Europe, 1500–1800*, Ashgate Variorum, Aldershot, pp. 1–27 and 159–180.
[20] *O Rosto Feminino da Expansão Portuguesa* (2004), Actas, 2 vols, Cadernos Condição Feminina 43, Edição da Comissão para a Igualdade e para os Direitos das Mulheres, Lisbon.

convent of Santa Maria.[21] More recently, international conferences titled 'Female Slavery, Orphanage and Poverty in the Portuguese Colonial Empire (XVI to XX Century),' held at Bahia in 2005 and Porto in 2006, included various presentations on Portuguese women in the era of the first colonial empire.[22] The most current volume to address this important topic is the edited collection by Clara Sarmento, which is available in substantially different Portuguese and English versions, *Condição Feminina no Império Colonial Português* (Porto: Centro de Estudos Interculturais, Instituto Superior de Contabilidade e Administração, Instituto Politécnico do Porto, 2008) and *Women in the Portuguese Colonial Empire: The Theatre of Shadows* (Newcastle-upon-Tyne: Cambridge Scholars Press, 2008). Both collections are somewhat uneven, but they do span the entire Portuguese Empire from the 16th to the 20th centuries. The Portuguese version includes 31 chapters, while the English edition includes only 21 chapters from the Portuguese collection, not all of them well translated. Only a few contributions deal with Portuguese women in the period of expansion, however; the remainder either focuses on slavery or the post-1800 periods. Although he does not include much information about women, Daviken Studnicki-Gizbert is keenly aware of their significance in securing the establishment of Portuguese families across the Atlantic world, a subject about which he writes impressively. He notes that 'it was imperative that certain family members settle down and establish households.' Even though female emigration was a comparatively rare event, he argues that 'women ensured the formation and continuity of the household. The emigration of women was thus a key condition for the long-term establishment of Portuguese sojourner communities.'[23] Much remains to be done on this front, however, although the universal recognition of the exceptional gender imbalance in favour of males during this era probably will continue to restrict scholarship on Portuguese women. Of course, the other side of the equation – the role of non-Portuguese women as go-betweens – is hinted at by Metcalf for early colonial Brazil and is taken up by several papers in the 1995 *Rosto Feminino* volumes.[24] Nevertheless, studies such as these

---

[21] Coates, *Convicts and Orphans*; Silva, M. B. Nizza da (2002), *Donas e Plebias na sociedade colonial*, Editorial Estampa, Lisbon; Maria, E. (2002), *Women in Portuguese Goa (1510–1835)*, Institute for Research in Social Sciences and Humanities, Tellicherry. See also Silva, M. B. Nizza da (1998), *História da Família no Brasil Colonial*, Nova Fronteira, Rio de Janeiro, which includes consideration of early settlement and royal schemes to settle families in Brazil.

[22] See the program for the 2006 conference, http://www.iscap.ipp.pt/congresso2006/eng/index_Eng.htm

[23] Studnicki-Gizbert, D. (2007), *A Nation upon the Ocean Sea: Portugal's Atlantic Diaspora and the Crisis of the Spanish Empire, 1492–1640*, Oxford University Press, New York, pp. 54–55.

[24] Metcalf, A. C. (2005), *Go-betweens and the Colonization of Brazil, 1500–1600*, University of Texas Press, Austin.

should remind us that we need to seek to understand the ways in which marrying local, a phenomenon that appears most often in the literature under the not very useful heading 'miscegenation,' enabled populations of Portuguese men to become indigenised while concomitantly retaining and exploiting their Portuguese identification when it served their needs. For studies like these perhaps the best place to look at what is possible are the early works of Allen Isaacman and Malyn Newitt on the *prazo* (feudal estate) system of Zambesia, even though they speak to a later period in the history of the Portuguese overseas empire.[25]

Another theme that has received much attention in recent years is the role played by New Christians, conversos, crypto-Jews, and Sephardic Jews in the early centuries of the Portuguese diaspora. This attention is not, of course, entirely new, Boxer having noted both the disparaging identification of Portuguese by other Europeans as Jews following the forced conversion of Portuguese Jews in 1497 and the presence of (and restrictions against) New Christians in the Portuguese overseas empire.[26] Perhaps the first major study of this phenomenon is Arnold Wiznitzer's *Jews in Colonial Brazil* (New York: Columbia University Press, 1960), followed by two studies from José Gonçalves Salvador, *Os cristãos-novos e o comércio do Atlântico meridional (com enfoque nas capitanias do sul) 1530–1680* (São Paulo: Livraria Pioneira Editora, 1978) and *Os Cristãos-Novos em Minas Gerais Durante o Ciclo do Ouro (1695–1755): Relações com a Inglaterra* (São Paulo: Livraria Pioneira Editora & São Bernardo do Campo: Instituto Metodista de Ensino Superior, 1992). The second of these contributions was followed the next year by the important study by James C. Boyajian, *Portuguese Trade in Asia under the Habsburgs, 1580–1640* (Baltimore: Johns Hopkins University Press, 1993), which emphasises the important role played by New Christians in creating the Portuguese maritime merchant empire. Drawing upon Inquisition records as far afield as Madrid and Mexico, Boyajian actually ranges across the entire Portuguese enterprise. In his recent book on the Portuguese Atlantic 'nation' in the context of Spanish America, Studnicki-Gizbert similarly draws upon Inquisition records to understand the many contributions of the more than half of the Portuguese involved in the Atlantic world who

---

[25] Isaacman, A. F. (1972), *Mozambique: The Africanization of a European Institution – the Zambesi Prazos, 1750–1902*, University of Wisconsin Press, Madison, especially pp. 56–63; Newitt, M. (1973), *Portuguese Settlement on the Zambesi*. Longman, Harlow.

[26] Boxer, C. R. (1965), *Portuguese Society in the Tropics: The Municipal Councils of Goa, Macao, Bahia, and Luanda, 1510–1800*, University of Wisconsin Press, Madison, pp. 8, 30, 112–113; Boxer, *Portuguese Seaborne Empire*, pp. 266–272, 281, 293, 331, 333–334, 336–337. This attention remains in the most recent surveys by Newitt, *History of Portuguese Expansion*, and Disney, *History of Portugal and the Portuguese Empire*, vol. 2, as well as the collection coedited by Bethencourt and Curto, *Portuguese Oceanic Expansion*; see the entries 'Jews' and 'New Christians' in all three.

were either Sephardic Jews or New Christians. A more broadly cast approach to this topic that is situated primarily in the growing field of Sephardic studies rather than that of Portuguese expansion is a recent volume edited by Joseph Abraham Levi, *Survival and Adaptation: The Portuguese Jewish Diaspora in Europe, Africa, and the New World* (New York: Sepher-Hermon Press for the American Society for Sephardic Studies, 2002).[27] Jonathan Israel takes up the same global challenge in his massive *Diasporas within a Diaspora: Jews, Crypto-Jews and the World Maritime Empires, 1540–1740* (Boston: Brill, 2002).[28] There is also a study of New Christians in the economy of colonial Buenos Aires.[29] The presence of Jewish children in the peopling of São Tomé in the early 16th century has also attracted some interest, while the topic of Sephardim on the Upper Guinea Coast is featured in a new book by Peter Mark and José da Silva Horta.[30]

Indeed, there now seems to be fairly broad consensus that the entire concept of Portuguese expansion as settlement or the Lusophone diaspora involves a much more nuanced and socially complex set of phenomena than simply tracking Portuguese emigrants across the globe. To take the most obvious case, it is well known that what might be called secondary Portuguese out-migration from the Atlantic islands was a critical component in the settlement of both other Atlantic islands and Brazil. And while

---

[27] See, especially, Levi's introduction, 'The Sephardic Diaspora in Europe and Beyond: The Case of Portuguese Jewry,' pp. 1–11, which has a valuable set of references, and his chapter, '"Out of Brazil": The Key Role of the Sephardim in (Trans)Atlantic Trade before and after 1654,' pp. 91–127. See also Ben Ur, A. (2006), 'Distingués des autres Juifs: Les Sépharades des Caraïbes,' in Trigano, S. (ed.), *Le Monde Sépharade*. Éditions du Seuil, Paris, vol. 1, pp. 279–328.

[28] See also Tavim, J. A. R. da Silva (2008), 'In the Shadow of Empire: Portuguese Jewish Communities in the Sixteenth Century,' in Brockey, L. M. (ed.), *Portuguese Colonial Cities in the Early Modern World*, Ashgate, Farnham, Surrey, and Burlington, VT, pp. 17–39.

[29] Garwich, A. (1987), *Los Cristianos nuevos portugueses y la economía de la colonia*, Sociedade Argentina de Historiadores, Buenos Aires.

[30] See Discussion Log for 'Jews in São Tomé' in the March 2008 log of H-Luso Africa and Sousa, I. B. de (2008), *São Tomé et Principe de 1485 à 1755: Une société coloniale, du Blanc au Noir*, L'Harmattan, Paris, pp. 24–29 (on European settlers) and 207–214 (on demography); see also notice of a 11 March 2008 lecture by Tobias Green (Birmingham University) at the Arquivo Histórico Ultramarino in Lisbon, 'Os Cristãos Novos e a Crioulização em Cabo Verde e nos Rios da Guiné, Séculos XVI–XVII,' at http://www2.iict.pot/?idc=138&idi=12998. Mark, P., and Horta, J. da Silva (2011), *The Forgotten Diaspora: Jewish Communities in West Africa and the Creation of the Atlantic World*, Cambridge University Press, Cambridge. For New Christian/Jews in the building of a colonial state apparatus in Cape Verde, see Cohen, Z. (2005), 'Cabo Verde: Da crioulização do homen à crioulização do aparelho de estado,' *Revista Científica. Revista de Estudos* – Universidade de Cabo Verde, no. 0, pp. 7–16.

it is equally acknowledged that the settlement of Brazil cannot be understood without appreciating the dominant demographic role of Central Africans, Russell-Wood, extending this observation, suggests, 'Persons of African descent became an integral part of the population of Portuguese cities and forts of the Estado da Índia, as well as in Brazil and Portugal.'[31] A different but related theme that seems to be receiving a lot of attention in more recent literature is the recognition that the Lusophone diaspora has been carried forward by many more people of mixed Portuguese ancestry than by those who claimed Portuguese parentage on both sides. Indeed, this raises the question of who is Portuguese or what does it mean to claim Portuguese identity?[32] To be sure, this is not an entirely new recognition, although Gilberto Freyre's notorious thesis about Lusotropicalism cast a long shadow over scholarship on Portuguese colonial and Brazilian studies for many years.[33] For example, the older *bandeirante* literature on Portuguese expansion into the Brazilian *sertão* usually highlights the pivotal role played by the *mameluco* (Luso-Indian frontiersman) in which the *bandeira* became a romantic symbol of Brazilian nationalism.[34] More broadly, however, we find Alida Metcalf's characterisation of the *mameluco* go-between as 'a chameleon in the wilderness, adapting to, and insinuating himself in, each new situation' to be particularly instructive.[35]

While we have already noted the Africanisation of the *prazo*-holders of Zambesia, Walter Rodney long ago drew attention to the so-called *lançados* (Afro-Portuguese of the Upper Guinea coast), a subject that has been explored in greater detail by Jean Boulègue, George Brooks and, most recently, Peter Mark.[36] Recent work on Angola promises to give us a much more complete

---

[31] Russell-Wood, 'Patterns of Settlement,' p. 177.
[32] See, e.g., Havik, P. J., and Newitt, M. (eds.) (2007), *Creole Societies in the Portuguese Colonial Empire*, Lusophone Studies 6, Seagull/Faoileán, Bristol.
[33] Freyre, G. (1933), *Casa grande e senzala*, Maia and Schmidt, Rio de Janeiro, and many subsequent editions in numerous languages. The featured theme of *Lusotopie* 1997 4, is 'Lusotropicalisme. Idéologies coloniales et identités nationales dans les mondes lusophones' (Couto, D., Enders, A., and Léonard, Y., eds.), and for a definitive critique, see Castelo, C. (1998), '*O modo português de estar no mundo*': *O luso-tropicalismo e o ideologia colonial portuguesa (1933–1961)*, Edições Afrontamento, Porto.
[34] See Taunay, A. de Escragnolle (1926–50), *História geral das bandeiras paulistas*, 11 vols., Typ. Ideal, H. L. Canton, São Paulo; Taunay, E. (1951), *História das bandeiras paulistas*, Edições Melhoramentos, São Paulo; Cortesão, J. (1958), *Rapôso Tavares e a formação territorial do Brasil*, 2 vols., Ministério da Educação e Cultura, Serviço e Documentação, Rio de Janeiro; and Cortesão, J. (1964), *Introdução à historia das bandeiras*, 2 vols, Portugalia, Lisbon. See also Morse, R. (ed.) (1965), *The Bandeirantes: The Historical Role of the Brazilian Pathfinders*, Knopf, New York.
[35] Metcalf, *Go-betweens*, p. 249.
[36] Rodney, W. (1970), *A History of the Upper Guinea Coast, 1545–1800*, Clarendon Press, Oxford; Boulègue, J. (1972), *Les Luso-Africains de Sénégambie, xvie–xixe siècles*,

picture of both the character of this strongly *mestiço* society and its transatlantic connections to Brazil.[37] For years, of course, researchers have written about the way in which many Goans, but especially elites, have identified themselves as Portuguese, particularly in their global diaspora. A pioneering essay by Kenneth McPherson on Luso-Indian origins has been followed by several contributions that look in greater detail at the various roles played by Luso-Asians.[38] Although we choose this terminology here rather than Indo-Portuguese, each identity probably was embraced by individuals and communities according to changing historical circumstances and contingencies. Essays by McPherson, Timothy Barnard, Radin Fernando, and a jointly authored chapter by Maria de Jesus dos Mártires Lopes and Paulo Lopes Matos demonstrate in unique ways how Luso-Asians maintained their Portuguese identity during this period while also using their local marital ties to confirm their presence in indigenous societies.[39] It is precisely their in-betweenness, as Metcalf notes, that enabled them to straddle and often to serve as interlocutors between these different worlds.

Université de Dakar, Dakar; Brooks, G. E. (1980), *Luso-African Commerce and Settlement in the Gambia and Guinea-Bissau Region*, Working Papers, no. 24, African Studies Center, Boston University, Brookline, MA; Mark, P. (2002), *'Portuguese' Style and Luso-African Identity: Precolonial Senegambia, Sixteenth–Nineteenth Centuries*, Indiana University Press, Bloomington. See also the paper by Green, T. (2010) 'L'évolution d'une identité "africaine" parmi les *lançados* de la Haute-Guinée du xvie siècle' for the Paris conference noted in footnote 3 above. For a different approach to the process of Atlanticisation in this period and one that focuses on African women traders, see Havik, P. J. (2004), *Silences and Soundbites: The Gendered Dynamics of Trade and Brokerage in the Pre-Colonial Guinea Bissau Region*, Lit Verlag, Münster.

[37] See, e.g., Heintze, B. (2002), 'Angola under Portuguese Rule: How It All Began. Settlement and Economic Policy, 1570–1607,' in Tavares, A. P., and Santos, C. Madeira (eds.), *Monumenta Africae–a Apropriação da Escrita pelos Africanos*, Fundação Portugal África, Lisbon, pp. 509–535; Santos, C. M. (2008), 'Luanda: A Colonial City between Africa and the Atlantic, Seventeenth and Eighteenth Centuries,' in Brockey (ed.), *Portuguese Colonial Cities*, pp. 249–272; Ferreira, R. A. (2012), *Atlantic Microhistory: Slaving, Transatlantic Networks, and Cultural Exchange in Angola (ca. 1700–ca. 1830)*, Cambridge University Press, Cambridge, and numerous articles by this author. For an important unpublished paper on the larger issue of what is meant by 'Luso-African', see Florescu, M. (2010), 'Cultural Identities in Historical Perspective: The Case of Northern Angola,' presented at the Paris conference noted in footnote 3 above.

[38] McPherson, K. (1987), 'A Secret People of South Asia. The Origins, Evolution and Role of the Luso-Indian Goan Community from the Sixteenth to Twentieth Centuries,' *Itinerario* 11, no. 2, pp. 72–86.

[39] McPherson, K. (1999), 'Trade and Traders in the Bay of Bengal: Fifteenth to Nineteenth Centuries,' in Mukherjee, R., and Subramanian, L. (eds.), *Politics and Trade in the Indian Ocean: Essays in Honour of Ashin Das Gupta*, Oxford University Press, Delhi and Oxford, pp. 183–209; Barnard, T. P. (2004), 'Mestizos as Middlemen:

A further development that emerges from the last several decades of scholarship on the classic period of Portuguese imperial expansion is the recourse to new sources of evidence. To be sure, in the hands of a new generation of historians the careful rereading of venerable Portuguese chronicles continues to yield valuable insights into the Portuguese diaspora. But new perspectives lead historians to new sources, just as new sources yield new questions. In particular, in addition to the scholars whose work specifically focuses on New Christians and Sephardim (Salvador, Boyajian, Studnicki-Gizbert), a number of other historians have made valuable use of Inquisition records.[40] Other kinds of sources that still remain to be exploited fully by historians are those produced by indigenous people. Here Subrahmanyam's previously cited study of the Portuguese Asian empire is notable for its use of Asian and African sources to understand both local agency and perceptions of 'the other.'[41] More recently, several articles in the Macau-based journal *Revista da Cultura* argue for the significance of Chinese sources for understanding the impact of the Portuguese in East Asia.[42] Russell-Wood makes an interesting point about the importance of the visual arts and architecture in understanding the permanency of the Portuguese impact overseas,

---

Tomas Días and His Travels in Eastern Sumatra,' in Borschberg, P. (ed.), *Iberians in the Singapore-Melaka Area (16th to 18th Century)*, Fundação Oriente, Lisbon, pp. 147–160; Fernando, F. (2004), 'Metamorphosis of the Luso-Asian Diaspora in the Malay Archipelago,' in ibid., pp. 161–184; Lopes, M. de J dos Martires, and Matos, P. L. (2006), 'Naturais, reinóis e luso-descendentes: A socialização consequida,' in Lopes, M. de J. dos Martires (ed.), *O Império Oriental, 1660–1820*, vol. 5:2 of Serrão and Marques (eds.), *Nova História*, pp. 15–70.

[40] See, e.g., Rodrigues, J. D. (1996), 'O Arquipélago dos Açores: A Sociedade,' in Matos (ed.), *A colonização Atlântica*, vol. 3:1, pp. 446–491; Silva, M. B. Nizza da (1992), 'Sociedade, Instituições e Cultura,' in Johnson, H., and Silva, M. B. Nizza da (eds.), *O Império Luso-Brasileiro 1500–1620*, vol. 6, pp. 303–551, in Serrão and Marques (eds.), *Nova História da Expansão Portuguesa*; Souza, L. de Melo e (1986), *O Diabo e a Terra da Santa Cruz: Feitiçaria e religiosidade popular no Brasil colonial*, Companhia das Letras, São Paulo.

[41] Cf. Reid, A. (2000), 'Early Southeast Asian Categorizations of Europeans,' in Reid, A. (ed.), *Charting the Shape of Early Modern Southeast Asia*, Institute of Southeast Asian Studies, Singapore, pp. 155–180. For a different approach to the question of seeing 'the other,' see Prestholdt, J. (2001), 'Portuguese Conceptual Categories and the "Other" Encounter on the Swahili Coast,' *Journal of Asian and African Studies* 36, no. 4, pp. 383–406.

[42] Wenyuan, C. (2002), 'Compilação de Dados Históricos sobre Portugal e Macau no *Registo da Dinastia Ming*,' *Revista da Cultura* 2, pp. 108–129; Kaijian, T. (2002), 'Referências Históricas Relativas a Macau nos Relatórios de Cantão,' *Revista da Cultura* 2, pp. 130–144; and Yingxia T. (2002), 'Apontamentos de Visitas a Macau durante as Dinastias Ming e Qing,' *Revista da Cultura* 2, pp. 145–160; Jinglian, L. (2003), 'As Relações Sino-Portuguesas durante a Dinastia Qing através dos Ofícios das Chapas Sínicas,' *Revista da Cultura* 8, pp. 112–130.

quoting the Portuguese architect Walter Rossa that 'nothing outlasts the urban and territorial structures of a culture, not even language.'[43] Thus, Russell-Wood concludes, 'Be it in Africa, Asia, or America, settlements bore the hallmark of being Portuguese and identified themselves and were identified by other Europeans and indigenous peoples as being Portuguese.'[44] Here the previously noted work of Peter Mark is joined by an article by an architect, Carlos Marreiros, on Macau.[45] We should also emphasise that Portuguese informal settlement was not restricted to the Portuguese Empire. Most notably, in South America there was an important Portuguese presence in Buenos Aires during this period, which was first studied by Ricardo de Lafuente Machain in *Los portugueses en Buenos Aires (siglo XVII)* (Madrid: Tipografía de Archivos, 1931). Subsequent studies by Macedo, Lewin, Saguier (who also draws comparisons with Portuguese in Cartagena, Veracruz, and Lima), and, most recently, Reitano reveal that this topic continues to attract scholarly attention from historians of colonial Argentina.[46]

---

[43] Russell-Wood, 'Patterns of Settlement,' p. 194, citing Rossa, W. (1997), *Cidades Indo-Portuguesa: Contribuições para o estudo do urbanismo português no Hindustão Ocidental/Indo-Portuguese Cities: A Contribution to the Study of Portuguese Urbanism in Western Hindustan*, Comissão Nacional para as Comemorações dos Descobrimentos Portugueses, Lisbon. See also Porter, J. (1996), *Macau the Imaginary City: Culture and Society, 1557 to the Present*, Westview Press, Boulder, CO; and chapters by Pereira, A. N. (1997), 'Goan and Christian Architecture of the 16th Century,' in Borges, C., and Feldmann, H. (eds.), *Portugal and Goa: Their Cultural Links*, Concept Publishing Company, New Delhi, and by Carita, H. (2001), 'Hindu Tradition of the Vastu Shastra in Indo-Portuguese Architecture,' in Mathew, K. S., Souza, T. R. de, and Melakandathil, P. (eds.), *The Portuguese and the Socio-Cultural Changes in India, 1500–1800*, Fundação Oriente and Institute for Research in Social Sciences and Humanities, MESHAR, Tellicherry, pp. 205–222.
[44] Russell-Wood, 'Patterns of Settlement,' p. 188.
[45] Mark, *'Portuguese' Style*; Marreiros, C. (2002), 'A Arquitectura Mista e a Urbanização,' *Revista da Cultura* 3, pp. 7–41.
[46] Macedo, C. L. de (1961), *Presencia e integración portuguesa en el Río de la Plata*, Nascimento, Santiago de Chile; Lewin, B. (1980), 'Los portugueses en Buenos Aires en el período colonial,' in VI Congreso Internacional de Historia de América, Academia Nacional de Historia, Buenos Aires, vol. 4, pp. 47–62; Saguier, E. (1985), 'The Social Impact of a Middleman Minority in a Divided Host Society: The Case of the Portuguese in Early Seventeenth Century Buenos Aires,' *Hispanic American Historical Review* 65, no. 3, pp. 467–491; Reitano, E. (2006), 'La inmigración antes de la inmigración: Buenos Aires y el movimiento migratorio portugués en el espacio atlántico en ellargo siglo XVIII,' *Portuguese Studies Review* 14, no. 2, pp. 1–37; and Reitano, E. (2005), 'Los portugueses del Buenos Aires tardocolonial: Immigración, sociedad, familia, vida cotidiana y religion,' Ph.D. dissertation, Universidad Nacional de la Plata. As well, there is Garwich's book on Portuguese New Christians, noted above.

'Portuguese' Diasporas: A Survey of the Scholarly Literature 43

We are well aware of how selective this review of the literature on the first centuries of the Portuguese diaspora is,[47] but we want now to leave this vast bibliography to turn our attention to the rather less studied but rapidly growing literature on the modern Portuguese diaspora, essentially from about 1800 to the demise of the Portuguese corporate state.

Phase II: Portuguese diasporas, 1800–1974

Although, depending on the historian and regional specificity, there is clearly some overlap in periodisation between the long period of late medieval and early modern Portuguese expansion and settlement and its modern counterpart, we suggest that the modern period begins roughly from about 1800. While professional historians continue to dominate the scholarly literature into the 20th century, anthropologists, sociologists, political scientists, and amateur historians emerge as major contributors to our understanding of the Portuguese diaspora as we approach the present. The modern Lusophone diaspora is also notable for the movement of people from Lusophone areas outside of Portugal, although metropolitan Portugal certainly continued (and continues) to be a major locus of overseas emigration. Similarly, although various official overseas settlement schemes appeared at various times in this period of almost two centuries, informal settlement definitely dominates the modern diaspora.

The modern literature on Portuguese emigration dates back to major studies by J. Oliveira Martins, *Fomento Rural e Emigração* (Lisbon: Guimarães Editores, 1956), and Joel Serrão, *Emigração portuguesa: Sondagem histórica* (Lisbon: Livros Horizonte, 1971), as well as the seminal article by Magalhães Godinho previously cited.[48] A parallel study by Carlos Almeida and António Barreto, *Capitalismo e emigração em Portugal* (Lisbon: Prelo Editora, 1970) was significantly revised in 1974, when it appeared after the Revolution of the Carnations. Considering the period from 1950 to 1974, Almeida and Barreto portray Portuguese emigration as being driven by an internal dynamic

---

[47] For example, we have not spoken about the end of Portuguese colonisation in Morocco, which provoked a very original migration: the 'transfer' of Mazagão, from the last Portuguese fortified city on the Moroccan coast, to the Brazilian Amazonia. See Vidal L. (2008), *Mazagão, la ville qui traversa l'Atlantique. Du Maroc à l'Amazonie, 1769–1783*, Flammarion, Paris.
[48] See Bretell, C. B. (1977–1978), 'Annotated Bibliography: Nineteenth and Twentieth Century Portuguese Emigration,' *Portuguese Studies Newsletter* 3, pp. 7–18; Rocha-Trinidade, M. B., and Arroteia, J. (1984), *Bibliografia da Emigração Portuguesa*, Instituto Português de Ensino a Distância, Lisbon. Portuguese emigration is also noted in Marques, A. H. de Oliveira (1972), *History of Portugal*, vol. 2: *From Empire to Corporate State*, Columbia University Press, New York and London, pp. 82–83, 120, 200–201, 223, 241.

rooted in an externally directed economy and see continued emigration as exacerbating Portuguese underdevelopment. The authors further advocate for agrarian reform as well as industrial restructuring as a way to address these problems. A second part of the book deals with emigrant characteristics and demographics, while a third part discusses emigration's links with capitalism. A regional study that echoes these same issues from the 1950s is Modesto Navarro's *Emigração e crise no nordeste transmontano* (Lisbon: Prelo Editora, 1973). In his *Origens e formas de emigração* (Lisbon: Iniciativas Editoriais, 1976), economist Eduardo de Sousa Ferreira also looks at Portuguese emigration as a consequence and cause of major Portuguese economic problems. The major indicator for this underdevelopment is a low per capita income increase. Three major questions guide this radical study: 1) the role of savings, investment, and capital formation in the growth process; 2) the function of the balance of payments and the ratio of capital importation to emigration; and 3) how these two questions impact the development of the population politically and economically. More recent studies include Miriam Halpern Pereira's important examination of emigration before the rise of the New State, *A Política Portuguesa de Emigração, 1850-1930* (Lisbon: A Regra do Jogo, 1981), in which the author remarks on Portugal's ambiguous policies towards emigration, combining repressive state policies with toleration for clandestine emigration. Her analysis of remittances shows that the largest number of emigrants who sent money home were from Porto and Braga.[49] Two decades later these same two issues are further explored by Maria Ioannis Baganha, who examines the ratio of science and technology workers to unskilled labour in the Portuguese economy and concludes that the *Estado Novo* both controlled emigration and used it to its advantage to encourage new revenues in the form of remittances.[50] A particularly valuable collection of essays that cover a wide range of specific issues and communities, both domestic and overseas, by authors whose individual work is discussed elsewhere in this review, is *Emigração/ Imigração em Portugal: Actas do 'Collóquio Internacional sobre Emigração e Imigração em Portugal (séc. XIX–XX)'* (Algés: Editorial Fragmentos, 1993).[51]

Two microstudies that explore the situation of women are Karin Wall's *A outra face da emigração: Estudo sobre a situação das mulheres que ficam no país de origem* (Lisbon: Edição Comissão da Condição Feminina, cadernos condição feminina 14, 1982) and Caroline B. Bretell's *Men Who Migrate, Women Who Wait: Population and History in a Portuguese Parish* (Princeton,

---

[49] This volume consists of some 60 pages of analysis and 200 pages of original documents.
[50] Baganha, M. I. (2003), 'From Closed to Open Doors: Portuguese Emigration under the Corporatist Regime,' *e-JPH* 1, pp. 1–16.
[51] The organisers of the conference were Maria Beatriz Nizza da Silva, Maria Ioannis Baganha, Maria José Maranhão, and Miriam Halpern Pereira.

NJ: Princeton University Press, 1986). Wall bases her short monograph on interviews in two Minho villages and Lisbon, focusing on the years since 1950, which witnessed the first rise in female emigration. Bretell undertakes an interesting ethnographic and microhistorical study of Lanheses 'to demonstrate the impact of emigration as both cultural ethos and social strategy of a range of other demographic phenomena, and thus its impact on the roles of women in northwestern Portuguese society' (p. 264). Using parish marriage registry data and other local archives, she analyses marriage patterns between 1700 and 1969, as well as records concerning children, to conclude that high emigration rates are correlated with high marriage ages, high celibacy rates, low fertility, and high illegitimacy. These kinds of microstudies help to put real flesh on some of the more global, less intimate studies of the impact of Portuguese emigration on the sending society.

The regional focus for modern overseas settlement is unquestionably the Atlantic world. With the ending of the legal slave trade from West Central Africa to Brazil in 1850, successive governments of the young Brazilian nation-state pursued a conscious policy to whiten the population, which from its late-16th-century origins until the mid-19th century had been dominated by African peoples. Both Portuguese and Brazilian scholars have studied this phenomenon; all examine both push and pull factors underlying Portuguese emigration to Brazil. An important work for the 19th century by Jorge Fernandes Alves, *Os Brasileiros: Emigração e Retorno no Porto Oitocentista* (Porto: n.p., 1994) traces the previously unexamined migration from Porto (and the region of the Douro) to Brazil, in particular between 1836 and 1879, and ends by examining those *retornos* from Brazil to Portugal. The regional (not local) approach allows for more complete series and a larger data set. One of the work's real contributions is the emphasis on returnees (Chapter 6), which looks at the different characteristics of *brasileiros* who returned to northeastern Portugal. As part of the international celebration of the quincentenary, the municipal government of Porto produced a major art exhibition accompanied by a valuable catalogue, *Os Brasileiros de Torna-Viagem no Noroeste de Portugal*, edited by Eugénio Santos (Câmara Municipal do Porto: CNCDP, 2000), that is largely based on Alves' research.

Curiously, one of the first historians to study this movement was the American Ann Pescatello, whose 1970 UCLA PhD dissertation is entitled 'Both Ends of the Journey: An Historical Study of Migration and Change in Brazil and Portugal, 1889–1914.' Pescatello employs statistical data from both Portuguese and Brazilian official sources and a wide range of other evidence on commerce and Portuguese business firms operating in Brazil. She focuses on the various push-pull factors involved in Portuguese emigration and the role that Portuguese immigrants played in the urbanisation of Rio de Janeiro. She also shows that although some Portuguese merchants experienced success in Brazil, their inability as a group to construct alliances with their Brazilian counterparts relegated them to a marginal role in shaping Brazil's future economy. In Portugal, she notes the negative effects of mostly male emigration. In the same decade two Brazilian students at the Universidade de São Paulo produced theses that addressed the place of Portuguese merchants and *caixeiros* (clerks) in the transition to and early years of Brazilian independence, although they were not published until the early 1990s.[52] Lenira Martinho demonstrates that the dominant position in the economy of Portuguese merchants and the mediating role played by Portuguese *caixeiros* created anti-Portuguese sentiments among both *libertos* and mulattos. Riva Gorenstein shows how the alliance between Portuguese merchants and the new Brazilian elite served as a counterbalance to more broadly based emerging anti-Portuguese feelings. Tania Penido Monteiro subsequently explores the same broad themes in her *Portugueses na Bahia na segunda metade do séc. XIX: Emigração e comércio* (Porto: Secretaria de Estado da Emigração Centro de Estudos, 1985). Exploiting rich sources relating to merchants in the Arquivo Nacional da Torre do Tombo and to immigration in Bahian archives (including Portuguese immigrants registered at the Portuguese consulate in Salvador), she finds that most Portuguese immigrants to Bahia were labourers, although many listed their profession as *caixeiro*. Most of the immigrants came from Porto and were young; more than 85 per cent of males were single and eventually married Brazilian women. Although Portuguese merchants were relatively successful, she argues, their activities did not transform the regional economy. Many had aspirations to return enriched to Portugal, but not all succeeded in attaining this dream. These issues are revisited by Rosana Barbosa in *Immigration and Xenophobia: Portuguese Immigrants in Early 19th Century Rio de Janeiro* (Lanham, MD: University Press of America, 2008). A focused case study is the investigation undertaken by Ana Silvia Volpi Scott and Oswaldo Mário Serra Truzzi on movement between Lousã, Portugal, and Nova Lousã, Brazil.[53] A valuable overview of these topics is Herbert Klein's essay 'The Social and Economic Integration of Portuguese Immigrants in Brazil in the late 19th and 20th centuries.'[54] Joaquim da Costa Leite's Columbia University PhD dissertation (1994), 'Portugal and Emigration, 1855–1914,' reexamines the period covered by Pescatello a quarter century earlier. For Leite, himself a native

---

[52] Martinho, L. M., and Gorenstein, R. (1993), *Negociantes e Caixeiros na Sociedade da Independência*, Secretaria Municipal de Cultura, Turismo e Esportes, Rio de Janeiro.
[53] Volpi Scott, A. S. (2006), 'Migração Portuguesa para São Paulo na segunda metade do século XIX: Um estudo de caso,' paper presented at the XV Encontro Nacional de Estudos de População, Caxambo MG, at http://www.abep.nepo.unicamp.br/encontro2006/docspdf/ABEP2006_481.pdf, and, with Truzzi, O. M. S. (2006), 'Redes de conterrâneos: A Imigração de Lousanenses ao Brasil imperial,' *Portuguese Studies Review* 14, no. 2, pp. 39–61.
[54] 1991 in *Journal of Latin American Studies* 23, pp. 309–337.

of northeastern Portugal, emigration was a by-product of lower transaction costs (more information flowing with smoother communication and better transportation) and higher wages, as well as a solution to the population stress felt in Portugal.

From the late 1990s on, there are a large number of studies of Portuguese immigration to Brazil. José Verdasco, a wealthy Portuguese who lives in Brazil, reveals a decidedly pro-Portuguese perspective that minimises the part played by non-Portuguese in the making of modern Brazil.[55] The state government of São Paulo decided in 1998 to celebrate its rich immigrant heritage in a series of short publications, one of which concerns the Portuguese, especially during the period 1875–1940.[56] The booklet answers specific questions concerning points of origin, ultimate destination, and type of journey, while also noting significant Portuguese cultural contributions to Brazil such as children's games, food, and religious festivals. The booklet ends on an interesting note, discussing reverse migration by Brazilians to Portugal since the 1970s, a period that we take up in the next section of the chapter, finding parallel motives for this movement to those that impelled Portuguese migration to Brazil in an earlier era. Going beyond the study of well-known push-pull effects, in a collection of essays on immigration to Rio de Janeiro, Lená Medeiros de Menezes adopts a more cultural history approach to Portuguese immigration by trying to understand the immigrant as agent. Following a group of young *caixeiros* from the 1870s, she finds that the search for success in Brazil was a key motivator underlying their decision to emigrate.[57]

The search for new methodologies to understand Portuguese immigration in Brazil is clearly part of a larger project in Brazilian social history that has emerged in the last decade and that also involves new collaborations between Portuguese and Brazilian scholars. One example of this kind of scholarly collaboration is the collection of essays edited by Maria Beatriz Rocha-Trindade and Maria Christina Siqueira de Souza Campos, *Olhares Lusos e Brasileiros* (São Paulo: Usina do Livro, 2003), which was organised by the Universidade de São Paulo's Centro de Estudos Rurais e Urbanos and the Centro de Estudos das Migrações e das Relações Interculturais of Portugal's Universidade Aberta. The focus of the collection is Portuguese migration to São Paulo from 1850 to 1965, with a comparative examination of push-pull

---

[55] Verdasco, J. (1997), *Raízes da Nação Brasileira: Os Portugueses no Brasil*, IBRASA, São Paulo.
[56] Governo do Estado do São Paulo (1999), *Imigração Portuguesa no Brasil*, Memorial do Imigrante/Museu da Imigração, São Paulo.
[57] Menezes, L. Medeiros de (2000), 'Jovens Portugueses: Histórias de Trabalho, Histórias de Sucessos, História de Fracassos,' in Gomes, A. de Castro (ed.), *Histórias de Imigrantes e de Imigração no Rio de Janeiro*, Viveiros de Castro Editora, Rio de Janeiro, pp. 164–182.

factors. The first section of the book uses traditional methodologies to look at Portuguese traces in the São Paulo state and why Portuguese decided to emigrate and includes an essay on returnees. The second section takes up the possibilities of nontraditional approaches, including visual anthropology, visual representations, oral history, and the interpretation of immigrant life histories. There are many fascinating threads in this rich collection, including the suggestion by Domingos Caeiro (pp. 13-46) that Brazilian promotion of immigration was a more powerful factor than Portuguese push factors; Maria Cristina Siqueira de Souza Campos' argument (pp. 67-98) that the motivations for migration, combined with whether one's destination was urban or rural, helped to define how strongly an immigrant identified with the country of origin; and the contention by Alice Beatriz da Silva Gordo Lang (pp. 99-130) that immigrant personal identity is often linked with a person's town of origin and an ambiguous sense of whether one is Brazilian or Portuguese. Clearly, issues of identity emerge as an important issue in these studies. In her own contribution to the collection coeditor Rocha-Trinidade (pp. 131-146) depicts the ambiguous reception of successful returnees to Portugal, who are sometimes ridiculed as *brasileiros*. A second collaboration between these two institutions of higher education is a follow-up volume edited by Rocha-Trinidade and Souza Campos entitled *História, Memória e Imagens nas Migrações* (Oeiras: Celta Editora, 2005), which features different methodological approaches to studying Portuguese emigration to Brazil. The first half of the volume features chapters on written sources for reconstructing this history, while the second focuses on unwritten sources (oral histories, images, and recorded sounds), all pointing to suggest ways to study identity in the immigration process.

In *Portugueses em São Paulo: A face feminina da Imigração* (São Paulo: Expressão e Arte Editora, 2005), Maria Aparecida Macedo Pascal provides both a solid overview of Portuguese immigration to the city in the period 1890 to 1930 and two valuable chapters on female immigration. In the former she notes that Portuguese immigration to São Paulo is often overshadowed by Italian immigration but that it formed part of the broader policy of whitening of Brazilian society. She also discusses the converging push factors of mechanisation of agriculture (which others note as being made possible by emigration), a new Portuguese emigration policy that was primarily aimed at Africa (about which more below), and improved shipping. While reiterating the well-known factor of male domination in Portuguese immigration, she adds that when Portuguese families immigrated together, they had smaller families than other immigrants, although Molly Ball's data from recording subsidised and sponsored immigration to São Paulo indicates that Portuguese families were larger than those of other national origins.[58] Pascal

---

[58] See Ball, M., 'Industrialization in São Paulo's Old Republic: A Wage Perspective', UCLA PhD diss., in progress.

also notes the way in which constraints operated on women, who required their husband's or father's permission to emigrate and who were prevented from migrating if their husband did not first return to Portugal. In seeking to appreciate the experiences of Portuguese immigrant women, she presents five oral histories of women who arrived after 1920, although the substance of their accounts extends beyond the study's nominal ending date of 1930.

We should also note the very different contributions by Douglas Mansur da Silva in *A Oposição ao Estado Novo no Exílio Brasileiro, 1956–1974* (Lisbon: Imprensa de Ciências Sociais, 2006), and Heloisa Paulo on exile activities in Brazil from the 1930s, which extend our understanding of the Portuguese diaspora beyond the usual boundaries of socioeconomic analysis by addressing the exiled opposition to the *Estado Novo*.[59] Similarly, Brazilian political exiles also migrated to France during the period of the military dictatorship.[60] Another new direction in Brazilian migration studies is suggested in a conference paper by Lisa Shaw, 'Black Brazil(ians) in Paris in the First Half of the Twentieth Century.'[61]

Until recently, Portuguese communities in Latin America outside of Brazil were seriously neglected in the literature. After Brazil, the main Portuguese community in Latin America is in Venezuela. Portuguese arrived there in the early and middle 20th century, mostly from Madeira Island. Madeirans in different areas started businesses such as bakeries, sandwich shops, juice bars, grocery shops, restaurants, construction companies, travel agencies, and transport companies, among others. The first academic book on the subject was probably Miguel Acosta Saignes' 1959 *Historia de los portugueses en Venezuela*, Caracas, Dirección de Cultura de la Universidade Central (3rd edn 1977, Caracas, Instituto Português de Cultura), but in recent years the literature has grown significantly.[62] For Argentina the pioneering work of Marcelo J. Borges, himself an Argentinian, is important and builds on

---

[59] Paulo, H. (2006), 'O exílio português no Brasil: Os "Budas" e a opposição antisalazarista,' *Portuguese Studies Review* 14, no. 2, pp. 125–142.

[60] Silva, H. Rodrigues da (2007), 'Os exílios dos intelectuais brasileiros e chilenos, na França, durante as ditaduras militares: Uma história cruzada,' *Nuevo Mundo, Mundos Nuevos*, http://nuevomundo.revues.org/5791.

[61] Presented at the conference 'Africans in Europe in the Long Twentieth Century: Transnationalism, Translation and Transfer,' held in Liverpool, 30–31 October 2009; an abstract is available at http://www.liv.ac.uk/soclas/conferences/AFE/abstracts2.htm.

[62] See also Morón, G. (1992), 'Los Portugueses en Venezuela' in I Encontro das Academias de História da Venezuela e de Portugal, Academia Portuguesa de História, Lisbon, pp. 37–43; Abreu Xavier, A. de (2007), *Con Portugal en la maleta: Histórias de vida de los portugueses en Venezuela: Siglo XX*. Caracas: Alfa For religious topics, see Gama, M. da Encarnação Nobrega da (2001) (with Garrett F. de Almeida, photogr.), *Padrões da fé: Erguidos pela comunidade portuguesa na Venezuela: Achegas para a historia*, Funchal: Editorial Eco do Funchal; as well as some recent unpublished studies which show the beginning of a renewed interest in Portugal

studies of Portuguese in colonial Argentina noted above. In his 1997 Rutgers University PhD dissertation, 'Portuguese in Two Worlds: A Historical Study of Migration from Algarve to Argentina,' Borges emphasises migratory and primary social networks in the process of movement and adaptation from southern Portugal to Argentina in the first half of the 20th century. This microhistory focuses on two parishes in the Algarve and two cities in Argentina, while also noting that many migrants to the Algarve from other parts of Portugal were redirected to Argentina.[63] Other scholars have written on Madeiran emigration to and incorporation into different Caribbean societies. Mary Noel Menezes writes about Guyana; Robert Ciski, Arnold Thomas, and João Ribeiro about St. Vincent; and Jo-Anne Ferreira about Trinidad and Tobago, while Ferreira provides a useful overview in a recent article in the *Portuguese Studies Review*.[64]

Compared with the Caribbean and even Venezuela, there are large numbers of recent Portuguese immigrants in Europe. An early study of this modern phenomenon is M. L. Martinho Antunes' *A Emigração Portuguesa desde*

---

in this community: Costa, J. Torres (1997), 'Percurso com regresso(s). Estratégias e trajectórias sociais num percurso local da emigração para Venezuela,' MA dissertation, Universidade Aberta, Porto; Costa, M. de la Assuncion da Silva Faria (2002), 'A comunidade portuguesa na Venezuela: Integração e retorno ao país de origem,' MA dissertation, Universidade Aberta, Porto; Silva do Nascimento, J. da (2009), 'Emigração madeirense para a Venezuela (1940–1974),' MA dissertation, Universidade da Madeira, Funchal.

[63] For publications based partly on his dissertation research, see Borges, M. J. (2003), 'Network Migration, Marriage Patterns, and Adaptation in Rural Portugal and among Portuguese Immigrants in Argentina, 1870–1980,' *The History of the Family: An International Quarterly* 8, no. 3, pp. 445–479; Borges, M. J. (2003), 'Many Americas: Patterns of Transatlantic Migration and Choice of Destination in Southern Portugal (19th–20th Centuries),' *Studi Emigrazione / Migration Studies* 40, no. 150, pp. 351–375; and Borges, M. J. (2006), 'Portuguese Migration in Argentina: Transatlantic Networks and Local Experiences,' *Portuguese Studies Review* 14, no. 2, pp. 87–123.

[64] Menezes, M. N. (1994), *Scenes from the History of the Portuguese in Guyana*, M. N. Menezes, London; and Menezes, M. N. (1994), *The Portuguese of Guyana: A Study in Culture and Conflict*, M. N. Menezes, London. Ciski, R. (1979), 'The Vincentian Portuguese: A Study in Ethnic Group Adaptation', PhD dissertation, University of Massachusetts; Thomas, A. (1999–2000), 'Portuguese and Indian Immigration to St. Vincent (1845–1890),' *Journal of Caribbean Studies* 14, nos. 1–2, pp. 41–59; Ribeiro, J. M. (2006), *A emigração de madeirenses para as Ilhas de São Vicente nas Antilhas*, Editorial Calcamar, Funchal. Ferreira, J.-A. S. (1994), *The Portuguese of Trinidad and Tobago: Portrait of an Ethnic Minority*, Institute of Social and Economic Research, University of the West Indies, St. Augustine; Ferreira, J.-A. S. (1999), 'The Portuguese Language in Trinidad and Tobago: A Study of Language Shift and Language Death', PhD dissertation, University of the West Indies at St. Augustine; Ferreira, J.-A. S. (2003), 'Preliminary Bibliography on the Madeiran Presbyterians: From Madeira to Trinidad and the U.S.,' http://homepages.rootsweb.com/~madeira/jobiblio.htm;

1950: Dados e Comentários (Lisbon: Gabinete de Investigações Sociais, 1973), which provides demographic data and statistics for all Portuguese emigration with a focus on France. This study is particularly useful in evaluating the available sources (it demonstrates, for example, that Portuguese and French emigration/immigration data do not match for the period 1964–1968) and suggests lines for future research. Antunes also provides a method for estimating clandestine immigration to France to confront the statistical anomalies. A few years later an edited volume by Eduardo da Sousa Ferreira sought to situate modern Portuguese emigration in a wider European context.[65] A decade later Sousa Ferreira and Guy Clausse edited a collection of essays on *Closing the Migratory Cycle: The Case of Portugal* (Fort Lauderdale, FL: Verlag Breitenbach Publishers, 1986) that places emphasis on return migration and locates Portuguese emigration in the wider context of its benefits for Europe as a whole. In two important articles Victor Pereira critically examines the role played by the state in Portuguese migration to France in a study of the last years of the *Estado Novo*, a subject that he explores in greater detail in his PhD dissertation.[66] Marie-Christine Volovitch-Tavares contributes a valuable complementary essay on the role played by the Catholic Church in integrating Portuguese immigrants in France during this same period.[67] A further piece coauthored by Volovitch-Tavares discusses the character of Portuguese culture in France, while another investigates relations among immigrants in France and their connections to their homelands.[68] Álvaro Villalobos contributes an interesting article on Portuguese entrepreneurs in

---

Ferreira, J.-A. S. (2006), 'Madeiran Portuguese Migration to Guyana, St. Vincent, Antigua and Trinidad,' *Portuguese Studies Review* 14, no. 2, pp. 63–85.

[65] Ferreira, E. de Sousa (ed.) (1977), *O Poder Europeu – 1: A emigração portuguesa e o seu contexto internacional*, Iniciativas editoriais, Lisbon, especially chapters by the editor, 'Actualidade e perspectivas da emigração portuguesa no contexto europeu,' pp. 11–27, and by Poinard, M. and Roux, M. (1977), 'Os casos português e jugoslavo: A emigração contra a desenvolvimento,' pp. 31–66, as well as appendices 1 and 2.

[66] Pereira, V. (2002), 'L'État portugais et les Portugais en France de 1958 à 1974,' *Lusotopie* 14, no. 2, pp. 9–27, and Pereira, V. (2005), 'La politique d'émigration de l'Estado Novo entre 1958 et 1974', *Cahiers de l'Urmis* [online], no. 9, http://urmis.revues.org/index31; Pereira, V. (2007), 'L'État portugais et les Portugais en France de 1957 à 1974,' PhD dissertation, Institut d'Études Politiques de Paris.

[67] Volovitch-Tavares, M.-C. (1999), 'L'Église de France et l'accueil des immigrés portugais (1960–1975),' *Le Mouvement social* no. 188, pp. 89–102.

[68] Volovitch-Tavares, M.-C., and Stonesco, D. (2007), 'Portuguese Immigrants and Portuguese Culture in France,' *Museum International* 59, nos. 1–2, pp. 30–40; Santos, I. S. dos (2004), 'The Descendants of Migrants in France: Bonds with Home Country and Belonging,' *AEMI Journal* 2, pp. 173–184. An early reflection of the Portuguese presence and of the nostalgic power of Portuguese culture for that community in Paris can be found in the 1957 concert by the great *fadista* Amalia Rodrigues at the Paris Olympic, Columbia 33CSX-11.

France that sets out some basic data on Portuguese immigration in France and provides a sense of the experience of these Portuguese businessmen through several interviews.[69] Elsewhere, Alexandre Afonso provides an overview of Portuguese immigration in Switzerland.[70] The Atlantic islands are well known as one of the major points of diaspora for Portuguese-speakers in the 19th and 20th centuries. Originally published in Portuguese in 1977, shortly after Cape Verdean independence, António Carreira's *The People of the Cape Verde Islands: Exploitation and Emigration*, trans. Christopher Fyfe (London: C. Hurst; Hamden, CT: Archon Book, 1982) provides a mass of statistical data on both voluntary and forced migration from this African archipelago. After a valuable chapter, 'The Making of Cape Verdean Society' that focuses on the environment, the slave trade, and the creation of a three-tiered society with whites on top and African slaves on the bottom, he turns to voluntary migration to Brazil and then to the United States, which dates to the later 18th century. His chapter on forced migration to both Guinea-Bissau in the Pombaline era and later to São Tomé and Príncipe is highly critical of the Portuguese government. He ends his study with a short discussion of returnees. In *Race, Culture, and Portuguese Colonialism in Cabo Verde* (Syracuse, NY: Maxwell School of Citizenship and Public Affairs, 1984) anthropologist Deirdre Meintel examines the history of Portuguese and African settlement, with its resulting creation of a *mestiço* population, and posits that Cape Verde exhibits a perception of race that parallels that of Brazil. The question of identity is also examined by Toby Green in a recent article.[71] A further valuable article by Jørgen Carling and Lisa Åkesson analyses the historical patterns of Cape Verdean migration and then discusses contemporary attitudes about migration and its impact

---

[69] Villalobos, A. (2007), 'A Minority within a Minority: The Portuguese Entrepreneurs of Paris,' Immigration Here and There, Northwestern University Medill School of Journalism, http://www.immigrationhereandthere.org/2007/05/a_minority_within_a_minority_t.php.
[70] Afonso, A. (2010), 'Permanently Provisional: History, Facts and Figures of Portuguese Immigration in Switzerland,' published online in *International Migration*, http://onlinelibrary.wiley.com/doi/10.1111/j.1468–2435.2010.00636.x/pdf.
[71] Green, T. (2010), 'The Evolution of a Creole Identity in Cape Verde,' in Cohen, R. A., and Toninato, P. (eds.), *The Creolization Reader: Studies in Mixed Identities and Cultures*, Routledge, London, pp. 157–167. For problems of assimilation and identity in colonial Mozambique, see Penvenne, J. M. (1989), '"We Are All Portuguese!": Challenging the Political Economy of Assimilation, Lourenço Marques, 1870 to 1933,' in Vail, L. (ed.), *The Creation of Tribalism in Southern Africa*, University of California, Berkeley, pp. 255–288, and Penvenne, J. M. (1996), 'João dos Santos Albasini (1876–1922); The Contradictions of Politics and Identity in Colonial Mozambique,' *Journal of African History* 37, no. 3, pp. 417–464.

'Portuguese' Diasporas: A Survey of the Scholarly Literature 53

on society.[72] In *O Sul da Diaspora: Cabo-Verdeanos em Plantações de S. Tomé e Principe e Moçambique* (Praia: Edição da Presidência da República de Cabo Verde, 2003), Augusto Nascimento reconstructs the history of forced-labour migration within the modern Portuguese African empire.[73] Alexander Keese contributes an important chapter on Cabo Verdeans in Portugal's other African colonies during the *Estado Novo* to this volume. Marta Maffia similarly looks at the historical formation and contemporary situation of Cape Verdeans in Argentina.[74]

An early exploration of Azorean emigration is Caetano Valadão Serpa's *A Gente dos Açores: Identificação, emigração e religiosidade, Séculos XVI–XX* (Lisbon: Prelo, 1978). Serpa specifically links religiosity with the Azorean emigration experience, looking as far back as the origins of the islands. The strongest chapters discuss immigration in the United States through a careful examination at the archives of the Boston archdiocese, school records, and individual testimonies. In the mid-1990s, a preliminary introduction to Azorean emigration was published by Victor Pereira da Rosa and Salvato Trigo that emphasises the economic influences on migration trends, although they acknowledge the significance of noneconomic factors, as well.[75] In *Tides of Migration: A Study of Migration Decision-Making and Social Progress in São Miguel, Azores* (New York: AMS Press, 1989), Francis W. Chapin combines historical analysis with anthropological fieldwork completed between 1976 and 1978. The ideas advanced by these authors for understanding Azorean emigration can also be assessed against the somewhat quirky *Jornal da emigração: A L(USA)lândia reinventada* (Angra do Heroísmo: Gabinete de Emigração e Apoio às Comunidades Açorianas, 1990). An interesting form of community witness is embodied in a large volume that brings together presentations at the first Congress of Azorean Communities, with representatives from the Azores, Bermuda, Brazil, California, Canada, Lisbon, New England, and Venezuela.[76] It is worth noting, too, that there

---

[72] Carling, J., and Åkesson, L. (2009), 'Mobility at the Heart of a Nation: Patterns and Meanings of Cape Verdean Migration,' *International Migration* (special issue on migration in the Lusophone world) 47, no. 3, pp. 123–155.
[73] See also Nascimento, A. (2002), *Vidas de S. Tomé segundo vozes de Soncente*, Ilhéu Editora, Praia, and Nascimento, A. (2007), *O fim do caminho longi*, Ilhéu Editora, Praia.
[74] Maffia, M. M. (2010), 'Migration and Identity of Cape Verdeans and Their Descendants in Argentina,' *African and Black Diaspora: An International Journal* 3, no. 2, pp. 169–180.
[75] Rosa, V. Pereira da, and Trigo, S. (1994), *Azorean Emigration: A Preliminary Overview*, Imprensa da Universidade Fernando Pessoa, Porto.
[76] 1978, *I Congresso de Comunidades Açorianas*, Angra do Heroísmo/Horta/Ponta Delgada.

have also been regular congresses of Cape Verdean communities since 1994.[77] In the last two centuries North America has proved to be a major destination of immigrants from Portugal, Cape Verde, and the Azores. The earliest academic study that we have found is a statistical analysis by Frederic Hoffman published at the end of the 19th century.[78] Nearly two decades later, in 1916, John Bannick wrote his MA thesis, which was published as *Portuguese Immigration to the United States: Its Distribution and Status* (San Francisco: R&E Research Associates, 1971). Bannick compiled comprehensive immigration data from a variety of sources starting in 1820 and identified what remain today the main areas of Portuguese settlement in the United States: Massachusetts, Rhode Island, California, and Hawaii. Bannick profiles the most typical immigrant as a young, male, illiterate, but with a high propensity for success in waged positions often associated with agriculture. He also notes that Cape Verdeans were referred to as Bravas (because many of them came from the southwestern island of Brava in the archipelago) or black Portuguese (in other sources they are referred to as brown Portuguese) and were frequently employed on cranberry bogs in New England. The first of what have proved to be numerous amateur histories of Portuguese immigrant communities in North America is Manoel da Silveira Cardozo's *The Portuguese in America: 590 B.C.–1974* (New York: Oceana Publications, 1976), which is essentially a chronology that begins with the Portuguese colonisation of Madeira in 1425 and carries through to the opening of the Fado Restaurant in Acushnet, Massachusetts, in 1975. A more serious attempt to provide an overview comes a few years later from Maria Baganha, whose *Portuguese Emigrations to the United States, 1820–1930* was published at the beginning of the 1990s (New York: Garland, 1990; London: Taylor and Francis, 1991).[79] Baganha argues that decisions to emigrate to the United States were based more on familial organisation and other social network factors, which often provided the funds to make immigration possible, than on economic opportunities. She distinguishes between the positive opportunities for upward mobility in California against those in Hawaii, where Portuguese families were contracted to work on sugar plantations.[80] She also pays attention to illegal, as well as legal, immigration.

---

[77] Cahen, M. (1995), 'À la recherche de la nation. Le congrès des cadres capverdiens de la diaspora,' *Lusotopie* 2, pp. 69–74.

[78] Hoffman, F. L. (1899), 'The Portuguese Population in the United States,' *Publications of the American Statistical Association* 6, no. 47.

[79] See also Baganha, M. (1991), 'The Social Mobility of Portuguese Immigrants in the United States at the Turn of the Nineteenth Century,' *International Migration Review* 25, no. 2, pp. 277–302.

[80] An interesting comparative line of research would be to look at contracted immigrant labour in Hawaii and in the coffee hinterland of São Paulo state.

There are several sociological studies of the Portuguese communities in the United States that examine the differences within the Portuguese American population. Sandra Knight Wolforth focuses on New England in *Portuguese Presence in America* (San Francisco: R&E Research Associates, 1978), where she finds that the indifference to education and acceptance of mediocrity relegated Portuguese to a lower-class position in the region. She also emphasises differences within the community, a position which sets her study apart from others on the subject. Leo Papp, a professor of linguistics, published a more broadly based study, entitled *The Portuguese Americans* (Boston: Twayne, 1981), in which he sought to establish that the Portuguese in the United States may have been primarily working class but were not 'a low grade people', Although an entertaining read, there is little of substantive scholarship in this study.

The largest Cape Verdean communities in the United States have established themselves in Rhode Island and Massachusetts, where many men first emigrated through their labour in the whaling industry. For a general overview of the archipelago and its long history of migrations, Richard A. Lobban's *Cape Verde: Crioulo Colony to Independent Nation* (Boulder: Westview Press, 1995) and, with Paul Khalil Saucier, *Historical Dictionary of the Republic of Cape Verde* (4th ed. Lanham, MD: Scarecrow Press, 2007) make an excellent beginning. Specifically for Cape Verdeans in the United States, there is an interesting collection of essays edited by Raymond Anthony Almeida entitled *Cape Verdeans in America, Our Story* (Boston: Tchuba, American Committee for Cape Verde, 1978), which is based on original manuscripts by Michael K. H. Platzer and Deirdre Meintel Machado. For a more academic approach to this topic, there is a valuable study based on oral histories and ships' records by the historian Marilyn Halter, *Between Race and Ethnicity: Cape Verdean American Immigrants, 1860–1965* (Urbana: University of Illinois Press, 1993).[81] Finally, moving away from these general works, there is the fascinating autobiography based on an oral life history collected by Maria Luisa Nunes from her aunt, *A Portuguese Colonial in America, Belmira Nunes Lopes: The Autobiography of a Cape Verdean American* (Pittsburgh, PA: Latin American Literary Review Press, 1982), while anthropologist Sam Beck provides a richly textured grassroots study of a longshoreman's hangout in the Fox Point neighbourhood of Providence, Rhode Island in *Manny Almeida's Ringside Lounge: The Cape Verdeans' Struggle for Their Neighborhood* (Providence, RI: Gávea-Brown Publications, 1992).

An interesting attempt to understand Portuguese sending communities is Jerry R. Williams' *And Yet They Come: Portuguese Immigration from the Azores to the United States* (New York: Center for Migration Studies, 1982). Williams

---

[81] See also Lopes, M. L. (2005), *Cape Verdean Americans in Rhode Island*, Arcadia, Charleston.

establishes three major periods of immigration (1800–1870, 1870–1920, and 1957–ca.1980), but his study is shaky on its evidential grounds, where he is not always able positively to distinguish mainland Portuguese from Azoreans or account for illegal immigration. The first wave of migrants was attracted by the pull of the American whaling industry as a consequence of the fortuitous location of the Azores Islands in the mid-Atlantic.[82] The California gold rush was a secondary pull factor. The migrants of the second wave found most of their employment in the booming textile industry of New England, where Fall River and Providence were centres. With the decline of the whaling industry and the gold rush, Portuguese immigrants in California turned to dairy farming in Marin County and later in the Central Valley before filtering out to the canning industries around Salinas and San Diego. More recently, environmental and demographic pressures continued to move Azorean emigrants towards the United States (and Canada), while the U.S. Azorean Refugee Acts of 1958 and 1960 were responses to the eruption of the Capelinhos volcano, which occurred off the coast of the island of Faial in 1957.

There are many more state-specific studies of Portuguese immigration to the United States; however, they are essentially the products of amateur, community-based historians. As early as the mid-1960s, a member of the Irmandade do Divino Espírito Santo, August Mark Vaz, produced *The Portuguese in California* (Oakland: IDES Supreme Council, 1965). Vaz argues that the strong Catholicism of the Portuguese community and its celebration of traditional festivals bound together that community. His focus is on Azorean, rather than mainland Portuguese, immigrants, and he provides a comprehensive list of contemporary Luso-related organisations in California. Helder Pinho's *Portugueses na Califórnia: A história e o quotidiano de uma das mais vivas comunidades lusas no Mundo* (Lisbon: Editorial Notícias, 1978) consists of a series of articles originally published in the Lisbon newspaper *A Capital*. The volume is bookended with a preface by the poet Jorge de Sena, who taught at the University of California, Santa Barbara, and a postscript by the linguist Eduardo Mayone Dias, who taught at UCLA. An interesting aspect of these essays is the distance the Portuguese in California sought to place between themselves and Mexicans, among other minority groups. Dias was himself a prolific author on different Portuguese communities in the western United States. His studies include *Açorianos na California* (Angra do Heroísmo: Secretaria Regional de Educação e Cultura, 1982;, *Miscelânia LUSAlendesa* (Lisbon: Edições Cosmos, 1997); *A Presença Portuguesa no Havai* (Lisbon: Separata do Boletim Cultural da Assembleia Distrital de Lisbon, 1981); *Crónicas da Diáspora* (Lisbon: Edições Salamandra, 1992);

---

[82] See, e.g., Warrin, D. (2010), *So Ends This Day: The Portuguese in American Whaling, 1765–1927*, Center for Portuguese Studies and Culture, Portuguese in America Series, Dartmouth, MA.

and *Portugueses na America do Norte* (Rumford, RI: Pereginação Publications, 1999 [1983]), a collection of essays from a UCLA conference that mainly featured scholars of Portuguese descent working in the United States. Much of Dias' work is based on oral interviews with Portuguese immigrants or their descendants. Two works that focus specifically on the Portuguese presence in Hawaii are J. H. Felix and P. F. Senecal, *The Portuguese in Hawaii* (Honolulu: Centenial, 1978), and R. Rocha, *Apontamentos sobre a comunidade portuguesa de Hawaii* (Lisbon: n.p., 1983).

A bibliography on the Portuguese in Canada published some 20 years ago includes 761 titles of varying provenance.[83] An early study is *Imigrantes Portugueses: 25 Anos no Canadá* (Toronto: Movimento Comunitário Português, 1978), which demonstrates the important role that the ethnic community has played in creating and maintaining a Portuguese identity in Canada; it focuses on the principal communities in Toronto and Montréal. The authors document that two-thirds of Portuguese immigrants originate from the Azores, most from the island of São Miguel. A few years later David Higgs published a pamphlet, *The Portuguese in Canada* (Ottawa: Canadian Historical Association, 1982), that, given its publisher, mainly serves to validate the study of the Portuguese as a constituent Canadian community.[84] A contemporary publication is João António Alpalhão and Victor M. Pereira da Rosa's *Les Portugais du Québec: Éléments socio-culturels* (Ottawa: Éditions de l'Université d'Ottawa, 1979).[85]

As part of the third Portuguese Empire, Africa constitutes an entirely different experience for the Portuguese diaspora.[86] Several official settlement schemes promoted colonisation in both Angola and Mozambique, one of which enticed several hundred Madeirans to southern Angola in the 1880s in what Cristiana Bastos calls 'engineered migration'.[87] The emergence of an Africanist historiography since the 1950s has, with few exceptions, caused scholars of these two vast African countries to neglect this phenomenon, although it receives narrative treatment in the relevant volumes of the *Nova História da Expansão Portuguesa* and other syntheses

---

[83] Teixeira, C., and Lavigne, G. (1992), *The Portuguese in Canada: A Bibliography/ Les Portugais au Canada: Une bibliographie*, Institute for Social Research, York University, Toronto.
[84] See also Higgs, D. (1990), *Portuguese Migration in Global Perspective*, Multicultural History Society of Ontario, Toronto, in which most chapters focus on Canada.
[85] A revised edition by the same authors appeared in 1980 as *A Minority in a Changing Society: The Portuguese Communities of Quebec*, University of Ottawa Press, Ottawa, followed by a somewhat expanded Portuguese version in 1983 as *Da emigração à aculturação: Portugal insular e continental no Quebeque*, Imprensa Nacional, Lisbon.
[86] See Clarence-Smith, W. G. (1985), *The Third Portuguese Empire, 1825–1975*, Manchester University Press, Manchester.
[87] Bastos, C. (2008), 'Migrants, Settlers and Colonists: The Biopolitics of Displaced Bodies', *International Migration* 46, pp. 27–54.

of both Angolan and Mozambican history. There are, of course, officially sanctioned studies, such as Ilídio do Amaral's *Aspectos do povoamento branco de Angola* (Lisbon: Junta de Investigações do Ultramar – Estudos, Ensaios e Documentos 74, 1960), which is valuable for the official data that it provides. Until recently, the dominant study, which also served as a definitive demolition of Lusotropicalism, has been Gerald J. Bender's *Angola under the Portuguese: The Myth and the Reality* (Berkeley and Los Angeles: University of California Press, 1978). An important breakthrough, however, is the monograph by Cláudia Castelo, *Passagens para África: O Povoamento de Angola e Moçambique com Naturais da Metrópole (1920–1974)* (Porto: Edições Afrontamento, 2007). Based upon extensive archival research in Portugal, Angola and Mozambique, this remarkable work of historical reconstruction sets a high standard for all future work on the Portuguese diaspora by combining a sophisticated understanding of policy, politics, and social conditions in both metropolitan Portugal and the two colonial territories with solid demographic data. She emphasises push factors and the possibilities of social mobility in encouraging Portuguese settler migration, the latter of which created serious problems for *retornados* (returnees) after the 1974 revolution (about *retornados*, see below). Complementing Castelo's contribution on Portuguese migration to the two major African colonies is Augusto Nascimento's book on forced migration from Mozambique to the plantations of São Tomé and Príncipe, which parallels his study of Cape Verdean labour migration to these island-colonies.[88]

One aspect of secondary migration within the Lusophone Atlantic that is a direct by-product of the emergence of an Africa-centred historiography is the return of Afro-Brazilians to coastal West Africa (especially the modern Republic of Benin) and their place in that society. This phenomenon belongs to scholarship on both the African and 'Portuguese' diasporas; for notorious slave-trading families such as the de Souzas and their descendants, the so-called Agudas, being marked as Afro-Brazilian is still an important social indicator.[89]

---

[88] Nascimento, A. (2002), *Desterro e Contrato: Moçambicanos a Caminho de S. Tomé e Príncipé (Anos 1940 a 1960)*, Arquivo Histórico de Moçambique, Maputo.
[89] For an early study, see Ross, D. A. (1965), 'The Career of Domingo Martinez in the Bight of Biafra 1833–64,' *Journal of African History* 6, no. 1, pp. 79–90, but the classic study is Verger, P. (1968), *Flux et reflux de la traite des nègres entre le Golfe de Bénin et Bahia de Todos os Santos, du xviie au xixe siècle*, Mouton, Paris and The Hague; for more recent treatments, see Krasnovolski M. (1987), *Les Afro-Brésiliens dans le processus de changement de la Côte des Esclaves*, Zakad Narodowy im. Ossolinkich, Wroclaw; Yai, O. B. (1997), 'Les "Aguda" (Afro-Brésiliens) du Golfe du Bénin. Identité, apports, idéologie: Essai de réinterprétation,' *Lusotopie* 4, pp. 275–284; Soumonni, E. (2003), 'Afro-Brazilian Communities of the Bight of Benin in the Nineteenth Century,' in Lovejoy, P. E., and Trotman, D.V. (eds.), *Trans-Atlantic Dimension of Ethnicity in the African Diaspora*, Continuum, London

One final area that remains to be discussed is the emigration of Asian colonial subjects east of the Cape of Good Hope, in particular the major diaspora of Goans, initially to Mozambique, then to British East Africa, and more recently to Europe, North America, and the Gulf. Although the role of Catholic Goans in 18th- and 19th-century Zambesia – where they were called Canarins – is well known and sporadically discussed in the literature, with the exception of broader contributions on Indians in Mozambique by António Rita Ferreira and Joana Pereira Leite and a useful article by Sharmila S. Karnik, there is no major study of their community during this period.[90] Similarly, while Goans are certainly accounted for in the general literature on India and East Africa, there are no major studies of their presence at Zanzibar. That said, the devotion of an issue of *Lusotopie* (2000) to the theme 'Lusophonie asiatiques, Asiatiques en lusophonie' that includes papers on Goa, Bengal, Macau, East Timor, Sri Lanka, and migrant communities in Mozambique, Brazil, and the Middle East suggests that a lively new interest is emerging. In addition, several more recent articles indicate that the modern Indian and Goan diaspora is continuing to attract the attention of researchers. Margret Frenz contributes an important overview in her 'Global Goans. Migration Movements and Identity in a Historical Perspective,' in which she also notes two unpublished manuscripts, 'Goans in Zanzibar' and 'Global Goans.'[91] She also authors a chapter in the present volume on Goan consuls in East Africa. Luisa Pinto Teixeira considers the role of Indian

---

and New York, pp. 11–194; Law, R. (2004), 'Francisco Felix de Souza in West Africa, 1820–1849,' and Strickrodt, S. (2004), '"Afro-Brazilians" of the Western Slave Coast in the Nineteenth Century,' both in Curto, J. C., and Lovejoy, P. E. (eds.), *Enslaving Connections: Changing Cultures of Africa and Brazil during the Era of Slavery*, Humanity Books, New York, pp. 187–211, 213–244; and Guran, M. (1999), *Agudás: Os 'brasileiros' do Benim*, Editora Nova Frontera, Rio de Janeiro, and Guran, M. (2006), 'De africanos no Brasil a "brasileiros" na África: Os agudás do Golfo do Benim,' in Chaves, R., et al. (eds.), *Brasil África: Como se o mar fosse mentira*, Editora UNESP, São Paulo, pp. 159–178.

[90] Ferreira, A. R. (1985), 'Moçambique e os naturais da Índia Portuguesa,' in Albuquerque, L. de, and Guerreiro, I. (eds.), *Actas do II Seminário Internacional de História Indo-Portuguesa*, Instituto de Investigação Cientifica Troplical/Centro de Estudos de História e Cartografia Antiga, Lisbon, pp. 615–648; Leite, J. Pereira, (1996), 'Diáspora Indiana em Moçambique,' *Economia Global e Gestão* 2, pp. 67–108; Karnik, S. S. (1998), 'Goans in Mozambique,' *Africa Quarterly* 38, no.3, pp. 96–118. See also the short article by Mudenge, I. S. G. (1984), 'Goans in the Zambezi Valley,' *Purabhilekh-Puratatva* 1, no. 2. There is nothing comparable for Goans like the outstanding study of Gujarati Hindu *vania* merchants by Machado, P. A. da Silva Rupino (2005), 'Gujarati Indian Merchant Networks in Mozambique, 1777–c.1830,' unpublished PhD dissertation, School of Oriental and African Studies, University of London.

[91] Frenz, M. (2008), *Lusotopie* 15, no. 1, pp. 183–202. The references to her unpublished works are at 200, n. 57.

traders, who were mainly British subjects from Gujarat and either Hindus or Muslims, in Zambesia in the late 19th and early 20th centuries.[92] Writing about elite Goan accounts of their East African experiences, Rochelle Pinto suggests that these testimonies reveal that Indians in Mozambique internalised the racial categories of the Portuguese colonial empire in Africa and understood their identity 'within the Portuguese Empire against that of the indigenous black population of Mozambique.'[93] In a companion article, Pamila Gupta sets forth a research agenda on Portuguese decolonisation in the Indian Ocean in which she plans to focus on Goan immigration to Mozambique. She notes that 'during its history of Portuguese colonialism in Mozambique, Goans were alternately labeled "white" or "less than white," but rarely "black."'[94]

Finally, their small numbers notwithstanding, there are interesting chapters on Portuguese settlers in a collection of essays on Iberians in early modern Southeast Asia. Kenneth McPherson writes about informal Portuguese presence in the Bay of Bengal and Southeast Asia in the 17th and 18th centuries, Timothy P. Barnard considers 'Mestizos as Middlemen' in Sumatra, and Radin Fernando seeks to appreciate the 'Metamorphosis of the Luso-Asian Diaspora in the Malay Archipelago, 1640–1795.'[95] In addition, an anthropological study of the Macanese community of Macau undertaken just prior to the transition from Portuguese to Chinese rule makes a number of useful points about how Portuguese identity has taken root over the centuries in this population, while Margaret Sarkissian emphasises the role of 'performing Portuguese' in writing about Melaka.[96]

---

[92] Teixeira, L. Pinto (2008), 'Partners in Business: The Workings of the Indian Traders of Zambezia, Mozambique, 1870s–1910s,' *Lusotopie* 15, no. 1, pp. 39–58.
[93] Pinto, R. (2007), 'Race and Imperial Loss: Accounts of East Africa in Goa,' *South African Historical Journal* 57, pp. 82–92, quoted from p. 91. See also Prinz, M. (1997), 'Intercultral Links between Goa and Mozambique in Their Colonial and Contemporary History,' in Borges and Feldmann (eds.), *Goa and Portugal*, pp. 111–127.
[94] Gupta, P. (2007), 'Mapping Portuguese Recolonisation in the Indian Ocean: A Research Agenda,' *South African Historical Journal* 57, pp. 93–112, quoted from pp. 105–106. For more on this project, see Gupta, P. (2009), 'The Disquieting of History: Portuguese (De)colonization and Goan Migration in the Indian Ocean,' *Journal of Asian and African Studies* 44, no. 1, pp. 19–47.
[95] In Borschberg, P. (ed.) (2004), *Iberians in the Singapore-Melaka Area and Adjacent Regions (16th to 18th Century)*, Harrassowitz Verlag, Wiesbaden & Fundação Oriente, Lisbon.
[96] Cabral, J. de Pina (2002), *Between China and Europe: Person, Culture and Emotion in Macao*, Continuum, New York; Sarkissian, M. (2002), 'Playing Portuguese: Constructing Identity in Malaysia's Portuguese Community,' *Diaspora: A Journal of Transnational Studies* 11, no. 2, pp. 215–32.

Phase III: globalisation and diaspora since 1974

The last section of our chapter discusses the rapidly growing scholarly output on 'Portuguese' emigration in all its many manifestations since the Revolution of the Carnations in 1974 and the end of the Portuguese corporate state. This period also marks a more multidirectional set of migratory movements that involve Portuguese, citizens of postcolonial Asian territories or African nation-states where Portuguese is an official language (PALOPs) even if most of their citizens do not primarily speak Portuguese, a new outflow of Brazilian emigrants, and the persistent questions of integration, identity, and return.

Although he includes only passing references to the migratory movements that are the focus of this chapter, W. M. Spellman's *Uncertain Identity: International Migration since 1945* (London: Reaktion Books, 2008) raises several important questions about recent trends in international migration, including the reality of disruption in both sending and (by new immigrants) receiving societies, as well as the consequent tightening of regulations to restrict migration. Portugal is unusual, if not unique, for being both a sending and receiving country and thus faces both sets of problems.[97] Understanding how these issues affect contemporary migrant communities occupies a central place in many of the studies about 'Portuguese' diasporas. Among studies on Portugal, Félix Neto's *A Migração Portuguesa Vivida e Representada: Contribuição para o estudo dos projectos migratórios* (Porto: Secretaria de Estado das Comunidades Portuguesas, Centro de Estudos, 1986) reflects an early attempt to develop both a theory and methodology for understanding post-1974 migration and its consequences. The first part of the book looks at the return of Portuguese emigrants from France, while the second section discusses how migration is seen by adolescents and pre-adolescents within these communities.[98] The problem of how to deal with returning emigrants, but in particular with *retornados* from the colonial settler societies of Angola and Mozambique, is addressed by Rui Pena Pires in *Os Retornados: Um Estudo Sociográfico* (Lisbon: Cadernos do Instituto para o Desenvolvimento, 1987) and Paolo Filipe Monteiro in *Emigração: O Eterno Mito do Retorno* (Oeiras: Celta Editora, 1994).[99] Stephen Lubkemann has

---

[97] Rocha-Trinidade, M. B. (2005), 'Portugal: Destination Countries for Emigrants; Immigrants['] Countries of Origin,' *AEMI Journal* 3, pp. 76–89.
[98] Cf. Klimt, A., and Lubkemann, S. (2002), 'Argument across the Portuguese-Speaking World: A Discursive Approach to Diaspora,' *Diaspora: A Journal of Transnational Studies* 11, no. 2, pp. 145–162.
[99] See also Carrington, W. J., and Lima, P. J. de (1996), 'The Impact of 1970's Repatriates from Africa on the Portuguese Labor Market,' *Industrial and Labor Relations Review* 49, pp. 330–347.

published a useful short history of the first quarter century of *retornados*, who have also been studied by anthropologist Cecile Øien.[100] The online journal *Janus*, published by the External Relations wing of the Autonomous University of Lisbon, devoted two parts of its annual publication in 2001 to Portuguese emigration (Part 3.2) and immigration to Portugal (Part 3.3), each covering a very wide range of destinations and departures.[101] It is evident, however, that France continues to occupy centre stage for the modern Portuguese diaspora, where issues of belonging and invisibility predominate.[102] Particularly noteworthy is a provocative PhD dissertation, 'Immigrant In/visibility: Portuguese and North Africans in Post-Colonial France' (University of California, Irvine, 2007), by Brigitte Jelen, who contrasts the agency exhibited by North Africans and the overall invisibility of the Portuguese immigrant communities in France. She finds that this distinction stems not from similarities between the French and Portuguese but rather from the Portuguese maintaining their religious and cultural identity so that they remain an insular community and do not easily assimilate. This phenomenon is especially interesting in comparison with Portuguese communities in both Canada and the United States, as we shall presently see.[103] Although France remains central to the diasporic experience of continental Portugal, Andrea Klimpt studies Portuguese in Germany in comparative context,[104] while a study of Portuguese immigrants in Spain edited by L. L. Trigal, *La Migración de Portugueses en España*

---

[100] Lubkemann, S. C. (2003), 'Race, Class, and Kin in the Negotiation of "internal strangerhood" among Portuguese Retornados, 1975–2000,' in Smith, A. L. (ed.), *Europe's Invisible Migrants*, Amsterdam University Press, Amsterdam, pp. 75–93; see also Lubkemann, S. C. (2002), 'The Moral Economy of Portuguese Postcolonial Return,' *Diaspora: A Journal of Transnational Studies* 11, no. 2, pp. 163–188; Øien, C. (2009), 'Of Homecomings and Homesickness: The Question of Retornados and White Angolans in Postcolonial Portugal,' presented at the conference 'Africans in Europe in the Long Twentieth Century: Transnationalism, Translation and Transfer,' Liverpool; an abstract is available at http://www.liv.ac.uk/soclas/conferences/AFE/abstracts2.htm. See also Rui Penas Pires (1999), 'O regresso das colonias,' in Bethencourt, F., and Chauduri, K. (eds.), *História da expansão portuguesa*, vol. 5, Círculo dos Leitores, Lisbon, pp. 182–196, 212–213.

[101] Available at http://www.janusonline.pt/2001/2001.html, including sixteen and eighteen articles, respectively.

[102] See the special 2004 issue on 'Portugais de France, immigrés et citoyens d'Europe', *Cahiers de l'Urmis*, vol. 9, which also includes one paper on Luxemburg. Also, Carreira, TP and Tomé, M-A 1994 & 2000, *Portugais et Luso-Français*, 2 vols., L'Harmattan, Paris, which discusses the double identity of being both French and Portuguese, as well as dual language acquisition.

[103] See also Santos, 'The Descendants of Migrants in France', and Volovitch-Tavares, 'Portuguese Immigrants and Portuguese Culture in France', cited above.

[104] Klimt, A 2003, 'Do National Narratives Matter? Identity Formation among Portuguese Migrants in France and Germany', in Ohliger, R et al (eds), *European*

'Portuguese' Diasporas: A Survey of the Scholarly Literature 63

(Leon: Universidad de Leon, 1994), provides a group profile based on municipal archives, interviews, and personal experience. Similarly, Portuguese communities in North America continue to draw scholarly attention. A major study edited by Carlos Teixeira and Victor Pereira da Rosa, *The Portuguese in Canada* (Buffalo: University of Toronto Press, 2000), includes substantive chapters by the editors, Gilles Lavigne, and David Higgs, as well as other contributions from a wider cohort of Portuguese and Canadian academics in a variety of social science and humanities disciplines. This is clearly a fundamental volume for the study of Portuguese communities in Canada that combines historical perspectives with sociological analyses. In addition, in 2003 the *Portuguese Studies Review* (11, no. 2) devoted an entire issue to Portuguese and Luso-Canadians.[105] A collection of essays on the civic attitudes of Portuguese-Americans in Massachusetts has also been published.[106] Rocha-Trinidade has an engaging short article on cultural aspects of Portuguese emigration.[107] Commentary on the Portuguese situation that also reflects how much the terrain has shifted in the past four decades can be found in essays on postcolonial Portuguese migrants in Mozambique and Angola and the somewhat painful situation of the Portuguese community in postapartheid South Africa.[108]

More recently, Rui Pena Pires has sought to develop a new approach to the question of integration in *Migrações e Integração: Teoria e Aplicações à*

Encounters: Migrants, Migration and European Societies since 1945, Ashgate, Aldershot & Burlington, VT, pp. 255–278 and Klimpt, A 2006, 'Divergent Trajectories: Identity and Community among Portuguese in Germany and the United States', *Portuguese Studies Review*, vol. 14, no. 2, pp. 211–240.

[105] See also Melo, P. M. (1997), 'The Life History of Portuguese Return Migrants: A Canadian-Azorean Case Study,' MA diss., York University.

[106] Barrow, C. W. (ed.) (2002), *Portuguese-Americans and Contemporary Civic Culture in Massachusetts*, Center for Portuguese Studies and Culture,Portuguese in America Series, Dartmouth, MA.

[107] Rocha-Trinidade, M. B. (2007), 'Cultural Issues in Portuguese Migrations: Tokens of Identity,' *AEMI Journal* 5, pp. 140–152.

[108] Matos, E. D. (2009), 'Post-Colonial Portuguese Migration to Mozambique: An Examination of Causes, Effects and Future Implications for Development,' *International Migration* 47, no. 3, pp. 157–184; Rosa, V. Pereira da, and Trigo, S. (1986), *Portugueses e moçambicanos no apartheid: da ficção à realidade*, Secretaria de Estado das Comunidades Portuguesas, Porto; Rosa, V. Pereira da, and Trigo, S. (1990), 'Islands in a Segregated Land: Portuguese in South Africa,' in Higgs, *Portuguese Migration in Global Perspective*, pp. 182–199; Cravinho, J. Gomes (1994), *Portugueses na África do Sul: retrato político de uma comunidade emigrante 1990–1994*, CIDAC, Lisbon; Cravinho, J. Gomes (1995), 'La communauté portugaise dans la nouvelle Afrique du Sud', *Lusotopie* 2, pp. 323–348; Bessa, P. (2009). 'A Diáspora Invisível? Política e lusitanidade na África do Sul, da descolonização à democratização', *Lusotopie* 16, no.1, pp.133–153. Finally, in addition to Clive Glaser's chapter in this book, see Glaser, C., (forthcoming), 'White but Illegal: Undocumented Madeiran Immigration to South Africa, 1920s–1970s', *Immigrants and Minorities*, Vol. 31.

Sociedade Portuguesa (Oeiras: Celta Editora, 2003). An important meeting in late January 2003 brought together official and unofficial women's advocates, as well as representatives of women's immigrant communities in Portugal, to debate the many issues affecting women migrants.[109] Further indication of the significance of the issues of identity and return for Portuguese in France was 'Lusodescendance: Représentations, pratiques et enjeux', a meeting held in Paris at the end of March 2003. The framework for this meeting included an important question: 'What does it mean to be "of Portuguese descent" and what are the social uses of this identity?'[110] A special issue of the journal *International Migration* is devoted to 'Migration in the Lusophone World.' General articles include Maria Baganha's 'The Lusophone Migratory System: Patterns and Trends,' (5–20); Pedro Góis and José Carlos Marques' 'Portugal as a Semi-peripheral Country in the Global Migration System' (21–50), and João Peixoto's 'New Migrations in Portugal: Labour Markets, Smuggling and Gender Segmentation' (185–210). There are also contributions on specific national issues.[111] Not least among these new communities are Brazilians.[112]

The problem of integrating colonial *retornados* with their settler racial attitudes, Brazilians, and postcolonial immigrants from India and Africa poses a major social challenge for Portuguese society.[113] Most studies initially focused on Indian immigrants in Portugal, but others have recently begun to look at African immigrants beyond those from Cape Verde, who in other, earlier, contexts might have considered themselves to be Portuguese. For Goans and other Indian communities in Portugal, the most important observer has been Jorge Macaísta Malheiros, who writes about the full range of Indian migrants in Portugal: Catholic Goans, Muslims (including Ismailis), and Hindus.[114] Further indication that not all Indian migrants to

---

[109] Cadernos Condição Feminina (2005), *Mulheres Migrantes: Duas Faces de Uma Realidade: Actas do Seminário, Lisboa, 30 e 31 de Janeiro de 2003*, Comissão para Igualdade e Para Os Direitos das Mulheres, Lisbon.

[110] H-Luso Africa, Wednesday, 5 March 2003 12:55 p.m., Conference on 'Lusodescendance' in Paris. The original quote is 'Que signifie "lusodescendance" et quels sont ses usages sociaux?'

[111] 2009, *International Migration* 47, no. 3; also available online at http://dx.doi.org/10.1111/j.1468-2435.2009.00521.x through to 00528.x.

[112] Machado, I. J. de Renó (2007), 'Reflexões sobre a imigração brasileira em Portugal,' *Nuevo Mundo, Mundos Nuevuos*, available at http://nuevomundo.revues.org/5889.

[113] See Rocha-Trinidade, M. B. (2008), 'Integration Policies for Immigrants in Portugal,' *AEMI Journal* 6, no. 7, pp. 20–30. For an important study of how racial attitudes were formed during the colonial period, see Matos, P. Ferraz de (2006), *As Côres do Império: Representações Raciais no Império Colonial Português*, Imprensa das Ciências Sociais, Lisbon.

[114] Malheiros, J. Macaísta (1996), *Imigrantes na Região de Lisboa: Os Anos da Mudança: Integração e Processo de Integração das Comunidades de Origem Indiana*, Edições

Portugal are Catholic Goans is found in a book by Susana Trovão Pereira Bastos and José Gabriel Pereira Bastos entitled *De Moçambique a Portugal: Reinterpretações identitárias do hinduismo em viagem* (Lisbon: Fundação Oriente, 2001). Caroline Bretell, who has previously written about Portuguese migration, adds an interesting article on Goans as Portugal's 'first postcolonials' in which she highlights the importance of a hybrid Indo-Luso identity among Goans living in Portugal.[115] A recent anthropological study by Luís Batalha, *The Cape Verdean Diaspora in Portugal: Colonial Subjects in a Postcolonial World* (Lanham, MD: Lexington Books, 2004), begins with Cape Verdean emigration to the United States and then zeros in on two different groups of Cape Verdeans living in Portugal: elites and labourers, paying special attention to racial constructs.[116] A more detailed anthropological exploration of a group of Cape Verdean women in Lisbon is Kesha Fikes' *Managing African Portugal: The Citizen-Migrant Distinction* (Durham: Duke University Press, 2009). Fikes pays special attention to the many challenges and racism faced by these women in their working conditions in Lisbon. In one of her published articles, Fikes also explores the way in which emigration produces differences in Cape Verdean society.[117] Studies on the new Angolan and Mozambican communities in Portugal are also quite recent and address the issues of integration and how transnational migration creates family tensions.[118] A related phenomenon is the more significant

---

Colibiri, Lisbon, and Malheiros, J. Macaísta (2000), 'Circulação migratória e estratégias de inserção local das comunidades católica goesa e ismaelita: Uma interpretação a partir de Lisboa,' *Lusotopie*, pp. 377–398. Concerning the migration of the Mozambican Ismaili community to Portugal in 1973–1976, see Melo, A. (2008), 'A diáspora ismaelita. Preparação e "partida", vivências da migração dos anos 70,' *Lusotopie* 15, no.1, pp. 97–102; Khouri, N., Pereira Leite, J., and Mascarenhas, M. J. (2008), 'De l'Ombre à la lumière: Femmes ismaili du Mozambique,' *Revue Outre-Mers*, pp. 17–62, 2008; from the same authors, beside their chapter in this book, look for several forthcoming publications about migrations of Ismaili from Gujarat to Mozambique and from Mozambique to Portugal.

[115] Bretell, C. (2006), 'Portugal's First Post-Colonials: Citizenship, Identity and the Repatriation of Goans,' *Portuguese Studies Review* 14, no. 2, pp. 143–170. See also the website www.goacom.com/casa-de-goa

[116] For a related short study, see Ferreira, M. M., and Cardoso, A. J. (2004), 'Second Generation Cape Verdean Immigrants in Portugal: Problems of School Integration,' *AEMI Journal* 2, pp. 79–85.

[117] Fikes, K. D. (2006), 'Emigration and the Spatial Production of Difference from Cape Verde,' in Clarke, K. M., and Thomas, D. A. (eds.), *Globalization and Race: Transformations in the Cultural Production of Blackness*. Duke University Press, Durham, pp. 154–170. See also Acker, A. (2011), 'Entre deux drapeaux: Les ouvriers Capverdiens au Portugal pendant la période révolutionnaire (1974–1976)', *Cadernos de Estudos Africanos* no. 21, pp. 123–145.

[118] See Khan, Sheila (2009), *Imigrantes Africanos Moçambicanos: Narrativa de imigração e de identidade e estratégia de aculturação em Portugal e na Inglaterra*. Edições Colibri, Lisboa.

presence in mainly Catholic Portugal of Muslims from both India and Africa. Although there is obviously an important earlier history of Muslims in Portugal, this new generation of immigrants poses a very different challenge to Portuguese society.[119]

When we look beyond Portugal and the Portuguese, we find that the same complex issues regarding identity and return prevail.[120] For the more recent Goan diaspora, there is a study by Stella Mascarenhas-Keyes, 'Migration and the International Catholic Goan Community' (PhD dissertation, School of Oriental and African Studies, University of London, 1987) that deserves mention.[121] In general, however, the best source for following the current evolution of the Goan diaspora, as with so many other contemporary phenomena, is the Internet, where there are many organisational web sites.[122] Since Goa was designated a state within India in 1987, however, Konkani nationalism has become a significant factor in Goan identity, at least for some, so that sorting out those Goans who see themselves as part of the Lusophone diaspora is made more difficult.

The global range of Cape Verdean migration was featured in two recent international conferences[123] and is vividly encapsulated in the collection of essays edited by Luís Batalha and Jørgen Carling, *Transnational Archipelago: Perspectives on Cape Verdean Migration and Diaspora* (Chicago: University of Chicago Press, 2008), which includes eight country-identified community studies and 11 chapters on migration and transnationalism. Recent articles by Wilson Trajano Filho and Heike Drotbohm analyse the conservative features of a religious mutual-aid society, on the one hand, and the value of a 'contributive family model' in a four-generation study of a Cape Verdean

---

[119] See the important set of six articles published in 2007 under the grouped heading of '«Peuple postcolonial» et «nouveaux» immigrants: L'Islam dans le Portugal contemporain,' *Lusotopie* 14, no.1, pp. 181–285. For the earlier period, see Von Kemnitz, E. M. (2007), 'Envoys, Princesses, Seamen, and Captives. The Muslim Presence in Portugal in the 18th and 19th Centuries,' *Lusotopie* 14, no. 1, pp. 105–113.

[120] See, e.g., Noivo, E. (2002), 'Towards a Cartography of Portugueseness: Challenging the Hegemonic Center,' *Diaspora: A Journal of Transnational Studies* 11, no. 2, pp. 255–275, using Canada and Australia as her examples.

[121] See also Mascarenhas-Keyes, S. (1987), 'Death Notices and Dispersal: International Migration among Catholics Goans,' in Eades, J. (ed.), *Migrants, Workers, and the Social Order*. Tavistock, London, pp. 82–98.

[122] See, e.g., The Goan Forum, http://www.colaco.net/1/tgf1.htm

[123] Conferência Internacional sobre Migração e Diáspora Cabo-verdiana, Lisbon, 2005; Connecting the Global Caboverdiano Nation, Washington, DC, 2005, organised by Friends of the Republic of Cabo-Verde, Inc (FORCV), the Embassy of the Republic of Cabo Verde.

family, on the other hand.[124] Farther afield Luso-African (Cape Verde, Angola, and Guinea-Bissau) integration around Birmingham, England, was the topic of a recent conference paper, while migration linking Mozambique to Cuba is the subject of another study.[125] The consequences of state-sponsored labour migration from Mozambique to the former German Democratic Republic has also been examined, as well as the movement of Angolan asylum seekers to the Netherlands.[126]

Brazil remains an important host country for immigrants from the southern hemisphere, if not from Portugal, although a book chapter by Ana Maria de Moura Nogueira is a microhistory based on a set of intensive oral histories from a group of musicians who formed the Banda Portuguesa in the Ponta d'Areia neighbourhood in Niterói. Building on the methodology developed by Paul Thompson, she sought to understand how these Portuguese immigrants construct their habits and identity as Portuguese in Brazil.[127] Another study that is influenced by Thompson's work on oral history is Sônia Maria de Freitas' *Presença Portuguesa em São Paulo*

---

[124] Filho, W. Trajano (2009), 'The Conservative Aspects of a Centripetal Diaspora: The Case of Cape Verdean Tabancas,' *Africa* 79, no. 4, pp. 520–542; Drotbohm, H. (2009), 'Horizons of Long Distance Intimacies. Reciprocity, Contribution and Disjuncture in Cape Verde,' *History of the Family: An International Quarterly* 14, no. 2, pp. 132–149. See also Marcelino, P.F. (2011), 'Processes of Arrival, Integration, and Exclusion: Exploring a New Migratory Corridor in West Africa,' in Marcelino, P.F. (ed.), *Home in Motion: The Shifting Grammars of Self and Stranger*, Inter-Disciplinary Press, Oxford.

[125] Nafafé, J. L. (2009), 'African Migrants: Rethinking Past and Integration in the West Midlands,' presented at the conference 'Africans in Europe in the Long Twentieth Century: Transnationalism, Translation and Transfer,' Liverpool (abstract available at http://www.liv.ac.uk/soclas/conferences/AFE/abstracts2.htm); Hansing, K. (2008), 'South-South Migration and Transnational Tiers between Cuba and Mozambique,' in Smith, M. P., and Eade, J. (eds.), *Transnational Ties: Cities, Migrations, and Identities*, Transaction Publishers, New Brunswick, NJ, pp. 77–90. Mozambican connections to Cuba are also the subject of graduate research by Abubakr Fofana, York University, Toronto, Canada.

[126] Oppenheimer, J. (2004), 'Magermanes. Os trabalhores moçambicanos na antiga República Democrática Alemã', *Lusotopie* 11, pp. 85–105 and 2004, 'Mozambican Worker Migration to the Former German Democratic Republic: Serving Socialism and Struggling under Democracy,' *Portuguese Studies Review* 12, no.1, pp. 163–187; Van Wijk, J. (2010), 'Luanda-Holanda: Irregular Migration from Angola to the Netherlands,' *International Migration* 48, no. 2, pp. 1–30.

[127] Nogueira, A. M. de Moura (2000), 'No Ritmo da Banda: Histórias da Comunidade Lusa da Ponta d'Areia', in Gomes (ed.), *Histórias de Imigrantes*, pp. 183–206. For her methodology, see Thompson, P. R. (1988), *The Voice of the Past: Oral History*, Oxford University Press, Oxford and New York.

(São Paulo: Imprensa Oficial, 2006), which was commissioned by the state and includes 38 oral histories from the 21st century, 31 from immigrants and 7 from their descendants. João Leal contributes a fascinating article on the Azoreanisation movement in Santa Catarina Province in the 1990s.[128] Issues of shifting identity are explored in an interesting piece on Portuguese and Portuguese-speaking Africans in São Paulo.[129] As Brazil continues to establish itself as a major player in the global economy and within the Lusophone world, we can anticipate studies to be produced that examine the growing presence of African students in Brazil. An early examination of this phenomenon is the article by Wangui Kimari titled 'Retaking the Middle Passage: Glimpses of a Modern African Diaspora in Brazil.'[130] Brazilian racism is discussed by a Senegalese academic in another essay.[131] Since 2001 the Comissão Nacional de População e Desenvolvimento (CNDP) in Brasilia has published *Migrações Internacionais: Contribuições para Políticas*, whose numbers include many important contributions on contemporary migration in and from Brazil.

A new phenomenon that has attracted scholarly attention is Brazilian emigration. In a pioneering essay Franklin Goza compares Brazilian immigrants in Canada and the United States following the rise in this population from the 1980s as a consequence of Brazil's economic crisis. One of Goza's important conclusions is that Brazilian immigrants in Canada intended to remain, while those in the United States had a goal of return migration.[132] More detailed ethnographic studies of Brazilian immigrants in New York (with a total Brazilian population of some 100,000) were produced at about the same time in two books by Maxine L. Margolis, *Little Brazil: An Ethnography of Brazilian Immigrants in New York City* (Princeton, NJ: Princeton University Press, 1994) and *An Invisible Minority: Brazilians in New York City* (Boston: Allyn and Bacon, 1998). Margolis suggests that traditional push-pull effects may not sufficiently explain Brazilian emigration to the United States, noting that the

---

[128] Leal, J. (2002), 'Identities and Imagined Homelands: Reinventing the Azores in Southern Brazil,' *Diaspora: A Journal of Transnational Studies* 11, no. 2, pp. 233–254,
[129] Demartini, Z. de Brito Fabri (2006), 'Trajetórias e identidades múltiplas dos portugueses e luso-africanos em São Paulo após 1974,' *Portuguese Studies Review* 14, no.2, pp. 171–210.
[130] In (2008) *Africa and the Black Diaspora: An International Journal* 1, no. 2, pp. 133–146.
[131] Kaly, A. P. (2001), 'L'Être noir africain au «Paradis terrestre» brésilien: Un sociologue sénégalais au Brésil,' *Lusotopie* 8, pp. 105–121.
[132] Goza, F. (1994), 'Brazilian Immigration to North America,' *International Migration Review* 28, no, 1, pp. 136–152.

'Portuguese' Diasporas: A Survey of the Scholarly Literature 69

general level of education among immigrant Brazilians is higher than most immigrants to the United States. She also argues that Brazilians are relatively invisible because they constitute a minority within a larger Latino minority, echoing what others have suggested about Portuguese in the United States.[133] A valuable comparison may also be found in the work of Ana Cristina Braga Martes, Gláucia de Oliveira Assis, and Sueli Siqueira on Brazilian communities in Massachusetts, their successes and their disappointments.[134] Quite a different study of the Brazilian diaspora is presented by Ronaldo Arouck on the large community of Brazilians in neighbouring French Guyana.[135] In July 2010 a major seminar took place in Tokyo to examine 20 years of Brazilian migration to Japan, a phenomenon that appears to be winding down for a variety of reasons in both Japan and Brazil.[136] A major Brazilian centre for the study of migration is NEPO, (Núcleo de Estudos de População) at the Universidade Estadual de Campinas (UNICAMP) in São Paulo, which has published a number of important monographs on all aspects of migration in its Textos NEPO series, including studies of Japanese Brazilian migrants, or *dekasseguis*, in

---

[133] See Falconi, J. L., and Mazzoti, J. A. (eds.) (2007), *The Other Latinos: Central and South Americans in the United States*, Harvard University Press, Cambridge, MA, and London.

[134] Martes, A. C. B. (1999), 'Os imigrantes Brasileiros e as igrejas em Massachusetts,' in Martes, A. C. B., et al (eds.), *Cenas do Brasil migrante*, Bomtempo, São Paulo, which includes several other useful essays on North American Brazilian communities; Assis, G. de Oliveira (2007), 'Do Governador Valadares e Criciúma: Os novos emigrantes brasileiros rumo aos EUA,' *Nuevo Mundo, Mundos Nuevos*, available at http://nuevomundo.revues.org/3754; Siqueira, S. (2007), 'O sonho frustrado e o sonho realizado: As duas faces da migração para os EUA,' *Nuevo Mundo, Mundos Neuvos*, http://nuevomundo.revues.org/5973

[135] Arouck, R. (2000), 'Des Brésiliens en Guyane française: Nouvelles migrations internationales ou exportation des tensions sociales de l'Amazonie,' *Lusotopie* 7, pp. 67–78.

[136] See www.brasileirosnojapao.jp/seminario.php; McKenzie, D., and Salcedo, A. (n.d.), 'Japanese-Brazilians and the Future of Brazilian Migration to Japan,' abstract available at http://www.stanford.edu/~salcedo/Research.htm; also Sasaki, E. M. (2002), 'Dekasseguis: Japanese-Brazilian Immigrants in Japan and the Question of Identity,' *Bulletin of Portuguese-Japanese Studies* 4, pp. 111–141; Nakamizu, E. (2003), 'Language Contact between Portuguese and Japanese. Functions of Code-Switching in the Speech of Brazilians Living in Japan,' *Bulletin of Portuguese-Japanese Studies* 6, pp. 73–91. In addition, see the special issue of *Cahiers du Brésil contemporain* (Paris, Maison des Sciences de l'homme), no. 71–72, edited by Schpun, M. R. (2008), '1908–2008. Le centenaire de l'immigration japonaise au Brésil. L'heure des bilans,' which includes articles about Japanese Brazilians coming back to Brazil.

Japan and their return to Brazil, Brazilian migration to the United States, and the presence of Latin Americans in São Paulo.[137]

Conclusions

First, anyone who seeks to understand the 'Portuguese' diaspora in all its many guises must come to grips with determining who exactly one proposes to study. Who are the emigrants/immigrants who identify themselves as part of this diaspora? Are there some whom we, as scholars, might not include in such an overview or others whom we would include? Where do mainland Portuguese, Madeirans, Azoreans, Cape Verdeans, and Brazilians, let alone Goans (only Catholic? only with Portuguese surnames?), Macanese, and Portuguese-speaking Africans (only *mestiços?*) fit into this broad historical and contemporary phenomenon? In this review we have sought to be inclusive, but we have almost certainly not been comprehensive. Second, a detailed history of the 'Portuguese' diaspora must think carefully about how to balance global with regional coverage and how to integrate this treatment with an appropriate periodisation. Here we have suggested a tripartite periodisation, although we recognise that this does not apply equally to all segments of the diaspora. Third, to what extent is the Lusophone diaspora synonymous with the existence of emigrant/immigrant Portuguese-speakers? And where do non-Lusophones from places such as Goa and Macau fit into this mosaic? Fourth, how does the survival of cultural practices that are no longer embedded in a Lusophone context relate to our measuring of the Lusophone diaspora? Here there is much that can be said about transatlantic religious practices, such as candomblé. Fifth, to what degree is it true that Portuguese and Brazilian immigrant communities in Europe and North America are 'silent minorities'? Sixth, there is much more work that needs to be done on Portuguese communities in Latin America for both the colonial and national periods, as well as on Brazilians in Hispano-America. Seventh, in the context of the long history of the 'Portuguese' diaspora women and the family remain understudied topics. Eighth, and finally, future scholars on the diaspora would do well

---

[137] Sasaki, E. M. (2009), *Dekasseguis: Trabalhadores Migrantes Nipo-Brasileiros no Japão*, Texto NEPO 39, Campinas; Hirano, F. Y. (2008), *O Caminho para Casa: O Retorno dos Dekasseguis*, Textos NEPO 54, Campinas; Assis, G. de Oliveira (2002), *Estar Aqui, Estar Lá... uma cartografia da vida entre o Brasil e os Estados Unidos*, Textos NEPO 41, Campinas; Fusco, W. (2007), *Capital Social e Dinâmica Migratória: Um Estudo sobre Brasileiros nos Estados Unidos*, Textos NEPO 52, Campinas; Pires, R. G. (2007), *Diferencias por Sexo no Retorno Migratório: O Fluxo Criciúma-Estados Unidos*, Textos NEPO 53, Campinas; Silva, S. A. da (2008), *Faces da Latinidade: Hispano-Americanos em São Paulo*, Textos NEPO 55, Campinas.

to cast their nets as broadly as possible for new sources, both emic and etic, to understand both how immigrant communities see themselves and how they are perceived by different components of their host societies over time. Here our decision not to include literature indicates one area that could be effectively exploited (and has been by literary critics). These questions notwithstanding, one fact surely emerges clearly from this survey: the study of the 'Portuguese' diaspora in all its guises remains a dynamic field of academic inquiry.

3
Africans in Portuguese Society: Classification Ambiguities and Colonial Realities

Isabel Castro Henriques

The presence of Africans in Portugal during the 19th and 20th centuries (marked by the 'rush' to Africa and by Europe's colonial domination) is too complex to be analysed as a migratory phenomenon only. Akin to the installation of nonautochthonous populations in 'Portuguese Africa',[1] the situation of Africans in the Portuguese territory requires in-depth reflection on their inclusion within classification categories, such as 'migration,' 'community,' and 'diaspora.' If these terms' etymological uncertainties demand the study of their development and modifications in consideration of their genealogies, they can also only be understood within the context of the various contextual scenarios that produce and uses them, thus ensuring their operability. To do the history of the secular presence of African populations in Portugal is crucial not only to define and analyse the ambiguities surrounding the subject of this study – African women and men located within the Portuguese society during colonial times – but also to deconstruct the representations of the Africans (characterised on the basis of somatic signs – 'Negro', 'black' and 'mulatto') that structure the Portuguese social imaginary. The complexity of these questions, the study of which demands intensive investigations, new theoretical and methodological approaches, and an intellectual availability free of secular stereotypes, is too broad for the nature and scope of this short text. The present chapter aims therefore, above all, to share some observations (resulting from current investigations and observations partially argued in other recent studies)[2] and to establish an inventory of issues related to the African in the representations constructed by the Portuguese.

Ambiguities and classification categories

The first major ambiguity is precisely the *origin* of the majority of these populations, an ambiguity which lies not in the fact that they migrated to Portugal at the end of the 19th century or in the colonial 20th century but in their physical markers – such as skin colour – which indicate the certainty of their origin. Yet history reveals to us that, since the end of the 18th century, when slavery was abolished in Portugal, the arrival of Africans diminished greatly, and the Negroes and mulattos living in Portugal were legally Portuguese. In other words, if we can attest the existence of a minority of Africans who settled in the country during the colonial 20th century, part of colonial urban social groups or part of the 'assimilated' (or *évolué*) group from the colonies, the majority of Africans, that is, the majority of Negroes or mulattos, were born as Portuguese nationals, and thus they are 'false' Africans.

The second important ambiguity resides in the *identification/classification* of the African. The contents contrived and attributed to this classification category – the African – result from the construction of a Portuguese *representation* of this Other, which has been structured over centuries. The prejudice against and devaluation of Africans, which characterise the reductive ways that Portuguese society adopted to define and represent these people, allows for their exclusion from the social imaginary and national norms and virtually integrates them back into the African spaces. Even to naturalised Portuguese, Africans remain 'tribalised': 'the nation is for *us*, whites and Portuguese while ethnicity is for *you*, Negroes, Mulattos and Africans.' Such representations reveal the construction of ethnicisation and racialisation to serve Portuguese ideologies and interests. Paraphrasing the French anthropologist Edouard Vincke (1995, 253), the central character in this notion is 'the Negro of the White person' or, expressed more rigorously, 'the Africans (Negroes) fabricated by the Portuguese (the Whites),' since the use of the plural form reflects the various contours adopted by the representations according to the different realities created within and for the Portuguese society. These realities, manifested in the hierarchy of representations of Negroes (slaves, natives, assimilated, colonised, etc.) confirmed the correctness and virtues of the choices made by Portuguese colonialism, and it allowed ideologues and political leaders of the Salazar regime to point out the positive difference of 'our Negroes' vis-à-vis 'the Negroes of the other' European colonisers.

If the purpose of all classification is to reduce differences so that the Other can be comprehended, integrated, or dominated, the intent of classification operations in the case of the European and the African (the Portuguese example serving as the metonymy of Europeans) was not only to eliminate sociocultural distances by integrating the Other into the Western system of values, beliefs, and ideas and into Western cultural and social practices. It was also to perform an amputation of the Other's cultural originality and sociopolitical identity and to deprive him of any historical autonomy. These assumptions evince the need to consider the classification of human organisations as a structured European path that presents continuity lines with the development of European science. These assumptions also require a careful reading of the articulation between the European fabrication of classification grids and the different historical moments and geographical spaces, bearers of new projects, which included Africa and Africans.

The historical dimension of the process of construction, consolidation, renewal, recovery, elimination, and modification of the classification categories permits us to comprehend the manner by which the European/Portuguese social imaginary has been organised since the 15th century and, more particularly, in the 19th and 20th centuries (Henriques 2009a) around the valuation of the Same and the devaluation of the Other African. The progressive reinforcement of the density of prejudice and the establishment of archetypes, whose codes (intended to ensure a reductive reading of the Negro, the mulatto/mestizo, and the African who is 'naturally black' or 'of color'[3]) have still not been entirely eliminated; they have instead been reclaimed and utilised again to define and manage today's African immigrant.

Paths and strategies for integrating the Africans (15th–18th centuries)

Even though Africans have been present in Portugal for many centuries, knowledge about their cultures and their forms of participation in Portuguese society constitutes an extraordinary gap in the Portuguese historiography. The same can be said of Europe, whose relations with Africa are also embedded in the *longue durée*.

This situation reveals the lack of interest in Africans as well as the failure to ascribe any value to them; it demands rethinking and, even more, a revision of the classification operations that marked and 'scientifically' placed human beings in a hierarchy, beginning with the 19th century.

Studying the singularity of this presence, which molded Portugal's cultural and historical heritage, requires a broad and rigorous analysis of Africans' multifaceted journey within the country in relation to Portuguese history as well as to Portugal's relations with Africa and the world. It must also take into account the fact that the written, iconographic, and plastic representations of these African men and women pertain to the European sphere, particularly Portugal, and led to the consolidation of images, stereotypes, and prejudices that have organically shaped the Portuguese social imaginary.

The opacities and silences of memory

Historically, the memory of the African presence in Portugal began to be organised in the 13th century, when references to this population were found on the Iberian Peninsula and, more particularly, in the Galician territory. It is a written memory, strengthened by very beautiful illuminated manuscripts.[4] These scripts had the capacity to define the conditions in which some prejudices were born that so exaggeratedly evoke the Africans' physical structure and devalue their bodies because of their dark or black colour or because of other somatic marks deemed negative (hair, mouth, nose, odour) which bring them closer to animals and places them in opposition to the superiority of the normal body, which could only be white. This logic of body and colour (Devisse and Mollat 1979) did not prevent Africans from organising their lives, but it prevented them from fully integrating into the society of the whites.

In the historical context in which populations arrived on the Iberian Peninsula by land or by sea (as in the case of two of the most significant colonisations, Roman and Arabic, which left countless marks on the country in different and relatively short periods), the duration and nature of the Africans' presence in Portugal constitutes a fundamental differentiating element which is inscribed in another civilisational logic after the 15th century, initiated by the Europeans. The majority of men, women, and children of Africa did not come willingly to Europe but were captured or purchased on the African coast and unloaded as slaves at the western end of the Iberian Peninsula.[5] Between the 15th and 19th centuries, thousands of Africans, native of diverse regions and cultures, deprived of everything, integrated into the country and became a presence that gave structure to Portuguese society and left direct or indirect marks in Portugal's memory, cultural iconography, linguistic formulas, and places. If the visibility of this presence does not always appear to be clearly delineated, a more systematic analysis exposes the density of a silent African legacy – almost always invoked to record negative phenomena – in the organisation of the country: in work and production, religion and magic, celebration, dance and music, the body and sexuality, language and toponymy.[6] Present throughout the country, the Africans performed an ample number of different and essential tasks in the organisation and administration of Portuguese society, whether in the fields, in the cities, or even in the maritime colonial enterprises organised by the Portuguese, and participated in the life of the communities where they were registered.

Integration strategies

After the mid-15th century, for over a three-hundred-year period African slaves arrived in Portugal. They tried to adhere to Portuguese social imaginary and religious customs; they accepted baptism and Christian names, a clothed body, the Portuguese language (even if labelled as 'Negro language'), the principles of a Christian marriage, affective relationships, Catholic organisations, practices, and holy days, as well as recreational, political, and military events, while introducing at the same time marks of their cultural individuality into Portuguese life.

This integration, which was necessary for their survival in an unknown area, highlights the Africans' strategies, which enabled them to create mechanisms to preserve some basic values of their identities and historical memories. They did so through festivals, dance, music, and religious demonstrations designated as 'sorcery', 'witchcraft', and 'magic', which stimulated the approval and enthusiasm of the Portuguese and led to the creation and consolidation of syncretic, religious, and cultural customs that persisted in Portuguese social imaginaries and practices.

Marked by the social integration of many Africans, enslaved or free (generally liberated through a letter of emancipation issued by their owners or acquired through integration into fraternities or religious brotherhoods that ensured their protection), this situation did not prevent a lack of recognition and status for these men and women nor the repression and dehumanisation of many Africans slaves, who were animalised and objectified. The breeding of slaves, as if they were animals was a common practice in various regions of the country. It manifested itself in the production and trading of men and women in view of supplying the Portuguese and Spanish markets.

In the second half of the 18th century, the number of black slaves was still significant not only because the children of enslaved parents inherited the same status but also because slave-breeding activity persisted, as corroborated by the legal stipulation of 16 January 1773, which denunciated the existence of persons, 'throughout the Kingdom of the Algarve, and in some provinces of Portugal, [who have] slaves for reproduction, some of whom are whiter than their owners, others who are Mulattos, and still others who are certainly black [all of whom are designated as Negroes or blacks], with the aim of perpetuating captives through their propagation' (Pimentel 1995, pp. 57–59).

The existence of collars (similar to the ones designed to identify animals), which were placed around the slaves' necks, is evidence of the brutal treatment of the Negroes. Leite de Vasconcelos, who completed a remarkable project of collection, identification, and interpretation of historical and ethnographic materials, discovered two collars at the end of the 19th century and added them to the collections at the National Archaeology Museum. Translating the violence of such 'pieces' into words, the ethnographer wrote, 'This object scalds the hands of the person who touches it! What abuses does it hide? What weeping did it not cause?' (Vasconcelos 1915, 36).

In this inventory of the African presence in Portugal, it is necessary to recall the unprecedented nature (probably unique within in Europe) of Lisbon's Mocambo neighbourhood, known today as the Madragoa. A city district, by royal license in 1593, whose designation refers to Umbundu (one of the languages of Angola, signifying 'place of refuge,' 'settlement locality,' 'small village,' 'encampment'), the Mocambo was, beginning with the end of the 16th century, an urban area where Africans, both free and enslaved, established themselves and where, starting in the 17th century, they lived together with other Portuguese, especially with people involved with activities of the sea. Little by little, the Africans left this urban space, particularly after the laws of the Marquis of Pombal, which prohibited the importation of African slaves and abolished slavery in Portugal (1773). The disappearance of Lisbon's Mocambo was progressive and rapid; it transformed itself first into a street and then into the Travessa do Mocambo in the 19th century and eventually vanished during the second half of the 19th century.[7]

Mulattos: prejudice and exclusion

One of the least-studied yet essential issues for understanding contemporary Portuguese history lies in the 'production of mulattos'. Their appearance, which, ever since the onset of the expansion caused significant bewilderment in Portuguese society, manifested in the organisation of a zoomorphic classification structure for the purpose of adding these mestizo men and women to the vast catalogue of mules and not accepting them as the Portuguese they were. One must add to this way of classifying them the notion of their sexual hyperactivity – especially of the mulatto females – which was attributed to their African blood, and which marked the construction of a long-lasting and devaluating archetype that has not yet fully disappeared.

If some mestizo Portuguese have imposed themselves in society – by means of marriage to a Portuguese person of high social status, as was the case with D. Simoa Godinho of Santomean origin (16th century), or by virtue of the prestige of the person's profession, as exemplified by the playwright Afonso Álvares and the painter Domingos Lourenço Pardo (17th century), or even by religious statute, as with Madre Cecília de Jesus (17th century) – it is only in the final decades of the 18th century that one saw two operations, the adversarial complementarity of which merits reference. First, gradually overcoming the severity of prejudices, many mestizos (children of white and socially acknowledged parents) obtained social and financial support to enter Portuguese universities or the clergy. If family protection, money, and literary and professional prestige, as well as careers in public administration, constituted factors of some dilution of the somatic stigma, they also caused headaches for the political leaders of subsequent centuries in so far as they succeeded in obtaining position of mediation within the networks of Portuguese society. Highly criticised by different sectors and persons in Portugal, notably the poet Bocage, who contributed significantly to the stabilisation of negative stereotypes that burdened the Negroes, mulattos (who were considered to be on the side of blacks rather than whites) were able to reinforce their position in the 19th and 20th centuries in spite of the emergence of scientific theories that legitimised the hierarchisation of races, geographies, and civilisations. From Pai Paulino to Fernanda do Vale (commonly known as 'Black Fernanda'), Honório Barreto, Sousa Martins, Gonçalves Crespo, Costa Alegre, Virgínia Quaresma, and many other intellectuals and professionals of the 20th century, we can verify, by observing their practices and reflections, how important their intense participation in the collective life of their country was.

This however did not eliminate the ferocity of discrimination against mestizos in Portuguese society. In 1925, the poet Mário Saa emphasised the 'influence of black blood in Portugal, [which] appears in very many persons, by the way they swayed their hips, by the black spots they have on their bodies (genipap), by their colour and tidy hair, by their large bronze-coloured eyes, by their noses that provide a larger surface in front than laterally, by their lips, by their fingernails, by their semi-ventriloquial voice that seems not to pass through the larynx, but primarily by the signs pertaining to their souls, their inclination to mimicry, their predilection for African dancing and drum[; and he adds that] Mestizos predominate within Portugal in terms of population more than in any other nation of Europe, with an increase in stupidity and a reduction of the encephalic index' (155). This value judgement (which became very popular) served to feed the fundamental principles of racism, which consider Africans to be

Figure 3.1 'The mulatto women'

Portugal and the Colonies. Lithography by Rafael Bordalo Pinheiro, published in 1902 in *A Paródia*. The struggle between Portugal and England, caused by the colonial dispute, gave rise to many unpleasant caricatures of Portugal. Depicted here is a staggering old man surrounded by five women who do not hesitate to court younger and more dynamic men. One must keep in mind the symbology that this represents for the Portuguese colonies – caricatured women and mulatto females who do not hesitate to 'court' the European colonists (Bordalo Pinheiro Museum, Lisbon).

a teratology; ultimately, the mulattos would be etched into the image of monstrosities capable of defiling the human species itself because, having a white father or mother, they reflected, above all, the inferiority and structure of Africans.

Colonial representations and their impact on Portuguese society (until 1974)

Portuguese plans for colonial domination (organised since the end of the 19th century and implemented during the first republic [1910-1926] and even more after the military coup of 1926, which installed a dictatorship in the country) reinforced the devaluation of Africans and their civilisational practices. At the same time they sought to attract the attention and support of the Portuguese populations for the colonial effort in Africa, broadly justified through the concept of a 'civilising mission.'

New colonial realities and degradation of the African

The politico-ideological review of the empire in the 19th century, which began slowly after Brazil's independence (1822), after the (legal) abolition of slavery in African areas controlled by the Portuguese and organised by Sá da Bandeira, and was affirmed in the international framework of the Berlin Conference (1884-1885), led the Portuguese authorities to venture, within a very short time period (between the years 1880 and 1910), into the construction of a colonial mythology. This mythology was designed to involve Portuguese society in the so-called African question, which had become a national issue as a result of Portugal's 'victimisation' by the major European powers, who allegedly had 'illegitimate' African appetites (since the Portuguese had been the first to set foot in sub-Saharan Africa). This ideological structure had to supply the tools capable of sustaining Portugal's intentions in the face of Europe, calling for a national effort of integration, which reflected the notion 'of a vast homeland' of Portugal, strengthened the concepts of Portuguese 'priority' and 'specificity' in relations to the Others, and legitimated the country's colonial choices involving violent conflicts in Africa, necessary to substantiate the Portuguese 'civilising mission'.

This situation led to the reinforcement of ideas and prejudices that had already taken root in Portuguese society, in which the somatic – the Negro – and the social – the slave – were articulated together to define the African. If Portuguese laws recognised Africans as free and theoretically Portuguese, the secular consolidation of the African's image as being *naturally* a slave made it difficult to consider a change in the African's status. This devaluation found new legitimacy during the final decades of the 19th century in the context of the development of a colonial science where various dimensions of knowledge of humanities, societies, and geographies intersected and translated into a scientific production that politicians and ideologues looked at with great interest as it permitted the justification of projects and practices of colonial expansion.

Oliveira Martins, a Portuguese thinker and intellectual who inserted himself into European scientific currents, in particular in physical anthropology and craniology (which showed that the cranium was one of the physical elements most capable of enabling human knowledge and organising classification grids), undertook in 1880 the task of scientifically demonstrating 'the congenital inferiority of Blacks' and the absurdity of their education. He argued:

> The Negro has always made this impression on everyone: The Negro is an adult child. Negroes do not lack a child's precocity, mobility and perspicacity: But these infantile qualities do not transform into higher intellectual faculties. Could there not be reasons however to presume that this fact, of the black races' limited intellectual capacity that was proven on so many occasions and in so many places, has an intimate and constitutional cause? There is certainly an abundance of documents showing us that the Black is anthropologically inferior, often close to the anthropoid, and is quite unworthy of the name of man. As we know, the transition from one to the other manifests itself through various signs: an increase in capacity of the cerebral cavity, a relative inverse diminution of the cranium and the face, an opening of the facial angle resulting there from, and the placement of the occipital orifice. In all of these indications, Blacks find themselves placed between man and the anthropoid.

And he adds:

> Will this evidence not be enough to demonstrate the chimera of the savages' civilisation? And if there are no relationships between the anatomy of the cranium and intellectual and moral competency, why should philanthropy cease at the Negroes? Why not teach the Bible to the gorilla or to the orang-utan which might not possess the ability to speak but have a sense of hearing, and could understand, everything almost as the Negro understands, the metaphysics of the Incarnation of the Word and the dogma of the Trinity? (Martins 1953, p. 263)

The officialisation of the degradation of Africans, considered to be close relatives of the great apes – a common viewpoint in Europe – was based on 'scientific' evidence which allegedly recovered and confirmed the Africans' prolonged zoomorphisation that prevented them from having a biological history identical to that of other human groups.

If Oliveira Martins provided the scientific record of degradation of the Negro –, that is, of the African – it was António Ennes who abruptly brought attention to the primitive/civilised dichotomy during the last years of the 19th century. Knowledgeable about Africa, Ennes was a central political figure of colonial thought and practices and one of the principal authors of legislation concerning native labour. Ennes considered Europeans to be the 'refined children of the sophisticated races' and Africans to be crude, 'almost unthinking, impulsive creatures, [...] primitive, [...] idle vagabonds.' Thus he completed, with the solidity and density of his lived experiences in Africa,[8] the theoretical assertions of Oliveira Martins. There is another contemporaneous fact that also played an important role in this process of devaluation of the African, namely the military operations to occupy African territories and the pacification campaigns (versus the resistance fights) initiated at the end of the 19th century. These events revealed Portuguese political choices and Portugal's colonial relations with Africa and contributed to highlighting the correctness of the 'scientific' assertions of Oliveira Martins: The 'war' in Africa was characterised by ferocious and barbarous practices, and the courageous Portuguese soldiers were victims who attempted to bring civilisation to the savages. The creation of Portuguese heroes was thereby assured. The most significant example, for his normalisation in society, for his place in Portuguese history, and for his persistence over time, was Mouzinho de Albuquerque, the man who fought in Mozambique the Nguni Chief Gungunhana who became the absolute symbol of African savagery.[9] For decades Gungunhana constituted the image of the vanquished monster – he was depicted in various media, from ceramics to cartoons, history guides (Ameal 1959, 191) and history textbooks, illustrations for children and adolescents – and his image served to exalt heroism and the conqueror's characteristics.[10]

The articulation of these three registers of the black person's inferiority – the 'scientific' register, resulting from the theoretical advancement of knowledge; the 'political' register, lived on the land and derived from contact and experience; and the 'military' register, evidenced in actual conflicts – not only permitted the highlighting of the African population's proximity to nature and animalism, but it also provided the 'ideological breath' that had been lacking to strengthen or update secular archetypes that had been more or less dormant. The spread of cultural markers attributed to Africans such as laziness, anthropophagy, brutality, physical strength, absence of intelligence, excessive sexuality, witchcraft and idolatry ensured the establishment of a colonial culture, and this culture marked not only the colonised/coloniser relations but also the Portuguese social imaginary, giving rise to new depictions of the African in Portuguese society.

If the proclamation of the republic (1910) led to a review of colonial policies under pressure from European economic circles regarding laws on native labour, the ideological situation remained faithful to the same mythological perspective. The latter was even reinforced with the introduction of ideas referring to the republican mindset, that is, liberty, progress,

Figure 3.2 The Portuguese Empire at the turn of the century

Historical Legacy – Banquet of Anthrophagi. This lithography by Rafael Bordalo Pinheiro, published in 1900 in the magazine *A Paródia*, reveals the trivialisation of the notion of the Negro-anthropophagus, providing a singular spectacle in which the devaluating stereotypes of Africans are utilised abundantly. On the pedestal is a voluminous golden calf full of nails used by the Congolese to deal with the spirits of ancestors. Collecting skulls was also an African practice, even more complex than is shown by the picture: adversaries and ancestors can be equally indispensable to the African religious system. In civilisational contrast, Bordalo Pinheiro draws a hut with a Black African seated at the door, almost in the shadow of a banana tree. The image (the friezes of which laterally depict monkeys, skull masks and grotesque figures, with missionaries above and helmeted colonisers below) could not leave aside political sarcasm: two Englishmen (John Bull and Cecil Rhodes) observe, with an ironic smile, the assiduousness with which Portuguese politicians, disguised as Africans, devour pieces of Africa in a spirit of competition (Bordalo Pinheiro Museum, Lisbon).

education, and employment, which were now seen as essential to the tasks of civilisation and legitimatised the difficult modernisation operations of the colonial economies on the basis of the imposition of work upon the colonised. The continuity and operability of this ideological construction, after the installation of the dictatorship and the creation of the New State (1933), which subscribed to many of the republican colonial plans, resulted from an effort to build an organised theoretical corpus. This corpus comprised ideas, myths, and representations centred on Portugal's 'historical rights' in Africa, on the absolute inferiority of the Negro, on the unequivocal superiority of the white person, on the Portuguese civilising endeavour, and on the singularity of a relationship of the Portuguese with the Others – without any 'stain of racism.'

The notion of a civilising mission by means of assimilation was solidified to justify Portuguese colonisation in Africa. It was estimated that the process of assimilation of Africans would take much time, because of their backwardness in relation to civilisation, as was declared by Armindo Monteiro, minister to the colonies, in 1933: 'We do not imagine that it is possible to move them away abruptly from their superstitions toward our civilisation. [...] It is not possible for them [the Africans] to traverse, in a single bound, this centuries-old situation' (Monteiro 1933, pp. 108–109). Armindo Monteiro clearly conflated here his role as theorist of colonisation and as owner of plantations in São Tomé.[11]

Beginning with the 1950s, in the context of a new international reality in support of the end of colonialism and in the face of Portugal's refusal to abandon the colonies, the Portuguese ideological system registered a theoretical 'refreshment,' followed by a legislative production – such as the *Organic Law on Portuguese Overseas Lands* published in 1953 – designed to disguise the persistence of existing forms of domination, and this was done thanks to the reappropriation of the theoretical proposals of Lusotropicalism made by the Brazilian sociologist Gilberto Freyre.[12]

If subsequent contexts brought new formulations, the depreciation of the Negro and the mulatto continued to mark the representations of Africans in 20th-century Portuguese society. Indeed, the essence of the colonial ideology maintained its theoretical density and intervening vitality and resulted in numerous propaganda operations organised by the New State to make the empire known to the Portuguese population.

Colonial exhibitions: 'To Show the Savages to the Civilised'

If, as early as the end of the 15th century, the blacks brought from Africa were displayed in the circles of the Portuguese court as a recently acquired curiosity, along with parrots and monkeys, the 19th century adhered to the practice of exhibiting Africans to point out the 'monstrosity' of their bodies. These exhibitions took place in Europe throughout the century; for example, in Manchester (1814) and Paris (1815) with a South African named Saartaje Baartman, who was put on display, naked, alongside caged exotic animals, and in Lisbon in 1896, with Gungunhana, who, after disembarkation, was transported on an open carriage for three hours through the streets of Lisbon so he could be shown to the Portuguese prior to being imprisoned at Fort Monsanto, from where he was eventually exiled to the Azores. The 20th century continued this tradition with exhibits that purported to associate the European's curiosity in the presence of the exotic, the 'scientific' nature of the 'show' (which provided improved understanding of this unknown world), and even the economic, political, and civilisational added values resulting from the 'colonial reality'.

The New State organised at the Crystal Palace of Porto in 1934 the Portuguese Colonial Exhibition and, in Lisbon, at the Colonial Garden (known today as the Tropical Botanical Garden) in 1940, the Exhibition of the Portuguese World.[13] Through these patriotic manifestations, the state aimed at showing the Portuguese how to look at all of their colonies, including the 'samples' of the various populations (Africans and Asians from Cape Verde to Timor), and it presented them with a global view of 'their' empire, particularly 'their' African territories. In addition to these events, the regime also organised other initiatives such as conferences, colloquies, publications, literary prizes, school contests, processions and commemorations, and smaller exhibitions targeting the adult or young public, all of which had the objective to mobilise public opinion in favour of the colonial plan that brought civilisation to the African continent and consolidated the greatness of the Portuguese nation. Meticulously prepared for years as 'human zoological gardens', both exhibitions were the subject of major advertising campaigns, whether in the press, on radio or through

Figure 3.3 'The little Negroes'

Chocolate Candies. This advertisement constituted one of the great surprises of the 1920s. One found within the box six candies, each in the shape of a head of an African baby, all destined to be eaten. The advertisement aimed at emphasising the charm of 'the little Negroes' (by transforming, in a paternalistic way, African children into playthings), yet it also made a reference to white people's anthropophagy. (Empreza do Bulhão. Private collection)

other means, be them celebrity visits, organised excursions, discounts on admission tickets, postcards and small promotional items. A high point of all this spectacle was the arrival in Portugal of Africans ('typical representatives of the colonies') and exotic animals. On 18 June 1934, the newspaper *O Século* published on its front page an article entitled '1st Portuguese Colonial Exhibition,' which included an image of African children with the following caption: 'Another curious aspect of the natives who arrived in Lisbon yesterday: The ebony "babies" are certain to be a fine attraction of the Exhibition.'

The processions that occurred during the time of exhibitions stimulated great support from the Portuguese population. The newspaper *Novidades*, on 1 July 1940, dedicated the front page to the ' ... procession of the Portuguese World [that] formed a dazzling spectacle in which the golden and highest periods of our History passed before us', reporting that 'our colonies, with all their attributes, also figured in the parade. [...] the King of the Congo, in all his splendour, also participated on a float pulled by a zebra'.

The 1934 Colonial Exhibition of Porto, organised on the model of the 1931 International Colonial Exhibition of Paris, was directed by Henrique Galvão, who had created the Portugal Pavilion at that Paris show. It glorified the Portuguese colonial project, bringing attention to the Portuguese epic, the two 'discoveries,' and the 'pacification' and 'education' of the Negroes. The imagery expressed these patriotic objectives: the African did not possess any autonomy, and Africa existed only thanks to the Portuguese presence. On the one hand, this served to demonstrate the importance of Portuguese expansion; on the other hand, it permitted the exaltation of the modern colonising effort, thanks in particular to the success of the cocoa bean crops on the islands of São Tomé and Príncipe and the cultivation of coffee and sisal in Angola. As was highlighted in the 18 June issue of *O Século*, 'The lessons of the exhibition, from an economic point of view, should be intended to contribute toward an improved utilisation of our potential.'

If the exhibitions highlighted Portugal's major dates and heroes, they also served to exhibit Africans' physical and cultural difference, using some of the negative false images of Africa's regions and populations that had taken root in the Portuguese social imaginary long ago. At the same time, the exhibitions were aimed at influencing people to accept the idea of civilising Africans through religion and work, thanks to the devotion of missionaries and Portugal's administrative body.

Men, women and children were presented 'live', installed in mini-villages and mini-landscapes that attempted to remake the *habitat* of Africans and, failing that, leading 'Blacks to die of pneumonia like thrushes' (Lopes 2007, 166). Thus, the Portuguese population was put in touch with Africans and could observe their behaviour, attitudes, and primitive customs.

In these 'villages', the Africans had to accept the joining together of those who were dressed, not without mimicking white people (Cape Verdeans, Santomeans, a few Bissau-Guineans, especially Islamised) and those who remained 'faithful' to the naked body: the Angolans, the Mozambicans and the 'animists' of Guinea-Bissau. Their connection with missionaries permitted to underline the importance of the religious intervention: All those who were learning a trade wore European apparel. The team formed by the administrators and the missionaries thereby became the only ones capable of ensuring the transformation of the bodies and the behaviour of the hardly 'civilised' Africans. One must remember that this operation also had the objective of reorienting Portuguese emigration, which continued to have Brazil as a preferred destination. The aim was to recycle this emigration, which could expand economic activity and change the urban settlements which were still mediocre. While the Portuguese Colonial Exhibition of 1934 represented the first synthesis of the Portuguese perspective on the empire and gave 'a physical and tangible body' to the foundations of the Portuguese ideological discourse, demonstrating the possibilities and economic opportunities resulting from colonial rule (not to mention education, scientific development, and the civilisational nature of the Portuguese operations), the Exhibition of the Portuguese World in Lisbon in 1940 sought to reinforce Portuguese legitimacy in Africa and the world, making use of historical arguments and the strength of the Portuguese civilisational power. Organised around three structural pillars, that is, civilising mission, education, and scientific and technical advancement, in a framework bolstered by the history of Portuguese expansion and by the notion of national unity including the metropolis and all overseas colonies, this colonial exhibition was the last one realised in Europe – the winds of irreversible change were approaching and would soon translate into the independence of colonised peoples. Still, on 12 November 1940, *O Primeiro de Janeiro* wrote that 'for us Portuguese, colonisation is essentially the elevation of native populations to our civilisation by teaching them our religion, our language and our customs. It is our spirit that we wish to transmit to the peoples of the colonies.'

The Negro: plaything, advertising illustration, anthropophagus

Various ways of degrading the African, black or mestizo were seen in images and in trivialised texts in Portugal. A vast iconographic production was infused with a new perspective on these men and women, the negativity of which was legitimated by political authority, scientific ideas, and the denouncement of freakish practices attributed to Africans. Newspapers, cartoons, advertisements and other iconographic productions targeted children, youth, and adults, literate and illiterate, that is, a significant segment of the Portuguese population, which had a secular intimacy with Africans marked by prejudice that was both somatic (the Negro) and social (the slave).

An article published in the newspaper *O Primeiro de Janeiro,* on 13 November 1940, exposes one of the central elements of Portuguese racial discrimination in this way:

> [...] no matter how brilliant and effective their professional and economic activity may and should be, they [the assimilated Africans] must never fill positions of general politics; except perhaps in cases of full identification with us in terms of temperament, volition, understanding, ideas; though [such] cases are quite uncommon and improbable.

There also was a reference to the mulattos, who, 'as human beings, because they are linked to our lineage through the sacred bonds of origin, have [...] a right to our sympathy and support'. If, discrimination resided officially in criteria of a cultural and social nature, in practice the somatic features determined the relationships between white Portuguese and Portuguese 'of color', between Portuguese and Africans, between colonisers and colonised, be they assimilated individuals or natives. This situation, depicted through an abundant collection of images that circulated within Portugal and the colonies, normalised a representation of the Africans who, even if they were 'assimilated', as Vicente Ferreira (a soldier and former governor-general of Angola) wrote in 1934, 'are no more than grotesque imitations of white men [keeping, in their majority] the mentality of the primitive, concealed poorly by words, gestures and clothing, copied from the European' (Ferreira 1946, pp. 255–270). The ridiculing of these Africans was widespread, whether in the colonies – as in Angola, where these men were given the caricatured designation of 'underpants' (to oust them from the urban and Portuguese space and force them to return to their status as 'savages') – or in the specifically Portuguese social fabric. The violence of caricatures continued for a long time, enabling the hierarchy of races to be the guarantor of Portuguese domination in the colonies exercised by men and women who were (almost) illiterate and had no significant technical or cultural abilities. In the metropole, trivialised images depicted Africans as a symbol of technical backwardness and of 'primitive' forms of social and cultural organisation, and it attached an intrinsic lack of quality to blacks and mulattos, who were often referred to in a caricatured form in advertising.

One of the most disturbing and constant representations of the African was that of the Negro anthropophagus, which the Portuguese social imaginary has still not completely abandoned.

The notion that alimentary anthropophagy existed was one of the notions relating to America – the Antilles Islands and Brazil – which propagated itself after the start of the European expansion, if endowed with particular characteristics: Travellers and missionaries were involved (and were eaten!) in these ritual practices.

88 Isabel Castro Henriques

In relation to Africa, however, reference to these a practices began to appear only during the last years of the 16th century.[14] The idea of African anthropophagy implanted itself progressively in certain sectors of European societies, particularly those associated with overseas activity, with a view of classifying some of Africa's populations. It grew stronger in the following centuries marked by the slave trade: it permitted the joint salvation of body and soul and legitimised the violence of slavery after the reduction of Africans to slavery, their removal from the continent and their installation in societies administered by Europeans (Brásio 1944). This image of the Negro anthropophagus, emphasising a savage nature devoid of the most basic humanity, an image which was absent from the social imaginary

Figure 3.4   Advertising: 'color' and 'vice'

Arêgos Soap... only half is missing... Advertising poster from 1917 that shows the somatic clash between Europeans and Africans: black skin refers to diabolical figure even though this blackness can be not only lessened but even changed, thanks to the use of a fine European soap. The caring ingenuity of a white child who uses the Arêgos soap enables the dissolution of a good part of the blackness of the 'ridiculous' African, shown wearing a tie and a top hat. The dream of becoming white, which was already present in 16th-century São Vicente theatre, is reenacted in this advertisement, which was common in Europe during the first half of the 20th century (Poster published by ETP, Empresa Técnica Publicitária, Film-Gráfica Caldevilla. Private collection.)

Africans in Portuguese Society 89

Figure 3.4 Continued

Advertising for Alcoholic beverage could not refrain from resorting to depictions of Africans. In the long history of prejudice vis-à-vis the African, the thirst for alcohol, (rum, liqueur wine, etc.), uncontrolled drinking, and constant drunkenness are all signs of the savage, primitive, and irrational nature of black and mulatto men and women. In this advertisement the man is presented with the physical and cultural indications that allow instantaneous and meaningful identification (Label of *Rhum Velho Pretinha* [*Little Black woman old rum*] from Fábrica Âncora. Label of *Rhum Velho* [*Old Rum*] from Fábrica Victoria. Advertising poster of *Africano* Liqueur from a private collection.)

of most Portuguese people during the long centuries of cohabitation with Africans in Portugal, imposed itself from the end of the 1800s and was recycled by the scientific discourse of the 19th century. European and Portuguese intellectuals and researchers, including Oliveira Martins, incorporated anthropophagy into their analysis and classification grids of the Other, accepting the simplistic truth that the African was a congenital anthropophagus. The colonial 20th century made use of this classification category, normalising it in a variety of ways and employing it constantly as a tool to justify the violence of colonial actions carried out against the African populations. Many oral or painted anecdotes insisted on highlighting the African taste for human flesh. This archetype was not exclusively Portuguese; rather, it was European, and it enabled one to contrast the brutality of African practices against the virtues of the white norm. This normalisation of African anthropophagy was directed at all peoples, children, adolescents, and adults and made use of stories, poems, and cartoons, as well as publications of a scientific nature, which supplied the incontrovertible proof of this terrifying and despicable truth of the human species. Within this 'anthropophage delirium', the Portuguese society was confronted with a flurry of images, information, and 'proof', which made it incapable of adopting any critical and rational attitude. Europeans and Portuguese did not hesitate in accepting Africans to work in their houses, where they clearly 'lost' any and all of their anthropophagical impulses! We are faced here with one of the most profound paradoxes in intercivilisational relations: The Europeans, who denounced the cannibalistic practices of Negroes, were also the ones who, without the least bit of trepidation, entrusted their own children to the care of these same Negroes. In this day-to-day context of the Portuguese people, always engaged in the distortion of words and phonetics, we find a Negro who became famous in the years between 1920 and 1960: the *Preto-Papusse-Papão* – an invention of the writer Augusto de Santa-Rita. The anthropophage nature of this 'animalised' representation of a black African was very evident because the painter emphasised the size of the eyes, mouth, and teeth, a graphic metonymy of the anthropophagical appetite, just as in the story of the Big Bad Wolf and the Little Red Riding Hood! This book of poems and drawings was first published in 1920, with illustrations by Cotinelli Telmo, and it was published again in 1951, with new illustrations. Aimed at children, it set the boundaries of an aberrant, dangerous black character who did not hesitate to eat disobedient or misbehaving boys. It seemed almost impossible to escape from these threats because truth led one to consider this attitude as a deeply ingrained African vice. The same was seen in a 1946 cartoon entitled *The Adventures of Valentim*,[15] very popular among adolescents of that era, in which a monstrous anthropophagus (the figure of an African resembling a gorilla), baring the signs of his savagery, prepares to eat two fragile white, blond babies for breakfast, victims of the appetite and brutality of the Negro.

Another anecdotal depiction aimed at adults and published 1934, 'The Anthropophagus' Lunch', a very short illustrated story about a black African in European-style clothing who enters a restaurant and wants to eat not only the 'normal' culinary preparations but also the 'groom', a young servant who, trembling with fear, comes over to help him take off his overcoat. Although *évolué*, as demonstrated by his clothing and the fact that he frequents the restaurant, this African had not lost his congenital signs of savagery and anthropophagy.[16] If literature persisted in underscoring the 'evidence' of African anthropophagical practices which became part of the negative mythicisation of Africans, this mythicisation was fortified by the proof provided by the 'scientific' studies that justified the veracity of such behaviours. This was the case with a thick book written in 1947 by Captain Henrique Galvão (chief inspector of the Ministry of the Colonies), who amassed 'proof' and more 'proof' of the anthropophagy of the populations in the north of Angola, This book assembled a vast set of texts written in the 1930s and 1940s and extracted from documents produced

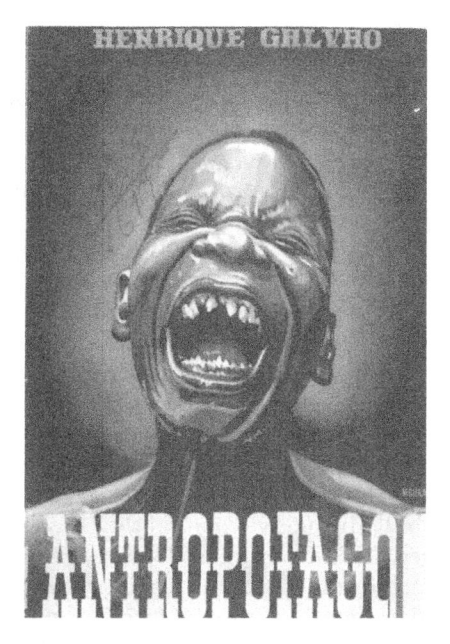

Figure 3.5 Anthropophagi

Anthropophagi. The cover of this book by Henrique Galvão (1947), designed by Moura, depicts a 'real cannibal Negro'; the ritually-modified teeth serve to underscore the violence of African anthropophagy. Ritual and the symbolic provide Portuguese and European designers the demonstration of this African practice, 'natural' and monstrous.

by Portuguese colonial administrative authorities with the intention to identify and prove the violent savagery of the Africans. Here, the anthropophagy is presented as a bloodcurdling reality in that region, legitimising the need to proceed with Portuguese civilising action, given the apparent inability of Africans to manage themselves autonomously.

The colonial war and the reinforcement of racism (1955–1975)

The theoretical solution to the late Portuguese 'colonial reality' – lasting when the cascade of independences had already occurred in Africa – came thanks to the Salazarist reappropriation of the Lusotropicalism theses of Freyre. These theses demonstrated a Portuguese superiority regarding the settlement of 'white persons' in the Tropics and even more in their relations with Africans. The Portuguese were among those who related most to African women, thereby engendering societies with a high degree of 'harmonious' relations that contributed to the multiplication of mulattos. Such a construct permitted the affirmation that the raison d'être of the Portuguese civilisational practices and colonial operations lay in the absence of Portuguese racist sentiments and practices (Freyre 1963, p. 45), something which differentiated them from other Europeans. This state of affair also permitted a strengthening of a large nation, unified and free of racism, 'from Minho to Timor' (a formula created in the 1950s and standardised beginning in 1961), thanks to the mechanism of assimilation, which ensured the homogeneity of humans and cultures.

The concept of a 'civilising mission' persisted and was reinforced at the end of the 1950s, when the majority of observers could not deny the need to define African political practices in a different manner. In a speech in 1957, Salazar asserted, 'we believe that there are races, decadent or crossbred, if you like, in relation to which we take on the duty of calling them to civilisation' (1957, p. 10). If this statement contains nothing really new, the context in which it was pronounced was fundamentally different. Salazar argued in favour of the only possible action from the point of view of the Portuguese: To continue with what was known as the 'civilising effort', since the Africans continued to remain faithful to their barbarism. Even Cunha Leal, the anti-Salazarist politician, possessed the same notions and, in 1961, wrote that only the interventions of the Europeans could wipe out the Africans' 'savagery', 'cannibalism', and 'nudity', without forgetting the need to eradicate 'sleeping sickness' and to eradicate 'witchcraft'. He invited Portuguese agents to vigorously affirm the specific rights of the Portuguese, who are the only ones capable of 'civilising' well (Leal 1961, p. 49). If, domestically, the politicians in charge relied on the diffuse racism that characterised relations between Portuguese and Africans, the Portuguese authorities (always supported by the opposition to the regime in colonial matters) mobilised internationally, without scruples, the old 'historical rights' and Lusotropicalism as a theory that 'scientifically' gave proof to the 'Lusitanian difference' in relations to the Others, serving to legitimise the righteousness of the continued Portuguese presence in Africa and the refusal to grant independence to subjugated peoples.

It is during the years 1955 to 1965 that another paradox occurred: On the one hand, Lusotropicalism was being invoked to justify the state's choices and solutions and the equality of Portuguese people from 'hither' and 'thither', while, on the other hand, one saw a proliferation of discriminatory laws in the colonies (now called overseas provinces) that would provoke violent responses from Africans. This discriminatory legislation must also be understood in the context of a highly aggressive plan to whiten the colonies, creating the necessary mechanisms to incentivise and support the emigration of Portuguese to Africa, especially to Angola. This option reinforced the obstinate nature of Portuguese colonialism, supported by an increasingly significant mass of settlers (the vast majority of whom, illiterate and very poor, came from rural areas of Portugal) who could aspire to a social and economic advancement in the overseas territories that was impossible to attain in Portugal: superior to the African savage or assimilated, these white settlers found in the Negroes the labourers indispensable to their rapid enrichment.

These actions significantly altered the opinion of Portuguese concerning the Africans who, having organised liberation movements, aimed at achieving independence. The African responses first manifested themselves through a multiplication of liberation movements, preceded by a few tragic events such as the so-called war of Batepá in São Tomé in February 1953, the massacre of Pidjiguiti in the port of Bissau in 1959, the workers' revolt in Baixa de Cassanje in January 1961, and the Angolan attempt to liberate the political prisoners detained at the S. Paulo jail in Luanda on 4 February 1961. The last incident, which was followed by attacks on Europeans and their property – residences, warehouses, plantation – signalled the start of the colonial war *versus* the struggle for national liberation. Almost immediately after, the Portuguese coined a new word – *turras*, an abbreviation in Portuguese of 'terrorists' (note the term's brutality; it also surrounds the image of the anthropophagus, foreshadowing the terrorists of today) – in order to decharacterise and caricature the African combatants; the Africans, in turn, retorted, creating the term *tugas* – an abbreviation of 'portugas' – to designate the Portuguese fighters. In this scenario of war and destruction, one saw the reinforcement of old myths of the 'savagising' of the Africans: The last operations linked to the normalisation of anthropophagy were certainly those that arose after acts of physical violence were perpetrated by the Africans of the UPA (Angolan Popular Union) beginning in March 1961 in the coffee zone of northern Angola – the news of this violence was broadly propagated by the Portuguese official services. The cruelty of these acts, which can be comprehended only against the backdrop of a military confrontation triggered by the refusal by Portuguese authorities to conduct

94 Isabel Castro Henriques

negotiations on the status to be granted to Africa's Portuguese colonies, led the leaders of the UPA to create the conditions of confrontation that implied a definitive rupture between the two communities. Countless Portuguese military companies could conjure up or even show 'cannibalistic acts', photographed by Portuguese soldiers who had been trained within the myth of an African anthropophagy. The turra was not only a terrorist but also a false combatant who did not hesitate to carry out the most hideous acts against Portuguese soldiers. But it was Portuguese photographs that showed decapitated bodies and the heads of Africans impaled on sticks for exhibition to the civilised world. In those days, the cruelty of torture and death was not enough; it was essential to guarantee that the images would last an eternity, proofs of the efficacy of violence, which showed that the only response to mythical anthropophagy was actual anthropophagy.

Despite the famous 'five centuries of colonisation' that even today are part of Portugal's mythical relationship with Africa, the Portuguese carried on until very late in the 20th century, the ghost of anthropophagy pushing Africans toward a continuous disqualification, as if this had been a contemporary practice among African populations. For more than thirteen years, the colonial war, which extended to Angola, Guinea, and Mozambique, could only sanction the negative image of the African, thus consolidating the harshest forms of racial and cultural prejudice, which translated in the establishment of a racist perspective on Africans in Portugal, who were silently discriminated against in jobs, daily practices, and social lives.

Visibility/invisibility of Africans in Portugal

In the 1960s agricultural engineer Daniel Nunes, a Cape Verdean who settled inland in Portugal to cultivate sugar beets, left his home at dusk and crossed paths with a housemaid who, breathless, fled screaming, 'He's the Devil, the Devil, the Devil!' In the same years, Paulo António dos Anjos, a mestizo journalist from Lisbon, was accosted in the street by a woman loaded with parcels that she held out, saying: 'You come with me and carry this to my house'.[17] One must highlight the fact that the two protagonists of these stories had a recognised social status: Even so, skin colour was the absolute marker. We could certainly report many other stories that demonstrate the Portuguese difficulty in acknowledging equality with the African.

The presence of Africans in Portuguese society during the 20 years that elapsed between 1955 (Bandung conference) and 1975 (birth of Lusophone Africa), a period marked by the colonial wars and African independences, has not aroused much interest within the academic community[18] and therefore not reduced the scarcity and fragility of our knowledge about migratory flows, types of settlement, and types of integration occurring in Portugal during that period. Let us begin by noting the arrival in Portugal of Portuguese whites, African mestizos, and Negroes from the colonies to study at university. Very few in number, these students settled in the Casa

Figure 3.6 'The Negro of Casa Africana'

The Negro of Casa Africana, a famous character who is a part of Lisbon's 20th-century memories, symbolised the Africans' physical strength – and, of course, their qualities as 'porters' – a strength that, by its brutality, could only defy the 'natural' intelligence of the Europeans.

dos Estudantes do Império (Residence of the Students from the Empire, CEI), which was established in Lisbon in 1944 by the Mocidade Portuguesa (Portuguese Youth – one of the regime's entities that managed national young people) and soon sought to denounce Portuguese colonialism.[19] During the 1950s, the CEI began to organise itself as an associative space for anti-Salazarist and anticolonial debate; it published texts, poems, testimonies, and essays in *Mensagem,* the organ of the CEI since 1948, and it created between 1951 and 1953, the Centre of African Studies, where many of the founding members of the independence movements collaborated. After 1961 various factors led to the end of CEI, which was closed by the Portuguese government in 1965: the arrival of new students from the colonies who had joined anti-regime organisations such as the Youth MUD (Movement of Democratic Unity) and the Portuguese Communist Party, the strictness of surveillance and political censorship, prisons and repression by the PIDE (the Portuguese secret police under Salazar), the flight of a significant portion of nationalist leaders (such as Amílcar Cabral, Agostinho Neto, Mário de Andrade, Vasco Cabral, among others), the struggle for independence that required another type of action and another type of education of leaders to ensure the liberation of the colonies. Though important in view of its role in training African elites, CEI's influence was limited in Portuguese society, which did not know how (and was not able) to build any social movement of an anticolonial nature. This being said, in spite of the colonial war which mobilised hundreds of thousands of Portuguese and affected national life, no explicit outbreaks of violence occurred in Portugal against the Africans who were living and working there – though this does not preclude the silent violence of prejudice. The African or Portuguese communities of African origin, whatever their social level, managed to live among the Portuguese without the fear of racist attacks from extremists. The fragile (and archaic) extreme right wing, which unconditionally supported the colonialist options, the incipient economy, and the rigid Portuguese social structure ('everyone in his/her place') kept peace, which relied also of course on political repression. In school, no Negro or mulatto student ever rejected the authority of the white teacher, just as the white students did not rebuff the authority of any Negro or mulatto teacher. To this set of elements that explain the social relationships in Portuguese society of those days, we must add the many forms of familiarity and complicity that marked the secular relationship between the Portuguese and the Africans in Portugal. This fact does not preclude the negative value judgements of the Portuguese regarding the Negro but allowed his integration in a natural way and in an almost invisible way because he was a contemptible element in the Portuguese landscape. On the other hand, in a society such as Portugal's, which was dominated by illiteracy and a lack of theoretical thought and scientific knowledge and aggravated by the censorship of the Salazar's regime, the only racism possible to be practiced and understood by the Portuguese population was an 'epidemic racism', or a naturally 'spontaneous' racism – to use an expression by Paul Mercier (1966, p. 15) to define a certain anthropological discourse prior to the creation of the discipline).[20]

In 1971, a Portuguese historian stated the following in a text devoted to *Escravatura* [slavery]:

> What was the consequence for the Country of this abundance of slaves? The bastardisation of customs [...,] a lack of moral discipline [...,] the desire for work and advancement did not develop in the Country [...] Production methods never progressed, and dependence on foreign industry increased. Idleness was another result. The most difficult tasks were abandoned, and free humans sought out the grand adventure of the sea [...,] male slaves [...] became vagabonds and thieves and [...] female slaves [...] became easy women (Miguel 1981, p. 423).

The vehemence of this opinion, in the second half of the 20th century, forces us to reflect on the Portuguese way of degrading the Other, who 'cannot be anything but the cause of all the misfortunes experienced in the country'!

The situation of African immigrants, who were Portuguese according to the logic of the regime, continued with hardly any changes until 1974. The arrival of African immigrants with no qualifications (one-third of whom came from Cape Verde) only began to have some impact after 1973 (INE, 1997). As Pires wrote (1999, pp. 198–199), until '1960, the majority of the nearly 30,000 foreigners residing in Portugal were Europeans (67%) and Brazilians (22%)'. Immigration increased slightly in the middle of the 1960s and in the early 1970s, thanks to a rapid acceleration of the economy, of civil

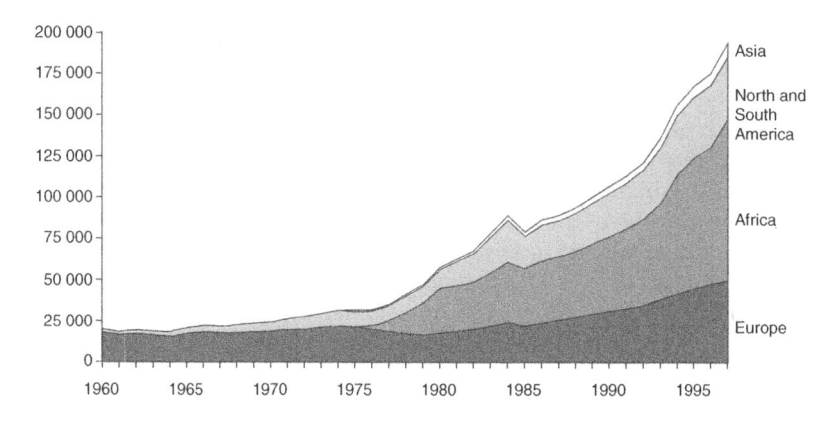

Figure 3.7 Evolution of the legally registered foreign population, 1960–1997

Note: Data for 1969, 1973, 1996, and 1997 are estimates, in the first two cases because there was no data at all and in the last two cases, so as to integrate the provisional information from an extraordinary legalisation of foreigners. The negative variation between 1984 and 1985 corresponds to an updating of the files of the Foreigners and Borders Services.

Source: Pires 1999, p. 197.

construction, and of tourism in particular. Pires adds that it was during the first years of the 1970s 'that one saw the start of some of the migratory flows originating from what were then African colonies [though it is] difficult to account for them [since] they were considered inter-regional migrations [...] that would bridge the scarcity of workers in economic sectors that were most affected by emigration to Europe and by military recruitment to the colonies' (pp. 198–199).

'African immigration, which followed de-colonisation, was relatively invisible for a few years, whether for the political authorities or for social scientists.' It was only mentioned occasionally by public opinion and by the media, 'African' often becoming synonymous with 'Cape Verdean'. Pires adds that 'this first migratory wave' included 'nationals from all the former colonies – approximately 45,000, according to data from the 1981 Census', and that it is 'very difficult to determine the precise number of Africans who immigrated into Portugal at the beginning of the 1980s' (1999, pp. 199–200). This first group included labourers without any technical skills but also students and, above all, 'the non-white returnees [who possessed] Portuguese nationality, some professional qualification and a level of education, all of which accelerated their integration [...] into Portuguese society, since they met the prerequisites of "civility" that were necessary for good social conviviality' (Gusmão 2004, pp. 136–137). Their social and economic position led to their separation not only from the black or mulatto communities that were already established in Lisbon's outlying districts but also from the African immigrants who came later on from various African countries[21] to supply the unskilled labour that was absorbed by the construction industry. Pires sees in this 'first phase of post-1974 African immigration, [the coexistence of] a *migration of refugees*, led by Angolans and Mozambicans, and a *migration of workers*', above all, Cape Verdeans. It is the significant increase in immigrants after 1980, visible in Portugal's labour sector and in the slums, which 'enable[d] [Portuguese society] to understand that the immigration of Africans was a wider, more heterogeneous and more dynamic process than it had imagined until then' (Pires 1999, 199). This observation, which reinforces the 'invisibility' of the African up to 1980, is surely one of the most disturbing elements of Portuguese society in the 20th century.

Conclusion

If the material built over centuries through images, texts, and iconographies does not depict reality, it does express metaphorical formulae and phantasmagorical visions of Africans, revealing not the Others but ourselves, the Europeans. The crucial problem with interpreting the representations of Africans created by the Portuguese, especially during the 19th and 20th centuries (marked by an efficacious panoply of technical and conceptual tools to fabricate the figure of the Other), is without any doubt the problem of deconstructing the Western/European/Portuguese paradigmatic discourse, of comprehending the view that was formed about the Negro and the mulatto, and of using/filtering/reinterpreting all the documentation produced (texts, photographs, advertisements, paintings, ceramics, drawings, engravings, films, etc.) in order to find in the web of prejudices the reality of the Other African. On 25 April 1974, the colonial war ended and opened the door for the possibility of a revision, so far rather modest, of the history of Portuguese relations with Africa and the history of the underlying concepts and prejudices which cemented them – an operation which demands a rigorous reading of the documents in order to reveal precisely the Africans' multicentury contribution to the building of the Portuguese society. The end of the Portuguese colonial process, taking place by means of the independences of the African colonies who had begun to balbutiate in Portuguese some centuries ago, allowed these new countries of Africa to incorporate the Portuguese language into their theoretical armour. The Portuguese disquiet manifested itself then in an attempt to secure the control of the Portuguese language, which is the only basis, so to speak, of 'lusophony' (Margarido 2000). Some people, still marked by the spectre of the empire and the ghost of (our) Elsenor Castle, tried to transform the latter into an arena isolated from the world, representing a Portuguese genius, supposedly well adapted to tropical structures. The last 20 years have shown a (slow) elimination of some forms of stereotypes that negatively labelled the African. But the strength of secular prejudice reemerges through the resurrection of old, absurd, and obsolete formulas and representations. These formulas and representations reinforce, in the context of new laws and new problems inherent to the globalisation that formatted the world beginning with the 1980s, innumerable acts of racial and social discrimination facing the many African immigrants who are seeking within Europe a place for survival and a new way of life.

Notes

1. According to Portuguese imperial logic, both Portuguese settlers and other populations coming from the colonies (who, until the 1950s, constituted 'Portuguese Africa', later referred to as 'overseas provinces' and integrated into the so-called 'Portugal from Minho to Timor') could not be, either theoretically or in the eyes of the law, 'emigrants' or 'foreigners', since, as Salazar said, Portugal was 'a nation spread around the world' (1963, p. 10) and the only nation where 'multiracialism' was practised (Nogueira 1967, pp. 197–198).
2. Besides the pioneering works of Vasconcelos (1942) and Tinhorão (1988) and of the most recent study (Henriques 2009a), other texts on some of the crucial issues in the study of Africans in the Portuguese social imaginary include Fonseca 2010; Gusmão 2004; Henriques 1993 and 2004; Lahon 1999; Lahon and Neto 1999; Margarido 1984; Pantoja 2011; Pimentel 1995, and 2010; Saunders 1994.
3. A racist formula, which still persists with some vigour in the Portuguese vocabulary for designating, in a 'politically correct manner', all nonwhites.
4. Afonso X, king of León and Castile, ordered a book of songs in honour of the Virgin Mary between 1252 and 1284; entitled *'Cantigas de Santa Maria'*, it served as the supporting text for illustrations made in Castile by local artists (El Escorial Library, Madrid). In the *'Cantiga de Maldizer'* (curse song), from the same king, studied by Margarido (2003, p. 138), is probably the first reference to an African woman; she is described as being 'black as coal.'
5. The first references to the significant presence of African populations in Portugal, and certainly in Europe, come from the chronicler Gomes Eanes de Zurara, who describes the first major load of slaves from Africa as arriving in the Portuguese city of Lagos (Algarve) in 1444. In 2009 archaeological research revealed a cemetery of black slaves to the north of the city of Lagos, outside its murals, which date back to the 15th century. The cemetery contained 155 skeletons of men, women, and children who seemed to have been thrown away like rubbish, some with their hands tied, in a natural pit used by the local population.
6. The Portuguese toponymy (Costa 1929–1949) reveals the African presence throughout the country, with somatic aspects constituting references to designations utilised, such as Rua das Pretas (Street of the Negresses) and Rua Poço dos Negros (Street of the Well of the Blacks) in Lisbon. New formulations in accordance with contemporary situations, referring to a kind of 'colonial urbanism,' remain in the Portuguese colonial memory – Rua da Cidade de Malanje (Malanje City Street), Rua Cidade de Cachéu (Cachéu City Street), and Rua Cidade de Inhambane (Inhambane City Street), and, after 1974, the terrorists of yesterday gave their names to Portuguese streets and public squares (Rua Agostinho Neto, Praça Eduardo Mondlane, Rua Amílcar Cabral).

7. The identification and explanation of the Mocambo district is a new interpretation put forward by Henriques (2009a, pp. 46–65).
8. Ennes directed the group that conducted the study entitled *Mozambique – Report Presented to the Government*. The report supplied indispensable information for labour laws and taxes on natives in 1891 and provided elements to find an institutional platform that enabled the exploitation of African men and territories, as well as the enrichment of Portuguese settlers (Ennes [1899] 1946, I, pp. 26–33).
9. For the theoretical question of constructing colonial heroes, see Henriques 2009b, pp. 337–351.
10. See the plastic works (engravings and ceramics) of Rafael Bordalo Pinheiro, produced between 1875 and 1900, which depict the Nguni chief in a caricatured manner that suggests not only his monstrous appearance but also his domestication.
11. Editors' note: Armindo Monteiro's wife had inherited a *roça* (cocoa plantation) from his father.
12. Gilberto Freyre furnished the theses that allowed the creation of the notion of Lusotropicalism, intended to designate what would be the exceptional Portuguese vocation to colonise without the stain of violence, renouncing 'the sword and the cross, to barely have recourse to sex' (Bastide 1971, p. 101). Freyre, who studied the singularity of social relationships in the formation of Brazilian society (1933) and showed his aversion to the Portuguese regime in 1945, was seduced by Salazar around the 1950s, issuing, at the time, dithyrambic praise regarding Portuguese colonising activities. According to Lusotropicalism, the Portuguese would have known how to create a perfect arrangement with the groups of 'colour,' giving birth to new situations in the colonies, characterised by a unique 'psychological and cultural unity' (1940, pp. 45–57). In the 1960s, Freyre strengthened these theses, seeking in the history of Portuguese expansion arguments to justify his statements (1961, p. 278). On Freyre and Lusotropicalism, see Alexandre 1995 and Moutinho 2000.
13. Some studies devoted totally or partially to the Portuguese colonial exhibitions have been published in the last decade. See Acciaiuoli 1998, Henriques 1993, João 2003, Matos 2006.
14. In the work of Duarte Lopes and Filippo Pigaffetta, *Relação do Reino do Congo e das Terras Circunvizinhas* (1591), Lisbon, Agência Geral do Ultramar, 1951, p. 43, which not only makes reference to anthropophagy as a practice that is highly prized by certain populations of the region but also presents an engraving in which one can see a depiction of a 'slice' of human flesh. Regarding this matter, see the article by I. Castro Henriques, 'A invenção da antropofagia africana,' in Henriques (2004, pp. 235–236 and 503).
15. Magazine *O Mosquito*, 11, n° 707, Lisbon, 3 April 1946, p. 5.
16. Magazine *O Senhor Doutor* [Mr. Doctor], A1, n° 46, Lisbon, 27 January 1934.
17. Both stories were recounted by the men themselves to Alfredo Margarido, around 1962.
18. See Pires 1999; Gusmão 2004; as well as the studies cited by these two researchers.
19. See the texts and various perspectives on the CEI on its 50th Anniversary in *Mensagem* (1997).
20. On the matter of 'Portuguese knowledge' relative to Africa and Africans, see Henriques 1997, pp. 40–56.
21. Since 1975 and especially 1980, the outskirts of Lisbon – which had already grown inordinately in the previous decade as a result of inland migrations (from the

countryside to the cities) – were progressively occupied by 'slums' or 'tents' that sheltered African immigrants. At first, they were often organised by nationality of origin but over time such distinction disappeared, with only a few nucleus of Cape Verdeans remaining (Gusmão 2004, chapter III).

References

Acciaiuoli, M. (1998), *Exposições do Estado Novo – 1934–1940*. Livros Horizonte, Lisbon.

Alexandre, V. (1995), 'A África no imaginário político português, séculos XIX-XX.' *Penélope* no. 15, pp. 39–52.

Ameal, J. (1959), *Obreiros do Império*. Direcção-Geral do Ensino Primário, Lisbon, série D, no. 5.

Associação Casa dos Estudantes do Império (1997), *Mensagem – Cinquentenário da fundação da Casa dos Estudantes do Império – 1944–1994*, Associação Casa dos Estudantes do Império, Lisbon.

Bastide, R. (1971), *Anthropologie Appliquée*. Payot, Paris.

Brásio, A. (1944), *Os Pretos em Portugal*. Agência Geral das Colónias, Lisbon.

Costa, A. (1929–1949), *Diccionário Corográfico de Portugal Continental e Insular*. 12 vols. Livraria Civilização, Porto.

Devisse, J., and Mollat, M. (1979), *L'Image du Noir dans l'art occidental*. 2 vols. Office du Livre, Paris.

Ferreira, V. (1946), 'Alguns aspectos da política indígena de Angola,' in *Antologia Colonial Portuguesa* I, Agência Geral das Colónias, Lisbon.

Fonseca, J. (2010), *Escravos e Senhores na Lisboa Quinhentista*. Colibri, Lisbon.

Freyre, G. (1933), *Casa Grande e Senzala*. Livros do Brasil, Lisbon.

—— (1940), *O mundo que o Português criou. Aspectos das relações sociais e de cultura do Brasil com Portugal e as colónias portuguesas*. Livraria José Olympio, Rio de Janeiro.

—— (1961), *O Luso e o Trópico*. Comemoração do V Centenário da Morte do Infante D. Henrique, Lisbon.

—— (1963), *O Brasil em face das Áfricas Negra e Mestiça*. Edição particular de um grupo de Amigos, Lisbon.

Galvão, H. (1947), *Antropófagos*. Editorial Jornal de Notícias, Lisbon.

Gusmão, N. M. Mendes (2004), *Os Filhos da África em Portugal. Antropologia, multiculturalidade e educação*. Imprensa de Ciências Sociais, Lisbon.

Henriques, I. Castro (1993), 'L'Afrique dans l'iconographie coloniale portugaise,' in P. Blanchard and A. Chatelier (eds.), *Images et Colonies*. Syros/Association pour la connaissance de l'Afrique contemporaine, Paris.

—— (1997), *Percursos da Modernidade em Angola. Dinâmicas Comerciais e transformações Sociais no Século XIX*. Instituto de Investigação Científica Tropical e Instituto da Cooperação Portuguesa, Lisbon (from the French original edition: 1995, *Commerce et changement en Angola au xixe siècle. Imbangala et Tshokwe face à la Modernité*. 2 vols. L'Harmattan, Paris).

—— (2004), *Os Pilares da Diferença. Relações Portugal – África (séculos XV–XX)*. Caleidoscópio, Lisbon.

—— (2009a), *A Herança Africana em Portugal – séculos XV–XX*. Correios de Portugal, Lisbon.

—— (2009b),'Construção e desconstrução do herói colonial – séculos XIX–XX,' in *Nações e Identidades Portugal, os Portugueses e os Outros*. Caleidoscópio (ed.), Lisbon, pp. 337–350.

INE (Instituto Nacional de Estatística) (1997), 'Evolução da população estrangeira em situação regular, segundo a origem, 1960–1997,' in *Estatísticas Demográficas, estatísticas e Relatórios Anuais*. Instituto Nacional de Estatística, Lisbon.
João, M. I. (2003), *Memória e Império. Comemorações em Portugal 1880–1960*. Gulbenkian, Lisbon.
Lahon, D. (1999), *O Negro no Coração do Império – Uma Memória a Resgatar. Séc. xv–xix*. Ministério da Educação, Lisbon.
Lahon, D. and Neto, M. C. (eds.) (1999), *Os Negros em Portugal – Sécs. XV a XIX*. Catálogo da Exposição, Comissão Nacional de Comemorações das Descobertas Portuguesas, Lisbon.
Leal, F. Pinto da Cunha (1961), *O Colonialismo dos Anticolonialistas*. s.n., Lisbon.
Lopes, Ó. (2007), *A Busca de Sentido*. Folio Edições, Porto.
Margarido, A. (1984), *La vision de l'Autre (africain et indien d'Amérique) dans la renaissance portugaise*. Fundação Gulbenkian, Paris.
—— (2000), *A Lusofonia e os Lusófonos. Novos Mitos Portugueses*. Edições Universitárias Lusófonas, Lisbon.
—— (2003), 'As normas somáticas de duas Cantigas de Maldizer.' *Revista de Humanidades e Tecnologias* no. 9, pp. 138–142.
Martins, J. P. de Oliveira (1953 [1880]), *O Brasil e as Colónias Portuguesas*. Guimarães Editora, Lisbon.
Matos, P. Ferraz (2006), *As Cores do Império. Representações Raciais no Império Colonial Português*. Instituto de Ciências Sociais, Lisbon.
Mercier, P. (1966), *Histoire de l'anthropologie*. Presses universitaires de France, Paris.
Miguel, C. F. Montenegro Sousa (1981), 'Escravatura,' in J. Serrão (ed.), *Dicionário de História de Portugal*, vol. 2, 2nd ed. Iniciativas Editoriais, Lisbon.
Monteiro, A. (1933), *Para uma política Imperial. Alguns discursos do Ministro das Colónias*. Agência Geral do Ultramar, Lisbon.
Moutinho, M. (2000), *O Indígena no Pensamento Colonial Português*. Edições Universitárias Lusófonas, Lisbon.
Nogueira, F. (1967), *The Third World*. Johnson, London.
Pantoja, S. (2011), *Negras em Terras de Brancas: As Africanas na Rede da Inquisição*. Edições Universidade de Brasilia, Brasília.
Pimentel, M. do Rosário (1995), *Viagem ao Fundo das Consciências. A Escravatura na Época Moderna*. Colibri, Lisbon.
—— (2010), *Chão de Sombras – Estudos sobe a Escravatura*. Colibri, Lisbon.
Pires, R. Pena (1999), 'A Imigração,' in F. Bethencourt and K. Chaudury (eds), *História da Expansão Portuguesa*. Vol. 5, Círculo dos Leitores, Lisbon, pp. 197–213.
Saa, M. (1925), *A Invasão dos Judeus*. s.n., Porto.
Salazar, A. Oliveira (1957), *A Atmosfera mundial e os Problemas Nacionais*. Serviço Nacional de Informação, Lisbon.
—— (1963), *Temos também o dever de ser orgulhosos dos vivos*. Serviço Nacional de Informação, Lisbon.
Santa-Rita, A. (1951 [1920]), *O Mundo dos meus Bonitos. Poemas*. Livraria Didáctica, Lisbon. Originally published in Rio de Janeiro.
Saunders, A. C. C. M. (1994 [1982]), *História Social dos Escravos e Libertos Negros em Portugal (1441–1555)*. Imprensa Nacional-Casa da Moeda, Lisbon.
Tinhorão, J. Ramos (1988), *Os Negros em Portugal. Uma Presença Silenciosa*. Caminho, Lisbon.

Vasconcelos, J. Leite de (1915), *De Campolide a Melrose. Relação de uma viagem de estudo (Filologia, Etnografia, Arqueologia)*. Imprensa Nacional, Lisbon.
—— (1942), *Etnografia portuguesa*. Vol. 3. Imprensa Nacional, Lisbon
Vincke, E. (1995), 'L'image du Noir dans les espaces publics,' in P. Blanchard et al. (eds.), *L'Autre et Nous. Scènes et Types*, Paris, Association pour la connaissance de l'Afrique contemporaine / Syros, pp. 253–259.
Zurara, Gomes Eanes de (1973), *Crónica de Guiné (1453)*. Livraria Civilização Editora, Lisbon.

Part II
Colonial Migrations in the Third Portuguese Empire

4
Colonial Migration to Angola and Mozambique: Constraints and Illusions

Cláudia Castelo[*]

The migration of nationals from European colonial powers to their possessions in Africa in the 19th and 20th centuries played a role in setting the socioeconomic, political, and administrative context of the colonial society, which rested on the exploitation of natural resources and bountiful, extremely cheap African labour.[1] As a rule, it was a temporary migration. Deadly diseases, intense heat, and high humidity made long-lasting settlement of Europeans difficult in the Tropics.

Only in certain colonies such as Algeria (from 1830), Southern Rhodesia, Kenya, Angola (from the late 19th century), and Mozambique (already in the 20th century) was it possible to combine definitive European settlement with a complete rule over African territories, labour, and indigenous peoples. In these places, one does not find a pure model of settler colonies but the combination of different aspects of settler colonies and exploitation colonies. In contrast with what went on in the colonies of European settlement in the New World (e.g., the United States and Australia), European colonisers in Africa in the 20th century were a minority which chose to reproduce itself by endogamy as much as it could and showed no impulse to eliminate the natives.

White settler colonies in Africa did not enjoy as much political autonomy from the imperial metropole as the colonial societies of the New World (with the important exception of South Africa, which was independent by 1910). They were marked by confrontations and negotiations between four key groups: the imperial metropole, which formally retained sovereignty; the local administration responsible for keeping authority and order on its behalf; the indigenous population; and the settlers' community, composed of both a minority established for several generations and more recent immigrants. Furthermore, they rested on a structure of privileges (political, economic, social, and symbolic) whose dividing line was the colour of one's skin. Despite the dominance and exploitation of the black majority by a white minority, the colonial societies built in Africa were intrinsically vulnerable (Elkins and Pedersen 2005, 2–4).

In Africa, colonial rule and (simultaneously or later) the presence of the settlers were successfully disputed by the majority of the native population. In Southern Rhodesia, the settlers achieved political independence from Great Britain in 1965 and went on to establish a racially segregated regime. Later, however, white dominance was also overcome – in 1980. In the remaining settlement colonies, the national liberation struggles led by indigenous movements led to the end of colonialism and, soon after, of white settlement. To a greater or lesser extent, there was an exodus of the settlers as they returned to their former imperial metropole.

Emigration and colonisation are two of the phenomena that have marked Portuguese society most in the long term. Interlinked between the European expansion begun in the 15th century and Brazil's independence in 1822, they were partially linked again during the last decades of the Portuguese Empire in Africa. Spatial and socioeconomic mobility between Portugal and its African colonies reached its peak between the end of the Second World War and 1974,[2] the destination being mainly Angola and Mozambique. It fits into a specific type of migratory movement: overseas migration of European population. Despite the extensive historiographic and sociological literature on Portuguese emigration, overseas migration has remained an almost unchartered territory until recently (countering this trend, see Castelo 2007).

The subject of study of this chapter is imperial migration and the communities of settlers that it generated in Angola and Mozambique.[3] In addition to expounding the ideological debate around overseas migration and the policy for the sector, I wish to analyse the evolution of the migratory flow into those territories and characterise Angola's and Mozambique's communities of settlers from a demographic, social, and cultural point of view.

Conflicting concepts on overseas migration

After the loss of the Brazilian Empire and a somewhat indecisive phase, the government in Lisbon started to see African colonies as a privileged field to assert the Portuguese nation. The European 'scramble' for Africa in the last quarter of the 19th century provided a decisive impetus to the interest of the Portuguese state towards gaining overseas territories. However, Brazil would continue until the early 1960s to be the preferential destination of Portuguese emigration – in 1963 it was supplanted by France. Emigrants were mainly males, of working age, who ensured Portugal's financial equilibrium through regular remittances to their families.

Since the last quarter of the 19th century at least, the peopling of Angola (mainly) and Mozambique with nationals from the motherland was a theme discussed in both the media and in political forums. In general terms, it was argued that Portuguese settlers would ensure national sovereignty and be a civilising factor over Africans as well as contribute to the economic progress of those territories. However, two concepts of empire conflicted ideologically and politically: that which advocated an intensive colonisation of wholesome areas (e.g., the Angolan plateau), with strong state investment and a view to transplanting chunks of rural Portugal to Africa; and that which argued for a colonisation of capital and factors based on private initiative.

With the establishment of the republic in Portugal in 1910, the preferential destination of Portuguese emigrants (Brazil) remained unchallenged. But some republican politicians continued to advocate the settlement of rural Portuguese families in the African colonies and the intensification of migration from every social extraction to Africa (e.g., Norton de Matos, High Commissioner for the Republic in Angola, 1921-1924).

In the early stages of the New State (an authoritarian, corporatist, and colonialist regime, 1933-1974), the concept which prevailed pointed to overseas migration being limited to specialist personnel, technical staff, and managers. The government considered the climate in the African colonies to be hostile and adaptation to the environment tough. It also thought that, even though black labour was plentiful, a limited number of white landowners and technicians could be enough to integrate black workers, ensure the development of the colonised peoples, and maintain national sovereignty.

In the 1930s and 1940s, the dictator Oliveira Salazar (president of the Council of Ministers, 1932-1968) considered colonial migration as a transfer of managers and specialist personnel to the colonies, and he rejected any state responsibility for routing and fixing settlers in Africa (Salazar 1937, 159-163). This did not mean that he did not attach importance to the permanent settling of Portuguese nationals in the colonies, only that the migrants had to be Portuguese with financial standing, initiative, and technical qualifications.

The idea of colonisation based on the economic exploitation of natural resources and of the indigenous peoples for the benefit of metropolitan interests was not consensual within the Salazar regime itself. In the post-Second World War context, in the face of external pressure for the self-determination of the colonies, the argument for this idea even became peripheral in the political and ideological discourse of the New State. In the 1951 review of its political constitution, Portugal no longer represented itself as a country possessing colonies but rather as a national unity scattered across several continents and, therefore, made up of metropolitan and overseas provinces. In practice, the economic exploitation of the overseas territories continued, largely for the benefit of the imperial metropole.

During this period, voices arose in favour of large-scale settlement strongly financed by the state – directly, in targeted colonisation programs and, indirectly, through support for free colonisation and economic development. Overseas settlement with Portuguese from the metropole was thought out alongside emigration issues and the national demographic surplus. Viewed as an extension of internal colonisation, migration to overseas territories was presented as one of the solutions for the excess of population in the metropole without the expatriation of nationals being required.

A nationalist and instrumental version of Lusotropicalism[4] served as the ideological prop for state white settlement projects, in particular, for settlements created in Cela and Cunene, in Angola, and in Limpopo, Mozambique, in the 1950s. It was argued that the creation of multiracial societies was underway in Africa, 'new Brazils' or 'new Lusotropical civilizations,' thanks to the increase in people of metropolitan origin, who were said to have all along shown special capabilities for human socialising with the peoples from the Tropics without any prejudice of colour. Such official discourse argued that the overseas provinces were an extension of mainland Portugal, where Portuguese populations settled in order to live, rather than dominate.

In the late stages of Portuguese colonialism, notwithstanding the great propaganda effort in favour of overseas settlement, credit for enticing vast segments of the metropolitan population to Africa should be given to the fast-paced economic development of Angola and Mozambique, lending this migratory flow characteristics that are quite different from emigration abroad and those idealised by the propagandists of rural colonisation.

The development of the overseas migration policy

The policy during the third Portuguese Empire for overseas migration was marked by material and symbolic constraints, as well as by indecision and mismatches between the discourse and the practice of the government.

It was in the mid-19th century that the Portuguese state took the first piecemeal measures to create agricultural settlements in Angola and to transport overseas a few hundred settlers free of charge. These undertakings faced various kinds of hindrances, and only the white settlements of Moçâmedes (1849–1850) and Lubango (1884–1885) had lasting consequences.

In view of the considerable growth of emigration to Brazil after the Paraguay war ended and the slave trade was abolished in 1870, the Portuguese government took measures to reroute part of the Portuguese emigration to Africa. Despite intentions however, the economic and demographic conditions in the colonies repelled would-be migrants and only the less able and prepared ones, who had nothing to lose, ventured to leave for the African continent, usually to undertake commercial activities on arrival.

In 1896, to stimulate the emigration of metropolitans, the passport for the Portuguese colonies in Africa became free of charge, and in 1907 it was abolished, the notion prevailing that it was actually not a migratory movement but a population move within an empire. Still, at the turn of the century, the white population in Angola and Mozambique remained relatively small: less than 10,000 individuals.

Military occupation, completed in the second decade of the 20th century, enabled the expansion of civil administration and white settlement. Propaganda around the colonisation of the empire continued in the press and in political debate. But Africa was not yet attractive in the eyes of prospective migrants, who saw it as a land of exile with a harsh climate, many dangers, and deadly diseases.

The high commissioners of the republic in Angola (mainly) and in Mozambique tried to promote the settlement of Portuguese nationals in the colonies in the early 20th century. In Angola, several measures were passed with this intention in mind. But they were discontinued in the 1930s owing to the 1929 world crisis and the subsequent imposition of budgetary equilibrium by Oliveira Salazar (minister of finance, 1928–1932).

Although the Colonial Act of 1930 stated that it was 'an organic essence of the Portuguese Nation to play the historic role of possessing and colonising overseas dominions,'[5] the truth is that tight restrictions were imposed on the entry of Portuguese migrants into Angola and Mozambique in the 1930s. Only those who had a high level of income or had received a 'call letter' guaranteeing employment or means of subsistence in the destination were allowed to travel to the Portuguese colonies. The model of economic development for the colonies put in place by the New State would not countenance mass migration to Angola and Mozambique. Thus, any migration that did take place was mainly migration by businessmen, managers, and qualified technical staff. This policy was endorsed by the colonial governments, which were deeply concerned with the eventual entry of migrants without capital and technical skills who might swell the ranks of the unemployed and heighten the ghost of poor whites, considered a serious sign of failure of any colonising and civilising work.[6] In addition to the obstacles for nationals from the motherland, the entry of foreign individuals was also discouraged, as the state viewed them as a threat to Portuguese sovereignty and a cause of Portuguese colonial unemployment.[7]

Portuguese migration to Angola and Mozambique only gained importance when the model for economic development and racial relationship implemented on the ground ceased to rest solely on the exploitation of local natural and human resources for the benefit of the metropolitan economy. The peak of Portuguese migration to Angola and Mozambique only occurred after the Second World War, thanks to the economic development brought about by the high value of colonial goods and, strangely enough, when the anticolonial movement was already underway. In this context, a timid reversal of the official policy for colonial migration was observed. In 1947, emigration abroad (at the time, still mostly to Brazil) was temporarily suspended.[8] The intention was to 'regulate Portuguese emigration, bearing in mind the protection owed to emigrants, the country's economic interests and the enhancement of the overseas territories by increasing the white population.'[9] In the following year, a decree was passed regulating the entry of nationals in the colonies, though with many reservations still.[10] Official opposition to the migration of foreigners to the Portuguese colonies in Africa was maintained, with the argument that it was necessary to prevent the denationalisation of the territories and to withhold the penetration of the 'red danger' (anticommunism being a central element in Salazar's ideology).

Asides being belated, overseas migration was lower than Portuguese emigration elsewhere, first to Brazil and, from 1963, to France. The settlement projects implemented by the New State in the 1950s (under the Planos de Fomento para o Ultramar [Overseas Development Plans]) and the official investment in the colonies, which intensified after the colonial wars started, were somewhat anachronistic by comparison with other colonial realities. In 1956, new conditions for entry in the colonies were introduced for Portuguese migrants, but it was only in 1962 that the 'entry and settlement of Portuguese citizens anywhere in the national territory' became free, following the creation of the 'Portuguese economic space,' which established the free circulation of goods within it.[11] Meanwhile, in 1961, after the start of the colonial war in Angola, provincial settlement boards for Angola and Mozambique were created whose role was to conduct and deal with any matters pertaining to settlement in those territories, from a perspective of multiracial integration and not just the settlement on the land of European families.[12]

The high flow of emigration in the mid-1960s worried the government, for whom settlement in the overseas provinces was a constitutional requirement, as there was a growing demand for economic progress in the Portuguese colonies (Ribeiro 1986, p. 45). This concern notwithstanding, 90,000 individuals emigrated in 1965, and over 120,000 in the following year. Because of the strong attraction of job opportunities in France and other central European countries, governmental measures were never able to reroute migratory flows.

In the early 1970s, the government tried to promote coordination between the National Secretariat for Emigration and the overseas agencies responsible for employment, with a view to increasing overseas settlment. In addition to being alert to the dangers of clandestine emigration, mostly to Europe, it stressed that the emigration movement had to fit the global context of the country's higher interests, of which the national priority was for the metropolitan labour surplus to emigrate to the overseas provinces (Ribeiro 1986, pp. 52–54). In order to reduce the emigration flow to European destinations and reroute it to Portuguese Africa, official information campaigns were launched, and job offers in the motherland and in the overseas provinces were publicised to attract emigrants. Neither the government concerns nor the government intentions managed to change the course of events, however.

Migratory flow to the colonies

In 1900, the white population in Angola was 9,198 and that of Mozambique (in the territory directly administered by Portugal) 2,064. As we saw earlier, the attempt to reroute emigration to Africa, in addition to the fact that it was not ideologically or politically consensual, also faced a number of obstacles of a symbolic, economic, and financial nature. These circumstances determined that the results achieved were quantitatively weak. Although there was considerable growth in the early 20th century, the contingent of migrants to Portuguese colonies would never exceed the flow to Brazil, and it remained a secondary destination until the mid-20th century.[13] In Portuguese Africa, there was insufficient need for European labour to enable the large-scale settlement of emigrants (Pereira 2001, p. 193).

Despite the indecision and ambiguities of the white colonisation policy between the last quarter of the 19th century and the 1920s, the evolution of the number of whites in Angola (mainly) and in Mozambique (marginally) was positive (see Table 4.1). At the time of the First World War, there were about 11,000 whites in Mozambique, and by 1920 some 20,700 whites lived in Angola. Most likely, such growth was due to the settlement in the colonies of the expeditionary forces, meanwhile demobilised, which were involved in the peacekeeping campaigns and the war; to the arrival of civil servants accompanied by their families; and to the progressive replacement of the gathering and exchange economic system with a system based on

Table 4.1 White population living in Angola and Mozambique, 1846–1973

Year	Angola	Mozambique
1846	1,830	
1900	9,198	2,064a
1910	12,000	11,000b
	1,920	20,700
1930c	30,000	
1935		23,131
1940	44,083	27,438
1950	78,826	48,213
1955		65,798
1960	172,529	97,245
1970	280,101	162,967
1973	324,000	190,000

(a) European inhabitants of the territory directly administrated by the Portuguese state only. (b) During First World War (Clarence-Smith 1990, p. 141). (c) Estimated numbers.

Source: Castelo 2007, pp. 59, 97, and 143.

the plantation economy, small agricultural production, and the mining sector (in Angola particularly). The vast distance between Portugal and Mozambique and the competition of Indian traders settled inland were important obstacles to white settlement in that colony.

The 1930s saw a clear retraction of overseas migration because of the world economic crisis and Oliveira Salazar's financial equilibrium policy. It should be noted, however, that the end of criminal deportation to Africa during this period and the strong investment to create an imperial mystique (instilled from school, in the Portuguese youth, through propaganda events, the press, etc.) would be factors promoting free migration in the medium term.

Even though the white population of Angola and Mozambique grew significantly in the 1950s, 1960s, and 1970s, 'both territories [remained] overwhelmingly black' (Penvenne 2005, p. 86) (see also Table 4.2).

The data available for analysing the migratory flow to the colonies – the movement by sea of metropolitan Portuguese between Portugal and its colonies – only covers the period between 1943 and 1974 in a systematic and relatively consistent way (Castelo 2007, pp. 167–168). This data reveals that, during the Second World War, the settlement of new migrants in Angola and Mozambique decreased owing to the war and its negative impact on sea transportation, especially in the Atlantic Ocean (see Table 4.3). When the war ended, the movement of passengers between Portugal and its overseas provinces showed an upward trend and a marked progressive expansion from 1947.

This rapid increase in population flow to Angola and Mozambique is linked to the economic growth of these territories in wartime, which made them attractive destinations in the eyes of prospective Portuguese emigrants. Added to the favourable economic situation in the colonies, the impact of the colonisation policy conducted by the Lisbon government on the volume of departure overseas should also be noted. Up to 1959, a considerable increase in the movement in both directions was observed. Both in absolute and relative terms, movement to Angola underwent a faster progression than movement to Mozambique owing to the stronger dynamics of the Angolan economy.

In 1960, the slowdown in the number of sea travellers to Angola that was observed reflected to a lesser degree the decrease in the number of overseas passengers in general. This decrease must be associated with the disquiet felt in Angola at the independence of the Belgian Congo. In 1961, the number of sea passengers from Angola clearly exceeded the number of people entering the colony, representing a negative balance of some 5,000 people who left the territory following the attacks on the northern farms by the UPA (União dos Povos de Angola [Union of the Peoples of Angola]) and the emotional and material insecurity felt then. The balance of the movement of passengers between Portugal and Angola had an obvious impact on the balance of the overseas provinces as a whole. The start of the

Table 4.2 Angola and Mozambique population by somatic groups, 1940–1970

Angola

Year	Total	White	%	Mestizos	%	Black	%
1940	3,738,010	44,083	1,18	28,035	0,75	3,665,829	98,07
1950	4,145,266	78,826	1,90	29,648	0,72	4,036,687	97,38
1960	4,830,449	172,529	3,57	53,392	1,11	4,604,362	95,32
1970*	5,669,504	280,101	4,94				

Mozambique

Year	Total	White	%	Mestizos	%	Black	%	Indians	%	Yellow	%
1940	5,085,627	27,438	0,54	15,641	0,31	5,031,955	98,94	9,144	0,18	1,449	0,03
1950	5,749,662	48,213	0,94	26,856	0,47	5,651,469	98,29	14,766	0,26	2,266	0,04
1960	6,603,653	97,245	1,47	31,455	0,48	6,455,614	97,76	17,241	0,26	2,098	0,03
1970	8,168,933	162,967	1,99	50,189	0,61	7,929,432	97,07	22,531	0,28	3,814	0,05

* Interim statistical summary.
Source: Castelo 2007, p. 216.

Table 4.3 Metropolitan passengers' arrivals and departures by steamer, 1943–1973

Year	Arrivals Angola	Departures Angola	Balance	Arrivals Mozambique	Departures Mozambique	Balance	Arrivals Empire	Departure Empire	Balance
1943	2,505	1,526	979	1,261	1,163	98	4,374	3,227	1,147
1944	2,180	1,489	691	1,595	1,000	595	4,267	2,929	1,338
1945	3,558	2,070	1,488	2,601	1,336	1,265	6,762	4,012	2,750
1946	3,983	2,211	1,772	3,167	1,563	1,604	8,021	4,780	3,241
1947	6,549	2,271	4,278	5,080	1,284	3,796	12,231	4,234	7,997
1948	6,549	3,216	3,333	4,159	1,953	2,206	11,547	5,721	5,826
1949	7,512	3,163	4,349	4,654	1,664	2,990	12,997	5,654	7,343
1950	10,335	3,525	6,810	4,725	1,954	2,771	15,735	6,012	9,723
1951	10,598	3,378	7,220	4,822	1,815	3,007	16,288	6,002	10,286
1952	14,483	4,505	9,978	5,441	2,132	3,309	21,224	7,477	13,747
1953	13,071	5,004	8,067	4,805	2,131	2,674	19,134	8,124	11,010
1954	13,739	5,172	8,567	4,865	2,231	2,634	19,839	8,507	11,332
1955	16,550	6,659	9,891	5,512	2,290	3,222	23,388	9,764	13,624
1956	15,139	6,493	8,646	6,927	2,072	4,855	23,366	9,567	13,799
1957	15,081	7,651	7,430	6,529	2,638	3,891	22,887	11,438	11,449
1958	16,906	8,725	8,181	8,032	2,705	5,327	26,349	12,505	13,844
1959	18,308	9,481	8,827	8,867	3,214	5,653	28,691	13,795	14,896
1960	14,731	9,976	4,755	9,522	2,991	6,531	26,157	14,311	11,846
1961	9,216	14,187	-4,971	6,752	3,721	3,031	17,345	19,803	-2,458
1962	19,965	8,967	10,998	6,512	3,672	2,840	27,803	14,374	13,429
1963	14,151	11,759	2,392	5,864	4,160	1,704	26,067	17,295	8,772

1964	16,031	10,674	5,357	6,795	4,312	2,483	23,766	16,178	7,588
1965	19,804	11,216	8,588	9,209	3,547	5,662	30,329	16,003	14,326
1966	19,793	11,610	8,183	6,973	3,481	3,492	27,853	16,108	11,745
1967	16,621	12,123	4,498	5,156	4,442	714	22,700	17,499	5,201
1968	19,140	11,589	7,551	5,917	3,682	2,235	26,032	16,165	9,867
1969	16,621	10,581	6,040	5,662	3,605	2,057	23,300	15,268	8,032
1970	14,173	10,542	3,631	4,708	3,185	1,523	19,619	14,588	5,031
1971	12,390	10,136	2,254	3,636	2,442	1,194	16,503	13,243	3,260
1972	12,639	7,864	4,775	2,305	1,561	744	15,362	9,924	5,438
1973	9,589	9,063	526	1,704	1,974	-270	11,572	11,591	-19
1974	5,215	8,247	-3,032	29	843	-814	5,331	9,295	-3,964
Total	397,125	235,073	162,052	163,786	80,763	83,023	596,839	345,393	251,446

Source: Castelo 2007, p. 177.

colonial war generated a climate of expectation and caution with consequences for departures to Mozambique, which decreased noticeably. The year 1962 records an unprecedented number of sea passengers to Angola, as a result of the many Portuguese who had left the previous year returning to the colony, the pledge by the government in Lisbon not to give in to the terrorists, and the full liberalisation of the migration regime in the national space.

Over the following years, there was an increase in the migratory contingents overseas bound, right up to 1965, when they reached a peak in Angola (with the exception of one abnormal year, 1962), in Mozambique, and in the other overseas provinces. This increase can be attributed to the development of the economies of Angola (stimulated by the war effort) and Mozambique, which were attracting a growing number of technical staff for the public administration, industry, and services. In the case of Mozambique, there was a clear fall in immigration after 1965, whereas in Angola the decrease fluctuated until 1969, only becoming definite after 1970. The peak in returns was in 1967 (with the exception of the abnormal year of 1961 in Angola). The subsequent decrease did not prevent a drop in the number of individuals settling every year, and the year 1974 dawned with a high negative balance for Angola. In Mozambique, the start of the colonial war in 1964 was paramount for the irreversible decrease in the arrivals of metropolitan subjects. The balance between inbound and outbound passengers saw a marked reversal in the case of Mozambique in 1972–1973, the balance in 1973 being already negative and worsening in 1974.

Comparing the overseas migratory flow with Portuguese emigration elsewhere, one should note that, with the exception of 1943–1945, the number of travellers to the colonies never exceeded the number of those leaving for elsewhere. Although an increase in departures to the colonies should be noted from 1945 to 1965/1969, this increase lost its impact within the emigration movement in general since Portuguese Africa was always a secondary destination in the overall picture of Portuguese emigration. Indeed, as noted by Cónim, 'in the period of 1961–1970, just over 1 million legal emigrants left the country [mainland Portugal], most of whom went to Western Europe, and the population of European origin in Angola and Mozambique in the late 1970s was about 443,000 people of both genders.' (Cónim 1990, p. 46).

Demographic and social characterisation of colonial migration

The migrants who settled in Angola and Mozambique were mainly from the districts of Lisbon, Porto, Viseu, and Guarda, as well as from the districts of Aveiro, Bragança, and Vila Real (in relation to Angola) and Coimbra and Santarém (for Mozambique). Bearing in mind the size of the population in these districts, we can say that most settlers came from the northern and central districts of Portugal. The prime role of the district of Lisbon (in absolute terms) must be linked to the fact that the capital was also the main recruiting centre for the colonial administration. Initially this migration was predominantly male, but with time the gap between genders diminished, and this contributed to a decrease in mixed-race unions. Individuals of working age always made up the biggest group, and in terms of marital status, most migrants were married. The level of education of the settlers was higher than that of metropolitan Portuguese as well as Portuguese emigrants abroad, even though there was a decrease in the average level of schooling during the golden age of the migratory flow overseas. More qualified individuals went to Mozambique than to Angola, first, because the ticket to Mozambique was more expensive and, second, because the railway and port activities in Mozambique in relation to South Africa and Southern Rhodesia required more skilled workers and engineers. Poorer settlers, mainly from Madeira Island, also came to Mozambique but often emigrated subsequently to South Africa, where the majority of the Portuguese community was made up of Madeirans (see Clive Glaser's chapter).

As for sectors of activity and professional situations, Angola attracted mainly people in trade – employers and freelancers were more represented. People working in the services and public administration mostly went to Mozambique, civil servants being particularly strongly represented. This situation reflected on how the journey was paid for: most people heading to Angola paid for the trip themselves or it was paid for by the head of the family; the expenses of most people going to Mozambique were covered by the state. For the whole of the overseas territories, between the mid-1950s and the mid-1960s, workers in the primary sector led the movement of passengers. It was during this period that overseas migration came nearest to the social pattern of emigration abroad. It is also in this period that the New State invested most intensively in the transportation of agricultural labourers to the settlements although, once there, they often turned their backs on the hoe and rejected the official projects.

If, in social terms, the migrants who settled in Angola and Mozambique cannot compare with the migratory elite who left Great Britain for Kenya, they also do not fully fit the profile of the Portuguese emigrant who travelled to Brazil or, later, to France. As in any migratory movement, push factors, usually of an economic nature, and pull factors influenced overseas migration. But in this case the latter factors seem to have been more determinant. Migrants – even during the expansion and consolidation of the colonial administration – were aware that they would be settling in a place of inequality in which they would be the privileged element in a permanent situation of superiority over the rest of the population. Their belonging to the settlers' community guaranteed preferential access to political, social, economic, and symbolic power.

Despite a few piecemeal measures against this trend, the Portuguese state tried until quite late to prevent migrants driven by push factors of an economic nature to come to the colonies. Although a gradual decrease in the migrants' social status was observed during the golden age of overseas migration (mid-1950s to mid-1960s), quite obvious in the contingents recruited for official settlements and agrarian communities, a longer-term analysis confirms a heterogeneous and, on average, socially higher migratory pattern towards the Portuguese colonies in Africa.

The white population of Angola and Mozambique revealed a clear tendency to concentrate in cities, contradicting the rural view disseminated by official propaganda (Pélissier 1978, p. 38). In 1950, 57 per cent of whites lived in the Angolan urban centres; in 1960, over 60 per cent; and in 1970, 77 per cent. In Mozambique, whites were mostly concentrated in the two main cities, Lourenço Marques and Beira. The growing urbanisation of the white population is linked to the kind of economic development that the territories underwent from the 1950s and was facilitated by the context of war in the 1960s. In psychological terms, the migration to Africa corresponded to the hope of ascendant social mobility and also to the wish to leave the countryside. Few metropolitan peasants wanted to remain peasants in Africa; many had previously migrated to the cities within Portugal. Only a tiny minority went to the state-sponsored rural settlements (*colonatos*) in Angola or Mozambique, and even then, a significant percentage eventually gave up and moved to the major cities.

By 1973 the white population in Angola and Mozambique numbered about 500,000, of whom only 35 per cent had been born in the colonies. It was a population in a fast-paced (though belated) root-taking process, mostly urban, not too mixed racially, and fairly balanced in gender terms, with a high percentage of young people, schooling levels above the national average, and people working mainly in the service sector. That is, it was a population for whom the colonies were not 'a hotel for a brief stay' but 'a family home to be lived in from generation to generation and passed on from parents to children.'[14]

On the culture of the settling communities

The way of thinking, acting, and interacting of the Portuguese from the metropole who settled in the colonies of Angola and Mozambique during the 20th century underwent changes and adjustments over time. It also varied according to the settlement area (coast/inland, urban/rural, old colonised cities/newly founded communities, and so on).

During the early decades of civil administration of the territories in particular, settlers faced a hostile or, at least, alien physical and human environment outside urban centres. This environment fascinated and scared them, and it demanded a great capacity to adapt. Both before departing and on arrival in Africa, the new residents were persuaded (by imperial propaganda) to feel superior to the local populations, to conform to social norms and the racial barriers put up by the settlers' community, and to replicate a number of daily routines of hygiene and protection from the climate and other dangers abounding outdoors. In this sense, the culture of the settling communities in the two main Portuguese colonies in Africa was no different from their counterparts in Algeria (Nora 1961), Kenya, or Rhodesia (Kennedy 1987). In fact, the notions and representations of the ideal settler, the African native, the climate, and the territory reveal great similarities, regardless of the national European reference context in which they were built and reproduced. And so did the norms and behaviours of racial discrimination and the social conflicts characterised and shaped by the relationships between settlers and native populations in the colonial dominions (Nora 1961, pp. 90–93).

The economic and social life of settlers in Angola and Mozambique relied on the existence of natives, who provided labour for farms, companies, industries, public works, house services, and so on. The wealth produced in the colonies was mainly the fruit of the work of the indigenous populations. The colonial economic system put African labourers and Portuguese employers, foremen, and supervisors in direct contact in the fields, in factories, in public offices, in shops, and at home. Physical proximity took place in a context of inequality and rigid racial barriers, even if it was to provide the social basis for the Portuguese nonracialist ideology.

Mechanisms leading to the stratification and segregation between whites and blacks applied to the home, labour, tax obligations, and the mobility of the natives. Although there was no formal apartheid system, there was a tacit segregation in public spaces, more marked in central and southern Mozambique because of the influence of neighbouring Rhodesia and South Africa and also because of the higher social level of the Portuguese in Lourenço Marques.

The behaviour of the settlers was conditioned by the colonial system and saw spatial and temporal variations, depending on the individual and the interpersonal relationships established. The fact that the overwhelming majority of natives had no access to Portuguese citizenship[15] placed them at the mercy of enforced recruiting, mandatory cultures, commercial exploitation, land occupation, discrimination in access to employment and upward social mobility, tyranny, and arbitrariness exercised by the colonial administration and the settlers themselves (Castelo 2007, pp. 283–330).

The cultures of the settler communities of Angola and Mozambique revealed – in certain moments, places, and/or aspects – specificities that set them apart from other colonial cultures, in particular the fact that there was no behavioural pattern as conservative and averse to change as that detected by Dane Kennedy in the colonial cultures in Kenya and Southern Rhodesia (Kennedy 1987, p. 191). On the one hand, until the 1940s at least, settlers were less racist and more permeable to exogenous influences (even taking on local colour in their eating habits, language, body, and everyday life) in the areas of oldest Portuguese colonisation (Luanda, Benguela, and their hinterlands), where the number of white men greatly exceeded the number of white women, and where less tightly knit relationships existed between Europeans and Africans.

On the other hand, the settler culture in the Portuguese territories of Africa was notable for its dynamics, boldness, and ambition, given that Portugal, during the years of strongest Portuguese migration to the colonies, was a country closed on itself, subject to an oppressive dictatorship which sought to instil in the Portuguese the values of work, discipline, and obedience. Instead of mimicking a rural, poor, and backward Portugal divided into small land parcels without much income or future, it aspired to create modern, progressive, and prosperous European societies in Africa. Reacting to their culture of origin, settlers valued private initiative (particularly in Angola, where there were more freelance workers); they were more liberal in their customs and more informal in social relationships between peers. They favoured spending and investing over saving (in the post–Second World War period in particular); they showed a higher predisposition for cultural, sporting, and recreational activities and for socialising and a greater appetite for adventure and risk, for the new and the modern; and they shared a more open view of the world (to which the wideness of spatial horizons was no stranger).

The political and economic relationship established by the Lisbon government with the Angolan and Mozambican colonial societies during the military dictatorship and the New State played a decisive role in the formation of their specific culture. Although patriotic and essentially Portuguese, this culture incorporated an aversion to the centralism of Lisbon, which was seen as interfering in issues pertaining to the colonies, hindering the freedom of action of settlers with red tape and bans, restricting their business opportunities to the advantage of metropolitan interests, and treating their children born in Africa as second-class citizens. The image of the 'deceptive motherland' eloquently reflects the disaffection of settlers in Angola and Mozambique who yearned to conduct their own destinies (political, administrative, and economic autonomy) without interference from the government in Lisbon. Most settlers probably voted in favour of the opposition candidate, Humberto Delgado, in the 1958 presidential elections. In spite of tricks, it was the case in Nova Lisboa (Huambo, Angola) and Beira (Mozambique). Such a vote did not represent an anticolonial stance but an anticentralist one, following a 'Brazilian' path. The small white bourgeoisie was becoming autonomist.

These common traits should not obscure the distinct images that the settlers' communities of Angola and Mozambique projected. Although written sources leave the issue virtually in shadow, oral memory provides clues that demand new research, namely on these distinctions: the settlers in Angola viewed themselves as entrepreneurial people, self-made men capable of facing adversity and deprivation to attain their goals, while the settlers in Mozambique tended to create a self-image of distinction in social and economic matters. The former emphasised achievement and merit; the latter, status and recognition. In addition, the image that each community projected of itself was built in opposition to the image that it made and disseminated of the other community. Thus, the Portuguese in Angola saw themselves as more tolerant on racial issues as opposed to the blatantly racist conceptions and practices they saw in the Portuguese in Mozambique (generalising the racial relations environment of southern and central Mozambique to the entire colony). The Portuguese in Mozambique, on the other hand, stressed their superiority over the Portuguese in Angola in educational and socioprofessional terms. The Portuguese in Angola considered the influence of South Africa and Rhodesia on Mozambique as negative since it exacerbated racism and a sense of superiority. On their side, the Portuguese in Mozambique prided themselves on maintaining a close relationship with neighbouring countries,[16] with whom they frequently compared themselves and whose British way of life on the dark continent they emulated (whisky drinking, bridge playing, clubs life, use of English words, etc.).

Conclusion

The white peopling of the Portuguese colonies did not correspond in practice to the whole rhetorical and ideological charge around the imperial calling of the Portuguese people (initially) and the creation in Portuguese Africa of multiracial societies, harmoniously integrated in a national unity (later). There was a gap between the ubiquity of the issue of white settlement in the national political and ideological discourse and the effective establishment of Portuguese from Europe in the colonies.

The Portuguese who settled in Africa after the end of the so-called pacification campaigns did not correspond exactly to the ideal advertised in dominant discourses throughout the period under study, neither in terms of social origin nor in terms of cultural practices at the destination. They did not correspond either to the misleading portrait that a historiography committed to the anticolonial movement made of them: *in loco* agents for colonialism. The situation experienced in the colonial context was more complex, despite the brutal, discriminating, and racist practices inherent in the colonial system and effectively conducted by the Portuguese who migrated to the colonies.

The presence until the first half of the 1970s of a white population in Angola and Mozambique was somewhat anachronistic in the international context (if we overlook the sui generis cases of South Africa and Rhodesia). It can be explained by the combination of three factors: 1) the near absence of anticolonial thinking in Portugal until the beginning of the national liberation wars in the African possessions; 2) the occurrence of mass migration to the colonies only after the Second World War; and 3) the existence in the metropole of an authoritarian and intrinsically colonialist regime (a characteristic assumed as part of the 'organic essence of the Portuguese nation') which used the school, censorship, repression, and propaganda to manufacture an imperial mystique, later reconverted into a 'Lusotropical vulgate' (Léonard 1997).

In contrast with what took place in the white settler territories of the other colonial powers, new Portuguese emigrants continued to settle in Angola (mainly) and Mozambique during the 13 years of colonial war, making use of the paradox economic development of those societies during that period. It could be speculated that those who kept on arriving did not believe that the 'unity of the Portuguese multicontinental nation' could be broken. Material evidence, that is, new construction, new shops and businesses, and market dynamics, also seemed to point to the permanence of the empire.

The societies created by the white settlement of Angola and Mozambique disappeared with decolonisation. Around half a million Portuguese who had been living in those territories flocked back to Portugal.[17] After the trauma and initial mistrust with which they were received back 'home,'[18] these individuals were usually capable of making use of or generating opportunities to build a new life in Portugal or the diaspora. Most of them had retained strong connections in their country of origin and were able to reactivate family and mutual-help networks.[19] Like any other Portuguese citizen who never left Portuguese soil, they are now an integral and active part of a democratic and plural Portuguese society. Despite the occasional regret or resentment (against those who led the liberation struggles and/or those who led the decolonisation process), what differentiates them is their identity forged in a 'double migration,'[20] first out of Portugal and then out of colonial Angola or Mozambique, as well as their African experiences, positively perceived and marshalled as social and cultural capital.[21] The majority still miss Africa, this all-significant Africa, which takes on various (and, at times, conflicting) meanings – the space, climate, landscape, exoticism, wealth, living standards, social prestige, power, childhood and youth, sociability, multiracial socialising and sex, and so on. In the domain of collective memories and shared feelings, Africa is invariably a paradise lost. While the overseas migratory cycle was definitely closed, the identities forged by the double migration remain open-ended.

Notes

* Translation by Isabel Alves/Bergen Peck, revised and edited by Eric Morier-Genoud. This chapter is based on the author's PhD thesis (University of Lisbon,

2005), published in 2007 as *Passagens para África: O povoamento de Angola e Moçambique com naturais da metrópole (1920–1974)*, Edições Afrontamento, Porto. It is dedicated to Valentim Alexandre.

1. Or even unpaid labour, in the case of forced labour, which persisted in the Portuguese Empire until 1961–1962 (abolition of the *indigenato* status and publication of a new rural labour code).
2. The military coup of April 1974 put an end to the dictatorship and opened the way for the end of the colonial wars (which had dragged on since 1961) and for decolonisation, which took place in 1975.
3. No other Portuguese colony in Africa was intended to be a settler colony or achieved that condition.
4. Lusotropicalism is a theory developed by the Brazilian social scientist Gilberto Freyre (1900–1987) according to which the Portuguese would have a special ability to relate to the people from the Tropics, through biological and cultural crossbreeding as well as through their ethnic past halfway between Europe and Africa. The New State appropriated Freyre's maxims in the 1950s and rewrote a simplified nationalistic and whitened version of Lusotropicalism to legitimise its external position in view of growing international pressure, particularly within the UN, in favour of the self-determination of colonies. It also used Lusotropicalism for the purpose of internal mobilisation towards the defence of the integrity of the 'Portuguese multicontinental nation.'
5. Decreto [Decree] no. 18570, *Diário do Governo* [*Government Gazette*], I Series, no. 156, 8 July 1930.
6. Portaria [Order] no. 676, 5 November 1930, of Angola's General Government (*Boletim Oficial da Colónia de Angola* [*Angola's Official Gazette*], I Series, no. 44, 15 November 1930); Diploma legislativo [Statute] no. 352, 23 July 1932, of Mozambique's General Government (*Boletim Oficial da Colónia de Moçambique* [*Mozambique's Offical Gazette*], no. 31, 30 July 1932); and no. 430, 13 January 1933, of Angola's General Government (*Boletim Oficial da Colónia de Angola*, I Series, no. 5, de 4 February 1933).
7. Diplomas Legislativos [Statutes] nos. 410 and 430, *Boletim Oficial de Angola*, no. 44, 29 October 1932, and no. 5 of 4 February 1933.
8. Portaria [Ministerial Order] no. 10919, *Diário do Governo*, I Series, no. 75, 9 April 1945, concerning the granting of free passage by the state to those travelling to the colonies in Africa.
9. Decreto no. 36199, *Diário do Governo*, I Series, no. 72, 29 March 1947.
10. Decreto no. 37196, *Diário do Governo*, I Series, no. 277, 27 November 1948.
11. Decreto-lei [Decree-law] no. 40610, *Diário do Governo*, I Series, no. 106, 25 May 1956; decreto no. 44171, *Diário do Governo*, I Series, no. 22, 1 February 1962.
12. Decreto no. 43895, *Diário do Governo*, I Series, no. 207, 6 September 1961. This decree is part of the reform package of Adriano Moreira (overseas minister, 1961–1962), which included the repeal of the Statute of Native Peoples of the Provinces of Guinea, Angola, and Mozambique; and the Regulation on Land Occupancy and Concession in the Overseas Provinces.
13. The emigration figures to Portuguese Africa and their weight in relation to the general Portuguese emigration is as follow: 1880–1890 – 5,087 (3.5 per cent); 1891–1900 – 12,046 (5.5 per cent); 1901–1907 – 10,506 (3.5 per cent).
14. Quotation from a news item published in the Belgian Congo newspaper *Cité Nouvelle*, brought to the knowledge of the Portuguese minister for the colonies, in which the high percentage of whites from Angola, determined in the 1940 census, was

highlighted. Portugal, Arquivo Histórico Ultramarino [Overseas Historical Archive], Gabinete do Ministro [Minister's Office], File 50/47. Various files – Room 6, no. 207.
15. When the Statute of Native Peoples of the Provinces of Guinea, Angola, and Mozambique was repealed, the number of *assimilados* (black Africans officially sanctioned as assimilated) was derisory: less than 1 per cent of Africans in Angola (Bender 1980, p. 11) and far less than 0.5 per cent of Africans in Mozambique (Newitt 1995, p. 475).
16. Middle- and upper-middle-class settlers from Lourenço Marques and Beira often went, respectively, to South Africa and Rhodesia, to shop, visit, or go to the doctor or the hospital. It was also fairly typical to enrol one's children in schools and universities in those countries. I believe that this heightened the cosmopolitan character of the settlers' community in Mozambique (who already socialised in the territory with different ethnic groups) and is a further trait that distinguished it from its Angolan counterpart.
17. Not all returnees (*retornados*) swere white: some were mestizos, black African *assimilados*, and Indians. An unspecified number of returnees migrated to South Africa, especially from Mozambique and southern Angola (see the chapter by Clive Glaser in the present volume); others went to Brazil, Australia, and Canada. About the emigration of former Portuguese settlers to Brazil, see Demartini, Z., and Cunha, D. (2008), 'Os colonos da África portuguesa sob o regime colonial e seu deslocamento para o Brasil no pós-independência,' *Cadernos CERU* (USP) 19, no. 1, pp. 121–137; Demartini, Z. (2009), 'Trajetórias e identidades múltiplas dos portugueses e luso-africanos em São Paulo após 1974,' *Portuguese Studies Review* 14, no. 2, pp. 171–210. See also the chapter by Lorenzo Macagno in the present volume.
18. Ovalle-Bahamon (2003, p. 165) stresses that returnees were poorly received in Portuguese society because they were regarded as agents of colonialism. I think that, although the author does not ignore the role of the economic crisis (pp. 159–160) in this unfavourable reception, he does not give due attention to the most decisive factor in the initial strain, namely: the fear felt in the host society of the potential competition in access to jobs and in career promotion posed by the new arrivals, all the more so since most returnees belonged to the service sector and had higher qualifications than most Portuguese.
19. Lubkemann (2005, p. 263) stresses (on the basis of fieldwork in a rural town in the district of Aveiro) that the reception of returnees by the families and communities of their origin was negative because, when they departed to Africa, these men and women had broken family and neighbourhood ties. I believe that the author makes the mistake of generalising on the basis of a very restricted reality. One should take into account the fact that overseas migration, in addition to being typically a family migration, fed on the 'call letter' addressed to family members, neighbours, and countrymen. Even after freedom of circulation between the imperial metropole and the overseas provinces was decreed, regional and local flows were not a matter of chance.
20. Katja Uusihakala uses the term 'double Diaspora' to describe the postcolonial identity of whites in Kenya, whereby departure from native England clearly configures a freely assumed experience of mobility in space and the 'desertion' of colonial Kenya underpins an imposed experience of mobility (Uusihakala 1999, p. 37).
21. 'Capital' understood here not as the ownership of cultural objects or school certificates but as forms of language, expression, knowledge, and know-how, which are 'incorporated cultural capital' (cf. Bourdieu 1979, pp. 3–6).

References

Alexandre, V. (2000), *Velho Brasil novas Áfricas: Portugal e o Império (1808–1975)*. Edições Afrontamento, Porto.
Amaral, I. (1960), *Aspectos do povoamento branco de Angola*. Junta de Investigações do Ultramar, Lisbon.
Bade, K. L. (2001), 'Migration History,' in N. J. Smelser and P. B. Baltes (eds.), *International Encyclopedia of the Social & Behavioral Sciences*. Vol. 14. Elsevier, Oxford, pp. 9809–9815.
Barata, O. Soares (1965), *Migrações e povoamento*. Sociedade de Geografia de Lisboa, Lisbon.
Bender, G. (1980), *Angola sob o domínio português: Mito e realidade*. Sá da Costa Editora, Lisbon.
Bourdieu, P. (1979), 'Les trois états du capital culturel.' *Actes de la Recherche en Sciences Sociales* no. 30, pp. 3–6.
Castelo, C. (1998), *'O modo português de estar no mundo': O luso-tropicalismo e a ideologia colonial portuguesa (1933–1961)*. Edições Afrontamento, Porto.
Castelo, C. (2007), *Passagens para África: O povoamento de Angola e Moçambique com naturais da metrópole (1920–1974)*. Edições Afrontamento, Porto.
Clarence-Smith, G. W. (1990), *O terceiro império português (1825–1975)*. Teorema, Lisbon.
Cónim, C. (1990), *Portugal e a sua população*. 2nd vol. Alfa, Lisbon.
Constantine, S. (1999), 'Migrants and settlers,' in J. Brown and W. R. Louis (eds.), *The Oxford History of the British Empire*. Vol. 4: *The Twentieth Century*. Oxford University Press, Oxford, pp. 163–187.
Elkins, C., and Pedersen, S. (eds.) (2005), *Settler Colonialism in the Twentieth Century: Projects, Practices, Legacies*. Routledge, New York.
Kennedy, D. (1987), *Islands of White: Settler Society and Culture in Kenya and Southern Rhodesia: 1890–1939*. Duke University Press, Durham (NC).
Léonard, Y. (1997), 'Salazarisme et lusotropicalisme: Histoire d'une appropriation,' *Lusotopie*, Karthala, Paris, pp. 211–226.
Lubkemann, S. (2005), 'Unsettling the Metropole: Race and Settler Reincorporation in Postcolonial Portugal,' in C. Elkins and S. Pedersen (eds.), *Settler Colonialism in the Twentieth Century: Projects, Practices, Legacies*. Routledge, New York, pp. 257–270.
Messiant, C. (2006), *1961: L'Angola colonial, histoire et société: Les prémisses du mouvement nationaliste*. P. Schlettwein, Basel.
Newitt, M. (1995), *A History of Mozambique*. C. Hurst and Co., London.
Nora, P. (1961), *Les français d'Algérie*. R. Julliard, Paris.
Ovalle-Bahamon, R. (2003), 'The Wrinkles of Decolonization and Nationness : White Angolans as Retornados in Portugal,' in A. Smith (ed.), *Europe's Invisible Migrants: Consequences of the Colonists Return*. Amsterdam University Press, Amsterdam, pp. 147–168.
Peixoto, J. (1999), 'A emigração,' in F. Bethencourt and K. Chaudhuri (eds.), *História da expansão portuguesa*. Vol. 5: *Último império e recentramento (1930–1998)*. Círculo de Leitores, Lisbon, pp. 152–181.
Pélissier, R. (1978), *La colonie du Minotaure: Nationalismes et révoltes en Angola: 1926–1961*, Author's Edition, Orgeval.
Penvenne, J. M. (2005), 'Settling against the Tide: The Layered Contradictions of Twentieth-Century Portuguese Settlement in Mozambique,' in C. Elkins and S. Pedersen (eds.), *Settler Colonialism in the Twentieth Century: Projects, Practices, Legacies*. Routledge, New York, pp. 79–94.

Pereira, M. Halpern (1981), *A política portuguesa de emigração: 1850-1930*. A Regra do Jogo, Lisbon.
Pereira, M. Halpern (2001), *Diversidade e assimetrias: Portugal nos séculos xix e xx*. Imprensa de Ciências Sociais, Lisbon.
Pimenta, F. Tavares (2008), *Angola, os brancos e a independência*. Edições Afrontamento, Porto.
Pires, R. Pena (2003), *Migrações e integração: Teoria e aplicações à sociedade portuguesa*. Celta Editora, Oeiras.
Ribeiro, F. G. Cassolo (1986), *Emigração portuguesa: Aspectos relevantes relativos às políticas adoptadas no domínio da emigração portuguesa, desde a última guerra: Contribuição para o seu estudo*. Secretaria de Estado das Comunidades Portuguesas, Lisbon.
Salazar, A. Oliveira (1937), *Discursos e notas políticas*. Vol. 2. Coimbra Editora, Coimbra.
Smith, A. (2003), *Europe's Invisible Migrants: Consequences of the Colonists Return*. Amsterdam University Press, Amsterdam.
Uusihakala, K. (1999), 'From Impulsive Adventure to Postcolonial Commitment: Making White Identity in Contemporary Kenya.' *European Journal of Cultural Studies* no. 2, pp. 27-46.

5
Imperial Actors? Cape Verdean Mentality in the Portuguese Empire under the *Estado Novo*, 1926–1974

Alexander Keese[1]

In July 1939, Mário Rogério Afonso Leite, the Cape Verdean administrator of Maio Island, one of the poorest of the isles of the archipelago, was invited to explain his activity in the first half of the year, described by his Portuguese superiors in the Praia administration as inadequate, even as 'apathy.' Afonso Leite's account of the situation on Maio was mainly an apology for his own failures to bring about change. However, he also commented on the nature of the ordinary islanders. According to the official, these islanders were living on a level that could 'hardly be called civilised'; their modes of production and attitudes seemed to be somewhat 'archaic':

> The people of this island show humility; they are respectful and earnest, for which I still regard them with an affectionate smile on my lips – the smile with which I am used to look at those who wish to be good... They remind me of those unhappy children we want to protect...[2]

This comment by Afonso Leite represents by and large the view of a corporate elite group of Cape Verdean officials, far removed from the interests and needs of rural Cape Verdeans. Having passed through secondary education via the higher education school (*liceu*) Gil Eanes, in Mindelo, São Vicente, and, later, via the higher education courses offered in Praia, on Santiago Island, members of this elite group filled many of the local administrative posts on the islands. From its inception in 1926, the authoritarian *Estado Novo* regime in Portugal had not touched these Cape Verdean careers. As in other cases of European colonial empires organising the education of a local elite through state schools, there was an effort to make these 'native' officials feel themselves to be imperial citizens.[3] In this respect, possibly the most impressive example for the whole of the African continent under colonial rule was the William-Ponty School, in French Senegal, where Africans were imbued with French metropolitan culture through much of the first half of the 20th century.[4] The organisation of Portugal's colonial empire in sub-Saharan Africa was undoubtedly more ambiguous and had more problems in integrating programs of 'assimilation', particularly in the 20th century. Thus, secondary education was very limited but theoretically available in other African territories, notably Angola. However, in Luanda, *liceus* were mainly built for the children of settlers who increasingly marginalised the existing urban African or mixed elite. In Lourenço Marques and Benguela, second to Luanda in their historical-cultural trajectory, conditions were similar (Newitt 1981, pp. 139–141). In this panorama, Cape Verde was an exception from several points of view: on the one hand, it did not have the character of a settler colony, and on the other, in the 19th century (and in earlier periods) it already had a reinforced Portuguese administrative presence, which had contributed to the creation of an early school infrastructure, at first in Mindelo (Moura 2009, pp. 110–124). Thus, Cape Verde was probably the only geographical area in Portugal's African empire where a small group of locals received access to a level of secondary education that allowed them to enter the administrative services at middle level (that is, as administrators of subdivision and directors or deputy directors within the central administration of the territorial government).[5] The members of this group were normally distinguished by relatively high social status and a particular physical appearance interpreted through a racial perspective – they usually had a rather fair skin colour – and came from families of the urban elite. Nevertheless, the very existence of this group in the Portuguese Empire is remarkable and more so for the period under the *Estado Novo* dictatorship, when the exclusion of Africans from any of the more important posts was intensified (Batalha 2004a, pp. 49–51, 60–70; Meintel 1984).

In contrast to these officials and the lawyers, doctors, and schoolteachers of Cape Verde, who also mostly belonged to the leading families of the islands, the peasants of the archipelago lived under far more difficult conditions. In 1941/42 and 1947/48, the islands were hit by droughts that killed tens of thousands of their inhabitants (Carreira 1984, 2nd edn, pp. 100–123). Such disasters, which the colonial administration was unable to handle before the late 1950s, caused widespread discontent and presented opportunities for anticolonial mobilisation that members of the Cape Verdean elite could have used. Moreover, a part of the Cape Verdean elite was strongly influenced by anticolonial tendencies which were prevalent in all European colonial metropolitan capitals from the end of the Second World War, and which did not spare Portugal despite the authoritarian nature of its political system and the activities of the secret police.[6] While Portuguese repression obviously accounts in part for the fact that there was no real revolt possible on the archipelago, we will have a closer look at signs (or the absence of signs) of any stronger activity in contestation, notably with regard to possible alliances between critics of the colonial system and the local populations.

This article will attempt to offer an explanation that goes beyond the usual narrative of Portuguese repression and the impossibility of Cape Verdeans on the islands to become active in political confrontation, whether through protest or even armed resistance. It analyses the situation in the archipelago during the 1960s and 1970s and takes into account the experiences of Cape Verdean presence on the African continent as a factor influencing the Cape Verdean attitudes on the islands. It also proceeds with the arguments I have presented in earlier work, where I insisted on the observation that Cape Verdean administrators within Portugal's colonial empire were, between 1961 and 1974, surprisingly loyal to the interests of the Portuguese authorities (Keese 2007). The current article now enlarges this perspective, questioning the situation on the islands and linking it to the behaviour of Cape Verdean settlers within other territories of the Portuguese Empire.

Our explanation is limited to making connections based on written, mainly archival, historical material. The conclusions thus won might be complemented or modified in the future by new results coming from oral history and interview-based sociology. There are, nevertheless, good reasons for elaborating, without further delay, a history of the Cape Verdean mentality under late colonial rule on the basis of an interpretation of contemporary archival material, which has not yet received sufficient attention. This is a particular need given the current political climate in which the diaspora experience plays a special role, the strong political importance still given to participation in the revolutionary struggle, and more general questions of political correctness (liberation struggle vs. colonial repression), all of which are likely to count for a great deal in establishing present-day political claims.[7] It is therefore necessary to provide a solid historical background, by first analysing the attitudes expressed in the enormous amounts of unexplored written material coming from Cape Verde and other parts of Portugal's colonial empire.

The Cape Verdeans and revolt in the 20th century

The Cape Verdean elite working for the Portuguese colonial power was not spared racist discrimination, and there was, in the early 1960s, a clear sense of anger about unequal treatment. In what was probably the most influential secret report on the attitudes of Cape Verdean administrators and the archipelago's elite in 1963, presented in much detail and with ample documentation by a colonial inspector, the discontent of many officials of Cape Verdean origin clearly transpired.[8] It would be easy and seemingly logical to link such experiences with the anticolonial revolts and wars in which Cape Verdeans were involved. Therefore, it is unsurprising that both Cape Verdean politicians and scholars working in the islands insist that the Cape Verdean population was very active in the liberation struggle of the

1960s and 1970s. While Cape Verde did not see its own revolt in the archipelago and obtained its independence as a by-product of the Portuguese Revolution of 1974, the Cape Verdean national myth insists on the active role of the islanders during the wars of liberation in Portugal's African empire. All over the empire – and particularly in Portuguese Guinea – Cape Verdeans are said to have contributed to the pace of events during the armed rebellions. In Cape Verde, this myth has long been a strong legitimising argument employed to justify the dominant position of the Partido Africano da Independência da Guiné e do Cabo Verde (PAIGC) – whose split-off, the Partido Africano da Independência de Cabo Verde (PAICV) ruled the archipelago from 1980 – in Cape Verde's political life after independence, especially before the introduction of a multiparty system in 1990 brought new and contested issues onto the agenda (Andrade 1996, pp. 287–290).

In part, the narrative defended by the ruling party is historically verifiable. It is beyond doubt that the PAICV, through the PAIGC, represented a tradition of defiance of the colonial power. However, it has to be asked in which arena this contestation took shape and under which particular circumstances. Much of the tradition is due to the fact that the PAIGC in Portuguese Guinea led a very efficient guerrilla war against the colonial power over 11 years, and obtained, by 1974, effective control over more than half of the territory of this Portuguese colony. Aristides Pereira, the first president of the Cape Verdean Islands, had been a leading personality during this war of liberation and thus personified the claim for Cape Verdean participation in the anticolonial struggle. Moreover, many other members of the leading group of the PAIGC in the 1960s and 1970s were indeed Cape Verdeans. When the Cape Verdean Luís Cabral was overthrown in 1980 as president of Guinea-Bissau (an event that provoked the final rupture of the PAICV with the federation project planned to keep Guinea-Bissau and Cape Verde in a federal state), the conspirators justified their decision on the basis of what they regarded as inappropriate Cape Verdean dominance in Guinean affairs (Chabal 2002, pp. 63–64).

However, the Cape Verdean involvement in the liberation process within the Portuguese Empire between, roughly, the end of the Second World War and independence is extremely complex and far more so when brought into the larger picture of the role of Cape Verdeans within the Portuguese late colonial state. There are several layers to this narrative, and the anticolonial involvement that some nationalist members of the Cape Verdean elite experienced is only one possible reaction to Portugal's imperial structures. The biographies of elite Cape Verdeans, such as Aristides Pereira, or of the PAIGC leader Amílcar Cabral or his brother and successor, Luís Cabral, are very well known but do not necessarily typify careers among the Cape Verdean social elite. In fact, their trajectories mainly represented the experience of students who had been socialised in Lisbon, where they became part of a broad Lusophone network of future radical leaders (MacQueen 1997, pp. 17–22; Chabal 1993, pp. 238–240).

Cape Verdeans studying in Portugal were frequently based in residences, such as the Casa dos Estudantes do Império (CEI) in Lisbon, where they enjoyed contacts with students from all over the Portuguese Empire. They were also connected with Portuguese groups of the political left, which, under the *Estado Novo*, operated underground. In this way, Cape Verdean students became part of the interterritorial networks of intellectuals evolving between 'radical' African students and former students – a tendency that increased until 1961. In particular, Amílcar Cabral was a very prominent figure in CEI activities. As an agronomist in the service of the Portuguese colonial government in Guinea-Bissau, Cabral managed to organise contacts with other left-leaning leaders of (future) liberation movements in Lusophone Africa, leaders who had been study colleagues in Lisbon or who had shared similar experiences. Those networks were very efficient. They created a strong group identity independent of the territorial origins of the respective leaders. Indeed, in the second half of the 1950s, Portuguese officials and secret-police informers were sometimes unable to distinguish between the personnel of different territorial anticolonial movements. Significantly, officers of the Portuguese secret police (*Polícia Internacional e de Defesa do Estado*; PIDE) used the names of Cabral and the Angolan 'radical' leader Mário Pinto de Andrade almost interchangeably. Cabral was reputed to be a mentor and even a founding father of the Angolan Movimento Popular da Libertação de Angola (MPLA), and Portuguese agents were convinced that he was extremely important for the opinion-building process within the MPLA. The latter is obviously an exaggeration and can be explained as resulting from a colonial misinterpretation of anticolonial networks. However, without doubt, the leader of the PAIGC was held in extremely high regard by MPLA leaders.[9]

Throughout much of the initial phase of the PAIGC movement, from the late 1950s until well into the period of armed rebellion against the Portuguese administration beginning in 1963, colonial officials and agents of the secret police found Amílcar Cabral's strategy difficult to understand. For much of this period, they believed that the PAIGC leader was only a puppet of Sékou Touré and the government of Guinea-Conakry, a puppet that could be removed from his post at will. However, while these erroneous interpretations relied on information distorted by a smokescreen of rumours, it remains clear that there always was a potential for internal unrest within the movement. Already in 1962, the Portuguese consul in Dakar and other colonial officials, basing themselves on credible information from Cape Verdean sources within the party, were convinced there would be a final (and fatal) clash between 'Cape Verdeans' and the 'Guineans' within the PAIGC.[10] However, while there clearly was an element of conflict within the movement, it was moderated by Cabral's abilities as a leader.

For many years, his qualities as the leader of the movement were sufficient to prevent any open internal strife. In that, obviously, Cabral was not only a successful Lusophone networker. He also was a genius in organising the local rebellion, and he not only enjoyed support in parts of the Cape Verdean community in Portuguese Guinea but was usually able to make his Guinean followers believe that rumors of Cape Verdean domination of the movement were groundless. Much of the success of the PAIGC can be accredited to this particular quality of its leader, as has been convincingly argued by Patrick Chabal (2002 [1983], pp. 138–141). In Portuguese Guinea, the broad support the rebel movement could enlist was rarely hampered by aversions against the Cape Verdean populations in the colony and their role in the leadership of the party, although potential for conflicts remained strong. However, to translate the success of Cape Verde–born leaders of the PAIGC into a broad mobilisation of Cape Verdean elites against the Portuguese colonial rulers would be to force the argument.

First, the activity of Amílcar and Luís Cabral and of Aristides Pereira within the PAIGC does not automatically mean that the islanders as a whole embraced the rebel attitude.[11] In the following section we will attempt to judge the situation in the archipelago between the early 1960s and 1974. In any case, the implantation of the PAIGC on the Cape Verdean Islands was a direct consequence of the victory of this rebel movement in Guinea-Bissau and of the 1974 revolution in Portugal (MacQueen 1997, pp. 110–115). Only the combination of these two factors after the revolution allowed the party, under the leadership of Aristides Pereira, not only to claim but to exercise control of the archipelago. Under the turbulent conditions of 1974/75, the Cape Verdean guerrilla warriors from the Guinean war theatre were able to monopolise the political and administrative posts (Anjos 2004, pp. 195–240). While there was widespread enthusiasm in 1974 for this unexpected situation, which initially brought the PAIGC a high level of popular support, this fact in itself does not tell us much about the pre-1974 attitudes of the Cape Verdeans in the archipelago.

Second, even in Portuguese Guinea the positions taken by members of the Cape Verdean community were far from coherent, and one needs to be careful in drawing conclusions. On the one hand, it is a fact that in the leading ranks of the PAIGC we find a considerable number of Cape Verdeans, and while – to our knowledge – no one has yet attempted to estimate the number of Cape Verdean guerrillas within the rebel movement, their number may have reached several hundreds. On the other hand, while the Cape Verdean community in Guinea-Bissau was observed distrustfully by the Portuguese colonial administrations and while Portuguese officials often suspected their Cape Verdean colleagues might be secret admirers of the guerrilla leaders, by the mid-1960s it had become clear that many Cape Verdeans in the small colony remained neutral. Also, there were comparatively few defections to the side of the rebel movement from among the administrative elite. So, while we have clear evidence for a larger Cape Verdean participation in the conflict in the colony of Portuguese Guinea, we still need to differentiate between very distinct trajectories within the community.

Third, the conditions of Portuguese Guinea, where a part of the Cape Verdean community was well integrated in the common struggle with other Guinean populations, cannot so easily be identified in other regional contexts. Even in Senegal, which besides Guinea-Conakry was a principal arena of PAIGC activity in exile and the home of a considerable Cape Verdean population, we can find these ambivalences. In Senegal the situation of the early 1970s was apparently characterised by internal fissures within the local PAIGC sections. Portuguese informants reported that the cells of the movement in that country were entirely dominated by Cape Verdean activists, who left little room for fellow members from Guinea-Bissau residing in Senegal. Therefore, Cape Verdeans and Guineans lived in an uneasy relationship in Dakar and Ziguinchor, and only the recurrent successes of the movement in the liberation struggle in Portuguese Guinea and the authority of Amílcar Cabral's leadership pushed the internal conflicts into the background and brought together the distinct currents.[12] Moreover, the relationship of the original Cape Verdean community in Dakar to the PAIGC and to the liberation movements in general adds to these complexities. In an environment where consecutive Senegalese governments sympathised with the liberation of Portuguese Guinea but remained for a long time lukewarm with regard to any open support for Amílcar Cabral (until the period when the movement of the latter began to monopolise the liberation struggle in the small territory under Portuguese colonial rule), the PAIGC had no control over this community. In 1971 and 1972, agents of the Portuguese secret police who had infiltrated the movement in Senegal reported that the leaders of the group in Dakar attempted to use the families of the Cape Verdean community in Senegal to gather information on the situation on the archipelago, information they obviously no longer had. However, these attempts met with very little success. PAIGC leaders appear to have been quite disappointed about their failure to mobilise Dakar's Cape Verdean community against the Portuguese government in the colony.[13]

Thus, while the military success of the PAIGC was outstanding during the 1960s and early 1970s, the same cannot be said about the party's achievements within the Cape Verdean communities of the Portuguese colony of Guinea-Bissau and of the neighbouring country of Senegal. We therefore have to be careful in making generalisations about Cape Verdean group behaviour during the anticolonial activities in Portugal's late colonial empire. In the following section, we will return to the situation in the archipelago itself.

At the brink of popular revolt? The war and the Cape Verdeans of the archipelago

During much of the 1960s and the early 1970s, the Portuguese authorities, in particular, agents of the secret police, remained convinced that there was a possibility of nationalist revolt in the archipelago. This idea remained alive although the representatives of the colonial state had rather early discarded the hypothesis of subversive involvement of the Cape Verdean officials on the islands. There were isolated accusations, however, but they did not always lead to interrogations or arrests, as in the case of Dr. Raul Querido Varela – the delegate of the public prosecutor for the Barlavento Islands of Cape Verde, in Mindelo – who was suspected of maintaining contacts with PAIGC members in Guinea-Bissau via his parents living in Dakar and of acting as a spokesmen of political prisoners in Praia.[14] The colonial power was unable to implicate this official, who was nonetheless removed to serve in Mozambique from 1964. Nor was there any sympathy for the revolt among the Cape Verdean officials within the colonial service. The obvious exceptions were the specialists who had joined Amílcar Cabral's rebel movement by the end of the 1950s but who were not normally *officials* of the colonial government.

With respect to the situation of the more modest social groups, there are several episodes illustrating the nervousness of the Portuguese colonial government (and of the Cape Verdean officials in the service of this government). The colonial officials interpreted various events, triggered by the experiences of hunger, poverty, and unemployment in the archipelago, as indications of possible popular unrest. The less accessible zones of the islands were as much an object of these comments as were the young populations of the suburbs of Praia and the seamen of the harbour areas of Mindelo and of the colonial capital. The following three episodes can be regarded as representative for the period between the late 1950s and the Carnation Revolution.

There was much speculation about attempts at intensifying propaganda among the 'common people,' particularly of Santiago and São Vicente islands. In September 1967, in Lem Ferreira, a suburb of Praia, adolescents and young male adults between 13 and 30 years of age participated in marches and exercises that appeared to be military training. The Portuguese secret police and regular police forces intervened; after some interrogation (which included violence) the officials were satisfied that these male participants only took part in plays 'of bad taste' referring to a local Catholic saint.[15] Even so, many of the young locals were increasingly frustrated by the lack of opportunities in the poorer neighbourhoods of Praia, whose population was steadily growing, and phenomena of this type became increasingly frequent.

Difficulties in the rural zones of Santiago Island were interpreted in similar ways. The most obvious case concerned religious dissidents in the mountainous interior of Santiago – the so-called *rabelados* – who openly defied the missions of hygiene and disinfection the colonial administration sent to their villages. The administrator of the *concelho* of Praia and a small medical mission were threatened and insulted by inhabitants of the villages of the highlands and had to withdraw without any further success. The officials involved were convinced that the *rabelados* were a potential basis for a separatist movement.[16] The following years saw repressive measures against the members of the group, though of a rather low level of intensity.

Mobile individuals who went back and forth between the archipelago and the West African coast seemed to be the ideal vehicle for the transfer of 'subversive propaganda' from Dakar to Mindelo.[17] Cape Verdean directors of theatre groups based in Dakar, such as 'Eddy Moreno' (alias Adolfo Capristano Silva), also appeared to be potentially dangerous individuals,[18] though proof was seldom established. While we know that seamen occasionally operated as message bearers for anticolonial groups, there were no particular findings by the police in Cape Verde.

For long periods, the subject of infiltration by armed groups reappeared occasionally, without being given any larger importance. There were now and again rumors of attempts by PAIGC leaders in Dakar to clandestinely transport weapons and material to the archipelago and to arm their sympathisers in the populous urban environment. In summer 1965 such rumours reached their first peak. However, there were no 'intellectuals' in Cape Verde who could be identified as followers of the plan of revolt, and while the propaganda that was efficiently diffused for some months in 1965 by the PAIGC seemed to indicate that the movement had some support base among the popular sectors of urban Praia and Mindelo, there was never any confirmation of the claims that a guerrilla war was planned.[19] Even though the level of nervousness among the agents of the colonial police remained constantly and curiously high, there were no signs whatsoever of organised popular discontent, and even the rumors about initiatives coming from outside became increasingly rare in the second half of the 1960s. It was only from 1970 that we again find police reports commenting upon an alleged conspiracy to arm local rebels to be recruited from the Cape Verdean (sub) urban populations. In June 1971 there was even unconfirmed information about a plan to ship trained rebels with their weapons from the PAIGC-controlled zone of Guinea-Bissau to Praia. This information seemed to be credible and led the armed forces of the colonial power on Cape Verde to take countermeasures and to anxiously wait for a rebellion that never materialised.[20] During much of 1971 and 1972, the Portuguese authorities continued to believe that the PAIGC would organise 'terrorist' surprise attacks on one of the major islands of the archipelago to boost its prestige among the islands' populations, which was regarded as minimal.[21]

We can therefore establish that the potential for a revolt in the archipelago was weaker than what existing ideas about the participation of Cape

Verdeans in the Guinean guerrilla movement would lead us to believe. We will need to analyse, in the next section, the type of information that inhabitants of the Cape Verdean Islands were likely to receive about other parts of sub-Saharan Africa. Apart from contacts to the Cape Verdean communities in Portuguese Guinea (and, with less impact, in Senegal), we will focus on Angola, São Tomé, and Príncipe as principal target regions of Cape Verdean settlement. Whenever the inhabitants of the islands obtained information about experiences with other Africans, these two geographical regions were most likely to receive comment.

Sympathy not included: the Cape Verdean settler experience in São Tomé and Príncipe, and Angola

The two deadly hunger crises in the archipelago in the 1940s and the inability of the Portuguese government to manage the drought or to support the starving inhabitants of the islands revived the theme of Cape Verdean emigration. Within the imperial logic, Portuguese officials made an attempt at channelling the streams of emigration towards the tropical colonies. We will in the following paragraphs analyse the conditions of this emigration and the ways in which it influenced the outlook of Cape Verdeans of the more modest social classes. Besides these settlers, we also find an 'elite' emigration of Cape Verdean administrators going to work in other parts of the empire; however, our perspective will mainly concern the experiences of the first group.

In Angola after the Second World War, while the turbulence of anticolonial rebellion was approaching, the presence of Cape Verdeans was intensified in parts of the colony. In addition to having a well-established community in Luanda, the Cape Verdeans also worked in the countryside as commanders of posts and subdistricts on the lowest administrative level. It is both obvious and remarkable that these officials supported the positions of the colonial state. During the early incidences of rebellion in the colony, that is, during the revolt in the Baixa de Cassange in January and February 1961, the Cape Verdean officials appeared as the loyal backbone of an administration under stress (Keese 2007, pp. 509–510).

Other, less well off Cape Verdeans came as settlers to Angolan territory; these initiatives of Cape Verdean settlement became increasingly important from the 1950s, although their influx remained in the shadow of the highly encouraged European settlement that accelerated during the same period. Peasants immigrating into Portugal's West Central African colony usually lived in agricultural model settlements in the Angolan interior, notably those in the fertile highlands of the Planalto. As Gerald Bender has pointed out, Cape Verdean settlers could be very unpopular with their Angolan neighbours (Bender 1978, pp. 119–120). The composition of these settler groups had a role in regional conflicts, and it must be said that the Portuguese organisation of immigration added to the problems. The Provincial Services of Settlement of Angola (Junta Provincial do Povoamento de Angola: JPPA) mainly received settlers from the islands of São Nicolau, Brava, and – to a much lesser degree – Fogo. These members of a rural 'proletariat,' as colonial officials labelled them, were to join the few existing Cape Verdean settlements or were sometimes instructed to create new villages. The Portuguese officials in Luanda had explicitly demanded complete families, which were seen as more likely to organise self-contained communities, but the administration of Cape Verde sent them complex groups of relatives and acquaintances. The social context had two main unplanned effects. First, to counter the centrifugal tendencies within the Cape Verdean settlements, Portuguese officials were active in indoctrinating the Cape Verdeans so that they felt themselves as a group to be separate from the Angolan Africans. Subsidies were employed to tie them emotionally to the Portuguese authorities, and the latter tried to make it clear to the settlers that their superiority as full imperial citizens entitled them to privileges that their Angolan neighbours could not claim. The end of the separate native code (*indigenato*) for Angolans could have modified this propaganda, but the Portuguese administration still insisted with the Cape Verdean settlers that they were morally if not legally superior. Second, the members of Cape Verdean settlements, with their very unstable socioeconomic structure, were far more likely to leave the family compounds, either to make their own living in an unwelcoming environment or, less frequently, to go back to the archipelago. The first created more risk of unfriendly encounters with locals, while the second enabled information of these experiences to be brought home to Cape Verde.

Cape Verdean settlers were very much dependent on imperial services in their everyday life. They also relied on the Junta Provincial when it came to repatriation, which was a constant issue for them. From the beginning, the Portuguese services had attempted to settle families in Angola that were less likely to return, but this issue was complicated, and, as we have seen, the unstable enlarged family groups sent over to Angolan soil were likely to explode, with individuals trying to return. Again and again, the specialists of the provincial government who were in charge of the settlement of Angola became desperate about the many Cape Verdeans who went back to the archipelago after only a couple of years in Angolan agriculture.[22] Yet originally the Portuguese administration was reluctant to implement a generous definition of education and grades, which would have allowed specialised Cape Verdean workers, for instance, artisans, the opportunity to earn better wages during service in Angola.[23] Also, there was little provision for social welfare in the sense of health coverage or even repatriation in the case of illness or old age, although this problem was actively debated in Portugal in the second half of the 1960s.[24] The absence of incentives motivated some Cape Verdeans to return to the archipelago, even if in the end they had to take on debts to finance the journey home.[25]

In the 1960s, the services of settler colonisation of the province of Angola, in the form of the Junta Provincial, regularly urged an intensification of Cape Verdean immigration to Angolan soil. Cape Verdean peasants were regarded as a positive factor in the stabilisation of Portuguese rule. To facilitate the transport of such settlers, the administrations of Cape Verde and Angola would pair these transports with shipment of plantation workers to São Tomé and Príncipe and combine them with the repatriation of labourers.[26] In years of promising agricultural productivity, the planners from the Junta also tried to counter the repatriation of Cape Verdean settlers – which was a particular problem with regard to candidates for settlement from Fogo – by offering more relaxed controls whenever heads of families asked to bring members to the Angolan settlement, such family members more often than not being merely acquaintances of the family.[27] These measures were successful, and they led to an even closer relationship between the Cape Verdean presence and the services of imperial control.

The relations between Cape Verdeans and their Angolan neighbours remained tense. The fact that the provincial government favoured Cape Verdean overseers in agricultural work over their Angolan colleagues did not improve matters.[28] Tensions appear to have been regular. Although most of the Cape Verdean settlers did not live in the regions touched by the war between 1961 and 1974, it can be argued that the image they had of their Angolan neighbours was clearly negative. Obviously, only part of this view was actively promoted by the propaganda of the provincial services. For the rest, the effect of Cape Verdeans living in a complicated environment and without a reliable status was sufficient to distance these settlers from involvement in anticolonial movements. The fact that individual Cape Verdean settlers who lived in Kwanza-Norte and Uíge had been killed by the União dos Povos de Angola (UPA) guerrillas in the early months of the war (from March 1961), was an additional reason to form a negative view of the anticolonial revolt in Angola.

The experience of intensified Cape Verdean settlement in São Tomé and Príncipe was different from that in Angola. First, there was an older tradition of drafting Cape Verdeans for the cocoa plantations (*roças*) although this practice before the Second World War was less well organised than the transport of Angolan labourers, or *serviçais*. Second, the organised emigration over much of the 1940s was a panic reaction prompted by Portuguese incapacity to respond to the famines in Cape Verde. This made a process of selection comparable to the efforts regarding emigration to Angola impossible. Third, although during the 1950s and 1960s the flux of emigration to the cocoa islands stabilised and Cape Verdeans were for these two decades the largest group of new settlers on the *roças*, the system remained less organised than were the structures of recruitment for agricultural labour in Angola.

The Cape Verdeans, immigrating into São Tomé and Príncipe in considerable strength in the 1940s and 1950s, did not form any relations with the *forros*, the urban 'autochthons' in São Tomé City and in the agricultural villages outside of the plantation zone, mainly in the Trindade region. This was primarily because of the clear geographical separation between the *roças* and the settlement zones of the *forros*. Also, they remained largely separated from the Angolan and Mozambican *serviçais*, who were the other more or less voluntary workers with whom they lived on the cocoa plantations.[29] Such separation, as in the case of Cape Verdean settlement in Angola, was indirectly encouraged by the colonial administration, and it was to have strong effects on the mentalities of the settlers.

For the early 1950s, reports suggest that many Cape Verdeans had little sympathy for emancipationist positions among the *forro* elite. In 1953, when Portuguese Governor Carlos da Sousa Gorgulho authorised brutal repression against the protests of *forros*, which led to a massacre on São Tomé, Cape Verdean labourers were regularly enlisted in the militia employed to quell the 'rebellion.' This Cape Verdean involvement in the countermeasures against the *forro* protests remained in the memories of the latter, and the Cape Verdeans would be farther than ever from any peaceful life with the populations living outside of the plantation system (Seibert 2002b; Eyzaguirre 1986, pp. 329–331).

During the second half of the 1950s and the early years of the 1960s, Portuguese officials were nevertheless convinced that the Cape Verdean presence could pose a threat to colonial rule in the province. These worries of the nervous Portuguese administration were expressed through a number of conjectures, which did not always make sense. In early 1961, the Portuguese authorities and secret police in São Tomé were occupied with crushing a (probably fictitious) rebellion plan of the *forros* of the villages of Santo Amaro, Vaz Monteiro, Guadelupe, and Santana, where there were widespread rumors of white Portuguese colonists poisoning the wells.[30] The presence of the exiled Angolan cleric Joaquim da Rocha Pinto de Andrade on Príncipe Island added to these worries. Portuguese police agents held that Pinto de Andrade incited individuals 'coming from the bush' to work against the colonial administration.[31] This was then connected to the economic problems many *roças* went through at the start of the new decade, which were seen to be the source of discontent for thousands, mainly Cape Verdean *serviçais* living under precarious conditions, who might be ready to ally themselves with subversive *forro* leaders.[32]

Indeed, Cape Verdeans had good reason to protest against the conditions of transport to and repatriation from São Tomé and Príncipe and the treatment on the *roças*; this protest was expressed in passive resistance and vandalism.[33] Even so, there was no significant rapprochement between Cape Verdean labourers and other groups working on the plantations, nor can we detect any sympathy among the Cape Verdeans for *forro* activism. By contrast, while the repatriation of these workers to Cape Verde was uncommon, their impressions were, nevertheless, easily transported back to the islands.[34] Opinions about fellow Africans encountered on the cocoa islands were largely negative. Such negativity was reinforced by the disastrous effects that work on the *roças* had on their health. In 1959, the administrator of Fogo Island commented that nearly all of these labourers returned either struggling to recuperate from illness or with their health already destroyed. Most of these former *serviçais* constructed their damning memory of life on the cocoa islands around the experience of illness: and those who wanted to accept new contracts were, by the Cape Verdean elite, held to be 'bewitched.'[35] The experiences with *forros* – often regarded as arrogant – and with Angolan, Mozambican, and *tonga* colleagues on the *roças* – frequently viewed as inferior – fitted with this memory of life in São Tomé and Príncipe being a disastrous experience.

Conclusion

This article works with a hypothesis which appears plausible in light of the empirical observations we can make about the behaviour of Cape Verdeans under the Portuguese late colonial state. While Cape Verdean leaders in Portuguese Guinea strongly engaged in the anticolonial struggle, it appears that there was no such engagement on the islands. This is to be explained not only by Portuguese repression but apparently also by a lack of sympathy for the African societies whose liberation movements were fighting against the Portuguese colonial system.

Only in Portuguese Guinea did these antipathies not have a negative moderating effect on the engagement of the Cape Verdean community; in the Guinean case, a Cape Verdean leader connected to an 'establishment' of African intellectuals who became, in part, guerrilla warriors, operated as a principal mediator between the Cape Verdean identity and a larger liberation project. Under such particular circumstances these antipathies did not have an effect on the engagement of the Cape Verdean community. However, even in Portuguese Guinea, the Cape Verdean community was divided into an active part and a hesitant group of which a good percentage of the members never embraced the guerrilla cause. In the end, it demonstrates the particular talent of the PAIGC leadership since they avoided being drawn into a conflict within their movement and with a group of its sympathisers, a conflict that could have questioned the eligibility of Cape Verdeans, as 'imperial auxiliaries,' for any anticolonial struggle.

In Angola and São Tomé and Príncipe, Cape Verdeans never found the cause of anticolonial movements attractive. Rather, Cape Verdean settlers who were part of the settlement schemes developed a stronger group feeling clearly distinct from and opposed to the other African groups from within the Portuguese Empire. Dependence on Portuguese services and a certain indoctrination, in addition to the experience of slowly improving conditions on the *roças* and in the Angolan model settlements, all had their role in this. The Cape Verdean elite living in these colonies could have instigated the settlers to sympathise with the cause of the rebellions, but instead these officials remained loyal servants of the empire. The effect of such experiences – told and retold by returnees from both provinces – on the mentality of the inhabitants of the archipelago cannot be underestimated. Intense research based in great part on oral interviews would be necessary in order to measure these effects accurately. Such research, it is to be feared, will only lead to clearer results under fortunate circumstances given the extreme significance of the issue for present-day politics and the complexities of restoring old opinions, from a period of four or five decades ago, through field interviews.

My interpretation shows the effects of late colonial empires, which in the case of the Portuguese colonial state have often been underrated. Even in the case of an authoritarian state and an underfunded metropolitan economy in the centre of the empire, the new, more professional services offered could emotionally bind populations or, if we wished to see it from such a perspective, manipulate them into taking their distance from anticolonial ventures. Cape Verdean administrators, although not treated on fair and nonracist terms within the colonial system, remained attached to the empire. Cape Verdean settlers, on the other hand, relied on improving imperial services under the late colonial state and 'learned', in this context, their otherness from potential African partners. This effect should warn us against drawing simplified conclusions about anticolonial revolt within colonial empires. Although Gerald Bender has efficiently demonstrated that the Portuguese colonial empire did not fulfil much of its propaganda with regard to 'multi-racial' participation within its structures, this is only one part of the colonial realities. These same structures had their effects in shaping the mentalities of colonial subjects.

Notes

1. Research for this chapter enjoyed at different stages the support of the University of Berne, the Holcim Foundation, and ERC Starting Grant n° 240898 within the Framework Programme 7 of the European Commission.
2. Arquivo Histórico Nacional de Cabo Verde, Praia, Cape Verde (AHNCV), Repartição Provincial dos Serviços da Administração Civil (RPSAC), SC:A\SR:C\ Cx124, 1499, Mário Rogério Afonso Leite, Administrator of the Sub-District (*concelho*) of Maio, Cape Verde, *Relatório respeitante ao ano de 1939 apresentado pela Administração do Concelho do Maio, Junho–Agosto 1939* (without number), 31 July 1939, p. 3.

144 Alexander Keese

3. An initial analysis of the complexities of 'imperial citizenship' has been made for the French case. See Cooper (2009, pp. 96–105).
4. Again, the better analytic coverage can be found for the French case, see Sabatier (1985) and Chafer (2002, 17–18).
5. With the notable exception of São Tomé and Príncipe, where the integration of the so-called *forros* – a local elite descended from the pre-19th-century inhabitants of this archipelago – was less pronounced and was further diminished by the new, repressive policy of the Gorgulho administration after 1945, see Seibert (2nd edition, 2002a, 71–93).
6. On the catalytic function of the Casa dos Estudantes do Império, see Mateus 1999, 66–78; Dáskalos 1983.
7. The point about the complexities of Cape Verdean identity with regard to the experience of emigration and cultural fusion is made, for the postcolonial period, in various books and articles. See, for instance, Gibau (2008, 261–262); Batalha (2004b, 209–211).
8. Arquivo Histórico Ultramarino, Lisbon, Portugal (AHU), MU/ISAU A2.49.003/49.00355, Nascimento Rodrigues, *Província Ultramarina de Cabo Verde – Relatório da Inspecção Administrativa ordinária a esta Província determinada por douto despacho de 19 de Fevereiro de 1963, de Sua Excelência o Sub-Secretario de Estado de Administração Ultramarina Pelo Inspector Administrativo do Quadro Comum do Ultramar António do Nascimento Rodrigues,* Vol. 1: *Província Ultramarina de Cabo Verde: Serviços de Inspecção Administrativa. – Inspecção Administrativa Ordinaria ao Concelho da Praia – Relatório N° 1, Ano de 1963* (n° 1), n.d., p. 54.
9. Arquivo Nacional da Torre do Tombo, Lisbon (ANTT), AOS/CO/UL-32A-1, Polícia Internacional e de Defesa do Estado (PIDE), *Informação – [Amilcar Cabral]* (n° 521/61-GU), 14 April 1961.
10. ANTT, AOS/CO/UL-32A-1, Portuguese Overseas Ministry, Cabinet of Political Affairs, *Apontamento: Amílcar Lopes Cabral, Secretário Geral do 'Partido Africano da Independência da Guiné e Cabo Verde' (PAIGC)* (without number), 24 July 1963, p. 7.
11. Such a vision has been strongly favoured in the account given by journalist, activist, and historian Basil Davidson (1989, 93–128).
12. ANTT, PIDE/DGS Del. CV Praia, SR, Proc. 62 (n° de unidade 5376), Commander of Directorate-General of Security (Direcção-Geral de Segurança: DGS) to Commander of DGS Post at Mindelo (n° 342/72–S.INF.), 11 September 1972.
13. ANTT, PIDE/DGS Del. CV Praia, SR, Proc. 62 (n° de unidade 5376), Miguel Henriques Nunes to Commander of Delegation of DGS in Praia, *Assunto: – P.A.I.G.C. – Referência: Colaborador 'Mascarenhas'.* (n° 2/72–S.R.), 6 January 1972.
14. ANTT, PIDE/DGS Del. CV Praia, SR, Proc. 62 (n° de unidade 5376), Commander of PIDE Post at Mindelo, *Assunto: – Raul Querido Varela* (n° 38/63–S.R.), 10 July 1963. Raul Querido Varela pursued the rest of his career under colonial rule as judge in Beira, Mozambique; after the independence of Cape Verde, he filled the highest diplomatic posts of the new republic, including ambassador to the United States (1975–1979); after a period of exile in Portugal (1979–1991), he reentered the public life of Cape Verde, now a multiparty democracy, as judge of the Supreme Court, nominated by the new Movimento para a Democracia (MpD) government.
15. ANTT, PIDE/DGS Del. CV Praia, SR, Proc. 83 (n° de unidade 5407), José Vasco Meireles, Inspector, Commander of the Subdelegation of PIDE in Cabo Verde, to Director-General of PIDE (n° 871/67-CI(2)), 20 October 1967, p. 1.

Imperial Actors? 145

16. AHU, MU/ISAU A2.49.003/49.00355, Ildo Maria Feijóo, Administrador of *concelho* of Praia to Director of Provincial Department of the Services of Civil Administration of Cape Verde (n° 638, Proc. 23, as Document n° 48), 26 June 1963, in *Província Ultramarina de Cabo Verde: Serviços de Inspecção Administrativa. – Inspecção Administrativa Ordinaria ao Concelho da Praia – Relatório N° 1, Ano de 1963*, which is part of *Província Ultramarina de Cabo Verde – Relatório da Inspecção Administrativa ordinária a esta Província determinada por douto despacho de 19 de Fevereiro de 1963, de Sua Excelência o Sub-Secretario de Estado de Administração Ultramarina Pelo Inspector Administrativo do Quadro Comum do Ultramar António do Nascimento Rodrigues, Volume 1*. (n° 1), n.d.
17. ANTT, PIDE/DGS Del. CV Praia, SR, Proc. 62 (n° de unidade 5376), Commander of PIDE Post at Mindelo to Commander of the Subdelegation of PIDE in Cape Verde (n° 454/63–S.R.), June 14, 1963; ANTT, PIDE/DGS Del. CV Praia, SR, Proc. 62 (n° de unidade 5376), António Lemos da Silva, Commander of the Subdelegation of PIDE in Cape Verde, to Commander of PIDE Post at Mindelo (n° 1295/63–S.R.), 3 July 1963.
18. ANTT, PIDE/DGS Del. CV Praia, SR, Proc. 62 (n° de unidade 5376), Commander of PIDE Post at Mindelo, *Informação: O Nacional: – Adolfo Capristano Silva 'Eddy Moreno'* (without number), 7 July 1963.
19. ANTT, PIDE/DGS Del. CV Praia, SR, Proc. 62 (n° de unidade 5376), António Manuel Cera Marques, Commander of Brigade, Commander of PIDE Post at Mindelo, to Commander of Subdelegation of PIDE in Cape Verde (n° 21/65), 16 August 1965, pp. 1–2.
20. ANTT, PIDE/DGS Del. CV Praia, SR, Proc. 62 (n° de unidade 5376), Miguel Henriques Nunes to Commander of Delegation of DGS in Praia, *Assunto: P.A.I.G.C. – Referência: Rádio cifrado deste Posto n° 459/71-GAB, de 16 do corrente* (n° 80/71–GAB), 16 June 1971, p. 1.
21. ANTT, PIDE/DGS Del. CV Praia, SR, Proc. 62 (n° de unidade 5376), PIDE, Subdelegation of Cape Verde in Praia, *Planos do P.A.I.G.C.* (n° 19/71–DN), 15 June 1971; ANTT, PIDE/DGS Del. CV Praia, SR, Proc. 62 (n° de unidade 5376), PIDE, Subdelegation of Cape Verde in Praia, *Boatos sobre um acto de terrorismo em Cabo Verde* (n° 97/72–S.R.), 14 February 1972.
22. AHNCV, Instituto do Trabalho, Previdência e Acção Social (ITPAS), SSC:F2\SR:E\ Cx170, Joaquim Pedro Monteiro de Vasconcelos Nogueira Jordão, Vice President of the Service of Rural Colonisation Issues of the Province of Angola, to Institute of Labour, Welfare and Social Action of Cape Verde (ITPASCV), *Condições a que deve obedecer a emigração de 200 famílias rurais caboverdeanas, para Angola, sob a égide da Junta Provincial de Povoamento* (without number), 9 December 1963, pp. 1–2. Bender holds that the larger percentage of the Cape Verdeans actually stayed in Angola until 1974, but whether the 30 to 40 per cent of returnees were many or few, depends on the point of view: Portuguese authorities in Angola obviously hoped for permanent settlement and were not content with return rates. See Bender, (1978, pp. 116–118).
23. See the discussion of a particular case in AHNCV, ITPAS, SSC:F2\SR:E\Cx170, Emílio Baptista Cerqueira, Head of Special Department of Social Action, Service of Rural Colonisation of the Province of Angola (JPP), to Anastácio Isidoro Costa, Forest Labourer in the *concelho* of Porto Novo, Santo Antão, Cape Verde (n° 12686/DAS/Proc°.1376), 17 November 1964; AHNCV, ITPAS, SSC:F2\SR:E\Cx170, A. Isidoro Costa to Silvino Silvério Marques, Governor-General of Angola, 1 October 1965.

146 Alexander Keese

24. AHNCV, ITPAS, SSC:F2\SR:E\Cx170, Lívio Borges, High Inspector of Health Affairs, for the Directorate-General of Health Issues and Social Assistance, to the President of ITPASCV, *Conferência de Imprensa* (without number), without date [November 1964], p. 6.
25. See a characteristic case in AHNCV, ITPAS, SSC:F2\SR:E\Cx170, Fernando Manuel Ferreira Borges Mouzinho, President of the Junta Províncial de Povoamento de Angola, to Marcos Pinto Basto, President of the ITPASCV (n° 1696/Col/68), 22 October 1968.
26. AHNCV, Instituto do Trabalho, Previdência e Acção Social (ITPAS), SSC:F2\ SR:E\Cx170, Marcos Pinto Basto to Abrantes Amaral, Governor of Cape Verde, *Informação* (n° 57/67), 6 October 1967, p. 1.
27. AHNCV, Instituto do Trabalho, Previdência e Acção Social (ITPAS), SSC:F2\SR:E\ Cx170, Marcos Pinto Basto to Peixoto Correia, Acting Governor of Cape Verde, *Informação* (n° 67/67), 7 December 1967, p. 2.
28. AHNCV, Instituto do Trabalho, Previdência e Acção Social (ITPAS), SSC:F2\SR:E\ Cx170, Joaquim Pedro Monteiro de Vasconcelos Nogueira Jordão to President of the ITPASCV, *Capatazes Agro-Pecuários da Escola de S. Jorge dos Orgãos* (n° 5117/731/ POV/67), 25 April 1967, p. 1.
29. Violence between Cape Verdeans, on the one hand, and Angolans, Mozambicans, and *tongas* (in this case, meaning children of Angolans and/or Mozambicans born on the plantations), on the other, was typical, and there is abundant information on armed and unarmed battles. Over the 1950s, however, this violence disappeared into the background, probably given the increased numbers of Cape Verdeans living on the *roças*. See, for a characteristic example, Arquivo Histórico de São Tomé e Príncipe, São Tomé (AHSTP), Curadoria Geral dos Serviçais e Indígenas, 189 (cota 3.27.2.14), Administrator of Companhia Ilha de São Tomé to Curator-General of Labourers and Natives (without number), 24 May 1949.
30. ANTT, AOS/CO/UL-32A-1, PIDE, *Informação – [São Tomé e Príncipe]* (n° 77/61-GU), 23 January 1961, p. 1; ANTT, AOS/CO/UL-32A-1, PIDE, *Informação – [São Tomé e Príncipe]* (n° 221/61-GU), 27 February 1961.
31. ANTT, AOS/CO/UL-32A-1, PIDE, *Informação – [São Tomé e Príncipe]* (n° 228/61-GU), 27 February 1961; ANTT, AOS/CO/UL-32A-1, PIDE, *Informação – [São Tomé e Príncipe]* (n° 538/61-G.U.), 18 April 1961.
32. ANTT, AOS/CO/UL-32A-1, PIDE, *Informação – [São Tomé e Príncipe]* (n° 438/61-GU), 5 April 1961.
33. AHNCV, Repartição Provincial dos Serviços da Administração Civil (RPSAC), SC:A\SR:A/Cx173 (0022), Adelino Macedo, Curator-General of Labourers and Natives of São Tomé and Príncipe, to Abrantes Amaral, Governor of Cape Verde, *Informação* (n° 23/957), 19 June 1957, pp. 1–3.
34. Early examples of letters sent back by Cape Verdean labourers from the *roças* to Cape Verde, including comments on hostile encounters of Cape Verdeans with other Africans, can be found in AHSTP, Vários, Secretaria Geral do Governo (Série D), 026 (cota 1.1.3.3.), A. Mendes Serra, Director of Services of the Provincial Department of Civil Administration, *Cópia de algumas passagens de dezoito cartas escritas pelos trabalhadores de Santo Antão, que prestam serviço em São Tomé e Príncipe, dirigidas às pessoas amigas e parentes da terra da naturalidade dos mesmos*: (without number), 8 April 1953.
35. AHNCV, Repartição Provincial dos Serviços da Administração Civil (RPSAC), SC:A\SR:C\Cx123, 1492, Luís Silva Rendall, Administrator of Sub-District (*concelho*) of Fogo, *Administração do Concelho do Fogo: Ano Civil de 1958* (without number), 24 February 1959, 66–67.

References

Andrade, E. S. (1996), *Les îles du Cap-Vert de la 'Découverte' à l'Indépendance Nationale (1460–1975)*. L'Harmattan, Paris.
Anjos, J. C. G. dos (2004), *Intelectuais, literatura e poder em Cabo Verde: lutas de definição da identidade nacional*. UFRGS/IFCH, Porto Alegre/Brazil – INIPC, Praia.
Batalha, L. (2004a), *The Cape Verdean Diaspora in Portugal. Colonial Subjects in a Postcolonial World*. Lexington Books, Lanham, MD, and Oxford.
Batalha, L. (2004b), 'A elite portuguesa-cabo-verdiana: ascensão e queda de um grupo colonial intermediário,' in C. Carvalho and J. de Pina Cabral (eds.), *A Persistência da História. Passado e Contemporaneidade em África*. Imprensa de Ciências Sociais, Lisbon, pp. 191–225.
Bender, G. (1978), *Angola under the Portuguese: The Myth and the Reality*. Heinemann, London.
Carreira, A. (1984), *Cabo Verde (Aspectos sociais, Secas e fomes do século XX)*. 2nd edn. Ulmeiro, Lisbon.
Chabal, P. (1993), 'Emergencies and Nationalist Wars in Portuguese Africa,' *Journal of Imperial and Commonwealth History* 21, no. 3, pp. 235–249.
Chabal, P. (2002 [1983]), *Amilcar Cabral: Revolutionary Leadership and People's War*. Hurst, London.
Chabal, P. (2002), 'Lusophone Africa in Historical and Comparative Perspective,' in P. Chabal (ed.), *A History of Postcolonial Lusophone Africa*. Indiana University Press, Bloomington and Indianapolis, pp. 3–134.
Chafer, T. (2002), *The End of Empire in French West Africa. France's Successful Decolonization?* Berg, Oxford and New York.
Cooper, F. (2009), 'From Imperial Inclusion to Republican Exclusion? France's Ambiguous Post-War Trajectory,' in C. Tshimanga-Kashama, D. Gondola, and P. Bloom (eds.), *Frenchness and the African Diaspora*. Indiana University Press, Bloomington, pp. 91–119.
Dáskalos, S. (1983), *A Casa dos Estudantes do Império – Fundação e Primeiros Anos de Vida*. Câmara Municipal de Lisboa, Lisbon.
Davidson, B. (1989), *The Fortunate Isles: A Study in African Transformation*. Africa World Press, Trenton, NJ.
Eyzaguirre, P. B. (1986), 'Small Farmers and Estates in São Tomé, West Africa.' PhD diss., Yale University.
Gibau, G. S. (2008), 'Cape Verdean Diasporic Identity Formation,' in L. Batalha and J. Carling (eds.), *Transnational Archipelago: Perspectives on Cape Verdean Migration and Diaspora*. Amsterdam University Press, pp. 255–268.
Keese, A. (2007), 'The Role of Cape Verdeans in War Mobilization and War Prevention in Portugal's African Empire, 1955–1965,' *International Journal of African Historical Studies* 40, no. 3, pp. 497–511.
MacQueen, N. (1997), *The Decolonization of Portuguese Africa: Metropolitan Revolution and the Dissolution of Empire*. Longman, London and New York.
Mateus, D. C. (1999), *A Luta pela Independência: A formação das elites fundadoras da Frelimo, MPLA e PAIGC*. Inquérito, Mem Martins.
Meintel, D. (1984), *Race, Culture, and Portuguese Colonialism in Cabo Verde*. Maxwell School of Citizenship and Public Affairs, Syracuse University, Syracuse, NY.
Moura, A. F. da, (2009), 'Eficácia social (qualidade e equidade) do sistema educativo en Cabo Verde.' PhD thesis, University of Santiago de Compostela.
Newitt, M. (1981), *Portugal in Africa: The Last Hundred Years*. Hurst, London.

Sabatier, P. (1985), 'Did Africans Really Learn to Be French? The Francophone Elite of the École William Ponty,' in G. W. Johnson (ed.), *Double Impact: France and Africa in the Age of Imperialism*. Greenwood Press, Westport, CT, and London, pp. 179–187.

Seibert, G., (2002a), *Camaradas, clientes e compadres: Colonialismo, socialismo e democratização em São Tomé e Príncipe*. 2nd edn. Vega, Lisbon.

Seibert, G., (2002b), 'The February 1953 Massacre in São Tomé: Crack in the Salazarist Image of Multiracial Harmony and Impetus for Nationalist Demands for Independence,' *Portuguese Studies Review* 10, no. 2, pp. 53–80.

6
Unlike the Other Whites? The Swiss in Mozambique under Colonialism

Sérgio Inácio Chichava

It is frequently said that the history of a country is influenced by its ruling elites. The history of Mozambique's Swiss community provides a good example of this statement. Analysis of its past will reveal much about the present state of this former African Portuguese colony.

In relation to the Swiss community in Mozambique (both colonial and postcolonial), it is necessary to say that it is probably the most thoroughly researched foreign community in the country (Harries 1989, 1994; Monnier 1995; Macamo 1998; Butselaar 1998; Ngoenha 1999; Silva 2001; Linder 2001). With the exception of Linder's study, however, almost all studies have centred not on the Swiss community in general but on the role of the Swiss mission (today's Presbyterian Church in Mozambique) in the formation of a certain identity amongst the Shangaan population of southern Mozambique and of an awareness of their colonised condition.

These studies analyse the links between the Swiss Protestant missionaries and the formation of a Shangaan identity and Mozambican nationalism, especially among those who led the Liberation Front of Mozambique (Frelimo), the movement which overthrew Portuguese colonialism and brought independence to Mozambique in 1975. These studies (with a few exception, e.g., Morier-Genoud 1998) are silent in relation to other missionaries, both Protestants (in particular evangelicals) and Catholics (e.g., White Fathers or Capuchins), Swiss and non-Swiss, who, even if in smaller numbers also made their presence felt in Mozambique and contributed to the training of local people and the development of knowledge about their culture. In addition, these studies do not assess, not even on a general level, the Frelimo discourse after independence, which consisted in marginalising religion, especially Catholicism, Islam, and Protestantism.

Looking at the centre of Mozambique, particularly the provinces of Zambézia, Manica, and Sofala, this chapter aims at showing and explaining, first, that, apart from the Swiss Protestants in the south, there were other Christian Protestant missions in the centre and north of the country that had an important role in training Mozambicans, some of whom would later join Frelimo. Second, it aims at showing and explaining that, even if the Swiss group most visible in the academic literature consisted of members of the Swiss mission, there were other Swiss people who were active outside the religious field too. The chapter will show that there were very important ties between parts of the Swiss community and colonial capitalism.

This chapter will focus in particular on the province of Zambézia. The former district of Quelimane is an interesting case study since it is the area where the largest capitalist companies established themselves after the Berlin Conference of 1884–1885 – the years marking the beginning of a more intensive and effective colonisation of present-day Mozambique and the setting up of colonial capitalism in the region. This is also an area where significant members of the Swiss bourgeoisie played an important role. Indeed, while the Swiss Protestant missionaries were active in 'humanising' the Africans and helping them discover the importance of their culture and identity, as it has been argued in the literature, the Swiss colonial bourgeoisie also participated in the conquest and exploitation of Africans, most evidently in the centre of Mozambique.

In this chapter, I will start by analysing the activities of the different Protestant congregations in Mozambique. I shall try to explain the reasons which led the Swiss community to be seen as different from other Europeans – as being more humane and kinder to African people than other settlers. I shall proceed in two steps. First, I will attempt to demonstrate that beyond the Swiss Protestant missionaries, other religious groups, notably Catholics, played an important role through religion and education in influencing the thinking and acting of Africans regarding their oppressed condition and the value of their culture. Second, I will discuss the Swiss involvement in colonial capitalism through a case study of the Boror Company and the Empresa Agrícola do Lugela, in the Zambézia region.

Overall, this chapter should demonstrate that the Swiss community was not very different from other European populations on the African continent during colonial times. My global discussion of the Swiss community should also help the understanding of the complex process of nation building in Mozambique (something that has relevance for all socially heterogeneous countries).

The Swiss mission: an exception among colonial Protestant missions?

The Swiss mission, whose community was estimated at 1,000 people between 1856 and 1975, is the institution that has been used to demonstrate the positive input of the Swiss community in Mozambique (Linder 2001, 12). Based in southern Mozambique since 1882, the Swiss mission played, according to several authors, a key role in raising the political consciousness of the people of this region. It did so, it is argued, by (a) training a small, educated black elite, (b) Africanising the Protestant Church before independence (consecration of African evangelists and pastors, prayers in local languages), and (c) producing an anticolonial discourse (Silva, 2001). Mozambican leaders and would-be leaders of Frelimo, such as Eduardo Mondlane,[1] Armando Guebuza,[2] and Pascoal Mocumbi[3] are seen as having developed a nationalist conscience under the influence of Swiss reformed Protestantism (ibid.). If the growth of Mozambican Protestantism in the south is often highlighted, its role sometimes even exaggerated, one should note that other Protestant influences, such as Anglicanism, Methodism, and Congregationalism, played a major role in the same way and in the same region as well as in other parts of the colony. To illustrate my point, I will discuss, first, the American Board Mission in the former colonial district of Manica and Sofala and, second, the Evangelical Mission of Nauela and the Seventh-Day Adventist Church, both in the colonial district of Zambézia. There is indeed a tendency to minimise the role of the American Board Mission, mostly in Machanga and Mambone, in the south of the former district of Manica and Sofala, in training an African elite that later played a major role in the creation of nationalist movements (Rennie 1973; Neves 1998; Spencer 2012). The same historical silence exists in relation to the Evangelical Mission of Nauela, in Alto-Molocué, and the Seventh-Day Adventist Church of Munguluni, in Lugela, which produced a black elite that took up important positions within the Frelimo leadership (Morier-Genoud 2000; Chichava 2007).

The American Board Mission

Established at the end of 19th century by American missionaries coming from Natal, South Africa, the American Board Mission (today's United Church of Christ in Mozambique) trained Mozambicans such as Kamba Simango, Bede Simango, Tapera Ncomo, and Sixpence Simango to become leaders of the mission in Mozambique (Rennie 1973; Neves 1998; Spencer 2012).

Amongst these figures, it is worth stressing the role of Kamba Columbus Simango. Kamba Simango, who studied at Hampton Institute, in Virginia (he graduated in 1919), and at Columbia University, in New York (where he obtained a teacher's degree in 1923), contributed to increasing the academic knowledge of African cultures in the United States (Curtis Burlin 1921; Andrade 1989; Morier-Genoud 2011; Spencer 2012). He worked closely with the American ethnomusicologist Natalie Curtis Burlin and with the American cultural anthropologist Franz Boas (Spencer 2012, 28). Kamba Simango was also close to W. E. B. Dubois and worked with him in the defence of black people (ibid., 32). He was the main source of inspiration of the Grémio Negrófilo de Manica e Sofala (later Núcleo Negrófilo de Manica e Sofala), an organisation which had as its main objective the dissemination of education through schools, conferences, meetings, and literary and religious propaganda (Protestant religion). With Sixpence Simango as its first leader (he was a follower of Kamba Simango), the organisation developed a political bent. In 1932, people from Machanga and Mambone were behind the Beira city demonstrations against the increase in tax rates by the Companhia de Moçambique – the majestic company ruling the territories of Manica and Sofala since 1890 – which was looking for ways to face the 1929 world economic crisis. In 1953, a mutiny took place in areas of Machanga and Mambone against the colonial administration and required military intervention. The Nucléo Negrófilo de Manica e Sofala was accused of being behind the mutiny, and, invoking national security, the Portuguese administration first banned the organisation and then dismantled it in 1956. Several of its members were deported, amongst them Uria Timóteo Simango, the father of Uria Simango, who subsequently became a very important figure in Frelimo (Cahen 1991; Chichava 2007, 232).[4]

Although ignored by most of the postcolonial historiography, some scholars consider these riots one of the most important forms of protonationalism in Mozambique (Andrade 1989) or a precocious form of African nationalism (Cahen 1991). According to Eduardo Mondlane (Wheeler 1969, 323), Kamba Simango had to go into exile first in Rhodesia and then in Ghana because of his activities, which the colonial authorities saw as politically dangerous. Others sources (Morier-Genoud 2011) suggest however that Kamba Simango left Mozambique for different reasons: (a) the existence of numerous barriers imposed by the Portuguese administration to prevent the growth of Protestantism in Mozambique and (b) his private life, which led to his eventual dismissal from the mission. Regarding this last issue, Simango seems to have had an extramarital affair with the wife of a fellow white missionary (Spencer 2012, 34).[5]

One needs to stress here that the Mozambican northern and central elites consider Kamba Simango as one of the main Mozambican heroes against Portuguese colonialism. The fact that Kamba Simango was never considered a national hero by the Mozambican state is seen as an act of ethnic discrimination (Adelino 2009). For those elites, another fact that shows discrimination is the nonconsideration of Kamba Simango as the first Mozambican black intellectual, before Frelimo's first leader, Eduardo Mondlane.[6] Ironically, although Kamba Simango was underplayed in the official historiography after Mozambique's independence, Mondlane himself considered Kamba one of the first Mozambican intellectuals to contribute to nationalism (Wheeler 1969, 323).

The only visible action taken by the postcolonial authorities to give some importance to Kamba Simango was the naming of a small street after him in the city of Maputo in 2009. This was not an isolated action, and it must be seen in the context of Frelimo's vast campaign under the presidency of Armando Guebuza to remember some people, mainly from the north and centre, who contributed to the struggle against Portuguese colonialism.

In addition to Kamba Simango, Faustino Vanombe and Kibiriti Diwane[7] also had streets named for them in Maputo. It is important to stress that this campaign was also responsible for renaming some regions or places with local names (Guebuza 2009). These actions could be read as an effort by Frelimo to attract the sympathies of some politically marginalised groups.

Last but not least, it is important to say that amongst the leaders trained by the American missionaries was Uria Simango, the future vice president of Frelimo during the anticolonial struggle. Uria Simango was expelled from Frelimo in 1969 after accusation that he was behind the plot that led to the death of Eduardo Mondlane, the first president of Frelimo, on 3 February 1969. Before his expulsion, Uria Simango published a text in which he accused the southern leaders of Frelimo of ethnic discrimination against the northern and central Mozambicans. Thereafter, Uria Simango was considered a reactionary and a threat, and Frelimo arrested him (with other Frelimo dissidents) after independence and killed him somewhere in Niassa in the late 1970s.

Although the American Board Mission was intensively involved in social and cultural improvement of the local community, its activities have been neglected by the postcolonial historiography. The mission can be considered as a space of confrontation between the southern Frelimo elites and those from Manica and Sofala. In 2005, during its centenary celebration, the United Church of Christ in Mozambique immortalised Uria Simango, Kamba Simango, Tapera Nkomo, and other local figures who are considered heroes (Craveirinha 2005). One can easily understand Frelimo's silence regarding this church.

The Seventh-Day Adventist Church of Munguluni

Established in 1935 by American Presbyterians coming from the Malamulo mission in Malawi (the request to establish a mission station was submitted in 1931),[8] the Seventh-Day Adventist Church of Munguluni is considered the first station of the Adventists in Mozambique (Simoque 2011).

The contribution of the Mozambican Adventist to the struggle against Portuguese colonialism is a fact that must be considered, and it is important to note that the Munguluni Adventist mission had always had problems with the Portuguese authorities, having even been threatened with closure at some point.

The colonial authorities, worried about the influence of this church on Africans, took a series of measures in order to counter it. One of the most important measures was the establishment of the São Gabriel de Munhamade Catholic mission in 1956, which was situated 20 kilometers away from the Adventist church. Concomitantly the authorities refused to allow the expansion of the Adventist church to Molumbo, in Milange, in Zambézia.[9]

In 1967, the authorities arrested the traditional authority of the area, dismantled the Nangoma *regedoria* (chieftaincy) and distributed its population to others traditional authorities because it considered that the latter, under Adventist influence, housed and fed the Sonte Machado brothers (Santos Machado brothers) as well as other Frelimo activists. To further demonstrate their indignation, the colonial authorities called the heads of the Adventist Church to an urgent meeting in Lourenço Marques, the capital (present day Maputo) and told them that, if the population continued to support Frelimo's activities, the church would be closed.[10]

The Portuguese authorities' perception was right concerning certain important Adventists members; the Santos Machado brothers, Alberto Mutumula, Alves Dulaudilo, Ernesto Evangué, Castro Evangué, Abílio Tungululo were indeed among the Frelimo activists in the area.[11] Of these nationalist figures trained by the Adventist mission at Munguluni, the role of Abílio Tungululo, Alberto Mutumula, and Alves Dulaudilo must be highlighted.

A member of Frelimo, Abílio Tungululo helped the guerrilla movement come in contact with the population of Munguluni and its surroundings, and he took part in Frelimo's Second Congress in 1968 (Simoque 2011, 31). Considered one of the first Frelimo members from the Adventist community of Munguluni, Tungululo was much respected in his local community (ibid., 30–32). His allegiance to Frelimo was considered one of the biggest assets of the movement in the area during the liberation war.

Alberto Mutumula, a former Adventist teacher in Munguluni and one of Frelimo's main figures at the beginning of the liberation war, was the political representative of Frelimo for the Zambézia front. Like Tungululo, Mutumula was much respected in his community, and he contributed by recruiting a sizeable number of Zambézians for Frelimo (Chichava 2007, 297). It was Alberto Mutumula who led the attack on the administrative post of Tacuane on 25 October 1964, marking the beginning of Frelimo's anticolonial struggle in Zambézia (ibid.). Mutumula was killed in 1968 in unclear circumstances. Frelimo attributed his death to the União Nacional Africana da Rombézia (UNAR), a dissident and regionalist movement.[12] At independence, President Samora Machel accused some Zambézian militants of the death of Mutumula and added that it was one of the reasons for the failure of the anticolonial war in the region (Machel 1983, pp. 27–29; Chichava 2007, pp. 331–332).

Alves Dulaudilo, who was a former teacher in the Adventist school of Munguluni, replaced Mutumula after his death as the head of Frelimo's front in Zambézia. But, because of internal conflicts in Frelimo between Mozambicans from the south and north or centre, the failure in opening the Zambézia Liberation Front in 1964 (leading to the defection of many of its militants, particularly Zambézians), and the psychological actions of the Portuguese services, Dulaudilo surrendered to the Portuguese authorities in

1973. Again, the action of Dulaudilo was presented as creating an obstacle to Frelimo in Zambézia (Chichava 2007, p. 298).

It is important to note that, at the time of independence, the Adventists of Munguluni were subjected to reprisal, like other religious confessions, from the new Marxist-Leninist Frelimo government. Accused of not respecting Frelimo's policy, some of its local representatives were arrested, and its head, Henrique Berg, a Brazilian missionary, was expelled from the country (Simoque 2011, p. 29). Henrique Berg was replaced by Armando Pires, whose harassment by the Frelimo administration led him to resign from his post and leave the country. The years after independence proved to be hard times for the Adventist Church of Munguluni, which was additionally confronted with internal conflicts, most church members demanding the nomination of a Mozambican to head the church. This led, after the departure of Armando Pires, to the nomination of Abílio Tungululo as head of the Seventh–Day Adventists in Mozambique (ibid., pp. 30–31). Thus, Tungululo became the first African leader of the Adventist Church in Mozambique. He died in 1980 in Malawi, where he had been living because of Frelimo's negative approach to religion (ibid., 32).

The Evangelical Mission of Nauela

The Evangelical Mission of Nauela (today called the Evangelical Church of Christ in Mozambique) was founded by Scottish Presbyterians coming from Malawi in 1913 (Reformed Online, n.d.). According to Morier-Genoud (2000, 625), who considers the history of this Protestant mission to be complicated, the Evangelical Mission of Nauela was not strictly a church but a missionary station where different Protestants organisations worked – the mission was in the hands of the South African General Mission (SAGM) in 1939, for example, and in the hands of the Scandinavian Independent Baptist Union in 1960 (ibid.).

An important event in the history of this mission has to do with its closure by the Portuguese colonial authorities in 1959. In that year, a missionary preacher killed a child at the mission clinic, claiming to have power to raise him back from the dead (Foster 2009; Alberto 2011). The church was also accused of protecting a Mozambican man who had stolen a large sum of money from the government (Alberto 2011). Both incidents led to the closure of the station and the expulsion of its foreign missionaries.

As complicated as its history may be, the Evangelical Mission of Nauela contributed to knowledge of the local culture. In the 1930s, one of its pastors, John C. Procter, translated the Psalms and the New Testament into Lomwe, one of the main local languages (Reformed Online, n.d.). Equally important, the mission trained several Mozambicans who later became Frelimo leaders, including Lourenço Mutaca and Eduardo da Silva Nihia.

Eduardo Silva Nihia (who is not a Zambézian, coming as he does from Malema, a northern district of Nampula Province neighbouring Alto-Molocué) held various positions in Frelimo and is to this day one of its main historical figures. Nihia studied at Nauela's school, where he came in contact with Lourenço Mutaca (Intetepe 2008). Even though Nihia is not a Zambézian, it is important to cite his name because it shows that the influence of this church went beyond the province where it is located.

One of the most prominent Frelimo leaders who came out of that church and was from Zambézia is Lourenço Mutaca. A former interpreter in the colonial administration of Alto-Molocue, Zambézia, Mutaca left Mozambique before independence to pursue his studies in Portugal. He later joined Frelimo in Tanzania and rapidly became one of the few leaders in this movement from the north of Mozambique. He was responsible for the finances of the liberation movement and later its representative in Sweden. Despite leaving Frelimo in 1969 after the expulsion of Uria Simango, he reconciled with the movement at the time of independence and was given a second chance by Frelimo. He went on to become Mozambique's representative at the UN High Commissioner for Refugees (UNHCR). In 1992 he was found dead in mysterious circumstances in the streets of Addis Ababa, apparently gunned down by unidentified men (Ncomo 2004, 241). Some Zambézians believed Mutaca was killed by Frelimo's southern leaders, who never forgave him for his support of Uria Simango.[13] In fact, Mutaca was killed in the town of Gode, Ogaden (not Addis Ababa) by one of the armed groups creating unrest in some parts of Ethiopia in the 1990s (Hiltzik 1992). Before Mutaca's death, another UNHCR worker had been killed in Ethiopia (ibid.).

At independence, the Evangelical Mission of Nauela was among the religious organisations directly affected by the actions of the Frelimo government. According to Alberto (2011), in 1977 the church's properties were ransacked by the soldiers of the regime, and its buildings were nationalised, except for the main church, when the government intensified its antireligious policy.

All this does not mean that the only Zambézians who joined Frelimo during the colonial struggle were coming from the Protestant community or even that they were the majority. Rather it shows that Zambézian Protestantism (even if it was a minority religion) was also a vector of recruitment for nationalism in Mozambique, much like the Swiss mission in southern Mozambique, in another area of the country.

The invisibility of other Protestants groups in the postcolonial historiography

How do we explain the relative invisibility in the historiography of the majority of Protestant groups? Or, better, how do we explain the importance given to the Swiss mission when we know that other Protestant groups also contributed to the formation of political consciousness, at least in the north and centre of Mozambique?

Frelimo's hostility toward religious groups when it took power in 1975 is one of the main explanations. Accusing religious groups of collaboration with Portuguese authorities in exploiting and colonising Mozambicans, Frelimo conducted an aggressive anticlerical policy, particularly in relation to the Catholic Church (considered the Portuguese state's right hand during colonialism) and Islamic organisations. One of the first major actions taken by the new government after independence was related to religion: the nationalisation in July 1975 of all schools and health facilities belonging to religious institutions and private entities. Religious institutions were further forbidden to teach children, because their teaching was seen as undermining the official program. For Frelimo (which declared itself Marxist-Leninist in 1977 at its third congress), the metaphysical concept of religion came in conflict with its materialist conception of the world and its desire to build a socialist state and a 'new man' in Mozambique.[14] Religious teaching would only divert people from the 'correct line' of the party (ibid.). As a result, more than 600 missionaries left Mozambique in the first year of the revolution, between 1975 and 1976, either because they felt uncomfortable or because they were harassed or expelled by the government (CEM 1976, 7).

It is important to note that, at that time, Frelimo antireligious discourse did not distinguish between different religious confessions – it opposed all of them. It is only after the Catholic Pastoral Assembly of 1978, which the new party-state perceived as starting a form of Catholic resistance against Frelimo's policies, that Frelimo's discourse started to distinguish between faiths and attacked the Catholic Church in particular. After 1981, Frelimo began to try to mend its differences with faith organisations, and so it started to develop a discourse favourable to the Protestants, who were said to be different from the 'racists and colonialists Catholics.' It is this dynamic which explains the development of the historiography, its silences, and the argument that there is a 'Protestant specificity' in Mozambique (Morier-Genoud 1998, pp. 416–418). But, as I have shown, it is really only the Swiss mission among the Protestants confessions which was put forward by the party-state. Other currents of Protestantism, especially those that developed in the northern and central regions of the country, were never mentioned.

A second explanation for the silence in the historiography about Protestants who do not belong to the Swiss mission has to do with the historical preeminence of the Swiss mission over other Protestant missions, at least in terms of its visibility. This, in turn, has to do with the historical socioeconomic inequalities that favoured southern Mozambique, particularly, the capital, Maputo (called Lourenço Marques during the colonial period), over other regions (Chichava 2007). Those sociohistorical inequalities have their origins in the late 19th century, the introduction of colonial capitalism, and the formation of the modern state in

Mozambique. They were symbolised by the move of the capital from Ilha de Moçambique, in the north, to Lourenço Marques in the south, and they had to do with the transformation of the Mozambican economy into an 'economy of services' (linked by ports and railways to South Africa and Rhodesia). They explain the domination of the southern elite within Frelimo; it was under this economy of services that the southern region became the most important economic region of Mozambique (Cahen 1994, 242).

Another explanation advanced by Morier-Genoud (1998) is a conflict that shook Frelimo in the mid-1960s and led to the marginalisation of religions within Frelimo. In this conflict, the central and northern nationalist elites within Frelimo, the majority of whom had been trained in Catholic missions, accused the southern and mostly Protestants leaders of tribalism, marginalisation, and anticlericalism. During this conflict the first president of Frelimo, Eduardo Mondlane, was killed, and the vice-president, Uria Simango, and other figures, including the Catholic priest Mateus Gwenjere, were expelled.[15] The conflict was resolved in favour of the southern elite, through the expulsion of many people and the silencing of difficult topics such as race and religion. This crisis helps explain, first, the coming to power within Frelimo of a southern elite, and second, the latter's difficult relations with religion and its particular view about the Swiss mission, with which many leaders had ties (Morier-Genoud 1998).

Finally, one must note, to complete the picture, that the central and northern nationalist elite, who were trained by the Catholic Church, the American Board Mission, the Evangelical Mission of Nauela, and the Seventh-Day Adventist Church of Munguluni, were accused after the internal crisis of treason and expelled from Frelimo. Many northern and central nationalists also deserted the liberation front, claiming discrimination on the part of the new Frelimo leadership. To Frelimo leaders, such desertions reinforced their view and their argument that the failure of the anticolonial war in Zambézia had to do with the region's men – Zambézia was the only military fronts where Frelimo's struggle clearly failed. In a well-known meeting held in 1983 in Quelimane, Zambézia's capital, the first president of independent Mozambique, Samora Machel, declared that Frelimo's anticolonial war had been compromised in this region by of the desertion of 2,000 Zambézians who later joined the colonial rows (Machel 1983, pp. 27–29; Chichava 2007, pp. 301–302). But in reality the Zambézians were not the only ones to leave Frelimo during this period. Many other Mozambicans, mostly from the centre and north of the country, left the movement. The reasons advanced by Frelimo's ex-members from Zambézia are the same as the ones mentioned by the other Mozambicans from the north and centre, namely the tribalism on the part of (the southern-dominated) Frelimo liberation movement (Chichava 2007, 303).

The Swiss colonial bourgeoisie: colonialism and capitalism

If the Swiss missionaries were not unique in relation to colonialism and African nationalism, neither were they more generally different from other settlers in relation to capitalism and colonial exploitation. Indeed the Swiss participated in the colonial enterprise in many regions of what constitutes today's Mozambique. To analyse this in detail, I will look in this section at the Swiss relation to colonial capitalism in the province of Zambézia. Among the biggest Swiss companies in that region, one finds the Boror Company, created in 1895 by Joseph Émile Stucky de Quay, and the Madal Company, created in 1903 by Gustave Bovay, both of which became major companies in colonial Mozambique (Vail and White 1980). Swiss individuals worked in other colonial companies too, including the Sena Sugar Estates, the Zambézia Company, and the Empresa Agrícola de Lugela (later Namagoa Plantations), where they often occupied positions of responsibility. As Adolphe Linder reported (2001, 24), the Swiss were considered good managers. In this section, we will focus specifically on the Boror Company and the Empresa Agrícola de Lugela.

Stucky de Quay and the conquest and exploitation of Africans

At the end of the 19th century, the political situation in northern Zambézia, where the 'brutal' Lomués lived, was not considered good for Portugal. While Portugal effectively dominated southern Zambézia, populated by the 'docile' Chuabos, the Lomué regions remained under the control of local chiefs who strongly rejected Portugal's authority.[16]

After 1885, Portugal launched a vast program to dominate and control such regions. Lacking the necessary capital and military power, Portugal relied on foreign companies to accomplish its mission, and so it rented huge tracks of the colony to majestic companies. These companies were expected to help pacify the rebels hostile to the new 'civilisation.' The Boror Company, created by the Swiss Joseph Émile Stucky de Quay in partnership with two other associates (Eigenman and Pereira, Swiss and Portuguese businessmen, respectively), took on this mission in 1895 (Cardoso 1943, 99, Vail and White 1980, pp. 117-120).

Initially, the company acquired concessions in the Boror and Tirre *prazos* belonging to the Eigenman, Pereira, and Stucky firm. It later acquired concessions from the Nameduro *prazo* of Amaral and Company and the Licungo and Macuse *prazos* that had belonged to Pedro Campos Valdez, a Portuguese entrepreneur. The activities it intended to develop included the production of coffee, sisal, coconut, sugar, and livestock, though only the cultures of coconuts and sisal became successful (Stucky de Quay 1928, 1943).

Like other colonial companies, the Boror Company was at its beginning only interested in *mussoco* collection (the indigenous tax). This situation led to several revolts in Zambézia, such as the 1893 uprising, when peasants in the Boror *prazo* attacked the company's tax collectors (Vail and White 1980, pp. 59–60; Pélissier 1988, pp. 356–357). In 1900, when the Boror Company began its vast plantation program, there was strong resistance on the part of natives.

The Boror Company was considered by the Portuguese as one of the most innovative companies and one that contributed most to the advancement of colonisation. For this reason, Prince Dom Luis Felipe knighted its founder, Joseph Émile in 1907, handing him the title of count in person during a visit to Quelimane in 1908 (Cardoso 1943, p. 101; Linder 2001, p. 41).

Georges Stucky, Joseph's younger brother and a partner in the company, also played a key role in extending Portuguese colonial authority over the Zambézia territory. Georges, with the participation of another Swiss (Victor Linder, who also received the Military Order of Christ and Portuguese nationality for his loyalty to the Portuguese authorities) led several military expeditions against the Maganjas and the Yao population of Niassa under the leadership of the Mataca chief, and they successfully defeated one of the most powerful chiefs of the Alto-Boror region, Chief Congone, who had caused many problems for the Portuguese authorities in the past.[17] George Stucky also participated in the campaign against one of the fiercest kingdoms in colonial central Mozambique, namely Barué, in 1902. As a reward for his loyal services to the empire, Georges Stucky was given one of the highest Portuguese rewards: the Knight of Christ medal (Cardoso 1943, 101; Linder 2001, 49).

The Swiss Boror Company was known for the abuses it committed against its African employees. It was amongst the companies accused in 1908 of not only not meeting the agricultural targets set by Portuguese law but also living off *mussoco* (customary tribute), making a fortune on the back of the indigenous population, without producing much.[18] This company was further accused of acting like a feudal lord; the imposition of too much hard labour in exchange for poor salaries caused huge migrations to Nyasaland and Rhodesia as people fled these terrible conditions (ibid.).

Despite (and thanks to) all these aspects, the Boror Company became one of the biggest companies of Mozambique. By the 1920s it had the world's largest coconut plantation in the world and was the biggest employer of Zambézia after the Sena Sugar Estates (Vail and White 1980, 117).[19]

In 1942, the Boror Company was still paying the same salaries as at the time of the *prazos*. With the natives unable to pay their taxes and deal with their family expenses, the Portuguese authorities urged the company to change its behaviour (Silva 1942). In spite of this urging from the government, the company, one of the most prosperous in Mozambique, did not change its policy. In 1964, a group of students from the Swiss Institut de Hautes Études

Internationales in Geneva found that the Boror Company, among all those companies visited in Angola and Mozambique, paid the lowest wages and gave no alimentation or clothes to its employees.[20]

It is no surprise that after the Lusaka Agreement between Frelimo and the Portuguese government in 1974 (an agreement which marked the end of the colonial war and the beginning of the Mozambique independence), the Boror Company was attacked by the local population, which demanded the restitution of land which had been expropriated from them years earlier (*Tempo* 1974).

In sum, like many other colonial companies, the Boror Company produced its wealth by exploiting the African population of Mozambique without investing much in return in the development of the colony. Unsurprisingly, the company went bankrupt shortly after the independence.

René Vuilleumier at Empresa Agrícola do Lugela

The Empresa Agrícola do Lugela was created in 1905, after the leasing of three *prazos* from Companhia da Zambezia by three men, namely Francisco Mantero (a big owner of cacao plantations in São Tomé), Carlos Masetti (a former agent of Companhia da Zambezia), and Pedro Gusmão (a former officer of the Portuguese marines). At first, the objective of Mantero was to provide its cacao plantations in São Tomé with Mozambican labour (Vail and White 1980, 167). In 1915, however, the company pioneered the cultivation and production of tea in colonial Mozambique. Tea production rapidly became the most successful product cultivated in Zambézia – the company's best-known brand was Chá Lugela. Aside from tea, the Empresa Agrícola do Lugela produced sisal.

Although the Empresa Agrícola do Lugela was not a Swiss company, its main shareholder was a Swiss man named René Vuilleumier – as mentioned earlier, the Swiss had the reputation of being excellent managers. Vuilleumier ran the company with an iron fist, from its creation until 1931, when he died in a car crash.[21] While the company was very successful, it was also one of the most feared by the local African population in the area – forced labour leading to population flight to Nyasaland. The situation was such that the Portuguese administration launched an official investigation in 1921 as it feared for the empire's stability.[22]

The resulting report found René Vuilleumier a 'criminal and colonial despot' and described the Lugela Company as a 'state within a state.' Vuilleumier was accused of committing grave abuses against the people of the Lugela and Lomué *prazos*. He was said to have forbidden indigenous people from selling their local produce outside of the *prazos*, to have forced those same people to sell their produce only to the Empresa Agrícola do Lugela, and to have demanded that they buy goods from this company only. People were also prohibited from leaving the *prazos*, or else they would face corporal punishment. The traditional Macua-Lomué chiefs, known as *muenes*, had orders in relation to the movement of population; should they not prevent people from leaving, the *mussoco* tax would be levied on them, and they would be beaten. Vuilleumier was also accused of sexually abusing local girls and forcing pregnant women to perform hard labour. Finally, he was accused of mistreating his workers and not giving them enough nourishment; they were allowed only one kilo of flour without curry and some salt every day.[23]

The brutality which Vuilleumier exercised against the people not only led many to flee abroad, they also allied themselves with the Germans when they invaded Zambézia in 1918. As a result, there was a greater loss of lives on the Portuguese side. Vuilleumier himself was hurt when commanding a group of African soldiers, the Sepoys, in defence of Portuguese sovereignty (Pélissier 1988, pp. 425–428; Linder 2001, p. 57). The people of the Lugela *prazo*, on their side, particularly in the Mutumula *muene* area, took advantage of the situation to loot and burn the Lugela Company's buildings at Bas-Lugela. Following these acts, Vuilleumier gave orders for many indigenous people to be arrested; those arrested were mistreated, some even killed, for example, the *samaçoas* (auxiliaries of traditional chiefs) of Murapa, Mahala and Vingoe (with his two wives) from the Lugela *prazo*, and Chief Ecaia and his son Mugabeque from the Lomué *prazo*. The land and huts of Chief Mualija and his people were also looted and burned by the company.[24]

Interestingly, it was in this area of Zambézia, particularly the area of the Mutumula *regulo*, that Frelimo was to find strong support in 1964 when it launched its liberation war against Portuguese colonialism. Like Alberto Mutumula, most of the Zambézian militants of Frelimo were from this region, which had also been influenced by the Seventh-day Adventist Church of Munguluni.

Conclusion

This chapter has looked at the Swiss relations to nationalism, capitalism, and colonialism by studying the Swiss in the province of Zambézia and comparing the Swiss mission activities in the south to those of Protestant churches in the centre and north. What the investigation revealed is that it is not possible to consider the Swiss community as a homogeneous entity or take the Swiss mission as the representative of all Swiss or all Protestants missionaries in Mozambique. It also revealed the manner in which Protestant institutions not based in the south of Mozambique contributed to the knowledge of local cultures, to the training of Africans in their church, and to the emergence of a small elite which went on to contest colonialism. The chapter gave also some explanations for the marginalisation of Protestantism (and other faiths) in Mozambique after independence.

The key factors explaining the marginalisation of religion after 1975 and the development of a discourse holding the Swiss mission as different in Mozambique can be summarised in the following way: (a) the implantation of the Swiss church in the south of Mozambique, which became the most important economic region of the country; (b) the internal conflicts within Frelimo between a southern elite, predominantly trained by the Swiss mission, while elites in the centre and north were trained in Catholic or other Protestant missions; (c) the attempt by Frelimo after 1981 to reverse its antireligious image while still trying to keep the Catholic Church under control.

Overall, there is no question that the Swiss Protestant missionaries were influential in creating an African elite in the south of Mozambique that played an important role in Mozambican nationalism and the liberation struggle. But it is equally true that other churches had a similar role and that the Swiss also played a role in the consolidation of the Portuguese Empire via their military and economic activities. While not exhaustive, the example of the province of Zambézia is sufficient to make the point.

Finally, we should note that the rhetoric consisting of painting the Swiss missionaries as different from the others and the Swiss as all pro-African if not pro-African nationalism is little more than the discourse of an African elite that was a product of these very missionaries and that aimed at consolidating its identity and reinforcing its hegemony. As I tried to show in this chapter, this discourse reflects a particular reality and particular interests and not the historical truth, nor the reality of the whole of Mozambique.

Notes

1. Frelimo's first president.
2. Mozambique's president.
3. A former prime minister.
4. A. Ivens-Ferraz de Freitas, Assunto: 'Distrito de Manica e Sofala. Subversão,' Informação n° 45/965, 4 November 1965, Lourenço Marques, Arquivo Histórico Ultramarino, Gabinete do Ministro, Gabinete dos Negócios Políticos/Situação subversiva em Moçambique, SR36, Pasta 3.
5. Morier-Genoud, pers. comm., June 2011.
6. Mondlane, who got his PhD in the United States, is often considered by local authorities to be the first black Mozambican intellectual, a fact which is strongly contested by the centre and northern elite.
7. Both linked to the Mueda massacre. See Cahen (1999).
8. For more information on the history of this mission, see Machado 1964.
9. F. N. Teixeira, 'Assunto: Relatório do Prelado de 1956,' Relatório dos Prelados (1947–1962), Maço 37, Processo no 55, I.3, Diocese de Quelimane, Quelimane, 8 March 1957, in Arquivo Histórico Ultramarino/Ministério do Ultramar/Direcção

Geral do Ensino; F. N. Teixeira, 'Assunto: Relatório do Prelado de 1958,' Relatório dos Prelados (1947–1962), Maço 37, Processo no 55, 1.3, Diocese de Quelimane, Quelimane, 8 March 1959, in Arquivo Histórico Ultramarino/Ministério do Ultramar/Direcção Geral do Ensino.
10. A. Ivens-Ferraz de Freitas, 'Assunto: Subversivo. Circunscrição do Lugela sede e seus Postos de Munhamade e Tacuane,' Informação n° 82/1964, período de 14 de Março 1963 a 20 de Fevereiro de 1965, Lourenço Marques, 5 November 1964, 1965, in Arquivo Histórico Ultramarino/Ministério do Ultramar/Gabinete do Ministro /Gabinete dos Negócios Políticos/SCCIM/Incidentes em Moçambique, SR053, Pasta 1.
11. Ibid.
12. UNAR was a movement formed in 1968 by Frelimo and Unami (União Nacional de Moçambique Independente) dissidents who claimed that southern leaders discriminated against Frelimo members from the north and centre. Unami was an old and small Zambézian group. UNAR required the liberation of the area between the Rovuma and Zambeze rivers, making the 'Rombézia' embrace five provinces (Cabo Delgado, Nampula, Niassa, Tete, and Zambézia).
13. C. Meragi, interviewed by Chichava, Quelimane, 2005.
14. Ministério do Interior, *I seminário nacional sobre questões das actividades associativas e religiosas*, Maputo, Arquivo do Governo da Zambézia, 4 July 1980.
15. Mateus Gwenjere, a Catholic priest from Manica and Sofala district had joined Frelimo in Tanzania in mid-1967, bringing with him a number of students from his mission station, after sending many more in previous years.
16. Unlike the southern part of Zambézia, which was under Portuguese authority since the 16th century under the *prazos* system, the northern Zambézia region was inhabited by the Lomué people, who resisted strongly the Portuguese and were the last ones in this area conquered by the Portuguese at the beginning of the 20th century. The *prazos* were concessions of land. Considered as backward and an obstacle to the development of the colony, they were replaced by capitalists companies. To learn more about *prazos*, see Isaacman (1972), Newitt (1973), Vail and White (1980).
17. To learn more about these two military expeditions, see Stucky de Quay (1940, 1944).
18. A. A. de Piedade, *Relatório do inquérito administrativo aos prazos arrendados à Empresa Agricola do Lugela*, Arquivo Histórico de Moçambique/Direcção dos Serviços Indígenas, Tete, 1921, Caixa 140.
19. Launched by a British citizen, John Peter Hornung, in 1890, Sena Sugar States was considered the most important company of Moçambique. See Vail and White (1980) and Pélissier (1988).
20. P. F. Pinto, 'Aspectos negativos da vista realizada recentemente a Moçambique com um grupo de estudantes do Instituto de Altos Estudos Internacionais de Genève,' Apontamentos Secretos, Lisbon, 26 October 1964, Arquivo Histórico Ultramarino, Caixa 6.
21. Two years after Vuilleumier's death, the Empresa Agrícola do Lugela was in dire financial straits, and it was bought by the Sena Sugar States.
22. A. A. de Piedade, *Relatório do inquérito administrativo aos prazos arrendados à Empresa Agricola do Lugela*, Arquivo Histórico de Moçambique/Direcção dos Serviços Indígenas, Tete, 1921, Caixa 140.
23. Ibid.
24. Ibid.

References

Adelino, T. (2009), 'Porquê os cidadãos do norte e centro são reaccionários e os do sul revolucionários?' *Canal de Moçambique*, 29 July.
Alberto, V. (2011), 'Working Hard' (accessed 21 July 2011), http://gatorinmozambique. blogspot.com /2011/04/working-hard-pastor-vicente.html.
Andrade, M. Pinto de (1989), 'Proto-nacionalismo em Moçambique: Um estudo de caso: Kamba Simango (c. 1890–1967),' *Arquivo* 6, pp. 127–148.
Butselaar, J. V. (1999), 'La culture des "gens de la prière": La vie d'une communauté protestante au Mozambique à la fin du xixe siècle: Dynamiques religieuses en lusophonie,' *Lusotopie* 6, pp. 439–450.
Cahen, M. (1991), 'Les mutineries de la Machanga et de Mambone (1953): Conflits sociaux, activisme associatif et tension religieuse dans la partie orientale de la "zone vandau"' (unpublished).
Cahen, M. (1994), 'Mozambique. Histoire géopolitique d'un pays sans nation,' *Lusotopie* 1, nos. 1–2, pp. 213–266.
Cahen, M. (1999), 'The Mueda Case and Maconde Political Ethnicity: Some Notes on a Work in Progress,' *Africana Studia* 2, pp. 29–46.
Cardoso, J. (1943), 'Companhia do Boror- Breve resenha da sua acção na ocupação e na exploração económica da Zambézia,' *Moçambique, Documentário Trimestral* 9, no. 35, pp. 91–111.
Chichava, S. (2007), '"Le vieux Mozambique". Étude sur l'identité politique de la Zambezie.' PhD thesis, University of Bordeaux, Bordeaux.
Conferência Episcopal de Moçambique (CEM) (1976), *Carta Pastoral do episcopado de Moçambique. Viver a fé no Moçambique de hoje*. Maputo.
Craveirinha, J. (2005), 'Uria Simango e companhia imortalizados na Beira,' *Zambeze*, 15 July.
Curtis Burlin, N. C. (1920), *Songs and Thales from the Dark Continent, Recorded from the Singing and the Sayings of C. Kamba Simango and Madikane Cele*. G. Schirmer, New York and Boston.
Foster, S. T. (2009), *Campos, Martinho Waphalac, 1925 to 1990. Igreja União Baptista (Union Baptist Church) Mozambique* (accessed 21 July 2011), http://www.dacb.org /stories/aa-print-stories/mozambique/ campos-martinho.html.
Guebuza, A. (2009), *Nova toponímia. Uma questão de auto-estima, identidade cultural e história* (accessed 9 August 2011), http://armandoguebuza.blogspot.com/2009/11 /toponimia-uma-questao-de-auto-estima.html.
Harries, P. (1989), 'Exclusion, Classification and Internal Colonialism: The Emergence of Ethnicity among the Tsonga Speakers of South Africa,' in L. Vail (ed.), *The Creation of Tribalism in Southern Africa*. James Currey, London; University of California Press, Berkeley, pp. 82–117.
Harries, (1994), *Work, Culture, and Identity. Migrant Laborers in Mozambique and South Africa, c. 1860–1910*. Heinemann, Portsmouth, NH; James Currey, London.
Hiltzik, M. A. (1992), 'Ethiopia Fears New Civil War, Loss of Its Aid,' *Los Angeles Times* (accessed 28 May 2011), http://articles.latimes.com/1992-04-15/news /mn-144_1_democratic-front/3
Intetepe, M. A. (2008), *Eduardo Silva Nihia – Patrono da Escola Secundária de Malema*. (accessed 22 July 2011), http://malemataus.blogspot.com/2010_08_01_archive. html
Isaacman, A. (1972), *Mozambique: The Africanization of a European Institution; The Zambesi Prazos, 1750–1902*, University of Wisconsin Press, Madison.

Linder, A. (2001), *Os suíços em Moçambique*. Arquivo Histórico de Moçambique, Maputo.
Macamo, E. (1998), 'A influência da religião na formação de identidades sociais,' in C. Serra (ed.), *Identidade, Moçambicanidade, Mocambicanização*. Livraria Universitária, Maputo, pp. 35–69.
Machel, S. (1983), *A nossa força está na unidade. Intervenção do presidente Samora Machel no comício realizado em Quelimane em 19 de Junho de 1983 para apresentação do novo dirigente da Província da Zambézia*. Instituto Nacional do Livro e do Disco, Maputo.
Newitt, M. (1973), *Portuguese Settlement on the Zambesi: Exploration, Land Tenure, and Colonial Rule in East Africa*. Longman, London.
Monnier, N. (1995), 'Stratégie missionnaire et tactiques d'appropriation indigènes: La Mission Romande au Mozambique 1888–1896,' *Le Fait Missionnaire* 1, Lausanne, p. 85.
Morier-Genoud, E. (1998), 'Y-a-t-il une spécificité protestante au Mozambique? Discours du pouvoir postcolonial et histoire des Églises chrétiennes,' *Lusotopie* 5, pp. 407–420.
Morier-Genoud, E. (2000), 'Archives, historiographie et Églises évangéliques au Mozambique,' *Lusotopie* 7, pp. 621–630.
Morier-Genoud, E. (2011), 'Columbus Kamba Simango,' *Dictionary of African Biography*. Oxford University Press, Oxford.
Ncomo, B. L. (2004), *Moçambique – Uria Simango – Um Homem, uma causa*. Nova África, Maputo.
Ngoenha, S. (1999), 'Os missionários suíços face ao nacionalismo moçambicano. Entre a tsonganidade e a moçambicanidade', *Lusotopie*, 6, pp. 425–436.
Neves, J. (1998), 'A American Board Mission e os desafios do protestantismo em Manica e Sofala (Moçambique), ca. 1900–1950,' *Lusotopie* 5, pp. 335–343.
Pélissier, R. (1988), *História de Moçambique. Formação e oposição 1854–1918*. Editorial Estampa, Lisbon.
Reformed Online (n.d.), 'Igreja Evangélica de Cristo em Moçambique' (accessed 21 July 2011), http://www.reformiert-online.net/adressen/detail.php?id=13228&lg=eng
Rennie, K. J. (1973), 'Christianity, Colonialism and the Origins of Nationalism among the Ndau of Southern Rhodesia, 1890–1935.' PhD thesis, Northwestern University, Evanston.
Silva, J. Castro e (1942), 'Nota nº 1:538/B/2/4 Ordem,' in Colónia de Moçambique, *Ordem da Província da Zambézia 1937–1943*. Quelimane.
Silva, T. Cruz e (2001) *Igrejas protestantes e consciência politica no sul de Moçambique (1930–1974)*. Promédia, Maputo.
Simoque, M. G. (2011), 'História da Igreja Adventista do 7º dia em Moçambique' (unpublished MS).
Spencer, L. P. (2012), *Toward an African Church in Mozambique: The Protestant Community in Manica and Sofala, 1892–1945*. Kachere Press, Zomba.
Stucky de Quay, G. (1928), *Vieux souvenirs de chasse au Zambèze, suivis d'une étude sur les Cafres de la région de Quelimane Zambézie. 1897–1915*. Aubanel Frères, Avignon.
Stucky de Quay, G. (1940), 'Diário de campanha da expedição contra o Mataca,' *Boletim Geral das Colónias* 175, pp. 35–70.
Stucky de Quay, G. (1943), *Compagnie du Boror 1898–1934*. Moullot, Marseille.
Stucky de Quay, G. (1944), 'Uma missão ao Lomué em 1902,' *Boletim Geral das Colónias* 224, pp. 30–59.

Tempo (1974), 'Democratas de Quelimane: Exploração latifundiária é responsável pelos distúrbios,' 25 August, pp. 32–36.

Vail, L., and White, L. (1980), *Capitalism and Colonialism in Mozambique. A study of Quelimane District*. Heinemann, London.

Wheeler, D. (1969), 'A Document for the History of African Nationalism: A Frelimo "White Paper" by Dr. Eduardo C. Mondlane (1920–1969),' *African Historical Studies* 2, no. 2, pp. 319–333.

7
The Ismailis of Mozambique: History of a Twofold Migration (late 19th century–1975)

Nicole Khouri and Joana Pereira Leite

The Ismaili community, which arrived in Mozambique between 1890 and 1920, is part of the history of the long presence of Indians in Mozambique and East Africa (Khouri and Leite 2008) but nonetheless presents distinctive features. On the one hand, the Ismailis arrived at a crucial period of Portuguese colonialism, namely that of the effective occupation of the territory. On the other hand, practically the entire community left Mozambique to settle in Portugal between 1973 and 1976 following a decision taken in 1972. The aim of this article is to analyse both the arrival and the departure of the Ismailis but with greater emphasis on their departure as it is the least well known and most controversial aspect.

For reasons specific to the history of the Portuguese Empire, Indians started settling in Mozambique as early as 1686.[1] They were either Portuguese Indians from the Portuguese territories along the west coast of India (Goa, Damão, and Diu) or British Indians, including the Ismailis, from Gujarat, a territory which from the mid-19th century was under British domination. The Ismailism practiced by the followers of Aga Khan is a branch of Shi'ism, the first roots of which were planted in Persia. The Ismailis discussed in this article, the Khojas, all come from the province of Gujarat, in India. They left initially for reasons related to the social and economic situation of India after consecutive years of drought and famine and also because they were hard hit by the consequences of the restructuring of land ownership under British colonisation, which transformed Gujarat into one vast cotton field, the industrialisation of which was managed exclusively in Great Britain. That change affected all classes, castes, and professions, including landowners, farmers, tax collectors, craftsmen, and shopkeepers. Subsequently, religious dissidences within the Ismaili community itself drove others to leave (Hollister 1953; Masselos 1973).[2] The Indian Ismailis are Hindus who converted to Ismailism from the 14th century. Some belonged to the caste of the Lohana tradespeople; others were farmers or belonged to the small number of the urban poor who, following the rural exodus, came to swell the population of the towns of Gujarat and were given over to the lowly tasks of collecting cow dung and burying corpses. Encouraged by their leader, Aga Khan, to emigrate to the East African coast, they went to territories which were under British, German, Portuguese, or French colonisation.

From Gujarat to Mozambique

Initially, only a handful of families were tradespeople, the vast majority knowing nothing of the world of trade and its culture. For the first generation of Ismaili migrants in Mozambique, however, trade appeared to be the only accessible professional niche. The Ismailis generally arrived with call letters, *cartas de chamada*, a kind of promise of employment written by those who had already settled to those seeking to emigrate, guaranteeing them work and accommodation. That requirement on the Portuguese side was even greater with the British, who kept tight control over emigration from India to prevent Indians from settling clandestinely in their colonies in eastern and southern Africa. That did not stop stowaways on ships and cargo boats from jumping into the water upon arrival in Delagoa Bay (Lourenço Marques bay), often at the risk of their lives, to swim to shore, where another Indian would be waiting to collect them and take them to their future employer.[3]

Settlement in Mozambique[4]

Whilst the pioneers started arriving around 1890, the greatest number of immigrants arrived between 1910 and 1920. It can be said that by 1930 immigration had stabilised and, according to those interviewed,[5] by 1960 they totalled nearly 1,000 people in the north and close to 500 people in the south of the colony. In the north of Mozambique, they settled in the district of Moçambique[6] (in coastal towns such as Ilha de Moçambique, Mossuril, Angoche, Nacala-a-Velha, and further inland, in places such as Nampula) or in the towns and villages along the railway line connecting Nacala to Nampula and the province of Niassa (as from the 1950s). Settlement in the south of the colony (provinces south of the Save) focused essentially on Inhambane and its hinterland, the capital Lourenço Marques, and various localities in the district of the same name.

The two sections of the community, in the north and in the south, were very different and had little contact with each other because of the distance between them and the scarcity of means of transport. The more 'modern' society in the south was given over to the South African economy of mining and services which had led to the expansion of an urban infrastructure and communication lines between the capital and Pretoria. In the capital, relations between the various groups making up the colonial society were extremely racially oriented, probably owing to the influence of neighbouring South Africa but also because it was a recent colonial settlement which had not experienced the phenomenon of the old creolised communities. The Ismaili community suffered from such racism, although it also inflicted it in turn upon the African population. Throughout its life in Lourenço Marques, that part of the community was more hardened and more pugnacious than the community which had settled in the north, where, given the extreme difficulty experienced by the colonial administration in enforcing law and order and where the action of the Catholic missions came up against the influence of Islam on the coast of the Macua region and with the Yaos of Niassa, matters were abandoned to regional administrators and governors who established special relationships with all the Indians, including the Ismailis. Paternalistic ties and patronage guaranteed their survival in a hostile environment in exchange for a certain complicity in business matters. Such instrumentalisation of relationships did not prevent ties of friendship and especially a high level of curiosity on the part of Portuguese officials for the specific culture of the Ismailis, who, moreover, saw themselves as heirs to a cultured tradition.

The first generation born in Mozambique

The first generation of Ismailis born in Mozambique extended the trade opportunities built by their parents. One of the keys to their success lay in the fact that they were bound together by very precise ties, whether in the retail, wholesale, or import and export trade, on a par with other established Indian Hindu and Muslim Sunni communities. The business network operated in the following manner: in the retail stores (*cantinas*), generally run by the latest arrivals and located in the far-flung towns and villages, the Ismailis bought oil and seed products (cashew nuts, copra, peanuts, sesame) from the Africans and sold them rice, cigarettes, and loincloths, to which other consumer goods were added over the years. Part of the products purchased found their way to the local market, the prosperity of which depended on the drive of the retail network, whilst another part went to the wholesale merchants (*armazenistas*) located in the intermediary and port towns. It was in the ports of Ilha de Moçambique and Angoche, in the north, and of Inhambane, in the south, that a few leading Ismaili families held the monopoly of the import/export trade (in particular, of cashew nuts) between Mozambique and the ports of the west coast of India (Leite 1995, 2000, 2001). Those families made the advance of goods to the managers of the *cantinas*. The type of contract that was established between the wholesale and retail traders guaranteed the supply of raw materials and implied immediate credit in exchange for future delivery and deferred payment. It was a time-honoured contractual form widely used in their home region of Gujarat which had lasted long after the arrival of the British and the Dutch.[7]

The end of the 1950s saw a very considerable concentration of capital in the hands of just a few families in the import/export business (two families in the south and two or three in the north), whilst the other members of the community benefited from an affluent lifestyle but without any great accumulation of wealth. Two major socioeconomic phenomena occurred in the 1960s. The first arrivals started to die off (life expectancy was relatively short at around 45–50 years), and their inheritances were passed on more according to the Hindu custom of joint possession of property than according to the division of assets under Muslim law. Anthropological factors were particularly important in the economic resurgence of the less well off who had suffered from the economic contingencies stemming from the crisis of 1929 and from the upset, not to say the halt, in business relations in the Indian Ocean during the Second World War. An uncle or a wealthier relative would intervene, seeking to expand his business and offering his material assistance and even his daughter in marriage to a future son-in-law, a trustworthy young man ready to take risks in occasionally inhospitable areas. This expansion of the trading firms also led to the appearance of management of the *cantinas* being entrusted to the Portuguese or Africans. It is important to stress the existence of commercial strategies based on matrimonial strategies in the handing over of capital to a son-in-law as an indirect form of the daughter's dowry. The new matrimonial tie thus ensured not only the enrichment of all those involved but above all the professional independence of an individual, provided he accepted a high level of involvement in the family and community ties.

Many members of the first generation born in Mozambique benefited from four years of primary school education. The eldest members of this generation were often sent to India to pursue their secondary and even higher education. Ismailis from this first generation continued to go to India to find their wives, although less often than the generation of their fathers. Others went to South Africa, where a sizeable community had already settled, while others found wives at home where they lived. According to the testimonies of their children (born between 1945 and 1955), whilst the eldest had rarely gone to school, they were nonetheless educated and had built up their reputation as exemplary figures of hard work and open-mindedness and with a capacity for mediation within the community and between the community and the outside world. They had a culture greater than that of the settlers, who were often ignorant and illiterate. In fact, the Ismailis spoke and wrote several languages, such as Gujarati and Kutchi (languages that they continued to use within the community) and frequently English. They rapidly learned Portuguese and the African language of the place where they settled. From their homeland, they continued to receive literature in Gujarati (newspapers, magazines, novels, poetry, and films), which they distributed to the members of the community.

Professional diversification in the 1950s, 1960s, and 1970s

On a par with other economic agents and with the Indians generally, the Ismailis benefited from the economic boom after the Second World War. Concomitant to the upswing in the export trade, especially of cashew nuts, the cornerstone of the accumulation of the wealth of the Indians, new trading opportunities appeared in the 1950s. From the mid-1950s, some ventured into livestock rearing and agribusiness (shelling of cashew nuts) for export or for the domestic market in industries based on oil seeds. Furthermore, the progressive urban and periurban expansion of the 1960s paved the way for shopkeepers keen to meet the demands of an increasingly large European and African clientele for consumer goods.

The 1960s were marked by a specific set of circumstances which resulted in new economic adjustments and a diversification of business. Faced with the fall (retrocession) of Goa in 1961 and the start of the wars for independence in Africa[8], a new colonial policy[9] organised the enlargement of the domestic market owing to the presence of the military and to the new influx of Portuguese immigrants from the mother country; in addition, the access to bank loans[10] encouraged industrialisation as a substitution for imports.[11] These changes enabled the Ismaili traders to set up businesses during the last years of colonisation in the production of consumer goods for the domestic market, an industrial sector requiring little capital (Leite 1989).

This idyllic vision of the golden era of trade and diversification in capital investment must be qualified by the fact that colonial society opted for national preference. The arrival of the 'petty whites' resulted in obstacles in obtaining the licenses required for the extension of the trade of the Indians and the permits for the investment of the capital already accumulated in the early days of industrialisation. In the colony, all the gestures of everyday life were marked by 'difference': official documents which had to be stamped 'Indian', exemption from military service until 1956 in exchange for the payment of a military tax, and common comments such as 'Indians are not called up for military service. Why were we not, if considered to be Portuguese?' There was also the real-life experience of racism aimed at the blacks:

> ...one day, when I was in Liupe, in the north, I heard someone screaming. I then saw four sepoys holding a naked man by all four limbs while a fifth one was beating him atrociously with a heavy pipe. That tortured me for a long time. I have relived that scene so often in my head...when we arrived in Lisbon, it was very different. I didn't feel the same things because here the people had also suffered a great deal under Salazar...that is the first time I've talked about those differences and about discrimination...you have to invent to survive.[12]

The Ismailis of Mozambique 173

During the 1960s, because of the strong community ties and their allegiance to Aga Khan, their chief with religious and temporal powers, the Ismaili families invested heavily in the education of their children.[13] They benefited from the new school system that had been set up, and from the end of the decade, their professional careers were successfully turned to banking, engineering, statistics, the civil services, social work, and so on.

The departure of the Ismailis from Mozambique – a problematic event[14]

The members of the Ismaili community, when questioned about their relationships with the various groups making up colonial society during the last decades of Portuguese colonisation, speak of their departure (spread over three years from 1973 to 1976) as a natural move which ended their two or three generations–old settlement in the colony. It remains very difficult for them to recognise that it was an organised community departure as if the attributes of the event referred to something forbidden or unspeakable to foreigners and, in this case, to researchers.

First of all, the mobilisation for a collective departure by the Ismaili community before 25 April 1974, proved to be extremely embarrassing for the Portuguese colonial regime, which did not yet believe that its end had come in Mozambique. Even if it was a question of moving from one part of the empire (Mozambique) to another (Portugal), it signalled the irreversibility of time and tolled the knell of colonial order. Might the Ismaili community have betrayed the colony's government by making such a move even before the fall of the colonial regime? Had not its leader, Sultan Mohamed Shah, Aga Khan III, assured the Salazar government of the ties of loyalty of his community with respect to Portuguese policy? [15]

Seen from the anticolonial viewpoint, was the collective departure not a betrayal of the African populations on whose land the community had prospered? Was it not also a betrayal of the white Mozambicans who remained after independence and thus made a different choice? It goes without saying that for the Frelimo party the departure clearly meant a betrayal of the ideals of the fight for independence.

Are we not faced here with a classic example of the construction of the figure of the foreigner taken in its representation by all the social groups and all the political forces which, in times of crisis, point an accusing finger at him and marginalise him? If one facet of the anthropological status of the foreigner refers to a dimension of potential betrayal in the way others see him, the other facet is that of the debt the foreigner owes to those who welcomed him.

Why, however, has there been no mention of betrayal with respect to the Sunni(te) Muslim Indians, other than the Ismailis, or to the Portuguese who left at the same time? Is it the specific feature of this collective, organised departure undertaken within a community reputed to be 'secret'[16] which makes a difference in the perception of the event, both for those outside and for its own members?

This article will not elucidate all the reasons for the taboo connected to this collective event. It nonetheless starts from the finding, when we pursued our discussions in Lisbon and in Maputo with members of the Ismaili community originally from Mozambique, that there is still a taboo thirty-five years after the event. It can be studied, firstly, starting from fragments of information from outside on the collective departure of the Ismailis from the Mozambique colony. We shall do so on the basis of rumours, of the sources of the DGS,[17] and of academic research. Secondly, the phenomenon of the departure of the Ismailis must be evaluated quantitatively according to the yardstick of the other departures from the colony from 1974 to 1975. Finally, for a better grasp of the breach of a secret over the years, we shall study the two extremes (what has been said and left unsaid about the collective, organised departure) between which those interviewed swung, namely the version they had experienced, which is covered by the secret, and the official version, aimed some twenty years later at revisiting the event and the history of the community for the benefit of the general public.

The interviews were conducted with the members of the community between 2005 and 2008 in Lisbon and Maputo. For all the accounts given by memory concerning the last two decades of the Portuguese colonisation (1955–1975), it was essential to situate what they said in an effort to revisit the events along two lines: that of an existential experience (their departure) and that of the discourse of the community (on the departure). Each line was further split as follows: the existential experience referred to a memory of the actual experience of life in Mozambique, which was not disconnected from the positive or negative connotation felt upon arrival and life in Portugal. The discourse of the community referred both to an order which circulated according to certain procedures within the community and to the much later interpretation of the event, aimed both at the outside world and at the Ismailis who interiorised it.

In the form of a conclusion, we shall highlight the specificity of the relationships between the individual or family departures, the departure of the community, and the question of the secret in that community.

Fragments of information on the event built from the outside

For the Sunni Indians from the colony,[18] as for the Hindu community, the order of departure for the Ismailis was given by their supreme leader, and some of the former even saw in that a form of protection from which they could not themselves benefit. Whilst they were without doubt an ethnic religious community, they did not have a leader who, in addition, was perceived as being anxious to ensure a better future for his followers. The sale of their property by the Ismailis, as a signal of a community about to leave and not as a series of individual decisions, was part of the rumours circulating in their society before April 1974.

As far as the political police were concerned, certain DGS sources explicitly refer to the preparations made by the Ismaili community for its departure; the regime faced that mobilisation with concern for its consequences and the possible destabilisation of the colonial society. An initial report, dated 6 July 1973,[19] states that 'Ali Khan (Ismaili prince living abroad) had sent instructions to the leaders of the Ismaili colony in Mozambique.' They included certain items of information, such as that the Ismailis of Mozambique should get ready to leave for new destinations (England, Venezuela, or Portugal) but Portugal was preferable as a destination for the transfer of capital. For that purpose, they were to sell all their property within the space of three years. The author of the report specified that a commission of Ismailis from Lourenço Marques had gone to the north of the colony in March 1973. Under the cover of spiritual meetings, the members of the commission passed on the message, following which many Ismailis sold property and businesses, after putting advertisements in the newspapers. Some went to Portugal, especially as pioneers were already there to set up business. The European friends of the Ismailis became increasingly worried and started returning to Portugal too.

Nevertheless, the police report only recommended supervision of the frontiers and of the drain of capital. On request from the governor-general, elements of the report were very rapidly verified by the DGS, which confirmed the financial mobilisation of the Ismailis (sale of various properties, clandestine passing of sums of money overseas, etc.) but was unable to refute or to confirm 'the sending of instructions or directives from Ismaili dignitaries living abroad.'[20] To date, the correctness of this police analysis has been difficult to establish insofar as it is not corroborated by any other official written source or from the community itself.[21]

After the archives became open to the public, this document scared the first person of confidence to whom we showed it. That person begged us not to mention it during the interviews as it was considered to be highly compromising. That led to the questions of the nature of the order (was it an injunction, a recommendation?) to leave the colony and how much the members of the community actually knew. What was the position of those in charge of disseminating the information? What information did they pass on to those around them? Were the people contacted sworn to secrecy? By what means was the order actually received?

These questions related to a sociology of secrecy within a community, which, as indicated above, had already turned away other researchers, do not invalidate the interest in more trivial questions and answers. Within the context of the colonial society and, above all, in wartime, the political police (which remained attentive to the mobilisation of the Ismailis up until July 1973)

> …had contacts with the leaders of the community, personal relationships of confidence or at the very least of mutual convenience. There is no doubt that the capacity of dissimulation triumphed over the laboured reasoning of the police. The DGS failed to clearly identify that the movements noticed were the beginning of the implementation of an irreversible plan for departure. (Melo 2008, p. 100)

Thirty-five years after this police report, António Melo's article (2008) constituted the first academic approach to this theme, based on an analysis of the Portuguese archives and with the enlightening input of reliable testimonies from members of the community living in Lisbon. Its reading by a few members of the community gave rise to some very different reactions. Some expressed a certain surprise with respect to the many elements exposed or revealed about the issues of the departure of the community and a curiosity concerning the documents and a desire to see the latter. Others were wary about the content of the article, which insinuated that the departure was collective and organised, and sought to rectify such a viewpoint, saying that the departure was no more than a recommendation from Aga Khan, an 'orientation' for his communities living in Africa. The decision to migrate was incumbent upon the families. Portugal as a destination was recommended because of the community's mastery of its language and culture. That became, moreover, the drift of the official discourse concerning the event from the 1990s. Nevertheless, even thirty-five years later, the event of the departure is still a source of upset for the members of the community who experienced it.

A living example of such unease occurred recently and, moreover, in Mozambique itself. At a press conference organised in 2007 in the Polana Hotel in Maputo on the occasion of the preparations for the imminent visit of Aga Khan to the country, a Mozambican journalist asked the following question: 'We know that practically all the Ismailis abandoned Mozambique at the time of independence. We are now seeing their massive return. Could you explain the reason for this change in decision?' The answer was: 'Chissano's sons studied in the schools of Aga Khan in Tanzania during the war of independence and one of his sons was given medical care in Aga Khan's hospital in Dar es Salaam.'

What that diplomatically correct reply implied was an element of continuity since 1974. To justify the return of the Ismailis to Mozambique after 1993,[22] another dimension was therefore indicated. For lack of being able to assert ideological proximity with the Frelimo party, proximity with the people holding political power was put forward to silence the impertinent journalist. What is new in this discourse is the invention of continuity in an independent Mozambique, a concept that the researchers could never have suspected before, since until the survey in 2008, they had only collated the accounts of the community living in Lisbon.

Whether in Portugal or in Mozambique, the issue of the collective departure of the community has proved to be the Gordian knot in all the accounts collated to expound a 'continuity' anchored in Portuguese or Mozambican history. Would it not be a better solution to put forward a 'noncontinuity,' positioning the issue of the departure as one link in a long chain of migrations?

Within the perspective of a return to Mozambique following a departure in a manner different from that of the other Indians, a distinction must be made between the individual returns and the drive for the settlement of Aga Khan's projects through the Aga Khan Development Network (AKDN). That is a difficult task because, just as the Ismailis returning individually from the early 1990s used their belonging to the community as leverage on which to base their projects, so those returning through the AKDN sought out the former to establish links with the population and those in power.

With the various rumours swirling around the departure of the Ismaili community as a collective, even organised move, the documents of the DGS and the work of researchers in social sciences have forced the Ismaili authorities to produce an intelligible interpretation of that crucial event taken in the new, postcolonial context. This new dimension in the official Ismaili reading now refers to an extremely important strategic reality insofar as Portugal was chosen at the strategic place for the AKDN projects for the whole of Africa and insofar as Africa was explicitly designated as a continent where it was once again possible and desirable to invest and prosper.

The quantitative evaluation of the departures of the Ismailis

According to the available data available in Melo's work (2008, p. 101), preparations for the departure began in December 1972, and the departure itself ended in December 1976. According to Melo, the departures concerned approximately 600 families, or 3,810 people. The majority of departures took place after June 1975 (3,000 people). Only 810 people had left before.

In the statistical processing of the *retornados*, or returnees (Esteves et al. 1991), the Indians of Mozambique (Avila and Alves 1993), including the Ismailis, were part of the flood (Franco 1991; Pires 2003) and were therefore counted as Portuguese.[23] In comparison with the massive exodus of the Portuguese colonists in 1975, that of the Ismailis is similar in proportion (3,000 of the 3,810 people according to the internal sources of the community) and covered the same period (from June 1975 to June 1976). It is hardly surprising that certain Ismailis talk of their leaving Mozambique as part of the general movement, thus closing the door on what they considered to be an intrusion by researchers into their privacy.

Whilst the parallelism is irrefutable in terms of proportions, it says nothing about the qualitative dimension specific to the community's departure. Three hundred and ten members, mobilised as from December 1972, left before 25 April 1974. It can be reasonably supposed that the period of the mass departures from June 1975 corresponded to the time required – roughly speaking a year – for the mobilisation of the entire community, for the sale and protection of property, for the settlement of the pioneer families in Portugal, and for the transfer of property by various means, even if the independence of Mozambique proclaimed on 25 June 1975, had without doubt an accelerating effect. That clearly indicates a collective and organised departure that no statistic can reveal. As Ali confided to us, '[we] had an initial orientation,' clearly implying that it came from Aga Khan.

Was His Highness advised?[24]

In our interviews between 2005 and 2008, the issue of the departure – whether described as personal, family, or collective – continued to preoccupy the members of the community. There were those who spoke of it as a personal or family departure, those who said it was an event related to the community as such, and finally, those for whom the departure of the community was also related to an injunction from Aga Khan. In all three cases, there was ample description of the difficulties associated with the intensification of the colonial wars, of the excellent awareness of the situations in central and eastern Africa following the declarations of independence (Africanisation of leaders in Kenya, nationalisation of the property of the Indians in Tanzania, expulsions from Uganda, economic and political difficulties in the Congo), of the chaos experienced in the district of Moçambique, of the violence of the ultras seeking to perpetuate the presence of the Portuguese colonists both in the north and in the south, and of the equally violent reaction of uncontrolled anticolonists – in short, all factors making up a set of circumstances lending legitimacy to the departure.

So be it. There are, however, two points that remain to be elucidated. Why did certain members of the community talk of a collective, organised departure in obedience to an injunction from superior, responsible bodies? Why does the secrecy, which is still present today, impose a form of silence on the members of the community when it is historically null and void?

All the accounts collated appear to be clearly structured, consciously or unconsciously, according to two divergent viewpoints but also according to a discourse always put forward by the supreme authorities of the community. The first viewpoint stems from the secret discourse addressed by the community leaders to their members in Mozambique from March 1973. The second stems from the new official discourse put forward in the 1990s in

Portugal,[25] aimed at providing a new interpretation of the event and of the history of the community for the general public.
These viewpoints can be illustrated by two interviews.

The departure was an order for the entire community that had to be persuaded and prepared

Ali[26] presents an account speaking as the living memory of his community, of which he considers himself to be the depositary. He was very close to the leaders who organised the departure from Mozambique and one of the first to scout for the settlement of his community in Lisbon.

> There was April 25 but our community had started leaving Mozambique long before that. Aga Khan recommended that Africa be forgotten. The question then arose – to go where? Neither India nor Pakistan, because they were under-developed countries, nor Brazil because that was a politically unstable country. That left Portugal which had advantages – we were familiar with the language and culture. [...] X paid a visit to Aga Khan and when he came back he passed on the advice first of all to the community Council in Lourenço Marques, and the message was subsequently disclosed to all the members of the community both in the south and in the north. We started talking about it and rumours rapidly spread outside of the community which is how the PIDE[27] had wind of the matter.... I must stress that there had been other presidents who passed on the advice but that never worked because nobody wanted to leave or nobody wanted to understand. Moreover, even that time round it was not easy to convince the families. So they reviewed the 600 families, one by one, I mean the heads of the families who represented the 3,000 members that made up the community at that time, and asked them to sell all their property. We all obeyed. Aga Khan spoke and we acted.[28]

The first part of this account deserves close attention. Recorded in 2005, it contrasts with another version given some years earlier by the same person.[29] According to the previous account, X did not 'pay a visit' to Aga Khan but was explicitly summoned by him. Was it a recommendation or an order? In all probability, Aga Khan had an overall plan for his African communities, and X no doubt also had his own idea.[30] Whilst it is true that the recommendation had already been given on several occasions, this time it took on the value of an injunction, and there is every reason to believe that the experience of Uganda in 1972 must have weighed heavily in the balance. The use of the expression 'they reviewed the 600 families' appears to refer to a tour of the community by the members of the council, whereas in the other version, it was X himself who went to see the families to convince them to sell up their property and leave. Are we faced with an account which is revisited over the years, moving from a personified presentation to an institutional affair incumbent upon the community council? It would be judicious to put that hypothesis up against the reaction of a member of the community who, when shown the document from the DGS, expressed his concern about the presence of names which could harm the relevant families. Who, however, would harm them, if not the other members of the community discovering facts hitherto kept secret from them?

When questioned about that document, Ali asserted that

> ties of friendship [existed with the leaders of the DGS], but nobody knew who was at the head of the PIDE [i.e., the DGS]. They would go together to the casino in Swaziland. One of the leaders of the PIDE asked X for an explanation on the rumours about the departure of the Ismailis. X replied that Aga Khan had advised the families living in the hinterland to go to Nampula, to Beira, to Lourenço Marques and to Portugal. But not all to Portugal. In fact, Aga Khan didn't say that but that's how X wriggled out of it!

Ali left Mozambique as a pioneer and scout to pave the way for the arrival of the others. He assumed both roles in Lisbon, operating out of a restaurant that he owned. He told the story of the history of his community to his Portuguese customers, the majority of them journalists. He carried out a kind of market survey and prospected for the imminent settlement of the Ismailis in the capital. He also acted as guarantor with owners for the rental of accommodation for the new arrivals. He enjoyed taking risks which enabled him to become self-sufficient and start new businesses. The Ismailis who came to settle from 1973, earlier than the others and thus not coming up against any clear competition, benefited from the professional niches opened up: '[W]e were given a very good reception.... Everything is better here than over there.'

Twenty five years later, however, the Ismailis went back to Mozambique:

> There are currently close on 300 Ismailis in Mozambique, 250 of whom arrived in the 1980s from the Indian sub-continent. No-one in the community remained after 1975.[31] Those who went to South Africa started coming back in 1986–87,[32] those who had settled in Lisbon were toing and froing as from 1998...I can't contemplate going back to earn money, that's not a sufficient reason.... As for the Aga Khan Foundation, it is investing in precise fields having studied the economic situation of the country and the needs of the populations.[33]

The departure was an orientation, everyone being responsible for making the right choice

The recommendation of Aga Khan, expressed by Kassam with a great deal of officialdom, aims first of all at silencing all the rumours, including the

The Ismailis of Mozambique 181

dubious archives on which academic research may be based, circulating on the supposedly collective and organised departure of the community, on the one hand, and on the distorted statement attributed to Aga Khan, on the other hand:

I don't know if the archives make any reference to that but people outside of the community are saying that we left because His Highness told us to leave. No, that does not correspond to the truth. When His Highness was approached,[34] at the time when the war was starting and becoming serious, he said to us: don't forget that Africa is a continent which will suffer from the transformations and that the African process is irreversible. I therefore advise you to take precautions in particular for your children in terms of education and university training. If you are obliged to leave, opt for a country where you will be able to be together, given that you are a small community. In a big country, you will be scattered. Consider the mother tongue, where you are, and which is Portuguese.... De facto, they all went to Portugal and then some to Canada or London.[35]

Thus, it would appear that the recommendation and lucid analysis of the leader had no coercive value. It was not a *farman* for his community. Moreover, Kassam himself states that the reasons for his departure in 1975–1976 had nothing to do with his community and stemmed from convenience for professional affairs. In a liberal and European context, it is therefore a question of avoiding painting the picture of blind obedience to the leader, as in a sect. The recommendation, as presented by Kassam, left everyone free to choose whether to leave or to stay according to his personal judgement enlightened by that of Aga Khan.

Finally, if there was no injunction to leave and the choice was dictated by a personal perception of the situation, that relieves the discourse of Aga Khan from the contradiction between his new measures of encouragement and action for a return to Africa in the early 1990s and the recommendation/order to leave given in 1972.

For a researcher, it is not so much the identification of the truthfulness of his word which matters as the way in which his followers perceived it, organised themselves (with an eye to a possible community sanction) and the effect this had on their lives. All this eventually positions Kassam's account, and for that matter all the accounts (cf. below), in a paradoxical tension: on the one hand, it refers to what was said and experienced at the time of the departure and, on the other hand, it adopts a new discourse, constructed over the last 15 years about the Mozambique to which they have returned as 'Portuguese born in Mozambique'.[36] Between these two moments in time, the community apparently simply migrated from one territory to another, following the course of processes which are reversible in time, whether it be the time of economic cycles or the time of generation-founded opportunities. According to that reading, the departure from Mozambique would have nothing to connect it with a particular issue attracting the attention of a researcher for whom there would be no point in digging into some secret or unspoken aspect. The departure would then be just part of a series of diaspora-like migrations, making it a banal everyday event.

Whilst Ali's account starts from the arrival in Portugal and is based on his experience in the peninsula, Kassam's account starts from the return to Mozambique. The redefinition of the departure for the community lies between two milestones formed by secrecy and linked to the issue not only of its departure but also of its return.

Those two very different accounts form the two explicit poles around which all the other accounts revolve. The first viewpoint remains hidden – deliberately or otherwise – a buried layer, the past knowledge and current expression of which depend on the place occupied by the faithful within the community.

The departures of the community and the issue of the secret

Why has the departure of the community as a whole and the way in which it was organised been considered a secret by those who were part of it? In 1973, the years of colonial warfare did not yet point to the end of the presence of the Portuguese colony in Mozambique, and the secrecy around the preparations could be temporarily justified by the need to ensure the essential safety of the community. That argument is perfectly well founded.

The DGS did not see the Ismailis as a secret society, the intrinsic feature of which would be to make itself invisible, but as relatively secretive where what was said about it outside called for verification. Two hypotheses to account for what got out can be put forward: either a leak, perhaps by one of the community who could not keep his or her mouth shut; or a more subtle relationship in the balance between the *visibility*, which was often even ostentatious and nurtured in its representations with all the political powers (a strategy found constantly and everywhere throughout the different colonised territories in Africa), and the sense of community which remained practically impenetrable for any outsider. The visibility would be all the greater when the *all in the family* had to be closely guarded. That is the more likely interpretation of the report of the DGS, which is based on the visibility for outsiders as opposed to the secrecy of what was happening on the inside.

It is therefore not so much a question of being able to hold one's tongue as the possible intelligence of having divulged information (the visible face) which definitely intrigued the colonial powers who sought to see the situation more clearly. The reply of X to the leader of the DGS, mentioned above, presupposes a community that was thoroughly versed in controlling everything that could be let out and that painstakingly arranged its words and actions intended to be made known to outsiders.

What took place between the visible and hidden faces of the community, as enacted by its leaders, is not, however, the same as what took place on the individual level. What did the risk of 'talking' hinge on at that level?

Practically all the people we interviewed spoke off the record. Social science researchers are familiar with such situations, which do not necessarily stem from a community-held secret but rather from situations stirred up by the telling of one's memories (resistance, aggressiveness, withholding of events, elements left unsaid, complicity, relief in talking, etc.). They are extraordinary situations with a complex interplay between the teller, the listener and the memory itself.

Finally, there are people who talked, spurred by another mechanism, such as the pleasure of admittance, which produces a feeling of power when it is let out, like the insistence of one of the members saying: 'I'm going to tell you what nobody in the community would ever tell you.' The secret, which puts the individual in an exceptional position when it is learned, also produces an exceptional feeling for the same individual when it is disclosed. There is a tension that is released at the time of the disclosure, a tension maintained over the years between the keeping and the telling of a secret.

A secret requires the ability to keep it. How can a moral solidarity be established between those who share that secret? Several methods can be deployed for the secret to remain unspoken with respect to outsiders: the strong or diffuse threat of punishment, and the learning by everyone of systematic silence. To that end, exercises in self-control (including meditation) and self-discipline are essential. As Simmel wrote, 'If you can succeed in remaining silent over the years, you are probably capable of resisting temptations other than gossiping' (1999, pp. 347–405, p. 383). That presupposes a community organised in line with such an objective in which newcomers are taken care of in an appropriate process of education and socialisation. Along their history, the Ismailis were constituted as small circles within wider circles (Sunni Islam and Shi'a Islam), and their existence in opposition could have been lastingly maintained only by processes of closure/protection. In the *farmans* on the secret of Sultan Mohamed Shah, Aga Khan III, concerning the modes of education within the Ismaili community,[37] silence is a virtue which encapsulates the faithful, convinced of belonging to a race of the chosen because they have with them Hazar Imam, the Living Imam of Time.

The Ismaili community is not a secret society even if it presents certain features of one. It has the capacity of accommodating adjustments, such as the issue of the departure, the secret of which in 1973 was able to become null and void in the mid 1990s. A revisiting of the events was then instigated with a shift in the story, a reconstruction of the meaning of the earlier events. The problem is no longer that of the capacity of keeping a secret but of persuading the faithful who had kept it that it is now better to get rid of it without actually disclosing it. How can they square that with the word of the Imam? How can they become convinced that what had been perceived as a *farman*[38] is (was) apparently no more than a simple recommendation? The figure of the Imam then becomes vital. It must be even more detached from human nature to give it its own aura, which is part of its divine nature and therefore imbued with foreknowledge in the conduct of his faithful. The institutions had to bear the historical weight of the avatars of the secrets.

Sociologically speaking, the pivotal position of the Imam's word is handled concretely by those within his closest inner circle. The extremely hierarchical nature of the community is based on circles of access to knowledge and decision making. It can be supposed that in crucial circumstances, such as those of Mozambique in 1973, the elite succeeded in handling the word of the Imam, stressing the force of a *farman* to ensure its impact upon the minds of the faithful. When the community of Lourenço Marques received the message in 1973, the faithful reported some hesitation as to the fidelity to the word of the Imam as brought by the leaders. Such hesitations were, however, rapidly dispelled.

One of the functions of a *farman* is based on the ambiguity, that is never dispelled, which refers both to a clear instruction and its coercive value, and to the reality of its much freer application (linked to the way it is disseminated and it is received among the faithful). In the example of the departure, that ambiguity impacted the crucial choice made by the faithful in two ways: on the one hand, their perception of the departure as a *farman* clashed with another, much older *farman*, which based their existence and prosperity in Africa on loyalty to the host country and its government; on the other hand, they were called upon to deny what they had experienced as a *farman* in order to lend legitimacy to a possible return to Africa.

The Ismaili community in Portugal, Khojas originally from Mozambique, now lives as an entrepreneurial diaspora integrated in globalisation. It nonetheless remains strongly attached to its religious dimension as an essential and a constituent part of its identity. It is in that context that its collective and organised departure from the colony of Mozambique lives on, thirty-five years later, as a significant fact that continues to resonate today.

Notes

1. According to recent historiography (in particular Antunes 1992), the creation of the Company of the Mahajans of Diu in 1686, to which the Portuguese government granted a monopoly over trade between the colonies of Mozambique and Diu, is considered as being the date of 'Banian settlement' in Mozambique.
2. From 1829, there were protest movements within the community. Some of the rich traders in the Bombay community refused to pay the amount of the tithe

demanded by the Imam, followed by a large number of believers who joined the ranks of the Twelver Shi'ites or the Sunnites. A series of dissident movements, excommunications, reintegrations, and normalisations followed in 1845, 1851, 1866, and 1908.
3. We present this data on the basis of a review of the existing historiography (archives, published documents, and books) and a comparison with verbal accounts from members of the Ismaili community in Lisbon and Maputo.
4. This first part of the article reprises, in a shorter form, a much more extensive study released in Portuguese as a working paper (Leite and Khouri 2011).
5. We have found no statistics.
6. To make the distinction between the colony (Mozambique) and the Island or District of Moçambique (former capital of the colony), we have kept the Portuguese spelling for the latter.
7. Goody (1996) tells of the system on which all cotton production relied in Gujarat in the 15th century, as told by many travellers in the 17th century. It was based on contracts implying immediate payments (advances in cash or in materials) from 'capitalists' and brokers to acquire commodities in exchange for future deliveries. These contracts, called *sillim* or *hundis*, bound the members of the same caste or of the same lineage on account of the great distances and large number of intermediaries.
8. 1961 in Angola, 1963 in Portuguese Guinea, and 1964 in Mozambique.
9. Decree-Law 44016 of 8 November 1961, introduced a policy for the integration of a Portuguese economic space, completed by Decree-Law 44652 of 27 October 1962, on economic growth for the overseas territories.
10. The establishment of the Commercial Bank dates back to the mid-1960s. On regulation of banking activities in the colonies, refer to Decree-Law 45296 of 8 October 1963, and on the regulation and application of foreign investments in the Portuguese space, to Decree-Law 45296 of 28 April 1965.
11. Decree-Law 177/71 prohibited import duties on foreign commodities supplying the colonial industry.
12. Interview with Ali, Lisbon, 28 September 2005.
13. Aga Khan, in the form of *farmans* (guidelines with the force of orders) addressed to followers from 1937 onwards, called upon the community to modernise (adopt European-style clothes, invest in the education of girls), diversify its professional occupations to avoid seeing its future in Africa merely in terms of 'dukawalla' or 'cantinas' (as they called the small retail trade posts in British East Africa and Mozambique), and integrate into this African colonial space through explicit loyalty to the Portuguese government, which had received them, as well as by adopting the Portuguese language and culture.
14. This part of the article is a simplified version of a much more extensive study released in French as a working paper (Khouri, Leite, and Mascarenhas 2011).
15. See the letter from Aga Khan assuring President Salazar of the community's loyalty in the crucial moments of the political history of modern India in its relations with the Portuguese. Letter from Aga Khan of 5 June 1951 (PIDE/DGS, processo 749/73. CI (2)).
16. The conclusion of Domingo José Soares Rebelo (1961, p. 87) in his memo on the Ismaili community of Mozambique can still be heard forty years on: 'We are allowed no access to any information whatsoever about the activities of this curious religious group of Indians. The individuals we interviewed proved to be very reserved as to the good intentions of the author. Very certainly, the

Supreme Council holds information of an economic nature. The mere fact of asking the members for it was met by a refusal, however, informing us that a part of the information would never be supplied to us. The author then turned to followers of Aga Khan, both young and old, who merely provided him with evasive responses on many an occasion.'

17. DGS, Direcção Geral de Segurança (General Directorate for Security), the political police of the New State.
18. Interviews with Sunni Indians from Mozambique were conducted in Portugal between 1993 and 2002, before we began our research on the members of the Ismaili community in Lisbon. It should be noted that between 1975 and 1982, the departure of many Sunni Indians (almost 10,000 out of an estimated 30,000 Indians of all confessions residing in Mozambique in 1974) did not have the appearance of a departure of a community. Of those that remained after the independence of Mozambique, many assumed the role of business entrepreneurs or political and administrative elites linked with Frelimo (Mozambique Liberation Front). Sunni Indian families have always kept close ties between Portugal and Mozambique (Carvalho 1999; Mira 2005) .
19. Arquivos Nacionais da Torre do Tombo (ANTT), Lisbon, PIDE, 'Ismaelitas em Moçambique,' Processo 749/73, CI(2), Cx 7864.
20. DGS memo of 20 July 1973, 'Estado de espírito das populações. Comunidade ismaelita de Moçambique,' PIDE/DGS, Processo 749/73, CI(2).
21. We shall see below that one of our contacts (Ali) confirmed the truth of these accounts.
22. It should be noted that black and white Mozambicans call the Ismailis who return Portuguese; white Mozambicans call them, more specifically, disciples of Aga Khan. For Mozambican Muslims and Indian Sunnites, they are *khojas*. White Mozambicans continue to be almost totally ignorant of this community, and the term *disciples of Aga Khan* conveys an idea of wealth they associate with the community. White Mozambicans are also ignorant of the religious foundations of this Shi'a Muslim community.
23. During the colonial period, Indians born in Mozambique were Portuguese by virtue of the *Ius Solis*. However, during the Carnation Revolution (1974) it was the criterion of *Ius Sanguinis* which became predominant for the conservation of Portuguese nationality by individuals born or resident in the colonies (Decree-Law n 308-A75/ 24 of June 1975, passed on the eve of the independence of Mozambique). This legislative decision to 'make the loss of nationality the operative principle' (Esteves et al. 1991, p. 32) was to deprive of Portuguese nationality (meaning they would not conserve it) not only blacks but also Asians – including the Ismailis – born in Mozambique of parents who were not born in Portugal (mainland and adjacent islands). An exceptional regime was granted, however, for those natives of the former 'state of India' (Goa) born before its annexation by India in 1961 who declared that they wished to retain Portuguese nationality (articles 1 (e) and (d), and article 4). Also, as provided by Article 5 of the law for special, duly justified cases of reacquisition of Portuguese nationality, a large number of applications were made for the conservation or concession of Portuguese nationality, notably by Ismailis from Mozambique who had recently arrived in Portugal and by *retornados* from the former colonies who found themselves stateless on arrival on account of Decree-Law n 308. Finally, the members of the Ismaili community who had left Mozambique and arrived in Portugal before the approval of the Decree-Law were also deprived of their nationality. It

was a traumatic experience for many Ismailis although they were able, once all the painstaking formalities required by the law had been completed, to acquire Portuguese nationality again.
24. 'A Sua Alteza aconselhou': in Portuguese, the verb *aconselhar (advise)* encompasses meanings ranging from the categorical imperative to mere suggestion, leaving the choice at the discretion of the listener. For the Ismaili community, which speaks Gujarati, was it presented as a *farman* or as a *talika*? That is to say, was it presented as a directive from the Imam addressing his followers directly, in which case the *farman* has the value of an injunction, or as written or spoken word of the Imam speaking to believers through the competent bodies? Regarding the way it is received by believers, a *farman*/directive or a *talika* that has been transmitted can, depending on the circumstances, have categorical imperative force, given that the followers are referred to as *farman dari* (those who follow the *farman*).
25. The Ismaili centre was inaugurated in 1998 and has enabled better visibility of the community in Lisbon.
26. At the request of the respondents, all the names have been changed.
27. PIDE, Polícia internacional e de defesa do estado (International and State Defense Police), former name for the DGS.
28. Interview of 22 June 2005.
29. Informal interviews held in Lisbon during the 1990s.
30. See the interpretation of Melo (2008, p. 100), which we share.
31. Thanks to a comparison of verbal accounts, we know that, in reality, half a dozen Ismailis stayed in Mozambique.
32. These years correspond to the opening of Mozambique to the market economy while the civil war continued between Frelimo and Renamo. The peace agreements came only in 1992 (Renamo, Mozambique National Resistance).
33. Ali, interview of 28 September 2005.
34. Note that in the expression 'when His Highness was approached' '(quando A Sua Alteza foi abordada'), the passive form makes it possible to give a subject to the statement without indicating who actually approached his highness. This leaves us ignorant of their religious standing, or possibly of their economic weight in the community and their establishment, on their return to Mozambique, as the persons responsible for mobilising and organising the departure of followers.
35. Interview, July 2008, Maputo.
36. Having left as the Portuguese had done and for the same reasons, they say they, like the Portuguese, are now returning to Mozambique.
37. Aga Khan (1926), see in particular the *farmans* addressed to Jangbar, on 6 July 1900, and 29 August 1905.
38. We should not confuse the perception of believers with the reality of what their leader might have said. What might appear to have the value of a *farman* for followers was not necessarily an actual *farman* for Aga Khan.

References

Primary sources

Oral Sources

Between 2005 and 2008, 33 interviews were recorded with 25 members of the Ismaili community living in Lisbon and Maputo, a community that had between 3,000 and 3,800 faithful members in 1975. In accordance with the wishes of those interviewed, all the names have been changed.

Written Sources: National Archives of Torre do Tombo (ANTT), Lisbon, PIDE-DGS.
Letter from the Aga Khan sent to Salazar, dated 5 June 1951, PIDE/DGS, processo 749/73. CI (2).
'Ismaelitas em Moçambique,' Processo 749/73, CI(2), Cx 7864.
Note of the DGS, dated 20 July 1973, 'Estado de espírito das populações. Comunidade ismaelita de Moçambique,' PIDE/DGS, Processo 749/73, CI(2).
Boletim Oficial de Moçambique (BOM) 1973–1974.

Secondary sources

Antunes, L. F. (1992), 'A actividade da companhia de comércio dos baneanes de Diu em Moçambique (1686–1777).' MA thesis, Universidade Nova de Lisboa, Lisbon.
Ávila, P., and Alves, M. (1993), 'Trajectorias sociais e estratégias colectivas dos comerciantes indianos,' *Sociologia, problemas e práticas* no. 13, pp. 115–133.
Carvalho, A. Soriano (1999), 'O empresariado islâmico em Moçambique no período pós-colonial, 1974–1994.' PhD diss., Universidade Técnica de Lisboa, Lisbon.
Esteves, M. do Céu (ed.), (1991), *Portugal, País de imigração*. Instituto de estudos do desenvolvimento, Lisbon.
Franco, V. (1991), 'A aquisição da nacionalidade portuguesa,' in M. do Céu Esteves et al. (eds.), *Portugal, País de imigração*. Instituto de estudos do desenvolvimento, Lisbon, pp. 119–144.
Goody, J. (1996), *The East in the West*. Cambridge University Press, London.
Hollister, J. N. (1953), *The Shi'a of India*. Luzac and Co., London.
Khouri, N., and Leite, J. Pereira (eds.) 2008, 'Indiens des cinq colonisations de l'Afrique Orientale: Mobilités et identités en diaspora de 1870 à nos jours,' *Lusotopie* 15, no. 2, pp. 27–207.
Khouri, N., Leite, J. Pereira, and Mascarenhas, M. J. (2011), 'Les départs des Ismailis du Mozambique : Réfléxions sur le départ d'une communauté et sa relation au secret,' *Documentos de Trabalho* no. 91, Centro de estudos sobre África e do desenvolvimento, Universidade Técnica de Lisboa, Lisbon.
Leite, J. Pereira (2001), 'Indo-britanniques et indo-portugais: Présence marchande au Sud de Mozambique au moment de l'implantation du système colonial, de la fin du XIXe siècle jusqu'aux années 1930,' *Outre-Mers Revue d'Histoire* no. 330–331, pp. 13–37.
―― (2000), 'A guerra do caju e as relações Moçambique-Índia na época pós-colonial,' *Lusotopie* 7, pp. 295–332.
―― (1995), 'A economia do caju em Moçambique e as relações com a Índia: dos anos 20 ao fim da época colonial,' in *Ensaios de Homenagem ao Professor Francisco Pereira de Moura*. Universidade Técnica de Lisboa, Lisbon (ed.), pp. 631–653.
―― (1989), 'La formation de l'économie coloniale au Mozambique. Pacte colonial et industrialisation. Du colonialisme portugais aux réseaux informels de sujétion marchande.' PhD diss., École des hautes études en sciences sociales, Paris.
Leite, J. Pereira, and Khouri, N. (2011), 'Historia social económica dos Ismailis de Moçambique, século XX,' *Documentos de Trabalho* no. 92, Centro de estudos sobre África e do desenvolvimento, Universidade Técnica de Lisboa, Lisbon.
Masselos, J. C. (1973), 'The Khojas of Bombay: The Defining of Formal Membership Criteria during the Nineteenth Century,' in I. Ahmad (ed.), *Caste and Social Stratification among the Muslims*. Manohar Book Service, Delhi, pp. 1–20.

Melo, A. (2008), 'A diáspora ismaelita – preparação e "partida", vivências da migração dos anos 70,' in Khouri and Leite (eds.), 'Indiens des cinq colonisations...,' pp. 97–102.

Mira, F. (2005), 'Les élites et les entrepreneurs au Mozambique: Globalisation, systèmes de pouvoir et reclassements sociaux, 1987–1999.' PhD diss., École des hautes études en sciences sociales, Paris – Universidade Técnica de Lisboa, Lisbon.

—— (2003), *Migrações e integração. Teoria e aplicações à sociedade portuguesa*. Celta editora, Lisbon.

Rebelo, D. J. Soares (1961), 'Breve apontamentos sobre um grupo de indianos em Moçambique, a Comunidade Ismailia Maometana,' *Boletim da Sociedade de Estudos da Colónia de Moçambique*, Lourenço Marques, 30, no. 128, pp. 83–89.

Shah, Sultan Muhammed (Aga Khan) (1952 [1926]), *Khangi Farman*. Khoja Sindhi Printing Press Department, Bombay. [second larger edition, without any author's or publisher's name, of the 1st edition printed by Rahemtullah Virji, Honory Secretary of the Press Department]

Simmel, G. (1999), *Sociologie. Études sur les formes de la socialisation*. PUF, Paris. [1st German ed., Leipzig, 1908].

Part III

Migrations at the Margins of the Third Empire

8
Representing the Portuguese Empire: Goan Consuls in British East Africa, c. 1910–1963

Margret Frenz

> I remember the Portuguese flag flying from the pole in front of our house, raised every morning and lowered each evening. (Ribeiro 1996, p. 23)
>
> It [the house] had the Portuguese flag just above it – because the Consulate was above – and papa also had a [car] which had a CD plate.[1]

How was it possible for Goans – such as those quoted above – to represent Portugal in East Africa? Dr. Rosendo A. Ribeiro was Portuguese vice-consul in Nairobi from 1914 to 1922, and Henry Figueiredo de Souza, was Portuguese consul in Kampala in the 1950s. These periods mark the early and the late years of the Portuguese government employing Goans in such positions. Why were Goans so attractive to the colonial Portuguese governments for these roles? In this paper I argue that the multitude of political, social, and cultural connections of Goans enabled them to negotiate and interact successfully across the political, social, and cultural boundaries set in place by the imperial powers in East Africa in the first half of the 20th century. Rather than analysing them in a translocal or transnational field, I argue that Goans in British East Africa, and in particular the Goan Portuguese consuls, were transimperial actors.

Migration movements lie at the heart of empires – be they the British, the Portuguese or any other. Without migrant groups and their expertise, these political entities would not have been sustainable – or only for short time periods. According to Burbank and Cooper (2010, p. 8), the 'empire-state declares the non-equivalence of multiple populations […] and draws, usually coercively, peoples whose difference is made explicit under its rule.' This happened on different scales in different empires; whilst the Portuguese Empire employed its overseas citizens as representatives of empire in their own colonies and in territories governed by other European empires, in the British Empire there are no examples of equivalent appointments of colonial subjects as representatives of their government to other countries. The Portuguese passed laws to introduce the full equality of Goans in the Estado da Índia with Portuguese-born citizens in the early 19th century, and this was finally implemented with the creation of the Portuguese republic in 1910. But in British India, Indians were perceived as colonial subordinates and were accorded British subject status, a kind of second-rate citizenship with limited rights. Only after independence could individuals of South Asia obtain full citizenship of the new states of India, Pakistan, and Ceylon. This was a fundamental difference between the Portuguese and British Empires: Goans from Portuguese India travelled by and large on Portuguese passports and were perceived and often perceived themselves as Portuguese citizens, whether travelling or living in South Asia, Africa, or elsewhere.[2]

Why was there such a considerable difference in how the two empires went about the management of their colonies? Recently, the historians Jane Burbank and Frederick Cooper (2010, p. 2) have pointed out how differently empires were ruled and how 'imperial practices, and imperial cultures have shaped the world we live in.' The case study of Goan consuls representing the Portuguese Empire in British East Africa provides an excellent window into analysing these different imperial practices and cultures. It also shows how these were understood and negotiated by a set of individuals who, through their migratory experience between two coexisting empires, took part in particular aspects of the political, economic, cultural, and social practices of both. In short, Goans, and especially their representatives in the roles of Portuguese consuls, were transimperial actors.

First, I set out the context of the migrations from Goa to East Africa, in order to highlight the physical move from one empire to another, and its connections to citizenship through passport issues. Then I sketch the historical context of the Portuguese and British experiences and conceptions of empire, as these crucially influenced how they conducted imperial politics and practices. In the third section, I look at the representation of the Indo-Portuguese or Goan community in British East Africa, exemplified by the appointment and role of Portuguese Goan consuls who took up office in Kampala, Nairobi, Dar es Salaam, and other East African cities during the first half of the 20th century. Finally, I show that the variations in imperial practices and cultures and the different conceptions of empire are due to the distinct historical experiences of Portugal and Britain. Both versions of empire, coexisting during the 19th and 20th centuries, became tangible in the perception and practice of Portuguese consular representation in British East Africa. Goans were transimperial actors at a particular historical juncture and the transformative process of Goan self-perception and political orientation – moving away from a rather firm identification with the Portuguese towards a more pronounced affinity to the British Empire – created a paradoxical situation of constant tension between their cultural and political communities. This tension was never fully resolved from within, but as an unexpected by-product of the integration of Goa, Daman, and Diu into the Indian Union, which ended the official Portuguese Empire in India in 1961.

Moving between empires: Goan/Indo-Portuguese migration to British East Africa

Predating the Portuguese presence, the number of Goans coming to East Africa steadily increased from the 16th century onwards.[3] It reached its first peak in the early 20th century, with a second high in the late 1940s and throughout the 1950s. East African Goans were known as Indo-Portuguese in Portuguese East Africa, but also in British East Africa during the earlier decades of migration.[4] In due course the growing Goan (Indo-Portuguese) community required some sort of representation.

East Africa was an attractive destination for Goans because it offered job opportunities not available in Goa at the time. Under Portuguese rule, Goa remained a largely agriculturally based society well into the 20th century. Its main crops were rice and coconuts. However, major parameters did change: the majority of Goans in the so-called old conquests – today's districts of Tiswadi, Bardez and Salcette – were converted to Catholicism, often as complete villages and, at times, under rather coercive and violent conditions, from the 16th century onwards. Portuguese officials retained a firm control over the army and administration. The colonial government introduced Portuguese and English medium schools in conjunction with missionary societies, and made schooling compulsory in the 19th century. Yet, in accordance with Portuguese policy, industrial development was kept at a bare minimum. Consequently, a growing number of school leavers could not find adequate work and started migrating to not-so-far-away Bombay or famously, worked as stewards and 'shippies'[5] aboard oceangoing ships plying under the Portuguese or British flags.

During the 19th century, Goan seamen tended to call at the island of Zanzibar. By the 1870s, quite a few of them had settled there and made the island their new home. Many Goans worked under or for the Sultan of Zanzibar, for example, as doctors or musicians, and in the administration, or opened their own businesses (Frenz 2005).[6] Over the years and with increasing job opportunities in Tanganyika, Kenya, and Uganda, more and more Goans either moved from Zanzibar to the mainland, or directly relocated there when they arrived from Goa. After the 1890s, the British Imperial East Africa Company, and following its demise a few years later, the British colonial government recruited Goans to work alongside Punjabis and Gujaratis on the construction of the Uganda Railway, and also in the emerging service sector and administration of the newly established colonial cities in East Africa. Written and oral evidence suggests that British officials perceived Goans as being comparatively well educated as well as being 'loyal and hard working'.[7] Thus, the period from the 1890s to about the 1920s saw a growing number of Goan and other Indian immigrants coming to British East Africa.[8] In contrast to the Punjabis and Gujaratis, who were British subjects from British India, Goans hailed from Portuguese India, with Portuguese passports, and therefore inhabited a different legal status. In addition, Goans had to adjust to a different imperial culture. The practices that were followed in British East Africa, at least with respect to work and to rules and regulations concerning their leisure, health, and education, were very different from those they had experienced in Goa. Goans had to negotiate between the economically driven, utilitarian and hierarchical approach from the British colonial government, which organised its administration along racial categories, and their 'home' empire, the Portuguese, whose emphasis was on the cultural, linguistic, and social aspects (see further below).

With the increasing numbers of Goan trade and retail businesses, and more and more Goans working in the administration and other parts of the service sector and in the professions, there arose a need for representation in and of this community. Because the Goans were classified by the British colonial government in a separate category from Indians, it was not clear who should represent them. Since hardly any suitable Portuguese citizens born in Portugal resided in British East Africa at the time (they were mostly to be found in Portuguese East Africa), the nearest possibility for the Portuguese government was to appoint consuls from the local communities who held Portuguese passports, most of whom had come from Goa.

Differing imperial practices: indications of Portuguese and British conceptions

The history of empires – in terms of the relationship between overseas regions (later colonies) and the metropole – underwent several phases: expansion and contraction, negotiation and domination, and all shades of grey in-between these outer points of the spectrum. Here, it will suffice to refer to developments during the 19th century in both Portugal and Britain and to sketch out the historical background of the situation on the ground in East Africa. Excellent analyses of the Portuguese Empire or its parts in its early incarnations up to about 1810 can be found particularly in the work of Sanjay Subrahmanyam (1993), A. J. R. Russell-Wood (1992), and A. R. Disney (2009) – not to forget Boxer's *Seaborne Empire* (1969) – as well as the collected works on the history of the Portuguese expansion (Bethencourt and Chaudhuri 1998; Albuquerque 1989). However, the 19th and 20th centuries have not yet received the necessary attention with respect to combining the histories of Portugal and its Empire with a few notable exceptions, for instance, Newitt (2009) and Clarence-Smith (1985). Therefore, I shall sketch a few important landmark developments in the history of Portugal to provide the context in which Portuguese imperial strategies and practices were put in place.

Nineteenth-century Portugal was a country in turmoil, in many respects: for example, it was one of Europe's main war theatres. Napoleon marched into Portugal in 1807, triggering the flight of the Portuguese royal family and the Portuguese government to Brazil.[9] Although peace was settled in Vienna in 1815, Dom João VI returned to Portugal only in 1821. In the fourteen years of his absence, Portugal functioned under the protective umbrella of the British. After João VI's death in 1826, a civil war broke out between liberal and conservative Portuguese factions, whose opposition had developed during the king's absence in Brazil. Returning soldiers contributed to the explosive mix in the weakened Portuguese society and state. Dom João's sons, Dom Pedro and Dom Miguel, headed the two sides in the civil war: Dom Pedro was at the centre of the liberal movement, which favoured a constitutional monarchy, and Dom Miguel led the conservatives, who preferred an absolutist state. At the beginning of the conflict the prospects of the conservatives had been much better as they were supported by the clergy, the old nobility, and the army. In 1834, however, the liberals under Dom Pedro won the civil war. Despite this, the political tensions calmed down only in 1851. Thereafter, internal policies in Portugal remained relatively calm until the late 1880s. While the country struggled to adjust to the new economic conditions in Europe, it remained more or less dependent on other European powers, particularly the British (Marques 1981, pp. 34–35; Newitt 2009, p. 174).

Portugal was declared a republic in 1910, but became an authoritarian regime, particularly with the introduction of the *Estado Novo* in 1932 by its prime minister, António de Oliveira Salazar, in the wake of the 1926 military coup. Following conservative, Roman Catholic family values, the regime was based on social, cultural, and economic control, reflected in its motto: *Deus, Pátria e Família*. True to his motto *Nada contra a Nação, tudo pela Nação* ('Nothing against the Nation. Everything for the Nation'), Salazar kept a strict hand on all overseas territories, which were seen as an integral part of the Portuguese Empire (Marques 1981, p. 372). As a result, Salazar was strongly opposed to decolonisation after World War II (Brettel 2006, p. 143).

Internal politics in Portugal affected how the colonies, or provinces, were perceived and governed. Although the Portuguese were active in their overseas territories throughout the 19th century, for instance in various expeditions, keeping colonies in Africa was mostly motivated by political considerations, less so by economic ones. According to the historian Oliveira Marques, it was 'national pride' to belong to the European powers who wielded an empire (Marques 1981, p. 157). In contrast, Gervase Clarence-Smith and others emphasise the economic importance of the empire to Portugal, although it was only under Salazar that an economic programme was created (Clarence-Smith 1985, pp. 146–191).[10] Across the Portuguese Empire, manpower was in short supply; the small country of Portugal could send only limited numbers of rulers, governors, and administrators to its overseas territories. For instance, only about 12,000 European Portuguese lived in Angola and 6,000 in Mozambique in 1910, of which only a small fraction was involved in governing the province (Marques 1981, p. 159). This might have been part of the motivation to include an article in the 1822 constitution that considered everyone within the realm of the Portuguese Empire a citizen, and defined the Portuguese nation as *'a união de todos os Portuguezes de ambos os hemisférios'* ('the union of all the Portuguese of both hemispheres') (Homem 2010, p. 65). With this came the Portugalisation of the overseas regions, which could be characterised as cultural imperialism, based on cultural and social practices, including the use of Portuguese, following Christianity, in particular, Roman Catholic norms.

Portugal remained the weakest competitor in the scramble for colonies and imperial power in Europe, frequently overruled by Britain's thirst for land (Newitt 1981, pp. 24–33). In the areas that remained Portuguese, legislative measures in Portugal were applied to the overseas provinces as well, at times with alterations according to local circumstances; there were various changes throughout the century with respect to the administrative structures. Overall, the instability in Portugal had its effects on the overseas regions; frequent changes of governors and moves to and fro between centralised and decentralised approaches to administration led to a limited rule (Marques 1981, pp. 178–182).

This brief outline shows that Portugal did not establish a coherent core ideology or a clear mission with respect to its colonies in the 19th century nor into the early decades of the 20th. Its internal conflicts, disparate forces, and plurality stood in the way of creating a comprehensive strategy. Portugal has been described as 'backward', with strong conservative forces at work – be they royals or Catholic clerics – and they suffered from the 'Napoleonic' trauma of 1807. In its foreign policy, Portugal was at the same time economically dependent on and a political as well as an imperial rival of Britain, with a marginal executive power and a need to count on allies and representatives (Osterhammel 2009, p. 682). Under Salazar's regime, this situation changed profoundly: Salazar developed a policy in which the overseas provinces were to be part of the Portuguese nation. He followed a strategy of establishing the *Estado Novo* as an authoritarian, pro-Catholic, and all-encompassing state by trying to revive an imagined glorious past with the aim of shaping Portugal's 'glorious global future.'

Britain's attitude to its empire was very different. In the 19th century, Britain moved towards a more and more systematic rule over India, its 'jewel in the crown.' Particularly after the so-called mutiny in 1857 and the proclamation of Victoria as the Empress of India in 1876, the colonies 'along with the pomp and grandeur created for such occasions, pumped up a new loyalist popularity in which the British Empire was the definitive symbol of British greatness' (Levine, 2007, p. 12). In the 19th century, this went along with Britain's push for industrialisation and a huge military power – the contributions of British India to the British economy and army could be measured in both kind and cash. Indian commercial enterprise opened up new markets, Indian labour provided cheap labour, and Indian taxpayers financed two-thirds of the British army (Darwin 2009, p. 183). Administrative structures and procedures were increasingly formalised and tailored to the perceived needs of the colonial government. For instance, the Indian Civil Service, formally established in 1854, effectively created a 'steel frame' and 'formed a ruling oligarchy' that held British India together (Darwin 2009, pp. 182, 186–187; Kennedy, 2002, p. 9; Wesselink, 2004). British administrators in India could build on the experiences of subjugating Scotland, Wales, and Ireland in the 18th century, such as the introduction of English as the language of law, policy, and education.[11]

Although the proclamation of 1858 had promised that no differences would be made with respect to race in the British Raj, the perception of Indians (and Africans in East Africa) as 'backward races' and the perceived need to 'civilise' the colonies contradicted this announcement. In both India and East Africa, the colonial government established a distinct difference between British citizens and its colonial subjects, who were accorded only subject status. This subordinate position was based on racial or other sociocultural categories (caste and religion in India). Despite the rhetoric of bringing 'moral and material progress' to their colonies, efforts in building a sound economy and offering adequate health, educational, and other facilities in South Asia and East Africa remained limited (Rich 1990; Thompson 2005; Dirks 2001). Although Indians and Africans were employed in the administration and other government services, their opportunities for promotions largely ended at the glass ceiling of the ranks created for them. The 'condescending attitude towards [...] Indian society' (Darwin 2009, p. 186) was manifested and perpetuated in the press. In India the struggle for freedom from British rule started in the late 19th century and finally led to independence for India and Pakistan in 1947; in East Africa, this happened roughly 15 years later: Tanzania, Uganda, and Kenya celebrated independence in 1961, 1962, and 1963 respectively.

In contrast to Portugal, Britain appeared as a progressive, secular state. It was at the forefront of the industrial revolution, including the push towards a technically sophisticated infrastructure with steamships and railways and an enormous military presence. Britain conducted its affairs in India through the India Office and in Africa through the Colonial Office, with specific sets of rules, maintaining the distance between the metropole and the colony clearly, as well as the perceived superiority of the colonial government vis-à-vis the populations in the colonies.

Using a simplified dichotomy, it could be argued that Britain was perceived as a modern, industrialised, progressive colonial state based on racial categories, whereas Portugal and its empire were largely seen as characterised by agriculture, conservative family values, the importance of language and culture, and an imagined community across the metropole and the overseas territories with a common language and shared sets of values. Whilst the emphasis in the Portuguese Empire was on a shared language and shared cultural values, the British Empire emphasised its economic interests and administrative superiority.

Against this backdrop of a mixed, shared, and competing history between the Portuguese and the British Empire, their position in Europe and towards overseas territories, I will look at the representation of the Portuguese in the British Empire by one of its 'colonised' communities: the Goans, whose negotiations across imperial boundaries crystallise these contrasts.

Representing the Portuguese Empire: Goan Consuls in British East Africa

Already in the late 19th century, Goans could be found in the position of a Portuguese consul in Zanzibar.[12] Further Portuguese consulates were opened in Mombasa, Nairobi, Kampala, and Dar es Salaam and the posts of consul filled with Goans.[13] In general, these were honorary posts which did not come with a regular salary. From the evidence available, it appears that most of the consuls were sufficiently well off to take on this additional position: they were often substantial retail traders, or medical doctors. This suggests that the Portuguese government selected their representatives carefully: they were generally of high social status, often with a university education; they spoke Portuguese and identified with what the Portuguese Governments regarded as the right cultural values and thus shared the same imagined community. In turn, these 'big men' accumulated an even higher status amongst Goans, as well as more respect from other communities in East Africa, and were appreciated in diplomatic circles in the British East African colonies.[14] It seems that, well into the 1920s, the self-perception of these Goan consuls was grounded in seeing themselves as Portuguese citizens.[15] In the absence of a sizeable group of Portuguese migrants from Portugal, and according to the policy of the Portuguese government to treat metropolitans and Indo-Portuguese alike, the employment of Goans as consuls and vice-consuls appears as a rational strategy. At the same time, the decision to employ Goans as representatives of the Portuguese Empire is remarkable: it instantiates in a very public way the idea of equality between all Portuguese citizens, be they originally from the metropole or the provinces.[16]

Portuguese Goan consuls in Zanzibar included Manuel Francisco de Albuquerque, who hailed from Anjuna, in Goa. He was a medical practitioner with a degree from Grant Medical College, Bombay, and lived for most of his life, from the late 19th century to 1946, in Zanzibar where he was personal physician of two subsequent sultans. For his services to the sultans and for his detection of and fight against bubonic plague in Zanzibar in 1903, he was honoured with the Order of the Brilliant Star of Zanzibar, the Order of Homoudieh, and presented with a Golden Sword. The Portuguese Government awarded him the Cavaleiro da Ordem de Christo for his services as Portuguese consul, a post he had held from 1916 to 1923 and 1928 to 1933.[17] His daughter-in-law, who (as of 2012) still lives in the house he built in Anjuna, initiated the sculpting and setting up of his statue in front of the house; it was unveiled by the dean of Goa Medical College on 27 March 2011.[18] Albuquerque was followed in office by another Goan, Justiniano Baltazar de Souza.[19]

In Nairobi, another medical practitioner, Dr. Rosendo Ayres Ribeiro, was Portuguese consul from 1914 to 1924.[20] He was famously known as the 'doctor on a zebra,' as he did his medical rounds on a zebra for several years before World War I (Ribeiro 1996, p. 23). Besides being the Portuguese consul in Nairobi, he was very active in his community, donating a major sum to build a Goan school named after him. A medical colleague of his, Dr. A. C. L. de Sousa, acted for him as a Portuguese consul in 1921 when Ribeiro was on home leave in Goa.[21] From May 1940 onwards, Gorgonio Tomaz Esperato da Cruz was the Portuguese consul at Nairobi. Most probably, he would have continued in this position, had he not died unexpectedly.[22] Justiniano Baltazar de Souza, consul in Zanzibar, acted as consul general immediately after da Cruz's death until a Portuguese successor was found, in June 1947, who came to Nairobi from Portugal to take up office.[23] Nairobi was the main office of the Portuguese representation in British East Africa; consuls there had jurisdiction over Kenya, Tanganyika, Uganda, Zanzibar, and the Seychelles.[24]

In Mombasa, Dr. Boaventura Pinto was honorary Portuguese consul.[25] Caetano Francis Martins acted as Portuguese consul in Dar es Salaam from 1947 to 1970.[26] In Uganda, Henry De Souza Figueiredo, a well-known retailer with a sizeable shop dealing in provisions, groceries, wines, and spirits, as well as a land and property owner, filled the post as a Portuguese consul from 1954 to the early 1960s.[27] De Souza Figueiredo also owned a radio company, and was a member of the Uganda Chamber of Commerce, as well as of several sports organisations – including the advisory board for cricket in Uganda, which was based in Jinja (Pandit 1963, p. 135). One of his children proudly remembers the Portuguese flag which flew above his shop (which also contained the Portuguese consulate office and their flat on the upper floor), the Corps Diplomatique plaque on his car, and the ceremony at which her father was awarded a medal. Furthermore, she recalls the celebration of Portuguese Independence Day.[28] Again, this suggests a close identification of the Goan consuls with Portuguese culture and politics – or at least, its imagined community of a shared set of cultural values and legal status which the Portuguese Empire provided.

The Portuguese consuls in East Africa had a variety of responsibilities. Frequently, they had to issue passports and translate documents into and from Portuguese. Some of the consulates also offered bursaries and grants to prospective students to study in British East Africa. Apart from these more formal responsibilities, informal duties were attached to this position on the part of the Goan community. These included, according to one of my interviewees,

> to keep the Portuguese influence [...] amongst the Goans [...] to remind them that their ancestry was Portuguese and Goa was a Portuguese colony.[29]

This statement is remarkable in its distinct expression of loyalty towards the Portuguese Empire. It alludes to a Portuguese ancestry, one that was imagined in combination with Portuguese culture, religion, and social norms. This arguably expresses a sense of belonging to a wider Lusotropical culture.

From the information material produced by the Portuguese consulate general in Nairobi, it becomes clear that the economic value of the Portuguese colonies was seen as their capacity to provide 'high returns with the tapping of their resourceful and extremely fertile lands.'[30] Imperial solidarity was emphasised and clearly stated as evidence – and 'not an empty phraseology' – with respect to the food supplies that went from Portugal to Goa in the late 1940s via Mozambique and Angola. This tied in with Salazar's economic strategy of trying to make Portugal self-sufficient by using all resources available within metropolitan Portugal and its provinces, all based on the idea of ruralism (Táboas et al. 2010, p. 1). On a political/ideological level, Salazar and his regime insisted on the Portuguese territories being 'overseas provinces,' not 'colonies'. Repercussions of this policy can be found in various instances in mid-20th-century British East Africa, for instance, in the communications of the Portuguese consulate general of September 1948:

> 1) GOA [sic] is an Overseas Province of Portugal and not a Colony or Dominion; 2) Consequently, the word 'GOAN' [sic] does not indicate a nationality but solely that one is a native from a Portuguese Province as the words 'Welsh' and 'Scotch' mean that persons so indicated are natives from such and such British Provinces.[31]

Accordingly, the Portuguese Consul advised the Chief Secretary of the British Government to use the latter interpretation in any official publications, such as the census: they should use either 'Portuguese citizen' or 'British subject' in the nationality column rather than 'Goan.'[32]

These statements highlight how a particular perspective on, and political use of, the empire became part and parcel of Portuguese politics under the

Estado Novo. This fitted well with the overall ideology of the *Estado Novo*, state, which has been characterised as an 'extremely conservative, catholic and corporative regime' (Táboas et al. 2010, p. 1; see also Pinto 2010; Cahen 2007). The idea of citizenship also included the idea of multiracialism, which was propagated by Salazar towards the end of his premiership, possibly triggered by the independence of Goa in 1961 and by the need to keep together what was left of the Portuguese Empire in the 1960s, and in the light of the colonial war in Africa between 1961 and 1974 and its consequences (Newitt 1981, p. 220).[33] The ideology of multiracialism was actively propagated by Portuguese consuls in British East Africa.[34] However, it seems that although the ideology was publicised widely, its implementation was limited – at least partly owing to the fact that the Portuguese consuls could not effectively influence British policies in British East Africa. These policies followed the idea of racial segregation, rather than multiracialism, constituting one of the main (and very visible) differences in imperial practice of the Portuguese and the British Empires, which the Goan Portuguese consuls negotiated.

Thus, the bulletins published by the consulate in Nairobi from 1948 onwards propagated an egalitarian perspective on metropolitans and Indo- or Afro-Portuguese alike. Moreover, the bulletins served as a propaganda medium, emphasising the all-embracing Portuguese Empire and its aspiration to encompass not only Portuguese citizens but members closely linked to the Portuguese cultural sphere. The following quote from the first issue of the bulletin illustrates this perspective:

> We felt it convenient to devise some method for placing before one and all the active and progressive work that is being carried out throughout the PORTUGUESE WORLD [sic] for the benefit of our citizens and others who, though not with us politically, still form part and parcel of our own family.[35]

The second part of the quote refers to the differentiation of the Portuguese speaking communities into those who were politically affiliated with the Portuguese Empire through their passports, and those who either spoke the language or nurtured close links with Portuguese culture, but were formally subject to another entity such as the British Empire. The bulletin also reflects Portugal's political strategy of increasingly incorporating the overseas territories, which reached a peak under Salazar's *Estado Novo*. From the late 1920s and particularly the 1930s onwards, the Portuguese government depicted its empire as a unitary entity, i.e. colonial policy perceived the African and Asian possessions to be part and parcel of the Portuguese state. The economic and jurisdictional integration of Portugal and its overseas provinces, as they were called from 1951 onwards, found its peak in 1961, when equal status with respect to citizenship was accorded to everyone in the provinces and in Portugal (Newitt 1981, pp. 184–186).[36] With this legislation, the understanding of the Portuguese Empire as a pluricontinental entity took formal shape. In recent years, the CPLP (Comunidade dos Países de Língua Portuguesa)[37] has implicitly reverted to some of these ideas. Its base is the Portuguese language and Lusotropical culture, including the construction of racial equality within the alliance. The outgoing president Luís Fonseca (Brandes 2008) emphasised the importance of this common platform for all member states, but particularly for Portugal, which perceives itself as a link between the global north and south – a role very much part of its initiative of founding and nurturing the CPLP (Teixeira 2008; Cahen 1997).[38]

Another instance illustrates the division into political and cultural community. Arguably, the distinction between political and cultural community which had already appeared 'on the ground' became more pronounced during the 1940s and 1950s. The correspondence between members of the Goan community and the Portuguese consuls at the time discusses the issue officially and seeks to find a workable solution for international travel and migration. Although for the time being, there seems to have been a political result – for instance, the category 'Goan' does not exist in any British East African census after 1948 – the differentiation between political and cultural community widened in the years to come. Although the majority of Goans by that time had become British subjects, they referred to the Portuguese consul in times of emergency. Apparently, the Portuguese consul was held in high esteem and therefore, the community was confident in his ability to reach a diplomatic understanding with the British colonial government with respect to its grievances; for example, it petitioned for a change in the route of steamers plying between British East Africa and Goa, and demanded separate quotas on Indian Ocean steamers for the Goan community.[39] In his turn, the Portuguese consul in his correspondence with the British colonial government in Nairobi referred to the Goan community as 'my nationals'.[40] Whereas throughout the early decades of the 20th century ships left Mombasa and sailed or steamed directly to Marmagoa, the Ministry of War Transport of the United Kingdom (Office of the Regional Representative for British East Africa) ended the direct service due to the shortage of space on ships during wartime.[41] Instead, ships harboured only at Karachi or Bombay. Having to change ships in either of these ports brought additional bureaucratic measures and costs, and thus created considerable anxiety and anger in the Goan community. For instance, in Bombay or Karachi they had to wait up to three weeks for a connection to Marmagoa, often caused by timetabling issues between British and Portuguese companies, the delay making a stay at expensive hotels necessary to bridge the gap in trans-shipment. Further problems were severe damage of luggage, additional custom duties, the need of getting new papers, and the requirement to obtain a transit visa to be allowed to wait in Bombay or Karachi until the connecting ship arrived.[42]

The Portuguese consul acted upon the grievances by reporting them to the British government. He tried to negotiate a deal for the Goans wishing to travel to Goa. But the British secretary declined any further compromise.[43] Finally, the Portuguese government in Portugal decided to send a Portuguese ship in January 1945 to relieve the numbers of passengers waiting for transport. The steamer was promised to take on 310 of his 'nationals' in Mombasa, that is, Goan passengers bound for Marmagoa.[44] Despite all his efforts, however, the representations by the Portuguese consul on behalf of the Goan community did not trigger a change in the practice of the British administration. This situation continued well into the 1950s, albeit under different international conditions. In 1947, India had become independent, and in 1949, after passing a new constitution, was in the process of integrating the various parts of the subcontinent, including the princely states, into the framework of the Indian Union. Goans travelling from East Africa to Goa via Bombay, as a consequence, had to gain permission to transit through India in order to enter Goa upon their trans-shipment in Bombay. In 1957, a number of Goans wrote letters to the Portuguese Consul at Mombasa and requested an intervention to ease their way from Bombay to Goa by the abolition of the permit system and to have the vessels stop at Marmagoa again. The Portuguese consul requested the British government in Kenya to intervene at the Indian High Commissioner's office to alleviate the travel difficulties of East African Goans, of whom the majority worked in the British government and held British subject passports.

Portugal decided to end diplomatic representation in East Africa when Tanganyika, Kenya, and Uganda became independent. For the years 1963 to 1966, the yearbook of the Foreign Ministry in Portugal mentions the consulates in all East African cities as being 'under revision', and by 1966, they disappear completely.[45] This also meant the end of the representation of Goan communities through a Portuguese consul.

It is noteworthy that the grievances were represented to the Portuguese consul rather than directly to the British government: Despite being British government servants holding British subject passports, these Goans apparently had more confidence in the Portuguese consul to undertake something on behalf of the Goan community than in the British government. Only with his 'protection' or on his behalf, would a presentation to the British government seem likely to be adequate and to promise success. Perhaps this reflects the close links of the community to Portuguese culture, the Catholic religion, and at least in the beginning, to the Portuguese language – apparently at such a high level that the Portuguese consul was willing to represent East African Goans to the British authorities, although these Goans had shifted their political alliance to a competing empire.

Paradoxically, it seems both strange and logical that Goans were employed as Portuguese consuls. On the one hand, the ideology of the Portuguese government emphasised the equality of all members of the empire. On the other hand, the Goan community became more and more Anglicised; not only were their passports British, but English was spoken at home, in school and at work. In stark contrast to the ambition of keeping up 'Portuguese culture' including regular church visits, cultural events, and the like, the majority of Goan families spoke English in their homes. While language is an important marker of identity – this seems to be one of the major points of the CPLP today – for the Goans in East Africa, this certainly was one of the factors that went most quickly out of fashion. The generation of Goans born in the 1940s and 1950s largely perceive English as their mother tongue. Sometimes, they know a few words in Portuguese, or have encountered the language as their parents' 'secret' language which sometimes also could be Konkani.[46] This major shift in the basis of communication shows a transformation away from the Portuguese Empire of Goan identity, which occurred slowly but surely towards the later 1950s. Particularly for East Africa-born Goans, English was the lingua franca which offered attractive job prospects and, with them, perceived high social status. Despite this shift to English in the linguistic sphere, representation by the Portuguese consul was thought to be essential. It might also have had a practical reason: representation through a consul was perceived to promise better results than a representation by the community on its own. This seems to suggest that the idea of a Lusotropical diaspora can be applied to the Goan community in British East Africa even if the people who belonged to it do not necessarily speak Portuguese, but have close cultural links to the Portuguese sphere. Here religion, specifically Catholicism, played an important role.

Conclusion: transimperial Goans

By exploring some aspects of the work and functions of Portuguese consuls of Goan origin this chapter has shown that East African Goans and especially their official representatives, the Portuguese Goan consuls, negotiated and interacted across imperial boundaries, cultures, and practices. Therefore, I term them transimperial actors. Through their negotiations they belonged to both empires in different ways: they moved to British East Africa for its economic opportunities and options for social mobility, but still felt culturally attached to the Portuguese empire, as the examples of letters I have cited have highlighted.

Moreover, Goan perceptions and identities underwent significant transformations in the first half of the 20th century. Goans tended to identify more and more with the British Empire – at least practically – as the majority of Goans worked for the British administration, took on British subject passports, and by and large spoke English, not only at work or at school, but at home as well. Moreover, job prospects and, with these, perceived status were closely linked to the British Empire. Thus, the 1910s to 1950s saw a major identity shift with respect to political affiliation away from the Portuguese Empire towards the British. Nevertheless, when it came to grievances, for instance, with respect to the routes of ships plying between East Africa and India, the Goans approached the Portuguese consul rather than the British authorities directly. This suggests that a perceived cultural closeness between Goans and Portuguese still existed. Their multiple identities were, for instance, reflected in the international travel issues in the 1940s and 1950s. Thus, they sought political representation through the institutions of the cultural rather than political community.

The conundrum for the Goan community, and in particular, their representatives, the Goan Portuguese consuls, was that they had to negotiate across quite different empires and imperial practices. On the one hand, they came from and often were citizens of an economically relatively weak empire, which offered strong cultural and social affinities (Catholicism, Portuguese language), as well as legal advantages in the form of citizenship; on the other hand, they had chosen to live in an empire which offered economic opportunities and social mobility – at least to a certain extent – but at the same time restricted their social and cultural life to a (racially segregated) prescribed niche, and, if they decided to take on British passports, limited their legal status to 'subject' status. These Goans in British East Africa constitute a unique group of transimperial actors, actors who were quite successful in the years until Indian and Pakistani independence in 1947, and East African independence in the early 1960s, but whose positions rapidly unravelled thereafter. Goans were caught in negotiations between the decline of the British and Portuguese Empires and the emergence of novel and mutually exclusive forms of citizenship in East Africa and South Asia with the establishment of nation-states. Thus, the Goan community was an 'anomaly' in the process of decolonisation but one that can reveal a lot about empires as well as the entanglement of political and cultural processes of identity formation.

Notes

1. Interview with Anna (London, 2005). The interviews quoted here are part of a body of about 220 interviews conducted with Goans in Goa, Zanzibar, Kenya, Uganda, Tanzania, Canada, Germany, and the UK between 2003 and 2009. I used open-ended semistructured interview guide. In general, I provide a pseudonym and the location and date of the interview. The names of all interviewees have been changed to protect their privacy. For the methodology of oral history, see Thompson (2000).
2. See the Passaportes series in the State Archives of Goa. The first passport in this series issued to a Goan to go to Mozambique dates from 1819. Passaportes series, Goa State Archives, serial no. 2572. For Goans in Goa, Siqueira (2002,

p. 212) states, 'Those from Goa who were and experienced assimilation (and they were always only a few) believed and do believe that they were and are Portuguese.'
3. See Karnik (1998) for early Goan migration to Portuguese East Africa. Cf. Pearson (1998, p. 237).
4. The terminology is varied; Goans are described or returned under different labels and categories in available archival documents, including the British East African census. They are either known as or subsumed under categories such as Indo-Portuguese, Portuguese, Goans, Christians, Asians, Christian Asians. Therefore, it is extremely difficult to arrive at exact statistics of their presence in the different East African countries. 'Asians' is used in East Africa to denote Indians and Pakistanis since 1947 and Bangladeshis since 1971. Prior to 1947, the term 'Indians' was usually used. 'Goans' constituted a separate category in British colonial administration, records, and daily use until shortly after the Second World War.
5. This term, still used in Goa today, denotes (young) men working on ships, also known as lascars. On Goans in Bombay, see Albuquerque (1986).
6. See also Zanzibar Official Gazette, throughout the 1890s. Furthermore, the British Consular General of Zanzibar prepared a list of European and Goan resident in Zanzibar. However, it is not clear how complete this list is (ZNA AB33/10).
7. See interviews passim.
8. Numbers of migration to East Africa: compilation of numbers from British census in Uganda, Kenya, Tanzania, and Zanzibar; see Frenz (2008, p. 187).
9. Apart from providing a place to stay for the exiled royal family and the Portuguese government, it seems that the arrival of these institutions in Brazil prevented a movement for independent Brazil at the time. See Newitt (2009, p. 170).
10. Clarence-Smith's account focuses on the economic exchanges between the Portuguese in Portugal, Mozambique, and Angola but does not refer to the economic conditions of Africans. This would have been significant for a more thorough understanding of the economies in Mozambique and Angola as a whole.
11. See the classic account on the utilitarians – Stokes (1959) and the Minute on Education, drafted by Thomas Babington Macaulay (1800–1859) in 1835 and agreed to by Governor-General William Bentinck (1774–1839) in Sharp (1920), pp. 107–117).
12. Ministério dos Negócios Estrangeiros, Anuário Diplomatico e Consular Portuguez. Relativo dos Annos de 1888 (Lisboa, 1889), p. 253. It has to be noted that the documents relating to Portuguese consuls in East Africa in the Arquivo Histórico-Diplomático, Ministério dos Negócios Estrangeiros, have not been opened to the public yet. Therefore, the Anuários are the main source of information at present.
13. Zanzibar Archives; Kenya National Archives; interviews, passim.
14. See correspondence of British government officials, KNA CS/2/7/16, passim.
15. Interview with Anna (London, 2005) and Emma (Goa, 2008).
16. The equality between Portuguese citizens was restricted to individuals who had the status of a citizen – for instance, the Portuguese, the Goans, the Chinese, mestiços, and assimilados – but it did not apply to every Portuguese national. In fact, the category of 'citizen' excluded about 98% of African Portuguese individuals in the overseas territories (Michel Cahen, personal communication).

Representing the Portuguese Empire 209

17. Ministério dos Negócios Estrangeiros, Anuário Diplomatico e Consular Portuguez. Relativo dos Annos de 1916–1917 and following through to 1933.
18. Born 14 August 1869, and died in Anjuna 8 April 1956. He lived in Zanzibar for nearly 50 years and returned to Goa in 1946. Apparently, he was given permission by the sultan to build a house for himself in Anjuna that had features of the Zanzibar sultan's palace. Interview with Pascal, May 2005; see also Das (2011) and TNN (2011).
19. KNA, CS/2/7/16. He is mentioned in the Kenya Gazette 51, no. 40 (30 August 1949, p. 685), as having been exempted from the Registration of Persons Ordinance of the British colonial government. See also Anuário 1934 through to 1948.
20. Born in Goa 17 February 1870, died in Nairobi 2 February 1951. He came to Mombasa in 1898 before moving to Nairobi in 1899, having undertaken his medical training at the Goa Medical College. See also Pandit (1963, p. 91) and Anuário 1914 through to 1924.
21. Dr A. C. L. de Sousa was born in 1883 in Goa and died in 1958 in Nairobi. He did his medical training at Grant Medical College, Bombay, and came to Kenya in 1915. See also Pandit (1963, pp. 71–72).
22. KNA, CS/2/7/16. G. T. Esperato da Cruz was acting consul at Nairobi from 1 May 1940 to 23 January 1946, when he died. KNA, CS/2/7/16.
23. Senhor Jose Leopoldo Lopes de Neiva; KNA, CS/2/7/16. See Anuário 1949.
24. Kenya Gazette 39, no. 2 (12 January 1937, p. 20). See Anuário, passim.
25. KNA CS/2/7/16. He was also on the Advisory Council on Goan Education. Kenya Gazette 60, no. 61, (16 December 1958, p. 1452). See Anuário 1949 through to 1951.
26. Caetano Francis Martins, born 26 August 1924, in Tanga; died March 17, 2007, in Vancouver. See Goa (2007) and Interview with Charlotte (London, 2006). See Anuário 1950 through to 1963.
27. De Souza Figueiredo was born in Kampala in 1920, educated in Bombay, Allahabad, and London (Pandit, 1963, p. 135). He married in 1942 in Goa, and returned with his wife and eldest son to Kampala in 1943 (Interview with Emma [Goa, 2008]). His father, Marshall de Souza Figueiredo, originally from Saligao, in Goa, came to Uganda in 1911 and was a founding member of the Goan Institutes in Kampala and Jinja, as well as a guarantor for the building loan of the Goan school in Jinja. For his time as consul, see Anuário 1954 through to 1963.
28. Interview with Anna (London, 2005). December 1, 1640, when Portugal became independent from Spain.
29. Interview with Anna (London, 2005). The description of this portfolio of responsibilities relates to the 1940s and 1950s.
30. Consulado de Portugal em Nairobi, Servico de Informacao [sic], no. 1, 8 March 1948, p. 2 (KNA CS/2/7/16).
31. Consulado de Portugal em Nairobi to the chief secretary, Nairobi, 6 September 1948 (KNA CS/2/7/16). Emphasis in original. See declaration of all Portuguese territories being overseas provinces in the Acto Colonial of 1930 and its 1951 incorporation into the new Portuguese constitution.
32. Letter from the consulado geral de Portugal to the chief secretary, Nairobi, 6 September 1948, (KNA, CS/2/7/16).
33. Newitt, Portugal in Africa, p. 220.
34. Consulado de Portugal em Nairobi, Servico de Informacao [sic], no. 1, 8 March 1948, p. 4 (KNA CS/2/7/16).

35. Consulado de Portugal em Nairobi, Servico de Informacao [sic], no. 1, 8 March 1948, p. 1 (KNA CS/2/7/16). Emphasis in original.
36. Although every individual now was a citizen legally, the right to vote was still restricted in practice; even in the local elections conducted by the Portuguese in Mozambique in 1973, only about 10% Mozambicans had the franchise.
37. The Community of the Portuguese Speaking Countries was formed in 1996. Members today are Portugal, Brazil, Angola, Mozambique, Cape Verde, São Tomé, Príncipe, East Timor. Mozambique is also a member of the Commonwealth.
38. The idea of racial equality emerged only after the idea of multiracialism had gained currency in Europe (Newitt 1981, p. 184).
39. Letter from the president of the Goan community, Luis Barreto, to the consul for Portugal in Mombasa, 29 May 1944 (KNA, CS/2/7/16).
40. Letter from the Portuguese consul in Mombasa to the chief secretary, Nairobi, 15 January 1945 (KNA, CS/2/7/16).
41. Letter of the regional representative, Ministry of War Transport of the United Kingdom, to the chief secretary, Nairobi, 23 August 1945 (KNA, CS/2/7/16).
42. Letters by various Goans to the Portuguese consul in the 1940s and 1950s (KNA CS/2/7/16; CS/2/9/37).
43. Letter from the British acting chief secretary to the consul for Portugal, 29 June 1944 (KNA CS/2/9/37).
44. Letter from the Portuguese consul to the chief secretary, 15 January 1945 (KNA CS/2/9/37). In this letter, the Portuguese consul calls the Goans 'my nationals'.
45. Anuário, 1963 through to 1966.
46. Interview with Anna (London, 2005): 'All that time while dad was a Portuguese consul, my mum and dad always spoke English at home to us – and if they wanted to talk something, they would talk in Portuguese between themselves so the children did not understand what they were saying.'

References

Albuquerque, L. de (ed.) (1989), *Portugal no mundo*. Alfa, Lisbon.
Albuquerque, T. (1986), *To Love Is to Serve. Catholics of Bombay*. Heras Institute of Indian History and Culture, Bombay.
Bethencourt, F., and K. N. Chaudhuri (eds.) (1998), *História da expansão portuguesa*. Temas e Debates, Lisbon.
Boxer, C. (1969), *The Portuguese Seaborne Empire 1415–1825*. Knopf, London.
Brandes, N. (2008), 'Schweres Erbe. Luis Fonseca kämpfte als Generalsekretär der Gemeinschaft portugiesischsprachiger Länder gegen das koloniale Gespenst. Jetzt endet seine Amtszeit,' *Süddeutsche Zeitung* no. 187, p. 13.
Brettel, C. B. (2006), 'Portugal's First Post-Colonials. Citizenship, Identity, and the Repatriation of Goans,' *Portuguese Studies Review* 14, no. 2, pp. 143–170.
Burbank, J., and Cooper F. (2010), *Empires in World History. Power and the Politics of Difference*. Princeton University Press, Princeton, NJ.
Cahen, M. (1997), 'Des caravelles pour le futur? Discours politique et idéologie dans l'institutionalisation' de la Communauté des pays de langue portugaise,' *Lusotopie* 4, pp. 391–433.
Cahen, M. (2007), 'Salazarisme, fascisme et colonialisme. Problèmes d'interprétation en sciences sociales, ou le sébastianisme de l'exception,' *Portuguese Studies Review* 15, no. 1, pp. 97–113.

Clarence-Smith, G. W. (1985), *The Third Portuguese Empire, 1825–1975: A Study in Economic Imperialism.* Manchester University Press, Manchester.
Darwin, J. (2009), *The Empire Project. The Rise and Fall of the British World-System, 1830–1970.* Cambridge University Press, Cambridge.
Das, A. (2011), 'A House Full of Memories,' *The Navhindtimes* [online], 25 March 2011, http://www.navhindtimes.in/ilive/house001Efull001Ememories, date accessed 27 April 2011.
Dirks, N. (2001), *Castes of Mind. Colonialism and the Making of Modern India.* Princeton University Press, Princeton, NJ.
Disney, A. R. (2009), *A History of Portugal and the Portuguese Empire.* 2 vols. Cambridge University Press, Cambridge.
Frenz, M. (2005), 'Moving Home, Settling In. Cosmopolitan Goans in Zanzibar.' Unpublished manuscript, Zanzibar.
Frenz, M. (2008), 'Global Goans. Migration Movements and Identity in a Historical Perspective,' *Lusotopie* 15, no. 1, pp. 183–202.
Homem, A. P. Barbas, et al. (eds.) (2010), *Textos constitucionais de Portugal e Espanha, 1808–1845*, vol. 13, in H. Dippel (ed.), *Constitutions of the World from the Late 18th Century to the Middle of the 19th Century.* De Gruyter, Berlin and New York.
Karnik, S. (1998), 'Goans in Mozambique,' *Africa Quarterly* 38, no. 3, pp. 95–118.
Kennedy, D. (2004), *Britain and Empire, 1880–1945.* Longman, Harlow.
Levine, P. (2007), *The British Empire. Sunrise to Sunset.* Longman, Harlow.
Marques, A. H. de Oliveira (1981), *História de Portugal.* Vol. 3: *Das Revoluções Liberais aos Nossos Dias.* 2nd ed.. Editorial Presença, Lisbon.
Newitt, M. (1981), *Portugal in Africa. The Last Hundred Years.* Longman, London.
Newitt, M. (2009), *Portugal in European and World History.* Reaktion Books, London.
Osterhammel, J. (2009), *Die Verwandlung der Welt. Eine Geschichte des 19. Jahrhunderts.* C. H. Beck, Munich.
Pandit, S. (1963), *Asians in East and Central Africa.* Panco Publications, Nairobi.
Pearson, M. N. (1998), 'Indians in East Africa: The Early Modern Period,' in R. Mukherjee and L. Subramanian (eds.), *Politics and Trade in the Indian Ocean World. Essays in Honour of Ashin Das Gupta.* Oxford University Press, New Delhi.
Pinto, A. Costa (2010), *Rethinking the Nature of Fascism: Comparative Perspectives.* Palgrave Macmillan, New York.
Ribeiro, A. (1996), 'Doctor on a Zebra,' in C. Salvadori (ed.), *We Came in Dhows* Vol. 1. Paperchase, Kenya Ltd., Nairobi.
Rich, P. B. (1990), *Race and Empire in British Politics.* Cambridge University Press, Cambridge.
Russell-Wood, A. J. R. (1992), *The Portuguese Empire, 1415–1808. A World on the Move.* Johns Hopkins University Press, Baltimore.
Sharp, H. (1920) *Selections from Educational Records, part 1: 1781–1839.* Superintendent Government Printing, Calcutta.
Siqueira, A. (2002), 'Postcolonial Portugal, Postcolonial Goa. A Note on Portuguese Identity and Its Resonance in Goa and India,' *Lusotopie* 10, no. 2, pp. 211–213.
Stokes, E. (1959), *The English Utilitarians and India.* Oxford University Press (Clarendon), Oxford.
Subrahmanyam, S. (1993), *The Portuguese Empire in Asia, 1500–1700. A Political and Economic History.* Longman, London.
Táboas, L., Táboas, D., and Casteleiro, A. Tabuada (2010), 'The Portuguese Estado Novo: Programmes and Hindrances for Agrarian Modernization (1933–1974).'

Paper presented at the Rural History Conference, University of Sussex, 13–16 September 2010.

Teixeira, L. Pinto (2008), 'Echoes or Transcendence? From Standards of Civilisation to EU Conditionality.' Paper presented at the workshop Echoes of Imperialism, University of Oxford, 9–10 May 2008.

Thompson, A. S. (2005), *The Empire Strikes Back? The Impact of Imperialism on Britain from the Mid-Nineteenth Century*. Longman, Harlow.

Thompson, P. (2000), *The Voice of the Past. Oral History*. 3rd edn. Oxford University Press, Oxford.

TNN (Times News Network) (2011), 'Star of Zanzibar Set to Shine in Anjuna,' *Times of India* [online], 27 March 2011, http://articles.timesofindia.indiatimes.com/2011001E03001E27/goa/29194722_1_anjuna001Esultan001Evillagers (accessed 27 April 2011).

Wesselink, H. L. (2004), *The European Colonial Empires, 1815–1919*. Longman, Harlow.

9
The Making of a Portuguese Community in South Africa, 1900–1994

Clive Glaser

Carlos Farinha was born into a large, poor farming family in the north of Madeira in 1933. He left school aged 14 and found work in a local registry office. But he was paid only 'a few cents a day' and started to look for alternatives. Two of his sisters and a brother had moved to South Africa during the 1940s seeking opportunities. In 1950 one of his brothers-in-law organised Carlos' papers to work in South Africa. Barely literate and unable to speak a word of English, he travelled by boat to Cape Town in February 1951 and made his way to the Witwatersrand. Carlos lived with his sisters and their families on their small farm and worked in the family shop. For many years the combined families lived off pooled resources from mine jobs, farming vegetables and running a small shop. When Carlos' father died in the mid 1950s, his mother and another little sister joined them in South Africa. By the early 1960s two more brothers had arrived from Madeira to join the family business. Throughout the 1960s Carlos got up before dawn to drive to the Johannesburg market to sell fresh produce from the farm and buy stock for the shop, working extraordinarily long hours. During the mid 1960s he married a young second generation Madeiran woman and during the 1970s and 1980s Carlos and his family were able to achieve a measure of prosperity and educate their children. He and his wife are now retired and living in a comfortable town-house on the East Rand. (Interview, Carlos Farinha 2009)

Maria Gonçalves was only eighteen in June 1953 when she stepped onto the dock in Cape Town to meet her 42 year-old husband for the first time. This was the first time she had left the island of Madeira and she spoke no English. She came from a relatively well-off family from a town close to Funchal, and she had been lucky enough to go to school for several years. Nevertheless, there were few opportunities for young women in Madeira and her parents decided to find her a South African husband.

João Gonçalves seemed a good match: he owned a shop and appeared to be doing well. It was an unhappy marriage: there was a big age gap and they had little in common. Maria had five children and worked extremely hard all her life, initially in João's various shops and later finding employment. João's business failed in Cape Town and they resettled first on a farm near the Witwatersrand and then moved to the city itself. She was always a devout Catholic but it was only after her husband's death in the early 1990s that she became more involved in the church. The church became a great comfort to her, providing her with a sense of purpose and a network of friends. In her mid 70s now, fiercely independent, still employed and highly active, Maria lives in a small Catholic retirement home on the East Rand. Her children and their families mostly also live on the Witwatersrand. (Interview, Maria Gonçalves 2010)

José Rodrigues, born in 1957, came to South Africa in 1965 from a village in the north of Portugal. José's father, like many from his region, left the repressive and economically depressing Portugal for South Africa in 1963 to find work. He was a painter, but dabbled in most aspects of the building trade. Two years later, José and his mother joined him. They lived in the south of Johannesburg, along with numerous other newly-immigrant Portuguese families. In 1972 his father was killed in a tragic motor accident. This caused great hardship and the family was initially only able to make ends meet with help from the local Portuguese community. José left school, aged 14, was apprenticed as a motor mechanic, and became the bread-winner in his family. After completing his apprenticeship and working for several small businesses run by Portuguese immigrants, he started up a practice of his own in his mid 20s. Through word of mouth, he built up the practice and was able to make a decent living. José married a woman whose family, like his own, immigrated from the north of Portugal in the 1960s. José and his family lived in the working class Bertrams area of south-eastern Johannesburg until the 1990s before moving to a nearby middle class suburb in the 2000s. (Interview, José Rodrigues 2009)

Ana Rocha, while still a toddler, left mainland Portugal for Mozambique with her family in 1963. Her father was a skilled boilermaker who made a good living in the colony. She and her parents lived a comfortable life in a spacious home in Lourenço Marques. In 1975, as conditions became more tenuous for white colonists, the family relocated to Johannesburg. It was a relatively easy transition because her father was re-employed by a company he had worked for in the early 1970s. Many other white Mozambican families she knew came with nothing and even had to live in temporary refugee camps in South Africa. Ana and her family lived in Rosettenville, the heart of the 'Portuguese belt' to the south of the city. Ana found the transition very difficult but it was made easier by the fact *that there were so many Portuguese Mozambicans living nearby and attending her high school. Ana went to the University of the Witwatersrand in 1979, majoring in Portuguese language studies. In the mid 1980s, along with many of her contemporaries, she went to Portugal for several years, but never felt at home in Europe and returned to South Africa in the early 1990s. She married an ex-Portuguese Mozambican and most of her good friends are originally from Mozambique or Angola. She lives in Johannesburg and teaches Portuguese at her alma mater.* (Interview, Ana Rocha 2011)

These fairly typical life stories offer some sense of the diversity of the origins of Portuguese South Africans. In spite of the fact that anywhere between 300,000 and 500,000 South Africans have 20th-century Portuguese origins and despite the long historical connection between the two countries, South Africa has been a relatively neglected corner of the Portuguese diaspora.[1] While the Portuguese government has recognised the importance of the community in recent decades, probably because of its sheer size, it has rarely been the subject of social or historical research.[2] In part, I would argue, this is because it is only ambiguously a 'community'. Rather, Portuguese South Africans have consisted historically of a series of tight ethnic networks and enclaves, separated along lines of regional background, occupation, and phase of migration. Some institutions began to work towards forging a broader national identity in the late 1960s and 1970s, but even in the 21st century it would be difficult to argue that Portuguese South Africans form a coherent community. It is incorrect to assume that people who share a common language and some sort of connection to the Portuguese state automatically 'imagine' themselves, in the term of Benedict Anderson, as a community. They continue to maintain a low profile, rarely projecting themselves as a group or asserting their interests as a bloc (as we see, for example, with the local Jewish community). While many of the internal divisions have eased, the outer boundaries have frayed through assimilation in the second and third generations. There has also been substantial emigration since the early 1990s. This chapter discusses the various historical strands which have made up this community-in-the-making and assesses some of the forces which have pulled it together and pulled it apart.

Three immigrant paths

As these individual profiles suggest, there were three quite distinct Portuguese groups that migrated to South Africa in the 20th century.[3] First, Madeirans, usually with very low levels of skill and literacy, trickled in steadily from the late 1800s until at least the 1970s. Second, relatively skilled artisans from the Portuguese mainland arrived from about 1940 to 1980, but mostly concentrated between 1963 and 1971. Third, Mozambican and Angolan colonists occasionally moved to South Africa for work or education throughout the 20th century, but their numbers became significant only when they fled from sudden political upheavals between 1974 and 1976.

From the island of Madeira

The Atlantic island of Madeira, first settled by Portuguese in the 1500s, was densely populated by the 20th century. Yet the mountainous terrain allowed little space for cultivation. The overwhelming majority of the population managed to subsist through small-scale farming, usually on terraced plots. Fishing was crucial for the coastal communities. Schooling and social services, beyond the capital, Funchal, were scarce. Migration, initiated by young men, became a way of life on the island.[4] Brazil, Venezuela and South Africa emerged as the most popular destinations for islanders.[5] South Africa was attractive for several reasons. There was a convenient shipping route which linked Lisbon, Funchal, Cape Town, and Lourenço Marques. News got back to Madeira from earlier pioneers that South Africa was a land of great opportunity. Once some became established in South Africa, the existence of a substantial Madeiran support network became an important attraction in itself. Mozambique's proximity to the Witwatersrand, South Africa's industrial hub, was also important. Portuguese East Africa, as it was called under colonial rule, was culturally and linguistically less intimidating, and entry visas into the colony were relatively easy to obtain; it was an ideal transitional base to enter South Africa.[6]

The union government of South Africa from 1910 was, on the whole, hostile to Madeiran immigration. Contrary to popular perceptions, the South African government was not unambiguously in favour of white immigration during the segregationist and apartheid years (See especially Peberdy 2009). The shape of white immigration was in fact heavily contested by competing political factions from the 1920s through to the 1970s. While the South African Party and United Party under the leadership of Smuts was generally sympathetic to most European immigration to offset racial demographic vulnerability and assist with the country's development goals, Afrikaner nationalists feared the dilution of Afrikaner culture and, more basically, the reduction of an Afrikaner majority in white politics. During the 1920s and 1930s governments were also convinced by powerful eugenicist and anti-Semitic lobbies to limit the entry of Jews and impoverished, illiterate, unskilled, darker-skinned southern Europeans. Successive alien immigration legislation in 1913, 1930, and 1937 gave immigration authorities increasingly wide discretion to exclude applicants on grounds of 'desirability'. As late as the 1960s most Afrikaner nationalists felt comfortable only with Dutch, German, and Flemish immigrants, who, they argued, could be assimilated as Afrikaners. When the Nationalists came to power in 1948, they quickly reversed the short-lived European immigrant-friendly policy of the postwar Smuts government. Only severe skills shortages in the

1960s forced the Nationalists to make compromises.[7] (It is important to note that Salazar's *Estado Novo* was itself hostile to emigration until a sudden reassessment of policy in the 1960s (See Baganha, c. 2000). Madeirans thus faced difficulties at both exit and entry.

For Madeirans to enter South Africa legally, they usually had to be able to demonstrate that they had some basic literacy, skills needed for the economy and an offer of employment. Women and children were allowed to join already established male family members. By 1904 there were officially just under a thousand Madeirans living in the Cape, mostly male. They were either market gardeners or fishermen. But the figure was almost certainly underestimated in the Cape census because many entered illegally (Rosa and Trigo 1990, p. 183). It is almost impossible to estimate how many had entered the Transvaal and Natal by that stage. But there was certainly a substantial presence by the time the Portuguese consulate started registering immigrants in 1909.[8] The Cape Madeiran community gradually established itself during the 1910s and 1920s. Hundreds of Madeirans were employed in the fishing industry or on farms, but a growing number owned or rented their own farms, shops, and coffee houses by the 1920s. This opened opportunities for new Madeirans who could find employment in these enterprises and, with local sponsorship, stand a good chance of gaining legal entry (Machado 1992, Tozzo 2005). In the Transvaal a small number of Madeirans were allowed in as mine or farm workers. According to official records, fewer than 200 Madeirans became legal residents per year during the 1920s and 1930s.[9]

In spite of official hostility, the legal Madeiran population continued to grow. Immigration records reveal that 14,000 Madeirans entered legally between 1940 and 1981 (Machado 1992, p. 5). Work permits were issued cautiously, and families were allowed to reunify. Perhaps more importantly, their birth rates were high, and very few reunited families returned to Madeira. Machado's (1992) micro-study of the Madeiran community in Woodstock, Cape Town, is illustrative. At the core of this community were Madeiran fishermen who found employment in fishing companies operating out of Cape Town and Luderitz, South West Africa (Namibia), and eventually brought their families to join them. From this base in fishing, many diversified into shops and restaurants and other small businesses and invested in their children's education. On a larger scale, a similar process was taking place throughout the Transvaal, but especially in the Witwatersrand/Pretoria/Vaal Triangle area. Here the economic base was small-scale fruit and vegetable farming on the outskirts of urban centres and, to an extent, employment in the mines. This allowed for investment in family shops and businesses. Madeirans also established a presence in Durban, Port Elizabeth, East London, and Bloemfontein (Tozzo 2005, Pereira 2000, Bartolo 1978, Van Rensburg 1968).

Most aspirant immigrants, however, struggled to fulfil the criteria for residency. Thousands, almost impossible to quantify, entered illegally.

Most settled in the Transvaal, where they could find fellow Madeirans to employ them quietly on their farms and in their shops. From as early as the mid 1920s, Union officials were disturbed by the number of Madeirans crossing illegally into the Transvaal (see Tozzo 2005, pp. 23–26). From the late 1930s to the early 1960s, it became a major issue for the Department of Immigration. The South African Police (SAP) and immigration authorities cooperated with the Portuguese East African police to stamp out highly organised smuggling syndicates which operated out of Madeira, Lourenço Marques (LM), and Johannesburg. The smugglers organised papers for prospective immigrants to go to LM, which was used as a base to cross into the Transvaal. Although the authorities on both sides of the border arrested numerous illegal residents and smugglers, they were ultimately unable to police the vast land border between Mozambique, Swaziland, and South Africa. On an almost daily basis Madeirans crossed over by foot, in hidden compartments of trains or trucks, even in banana crates. The syndicates bribed border officials and employed guides to lead groups along smuggling routes.[10] Although the documentary record seems to stop (or has been lost) after the early 1960s, oral testimony suggests that this process continued well into the 1960s and 1970s. As I have discussed elsewhere (Glaser 2013 forthcoming), illegality was central to the Madeiran immigrant experience in South Africa. Virtually all first-generation Madeirans, at some point in their lives, had direct or indirect experiences of illegal residency. Many illegal Madeirans crossed the Mozambique–South African border several times. In some cases they returned after deportation, in other cases they continued to work in South Africa while trying to secure legal papers in the Portuguese colony. There were cases of illegal Madeirans working for many years in South Africa before being detected. Some were even able to establish businesses, using the names of legal residents to secure licenses, bank accounts, and so on. According to both oral testimony and the documentary record, illegal workers were often exploited. After being fleeced by the smuggling syndicates, their vulnerability was regularly exploited by employers, usually fellow Madeirans, who paid them meagre wages. Stories abound of employers tipping off police about illegal workers just before their wages were due. But Madeirans generally protected each other from the scrutiny of the immigration authorities. After working illegally in the country, a large number were able to secure legal papers. Ironically, many felt that their best chance to secure residency rights was through entering illegally, working for a few years, improving their English or Afrikaans, and then applying for legal papers from within the country. Several Portuguese organisations helped these illegal residents to get their papers sorted out once they came out into the open and applied for temporary permits.[11]

From the 1890s through to the 1970s, men led the migration from Madeira to South Africa. Women could not migrate without a formal attachment to a man. There were often long periods of separation as the men tried to establish themselves in the host country. When the men felt relatively secure, the married ones brought their wives and children over. Until at least the mid 1960s, the pool of eligible second-generation Madeiran women in South Africa was small, and so single men often arranged marriages with women back in Madeira. Many of these Madeiran women married by proxy and met their husbands for the first time on arrival in South Africa. It was also common for men, once they had saved enough, to return briefly to Madeira to 'find' a wife to take back to South Africa. In both cases wives found themselves culturally and socially isolated, quite often in unhappy marriages with virtual strangers. There was great stigma associated with divorce. They could not speak the local language and depended heavily on their husbands to mediate their access to services and resources. Not surprisingly, Madeiran immigrant women were usually tied closely to their communities, and they were known by authorities to be slow to integrate into South African society. Madeiran families tended to be highly patriarchal and conservative; the mobility of girl children was tightly monitored. Although they were largely involved in domestic work, women also played a crucial, largely unrecognised, role as unpaid labour on the farms and in the vegetable shops and cafés[12] which formed the basis of the Madeiran immigrant economy.[13]

Madeirans found themselves on the margins of white society. The first generation faced severe language difficulties and high levels of illiteracy. Very few were educated beyond the most basic years of schooling. Their shops and farms were subjected to routine raids for illegal residents. They often faced derision and insulting behaviour from established local, especially Afrikaner, white residents. Nevertheless, they managed to achieve substantial upward mobility during the 20th century. This was in part due to extremely hard work and determination, the mutual support of ethnic networks, and the developing of a key economic niche in the fresh fruit and vegetable trade.[14] But it was also made possible by their official white status. Although some Afrikaner nationalists questioned their whiteness (since poverty, linguistic difficulty in the two main white languages, low levels of education, and a non-Protestant culture were associated with blackness), they were classified as European, or white, a status that came with many advantages.[15] Madeiran residents could get access to virtually free state schooling and health and welfare services. Perhaps more importantly, they could live, own property, and obtain business licenses in white areas. This meant that their properties could appreciate in value and their businesses could tap into a growing white middle-class market. As the cities expanded, small farms, which used to be on the urban peripheries and which had been purchased very cheaply in the first half of the 20th century, became increasingly valuable.[16] Although a small minority of Madeirans continued to farm, most had invested in urban businesses or become professionals by the 1980s and 1990s.

From Mainland Portugal

Those who came from the mainland of Portugal were escaping for similar reasons: economic stagnation, poor social services, and political repression. By the 1960s, as colonial wars intensified, many young men wanted to avoid military conscription. But the experience of the mainland immigrants was very different. They were mostly literate and, even if only schooled to fairly low levels, skilled. South Africa needed artisans, particularly those involved in the building, engineering, or steel industries. Consequently, between 1940 and the early 1960s a few hundred Portuguese artisans – mostly bricklayers, carpenters, fitter-and-turners, boilermakers, and mechanics – were allowed into South Africa every year. The mainlanders were generally seen by the immigration authorities as somewhat more desirable than the Madeirans; not only were they more literate and skilled but they were also somehow more 'European'. In the early 1960s, the nationalist government had to concede that there was a skilled-labour crisis and, since the alternative would have been to relax the colour bar on skilled labour (a central feature of apartheid), it began actively recruiting skilled European workers from wherever they could be found. At more or less the same time, the Salazar regime in Portugal changed its attitude and started to encourage emigration.[17] In spite of its instinctive suspicion of southern European Catholics, the South African government even set up a recruitment office in Lisbon. This allowed for a spate of Portuguese migration to South Africa from 1963 until a nationalist backlash towards the end of the decade forced a striking deceleration in the early 1970s.[18]

The skilled mainlanders were absorbed almost immediately as formal employees in the mainstream of the economy. Most of the big construction projects in the Pretoria/Johannesburg/Vaal Triangle industrial hub during the economic boom of the 1960s employed skilled Portuguese workers. In the 1960s the immigration authorities even subsidised the move of these skilled mainlanders to South Africa and often provided assistance, such as translators and temporary accommodation, on arrival. The majority arrived directly in Johannesburg by air. A significant minority, though, came via Mozambique. Families either came together, or if men came ahead of their families, the separation was rarely longer than a year or two.[19]

Compared with Portugal in the 1950s and 1960s, South Africa offered enormous opportunity; skilled workers could find work easily and command good wages, housing was spacious and reasonably priced, and schooling and healthcare were decent, accessible, and almost free. Nevertheless, compared with that of other European immigrants in the 1960s and 1970s, their income was relatively low. The British and German immigrants, for example, tended to be highly paid professionals who moved quickly into the elite of South African society (Van Rensburg, 1968, pp. 136–147; Botha, 1971, pp. 33–39). During the 1960s the mainland Portuguese immigrants transformed several shabby suburbs in the south of Johannesburg – La Rochelle, Turfontein, Regents Park, Rosettenville, and Kenilworth – into what became known as Little Portugal. Housing in this area was run-down and cheap in the early 1960s and conveniently close to the centre of town. It made a lot of sense to buy and rent houses there, especially once the ethnic enclave in itself became a drawing card. For immigrants who spoke little English, it was comforting to be able to socialise, shop, and attend church services in Portuguese. As skilled artisans, they put a lot of effort into improving their own homes, often with the help of fellow immigrants who worked on the basis of reciprocity (Cohen 1971, Botha 1971; interviews: Silvério da Silva 2011, Caetano 2011).

Portuguese immigrants in Johannesburg faced a great deal of hostility and abuse from white, especially Afrikaans-speaking, locals in the 1960s and 1970s. Not only did Afrikaner working class families often live in the same parts of town and encounter huge language and cultural barriers, but they were often competing for the same jobs. They almost certainly felt threatened by the immigrants' relentless work ethic and skills, which gave them access to better employment. Perhaps the improvement of the Portuguese homes and neighbourhoods emphasised their own blunted aspirations (Rosa and Trigo, 1990; interviews: Caetano 2011, Galego 2010, Quintal 2011). These threats fuelled Afrikaner nationalist prejudices towards non-Protestant southern European immigrants and led ultimately to the tightening of Portuguese immigration by the early 1970s (Glaser 2013 forthcoming; Peberdy 2009, pp. 126–134).

Like the Madeirans, the mainland Portuguese were upwardly mobile by the mid-1970s, but they operated in a different sector of the economy. A few small Portuguese-owned engineering and construction businesses had established themselves in the 1940s and 1950s. They were, not surprisingly, among the most enthusiastic employers of new Portuguese immigrants in the 1960s. Nevertheless, it was only in the 1970s that Portuguese-owned companies became significant. The new immigrants worked their way up the employment ladder from foremen to supervisors and into middle management. Increasingly, they started up their own small businesses. Eventually some of these businessmen became big players in the engineering and construction sector. The majority, however, crept into the middle classes as employed skilled artisans or by running small private businesses. The children of the second generation, much more educated than their parents, successfully entered a range of professions in the 1980s and beyond (Rosa and Trigo 1990; interviews: Silvério da Silva 2011, George da Silva 2011). Communal solidarity and a powerful work ethic, no doubt, played a big part in the story of upward mobility. But the mainland Portuguese, in spite of local prejudices and often tough early conditions, benefited enormously from the peculiar intersection of racial advantage and a dire skills shortage within a growing industrial economy.

From Mozambique and Angola

The sudden decolonisation of Mozambique and Angola, following the collapse of the Salazar regime in Portugal, led to another wave of Portuguese migration to South Africa between 1974 and 1976. While most of these colonists, especially from Angola, returned to Portugal, a substantial proportion moved to South Africa. Unlike the other Portuguese immigrants to South Africa, the Mozambicans and Angolans had been a privileged elite in the colonies and lost a great deal, in terms of both material possessions and status, in the transition. During the chaotic aftermath of the revolutions, colonial families who stayed on were vulnerable to violent attacks and confiscations. Although some had foreseen the inevitable in the preceding years and prepared their move quite carefully by, for example, buying property in South Africa or establishing business connections, the transition was traumatic. Properties, businesses, familiar neighbourhoods, and friendship networks were abandoned in haste. The fleeing colonists were left feeling bitter about the chaotic capitulation of the Caetano government and its failure to provide them with adequate protection and compensation. Portugal, they felt, had turned its back on them.[20]

Flights out of Lourenço Marques and Luanda were limited. While the upper echelons of society were swiftly airlifted to Lisbon, most of the colonial families had to wait anxiously for flights or make a hazardous overland journey to South Africa. The remnants of the Portuguese colonial army, in a last act of protection, organised armed convoys to guide civilians through to the South African or Namibian borders.[21] The South African government, sympathetic to white colonists fleeing black rule, set up a series of refugee camps in Namibia and the Transvaal to absorb them. These camps provided temporary shelter while they tried to find employment and accommodation in South Africa. The immigration authorities also arranged language courses and lectures at these camps to help the new arrivals prepare for South African life (Gupta 2011). South African Portuguese organisations helped to integrate the refugees, providing food parcels, accommodation, assistance with immigration paperwork, and translation services (interviews: Gouveia 2008, Silvério da Silva 2011). On the whole, the South African government did not make it difficult for them to obtain residency rights.

The Mozambican and Angolan Portuguese immigrants were far more skilled and educated than the Madeiran or mainland Portuguese immigrant communities. They tended to be professionals, administrators, or commercial farmers or established in businesses with links to South Africa. Rosa and Trigo (1990, pp. 183, 188) argue that this more educated wave of immigrants helped shift the image of the local Portuguese away from the farming, artisan, and petty trader stereotype. In spite of the initial trauma of departure, they found their feet quickly in South Africa, brought valuable skills into the country, and became something of an elite within local Portuguese society by the 1980s. They set up their own clubs and societies, partly dedicated to getting compensation for their confiscated property in Mozambique (Pereira 2000, pp. 53–56). While a minority of the new arrivals went to other centres, such as Durban, most initially found homes in the south of Johannesburg, where they consolidated the Portuguese character of the 'Portuguese belt'. At least two English-speaking high schools in the south of Johannesburg were dominated by Portuguese students during the 1980s. (Interviews: Rocha 2011, Caetano 2011; conversation, Peres 2011).

Former colonial immigrants from Mozambique and Angola, though identifying strongly with Portugal, were proud of their separate 'African' identity. Most had grown up in settled, privileged communities in the colonies. A substantial portion were born in Africa or had emigrated when they were too young to have memories of Portugal. Ex-Mozambicans, in particular, felt a powerful nostalgia for their former colony. Although they often felt displaced in South Africa, it felt more familiar than Portugal.[22] They were initially surprised by the rigidity of apartheid South Africa; the strict, formalised racial segregation of schools, social interaction, and public facilities was different from the colonies, where segregation was more relaxed and customary (even if exploitation of labour and political repression was equally harsh). Nevertheless, the overwhelming majority, scarred by the revolutionary process in the colonies, rejected democratic transformation in South Africa during the 1980s and early 1990s. Many even joined and donated money to the Nationalist Party (Cravinho 1993, 1995; Bessa 2009, pp. 137–142).

According to official immigration figures, 33,000 Mozambican and 4,000 Angolan former colonials settled permanently in South Africa between 1974 and 1980 (McDuling 1995, p. 10). This is, however, probably an underestimate of the actual numbers. During the chaotic years of transition, thousands entered without proper documentation. Angry with the new Portuguese government, which they felt had abandoned them, many did not bother to register with the Portuguese consulate (Bessa 2009, p. 139; conversation, Peres 2011). A large number, difficult to estimate, spent several years in South Africa before moving on to other destinations.

Portuguese community

Portuguese neighbourhoods and social networks

The establishment of ethnic enclaves is often a good indicator of community cohesion and identity. By the mid-1960s these enclaves were certainly present in the case of Portuguese South Africans. The best-known and the largest Little Portugal, as I have discussed earlier, was in the south of Johannesburg (Botha 1971, Cohen 1971). But there were also noteworthy enclaves in Pretoria (interviews, Silvério da Silva 2011, George da Silva 2011), Vaal Triangle (conversation, de Andrade 2009), Cape Town (Machado 1992), Durban (Tozzo 2000) and Bloemfontein (Van Rensburg 1968). Former residents recall that there was a strong spirit of community among the Portuguese in Johannesburg's south during the 1960s, 1970s, and 1980s. Nobody was wealthy but neighbours helped each other with home improvements, and they were very sociable. It was safe to walk several miles at night to clubs or community centres where Portuguese movies were showing or live *Fado* bands playing. New immigrants could get by without ever having to speak English. If disaster struck a local Portuguese family, community organisations would help to raise money (Interviews: Rodrigues 2009, Caetano 2011, Galego 2010, Silvério da Silva 2011). The emergence of the feared La Rochelle United gang in the late 1970s and early 1980s was perhaps another interesting indication of tight neighbourhood identity. Some claimed that there were as many as 1 000 gang members by 1980 (*Sunday Express*, July 19, 1980). It started as a defensive response by Portuguese immigrant youth who felt excluded and disparaged by wider white South African society and tried to assert their masculinity through a close identification with their neighbourhood and ethnicity.[23]

It is important to note, however, that enclaves did not necessarily indicate a wider Portuguese identity. These enclaves were mostly regionally constituted. There was, for example, only a minor Madeiran presence in Johannesburg's Little Portugal. In Cohen's sample of residents of La Rochelle, at the epicentre of the enclave, only 9 per cent had Madeiran origins (Cohen 1971, p. 12). The enclave was essentially developed by mainlanders during the 1960s and early 1970s and then consolidated by the arrival of Mozambican and Angolan Portuguese in the second half of the 1970s. Some of the shops and restaurants in the area were owned by Madeirans, but they were never a central part of this community. From the early 20th century, the Madeiran population was scattered. A good number worked and lived on farms or ran shops in small towns. Those in the cities, the majority, tended to be dispersed, unless they concentrated around specific occupations, for example, the fishing community of Woodstock (Machado 1992) or the mining community of Krugersdorp on the West Rand from the 1930s to the 1940s (interview, Nobrega 2009). Small fruit and vegetable farms were located on urban peripheries, while the shops, possibly to avoid competing with one another, were not concentrated. Woodstock is probably the only example of a 'Little Madeira'. Madeirans maintained strong familial support networks and business connections. But, aside perhaps from weddings and funerals and big church feast days, they did not actually see a lot of one another. This was especially the case for women, who were largely bound to the home or a shop (Glaser 2011). Johannesburg's fruit and vegetable market, initially in Newtown before moving to City Deep in the 1970s, was probably a more important space, albeit a male-dominated one, for Madeiran sociality than any specific neighbourhood. Newly arrived Madeiran men knew that the market was the best place to connect with countrymen.[24]

It should also be noted that the Mozambique/Angola arrival, though adding numerically, did not necessarily strengthen the sense of Portuguese community in the south of Johannesburg. In fact, one former resident suggests that community unity was weakened by their arrival because it created social divisions (interview, Caetano 2011). Certainly there was not a great deal of social interaction between the older mainlanders and newer ex-colonial immigrants in the 1980s (interview, Rocha 2011).

Johannesburg's Little Portugal began to disperse significantly in the 1990s. This was due, in part, to greater prosperity, which allowed residents to buy more expensive property in other parts of town. Thousands also emigrated in fear of crime and political instability. Equally importantly, the area became a popular neighbourhood for poor black immigrants who flooded into South Africa in the 1990s. They tended to let and sublet properties, creating denser living spaces and allowing housing stock to deteriorate. With 'white flight', property prices slumped, and banks became increasingly reluctant to offer housing loans in the area. Many Portuguese South Africans still live and run businesses in the 'old south', particularly in La Rochelle, Turfontein, and Regents Park, but it can no longer be thought of as a Little Portugal. Interestingly, most of the new black residents in suburbs such as Turfontein and Rosettenville are Portuguese-speaking Mozambicans, so the area has maintained a different kind of Portuguese character.[25] While the majority of the Portuguese on the Witwatersrand still live in the southern, though more middle class, parts of Johannesburg and the East Rand, there are no longer any dense ethnic Portuguese neighbourhoods.

Although contemporary observers in the 1990s (Rosa and Trigo 1990, McDuling 1995, Pereira 2000) dismissed internal regional tensions in the Portuguese community as irrelevant, deep social divisions persisted between first-generation Madeirans, mainlanders, and former Mozambican and Angolan colonists throughout the 1970s and 1980s. They were divided along lines of class, educational levels, professions, culture, and even regional dialects. Generally these were relationships not of conflict but of indifference. Madeirans, in particular, were regarded by the other groups as a separate community whose members 'stuck to themselves'. Most Madeirans arrived with almost no education and were skilled only in small farming or fishing. Although they had mostly clawed their way out of poverty by the mid 1970s, they often felt that mainlanders and especially the ex-colonists looked down on them. Their professional lives very rarely brought them into contact with other Portuguese, aside perhaps as customers in their shops, and they felt insufficient familiarity or trust to establish business partnerships with non-Madeirans. Mainlanders recall having little contact with Madeirans when they arrived in the 1960s. Madeirans, from their perspective, had a longer history in South Africa; they worked extremely hard, focused inwards, and seemed to have little interest in new arrivals from the mainland. Not surprisingly, it was very unusual for first-generation Madeirans to socialise with or marry other Portuguese immigrants. Even in the 1990s such behaviour was regarded as unusual, something to be remarked upon, even if not necessarily frowned upon.[26]

There was a widespread belief among ex-colonists that Madeirans, with their apparent lack of education and sophistication, encouraged a negative stereotype of Portuguese South Africans. One ex-colonial Mozambican recalls being angered that the Madeirans did nothing to challenge this negative image, which in turn rubbed off on all Portuguese immigrants. In spite of the fact that they came from privileged, professional backgrounds, Mozambique and Angolan Portuguese were teased at school along with the others: 'Hey, Porra, does your dad have a fruit shop?' She wanted to be recognised as 'proudly Portuguese' (Rocha 2011). Like Madeirans, they tended to socialise and marry among themselves. Local Portuguese organisations mobilised to assist the ex-colonial refugees when they arrived in the mid 1970s, but this did not necessarily break down social barriers. Mainlanders and Madeirans, after offering a great deal of sympathy in the refugee phase, often came to perceive Portuguese from Mozambique and Angola as rather uppity, with their better education, their experience of privilege, and their more cosmopolitan and permissive culture (interview, Caetano 2011).

Institutions

A number of ethnic institutions which were established from the 1930s onwards strengthened Portuguese identity. The Catholic Church played an important role in bringing people together. First-generation Portuguese immigrants were mostly observant Catholics. Church services, especially traditional feast days and weddings and funerals, drew Portuguese speakers together in large numbers. Numerous Catholic churches provided dedicated Portuguese services and even hired priests from Portuguese-speaking countries. Several churches became essentially Portuguese community churches. A cathedral in Mayfair (in western Johannesburg), initially catering to black Mozambican migrants, was transformed into a Portuguese community church by the 1950s. The Madeiran community raised funds to build a dedicated Portuguese cathedral in Benoni (on the East Rand) in the 1940s. Another Portuguese cathedral was built more recently in Pretoria. Religion and ethnic identity were closely interwoven. Aside from providing Portuguese-language services, these churches maintained specific regional customs and feast days and served in many ways as community centres. Portuguese churches, particularly the big cathedrals, have been well attended since the 1950s and continue to function as crucial community meeting points.[27]

While the Catholic Church clearly served to strengthen localised Portuguese-speaking communities, it is questionable whether it galvanised a *wider* Portuguese identity. For the most part, church affiliation mimicked the social patterns discussed in the previous section. The Mayfair and Benoni churches, for example, were and continue to be Madeiran dominated. The residents of Johannesburg's Little Portugal generally attended smaller local churches. Scattered Madeirans, aside perhaps from special occasions, attended the most convenient (usually mixed-ethnic English-medium) Catholic churches. There is little evidence to suggest that the church substantially broke down internal Portuguese barriers. While the church seemed to retain its powerful ethnic character for Madeirans well into the 21st century, for most second- and third-generation Portuguese, the Catholic Church gradually became both less significant and less ethnically specific (interview, George da Silva 2011; McDuling 1995, pp. 182–183).

The first noteworthy Portuguese social club, Casa da Madeira, was established in western Johannesburg in 1938. Shortly thereafter the Associação da Colónia Portuguesa (Portuguese Association) broke away, catering mostly to non-Madeirans (interview, Quintal 2011). Over the next 40 to 50 years Portuguese social clubs sprang up wherever there were concentrations of Portuguese immigrants. Clubs tended to be either social gathering points which involved a hall, with perhaps a bar and restaurant, or sports clubs. Some combined the two. Football was the dominant sport, although roller hockey was introduced with the arrival of the Mozambican colonists in the mid-1970s and became increasingly popular. Portuguese clubs participated in competitive football and, later, roller hockey leagues. Football clubs, such as Marítimo, set up official links with popular regional football clubs in Madeira or mainland Portugal. Following Portuguese and European club football, initially through newspapers and radio and later satellite television, became a focal point, especially for men, of sociality. Club halls were hired for weddings, private parties, and live music or folk dancing performances. Club bars and restaurants attracted regular customers.

Clubs were probably more effective than churches in forging cross-regional social spaces, but with some exceptions, they were also constituted in line with regional networks or neighbourhoods. By the 1990s some of the big recreational clubs, such as União in Turfontein, had a diverse membership, but most retained a regional character well into the 21st century (Silvério da Silva 2011, George da Silva 2011, Quintal 2011). For example, folklore and folk dancing clubs tended to preserve and promote regionally specific culture.[28]

The Casa da Madeira and the Portuguese Association often came across as 'representing' the Portuguese community during moments of crisis or threat, such as the late-1960s Afrikaner nationalist anti-immigrant backlash or the mid-1970s ex-colonial refugee crisis. They also assisted legal and illegal immigrants with a range of problems from the late 1930s to the 1970s and helped to negotiate amnesties for illegal immigrants. But, although they occasionally claimed to speak on behalf of the community and probably received broad support, it was never clear exactly who they represented or how their mandate was constituted.

Portuguese welfare organisations were probably the most broadly constituted community institutions. The Academia do Bacalhau (Codfish Academy) started in 1968 when a group of friends, with mostly mainland origins, came together to celebrate the national Portuguese day by eating traditional rock cod. They met more regularly and developed a charitable arm, with affiliates scattered throughout southern Africa, known as the Academia. The Sociedade Portuguesa de Beneficência (Portuguese Welfare Society) emerged out of this in the mid-1970s initially to help destitute ex-colonials from Mozambique and Angola refugees and then to establish a Portuguese home for the aged in Johannesburg (interviews: George da Silva 2011, Galego 2010). The Lusito School was established in Johannesburg in the late 1970s to cater to the needs of handicapped children of Portuguese origin. Like the Academia the school was initially galvanised by the Mozambican and Angolan refugee crisis, and much of the early work was focused on refugee children. But it developed into a crucial community institution during the 1980s and 1990s and, significantly, spawned the famous annual Lusito festival, which takes place in the south of Johannesburg, as a community fund-raiser (interview, Gouveia 2008). The latter has become probably the single most visible icon of local Portuguese identity. It is one of the few instances where a Portuguese community projects itself to a wider South African public. Organisations such as the Portuguese Welfare Association and the Lusito School continue to be managed by Portuguese South Africans of diverse origins. They provide services for all in need and certainly helped to foster a sense of broader communal identity over the last three decades.

Leaders who have tried to get the community to speak with one voice, however, have generally met with frustration. An umbrella body, the Federação das Associações Portuguesas na República da África do Sul (FAPRAS, Federation of Portuguese Associations of South Africa), was established in the 1990s to represent the wider Portuguese community. Over 30 clubs have affiliated, but the federation has never really succeeded in establishing unity. The various clubs resist any intrusions on their autonomy. Club presidents tend to prefer dealing directly with the Portuguese consulate rather than work through FAPRAS. 'I don't think the Portuguese community binds together the way it should,' commented George da Silva (interview 2011), the current general secretary of FAPRAS. Some community leaders have worked hard to establish a single Casa de Portugal, but they have never met with success because, as one of the leaders puts it, 'people like to hang on to their own piece of Portugal' (interview, Silvério da Silva 2011).

Language and media

The Portuguese language, irrespective of dialectic variations or social background, played a vital role in connecting first- and, to a large extent, second-generation Portuguese immigrants. New immigrants inevitably found their weakness in English and Afrikaans a huge barrier to social integration. The fact that there were already established communities of Portuguese speakers by the 1950s allowed them to insulate themselves; it simultaneously eased their transition into the host country but slowed their acquisition of local languages (see Van Rensburg 1968, pp. 151–152, 171–175; Botha 1971, pp. 86–89). The language was important not only as a social discourse but also as a symbol of identity. First-generation immigrants were anxious for their children and grandchildren to continue speaking Portuguese. This was not merely a question of easing personal communication with them but of maintaining a sense of national identity. They therefore tried to ensure that their children attended Portuguese classes, organised privately or through the Portuguese consulate, over and above their normal schooling. Churches and social clubs often provided venues. Although these Portuguese schools were primarily concerned to preserve the language, they also taught students about Portuguese culture and history. For some, it was an important meeting space, where people of similar age could share experiences and reinforce identity. The majority of second-generation children attended Portuguese afternoon classes for at least a few years.[29]

Literate immigrants read, when available, Portuguese or Mozambican newspapers to keep in touch with the news from home. Once the market was big enough, local Portuguese publications started to emerge. The most important of these was *O Século de Joanesburgo*, a Portuguese language newspaper based in Johannesburg. It was established in 1963 and grew substantially throughout the 1970s and 1980s. By the mid-1990s it claimed a circulation of 40,000 and a readership of well over 200,000. The columns include news from Portugal and the Portuguese diaspora, local community news, gossip, small-business advertising and classifieds and, most popularly, Portuguese football coverage. A number of smaller Portuguese language newspapers have been established since the 1970s but with less impact. In 1976 a regional Portuguese language radio station was launched. It was modernised and restructured in the early 1990s as Radio Cidade. The station, which is now predominantly in English, claims a listenership of two-thirds of the South African Portuguese community. In 1989 Portuguese media expanded into television with the launch of M-Net Portuguesa. By the mid-1990s they claimed 80,000 subscribers (McDuling 1995, pp. 223–230). Satellite television and the Internet have subsequently opened new spaces of shared communication. It has obviously been in the interests of commercial media to appeal to as broad a Portuguese-speaking market as possible. In the process, they have created a far wider base of shared knowledge and experience and encouraged more Portuguese South Africans to imagine themselves as a community.

Generations

The children of first-generation Portuguese immigrants, not surprisingly, integrated into white South African society far more effectively than their forebears.[30] They received their schooling in English or, for a small minority, Afrikaans. Although the children of immigrants continued to speak Portuguese in their homes, English became their primary language of communication. Through schools, sometimes universities, and their professional lives, they interacted with a wide cross section of white South Africans. (Classified as whites, their interaction with other races was circumscribed through residential, educational, and professional segregation.) Madeirans, who have the longest immigrant history in the country, were the earliest to integrate. By the time the bulk of the mainlanders arrived in the 1960s, there was already an established Madeiran community, sometimes two to three generations old. Although Madeirans continued to arrive in large numbers in the 1960s and 1970s, the integration of the previous generations assisted, to some extent, in the integration of the newer arrivals. By the 1980s the second generation of the mainland immigrants was well established. In spite of attempts by their parents to retain a sense of national identity and culture, second- and third-generation immigrants increasingly secularised and married non-Portuguese South Africans.[31] As they immersed themselves in wider society, socialised more widely, intermarried, and became more secular, their identities became increasingly South African or at least hybridised.[32]

On one level, the settling in of second- and third-generation immigrants broadened Portuguese identity. As their class differences flattened out and as they lost touch with regional home cultures, interaction across regional lines eased. For example, cross-marriages between people from mainland and island backgrounds were much more common. Identification with Portugal and the Lusophone world, it could be argued, became more significant than narrow regional affiliations. The new prosperity of Portugal and its full integration as a European Union (EU) member in the 1990s generally encouraged Portuguese identification even among those who had no memory or experience of the place. Not only did Portugal seem a country to be proud of in those years, but a Portuguese passport became a valuable possession, easing access to the whole of the European Union. Nevertheless, assimilation simultaneously led to a weakening of Portuguese communal identity. The 'community', in a sense, broadened but weakened; internal divisions became less pronounced, but the intensity of identity declined. Significant emigration and dispersal during the 1990s also depleted many tightly bound networks and enclaves. Younger people were more apathetic about joining ethnic clubs and learning Portuguese. Community events drew fewer people. Though club managers tried to introduce new blood, memberships were aging by the 1990s (interviews: Quintal 2011, Silvério da Silva 2011). Community leaders, however, do detect something of a revival in recent years. The 2010 World Cup galvanised community interest in the Portuguese football team and an energetic new consul general in Johannesburg has worked hard to revive Portuguese identity (interviews: George da Silva 2011, Ângela Gonçalves 2011, Farinha family 2009).

Cohesion and identity in South Africa

Although South Africans of Portuguese origin display some elements of a coherent community and have at certain times and in certain spaces bound together, they have lacked the kind of cohesion we see in other immigrant groups such as Jews[33] and Greeks. Most Portuguese immigrants, aside from Madeirans, arrived relatively late and in very divergent waves. They often faced hostility and even humiliation, and a sense of crisis did at times draw the community closer, but only transiently. They relied on substantial regional networks to ease their entry into South Africa, which offset the necessity to forge a wider community. As marginal whites, often faced with problems of illegality, they tended to adopt a strategy of not drawing too much attention to themselves. They were mostly politically conservative but not vocal about it. If they voted at all during the apartheid years, constituency patterns suggest that they mostly voted for the ruling party.[34] I would argue that their political quiescence was not greatly different from that of other white immigrant groups, including the Jewish community, which is sometimes noted for its antiapartheid stance. While a disproportionate number of antiapartheid activists did emerge from the community, mainstream representative Jewish organisations consistently avoided criticism of the apartheid government and carefully distanced themselves from individual extra parliamentary activists who had a Jewish background. Like other immigrants, Portuguese South Africans worked extremely hard at their businesses and jobs, quietly supporting or accepting a racial order which brought them tangible benefits. Most Portuguese immigrants were observant Catholics and generally proud of their Portuguese culture, but unlike Jews with their postwar Zionism, they lacked a unifying ideology. The idea of Portuguese nationhood, especially under Salazar, was not an inspiring one for much of the 20th century. At least until the 1980s Portugal was regarded as a poor cousin of Europe: underdeveloped, stagnant, and repressive. Second- and third-generation immigrants held on to their language and culture very unevenly. Most were comfortable with their Portuguese origins but were eager to become ordinary white South Africans.

Conclusion

South Africans of Portuguese origin have never formed an easily identifiable, homogenous community. Immigrants arrived in historically and geographically distinct waves over many decades. It could even be argued that three Portuguese communities formed rather than one. Any analysis of Portuguese immigration into South Africa must pay careful attention to gender; patriarchal family structures and gendered socialisation intimately shaped both the patterns of migration and the social life of immigrant communities. Generational dynamics are equally important. I have argued that internal regional and historical divisions gradually blurred among the second and third generation, allowing for the emergence of a broader pan-ethnic identity. Yet, simultaneously, while internal barriers came down, the sense of distinctiveness within South African society gradually eroded. Although sporadic revivals of intense feelings of identity among later generations are not uncommon, the trend appears to be towards assimilation, secularisation, language loss, and exogamous marriage. To what extent then is it useful to think of this community (or these communities) as part of a Portuguese 'diaspora'? Those born in South Africa are usually aware of, even proud of, their Portuguese origins. But they have become a diverse, mobile, transnational group with often hybrid, fluid identities. If the concept of diaspora requires the retention of strong national identity into the second and third generation, it may be too blunt a term to capture the Portuguese immigrant experience in South Africa.

Notes

1. Estimates of their numbers by the 1990s vary from 300,000 to 700,000. *The Star* (21 February 1979) reported: 'Now the Portuguese population is more than 600,000 – one-seventh of the white population.' The following year an article in the *Sunday Times* (10 August 1980) estimated 'at least 400,000' and the magazine *To the Point* (14 March 1980), referred to 'reliable estimates' of 'more than 600,000'. My interviewees estimate anything from 400,000 to a million by the early 1990s. Rosa and Trigo (1990, pp. 185–186), weighing their various pieces of evidence, suggest a figure of half a million. This may not be unrealistic if second- and third-generation immigrants are included, although the figure remains in dispute. Formal immigration figures and consular registrations suggest a far lower number. Most agree that the population declined significantly through emigration from the mid-1990s. For an almost encyclopaedic collection of connections between South Africa and Portugal, see Ferreira and Le Roux (2009).
2. A great deal has been written about *earlier* Portuguese involvement with the subcontinent dating back as far as the late-15th-century 'discoveries' (see, for example, the prolific work of Eric Axelson). But the numerically and socially more significant migrations of the 20th century have been neglected. Even in the growing field of Portuguese diasporic studies, South Africa has received little attention. For a more detailed discussion of the historiography, see Glaser (2010). Published academic work dealing with various aspects of 20th-century Portuguese immigrant life in South Africa includes Leal (1977), Groenewald and Smedley (1977), Schutte (1990), Rosa and Trigo (1990), Cravinho (1993, 1995), Pereira (2001), Bessa (2009), Gupta (2009, 2011), Glaser (2013 forthcoming). Published work aiming at a nonacademic audience includes Bartolo (1978), Pereira (2008), Ferreira and Le Roux (2009). Unpublished work includes Van Rensburg (1968), Botha (1971), Cohen (1971), Pereira (2000), McDuling (1995). Two excellent BA Honours dissertations, both local studies which make use of

archival sources and life history interviews, stand out. Machado (1992) has made a fascinating micro-study of the Madeiran community of Woodstock, Cape Town, while Tozzo's pioneering work (2005) focuses on the Durban community but offers broader insights into Portuguese immigration into South Africa in general.
3. Note that a small number of Portuguese travellers and merchants integrated into Afrikaner society from the 1700s until the mid-1800s. For short overviews of these figures, see Ferreira and Le Roux (2009). If traces of Portuguese identity survive in these groups (an interesting historical question in itself), it is not the subject of this more contemporary overview.
4. According to Machado (1992, p. 8), the island exported 316,000 people between 1940 and 1970, while its total resident population remained virtually stagnant at around a quarter of a million between 1940 and 1980.
5. The Azores has a similar history, but, probably because of its location and the direction of shipping routes, the United States was a much more popular destination for Azoris; few went to Africa.
6. One or more of these points is raised regularly in interviews with Madeiran expatriates: Gouveia 2009, Melim 2009, Farinha family 2009, Carlos Farinha 2009, Castro 2009, Pestana 2010, Fiandeiro 2010, Beatrice da Silva 2011, Teixeira 2011, Jardim 2011, Duarte 2011, Ângela Gonçalves 2011, Quintal 2011.
7. For more detail on white immigration policy in 20th-century South Africa, see Peberdy 2009, Donsky 1989, and Glaser 2013 forthcoming.
8. I would like to thank the Portuguese consul general in Johannesburg, Carlos Marques, for allowing me access to consul records. There are still well-preserved registration records from 1909 to 1946. The overwhelming majority of these early Portuguese immigrants were from Madeira.
9. See Union Census Reports: 1921 (UG37–1924), 1926 (UG 32–1927), 1936 (UG 21–1938). See also Archive of the Portugal Consul, Johannesburg, registration documentation, 1920–1940.
10. This is all clearly illustrated in dozens of documents housed at the Central Archive Depot, Pretoria (CAD): South African Police (SAP), Vol. 338, File 18/36/40; Commissioner for Immigration and Asiatic Affairs (CIAA), Vol. 65, File M 716; Department of Foreign Affairs (BLB) Vol. 3, File 11/5. For much more detail, see Glaser (2013 forthcoming).
11. Interviews: Castro 2009, Fiandeiro 2010, Carlos Farinha 2009, Farinha family 2009, Pestana 2010, Quintal 2011, Silverio da Silva 2011, Ângela Gonçalves 2011, Galego 2010, Jardim 2010. See also CAD CIAA,Vol. 65, File M 716: several letters from the Portuguese Association and Casa da Madeira to the Commissioner for Immigration.
12. In South Africa 'cafés' are understood to be small corner grocery stores which sell anything from fruit and vegetables to bread, cigarettes, sweets, and even takeout.
13. This is discussed in more detail in a recent paper on Madeiran women in South Africa (Glaser 2011). For some more general reflections on the issue of women and migration, see, for example, Kofman (2004), Williams (2010), Morokvasic (1984).
14. In its 14 March 1980 edition, To the Point reported that 'Portuguese are believed to account for 85% of the fresh produce supplied to South African homes.' No source for this information, however, is given. The article does not distinguish between Madeirans and other Portuguese immigrants, but it is safe to assume

that Madeirans dominated this sector. Silvério da Silva (interview 2011) claims that by the 1980s 80% of the stalls in Johannesburg's fruit and vegetable market in City Deep was run by Madeirans.
15. See Glaser (2013 forthcoming) for a discussion on Portuguese, especially Madeiran, whiteness and Afrikaner nationalist suspicion. As I suggested in an earlier article (Glaser 2010), fruitful comparisons can be made with Irish immigrants to the United States in the 19th century. Their whiteness also came into question, but it was important for them to emphasise their white status to give them a competitive advantage in the labour market. For a fascinating discussion of whiteness in the United States, see, for example, Ignatiev (1995), Roediger (1994), and Spickard (2007).
16. Madeiran marginality and upward mobility is discussed in more detail in Glaser (2013 forthcoming).
17. This had to do with a combination of high local unemployment and the huge benefits of remittance. See Baganha (c. 2000).
18. According to official statistics about 22,000 immigrants arrived in South Africa from the Portuguese mainland between 1963 and 1971 (Leal 1977, 37). Before and after this period mainland immigration was fairly thin, usually less than 500 a year, aside from an anomalous burst of around 2,300, who arrived in 1975 following the uncertainty of the 1974 coup d'état. See Union Census report 1951 (UG 34–1954) and Department of Immigration: Reports: 1961–1968 (RP 31–1969), 1972 (RP 1973–21), 1972–1974 (RP 41–1975).
19. Though individual details differ slightly, this is a composite picture drawn from interviews: Rodrigues 2009, Galego 2010, Silvério da Silva 2011, Caetano 2011, George da Silva 2011.
20. Interviews: Rocha 2011; conversation, Peres 2011. See also the stories of, among others, Maria Fereira, Maria J. G. C. Pereira in Pereira (2008), and the story of Carlos Garção in Gordon (1988).
21. Note that Namibia (known as South West Africa at the time) was a South African possession until 1990. Some of the Angolan refugees stayed for several years or even settled permanently in Namibia. For a graphic account of the flight of three families from Angola, see Gupta (2011).
22. Interview: Rocha 2011. See the stories of Maria Fereira, Maria João Pereira, Maria Victória Pereira, Micaela de Freitas, and other contributions in Pereira (2008).
23. Interviews: Rocha 2011, Caetano 2011, and Peres (conversation) 2011. I intend developing this theme in future research.
24. This is mentioned repeatedly in interviews and in illegal immigrant affidavits in CAD SAP, Vol. 338, File 18/36/40 and CAD CIAA, Vol. 65, File M 716.
25. It is not clear why this is the case. Certainly a large number of black Mozambicans, largely because of language familiarity, were employed in Portuguese businesses. Services were also often available in Portuguese. This may have established a connection to the southern suburbs which strengthened through chain migration. This is, however, a subject for another research project.
26. This is a generalised picture drawn from interviews: Ângela Gonçalves, Beatrice da Silva 2011, George da Silva 2011, Castro 2009, Quintal 2011, Melim 2010, Carlos Farinha 2009, Farinha family 2009, Fiandeiro 2010, Galego 2010, Rodrigues 2009, Maria Gonçalves 2010, Victor de Andrade (conversation) 2009, Rocha 2011. See also Van Rensburg (1968, 184–186) and Pereira (2000, 119–120).
27. On the role of the church in Portuguese communities, see Machado 1992, 45–48; Pereira 2000; McDuling 1995, 232–234; Botha 1971, 80–85. A general picture is

Making of a Portuguese Community in South Africa 235

  also drawn from interviews: Farinha family 2009, Melim 2010, Maria Gonçalves 2010, Nobrega 2009, Fiandeiro 2010, Beatrice da Silva 2011; and conversation, Victor de Andrade 2009.
28. For a thorough list of Portuguese clubs in the Witwatersrand area in 1995, see McDuling (1995, 218–221).
29. See McDuling (1995, 173–176), Pereira (2000, 53–54, 125); interviews: Fiandeiro (2010), Beatrice da Silva (2011), Rocha (2011), Rodrigues (2009), Gouveia (2008), Castro (2009).
30. It should be noted here, however, that I am thinking here of children who were either born in South Africa or who arrived as young children. It has been noted that children who immigrated to the United States at ages 13 to 17, what Rumbaut refers to as the '1.25 generation', often had great difficulties in adapting. They often struggled to acquire a new language and integrate socially (see Rumbaut 2007.) A similar argument could be made for Portuguese immigrants in South Africa.
31. Pereira also notes a significant minority trend towards Protestant conversion, usually resulting from intermarriage or, more recently, the growing influence of evangelical churches. (Pereira 2000, 43, 89; see also McDuling 1995, 182.)
32. Virtually all of my interviewees confirmed this picture. See especially Gouveia 2008, Mario de Andrade 2010, Victor de Andrade (conversation) 2009, Castro 2009, Farinha family 2009, Silvério da Silva 2011, George da Silva 2011, Beatrice da Silva 2011, Fiandeiro 2010, Teixeira 2011, Jardim 2011, Galego 2010, Quintal 2011, Ângela Gonçalves 2011, Pestana 2010, Caetano 2011.
33. There is a very well developed literature on South African Jewish history, which, in itself, makes an interesting contrast from South African Portuguese immigrant writing. Although there are still big gaps in the Jewish historiography, there are numerous relevant academic publications, biographies, and autobiographies. For a small sample, see Shimoni 1980, Krut 1987, Shane and Mendelsohn 2000.
34. For more detail on political inclinations, see Bessa (2009) and Cravinho (1993, 1995).

References

Primary sources

Central Archive Depot, Pretoria (CAD), Commissioner for Immigration and Asiatic Affairs (CIAA), Vol. 65, File M716.
Department of Foreign Affairs (BLB), Vol. 3, File 11/5.
South African Police (SAP), Vol. 338, File 18/36/40.

Government Publications

Census reports: Cape Census 1904, UG19–1905; Union Census reports: 1911 (UG32–1912), 1918 (UG50–1919), 1921 (UG37–1924), 1926 (UG 32–1927), 1936 (UG 21–1938), 1951 (UG 34–1954).
Department of Immigration: Reports: 1961–1968 (RP 31–1969), 1972 (RP 1973–21), 1972–1974 (RP 41–1975).
Department of Interior: Annual Reports: 1913 (UG 24–1914), 1916 (UG50–1917), 1973 (RP47–1973)

Portuguese Consulate, Johannesburg (PCJ)

Registration certificates 1909–1946

Interviews

Andrade, Maria Goretti de (Johannesburg, 17 March 2010)
Andrade, Victor de (Conversation and notes during 'tour' of the south of Johannesburg, 13 June 2009, with Pamila Gupta)
Caetano, José (Johannesburg, 19 March 2011)
Castro, Victor (Johannesburg 3 December 2009)
Duarte, John (Johannesburg, 11 February 2011)
Farinha, Carlos (East Rand, 10 December 2009)
Farinha family (East Rand, 10 December 2009)
Fiandeiro, Natália (Johannesburg, 4 August 2010)
Galego, Rudy (Johannesburg, 3 August 2010)
Gonçalves, 'Mariazinha' (East Rand, 23 January 23, 2010)
Gonçalves, Luís (Johannesburg, 7 February 2011)
Gonçalves, Ângela (Johannesburg, 19 March 2011)
Gouveia, Valentina (East Rand, 1 May 2008)
Jardim, Abel and Connie (Johannesburg, 3 April 2011)
Melim, Maria Ferreira de (Johannesburg, 17 March 2010)
Marques, Carlos (conversation with Portuguese consul general, Johannesburg)
Nobrega, Father John de (Johannesburg, 9 December 2009)
Peres, Michael (conversation, Johannesburg, 27 April 2011)
Pestana, Tony (Johannesburg, 29 July 2010)
Quintal, José (Johannesburg, 8 March 2011)
Rocha, Ana (Johannesburg, 16 March 2011)
Rodrigues, José (Johannesburg, 27 November 2009)
Silva, Beatrice de (Johannesburg 21 January 2011)
Silva, George da (Johannesburg 8 March 2011)
Silva, Slivério da (Johannesburg 7 March 2011)
Teixeira, Alcinda (Roodepoort 4 April 2011)

Secondary sources

Baganha, M. I. B. (c. 2000), 'From Closed to Open Doors: Portuguese Emigration under the Corporatist Regime,' http://ies.berkeley.edu/research/files (accessed October 2008).
Bartolo, C. (1978), *Portugal no Mundo, Portugal in the World: Republic of South Africa 1485–1978*. Editorial Publishers, Johannesburg.
Bessa, P. (2009), 'A Diáspora Invisível? Política e lusitanidade na África do Sul, da descolonização à democratização,' *Lusotopie* 16, no. 1, pp. 133–153.
Botha, S. J. (1971), 'Enkele faktore wat die inskakelingsvatbaarheid van 'n groep Portuguese immigrante aan die Witwatersrand bepaal.' MA thesis, Potchefstroom University.
Cohen, S. (1971), 'Clustering Characteristics of a Migrant Population in the Core of a Primate Centre.' BA (Hons) dissertation, University of the Witwatersrand.
Cravinho, J. Gomes(1993), 'A Comunidade portuguesa na África do Sul: Retrato político de uma comunidade emigrante,' *L'Année Africaine 1992–1993*. Pedone. Bordeaux and Paris, pp. 411–430.

Cravinho, J. Gomes (1995), 'La communauté portugaise dans la nouvelle Afrique du Sud,' *Lusotopie* 2, pp. 323–348.
Donsky, I. (1989), 'Aspects of the Immigration of Europeans to South Africa 1946–1970.' MA thesis, Rand Afrikaans University.
Ferreira, O. J. O., and Le Roux, S. W. (2009), *Sagres & Suidekruis: Raakpunte tussen Portugal en Suid Afrika deur Vyf Eeue*. Adamastor: Gordons Bay.
Glaser, C. (2010), 'Portuguese Immigrant History in Twentieth Century South Africa: A Preliminary Overview,' *African Historical Review* 42, no. 2, pp. 61–83.
Glaser, C.(2011), 'Home, Farm and Shop: The Migration of Madeiran Women to South Africa, 1900–1980,' Paper presented to the South African Historical Society Conference, Durban, 27–29 June.
Glaser, C. (2013 forthcoming), 'White but Illegal: Undocumented Madeiran Immigration to South Africa, 1920s–1970s,' *Immigrants and Minorities*.
Gordon, S. (1988), *Under the Harrow: Lives of White South Africans Today*. Heinemann, London.
Groenewald, D., and Smedley, L. N. (1977), *Attitudes of the White Population in South Africa towards Immigrants in General and the Main immigrant Groups in Particular*. South African Human Sciences Research Council, Pretoria.
Gupta, P. (2009), 'The Disquieting of History: Portuguese (De)colonization and Goan Migration in the Indian Ocean,' *Journal of Asian and African Studies* 44, no.1, pp. 19–47.
Gupta, P. (2011), '"Going for a Sunday Drive": Angolan Decolonization, Learning to Be "White", and the Portuguese Diaspora of South Africa,' in F. Cota Fagundes, I. Blayer, T. Alves, T. Cid (eds.), *Storytelling the Portuguese Diaspora: Piecing Things Together*. Peter Lang, New York.
Ignatiev, N. (1995), *How the Irish Became White*. Routledge, New York.
Kofman, E. (2004), 'Family-related Migration: A Critical Review of European Studies,' *Journal of Ethnic and Migration Studies* 30, no. 2, pp. 243–262.
Krut, R. (1987), 'The Making of a South African Jewish Community in Johannesburg, 1886–1914,' in B. Bozzoli (ed.), *Class, Community and Conflict: South African Perspectives*. Ravan Press, Johannesburg, pp. 135–159.
Leal, L. (1977), *Breve Historia dos Portugueses na África do Sul*. Potchefstroomse Universiteit vir Christelike Hoër Onderwys (PUCHO), Potchefstroom.
Machado, P. (1992), '"Little Madeira": The Portuguese in Woodstock c. 1940–1980.' BA (Hons) dissertation, Department of History, University of Cape Town, Cape Town.
McDuling, A. J. (1995), 'Language Shift and Maintenance in the Portuguese Community of Johannesburg.' MA thesis, University of South Africa, Pretoria.
Morokvasic, M. (1984), 'Birds of Passage Are Also Women … ,' *International Migration Review* 18, no. 4, special issue, *Women in Migration*, pp. 886–907.
Peberdy, S. (2009), *Selecting Immigrants: National Identity and South Africa's Immigration Policies 1910–2008*. Wits University Press, Johannesburg.
Pereira, M. V. (ed.) (2008), *Pathways of Feeling: Stories Told by Portuguese Women in Africa*. Portuguese Women's League of South Africa, Johannesburg.
Pereira, M. V. (2000), 'Religion, Identity and Community: The religious Life of Portuguese Women in Durban.' MA thesis, University of South Africa, Pretoria.
Pereira, M. V. (2001), 'The Religion of Portuguese Women in Durban,' *Journal of Constructive Theology* 7, no. 2.
Roediger, D. (1994), 'Whiteness and Ethnicity in the History of "White Ethnics" in the United States,' in Roediger, D., *Towards the Abolition of Whiteness*. Verso, London, pp. 181–198.

Rosa, V. M. Pereira da, and Trigo, S. V. P. (1990), 'Islands in a Segregated Land: Portuguese in South Africa,' in David Higgs (ed.), *Portuguese Migration in Global Perspective*. Multicultural History Society of Ontario, Toronto, pp. 182–199.

Rumbaut, R. (2007), 'Ages, Life Stages, and Generational Cohorts: Decomposing the Immigrant First and Second Generations in the United States,' in A. Portes and J. DeWind (eds.), *Rethinking Migration: New Theoretical and Empirical Perspectives*. Berghahn Books, New York, pp. 342–387.

Schutte, C. D. (1990), 'Some Attitudes of Portuguese Immigrants to South Africa regarding Re-migration,' *South African Journal of Sociology* 21, no. 3, pp. 157–166.

Shane, M., and Mendelsohn, R. (eds.) (2000), *Memories, Realities and Dreams: Aspects of the Jewish South African Experience*. Jonathan Ball, Johannesburg.

Shimoni, G. (1980), *Jews and Zionism: The South African Experience (1910–1967)*. Oxford University Press, Cape Town.

Spickard, P. (2007), *Almost All Aliens: Immigration, Race, and Colonialism in American History and Identity*. Routledge, New York.

Tozzo, D. (2005), 'People in Transition between Africa and Europe: Cultural, Social and Economic Aspects of Portuguese Immigration into South Africa from 1926 to 1975.' BA (Hons) dissertation, Department of History, University of KwaZulu-Natal, Durban.

Van Rensburg, H. C. J. (1968), ''n Sosiologies-vergelykende ondersoek van die aanpassing van Britse en Portuguese immigrante in Bloemfontein.' MA thesis, University of Orange Free State, Bloemfontein.

Williams, L. (2010). *Global Marriage*. Palgrave Macmillan, Basingstoke.

10
From Mozambique to Brazil: The 'Good Portuguese' of the Chinese Athletic Club

Lorenzo Macagno[1]

> Sometimes, on Sundays, Ching and I would ride by donkey (that's what we called our bicycles) along the banks of the Chiveve, to see the *mussopo* fishermen off and the *marora* sellers. The little Chinese man looked westward across the muddy waters and his narrow eyes seemed to see the landscape beyond the ocean. One day, he invited me to watch a basketball match. His favorite club was playing, the Atlético Chinês [Chinese Athletic Club]. 'My father would not let me utter the name of the Club in Portuguese,' he confided. 'And what other name does the Club have?' 'It's the Tung Hua Athletic Club.'
>
> Mia Couto, 'A China dentro de nós'
> *Pensageiro frequente*, 2010, p. 40.

During his famous journey to the 'Portuguese lands' of Asia and Africa at the invitation of the overseas minister Sarmento Rodrigues, Gilberto Freyre stayed in the Mozambican city of Beira. On this occasion, in 1952, at the premises of the so-called Clube Chinês (Chee Kung Tong), the directors of that growing and active Chinese community listened with admiration to what the Brazilian writer had to say. This was a time when Freyre was increasingly moving away from the innovative provocations of the *Casa Grande & Senzala* (1933), to definitively embrace the Luso-Tropicalist creed.[2] Obviously, he could never have imagined that his listeners that day, these 'Luso-Chinese', and their descendants would settle in Brazil nearly twenty years after that meeting.

This article reconstructs the tenuous and paradoxical incorporation of the Chinese of Beira into the 'Portuguese family', particularly after 1950, when Portugal sought to strengthen its ideology with references to multiracialism and tolerance in the so-called overseas provinces. At the end of this essay, I discuss the narratives of deception that emerged after the independence of Mozambique in 1975, when the Chinese had to abandon the possibility of a Portuguese future for their lives. Indeed, once considered 'good Portuguese', the new context that emerged out of the independence of Mozambique and the end of the colonial empire forced these Chinese to 'choose' the route of the diaspora. Many settled in Portugal, Canada, the United States, and Australia. But the majority, as we shall see, chose Brazil and, in particular, the city of Curitiba in the State of Paraná. Here they became engaged in commercial and professional activities, and in 1989 they founded the Associação Cultural Chinesa do Paraná (Cultural Chinese Association of Paraná).

From Guangdong to Mozambique

In the second half of the 19th century, as a consequence of the end of the slave trade, the world's large companies and plantation owners began to hire Chinese labourers, mainly from Guangdong Province in the south of China. Around that time, the islands in the Indian Ocean and the Caribbean received their first coolies.[3] It was in this same period that Chinese labourers began to arrive in East Africa and South Africa (Ly-Tio-Fane Pineo 1981, Wong-Hee-Kam 1996). The Companhia de Moçambique (1891–1942) was granted the concession for the territories of Manica and Sofala, whose capital was Beira. Before the city became the capital of the territory in 1892, the administrative institutions and headquarters of the District of Sofala operated from Chiloane Island (Liesegang 1989), where, it seems, some groups of Chinese were already living.[4] Meanwhile, the Chinese who arrived in the south of Mozambique (Lourenço Marques) established links with their colleagues in the city of Johannesburg, where Chinese nationalists linked to the Kuomintang had diplomatic representation. It should be noted that, at the end of the 19th century, the discovery of gold in the mines of Witwatersrand in the Transvaal led, in that part of South Africa, to a race to recruit Chinese labourers (Richardson 1977).

The first contingents of Chinese to arrive in Mozambique were mainly small craftsmen and carpenters; others dedicated themselves to fishing and horticulture. Over the decades, a number of British-owned companies, such as South African Timbu, East African Shipping, Allen Wack, and the Beira Boating Company, set up branches in the region, encouraged by the existence of the Beira Corridor[5] between Rhodesia and Beira, whose port was the only sea route for the neighbouring country. Many Chinese and their descendants found work in these companies.[6] The children of those early pioneers, born in Mozambique, became successful business owners, and many opened restaurants and *casas de pasto*.[7] Some found work as low-level employees of the colonial administration in the port and customs warehouses. Later, the more successful ones managed to make their fortunes by becoming businessmen and builders.

Many of the first families to arrive in Mozambique, both in the city of Beira and in Lourenço Marques, did not cut their ties with Guangdong or with China more generally. Some of the children and grandchildren of this first generation were sent home to study or to spend time with family members in Macau and Hong Kong who were unable to travel to Africa. In the 1930s, the violent Japanese attacks on the villages of Guangdong during the Sino-Japanese War caused those who had still hoped to return to China to change their minds. Thus, Africa became a destination of permanent settlement.

It should be recalled that the history of the province of Guangdong is closely related to the complex process of the formation of Chinese nationalism, which had, in turn, far-reaching repercussions among the Chinese communities of the Portuguese overseas provinces (Pan 1999). In 1895, after forming the Revive China Society (Xingzhong Hui), Sun Yat Sen decided that Guangdong Province would become the base for revolutionary activities. The role played by the Chinese associations abroad was to be fundamental for promoting the republican cause linked to the Kuomintang. The most important of these associations, with branches on various continents, was the Chee Kung Tong, whose codes and membership practices followed the principles of freemasonry. Its origins go back to the 18th century, when its members sought to conspire against the Qing dynasty, which was related to the Manchus. From the 19th century, the branches of Chee Kung Tong extended throughout Southeast Asia, America, Canada, Australia, South Africa, and Mozambique.

The early days

The period that we can call the prehistory of the Clube Atlético Chinês (Chinese Athletic Club) goes back to the first half of the 1920s, with the creation of the Chee Kung Tong Club association in the city of Beira. This association was created in the overseas province of Mozambique in response to the above-mentioned republican and nationalist loyalties inspired by Sun Yat Sen. Its statutes were legally approved on 22 February 1923, through Order no. 4449 of the government of the territory of the Companhia de Moçambique (the Mozambique Company). According to this regulation, the Chee Kung Tong was considered a charitable and educational association, the purpose of which was to promote the moral and material well-being of the Chinese community. After the 1930s, with the administrative reform of the overseas provinces, it was classified as an 'administrative corporation'. At the end of 1923, the association managed to complete the construction of its headquarters; this important building was situated in the *baixa* (downtown) region of the city, which came to be popularly known as the Clube Chinês (Chinese Club).

In 1943, the Chee Kung Tong Club applied to the Administrative Committee of the Municipal Chamber of Beira for an authorisation to use the two plots of land adjacent to it to create a space for 'physical exercises and sport'.[8] Authorisation was granted the same year, albeit for a temporary period. At that time, the Chee Kung Tong Club was considered an institution with the aim of promoting the 'welfare, recreation, education, and instruction of the Chinese community' living in Beira. In 1944, following a public tender, the land was granted definitively to the institution, and the Escola Chinesa (Chinese School) and a basketball court were built at the start of the 1950s.[9] Thus, out of the initial nucleus that was the Chee Kung Tong Club, the acquisition of this land led to the emergence of another two institutions of equal importance: the Escola Chinesa and the Chinese Athletic Club (Tung Hua Athletic Club). Since the 1950s these two institutions have been administrated by the so-called Associação Chinesa. One of the chief directors involved in this process was Eginwo Shung Chin, who was the father of João Ping,[10] one of the first and most well-known players of the Chinese Athletic Club men's basketball team. This family owned one of the principal photographic studios in the city of Beira: Foto Estúdio. The family also owned a farm in Massaquece, near the border with Rhodesia. From the end of 1940, the founders of the Chee Kung Tong gradually began to give way to a new generation of young businessmen who, from the beginning of the 1950s, would carry on the work of the Escola Chinesa, the Tung Hua Athletic Club, and the Associação Chinesa. But in the near future, the Chee Kung Tong and the Associação Chinesa will separate from each other.

Until the end of the 1940s, however, the Chee Kung Tong continued to be the sole institutional representative of the Chinese community recognised by the colonial administration. After the permanent acquisition of the plots of land in July 1947, the young businessmen generation compromised with the future Associação Chinesa requested the administration an approval of the statutes of a new club: the Tung Hua Athletic Club (or Chinese Athletic Club) that will be linked, beginning in the fifties, to the Associação Chinesa. The request was denied, under the argument that 'the Chinese colony has already had in the city, for many years, a club called the Chee Kung Tong Club,...and it is noted that its bylaws could be dedicated to the practice of sports...' (cited in Medeiros, 1998, p. 30). In other words, there is every indication that in the early days, the Tung Hua Athletic Club (new generation) needed institutional support from the Chee Kung Tong (old generation), which was, at least at that time, the only institution of the Chinese community to be recognised by the colonial administration.[11]

Throughout the 1950s and 1960s, the Chinese Athletic Club maintained its intensive sporting and associative activity; in 1974–1975, for reasons I shall analyse at the end of this essay, the 'Luso-Chinese'[12] began to leave the colony. In 1952, Kwin Yin became one of the first presidents of the Associação Chinesa and the Chinese Athletic Club. The presidency subsequently passed to Chin Yok Chong, popularly known as Chong. After his death from a disease, the Chinese Athletic Club came to be presided over by José Sousa Low and, finally, by Poo Quin at the start of the 1970s.[13]

It should be noted that basketball was not the only sport practiced by the Chinese of Beira. Between 1950 and 1960, table tennis, badminton, and the martial arts were also very popular. Some members even managed to play for the local football clubs. But it was through basketball that the Chinese gained notoriety. We do not know exactly why this sport was chosen, far less the reason for the initiative to build a basketball court at the Clube Chinês, but it is possible that this decision was related to the close personal, associative and political ties that the Chinese of Beira maintained with their colleagues in Rhodesia and South Africa, where there were similar associations, clubs, and schools. In Johannesburg, for example, the Chinese community managed to build a basketball court close to the facilities of the Overseas Chinese School, also known as the Johannesburg Chinese School. In 1939, its pupils, thanks to the initiatives of Fok Yu Kam and Leong Pak Seong, managed to form a team called 629, which played against a team from Pretoria (Yap and Leong Man 1996, p. 290). From 1950 onwards, the segregationist tendencies of the 'Group Areas and the Reservation of Separate Amenities' prohibited the Chinese in South Africa from taking part in tournaments with other 'racial groups' (to use the language of apartheid). At that time, to counter the ostracism caused by this segregationist measure, the Chinese Atlhetic Club of Beira, together with its counterparts in South Africa and the Federation of Rhodesia and Nyasaland, began to organise regional basketball tournaments. As a result, the Chinese of Beira began to travel more frequently to Salisbury, Pretoria, and Johannesburg.

According to Soares Rebelo (1970, p. 136), nearly 60 per cent of the Chinese of Mozambique had Portuguese nationality in 1955. The last census carried out in the colonial period, in 1970, showed a total of 3,814 Chinese individuals (see Table 10.1).[14]

In organisational and associative terms, the Chinese community of Beira was very similar to that of Lourenço Marques (present-day Maputo). In Lourenço Marques, there was a headquarters of the Chee Kung Tong (whose building is located in what is now Avenida Josina Machel) and a Chinese School (in what is now Avenida Fernão Magalhães). Each of the communities came from a different villages in Guangdong. While the majority of Beira inhabitants came from Toi San (or Taishan), the Chinese living in Lourenço Marques came from Suntak.[15] These differences in origin were reflected in differences in dialect within the Cantonese language itself. Moreover, following the independence of Mozambique, the majority of Chinese from Beira settled in the city of Curitiba, while the majority of those from Lourenço Marques went to São Paulo.[16]

Table 10.1 Census of the Chinese group individuals, 1928–1960 – Mozambique

Census Years	Total	Males	Females	Lourenço Marques	Beira
1928	896	750	146	314	403
1935	1,056	818	238	483	399
1940	1,449	1,011	438	570	593
1945	1,565	1,006	559	677	659
1950	1,613	997	616	709	665
1955	1,945	1,141	804	845	888
1960	2,098	1,136	962	992*	1,027**

*Corresponding Chinese individuals in the district of Lourenço Marques.
**Corresponding Chinese individuals in the district of Beira.
Source: Rebelo 1970, p. 134.

The 'good Portuguese' of the Atlético

From 1950 to 1960, the newspapers *Notícias da Beira* and *Diário de Moçambique* began to cover events related to the Chinese community more closely: sports events, meetings with local authorities, festivities, interviews, and deaths. The newspaper articles were marked by a celebratory and flattering tone. Learning to accept 'their place' and diligently collaborate with the society of Beira, these Chinese became, in the eyes of their admirers, 'good Portuguese' and good citizens.

An example is the obituary published in 1958, on the death of Mon Man, the director of the Chinese Association and the Chinese School: 'After prolonged suffering, the old settler Mon Man died yesterday at the Casa de Saúde. The deceased was born in Toi Shan – Canton – and was 66 years of age, having spent 42 years in our city, where he was a businessman. He was also Vice-president of the Chinese Association, where he had been President, and he was a great worker of the new School of that amiable Association.'[17] In this note of 'recognition', one of the aspects that stands out most is, perhaps, the use of the adjective 'amiable' (*simpático* in Portuguese)[18] to refer to the Chinese Association. This type of statement – the allusion to amiability – was no isolated occurrence. On the contrary, it was part of a late-colonial narrative in which praise and flattery, at least in relation to the potential allies, were an omnipresent feature. As a kind of ritual of public recognition that is played out in the newspaper articles dedicated to the Chinese community, it is possible to identify these narratives of compatibility and affinity.

On another occasion, the object of the attribution of amiability was the Associação da Juventude Católica Chinesa da Beira (Association of Chinese Catholic Youth of Beira). The journalist emphasises the values of 'elevation', 'simplicity', and 'happiness' that surrounded that group. The article came out on the occasion of the commemoration of the fourth anniversary of the association. The newspaper commented, 'Celebrating the anniversary of its foundation, and in honor of its Patron Saint, Our Lady of Conception, the Association of the Chinese Catholic Youth of Beira held an interesting party, in the hall of the Acção Católica building, which took place in an atmosphere of high spirits, simplicity and happiness. It was three o'clock in the afternoon when the president of the Association, Luis Chin, gave a speech in which he greeted all those present, explained the reason for the celebration, and thanked all those who had dedicated their time and efforts to this young but diligent and amiable fellowship, aimed at uniting, supporting and encouraging young Chinese Christians of Beira.'[19] In the text just cited, the attributions of 'young' and 'diligent' were added to that of 'amiable'.

It was without doubts in the area of sports, however, that the adjective 'amiable' was expanded and reproduced most, specifically around the growing protagonism that the Chinese of Beira were acquiring as basketball players. In 1960, when the women's basketball team won the Beira championship, the journalist reporting on the event described the team as 'champions of amiability'.[20] In its classificatory dynamic attributing a character, an ethos, or a style, the term was to become a kind of recurrent ethnic device, used to refer to the Chinese of Beira as a whole.

In 1954, Agostinho de Campos, a journalist with the *Diário de Moçambique* newspaper, held a long interview with the right forward of the Chinese Athletic Club, João Ping. At that time, João Ping was only 22 years old, but he was a great sports star. In the interview, which was accompanied by a photograph, the journalist referred to Jõao Ping as 'Player No. 4 of the amiable *Atlético*' (Chinese Athletic Club).[21]

Before that, around 1953, the *Diário de Moçambique* had begun publishing a regular section dedicated to the basketball teams of Beira, entitled 'Galeria dos Campeões' (Gallery of Champions). The section covered the activities of the men's team of 'honors' of the Chinese Athletic Club (i.e., the club's main team), as well as those of the women's and junior teams. The title that accompanied the text on the men's team was full of praise: 'This is our best basketball team: *Atlético Chinês*'. The group was presented as 'responsible' and 'amiable'.[22] Nearly two weeks later, it was the turn of the junior team of the Atlético to receive high praise. Once again, the 'Two words' in the introductory note begin with the flattering tone, repeated many times: 'The junior team of the amiable *Atlético Chinês* is, without any shadow of a doubt, a team of the future'.[23]

A few days later, the same newspaper praised the women's team of the *Atlético*. On that occasion, the members were described as 'lively', 'upright', and 'good sportswomen'. The attribute of 'amiable' appeared once again. This time, it appeared throughout the text itself, once referring to Chinese

Athletic Club as a whole, and the other two times to describe the captain of the women's team: Julieta Yee.[24]

Nearly a year later, the *Diário de Moçambique* dedicated a full report to Julieta Yee, who now lives in Curitiba. On that occasion, the first attribute announced in the title of the text, in reference to this sportswoman, was 'amiable'. At the end of the first column, we can read, 'It is evident that local sports players will be very familiar with the name of Julieta Yee, the friendly captain of the very amiable Basketball team of the *Atlético Chinês*…'. Further on in the text, the interviewer describes the context and the moment when the interview was given (during a break in a training session), adding: 'Now the whole team has left off their training. The group around us has grown. Ideas are exchanged. There is a sincere willingness. These young women of the *Atlético Chinês* are amiable – very amiable'.[25]

From the end of 1950 to the beginning of 1960, some players of the Chinese Athletic Club began to earn recognition at a national level. Some were even invited by the directors of the Portuguese clubs to continue their professional basketball careers in Portugal. This was the case for Quen Gui, who was signed up to play for the Associação Acadêmica Club of Coimbra in 1964. Some time later, during the colonial war, he was recruited to defend the Portuguese flag. And, from 1972 to 1974, he acted as a quartermaster for the army in the province of Tete, one of the regions of Mozambique where the fighting against the armed liberation movement was most intense. Quen Gui took part in numerous national championships in Portugal, and he is still remembered as one of the great historical figures of Acadêmica, as the Associação Acadêmica is popularly known.[26]

The above-mentioned newspaper narratives were written in a period when Portugal was attempting to demonstrate to the international community its special overseas vocation. This position became more radical when, faced with anticolonial international pressures, Portugal resorted to an argument of the existence of an irreversible emotional tie between the mother country and its colonies. It was a kind of 'colonial policy of feelings' that drank enthusiastically from the Luso-Tropicalist wellsprings created by Gilberto Freyre: 'We are materially poor, but rich in spirit' or 'We are a small country, but our heart is big' claimed some of the preferred slogans of the time. This dimension of emotionally driven rhetoric enabled the processes of a new construction of the Other – as a 'near-distant' and a virtual member of the Portuguese 'family' to be addressed in a unique way.

In the case of the Chinese of Beira, their talent in exercising the role of 'good Portuguese', exemplary citizens, lay in another two positive attributes that were equally valuable for the colonial administration. First of all, it was a community that was descended from the old chinese Republican, who was later opposed to the communist rule in China . They were therefore located on the opposite side of the 'communist threat'. Secondly, the habitus of the Chinese of Beira and their ethos, which was always focused on improving socially and economically, readily embraced the modernising efforts of the Portuguese administration of the time. The exercise of this modernity did not contradict the maintenance of tradition, for example, certain public festivities, or the preservation of an oriental memory in public and family rituals, such as the commemoration of the Chinese New year in Beira. These practices became ethnically inoffensive for the assimilationist aims of Portugal; it was, without doubt, nothing more than a ceremonial 'return' to China. However, the symbolic incorporation of this past was in keeping with the Portuguese civilising ideal, which was often permeated by a singular orientalist admiration. Both of the civilising worlds, far from cancelling each other out, could thus be admired and mutually recognised.

Hence, marriages and networks of family and kin relationships followed a pattern that was officially endogamous and that reinforced the reproduction of a differentiated ethnicity. However, the first contingents – the majority of which arrived without their Chinese womenfolk – had relations with African women that were almost never publicly recognised. This dimension of interethnic and interracial relationships involved complex dynamics. In fact there is nowadays a significant mixed-race population established in the Mozambican territory (notably in Inhassoro). These individuals, locally known as misto-chinas, obviously did not form part of the diaspora that left Mozambique to go to Brazil. Eduardo Medeiros (2007), in an article on the subject, prefers to resolve these mixing dynamics by appealing to hyphenated categories such as Sino-Africans, Afro-Asians, and Sino-Asians.

Gilberto Freyre at the Chee Kung Tong Club

As I stated in the introduction, the inventor of the Luso-Tropicalist doctrine, Gilberto Freyre, visited the 'Luso-Chinese' in Beira in 1952. The visit was part of the journey made by the Brazilian writer to various overseas territories at the invitation of the overseas minister at that time, Sarmento Rodrigues. The place where Freyre met with the 'Luso-Chinese' was the Chee Kung Tong Club – in the old building constructed by the Chinese in Beira in 1923. There, in the presence of the governor of Manica and Sofala and various local dignitaries, the president of the Chinese Association, Shung Chin, gave a welcome speech to Gilberto Freyre, worded as follows:

> We, the Chinese, immigrated to this city of Beira fifty years ago, in the struggle for survival. Through our arduous but patient work, in a spirit of abiding by the law and winning friends, enjoying the good administration of the Portuguese Government and its rights and freedoms, where there is no place for unjust discrimination of creed or race, we have always strived for the development and progress of this land, and our contribution in this regard is deemed considerable. So it was last year, so it is now, and so it will be in the future. (Shung Chin 1953, p. 336)

There is no doubt that these words were carefully chosen to flatter not only the guest of honor, Freyre, but also the colonial dignitaries who were gathered there. In his speech, the president of the Chinese Association sought, above all, to convey an image of responsibility and commitment on the part of the Chinese to the future of Portugal in Mozambique. The assumed tone corroborated, once again, the efforts of the members of the Chinese community to become obedient citizens and 'good Portuguese'. The president of the Chinese Association then took the opportunity to inform his audience about a project that was taking place next to the facilities of the Chee Kung Tong, to build the Chinese School. Indirectly, the report also conveyed the statistics of the Chinese community living in Beira in 1952:

> In this city, we have more than two hundred children of school age. We need to construct a convenient school building, where our children can, alongside the Chinese culture, benefit from a Portuguese education. The work to build this School had already used more than two thousand *contos*, and more than a thousand more are needed to complete the project. The work is massive, but essential. But it is a heavy burden for a hundred and something families, or around eight hundred people, many of whom live off their work and toil with many difficulties... We aspire to love, agreement and brotherhood between peoples, as well as between individuals. But for this, instruction and education are essential. And because we know that these things are of interest to Dr. Gilberto Freyre, we refer to them as a factor of progress and cultural development of this progressive city of Beira (Shung Chin1953, p. 337).

Despite the reality of forced labour and the persistence of the *regime de indigenato* (native statute), Gilberto Freyre insisted, at that time, on announcing to the world a supposed Portuguese 'uniqueness'. In spite of the triumph of the National Party in South Africa in 1948 and the consequent onset of apartheid, the Luso-Tropical discourse managed, at least for several years, to maintain its effectiveness. We should not forget that at that time UNESCO carried out a major research project on race relations in Brazil, together with various sociologists and anthropologists from the United States and Brazil. In view of the postwar trauma resulting from the Holocaust in Europe and the continued racial segregation in the United States, the UNESCO study sought to test, 'in the field', the scope and limits of the Luso-Tropicalist invention (Chor Maio, 1999).

In any case, the peak of the Luso-Tropicalist narrative occurred a little later, between the end of 1950 and the start of 1960. In 1947, the independence of India, the subsequent rise of pan-Arab nationalism, and the growing Afro-Asiatic movement (the outstanding antecedent of which was the Bandung conference) put Portugal on a state of alert. Effectively, Portugal would later lose Goa, and the Indians of Mozambique would come to be considered as enemies. In the 1950s, a new danger was added to the Asian denationalising threat: the imminent influence of the Arab-Muslim world in the processes of colonial emancipation. Portugal tried to react to all these new threats. In 1961, faced with international pressure, the Native Statute, which legally separated natives from the *assimilados*, was abolished. Through this measure, at least in terms of documentation, all the inhabitants of the so-called overseas provinces became Portuguese citizens.

It was in this period that Freyre's Luso-Tropicalism made its triumphal entry. The person who promoted the incorporation of his ideas into the colonial imagination of Portugal was the overseas minister Adriano Moreira – a specialist in international law, writer of the above-mentioned decree of abolition of the Native Statute, and professor at the Instituto Superior de Estudos Ultramarinos. However, a notable predecessor of the Luso-Tropicalist invention can be seen in the discourses of Freyre during his above-mentioned journey to the overseas colonies in the 1950s. In that meeting with the 'Luso-Chinese' in Beira, Freyre thanked them for the hospitality he had received at the Chee Kong Tong in an undeniably Luso-Tropicalist tone:

> There must be some similarity between Brazil and the ancient, but ever youthful Chinese Civilization, through which the Portuguese established in Macau a deep alliance, built not on strength but on fraternal love, not on imperial power, one over the other, but on mutual understanding. There must be some similarity between the so-called eternal China and the young, still green Brazil.... I feel at home in this ancient and historical Portuguese province, in relations of the most loving understanding with the Portuguese people and culture. I thank you for your words of praise and cordiality, and the care with which you welcomed a Brazilian: a son of the so-called 'China of America'. (Freyre 1953, p. 240)

In his speech, the president of the Chinese community stated, 'We aspire to love, agreement and brotherhood between peoples.' Meanwhile, Freyre insisted on this fraternal love that characterised the relationship between the Portuguese and the Chinese in Macau. Asides being a kind of 'colonial construction of amiability', Luso-Tropicalism here takes the form – recalling the work of Christian Geffray (1997) – of a 'discourse of love in servitude'. Without doubt, Freyre could never at that time have imagined that twenty years later, many of these 'Luso-Chinese' and their children would settle in Brazil.[27] The destination would be a city in the south of Brazil that many Chinese from Beira came to recognise as a second Beira: Curitiba.

The 'good tenants' on the eve of war

'Young', 'attentive', 'responsible', 'lively', 'upright', 'good sportsmen and sportswomen', 'orderly', 'hardworking', 'disciplined', and above all 'amiable'.

These are the adjectives that appeared most frequently in the newspaper chronicles of 1950 and 1960 to characterise the Chinese of Beira. They played the role of categories of flattery and praise and therefore, as a means of classifying and creating meaning. The Chinese community of Beira came to exist through this system of flattery. For the chroniclers of the time, sport was a kind of map on which it was possible to read and interpret the character, the way of being, the ethos of the Chinese. These narratives of affinity were not produced in a neutral political environment. It was a period when Portugal was becoming more radical in its multiracialist discourse, in a context of growing international pressure to put an end to the colonial presence in its overseas territories. But at the same time, it was also a period when the young people of the Chinese community were increasingly following the causes of the local Catholic Church.

The Catholic diocese of Beira was created in 1943. As Eduardo Medeiros rightly mentions,[28] in the 1950s, many 'Luso-Chinese' youth converted to Catholicism. One of the factors that favored these conversions was the action, at the heart of the Chinese community, of Father Serafin Bruno Amaral, who was linked to the famous Bishop of Beira, Dom Sebastião Soares de Resende. Through Father Amaral's intervention, the Associação da Juventude Católica Chinesa was formed in 1954. The priest was also the organiser of the above-mentioned visit of to the Clube Chinês.[29] To these actions of conversion need to be added, after 1955, those of the Jesuit priest Ferreira da Silva, who had taken part of his apprenticeship in Canton and was recruited by the bishop to look after the Chinese Catholic community (Medeiros n.d., p. 11).[30]

The attribution of amiability, seen in the above-mentioned newspaper texts, creates an expectation of imminent reciprocity and therefore the possibility of constructing a moral link. The object of praise should respond with a firm and unequivocal gesture in order to return the trust placed in the individual. Therefore, the categories of flattery created a virtual commitment to 'collaboration'. In other words, the metalanguage involved in this dynamic of potential affinities could be conveyed in the following imperative: 'You may be one of ours, but you need to prove it.' In fact, from the first events in the struggle for independence against Portugal in Africa and at a time when Maoist China was beginning to support these movements (particularly in Angola),[31], the Chinese of Mozambique had to make a clear gesture to show their vocation as 'good Portuguese'.

In that tense period for Portugal, marked by conflicts, the Chinese community of Beira could not destroy the trust that had been placed in them as good citizens. Thus, an event that led to a grand gesture of support for Portugal on the part of the Chinese of Beira was the start of the struggle for Angolan independence in 1961. The death of some settlers in that country – at the hand of the followers of Holden Roberto of the UPA and subsequent founder of the FNLA[32] – led to disturbances throughout the overseas colonies. Following these incidents, in November 1961, a contingent of directors of the Atlético Chinês, together with members of the Juventude Católica Chinesa da Beira decided to express publicly their solidarity with the 'Portuguese family' by personally presenting a sum of money (in the form of a check) to the governor of the province of Manica and Sofala, Commander Lopes Praça, for the 'victims of terrorism' of Angola. The presentation ceremony, which was reported on the first page of the newspaper *Notícias da Beira*, was attended by various members of the Atlético Chinês – its president Po Quin, as well as the president of the Juventude Chinesa Católica da Beira, Hon Quin Chee. On that occasion, Chee, entrusted with the task of giving a speech before the governor, referred to Mozambique as a 'piece of the Portuguese territory that is also ours'.[33] At the end of the text, the newspaper stated that after the check ceremony, 'Mr, Commander Lopes Praça, in a brilliant and sensitive improvised speech, thanked the initiative of the Chinese youth, to whose community he gave direct praise.' Some months before, the first page of the newspaper *Notícias da Beira* had published a photograph in which Po Quin was pictured presenting a sporting shield of the club to the governor of Manica and Sofala.[34] It was a welcome gesture to the new governor, who had just taken office.

These public expressions of solidarity with Portugal manifested by the Chinese community of Beira were a kind of metaphor for the colonial construction of amiability to which I referred above. It was clear that, in the case of the Chinese of Mozambique, the attribution of amiability may have also acted as a mechanism for the creation, in the near future, of a commitment of reciprocity implicitly obliging the Chinese to return the flattery and praise received in the form of unswerving loyalty. Here, in a dangerously seductive way, the gestures that convey the recognition of the Other – and its respective categories of flattery – include another metalanguage, one that enables this relation to be seen as a kind of 'double bind'. Neither fully Portuguese nor fully Chinese, when the political winds changed direction both in the metropole and in the overseas colonies, the only possible route left for the 'Luso-Chinese' was the diaspora. With the independence of Mozambique and the movement of 25 April in Portugal, the former flatterers of these 'good tenants' lost their place in the new local and international scenario. Without a 'father', or a 'mother', to shower them with praise, the Chinese of Beira became, in a manner of speaking, orphans. Overnight, those 'kind' friends turned into threatening enemies. They continued, undoubtedly influenced by an anticommunist feeling inherited from their ancestors. Perhaps for this reason, the Portugal of the Revolução dos Cravos (Carnation Revolution) was not necessarily the best option for their near future. While some families settled in Portugal most of them opted for Brazil, a country that at the time was still ruled by a military government and therefore, was far from a communist threat.

Diaspora and narratives of deception

From the end of the 1960s to the beginning of the 1970s, when the war between the Mozambique Liberation Front (FRELIMO) and the Portuguese army became more intense, the Chinese of Beira, as citizens of Portugal, began to be called up for military service to defend the Portuguese flag. Some time afterwards, with the defeat of the Portuguese army, independence negotiations began in Lusaka. As capitalist 'owners' and because they were suspected of complicity with the regime, the Chinese community began to feel, from 1974 (i.e., during the transition government), a growing hostility towards them. With the arrival of independence, this mistrust grew; unpredictable armed night searches for 'hidden goods' took place, and the Chinese were forced to do manual labour at arbitrarily assigned moments (sweeping the street and digging wells were some of the tasks imposed, according to statements by those interviewed in Curitiba), as well as to take part in the daily public demonstrations of the dynamising groups (Grupos Dinamizadores).[35] Within a short space of time, a law of nationalisations came into force. And, after the 3rd Congress of 1977, FRELIMO transformed into a party-state and adhered officially to Marxism-Leninism. Although there was no deliberate expulsion of the Chinese community, these political changes meant that within a short space of time, the Chinese went from being 'amiable owners' to 'undesirable tenants'. After independence, the abandonment of the country which had begun in 1973 and 1974 intensified.

In some cases, the departure was planned in advance, through the activation of respective contacts and networks of external relations. Macau and Taiwan were some of the initial destinations; however, the majority headed for Brazil, more specifically for the city of Curitiba.[36] Others dispersed to Portugal, Australia, Canada, and the United States. Some, for specific reasons, decided to stay in Mozambique. One of the few who stayed in Beira, Chin Kock Saum, died in 2009. In Lourenço Marques (Maputo), more families seem to have remained; among them was one linked to the Ho Ling, a shop located downtown (in the *baixa*), which was run by Yum Man Wah, who, aside from being a businessman, also owned a *machamba* (small farm) in Manhiça, near Maputo.[37]

With the independence of Mozambique, the tenuous link of the amiability, that which made the Chinese 'good Portuguese', was broken. The political circumstances had changed. In Portugal, at the time of the Carnation Revolution, the *retornados* (those who returned to Portugal from the overseas territories), including the 'Sino-Mozambicans', became an inconvenience. As I said previously, for those whose anticommunist feelings were more explicit, Brazil seemed a good destination., At that time, the Brazilian military regime – ruled by Ernesto Geisel – granted access to residence visas and work permits to attract the *retornados* from Portuguese Africa.

Could it be that the dispersion which the Chinese of Beira began to experience after 1975 became a kind of self-fulfilling prophesy, fed by their perpetual condition of 'close-distant Others'? As they were never fully Portuguese and never fully Chinese, the possibility of a future for these 'amiable' foreigners in Mozambique ended up becoming a fantasy at the start of the process of independence. 'Now I'm an African of Chinese origin, with Portuguese nationality, and naturalized Brazilian,' said one of my interlocutors in Curitiba, recalling his peaceful life in Beira in the 1960s.

Why did the majority of the Chinese of Beira choose to settle in Curitiba? In the conversations and interviews I held, the response almost always led to the figure of the pioneer Chin Fai Lai. He had arrived in Brazil before 1975 in the major port city of Santos to visit his sick father, who was working there at that time.

Chin Fai Lai's father had arrived in Santos directly from China. After inheriting some money on his father's death (and after having spent some time in various Brazilian cities), Chin Fai Lai settled on Curitiba as his place of permanent residence and opened a fast-food restaurant in the center of the city. When the Chinese of Mozambique, looking for a place to settle, began to contact their family networks outside the country, the news began to spread that Curitiba could be a good destination.

Although convenient from the native's point of view, this narrative of the pioneer does little to explain the structural and political conditions that motivated this choice. Other responses given by the Chinese from Beira refer to a kind of social-cultural compatibility between the two cities. There were, according to my interlocutors, many similarities between the Beira of the late colonial period, with its hotels, clubs, cafés, and networks of sociability, and the Curitiba of the 1970s, which was undergoing rapid urban expansion:

> Curitiba became like a second Beira. Here [in Curitiba] people were very close to each other. It was the same in Beira. We lived in harmony. It's a family atmosphere; when there's a celebration, everybody gets together. We communicate a lot with each other. Lots of people [Chinese of Beira from overseas] came here to visit us, and it reminded them of Beira, they would say 'it's just like a second Beira here'. Lots of things are similar to Beira. The *Cultural Chinese Association of Paraná*, for example, was 80% percent built by people from Beira.[38]

Perhaps it is no mere coincidence that the Chinese from Beira chose one of the least 'African' cities of Brazil. However, in their status as former colonial settlers in search of a new place (a kind of lost colonial paradise), it is possible that this search for points of compatibility between Beira and Curitiba was merely a justification elaborated a posteriori, or merely – in the words of Franz Boas – a 'secondary explanation'. It is probable that one of the key protagonists in the choice of Curitiba was Brother Cordeiro, a known figure in the 1960s and 1970s of the Colégio Marista da Beira, a high school where many Chinese studied.

Born in the south of Brazil, Brother Armando Corbellini, better known in Beira as Brother Cordeiro, left for Africa in 1948 after finishing his Marist studies at the Escola Normal Superior of the Instituto Champagnat de Porto Alegre (Brazil). Before arriving in Mozambique, he spent some time in Angola. On the eve of independence of Mozambique, he escaped to the border and managed to reach Rhodesia, from where he took a flight to Portugal. He stayed with the Marist Brothers of Portugal for a while, but in 1975 he returned to Brazil and settled in Rio de Janeiro. One of the jobs of Brother Cordeiro in Rio de Janeiro was to receive and assign *retornados* to appropriate places, particularly those coming from Mozambique and Angola. This task was carried out in the context of the *Movimento de apoio ao emigrante portugués* (MAEP, Support Movement for Portuguese Emigrants), which was set up in Rio de Janeiro in September 1975.[39] At that time, this city was the compulsory destination for the majority of 'refugees' and former Portuguese colonials. It is where all the newly arrived would put their documentation in order before dispersing throughout Brazil. Brother Cordeiro, who was also a pilot and a parachuting instructor, died in Rio de Janeiro in June 1996.[40]

There is no discernable common pattern in the dispersion experience of the Chinese from Beira. Those whose families had a network of cultural and commercial relations in places such as Hong Kong, Taiwan, and Singapore managed to build strategies for departure and prepare their lives outside Mozambique with more material planning. But those who, at the time of the dispersion, did not have help from distant relatives received only some assistance from consular employees in their country of destination, particularly Brazil, where the above-mentioned agreement with Portugal and the MAEP in Rio de Janeiro gave the returnees from the former colonies, including the Chinese from Beira, some degree of diplomatic protection. As one of these Chinese now living in Curitiba recalls, 'we were first degree refugees'. Those who managed to leave in more favorable financial conditions were able to take some personal belongings with them, including family photographs.

The photographic images that accompanied the newspaper article about the Atlético Chinês published in the *Diário de Moçambique* and *Notícias da Beira* are not simply images of a public nature. In that period, those pictures were reproduced and distributed among the families. They emerge from the intimate family world of the Chinese of Beira; they are, as such, part of the archive of memories protected by the diaspora itself.

Photography, with its practices and representations, occupies a central place in the constitution of the cultural and class habitus of the Chinese of

Beira. Around 1950, there were three photographic studios in the city, whose owners belonged to this community: Foto Estúdio, which was owned by Eginwo Shung Chin (the father of the basketball player João Ping mentioned earlier, who died in 1984); Foto Beira, which was owned by Lee King Wing, and Foto Central, which belonged to Kom Loom, who now lives in Australia. Much of the social and sporting and cultural life of the Chinese was portrayed by these photographic studios. But the photographs kept by these families who spread throughout the world were not only 'studio' pictures. Between the end of 1940 and start of the 1950s, many of the Chinese immigrants, now successful businessmen, began to acquire consumer goods such as radios, cars, record players, and cameras. Thus, cameras gradually left the studios and entered daily life. It became possible to travel and record images of the community at various activities, such as picnics, dancing and parties of the Escola Chinesa, sports meetings, outings, hunting and fishing trips in the *mato* (countryside), official ceremonies, and so on. My meeting with the 'Sino-Mozambican' diaspora was, I may say, very much a meeting with photographic images, too.

Some time after my interviews and conversations with the Chinese from Beira in Curitiba, between 2005 and 2009, I returned to Mozambique, taking the reverse route to the one they had taken more than thirty years earlier. I thus discovered that the Agostinho Neto state school now operates in the building of the old Escola Chinesa. The old building of the Clube Chinês now serves as a regional headquarters of ARPAC (Cultural Patrimony Archive). Beyond the experience of traveling to places about which I had heard so much in Curitiba, it was necessary for me to confirm, through the sources of the time, the social prominence that appeared self-evident in the narratives of the Chinese diaspora. In the newspapers I consulted in the Historical Archive of Mozambique (AHM), I found various blurry images, the same ones that I had seen in Curitiba, among so many others, in their clear original form. In Mozambique these photographs were merely historical artifacts deposited in the archives, while in Brazil they formed part of a vivid contemporary universe of references, and they had, to paraphrase Arjun Appadurai (1986), a 'social life' of their own. These images constitute, for the diaspora of the Chinese of Beira, a place of memories to which it is possible to return indefinitely. The fact that they belong to both a public record (the newspapers) and a private one (family albums) makes them essential testimonies of the protagonism that these 'good Portuguese' had in the colonial modernity of Beira from the 1950s and 1960s – a modernity which, incidentally, they were never able to abandon.

Even though some of the Chinese of Beira, particularly the older ones, had managed to maintain Portuguese nationality after leaving Mozambique, many of them were denied this nationality when attempting to renew their passports at the Portuguese consulates of the countries where they settled.

This denial of Portuguese nationality produced various narratives that circulated within the community of the Chinese of Beira and spread throughout the world – narratives of disappointment, told and retold a thousand times. One of the most well known and illustrative of these narratives relates to what I shall call here 'the passport incident'. The event that provoked this incident took place at the Portuguese consulate in Curitiba; a Chinese man of the diaspora, one of the Chinese of Beira, was denied the renewal of his Portuguese passport. The reaction to this rejection was immediate; right there, at the counter, this 'African of Chinese origin and Portuguese nationality' tore the pages of his old Portuguese passport, one by one, flinging them into the face of the consular employee. The once 'amiable' Chinese had now become undesirable and aggressive.

The emotional inconvenience of these Chinese of Beira is reinforced by the apparent paradox that many of them had defended the Portuguese flag during the war against the FRELIMO. As one Chinese from Beira, now living in Curitiba, said, 'I served in the army for forty five months. I tried to renew my Portuguese passport and was refused! They do not recognize me as a Portuguese citizen. This was one of the reasons I became a naturalized Brazilian. They do not recognize me. I was born in Mozambique, I fought in Mozambique, I had to swear allegiance to the Portuguese flag, as all Portuguese did before serving in the army. And after all that, they don't recognize me.' The objective and political criteria that defined 'national' had obviously changed. With this change, the subjectivity of those actors, now targets of new identity denominations, moved from a confused sense of 'affinity' to a clear 'elective' decision: 'now I feel more Brazilian, that is why I became a naturalized Brazilian'.

Finally, there is the question of the scope and comparative limits of this case study in relation to other similar diasporas. It might be a little hasty to extrapolate on the basis of the example of the 'Sino-Mozambicans' to make them part of a wider, extensively analysed, problem subsumed under the heading 'Chinese diaspora'. It is possible, however, that the comparison would become more fruitful in an analogy with other Asian minorities of Mozambique, such as the Ismailis, whose leaders managed to carefully prepare and coordinate the departure of their community from Mozambique before 1974 (Melo 2008, Leite and Khouri 2008 and their chapter in this volume).

'...that land belongs to the *gajos*...'

With the changes that took place in the postcolonial period, the statute of the Chinese of Beira changed. The independence of Mozambique and the end of the dictatorship in Portugal brought new spokespersons to a scenario that was already tainted by feelings of mistrust and apprehension towards these once 'good Portuguese'. These feelings were partly due to new circumstances born out of the defeat of the Portuguese military and police forces in the overseas territories; it was a period in which the very substance that fed the idea of nation was undergoing a major change and urgently needed to recompose itself under a new identity and on new political bases. Portugal was on the threshold of abandoning the designs of its imperial vocation and was beginning to face the challenges of an imminent European future. As holders of an ambiguous citizenship, the Chinese of Beira also had to reinvent their condition as former Portuguese born in Mozambique. However, the memories surrounding the Chinese Athletic Club, as well as the family photographs that evoked their sporting past were, for the Chinese of Beira of the diaspora, a rich and significant source for the production and reproduction of this reinvention of identity.

From the end of 1940 to the beginning of 1950, owing perhaps to the administrative requirements ruled by a growing assimilationism, the Thung Hua Athletic Club was renamed the *Clube Atlético Chinês* (Chinese Athletic Club). This metonymic shift was no mere detail. As illustrated in the epigraph at the beginning of this text, in which the Mozambican writer Mia Couto records his childhood journeys in Beira together with his Chinese friend, the 'Portuguese world' and China were two universes between which the Chinese community and their descendants debated. When the invitation to assume the role of 'good Portuguese' was presented explicitly to them, so to speak, the Chinese of Beira did not find any obstacle in accepting it. However, the sociopolitical circumstances that followed meant that they were unable to assume, until the ultimate consequences, a 'Portuguese-ness' that was now denied to them with the same emphasis that it had originally been offered. Instead, they had to adapt, as Aihwa Ong (1999) states, to a 'flexible citizenship'.

'That land belongs to the *gajos* [guys]', a Chinese from Beira currently living in Lisbon told me in reference to Mozambique. I noticed that this phrase, pronounced with a tone of weakness and confession, contained a wealth of significances concerning the problems dealt with. It may not be necessary to emphasise here that, in the words of my interlocutor, *gajos* meant 'autochthonous Africans'. However, beyond the clear and reassuring acceptance of the circumstances, the phrase appears to include another, more melancholic message. Something like a kind of fantasy that it was not, but might have been, had 'our predecessors not left China'. Now, this imaginary and almost unconscious return to a lost primordialism offers, paradoxically, the keys to understanding the dispersion of the Chinese of Beira; a dispersion which, it should be remembered, was marked by two key periods and movements: the departure from Guangdong to Mozambique and the departure from Mozambique to the world (particularly Brazil). It is precisely in this second period that the disturbing self-fulfilling prophesy comes full circle.

In the first movement (with the arrival in Mozambique), the label 'expatriates' dissapeared as the Chinese became part of the Portuguese family; in the second movement, this label becomes ever more indelible on the 'skin' of the Chinese of Beira.

Notes

1. I would like to thank António Sopa, former director of the Arquivo Histórico de Moçambique (Historical Archive of Mozambique) for his immense help in July 2009 when I consulted – still in the old building of the Arquivo Histórico in Maputo – the journals cited in this work. I also thank the 'Chinese from Beira' of Curitiba, Lisbon, New York, and Beira who, over the years, kindly agreed to talk to me.
2. Between the 'younger' Gilberto Freyre of the *Casa Grande & Senzala* and the more 'mature' Gilberto Freyre of Luso-Tropicalism, there are continuities and ruptures. I do not deny that *Casa Grande & Senzala* can be considered as the embryo of Luso-Tropicalism, but both periods correspond to different political and intellectual projects. The debate, certainly, is immense and rich, and the bibliography on the subject is vast. For an analysis of the internal tensions of the *Casa Grande & Senzala*, I recommend the book by Ricardo Benzaquen de Araújo (1994). To understand the modern-day consequences of Luso-Tropicalism in the framework of 'institutionalisation' of the CPLP (Comunidade de Países de Língua Portuguesa – Community of Portuguese-Speaking Countries), see Michel Cahen (1997).
3. The term '*coolie*' comes probably from the Hindi '*quli*,' which means 'seasonal worker'. Throughout the 18th and 19th centuries, the term was used to appoint low-status workers from Asia and India. Over time, it took on the biased meaning of a racial epithet.
4. See, in particular, Medeiros 2007, p. 182, note 55.
5. The short route which connected Beira to Mutare in Rhodesia (Zimbabwe) came to be known as the Beira Corridor.
6. These companies offered economic stability to their Chinese employees, generally paying them in escudos, pound sterling, and gold (personal information of A. Y., New York, 28 May 2010).
7. In colonial Mozambique, this was the term used to refer to the places where the Africans took their meals.
8. Arquivo Histórico de Moçambique (AHM), Fundo do Governo do Distrito da Beira, Assuntos Municipais e dos seus Organismos Autónomos, Actas 1942–1944, cx 92 – Acta n 55, Sessão Ordinária da Comissão Administrativa da Câmara Municipal da Beira de 23 de Dezembro de 1943, p. 4.
9. This refers to form no. 223. The individual Augusto Ramos de Pádua, and the firm Ebrahim Noormahomed & Irmãos also took part in the public tender. The basis of the tender was 6,025$00 and the Chee Kung Tong Club offered 6,424$00. AHM, Fundo do Governo do Distrito da Beira, Assuntos Municipais e dos seus Organismos Autónomos, Actas, 1942–1944, cx. 92 – Acta no. 17, Sessão Ordinária da Comissão Administrativa da Câmara Municipal da Beira de 20 de Abril de 1944, p. 22.
10. Sometimes in the sources the name appears as John Ping.
11. Information confirmed during an interview with Mr. N. H. in Curitiba (Brazil), on 12 April, 2011. Mr. N. H., aged 83, is one of the oldest members of the 'diaspora' of Chinese from Beira who lives in Brazil.

From Mozambique to Brazil 259

12. In the colonial sources, the members of this group are generally called 'Chinese' (*Chineses*), and on other occasions 'Chinese subjects' (*Súbditos chineses*). But in some cases, 'Luso-Chinese' is also used. In the colonial censuses, they were classified as 'yellow' (*amarelos*). Eduardo Medeiros, in his pioneering work (unfortunately still little publicised), prefers to speak in terms of 'Sino-Mozambicans'. It should be noted that the term 'China' (in plural, '*Os chinas*') was also used in the colonial period, sometimes as a stigmatising epithet. The native category – that used by the Chinese in Beira in their intimate circles – is '*bei-la yan*,' which in Cantonese means 'people of Beira'. Throughout this work, I will use a combination of two native categories, that of 'colonial rule', which emphasises the ethnonational aspect (Chinese) and that of the Chinese themselves, which places the emphasis on the place of birth: Beira. I therefore refer to them as the 'Chinese of Beira'. When referring to 'Luso-Chinese' or 'Sino-Mozambicans', I will place the terms in inverted commas (quotes).
13. Curitiba, interviews with K. V. Q., held between 2006 and 2009.
14. According to statistics reproduced by Castelo (2007, p. 216).
15. Curitiba, interview with H. M., 14 February 2009.
16. There is not enough space here to elaborate a systematic comparison between the Chinese community of Beira and that of Lourenço Marques. The motives that led those from Beira to choose Curitiba while those from Lourenço Marques chose São Paulo will hopefully be analysed in other works.
17. 'Necrologia: Mon Man,' *Diário de Moçambique*, Beira, 2 September 1958, p. 7 (author's translation).
18. The term that appeared in the newspapers, in Portuguese, was '*simpático*', conveying the idea that the Chinese of Beira were friendly, kind, and pleasant people. I have chosen to translate this term as 'amiable'. The advantage of the term '*amiable*' (derived from the Latin '*amicabilis*') is that it helps evoke one of the central issues addressed in this article: the colonial construction of the tension between the categories of 'friend' and 'enemy'.
19. 'A Associação da Juventude Católica Chinesa em festa,' *Diário de Moçambique*, Beira, 10 December 1958, p. 9.
20. 'Basquetebol. O Sporting em honras e A. Chinês em femininos são os novos campeões da Beira,' *Notícias da Beira*, February 1960.
21. 'Ouvindo um ás. John Ping. Um nome que é uma legenda do nosso basquetebol,' *Diário de Moçambique*, Beira, 15 March 1954, p. 6.
22. Galeria dos Campeões. 'Esta é a nossa melhor equipa de basquetebol: O Atlético Chinês', *Diário de Moçambique*, Beira, 9 April 1953.
23. 'Galeria dos Campeões. Eis um combinado do futuro: Os juniores do Atlético Chinês', *Diário de Moçambique*, Beira, 24 April 1953, p. 4.
24. 'Valores do Desporto Beirense. O grupo feminino do Atlético Chinês,' *Diário de Moçambique*, Beira, 28 April 1953, p. 4.
25. 'Uma simpatia, uma esportista e um valor são atributos de Julieta Yee capitã do "cinco" de basquetebol do Atlético Chinês,' *Diário de Moçambique*, Beira, 24 July 1954.
26. Quen Gui died on 30 April 2011, at the Hospital of the University of Coimbra.
27. Some years after his meeting with the Chinese of Beira, Freyre published an essay entitled 'Por que China Tropical?' In it, he emphasised the compatibilities between the 'Orient' and the 'Portuguese world', this time looking for analogies between the Chinese civilisation and Brazil ('Tropical China') – two Chinas '...whose presence in the modern world is becoming increasingly significant' (2003, 228). The essay was originally published in English in the book *New World*

in the Tropics (1959). In 2003, it was republished in Portuguese in the volume *China Tropical*, by the University of Brasília.
28. Medeiros, E. (n.d.).
29. Eric Morier-Genoud provided me with this information from the *Diário pessoal* (Personal diary) of Dom Sebastião Soares de Resende. Portions of this diary were widely used (also thanks to the generosity of Eric Morier-Genoud) and reproduced by Eduardo Medeiros; see Medeiros (n.d.).
30. Medeiros (n.d., p. 10) also emphasises the influence of some Portuguese families, together with their Chinese neighbours, particularly in the parish of S. João Baptista de Matacuane, created on 1 September 1963, under the leadership of the Companhia de Jesus, as well as the parish of the Imaculado Coração de Maria, in Alto da Manga, directed after 1967 by the Combonian missionaries. The college for boys, particularly that for children of mixed race, directed by the female Missionary Franciscans of Calais, in the Parish of Alto da Manga, was also very important.
31. Mario Pinto de Andrade, one of the founders of the MPLA, confirms this support in an interview given to Michel Laban: 'Our first money did not come, therefore, from Moscow but from China. ... This story has never been truthfully told. I have said it several times: I said it in the book on Cabral, I also said it in the courses in Mozambique, to the young generations. But in general, it has been officially hidden: Because of the Sino-Soviet conflict, and the fact that the Soviet Union had taken the first place in the scenario of direct help' (Andrade 1997, pp. 162–163; author's translation from the original Portuguese).
32. UPA, União dos Povos de Angola (Angola Peoples Union); FNLA, Frente Nacional de Libertação de Angola (Angolan National Liberation Front)
33. See 'A Juventude Chinesa contribuiu com o seu auxílio para as vítimas do terrorismo em Angola. Os dirigentes do Atlético Chinês entregaram um cheque ao Governador de Manica e Sofala,' *Notícias da Beira*, 25 November 1961, p. 1.
34. *Notícias da Beira*, 4 February 1961.
35. The dynamising groups (Grupos Dinamizadores, GDs) were mobilisation groups created (in the factories districts and neighborhoods) soon after independence. According with Newitt (1995, p. 543), in many areas ' ... the GDs acted as popular tribunals until a new legal system could be created. Later a greater distinction was to emerge between party, state and industrial management, but it had not been a satisfactory way to begin the new social and economic order'.
36. Currently, according to statistics that need to be improved, Curitiba has approximately 150 'Sino-Mozambican' families, totalling around 1,000 individuals. In São Paulo, according to a statement from the 'Sino-Mozambicans' themselves, there are around 50 families.
37. In Maputo there are also a few 'Sino-Mozambicans' that have remained in the country and supported FRELIMO. This is the case of Kok Nam (born in 1939). He is, perhaps, one of the most illustrious Mozambicans of Chinese ascendency. Son of Cantonese parents, he is, together with Richardo Rangel, one of the most important Mozambican photographers of the country. Kok Nam had a long and rich career in photographic journalism (in Mozambican media such as *Diário de Moçambique*, *Voz Africana*, *Revista Tempo*, and *Savana*). His photographic works have been published in many newspapers and international magazines, including the *New York Times*, *Time Magazine*, the *Observer*, *The Independent*, and *Expresso*, among others. For more information see *Kok Nam, o homem por detrás da câmara*, EPM-CELP, Maputo, 2010.
38. Curitiba, interview with K.V.Q., 17 May 2008.

39. 'Imigrantes tem ajuda no Rio,' *Jornal do Brasil*, Rio de Janeiro, 29 September 1975, p. 9. See also 'Curriculum Vitae (Irmão Armando Corbellini),' http://bernardetezanatta.blogspot.com/2009/10/curriculum-vitae-irmao-armando.html
40. For more information, see http://familiazanattah.blogspot.com/2007/05/vida-do-irmo-armando-corbellini.html

References

Andrade, M. P. (1997), *Uma entrevista dada a Michel Laban*. Edições João Sá da Costa, Lisbon.
Appadurai, A. (ed.) (1986), *The Social Life of Things. Commodities in Cultural Perspective*. Cambridge University Press, Cambridge, UK.
Araújo, R. B. (1994), *Guerra e Paz. Casa-Grande & Senzala e a obra de Gilberto Freyre nos anos 30*. Editora 34, Rio de Janeiro.
Cahen, M. (1997), 'Des caravelles pour le futur? Discours politique et idéologique dans l'"institutionnalisation" de la Communauté des pays de langue portugaise,' *Lusotopie* 4, pp. 391–433.
Castelo, C. (2007), *Passagens para África. O povoamento de Angola e Moçambique com Naturais da Metrópole (1920–1974)*. Edições Afrontamento, Oporto
Chin, S. (1953), 'Discurso do Sr. Shung Chin, presidente da Comunidade Chinesa de Sofala e Manica, no Clube Chee Kung Tong, da Beira,' in G. Freyre (1953, pp. 335–337).
Chor Maio, M. (1999), 'Tempo controverso. Gilberto Freyre e o Projeto Unesco,' *Tempo Social. Revista de Sociologia* 11, no.1, pp. 111–136.
Freyre, G. (1953), *Um Brasileiro em Terras Portuguesas*. Livraria José Olympio Editora, Rio de Janeiro.
—— (2003), *China Tropical, e outros escritos sobre a influência do Oriente na cultura luso-brasileira*. Editora UnB, Brasília.
Geffray, C. (1997), 'Le lusotropicalisme comme discours de l'amour dans la servitude,' *Lusotopie* 4, pp. 361–371.
Leite, J. Pereira, and Khouri, N. (eds.) (2008), 'Indiens du Mozambique et d'Afrique orientale,' *Lusotopie* 15, no. 1, pp. 27–207.
Liesegang, G. (1989), 'Sofala, Beira e a sua zona (c. 900–1894),' *Arquivo. Boletim do Arquivo Histórico de Moçambique* no. 6, pp. 21–64.
Ly-Tio-Fane-Pineo, H. 1981, *La diaspora chinoise dans l'océan Indien occidental*. Association des Chercheurs de l'océan Indien/Institut d'histoire des pays d'Outre-Mer, Aix-en-Provence.
Medeiros, E. (n.d.), 'Crenças e práticas religiosas entre os sino-moçambicanos da Beira (Moçambique).' Unpublished MS.
—— (1998), 'O Clube Chinês da Beira (Moçambique),' *Macau*, II Series, no. 73, pp. 26–33.
—— (2007), 'Os sino-moçambicanos da Beira. Mestiçagens várias,' *Caderno de Estudos Africanos* nos. 13–14, pp. 155–187.
Melo, A. (2008), 'A diáspora ismaelita – preparação e "partida", vivências da migração dos anos 70,' *Lusotopie* 15, no. 1, pp. 97–102.
Newitt, M. (1995), *A History of Mozambique*, Indiana University Press, Bloomington and Indianapolis.
Ong, A. (1999), *Flexible Citizenship. The Cultural Logics of Transnationality*. Duke University Press, Durham, NC, and London.

Pan, L. (ed.) (1999), *The Encyclopedia of the Chinese Overseas*. Harvard University Press, Cambridge, MA.
Rebelo, D. J. Soares (1970), 'The Chinese Extraction Group in Mozambique,' *Boletim da Sociedade de Estudos de Moçambique* 39, nos. 164–165, pp. 133–42.
Richardson, P. (1977), 'The Recruiting of Chinese Indentured Labour for the South African Gold-Mines, 1903–1980,' *Journal of African History* 18, no. 1, pp. 85–108.
Wong-Hee-Kam, E. (1996), *La diaspora chinoise aux Mascareignes: Le cas de la Réunion*. L'Harmattan, Paris.
Yap, M., and Leong Man, D. (1996), *Color, Confusion and Concessions: The History of the Chinese in South Africa*. Hong Kong University Press, Hong Kong.

Part IV
Ideology and Heritage

11
Luso-African Intimacies: Conceptions of National and Transnational Community

Rosa Williams

Rogers Brubaker (2005, pp. 6–7) has observed of the recent 'proliferation of diasporas and of diaspora-talk' the tendency for scholarship on transnationalism and diaspora to 'fuse'. The growing literature on transnationalism, he suggests, have contributed to a 'counter-current' which highlights the role of processes of 'boundary-*erosion*' as well as 'boundary-*maintenance*' in the construction of diasporic ties. Brubaker appears to see this 'interesting ambivalence' as a symptom of the analytical incoherence of the concept of diaspora. Yet he himself invites scholars to think of diaspora as a category of practice rather than a category of analysis: to look not at what it 'is' but at what it 'does' (p. 13).

I suggest that the tension which Brubaker identifies captures the contradictory nature of diasporic belonging, founded on both a purist understanding of a shared culture which must be preserved and a more fluid and inclusive account of a community developing out of common historical experience. Paul Gilroy (1993) points to these conflicting tendencies in his influential account of the 'black Atlantic' as a 'counter culture of modernity' which has the potential to displace empire, slavery, or even Africa as a means for imagining a more open-ended form of transnational community. While highlighting the challenge that this cultural formation presents to essentialised notions of national or racial identity, Gilroy also acknowledges within this oppositional stance the potential for a 'volkish popular cultural nationalism', which at times has overlapped aesthetically and politically with fascism (p. 15).[1]

Like 'diaspora', the concept of a Lusophone world or *Lusofonia* provides a framework for describing affective ties, forms of belonging, and relationships of mutuality that span noncontiguous territories, complicating conventional notions of national identity. I suggest that it is also similarly ambivalent – while the notion of *Lusofonia* has been adopted by artists, writers, politicians, and policy makers as a way of imagining new forms of transnational aesthetic and political community, it is has yet to be freed of the remnants of an already existing imperial narrative of transcontinental connection which put the Portuguese nation and Portuguese subjects at its centre. I argue that the content of that narrative itself serves as an obstacle for emerging accounts of a Lusophone world to reframe the relationship between Portugal and its former colonies. In both popular and scholarly accounts, the Portuguese character has been celebrated and condemned for its supposed capacity for cross-cultural intimacy, whether familial or sexual, affectionate or violent. This chapter examines the reoccurring metaphors of Portuguese proximity, excessive or exemplary, found in discussions of Portugal's colonial and postcolonial relationships with Africa.

Rhetoric and reality

In an article based on the premise of exposing the gap between the 'rhetoric and reality' of 'Portugal's civilizing mission in Guinea-Bissau', Peter Mendy draws on a curious example from a 1950s school textbook to demonstrate the parallels between the policies of assimilation in French and Portuguese Africa:

> Just as assimilated Africans in French colonies were made to recite 'Our forefathers, the Gauls,' the children of assimilados in Portuguese colonies were forced to chant: 'Who are we, the Portuguese who, for so many centuries, live in this western corner of Europe? History says that we are descendants of many ancient peoples who intermixed and intermingled.'
> (Mendy 2003, p. 50, author's translation)

In both the occasions which Mendy describes, the incongruity between the colonial and geographical situation of the speaking schoolchild and the national claim to a shared genealogical connection with Europe which they enunciate is stark. In his account of the formation of colonial French Caribbean identities, Frantz Fanon (1971 [1952], p. 120, n. 9) notes that the story of the *Antillais* child dutifully repeating *'nos pères, les Gaulois'* provokes a smile but should also provoke us to consider the power of the assimilationist myth which that act of speaking indexes. As readers we see the absurdity in this moment; we understand that the child cannot be and yet is required to be at once liberal citizen and racial subject.[2] Still, the other side to this story is that in the classroom everyone has a straight face; the state is in all seriousness demanding the performance of this contradiction.

Though presented by Mendy as if commensurate with the notorious French phrase, the myth of national origins presented in this Portuguese textbook (Ministério da Educação Nacional 1958) introduces a further dimension to the strange disconnection between speaking child and spoken text. It describes a national community located in a small corner of the world which has been produced through the merging of the societies which came before them. The racial and cultural form – now fixed – of the homogeneous, essentially European, Portuguese subject is ascribed a heterogeneous genealogy. This particular story of reciprocal adaptation and assimilation could enable a more intimate relationship between Africa and Portugal to be imagined. At the same time, the location of that process in a distant past and place maintains the historical disjuncture between the metropolitan subject and the colonial child who tells that subject's myth of origins.

The origin story that Mendy cites echoes earlier Portuguese accounts of the diversity of national racial types (Costa Ferreira 1902; Williams 2007). But in 1950s Guinea Bissau that narrative would have had a particular salience. The Brazilian sociologist Gilberto Freyre (1946 [1933]) employed the idea of miscegenation as both a metaphor and an explanation for the successful development of a New World culture. In his writing from the 1930s, Freyre represented sexual and familial relations in Brazil between Portuguese slave-owning patriarchs and Amerindian and African women as the locus of the production of a new society of mixed and mixable people. As elsewhere, interracial intimacy was understood as a challenge to colonial authority in Portuguese Africa. The *Estado Novo* administration initially regarded Freyre's research with suspicion, and only in the 1950s was he invited by the Portuguese state to extend his research beyond Brazil. Thereafter, the notion of an exceptionally adaptable and genial Lusophone subject and an exceptionally harmonious Lusotropical society, stripped – at least to some extent – of its overtones of sexual license and racial instability, was adopted to shore up the national narrative (Freyre 1958; Castelo 1998; Fikes 2009, pp. 37–39).

Before 1960, the visions which different European powers maintained for the future of their African colonies varied. As John Illife (1995, p. 246) explains, 'Britain planned gradual devolution to friendly successor states. France and Portugal planned ever closer integration between colonies and metropoles. Belgium scarcely thought about the matter.' From the late 1950s European colonial powers began handing over – or reluctantly giving up – power to anticolonial parties, and independent African nations were being recognised by the international community. France and Portugal parted ways once the Front de Libération National had forced de Gaulle to accept an independent Algeria in 1962. Portugal under the *Estado Novo* maintained its commitment to a political presence in Africa, sustained only through brutal colonial wars fought by young Portuguese and African conscripts.[3] Portugal's colonial representatives were engaged in reaffirming a national historical narrative of continuity and cross-continental connections just as the births of new nations in Africa were being celebrated.

Stories of the distinctiveness of Portuguese rule which centred on interpersonal relationships supplemented the notion of a transglobal Portuguese territory drawing distant communities into close connections with one another. This conception of the Portuguese nation was made explicit in official discourse from the beginning of the 1950s when the Portuguese colonies were renamed overseas provinces (*províncias ultramarinas*). So, for example, on the occasion of a visit from the Portuguese president Américo Thomaz in 1964, shortly before the outbreak of armed resistance to colonial rule, the governor-general of Mozambique described the president's 'voyage from Portugal to Portugal' as an 'object lesson in national unity', identifying that nation as 'the pluri-continental and pluri-racial fatherland that God has given to us'[4] (José da Costa Almeida, quoted in Patrício 1965, p. 95).

Much of mid- to late-20th-century scholarship on Portuguese imperialism in Africa focused on disputing accounts of the particularity of Portugal's colonial practices. From the 1950s on, historians and other social scientists challenged the concept of Lusotropicalism by seeking to expose the gap between the rhetoric of the nonracial society and the reality of colonial racism – located in structural inequalities, coercive labour practices, and abusive interpersonal relations (see Andrade 1955, Harris 1958, Boxer 1963, Mondlane 1969, Davidson 1972, Bender 1978). Discursive illusion, or delusion, contrasted by the facts uncovered by the historian or the stories told by those who were there – the tension between rhetoric and reality, ideology and practice – was a persistent theme in this writing.

Yet, even as they were challenging the rhetoric of the Portuguese state, scholars were also critically examining one another's depictions of that state and its agents. Historians sought to move beyond the notion of Portuguese ultracolonialism, which Perry Anderson (1962, pp. 97–98) described as 'both the most extreme and the most primitive modality of colonialism' in which forced labour was the 'ramshackle instrument of a [weak] colonial power.'[5] They lost patience with the 'the cliché of corrupt, inefficient and pompous Portuguese' and analyses of forced labour which reduced the Portuguese to 'mere monsters' (Penvenne 1985, p. 107; White 1985, p. 325). Douglas Wheeler (1976, p. 465) argued that what he termed Marxist 'ideological superstition' could obscure in less careful scholarship 'the extent to which much of official activity was an expression of Lusitanian nationalism.' Gervase Clarence-Smith (1979, 1985) responded to R. J. Hammond's (1966) depiction of a politically driven and economically irrational 'uneconomic imperialism' in an article which questioned this 'myth', followed by a monograph on Portugal's modern empire subtitled 'a study in economic imperialism'.

These myths about Portuguese colonialism perpetuated and debunked in both historical sources and the writing of history have some commonalities. The distinct and powerful fictions of nonracialism, Lusotropicalism, ultracolonialism, and uneconomic imperialism either called into question or defended the capability of this European state and of these European subjects to participate fully in the project of exporting European modernity. Whether describing the development of a distinct form of modernity or a failure to be modern, they emphasised the place of emotions over rationality and affective interpersonal relationships over indifferent institutional ones.

Colonialism-in-the-hammock: intimacy, brutality, disorder

Reading late-19th- and early-20th-century historical scholarship, Sanjay Subrahmanyam (1993) draws out a prevailing account of the perfecting of European imperialism. He paraphrases a conventional depiction of the ascendance of northwestern European imperial powers in Asia during the 17th and 18th centuries as a story in which 'colonialism-in-the-hammock' was trumped by 'colonialism-from-a-distance, wherein the "natives" were separated from the rulers, so that the pure characteristics of both could be preserved for their mutual benefit' (1993, p. 139). That narrative was later 'internalised but inverted' in 'the Portuguese claim to being non-racist colonisers' (p. 141). Subrahmanyam notes that this account has obscured the extent to which, in their methods and philosophies of rule, 'the Dutch and English in Asia were apprentices of the Portuguese' (1993, p. 142). This retrospective distinction between cold, rational northerners and impulsive, emotional southerners, between efficient distance and dangerous proximity was, he suggest, inaccurate but enduring.

Tales of intimacy between Portuguese and indigenous subjects in Asia and Africa alike threatened the security of the Portuguese imperial narrative because they were so familiar and uncomfortable. British and American accounts of a Portuguese capacity for forming close cross-cultural personal relationships was often characterised as curious, even commendable, but it was at the same time understood as the basis for social disorder. Assertions of the distinctive warmth of those relationships marked ambivalence about Portugal's capability of acting as a modern European custodian of its African subjects. We can find in them a suspicion of *immoderate* affection and the confusion of racial or cultural boundaries, threatening the insufficient marking of difference in social and intimate contexts. These forms of proximity were also associated with the improper use of force and, in particular, the violent coercion of African labour. In the ongoing reproduction of a paired set of portrayals of a backward, not quite modern, colonial nation which Jeanne Penvenne (1979, p. 97) refers to as 'the equally romantic caricatures of the Portuguese as decadent, drunken slave dealers or as the benevolent, humble, tolerant "civilizers" of their black brethren', Portugal could be characterised even within the same text as both the kindest and the cruelest coloniser.

David Livingstone (1875, p. 210), the mid-19th-century British missionary and explorer, was intensely critical of the Portuguese slave traders he met on his travels on the east coast of Africa, describing them as 'the vilest of the vile' and representing them as a long-established part of the landscape he encountered.[6] On the Central West African coast he found a terrain ripe for improvement, and while the Portuguese were integrated into the economy of the region, he felt that they had failed to 'develop [its] resources' (1858, p. 477). Yet, with some admiration he commented on the Portuguese men he met in Luanda:

> It was particularly gratifying to me...to view the liberality with which people of color were treated by the Portuguese. Instances, so common in the South, in which half-caste children are abandoned, are here extremely rare. They are acknowledged at table, and provided for by their fathers as if European. The colored clerks of the merchants sit at the same table with their employers without any embarrassment...nowhere else in Africa is there such goodwill between European and natives as here (1858, p. 399).

Nevertheless, Livingstone also stressed the necessity of maintaining the limits to European subjecthood in contesting Portugal's claim over an overland journey coast to coast recorded in the early 19th century. He noted that it was achieved merely by 'native Portuguese subjects', contending, 'No European ever accomplished it, though this fact has lately been quoted as if the men had been *"Portuguese"*' (1858, p. 472, emphasis in original).

Livingstone's double-edged portrayal of the Portuguese and their colonial practices is echoed in the writings of a late-19th-century visitor to Angola, Joachim John Monteiro, a British subject of Portuguese descent working as a mine geologist and prospector. Monteiro published a travel narrative for a British audience which told familiar stories about the failures of Portuguese administration at home and abroad:

> Whilst in Portugal itself patriotism and public morality are debased by an unchecked system of bribery and greed of money and power, it is too much to expect that the rich colonies will be purged of their long-existing abuses (1875, p. 59).

But he included amongst his tales of the venality and disorder inherent to Portuguese rule comments on the conspicuous absence of brutality in relationships between Portuguese masters and their servants (p. 188). C. P. Daly (1884, pp. 93–94) also restated this dual description in an address on the commercial potential of the Congo given before the American Geographical Society, of which he was president. Drawing on the descriptions of Monteiro and other visitors to the region, he described the Portuguese as 'the chief supporters of the slave trade...the first to begin it, and...the last to adhere to it' and concluded, 'Instead, therefore, of advancing, they have retarded civilization.' Nonetheless, he noted that 'in justice to the Portuguese' they should be recognised for having been 'kind masters to the Africans there who were about them, treating them, not only with kindness, but even equality.'

In the first decade of the 20th century, two articles published in the *Transvaal Leader* described Portuguese attitude towards racial difference in distinct terms. One, from 1911, reproduced a speech made by Mozambique's former governor-general Major Freire de Andrade on his return to Lisbon. Admiring his expression of concern for the treatment, in South Africa, the journalist asked his audience to

> Note his arresting phrase, 'these millions of natives, Portuguese like ourselves,' and consider the ideal which it connotes. Imagine a Union politician speaking of 'these millions of natives, South African like ourselves!'... [This phrase] gives us in a flash the difference between the Latin point of view and the Teutonic. (quoted in 'Mozambique natives,' *Lourenço Marques Guardian*, 27 February 1911)

Still, that difference – between northern and southern Europe, the inclusive and exclusive model of the nation – while here considered commendable, had not only a geographical but also a temporal referent. Portugal was described as a European power whose imperial vitality was of a different era and whose methods of administration were those of the past.

By contrast, an earlier article, possibly authored by the same sympathetic journalist, had defended Portuguese policy in Mozambique in terms of its movement *away* from the 'Latin point of view'. The author disputed the British assumption that Mozambique's capital was host to 'all the vices peculiar to an easy going southern race [and] that the people are corrupt and indolent' (Edwards 1907, p. 7). Instead, he averred, 'Mozambique is stepping into line with British South Africa', and he promised to demonstrate 'the extent to which the Portuguese Province is preparing to proceed along the path of Colonial progress' (p. 11). Freire de Andrade, as governor-general, was figured as advancing quickly in this process of becoming a civilised civiliser, having 'lived long enough in the Province of Mozambique to have become imbued with the British ideal of colonial government' (p. 13).

This friendly condescension referencing Portugal's position in a European colonial hierarchy was mirrored by turn-of-the-century Portuguese intellectuals who maintained an 'almost obsessive...preoccupation with national decadence' (Freeland 1995, p. 205). One of the most prominent members of that group, the novelist Eça de Queirós, emphasised the need to reform and modernise away from the gaze of foreign commentators, in a country that 'is backward, brutalized, dirty, insipid. [Portugal] needs to shut itself from within and close the curtains' (quoted in Wheeler 1997 p. 11, author's translation). With regard to Africa, while colonial officials emphasised the uniqueness of the time span over which Portugal had maintained connections with the continent, Europe's 'scramble for Africa' saw them redefining that relationship as one of direct colonial administration. One former governor of São Tomé e Príncipe wrote in 1885 of the Berlin conference that it should be taken by Portugal as both 'a lesson and the start of a new period of colonial administration' (Pinheiro 1885, p. 4).

Ways of seeing: science and colonial administration

For many Portuguese colonial officials, establishing the 'effective occupation' required by the General Act of the Berlin conference meant breaking from the past, laying the groundwork of administrative rationality, and cleaning out the remnants of former corruption. A Portuguese intellectual closely associated with Eça, the journalist and diplomat Jaime Batalha Reis, sought instead to look back on that past in order to recover a tradition of disinterested, scientific observation that could be put at the service of this new kind of colony. He did so in the context of a particular political project, conducting research in support of Portugal's claims to sovereignty over the Shire highlands close to what is now Lake Malawi that were challenged by the British.[7] In an article published in the *Scottish Geographical Magazine* in 1889,[8] Batalha Reis drew on evidence from Portuguese texts dating back to the 17th century in order to challenge: 'a settled opinion in England and Scotland that their travellers discovered, visited, explored, what they all style "Nyassaland" before the Portuguese did, and that therefore Great Britain has a superior right over Portugal to political sway in these territories' (Batalha Reis 1889a, p. 259). The geographical knowledge of the region demonstrated by the minute descriptions of these Portuguese writers, he argued, established 'priority of discovery, priority of exploration and priority of trade' in the contested areas (Batalha Reis 1889a, p. 268).

Batalha Reis' argument for the Portuguese having established their authority in the region was more tenuous. According to the recently established principle of effective occupation, the historical relationship which he set out to establish could not be the basis for Portugal's claim to the territory. Verney Lovett Cameron (1890), who led a Royal Geographical Society expedition across central Africa in 1873, called attention to this in a response published some months later. Cameron not only pointed out the irrelevance of Batalha Reis' evidence but also brought the reliability of the texts which he cited into question. While accepting the existence of already existing Portuguese records of 'the Shire and Lake Nyassa previous to their being, I will not say discovered but visited by Doctor Livingstone', he questioned whether the travellers referred to in these texts were European subjects: 'there is nothing to show that they were not merely slaves, or native agents, trading in the names of their masters' (Cameron, 1890, p. 585). Cameron further cast doubt on the quality of their observations, citing a later Portuguese source which disparaged these authors for 'disfiguring the face of the earth, describing whatever their fancies (heated with rum and strong liquors imbibed against the cold) painted during sleep' (Francisco José Maria de Lacera e Almeida, quoted in Cameron 1890, p. 585).

Livingstone's biographer Harry Johnston, who was involved in negotiating for British control of Mashonaland and the Shire highlands, also questioned whether the writers or subjects of these Portuguese narratives were genuine explorers. Johnston (1891, p. 39) described the two men, referred to by Livingstone, who travelled from the Angolan to the Mozambican coast at the start of the 19th century as 'half-caste Portuguese' who were not 'scientific observers' and whose journey 'left geographers almost as much in the dark as to Inner African geography as if it had never been undertaken'. He commented that these and other Portuguese travellers 'picked their way among great lakes and saw none of them'. What made travel or exploration significant, he indicated, was the production of knowledge based on disinterested and skilled observation.

Addressing the readers of a Portuguese journal of colonial administration a few years later, Batalha Reis (1897, pp. 13–14) in turn echoed Johnston's language. He suggested that despite the existence of records of 'the old heroic times of our explorations', the failure to take proper notice of the right kinds of information had put the legitimacy of Portuguese discoveries into doubt: 'the voyagers paid a great deal more attention to the men of foreign races that they met – looking at them, sometimes, with excessively European eyes – than to the animals, the plants, the rocks, the flow of the rivers, and the direction and height of the mountains'. This misjudged focus on the particularities of human societies was continued, he argued, even in the present. According to him, the numerous and extensive articles in Portuguese newspapers by correspondents sent to the colonies were far too interested in 'absorbing and insignificant *Politics*' and had nothing to say about 'geography, the products of the country, the progress of the study of land, that which must be constantly observed, explored and described'.[9]

Batalha Reis (1897, p. 12) asserted that this lack of proper scientific observation reflected the absence of interest in developing geographical research amongst Portugal's educated classes. In comparison, the 'English, Germans, – and to a lesser degree French and Italians' who travelled had both learned the means and developed the interest that would lead them to 'observe, write and publish their observations'. Skills in classifying minerals and organisms and in understanding maps and cartography were the foundation for the proper ways of seeing. They were complemented by mastery of a technology that had transformed the experience of travel: 'already everybody out there takes photographs just like they read and write'. In contrast, Portuguese travellers could not engage in the systematic observation of discrete analytical objects. Batalha Reis lamented that, lacking both scientific knowledge and tools, they 'look without seeing, or see without understanding', having nothing to relate on their return but 'some picturesque observations about the customs of the natives'.

In his account, the distinctiveness of the Portuguese character was its shortcoming. Like Johnston, he implied that the capacity to produce disinterested scientific knowledge separated those who could take responsibility for administration and those for whom the administration was responsible. The modern, secular state was called upon to perform effective government in accordance with impersonal laws and procedures. This aspiration was countered within by a conception of native administration appealing to the salience of traditional law and authority in exercising colonial rule. Within the colonial state itself were cross-cutting jurisdictions, each with their own claims to expertise in administering colonial subjects and their own conception of the moral obligations entailed by their responsibilities (Weber 1978 [1922], pp. 213–216, 956–958; 1946 [1919], pp. 116–119).

In November 1914 Mozambique's Board of Health (*Junta de Saúde*) considered a proposal submitted by the Director of Emigration (*Intendente da Emigração*), who worked closely with the Secretary for Native Affairs (*Secretário dos Negócios Indígenas*), that, given the colony's lack of success in providing 'the medical assistance owed to the native' (*indígena*), the state regularise the operation of the work of 'native medicine', practiced by *curandeiros* (a term connoting both 'healers' and 'charlatans'). This regularisation included limiting who practiced and where and what could be charged for treatment. It would also set parameters on what could be prescribed; love potions and poisons could not be sold. It provided the promise of criminal prosecution for the families of those who died as a result of the healer's negligence. The response of the junta was one of incredulity at the suggestion that therapeutic practices that were performed without adherence to scientific principles should be endorsed by the state. To do so, they argued, would be to undermine the qualifications of the graduates of the recently established course to train 'native nurses' who were expected to take the place of the *curandeiros* that such legislation would legitimise (Arquivo Histórico de Moçambique, Repartição de Saúde, Caixa 118).

Following the military coup in 1926, which toppled a republican government, the corporatist *Estado Novo* was established in 1928 under the authoritarian control of Antonio de Oliveira Salazar. As Norrie MacQueen (1999, p. 210) notes, Salazar's Colonial Act of 1930 'combined a strong element of economic protectionism with an assertion of the essential, "pluricontinental" unity (*portugalidade*).' Under the *Estado Novo* the form of the Portuguese narrative of national colonial modernity shifted. This new account described Portugal as just as civilised and rational as any other European colonising power, but *differently* modern.

Who speaks for *Lusofonia*?

Kesha Fikes' (2009) analysis of the everyday discourses of race in postcolonial Portugal reveals how ways of referencing racial difference are marked as socially acceptable or as offensive and confrontational. Her ethnographic observations of female Cape Verdean fish sellers (*peixeiras*) buying fish from male Portuguese wholesalers to sell on the streets of Lisbon in the early 1990s convey a sense of some of the ways in which colonial histories have been engaged in postcolonial and post-Salazarist Portugal. The terms of these negotiations lay both in the residual colonial narratives of Portuguese nonracialism sanctioned by the Salazarist state and in emerging notions of political correctness governing public discourse about race. In an effort to strike up conversation with potential customers, the Portuguese vendors would often refer to or ask questions about aspects of Cape Verdean culture, especially cuisine. In doing so, they would conspicuously acknowledge difference and demonstrate their comfort with it. On the other hand, *peixeiras* who felt they were not being treated fairly or with respect by vendors could publically accuse their Portuguese interlocutors of racism. Fikes notes that this would not only disrupt business but could also pose a threat to what she terms, following Erving Goffman, the 'social face' of the men accused, who in turn often defended themselves publically against such charges by referencing their own past ties with Africa: 'Racist? WHAT!? You really are crazy! I'm Mozambican!! How am I racist?' (p. 78, author's translation).

Fikes argues that the myth of the absence of racism in Portugal's colonial relationships with Africa was grounded in claims not of juridical or material equality but of the presence of affective relationships between Portuguese and African subjects (p. 39). While this continued to hold as *the* framework for talking about racism in Portugal until the early 1990s, she explains, since beginning her fieldwork, she has seen a discursive shift in line with changes in Portugal's relationship with Europe. *Lusofonia* is often seen as synonymous with a geopolitical project closely tied to the founding of the CPLP (Comunidade dos Países de Língua Portuguesa). Fikes argues that this term took on particular local meanings in Portugal in the late 1990s within the context of state discourses which distinguished between black migrants and white citizens, where, by promoting African cultural activities, the state addressed the racism of a modern, multicultural European nation. She suggests that the term began to circulate in Portuguese public discourse following the establishment of public programs in Portugal, in Lisbon in particular, that lent support to the cultural production of African and Brazilian migrant communities and engendered a new 'black cultural movement'. State support for preserving and performing traditions, was now 'tied to the subject of diversity', where once it would have affirmed or recalled a far-reaching Portuguese national space. The focus on culture, she suggests, enabled 'an evasion of talk of blood or race' (p. 48).

Not everyone engaged in the creative community producing and writing in Portuguese accepted the implications of the terminology of *Lusofonia*. Fikes alludes to the Angolan poet Ondjaki criticising *Lusofonia* as a 'convenient Portuguese descriptor that included Africans, for instance, but not the Portuguese' (p. 48). As Oliver Milhaud (2006) argues in regards to *Francophonie*, in order for that notion to be 'decolonised' its everyday use in France as a term 'for everything that is written in French but that is not French' must be challenged, or else the term merely reasserts the 'imperial dichotomy between France and "the rest"'. Likewise, in order for the conception of a Lusophone world to challenge the colonial framework of centre and periphery, Portugal would have to be understood as having no greater importance to that world than, for example, Mozambique. The limits to realising such an understanding are highlighted by the choice of then President Jorge Sampaio, introducing a literature prize in 2004 to employ a benign image of the global connections formed through the Portuguese language, which he called 'the great civilizational link with which Portugal has left its imprint on the world' (in *Público*, 1 August 2004; quoted in Almeida 2005, author's translation).

The term Lusophone itself has an ambiguous relationship with its imperial past. It has frequently proved contentious both for the 'luso' and for the 'phone'. The Angolan novelist José Eduardo Agualusa corrected an interviewer for a Brazilian literary journal who asked him how he understood *Lusofonia* – a term describing a global Lusophone 'space': 'No, no I don't like that expression…because I find it reductive. *Lusofonia* is a term which only speaks of Portugal and not even of Portugal really; Portugal only exists because the Roman campaign succeeded' (quoted in Polzonoff 2004, p. 20). Agualusa rejected the association between contemporary Portuguese and the Roman Lusitanian community, suggesting the Portuguese language should not be taken to be a marker of shared ancestry or a filial relationship with Europe and its distant past. In explaining his response, Agualusa repeated an argument he had made in a Portuguese newspaper column (Agualusa 2003), where he lent his support to an alternative term proposed by the Timorese author Luis Cardoso: *a fraternidade da fala* (the fraternity of speaking). Although Agualusa considers commonwealth a 'beautiful word', Cardoso's choice of words directly echoes the French republican conception of political community, taking as its foundation not liberty or equality but the affective claims of fraternity.

Agualusa's point is complicated by the fact that 'the Lusophone world' is often used to describe a community of people who certainly don't all speak Portuguese. Hence PALOP, the handy acronym which describes African countries with Portuguese as an official language (Países Africanos de Língua Oficial Portuguesa) and provides a 'decolonised' way to refer to the connections between nations born out of a shared colonial experience (Cahen 2003). The Mozambican author Mia Couto, like Agualusa, an African novelist of Portuguese descent, acknowledges this in explaining to a Mozambican journalist his own ambivalence about the term *Lusofonia*. While the existence of an institution called the Community of Portuguese Language Countries (*Comunidade dos Países de Língua Portuguesa*) is not in question, he argues, we should not take for granted that this political alliance 'corresponds to an affective community, a community of interaction'.

Couto's belief is that such a community does exist though 'not in the manner in which the politicians want to present it.' He cautions that although the 'Portuguese language gives us a certain historical affinity' ,the question of language itself is a delicate one 'because if we want to construct a family, a community ... [w]e have to remember that some Mozambicans, some Angolans and some Bissau-Guineans, don't speak Portuguese.' While noting how the idea of a language community can be exclusive and disregard difference, Couto cautiously suggests that the notion of a Lusophone world might be capable of describing more than a common linguistic landscape but also one constituted through a shared history and relations of reciprocity (quoted in Filipe 2008).

Taking an influential essay by the Portuguese sociologist Boaventura de Sousa Santos (2002)[10] as representative of an 'incipient Lusophone postcolonialism', Luis Madureira (2008, p. 203) argues that the task of explaining the distinctiveness of Portugal's colonial past continues to obscure more productive, politically radical inquiry. Sousa Santos provocatively describes Portugal as a 'Calibanized-Prospero' (p. 24) and argues that in 'the space of official Portuguese language ... postcolonialism must paradoxically focus on the weaknesses of the Portuguese Prospero' (p. 36). Madureira recognises in Sousa Santos' essay something of his own 'early epistemological crisis', in which he, a Portuguese schoolboy in Mozambique in 1974, was filled with adolescent rage as he discovered that Portugal was a far smaller country than he had been led to believe (pp. 200–202). The research agenda which Sousa Santos proposes, he suggests, leads to scholarship which only 'reproduces in a postcolonial register and epoch the *estadonovista* rhetoric of colonial difference' (p. 202). Madureira suggests instead that a genuinely Lusophone critical project must be grounded in the philosophical contributions of anticolonial nationalisms, which Couto's writing draws upon.

Acordos and *abraços*

In the wake of the Carnation Revolution, divisions emerged between President Ramalho Eanes and his prime minister and future successor Mario Soares over the terms of Portugal's relationship with its former colonies. Eanes followed the 'Third-Worldist' orientation of the Movimento das Forças Armadas. As Norrie MacQueen (2003, p. 189) explains, he was 'committed to an image of Portugal as a unique "bridge" between Africa and Europe' through Portugal's engagement with its former African colonies as another new democracy becoming integrated with an international community. He reworked the narrative of Luso-African proximity by describing Portugal as occupying a particular, shared, historical moment with his former colonies. Soares' vision, in contrast, was Europeanist and directed towards Portugal's integration into the European community, and this orientation directed Portugal's eventual entry into the European Economic Community in 1986. Soares has nonetheless since demonstrated his own continued attachment to the idea that the shared experience of political oppression under the *Estado Novo* had bound together the people of Portugal and its former colonial subjects. According to anthropologist Peter Fry (2000, p. 117), Soares' 'dream that the "affection" (*afeto*)[11] he believes to be a characteristic of the Portuguese and their former subject peoples [would] become a powerful counterpoint to the dominant power blocs of the world' was irreparably damaged when Mozambique joined the British Commonwealth in 1995. Fry knowingly re-presents Soares' aspiration for this small, poor, and politically marginalised nation for a scholarly audience more likely to associate Portugal's past in Africa with forced labour, excessive use of violence, and a failure to establish basic infrastructure. Rooted in the realities of Portugal's colonial history, these connections are also often drawn upon to signal the limits to the rationality of that colonial project. For some readers, Soares' term may also bring to mind other images of *immoderate* affection: the insufficient marking of difference characterising Portugal's historical relationship with Africa, found in the perceived confusion of racial or cultural boundaries.

Visiting Mozambique in 2005 for the occasion of 30 years of independence, Soares (2005), political dissident turned elder statesman, spoke of the connection he felt with the country and his pleasure in returning there. Rather than recount his presence in September 1974 at the signing of the Lusaka accords (*acordos de Lusaka*), in which the Portuguese agreed to cede power to a provisional Frelimo government, he spoke instead of the 'celebrated "Lusaka embrace [*abraço de Lusaka*]"' (p. 1). This was a reference to an event three months prior to the agreement, in June 1974, when the representatives of a postrevolutionary Portuguese state and those of the Mozambican liberation movement met for the first time on the neutral ground of Zambia's capital city.

As Frelimo cadre Oscar Monteiro (2005) recalls it, Soares broke the tense atmosphere in the main room of Lusaka's imposing state house by foregoing a handshake to walk instead to the other side of the table and say to Samora Machel, 'let me give you a hug [*Deixe-me dar um abraço*].'[12] It was a gesture, asserts Monteiro, of 'magnitude and symbolic value', where, 'In embracing Samora, the [new] Portuguese government signalled that it was renouncing the legacy of the colonial war and that Frelimo was not a terrorist movement.' According to Soares (2005, p. 1), in contrast, it symbolised 'that solidarity, in a common struggle, across great distance', an alliance between the antifascist and the anticolonial movements. Soares explained elsewhere that this embrace also spoke of something which endured in the Portuguese character, located in Machel as much as in Soares:

> It was a wonderful and unexpected thing, because (Zambia's ex-president Kenneth) Kaunda was expecting that here was a formal English-style affair...and we approached each other and embraced with the utmost fraternity. (quoted in Chale 2005)

For Soares the affectionate and quintessentially Portuguese gesture embodied the affinity between people on both continents oppressed by the same authoritarian regime. Soares' anecdote – the physical gesture itself, the common struggle, the shared historical narrative – all invoke a particular proximity between Portugal and Southeast Africa. Yet, for many Mozambicans winning independence meant severing cross-continental connections, and that is how they prefer to remember it. The climax of Oscar Monteiro's narrative, published in the state-sponsored daily newspaper *Notícias* the day of the anniversary of independence in 2005, was neither the *abraço* nor the *acordos de Lusaka* but the official announcement of independence the following year, the 25 June 1975. This was the moment from which Mozambicans were no longer to understand their national history as annexed to that of Portugal.

In an article published a year earlier than Monteiro's, in *Le Monde Diplomatique*, Mia Couto (2004) looked towards the independence celebrations in Mozambique, politely making a similar critique of Portuguese assumptions about Lusophone community:

> In 1999 my Portuguese publisher asked me to write a piece for an anthology commemorating the 25th anniversary of the April revolution [25 April 1974]. I refused, and explained why. The Mozambique anniversary commemorates a 25th day, but not that of April. I said this to a range of media and was not always understood. Some were hurt, thinking that I was distancing myself from Portugal because of resentment. That is not the case. But Africans cannot be expected to celebrate 25 April as the Portuguese do. It is an important anniversary for us and we celebrate it. But we do so with the respectful attitude of a guest, not the exhilaration of a host.

Couto and Monteiro displace the narratives of cross-continental proximity that place Portugal and Portuguese culture at their centre by engaging instead the romance of *national* culture articulated by Frantz Fanon (1961) and Amilcar Cabral (1974). This is a story organised not around authenticity but rather creativity. It describes the dialectical production of new and meaningful connections between individuals in the context of political independence. Thus, we can read these Mozambican texts as both reconstructions of nationalist clichés and nuanced critical interventions.

Bridging Europe and Africa

In December 2007, during the period of Portugal's European presidency, Portuguese Prime Minister José Sócrates (2007) opened the EU-Africa Summit in Lisbon by first reminding his audience of the temporal depth of Portugal's ties to the African continent. Transforming the conventional account of Vasco da Gama's journey as a 'voyage of discovery', where European scientific knowledge conquered the unknown, into one which described a shared moment of encounter, he declared 'It was through Lisbon that Europe met Africa. And it is in Lisbon that we are meeting again.' The lines that followed extended this idea of Portugal – a nation, a culture, and a people – as reprising this particular historical role: 'My country is proud to be today, once again, the perfect bridge between Europe and Africa. Once again, it is the Portuguese language that unites the two continents.'

The premise of the summit itself was the forging of a new form of partnership between Europe and Africa. Opening another meeting in Lisbon on the Joint European-Union Africa Strategy two years later, Socrates' Secretary of State for Foreign Affairs, João Gomes Cravinho (2009), described the Lisbon summit as the site of 'the launching of a new framework of relations – a partnership of equals' signalling 'a shift in Euro-African relations beyond what we could call a post-colonial donor-recipient approach.' In an interview with an online arts magazine, José António Fernandes Dias, anthropologist, lecturer in curatorial studies and professor of fine arts, articulated a similar explanation: 'For the first time, in a summit between Africa and the western world, there are no longer relations of paternalism, in return for the concession of loans, but actually relations of parity, of partnership.' Dias spoke about the summit in the context of explaining why he took on the role of consulting on a project for establishing a centre of African arts and culture in Lisbon called África.cont. What he found promising in this venture, he explained, was 'a desire to reorient Portugal's diplomatic policy towards Africa, that since the 25th of April [1974] has been restricted to the African countries with Portuguese as an official language, and broadening the network of relations to the rest of the countries of the continent' (quoted in Jürgens 2009).

The África.cont project was launched at a dinner with ambassadors of African nations and representatives of various Portuguese and African companies by Socrates, exactly one year after the opening of the EU-Africa Summit. Two sound bites printed in an article on the upcoming launch in the Portuguese newspaper *Público* described the intent of the project in distinct terms. Cravinho told *Público* that the centre would provide an opportunity for 'the consolidation of Lisbon as a Euro-African space' (quoted in Coelho 2008). Antonio Costa, the mayor of Lisbon who initiated the project, took up Socrates' language from the previous year, suggesting it would 'maintain this reality of Lisbon being a bridge between Europe and Africa' (quoted in Coelho 2008). Taken together, these two statements demonstrate the ways in which the partnerships marked by both the European Union strategy and the Lisbon arts centre, neither one directed only towards Lusophone Africa, were simultaneously being celebrated as creating something entirely new and as continuing Portugal's historical relationship with Africa.

Stories of interpersonal intimacy thread through narratives, both celebratory and critical, of Portuguese Empire or of the postimperial Lusophone world. The romance of a cross-continental imperial culture continues to endure, supported by metaphors of proximity that suggest connections not only historical and geographical but also emotional. That notion is born out of and closely tied to conflicting but related narratives of the particularity of Portuguese colonial practices used by the contemporary critics and supporters of that colonial project. These narratives in turn continue to be repeated in histories – popular and academic – of Portuguese imperialism and in contemporary representations of the Lusophone present. The idea of a Lusophone world as an affective community being formed through – or in spite of – violent imperial strategies of rule has not, or has not yet, displaced an enduring imperial narrative which puts the Portuguese nation at the centre of such a community.

Notes

1. Gilroy (2000, p. 8) examines the ominous implications of this ambivalence in more depth in *Against Race,* where he argues 'if ultranationalism, fraternalism and militarism can take hold, unidentified, among the descendants of slaves, they can enter anywhere. Past victimisation affords no protection against the allure of automatic, prepolitical uniformity.'
2. See Jean and John Comaroff's discussion of the contradictory colonial construction of Africans as both 'liberal citizen' and 'ethnic subject' (1997, pp. 395–397).
3. Marcus Power (2001, p. 462) notes that between 1961 and 1974 'nearly a million Portuguese people,' both men and women, were involved in the conflicts. Furthermore, 'the total number of African conscripts active in the three colonies in 1973 (87,716) was roughly similar to the total number of troops (87, 274) mobilised in the Metropole in the same year' (p. 484).
4. Translated from Portuguese. Unless otherwise stated, all translations are my own.
5. More recently, Eric Allina-Pisano (2002, p. 11) has commented on the longevity of Anderson's paradigm and argues that to represent the Portuguese state as singularly weak presupposes a metropolitan perspective focused on the power imbalance between colonial powers at the expense of that between coloniser and colonised.
6. Teresa Pinto Coelho (1990, p. 176) notes that in Britain 'Livingstone's travel writing...brought the continent, particularly Mozambique, to the public's attention and propagated the image of Portuguese maladministration in Africa.'
7. For an account of the negotiations over Mozambique's borders with Britain following the Berlin Conference, see Smith and Clarence-Smith (1985, pp. 501–506). For discussion of the treatment of the controversy in both the British and Portuguese Press, see Coelho (1990).
8. A Portuguese translation was published in Lisbon the same year (Batalha Reis 1889b).
9. It is not clear what Batalha Reis means by 'excessively European eyes'. Rather than criticising Portuguese travellers for exotifying African people, it may be

more likely that he considered those writers to have not sufficiently marked the differences between the people that they met and Europeans.
10. Madureira primarily focuses on the translated version of the essay. For a somewhat more extended version see Santos (2001).
11. This is the Brazilian spelling. In Soares' own continental Portuguese orthography, *'afecto'*.
12. Machel was then Frelimo's commander in chief and was later Mozambique's first president.

References

Agualusa, J. E. (2003), 'A Fraternidade de Fala,' *Público* (Lisbon), 28 July.
Allina-Pisano, E. (2002), 'Negotiating Colonialism: Africans, the State, and the Market in Manica District, Mozambique, 1895–c. 1935.' PhD diss., Yale University.
Almeida, O. T. (2005), 'Lusofonia – Some Thoughts on Language,' Institute of European Studies, University of California Berkeley, available at http://www.escholarship.org/uc/item/6sp4b6j6 (accessed 21 June 2011).
Anderson, P. (1962), 'Portugal and the End of Ultra-Colonialism 2,' *New Left Review* 1, no. 16, pp. 88–123.
Andrade, M. P. de (Buanga Fele) (1955), 'Qu'est-ce que le "lusotropicalisme"?' *Présence Africaine* no. 4, pp. 24–35.
Arquivo Histórico de Moçambique, Fundo da Repartição de Saúde, Caixa 118, Processo 102/7 'Intendencia de Emigração 1914', Intendente da Emigração to Chefe do Serviço de Saúde, Lourenço Marques, 28 October 1914, and response 7 November 1914, enclosing Acta da Junta de Saúde no. 92, 6 November 1914.
Bender, G. J. (1978), *Angola under the Portuguese: The Myth and the Reality*. University of California Press, Berkeley.
Boxer, C. R. (1963), *Race Relations in the Portuguese Colonial Empire*. Clarendon Press, Oxford.
Brubaker, R. (2005), 'The "Diaspora" Diaspora,' *Ethnic and Racial Studies* 28, no. 1, pp. 1–19.
Cabral, A. (1974), 'National Liberation and Culture,' *Transition* 45, pp. 12–17.
Cahen, M. (2003), 'What Use Is Portugal to an African?,' in S. Lloyd-Jones and A. C. Pinto (eds.), *The Last Empire: Thirty Years of Portuguese Decolonisation*. Intellect Books, Portland, OR, pp. 83–98.
Cameron, V. L. (1890), 'Portuguese Claims in Africa,' *National Review* 14, pp. 583–591.
Castelo, C. (1998). *'O modo português de estar no mundo': O luso-tropicalismo e a ideologia colonial portuguesa (1933–1961)*. Afrontamento, Porto.
Chale, M. (2005), 'O abraço de Lusaka,' interview with Mário Soares, *Expresso África* (online news source), 24 June, available at http://macua.blogs.com/moambique_para_todos/2005/06/mrio_soares_E_o.html (accessed 21 June 2011).
Clarence-Smith, W. G. (1979), 'The Myth of Uneconomic Imperialism: The Portuguese in Angola, 1836–1926,' *Journal of Southern African Studies* 5, no. 2, pp. 165–180.
Clarence-Smith, W. G. (1985). *The Third Portuguese Empire, 1825–1975: A Study in Economic Imperialism*. Manchester University Press, Manchester.
Clifford, J. (1994), 'Diasporas,' *Cultural Anthropology* 9, no. 3, pp. 302–338.
Coelho, A. P. (2008), 'Centro de arte africana contemporânea é aposta estratégica do Governo,' *Público* (Lisbon), 29 November.

Coelho, M. T. Pinto (1990), '"Pérfida Albion" and "Little Portugal": The Role of the Press in British and Portuguese National Perceptions of the 1890 Ultimatum,' *Portuguese Studies* 6, pp. 173–190.

Comaroff, J., and Comaroff, J. L. (1997), *Of Revelation and Revolution: The Dialectics of Modernity on a South African Frontier*. University of Chicago Press, Chicago.

Costa Ferreira, A. A. (1902), 'Sur la capacité des crânes portugais,' in *Congrès international d'anthropologie et d'archéologie préhistoriques. Compte rendu de la douzième session à Paris 1900*. Masson et Cie, Paris, pp. 474–475.

Couto, M. (2004), 'Carnation Revolution,' Trans. G. Cragg, *Le Monde diplomatique – English Edition*, April, available at http://mondediplo.com/2004/04/15mozambique (accessed 21 June 2011).

Cravinho, J. G. (2009), paper given at opening session of European Centre for Development Policy Management, 'The Partnership on Peace and Security in the Joint EU-Africa Strategy: Progresses and Challenges,' National Defense Institute, Lisbon, 26th November, available at http://www.ieei.pt/files/20091126_EARN_SENEC.pdf (accessed 21 June 2011).

Daly, C. P. (1884), 'Recent Developments in Central Africa and the Valley of the Congo,' *Journal of the American Geographical Society of New York* 16, pp. 89–159.

Davidson, B. (1972), *In the Eye of the Storm: Angola's People*. Longman, London.

Edwards, B. H. (2001). 'The Uses of Diaspora,' *Social Text* 19, no.1, pp. 45–73.

Edwards, E. J. (1907), 'Delagoa Bay and the Transvaal: Portugal's Claim for Fair Play', *Transvaal Leader*, Johannesburg.

Fanon, F. (1961), *Les damnés de la terre*. Maspéro, Paris.

Fanon, F. (1971 [1952]), *Peau noire, masques blancs*. Éditions du Seuil, Paris.

Fikes, K. (2009), *Managing African Portugal: The Citizen-Migrant Distinction*. Duke University Press, Durham, NC.

Filipe, G. (2008), 'Mia Couto e a CPLP: Moçambique é e não é país de língua portuguesa,' *Notícias* (Maputo), 25 June.

Freeland, A. (1995), '"The Sick Man of the West": A Late Nineteenth-Century diagnosis of Portugal,' in T. F. Earle and N. Griffin (eds.), *Portuguese, Brazilian and African Studies: Studies Presented to Clive Willis on His Retirement*. Aris and Phillips, Warminster, pp. 205–216.

Freyre, G. (1946 [1933]), *Casa-grande & senzala: formação da família brasileira sob o regime de economia patriarcal*. J. Olympio, Rio de Janeiro.

Freyre, G. (1958), *Integração portuguesa nos trópicos: Portuguese integration in the tropics*. Ministério do Ultramar, Junta de Investigações do Ultramar, Lisbon.

Fry, P. (2000), 'Cultures of Difference. The Aftermath of Portuguese and British Colonial Policies in Southern Africa,' *Social Anthropology* 8, no. 2, pp. 117–143.

Gilroy, P. (1993), *The Black Atlantic: Modernity and Double Consciousness*. Harvard University Press, Cambridge MA.

Gilroy, P. (2000), *Against Race: Imagining Political Culture beyond the Color Line*. Harvard University Press, Cambridge MA.

Hammond, R. J. (1966), *Portugal and Africa, 1815–1910: A Study in Uneconomic Imperialism*. Stanford University Press, Stanford, CA.

Harris, M. (1958), 'Portugal's African "Wards": A First-Hand Report on Labor and Education in Moçambique,' *Africa Today* 5, no.6, pp. 3–36.

Illife, J. (1995), *Africans: The History of a Continent*. Cambridge University Press, Cambridge.

Johnston, H. H. (1891), *Livingston and the Explorations of Central Africa*. G. Philip and Son, London.

Jürgens, S. V. (2009), 'Entrevista: José António Fernandes Dias,' *ArteCapital* (online magazine), available at http://www.artecapital.net/entrevistas.php?entrevista=64 (accessed 21 June 2011).
Livingstone, D. (1858), *Missionary Travels and Researches in South Africa; Including a Sketch of Sixteen Years' Residence in the Interior of Africa, and a Journey from the Cape of Good Hope to Loanda on the West Coast, Thence across the Continent, Down the River Zambesi, to the Eastern Ocean.* Harper, New York.
Livingstone, D. (1875), *The Last Journals of David Livingstone, in Central Africa, from 1865 to His Death.* Horace Waller (ed.). Harper, New York.
MacQueen, N. (1999), 'Portugal's First Domino: "Pluricontinentalism" and Colonial War in Guiné-Bissau, 1963–1974,' *Contemporary European History* 8 no. 2, pp. 209–230.
MacQueen, N. (2003) 'Re-Defining the "African Vocation": Portugal's Post-Colonial Identity Crisis,' *Journal of Contemporary European Studies* 11, no. 2, pp. 181–199.
Madureira, L. (2008) 'Nation, Identity and Loss of Footing: Mia Couto's "O Outro Pé da Sereia" and the Question of Lusophone Postcolonialism,' *Novel: A Forum on Fiction* 41, no. 2/3, pp. 200–228.
Mendy, P. K. (2003), 'Portugal's Civilizing Mission in Colonial Guinea-Bissau: Rhetoric and Reality,' *International Journal of African Historical Studies* 36, no. 1, pp. 35–58.
Milhaud, O. (2006), 'Post-Francophonie?,' *EspacesTemps.net*, 7 August, available at http://www.espacestemps.net/document2077.html (accessed 21 June 2011).
Ministério da Educação Nacional. (1958), *Ensino Primário Elementar. Livro da Leitura da Terceira Classe.* 4th edition, Livraria Bertrand, Lisbon.
Mondlane, E. (1969), *The Struggle for Mozambique.* Penguin, Harmondsworth.
Monteiro, J. J. (1875), *Angola and the River Congo.* Macmillan, London.
Monteiro, J. O. (2005), 'Testemunho de um jovem nas negociações para a independência de Moçambique,' *Notícias* (Maputo) 25 June 2005.
Patrício J. (1965), *Diário da viagem do Presidente Américo Thomaz a Moçambique e Ilha do Príncipe, 1964.* Agencia-Geral do Ultramar, Lisbon.
Penvenne, J. (1979), review of *Angola under the Portuguese: The Myth and the Reality* by Gerald J. Bender, *International Journal of African Historical Studies* 12, no. 1, pp. 96–105.
Penvenne, J (1985), review of *South Africa and Southern Mozambique: Labour, Railways and Trade in the Making of a Relationship* by Simon E. Katzenellenbogen, *Africa: Journal of the International African Institute* 55, no.1, pp. 106–107.
Pinheiro, V. (1885), *Politica colonial: Discussão do acto geral da Conferência de Berlim. Discurso proferido nas sessões de 10 e 11 de Junho de 1885.* Imprensa Nacional, Lisbon.
Pitcher, M. A. (1993), *Politics in the Portuguese Empire: The State, Industry, and Cotton, 1926–1974.* Clarendon Press, Oxford.
Polzonoff, P. (2004), '"Os bons livros são uma mentira". Interview with José Eduardo Agualusa,' *Rascunho* 5, no. 53, pp. 20–21.
Power, M. (2001), 'Geo-politics and the Representation of Portugal's African Colonial Wars: Examining the Limits of "Vietnam Syndrome",' *Political Geography* 20, no. 4, pp. 461–491.
Reis, J. Batalha (1889a), 'The Portuguese in Nyassaland,' *Scottish Geographical Magazine* 5, no.1, pp. 256–268.
Reis, J. Batalha (1889b), *Os Portuguezes na região do Nyassa*, Imprensa Nacional, Lisbon.

Reis, J. Batalha (1897), 'Algumas Particularidades da Colonisação Portuguesa,' *Revista Portugueza Colonial e Marítima* 1, no. 1, pp. 9–14.
Santos, B. de Sousa (2001), 'Entre Prospero e Caliban: Colonialismo, pós-colonialismo e inter-identidade,' in M. I. Ramalho and A. Sousa Ribeiro (eds.), *Entre ser e estar: raízes, percursos e discursos de identidade*, Afrontamento, Porto, pp. 23–85.
Santos, B. de Sousa (2002), 'Between Prospero and Caliban: Colonialism, Postcolonialism, and Inter-identity,' *Luso-Brazilian Review* 39, pp. 9–43.
Smith, A., and Clarence-Smith, W. G. (1985), 'Portuguese Colonies and Madagascar: Angola and Mozambique, 1870–1905,' in R. Oliver and G. N. Sanderson (eds.), *The Cambridge History of Africa*. Vol. 6: *From 1870 to 1905*. Cambridge University Press, Cambridge, pp. 493–521.
Soares, M. (2005), lecture given at Universidade Eduardo Mondlane, Maputo, 23 June, available at http://www.fmsoares.pt/mario_soares/textos_ms/007/7.pdf (accessed 21 June 2011).
Sócrates, J. (2007), speech given at the opening session of the European Union – Africa Summit, Lisbon, 8 December, available at http://www.eu2007.pt/UE/vPT/Noticias_Documentos/20071208DiscursoSocratesUEAFRICA.htm (accessed 21 June 2011).
Subrahmanyam, S. (1993), 'The "Kaffirs of Europe": A Comment on Portugal and the Historiography of European Expansion in Asia,' *Studies in History* 9, no. 1, pp. 131–146.
Weber, M. (1946 [1919]), 'Politics as a Vocation,' in H. H. Gerth and C. W. Mills (eds.), *From Max Weber: Essays in Sociology*. Macmillan, New York, pp. 26–45.
Weber, M. (1978 [1922]), *Economy and Society: An Outline of Interpretive Sociology*, 2 vols. University of California Press, Berkeley.
Wheeler, D. L. (1976), review of *Portuguese Colonialism in Africa: The End of an Era* by Eduardo de Sousa Ferreira, *International Journal of African Historical Studies* 9, no. 3, pp. 465–467.
Wheeler, D. L. (1996), 'Letter to the Membership: Remembering Portugal,' *Portuguese Studies Review* 5, no. 2, pp. 4–20.
White, L. (1985), 'Review Article: The Revolutions Ten Years On,' *Journal of Southern African Studies* 11, no. 2, pp. 320–332.
Williams R. (2007), 'Migration and Miscegenation: Maintaining Boundaries of Whiteness in the Narratives of the Angolan Colonial State 1875–1912,' in P. J. Havik and M. D. Newitt (eds.), *Creole Societies in the Portuguese Colonial Empire*. University of Bristol, Department of Hispanic, Portuguese and Latin American Studies, Bristol.

12
Mundo Pretuguês: Colonial and Postcolonial Diasporic Dis/articulations

AbdoolKarim Vakil

> Koração lá e korpo ká em pretugal
> mentalmente enkkarcerados ká em pretugal
> sem pão, mas kon veneno e armas p'ra morrermos em pretugal
> segregados p'ra n sermos ninguém em Portugal
>
> Chullage, 'Pretugal' (*Rapensar: Passado, presente, futuro*, 2004)[1]

There is a sense in which we've arrived at a point where the critique of *Lusofonia* and the Lusophone has become too attached to that of *Lusotopicalismo* and of a somewhat complacent and tiresomely repeated critique of Lusotropicalism at that. Each new critique exposes anew the same neotropicalism cum neocolonialist design in the rhetoric or project of state and public diplomacy institutions, primarily Portuguese, but also extended to postcolonial African elites, while these entities and institutions in turn continue to invest and peddle the same discourses by reference to the same worn clichés. Meanwhile, back in back-to-the-future post-1974 Portugal, the no less tiresome and timelessly impervious dressing up of ideology as philosophy that passes for linguistically determined *filosofia portuguesa* [Portuguese philosophy] and its neotraditionalist avatars continues to feed renascentist dreams of a 'Portuguese World' born of a world in Portuguese[2], while cutting-edge literary, cultural, and postcolonial studies exalt and nurture the linguistic play and hybridity which in fiction and the visual arts deconstructively challenges the Luso-centric conceptions of Lusophony.[3] But should they be our focus?

What I want to propose here is a different point of departure by way of exploring the unfinished business of empire and the Portuguese postcolonial condition, which builds on previous critiques, while sidestepping some of the agreed-upon wisdom. And to do so by taking a political postcolonial perspective on the diasporic.[4]

Take *Lusofonia, A [R]evolução/ Lusophony, the [R]evolution*, a documentary film produced by the Red Bull Music Academy (2006) which celebrates the historical roots and contemporary emergence of what it describes as new and hybrid popular musical forms 'inspired by Lusophone culture'.[5] It is only too easy to dismiss it as a new spin on an old story – Lusotropicalism repackaged as cool for the music video generation. The title alone, with its bracketing of revolution into evolution would give good cause for scepticism, all the more so coming as it did so close upon the polemical debates over the similar taming of the revolutionary legacy of 1974 in the official slogan adopted for the 30th anniversary commemorations of the 25 April Revolution (*Abril é Evolução* [April Is Evolution]) in 2004.[6] Stressing continuities over discontinuities presages Luso-centric Lusophony and its ideological entanglements further in evidence: the English blurb packaging of the DVD for the international festival circuit describes it as a 'unique portrayal of the essence and the magic of Lusophony'; free distribution was contracted through the Instituto Camões (the Portuguese equivalent of the British Council, and a dependency of the Ministry of Foreign Affairs) and CPLP (the Community of Portuguese Language Countries which anchors the institutional discourse of Lusophony); reinforced by a revealing faux pas in the voice-over opening line: 'está em movimento no mundo uma nova imagem da música *portuguesa*' [a new image of *Portuguese* music is in motion all around the world].[7] But even for all the confused and ideologically charged rhetoric of the talking heads, the history and critical import is in the music, not the narrative: the revolution is live, not televised.

Os rappers são os novos punks meu, além de serem os novos Camões e quê...

In the documentary, the take off of hip-hop in the 1990s is seen as one of the crucial developments of this urban (and mostly) Lisbon-based musical phenomenon, represented among others by Chullage, one of the pioneers of the genre and one of the outstanding MCs in the contemporary *tuga* [from *portuga*, i.e., Portuguese] hip-hop musicscape. Both in his trajectory to solo artist and in his two solo albums to date, *Rapresálias: Sangue, Lágrimas, Suor* (2001) and *Rapensar: Passado, Presente, Futuro* (2004), Chullage has fashioned himself, much like his name (a creolisation of the nickname *chulo* [pimp]), as an organic intellectual who puts his art at the service of his message, describing hip-hop as an alternative education in citizenship for the hood.[8]

Four general points need brief remarking. In keeping with the hip-hop emphasis on authenticity, Chullage's lyrics repeatedly assert his keeping faith with the truth of the ghetto and denounce the logic of the market and the sellouts who rhyme without reason for airtime and contracts or sell themselves and their people short by trading in blaxploitative bling.[9]

Second, and relatedly, this wordsmith's rap is a force in and of the community, denouncing exploitation, consumerism, racism, and the ideologies at work in the divide-and-rule disempowerment of the disenfranchised. Third, in the context of hegemonic framings in which nation-states and majoritarian citizens have history, and diasporians have cultural baggage, History and the memory of colonialism – no less than the anticolonial struggle – is central to the message, whether it be in terms of a counter discourse to the whitewashed narratives of the Portuguese 'discoveries' and 'expansion',[10] the translation of the Middle Passage into the inner city ghettos of the New World and the run-down estates of European suburbs, or the transposition of the spatial reproduction of coloniality in urban marginalisation and criminalisation.[11] But while firmly grounded in the localised specificity of his Arrentela suburb of Lisbon, the Arrentela is also the localised iteration of the universal ghetto and hence the authenticity of the U.S.-based 'ghettocentric' worldview culled from the U.S. underground and French hip-hop scenes which inform his lyrics and message.[12] Hence also the articulation of overlaying diasporic roots and shoots from Cape Verdean, Angolan, Brazilian, and Portuguese musical forms with African American forged black consciousness and Afrocentric references. Conspicuously, this political consciousness-raising and strongly interventionist critique is entirely absent both from Chullage's own participation and the Red Bull Academy documentary as a whole, which focuses rather on the celebratory hybridity of musical forms which Lisbon, as a diasporic hub, is stage to. Be that as it may, to a productive critical reading, the point, it seems to me, cannot be to dismissively reduce the documentary to merely another variation of the Lusophonic Lusotropicalist difference engine, but rather and precisely to read from it the very dynamics and dialectics of diasporic consciousness, transnational musical subcultures and networks, vernacular formations, the market logic of the music industry, and national cultural formations and structures. A dynamic which hip-hop's creative focus on authenticity itself exemplifies.

The point, in short, in the context of this volume's focus is twofold. Firstly, while we need to heed Michel Cahen's warning that the '[t]he concept of "lusophony" [...] is a simple blanket term that smothers some extremely different social realities and incomparable social statuses' in each of the postcolonial contexts[13], the same must, of course, apply also to 'Portugal' and 'Portuguese', where the retrospective and teleological identitarian illusion of the name (Balibar 1991, Vakil 1996) tends to conflate and erase the different statuses, social formations, identifications, and investments with the name and the language.[14] Something which, perversely, postcolonial critiques of Portugal and the Portuguese wilfully tend to ignore. And here is where both the more general tag of *tuga* hip-hop and Chullage's counter discursive *Pretugal* constitute effective and usefully disruptive performative postcolonial acts of writing back to the centre.[15] Portuguese hip-hop artists may have just produced to order a *Hip-hop Pessoa* album (in celebration of the 120 years of the birth of the iconic Portuguese modernist poet Fernando Pessoa, under an initiative of the Lisbon municipal government and Casa Fernando Pessoa), but Chullage's 'minha poesia tem o Camões eskecido numa kampa dos Jerónimos' [my poetry consigns Camões to oblivion in his tomb in the Jerónimos][16] problematises the very notion of co-optation; this is not an 'anxiety of influence' Camões – as Pessoa's own super-Camões was; it is, rather, an iconoclastic assault on the canon, closer to punk, which playfully and subversively strikes at the very heart of both the Portuguese (imperial) epic and the epic poet's own memorialisation in the pantheon of the Jeronimos.[17] 'The Portuguese imaginary' is indeed, as critics argue, 'only partially decolonised',[18] but that is a literary-political and institutional Portuguese imaginary; it may be the imaginary of the official curriculum, but it is one that is largely irrelevant to bricolaging and transnational youth cultures, which are far less shaped by the nation-state and territorial borders than these critics assume.

Second, as a cultural form which combines word sound, visual inscriptions, strongly embedded spatial locations in globalised circuits, and embodied performance – from gesture, movement, and rhythm to apparel – in short, a landscape and body politics, hip-hop, like popular culture in general, refers to a logic which rides on and continuously seeks to stay ahead of the colonising drive of the market and domesticating appropriations in and as 'culture'.[19] Its negotiations of *Lusofonia* usefully shift the focus of critical discourse from word to street, from the culture industry to its subversive sampling, from lazy postcolonial critiques of Portuguese institutionalised discourse to the contending sites and discourses of both artful and artless everyday imaginings, productions, and negotiations of history and identity in Portugal.[20]

Good diasporas, bad diasporas

Two key points are worth retaining from Katharina Schramm's synthetic overview of the fortunes of the concept of diaspora in relation to its popularisation in the 1960s (Schramm 2008). First, the crucial articulation between African independence and the American civil rights movements in terms of both political consciousness of solidarity, and cultural Africanness (though, in truth, it seems to me, it is in the Black Power movement, somewhat in tension with the civil rights movement, that the pan-African political articulation of common cause, not least around the issue of the Portuguese colonies culminating in the 1972–74 African liberation marches, was most strongly expressed).[21] Second, the historiographical take up of the conceptual purchase of diaspora at the 1965 Congress of African Historians. These genealogical considerations of the concept of diaspora allow us to move beyond the stale preoccupation with etymological and normative foundational diasporas towards its political conceptualisation in relation to the political and revolutionary role of diaspora and diasporic mobilisations, on the one hand, and its conceptual demarcation in relation to immigration and transnationalism and the structures, juridical and political, of nation-states, on the other.[22]

With reference to *Lusofonia*, diaspora, and the Portuguese context, two outrageously generalising points may be advanced for discussion. First, we may have become, partisans and critics alike, too complacent as to the received history of the Lusophone project we have settled for. The focus on state-sponsored Lusotropicalism and its colonial and neocolonial ideology, however peppered with exotic references to its left-wing mirror images, though both understandable and a necessary critique in its time, left plenty of work still to be done on transversal projects with unfinished business to be explored for alternative histories and configurations of Lusophony.[23] Part of this process, necessarily, given the historical role and archival function of literature in the formation of national cultures and imagined communities, will be fought over the reconstitution of national literary corpuses and canons in the postcolonial nations.[24] And with these, to draw on Biodun Jeyifo's exploration of postcolonial genealogical fiction's determined rememberings, a correspondingly fraught process of reconciliation, recognition, and accommodation of what he calls the 'African "enthusiast" of colonial hegemony'[25] written out of the postcolonial nationalist stories. Among them, the diasporic intellectuals Amilcar Cabral sanitised from the national culture preserved among the popular masses.[26] This too is a useful reminder to problematise the memories of colonialism of and in the diaspora and for the diaspora. And not least, for rethinking the contemporary meanings of 'return(s) to the source', as Cabral, ever the theorist of 'feet planted on the ground' would be the first to demand. Thus, if literature and history for the nation are one part of the process, another is at work in the reconstitution of the memory of colonialism in the life, arts, and civic struggles of the African diaspora in Portugal, not least over racialised citizenship and belonging and over the meaning of diaspora as belonging waged around usable pasts.

Second, and again generalising, the counterpart to this is a Manichean framing of 'diaspora' in Portuguese official rhetoric and policies. There is, on the one hand, a strong investment in the transnational links and memories of the Portuguese emigrant communities and *Luso-descendentes* fostered in external relations and foreign policy since the days of Adriano Moreira's Congresses of the Portuguese Communities, under the previous regime, and of Francisco Sá Carneiro's projects postrevolution. This positive view of the mobilisational and lobbying potential (not to mention the economic) of transnational ties and its soft power deployment can be said to continue as a dominant note into the present.[27] In contrast, on the other hand, what scant governmental and political attention is paid to diasporic communities in Portugal is perhaps most prominent in terms of security and policing concerns over integration, marginalisation, transnational criminality, and terrorism, of which the Ministry of Internal Administration's *Annual Reports on National Security* provide a good example.[28] The full significance of this, I would argue, is underlined by a retrenchment in the securitisation of national identity, conceived around converging notions of common culture, national history, heritage, and symbols, which reflects a wider European populist nativist inflection in the response to the ethnic and religious diversification of European societies and, with it, the challenge to the established and racialised narratives of the unreconstructed national-colonial cultural formation (Vakil 2006). In both governmental and public discourses heavily skewed by ideological panderings to moral panics on immigration, cohesion, security, and welfare, bonds of Portuguese-ness and Portugal-centred transnational imagined Portuguese community are benignly encouraged as good, while corresponding bonds of transnational non-Portuguese diasporic identities in Portugal are derided as disruptive and a threat.

It is in this regard that the concept of a *Mundo Pretuguês*, drawing on Chullage's 'Pretugal' and 'Kem Somos Nós',[29] with their explicit political theorisation of the logics of diaspora, coloniality, and Lusophony are good to think with and beyond the debunking critiques which put the lie to both the colonialist *Mundo Português* and the Lusotropicalist *Mundo que o Português Criou*.[30] Historians and postcolonial cultural critics would do well to listen.

Notes

1. 'Heart there body here in *Pretugal*/mentally incarcerated here in *Pretugal*/Without bread but with poison and weapons to die in *Pretugal*/segregated to be nobodies in *Portugal*' (Chullage, 'Pretugal', from the album *Rapensar*, extended edition, Lisafonia, 2004. *Pretugal* is a neologism coined by meshing *preto* [black] and *Portugal*, here to signify the black experience of Portugal as a parallel country or the internal colony of lives lived under 'the color line'. All the translations from the Portuguese in this chapter are my own.
2. While the Portuguese project of (elite) liberal political modernity has historically successively manifested itself under the name of Regeneration, (elite) Portuguese cultural traditionalism has similarly manifested itself under the name or spirit of Renascence/Renaissance. For a critique of *filosofia portuguesa* as ideology, see Onésimo Teotónio Pereira (1985).
3. For an excellent example of literary critical approaches, see Laura Cavalcante Padilha (2005).
4. On the 'political postcolonial' and the diasporic condition as it informs this chapter, see Hesse and Sayyid (2006, p. 17).
5. From the Red Bull Music Academy Portugal Press Release for *Lusofonia, A [R]evolução/Lusophony, The [R]evolution*, 2006.
6. Especially since the guerrilla response at the time was to paint the R back on: see http://graodeareia-attac.weblog.com.pt/arquivo/25A.jpg
7. A promotional short version of the documentary is available to watch online and download at http://www.redbullmusicacademy.com/video-archive/documentaries/3.

8. *Represálias: Sangue, Lágrimas, Suor* [Raprisals: Blood, Tears, Sweat] (2001), and *Rapensar: Passado, Presente, Futuro* [Rapthinking: Past, Present Future] (2004), both with the Lisafonia label. For a bio note and discography, see Chullage's MySpace 'about me' entry at http://profile.myspace.com/index.cfm?fuseaction=user.viewprofile&friendid=134988607

9. See 'Tu (és uma hoe…)' and especially 'Nomenklatura' from the album *Rapensar*; on the theme of authenticity, see the contributions by Neal (2004), Gilroy (2004), and Kelley (2004).

10. 'Lágrimas e Suor. É o resumo da vida do meu povo desde os descobrimentos até aqui, é isso. Por aí dá para tirar as ilações todas que quisermos. É escravatura, colonialismo, é o neo-colonialismo' [Tears and Sweat. This is the sum of the life of my people from the Discoveries till now, that's it. From this we can draw all the conclusions we need], Chullage interviewed in *Reportagem Sol Música*: available on youtube: http://www.youtube.com/watch?v=Tlj938QClPE&feature=related; see also the intro video piece to *Rapensar*, also at http://www.youtube.com/watch?v=nEPVGMDLm1Q&feature=related.

11. 'os ghettos kontinuam a ser slave ships/ k mantém niggas sonhando kom Bloods e Crips' [the ghettos are the new slave ships / which keep Niggas dreaming of Bloods and Crips], from the track 'Ignorância XL' [Ignorance XL], in *Rapensar*, one of the two tracks from the album also released as music videos, see: http://www.youtube.com/watch?v=PGhNnghCnVQ.

12. Loïc Wacquant's discussion of the disparate social formations of 'ghetto, banlieue, favela, et caetera' is useful here (Wacquant 2008).

13. See Michel Cahen's chapter in this book.

14. 'N precisamos forçosamente de ser e pensar como portugueses, mas talvez como afrikanos, brasileiros e ucranianos em Portugal. N podemos kontinuar a ser kontrolados pelas politikas judiciais, politikas de imigração, politikas de integração, politicas de edukação, políticas ekonomikas e restantes polítikkas k nos mantêm na condição social em k nos enkontramos' [We needn't necessarily be and think of ourselves as Portuguese, but as Afrikans, Brazilians, and Ukrainians in Portugal. We kannot allow ourselves to kontinue to be subjekt to kontrol by juridikal policies, immigration policies, integration policies, edukation policies, economik policies, and sundry other policies which keep us in the social condition in which we find ourselves], 'Kontrol' album note to 'Knowledge & Kontrol', in *Rapensar*.

15. Compare Sayyid's (2006) theorisation of the category of 'Brasians'.

16. In 'Tu (és uma hoe…)', op. cit.

17. 'Os rappers são os novos punks meu. Além de serem os novos Camões e quê porque nós pomos bué de palavra, bué de poesia naquilo que dizemos. Mas além disso também somos os novos punks é mais os novos punks' [rappers are the new punks bro, besides being the new Camões and what not, because we put loads of poetry in what we say. Beside that we are also the new punks, more the new punks], Chullage interview in *Reportagem Sol Música*, op cit. The Manueline Jerónimos [Hieronimite] Monastery of Belém, historically and mythically associated with the discovery of the sea route to India, emerged out of the nineteenth-century confluence of Romanticism and positivism as a nationalist-cultural pantheon housing the tombs of Camoes and Vasco da Gama (and Fernando Pessoa, among others).

18. Cahen, op. cit.

19. See in particular the discussion of the French case in Rupa Huq (2006).

20. At the time this text was written for presentation (in the form here published), I had not had access to the excellent ethnographic literature on hip-hop in Portugal (Contador & Ferreira 1997, Contador 2001, Fradique 2003, and especially Raposo 2010a and 2010b), to which the reader is referred for overviews and contextualisation.
21. On the African Liberation Support Committee's African Liberation Day mobilisations of 1972–1974, see Johnson (2003) and Frazier (2006).
22. See in particular Kalra, Kaur, and Hutnyk (2005) for critical exploration of this argument; compare Sayyid (2000) for the same political logic at work in a conceptualisation of the diasporic form of the Muslim Umma.
23. A case in point (if we are to believe the testimony of Manuel Alegre) would be the surprising inclusion of Amilcar Cabral among such visionaries of Lusophonic community: 'Podíamos fazer uma revolução única no mundo, uma revolução multicontinental e multiracial, brasileiros, africanos, portugueses, uma capital itinerante, uma presidência rotativa' [We could make a unique revolution in the world, a multicontinental and multiracial revolution, Brazilians, Africans, Portuguese, a peripatetic capital, a rotating presidency.] [Cabral, from a conversation with Alegre on the banks of the Nile on 12 February 1969, cited in Alegre (1994)]. My thanks to Margarida Calafate Ribeiro for supplying the article to assuage my scepticism over her inclusion of Cabral among such dreamers and schemers in her outstanding critical survey of the Portuguese colonial and postcolonial African imaginary (Ribeiro 2004, p. 164). Many other such visions and schemes spanning left and right political positionings, from Vasco da Gama Fernandes' Luso-Brasileirismo to Silvino Silvério Marques' pre- and post-1974 visions of/for Portugal, await critical discussion.
24. A deliberately provocative example is given by José Luandino Vieira in his intervention '"Angolan" Literature' on the 'Curso de Literatura Angolana' at the Centro de Estudos Sociais in Coimbra, June 2007 (published as Vieira 2008).
25. 'the vast complement of Africans who "embraced" colonialism, who adapted vigorously sometimes enthusiastically, to the invented traditions of the hegemonising imperative of European colonization' (Jeyifo 1997, p. 114).
26. See Cabral's remarks on the 'diásporas coloniais' and 'diásporas africanas implantadas nas metrópoles colonialistas e racistas' [colonial diasporas and African diasporas implanted in racist and colonialist metropoles] in Cabral (1999, pp. 127, 130). Some pertinent examples of diasporic intellectuals I have discussed elsewhere (Vakil 2000, 2001) include reimaginings of 'Greater Portugal' in the *Tribuna d'África: Orgão Nacional e Internacional dos Africanos* commentary on the Semana das Colónias (Semana das Colónias 1932) and Mário Domingues and Vianna de Almeida's *África Magazine* (nos. 1 and 2, March (Almeida and Domingues 1932) and April (Domingues 1932)), and Fausto Duarte's colonial literature (1934–1945), especially *Auá* (Duarte 1934).
27. See, for example, the survey review article by Joana Fisher in the journal of the Portuguese Ministry of Foreign Affairs (Fisher 2008).
28. The Report for the year 2001 (Ministério da Administração Interna 2002, p. 2) identifies 'multiculturalidade como potencial conflituante' [multiculturalism as a potential source of conflict] among the security risk factors of the new conjuncture; in the Report for 2005 (Ministério da Administração Interna 2006, p. 253), under the rubric of Urban Insecurity, along with organised crime the first threat to security is named as the 'proliferation of enclaves of insufficiently integrated people' classed as 'no-go areas', and the 'marginality and juvenile delinquency

typical of poorly integrated "second generation" immigrant communities', which have developed into criminal sanctuaries, concluding that 'é de esperar, a curto prazo, a emergência de reacções organizadas de natureza xenófoba, ainda que de uma forma todavia incipiente' [the emergence of organised xenophobic reaction albeit incipient is a short-term prospect].
29. 'Kem Somos Nós' [Who Are We], in *Rapensar*.
30. *Mundo Português* [Portuguese World] was the ideologically charged title of the grand 1940 Exposition organised by the Salazarist New State to celebrate its nationalist-colonialist teleological vision of 800 years of Portuguese history; it was the title of one of the most emblematic and important propaganda periodicals of the regime, published by the Secretariat for National Propagand Information and the National Agency for the Colonies (SPN/SNI, AGC) from 1934–1947; it is today the title of a periodical dedicated and directed to the Portuguese emigrant and diasporic communities. *O Mundo que o Português Criou* [The World the Portuguese Created] (Freyre n.d. [1940]), is the title of a collection of essays by the Brazilian sociologist and theorist of Lusotropicalism Gilberto Freyre on the cultural unity of the Lusophone world, published the same year (1940), with an important critical preface by the oppositional Portuguese intellectual António Sérgio.

References

Alegre, M. (1994), 'O Outro Lado da Alma,' *Jornal de Letras*, 22 June, p. xxxi.
Ali, N, Kalra, V. S., and Sayyid, S. (eds.) (2006), *A Postcolonial People: South Asians in Britain*. Hurst, London.
Almeida, M. V. (1932), 'Portugal Melhor. Conferência proferida pelo nosso director Sr. Viana de Almeida em terra de África,' *África Magazine* no. 1, pp. 30–33.
Almeida, M. V., and Domingues, M. (1932), 'África Magazine,' *África Magazine* no. 1, pp. 10–11.
Balibar, E. (1991), 'The Nation Form: History and Ideology,' in E. Balibar and I. Wallerstein (eds.), *Race, Nation, Class: Ambiguous Identities*. Verso, London, pp. 86–106.
Cabral, A. (1999 [1972]), 'O Papel da Cultura na Luta pela Independência,' in X. L. García (ed.), *Nacionalismo e Cultura*. Laiovento' Santiago de Compostela, pp. 123–142.
Contador, A. C., and Ferreira, E. L. (1997), *Ritmo & Poesia: Os Caminhos do Rap*. Assírio and Alvim, Lisbon.
Contador, A. C. (2001), *Cultura Juvenil Negra em Portugal*. Celta, Oeiras.
Domingues, M. (1932), 'Brancos e Pretos,' *África Magazine* 2, pp. 12–13.
Duarte, F. (1934), *Auá*. Livraria Clássica Editora, Lisbon.
Fisher, J. (2008), 'Diásporas,' *Negócios Estrangeiros* no. 12, pp. 100–126.
Fradique, T. (2003), *Fixar o Movimento: Representações da música rap em Portugal*. Dom Quixote, Lisbon.
Frazier, R. T. P. (2006), 'The Congress of African People: Baraka, Brother Mao and the Year of "74,"' *Souls* 8, no. 3, pp. 142–159.
Freyre, G. (n.d. [1940]), *O Mundo que o Português Criou*. Livros do Brasil, Lisbon.
Gilroy, P. (2004 [1992]), 'It's a Family Affair,' in N. Forman and M. A. Neal (eds.), *That's the Joint! The Hip-Hop Studies Reader*. Routledge, New York, pp. 87–94.
Hesse, B., and Sayyid, S. (2006), 'Narrating the Postcolonial Political and the Immigrant Imaginary,' in N. Ali, V. S. Kalra, and S. Sayyid (eds.), *A Postcolonial People: South Asians in Britain*. Hurst, London, pp. 13–31.

Huq, R. (2006), *Beyond Subculture: Pop, Youth and Identity in a Postcolonial World*. Routledge, Abingdon.

Jeyifo, B. (1997), 'Determining Remembering: Postcolonial Fictional Genealogies of Colonialism in Africa,' in P. Palumbo-Liu and H. U. Gumbrecht (eds.), *Streams of Cultural Capital: Transnational Cultural Studies*. Stanford University Press, Stanford, CA.

Johnson, C. (2003), 'From Popular Anti-Imperialism to Sectarianism: The African Liberation Support Committee and Black Power Radicals,' *New Political Science* 25, no. 4, (December), pp. 477–507.

Kalra, V. S., Kaur, R., and Hutnyk, J. (2005), *Diaspora & Hybridity*. Sage, London.

Kelley, R. D. G. (2004 [1997]), 'Looking for the "Real Nigga": Social Scientists Construct the Ghetto,' in M. Forman and M. A. Neal (eds.), *That's the Joint!: The Hip-Hop Studies Reader*. Routledge, New York, pp. 119–136.

Ministério da Administração Interna (2002), *Relatório Anual de Segurança Interna – Ano de 2001*, Lisbon.

Ministério da Administração Interna (2006), *Relatório Anual de Segurança Interna – Ano de 2005*, Lisbon.

Neal, M. A. (2004), 'No Time for Fake Niggas: Hip-hop Culture and the Authenticity Debates,' in M. Forman and M. A. Neal (eds.), *That's the Joint! The Hip-Hop Studies Reader*. Routledge, New York, pp. 57–60.

Padilha, L. C. (2005), 'Da Construção Identitária a Uma Trama de Diferenças: Um olhar sobre as literaturas de língua portuguesa,' *Revista Crítica de Ciências Sociais* no. 73, pp. 3–28.

Padilha, L. C., and Ribeiro, M. C. (eds.) (2008), *Lendo Angola*. Afrontamento, Porto.

Pereira, O. T. (1985), 'Filosofia Portuguesa – alguns equívocos,' *Cultura, História, Filosofia* Vol. 4, pp. 219–255.

Raposo, O. (2010a), '"Tu és *Rapper*, Representa Arrentela, és *Red Eyes Gang*": Sociabilidades e estilos de vida de jovens do subúrbio de Lisboa,' *Sociologia, Problemas e Práticas* no. 64, pp. 127–147.

Raposo, O. (2010b), '"Heart There and Body Here in Pretugal": In Between Mestizagem and the Affirmation of Blackness,' *Buala: African Contemporary Culture*, available at http://www.buala.org/en/to-read/heart-there-and-body-here-in-pretugal-in-between-mestizagem-and-the-affirmation-of-blackness.

Ribeiro, M. C. (2004), *Uma História de Regressos: Império, Guerra Colonial e Pós-colonialismo*. Afrontamento, Porto.

Sayyid, S. (2000), 'Beyond Westphalia: Nations and Diasporas – the case of the Muslim Umma,' in B. Hesse (ed.), *Un/settled Multiculturalisms: Diasporas, Entanglements, Transruptions*. Zed, London, pp. 33–50.

Sayyid, S. (2006), 'Brasians: Postcolonial People, Ironic Citizens,' in N. Ali, V. S. Kalra, and S. Sayyid (eds.), *A Postcolonial People: South Asians in Britain*. Hurst, London, pp. 1–10.

Schramm, K. (2008), 'Leaving Diaspora Behind: The Challenge of Diasporic Connections in the Field of African Studies,' *African and Black Diaspora: An International Journal* 1, no. 1, pp. 1–12.

'Semana das Colónias (A)' (1932), *Tribuna d'África*, 14 March, p. 1.

Vakil, A. (1996), 'Nationalising Cultural Politics: Representations of the Portuguese "Discoveries" and the Rhetoric of Identitarianism, 1880–1926,' in C. Mar-Molinero and A. Smith (eds.), *Nationalism and the Nation in the Iberian Peninsula: Competing and Conflicting Identities*. Berg, Oxford, pp. 33–52.

Vakil, A. (2000), 'Guinean Princes and Portuguese Pilgrims: Race, Religion and Politics in the Forging of a Portuguese Colonial Culture,' unpublished conference paper presented at *New Perspectives on Cultural Studies in Portuguese*, 19 May, Institute of Romance Studies, London.

Vakil A. (2001), 'O Portugal dos Outros, os Outros de Portugal e Outros Portugais: Achegas para uma re-leitura ex-cêntrica da historiografia do século XX português,' unpublished paper presented at *Congresso Portugal no Século XX*, Associação de Professores de História, 14–16 November, Lisbon.

Vakil, A. (2006), 'Heróis do Lar, Nação AmbiValente: Portugalidade e Identidade Nacional nos tempos dos *pós*,' in M. C. Meireles Pereira and M. Loff (eds.), *Portugal: 30 Anos de Democracia*. Faculdade de Letras da Universidade do Porto, Porto, pp. 73–101.

Vieira, J. L. (2008), 'Literatura Angolana: Estoriando a partir do que não se vê,' in L. C. Padilha and M. C. Ribeiro (eds.), *Lendo Angola*. Afrontamento, Porto, pp. 31–37.

Wacquant, L. (2008), *Urban Outcasts: A Comparative Sociology of Advanced Marginality*. Polity, Oxford.

13
'Portugal Is in the Sky': Conceptual Considerations on Communities, Lusitanity, and Lusophony

Michel Cahen

This contribution is that of a historian rather than a specialist of the literature on Lusophone culture. It therefore comes as no surprise that this piece starts by stating that such a culture does not exist. While there are indeed various cultures that can be described as Lusophone because they are expressed in the Portuguese language, the fact that they are expressed in Portuguese does not make them 'sister', or twin, cultures. Furthermore, does the fact that they use Portuguese make these phenomena specifically Lusophone? Are the Portuguese Lusophone? Are the French Francophone? We need to start by looking at the meaning of words. The aim of this piece is to deconstruct, but necessarily in full, and so partially to deconstruct the deconstruction itself.

On 17 July 1996, in Lisbon, a new interstate organisation was 'institutionalised', the Community of Portuguese Language Countries (Comunidades dos Paises de Língua Portuguesa, CPLP). This was not merely a technical meeting between the leaders of states whose official language was Portuguese but an initiative with weighty ideological content. Incidentally, this was one reason why the process was so long and drawn out and why it almost failed. We cannot go into too much detail here,[1] but we should at least examine the meaning of the letters C, P, L, and P in the Portuguese acronym. This new organisation did not call itself an *organisation*, like the UN, the OAU, or the OEI, but a *community* (hence the C); it did not call itself an organisation of states but of countries (and one early project proposed 'peoples'; hence the P, for *paises*); and it did not indicate that its members were countries with Portuguese as an official language – which was true at least of the seven founding states, as well as East Timor, which joined them in 2000 – but instead Portuguese-language countries, as if Portuguese were the language of the Mozambicans, Angolans, and today, the Timorese (hence the L and P). Lastly, what was announced was not the creation of the CPLP but its 'institutionalisation', with impassioned speeches from the Portuguese and

Brazilian leaders (although not the Africans) about the fact that the community had actually existed 'forever' thanks to 'centuries of fraternal bonds' and that the act of 17 July 1996, merely gave it official form. This discourse was evidently unacceptable to the Africans and, in striking contrast to its effect in Portugal, was only of minimal interest to the Brazilian intelligentsia.

So the debate in Africa revolved around the relationship with the former coloniser's language and the relationship with the former coloniser himself, but it was above all an intra-African debate on the *African social milieus* produced by colonisation. Inevitably, the Creole milieus were accused by the native movements (by which we should understand 'black', or even 'pro-authenticity') of not really being African because they were integrated into the CPLP culture.[2] The debate surrounding adhesion to the CPLP was one that focused on internal issues of power between social groups with different historical trajectories. Nonetheless, Portugal always stood in the dock as the accused, while Brazil, which had pretty much the same official discourse, was spared.[3] This differing attitudes on the part of PALOP[4] towards Portuguese and Brazilian discourse obviously expressed rancor against the most recent coloniser, as well as a certain southern solidarity with this other former colony of Portugal. But this solidarity overlooked the totally different nature of the colonisations: in Africa, the societies were invaded, exploited, oppressed, and partially acculturated by the coloniser, but they were maintained as African societies; Brazil, with the exception of the Indian populations, was a colonial society that acquired its independence without decolonisation[5] – it was a society maintained as a colony.[6]

Brazil could thus join Portugal in its Lusotropicalist discourse[7] on 'common origins', while the Africans vehemently rejected this line and pointed the finger only at Portugal. As we can see, Lusophony is an eminently political and ideological concept.

Lusitanity, Lusophony, empire

It has been widely observed that a number of colonial concepts have comfortably survived decolonisation, in that what was condemned with *Estado Novo* was much more its colonialism, as in policy, than the act of colonisation.

A lively colonial imaginary

The Portuguese imaginary has only been partially decolonised. In the popular speak of today, it is not uncommon to hear an expression such as *'a África nossa'* ('our Africa'). Many Portuguese, including a number of academics, often use the term *Países africanos de expressão portuguesa* ('African countries of Portuguese expression') without seeming to have noticed that these African countries have themselves adopted the term PALOP, a description that is both neutral and very different since it states that it is perfectly possible to use the Portuguese language without the *expression* being Portuguese: the expression is African.[8] The situation is the same in France with the poorly named *Afrique d'expression française* ('Africa of French expression'), which has however been more readily accepted thanks to the backing of Senghor.

Let us take just a few recent examples. We saw the way Lusotropicalist myths have persisted with the 1998 Universal Exhibition in Lisbon. The political objective of Expo'98 for the Portuguese government was in itself very interesting; just 12 years after the country's integration into the European Union, the idea was to bring millions of tourists from Europe and elsewhere to the capital and show them that Portugal had truly become a modern European nation with more to offer than *saudade*,[9] fado,[10] poetry, Fátima,[11] and caravels. But the message was soon lost with the choice of 'oceans' as the underlying theme, which, although attempting (and managing) to offer a modern portrayal (sustainable development, protection of the planet, etc.), immediately and inevitably brought to mind a powerful image of the caravel: the roof of the main Expo hall symbolising a sail (quite a technical feat, incidentally), the new bridge over the Tagus (Vasco da Gama), the new train station (Oriente), the street lamps and paving stones sketching the outline of caravels (Manya 1998), and so on, not to mention the concomitant existence of the National Commission for Commemoration of Portuguese Discoveries, as well as anti-Spanish polemic accusing the burdensome Iberian neighbour of doing yet more damage to Portugal's expression of exceptionality. However, the Expo commission was careful not to include a pavilion specially dedicated to the discoveries and, in so doing, incurred the wrath of a section of the intelligentsia.

But no-one, not even the far left, noticed that a pavilion was missing at the Expo, one dedicated to slavery and the slave trade. While a Universal Exhibition in Lisbon could do quite well without a Discoveries pavilion, it should never, given the government's political objective, have ignored the question of the slave trade – if for no other reason than to change the image that Africans have of modern Portugal (Cahen 1998).

África nossa, Ásia nossa

The colonial imaginary has not only persisted in the mind of the populace; it can be detected just as widely, although differently, among political leaders from both the right and the left. This is spectacularly apparent in Portuguese policy on Angola. Every government – with the semi-exception of certain periods of the Mário Soares presidency – has in practice almost unconditionally supported the MPLA political regime,[12] under cover of the fact that Angola was 'very important to Portugal'. While it is perfectly logical that African former colonies should be a matter of interest to Portugal, this importance did not necessarily imply exclusive support for only one of the political forces present (MPLA against Unita[13]) and abandonment of the Angolan civil society (churches, NGOs) in its efforts to reach a negotiated end to the civil war. This 'MPLA = Angola' equation goes back a long way, to the time when the MFA[14] openly helped the MPLA throw the other two fronts (FNLA[15] and Unita) out of Luanda. There was obviously a (left-wing) political bond but probably even more of a cultural and linguistic bond; the Portuguese soldiers of the MFA were delighted to discover that the MPLA leaders were like them, that is, having Portuguese as their mother tongue, from a similar educational background, city dwellers, hostile to African ethnicities, Third-Worldist, and so on. The MPLA was not perceived as part of a 'foreign' world by the MFA, unlike the FNLA and Unita with their discourse on African authenticity and blackness. Despite the massive tensions surrounding the unilateral proclamation of independence, which was made solely by the MPLA on 11 November 1975, Lisbon recognised its government quite soon, on 23 February 1976 – but even then, it was only the 82nd state to do so, thus heightening the MPLA government's contempt. Because while Angola was very important to Portugal, Portugal had never been very important to Angola. The Angolan government had always been extremely rigid and often scornful towards Portugal, despite Lisbon's increasingly generous concessions (Cahen 2001a; Messiant 1997, 2000, 2004).[16] But Portugal wanted to stick with Angola, the jewel in the empire's crown, in a way that it never did with Mozambique or Guinea-Bissau.

Another area in which the lasting legacy of the colonial imaginary can be measured is the mistrust of French cultural activism in the PALOP. As early as 1975, France included the PALOP among the African countries covered by its then Cooperation Ministry,[17] which usually included only former French colonies. Paris was clearly showing that it wished to annex the former Portuguese colonies and include them in the Francophone world, and the whole process was embellished with discourse as grandiloquent as it was abstract about the necessary solidarity between 'Latinophone' countries. Additionally, the material means at France's disposal to build the magnificent cultural center of Maputo and the activism of the more modest one in Bissau aroused anxiety and jealousy. And yet the French threat was largely baseless. If one language was a threat to Portuguese in Mozambique, it was English. Meanwhile, in Guinea-Bissau, the inexorable progress made by the French language, owing to the geopolitical context and the country's adhesion to Francophony, did not automatically mean that Portuguese was in decline; indeed, Portuguese was a founding language in Guinea-Bissau, while French was merely one instrument among others. And it was not the Portuguese cultural centre that was burned down by the crowd in the war of 1998 – it was the French one. The problem is thus largely imaginary; somehow, the cultural activity of France has always been seen as somewhat invasive in a part of Africa which is not part of Paris but of Lisbon.

A third example is the tremendous mobilisation of the Portuguese nation in a show of solidarity with the Timorese people during the Indonesian militia massacres following the referendum of 30 August 1999. This extraordinary movement (which went largely unnoticed outside Portugal and, when all is said and done, was incomprehensible to the rest of the world) was the result of a unification of the Portuguese nation due to the exceptional conjunction of three distinct, even opposing, historical trends. First, the Indonesian massacres rekindled the Portuguese national(ist) tradition, which recalled the shame of 7 December 1975, when Portuguese troops withdrew without combat against the Djakarta military offensive.[18] Second was the (often Christian) anticolonialist tradition; the Portuguese people were in favour of this end of decolonisation in their former empire. Third, and conversely, there was the Portuguese imperial and colonial tradition; a Portuguese territory of Asia was being invaded. They had to help the Timorese – Catholics, no less – who for years now, *'à noite, rezavam às escondidas em português'* ('had hidden away at night to pray in Portuguese'). In the historical contradiction between coloniser and colonised,[19] Indonesia had emerged as a stranger in the 'usual conflict' between the two traditional partners, perpetrating a war against the 'identity of the conflict' and thus allowing the symbolic reunification of the old enemies against the intruder (Cahen 2001c, p. 129). From the Partido Popular (People's Party[20]) to the Bloco de Esquerda (Left Bloc[21]), the *entire* Portuguese nation came together on this issue.

Meanwhile, the third Angolan civil war was producing 800,000 casualties, more than 20 times the Timor number. Nobody (apart from a few *Público* journalists) got excited about it, at least not to the extent of developing a mass solidarity movement. The problem was that the Portuguese nation was divided on the Angola issue and could therefore not speak to itself in the same way as with Timor. It could not really bring Angola into the Portuguese national imaginary, whereas it had no trouble doing so with Timor.

Lastly, we should mention the use and misuse of some fine expressions (or even book titles) by great writers, often taken out of context. While *O mundo que o português criou* (The world that the Portuguese created, Freyre 1940) is unequivocally a founder of Brazilian Lusotropicalism and more generally typical of the ideology of the 'discoveries' (relating to worlds created and 'invented' by the coloniser by negating the very existence of the societies conquered), and while the same can be said of still common expressions such as *Portugal deu novos mundos ao mundo* (Portugal gave new worlds to the world), what about the very famous declaration by Fernando Pessoa, *Minha pátria é a língua portuguesa* (My homeland is the Portuguese language), the meaning of which is almost completely turned on its head in its current (mis)use? It is worth quoting the passage almost in full:

> I don't have any political or social sentiment. Rather, in a sense, I have a patriotic feeling. *My homeland is the Portuguese language.* It wouldn't grieve me if Portugal were invaded or taken over, because this wouldn't

bother me, personally. However, I abhor, with real hatred – and this is the only hatred I feel – not those who write poorly in Portuguese, not those who don't understand syntax, not those who write with simplified spelling, but rather I hate the page that is written poorly by an individual; moreover, I hate incorrect syntax – which is akin to people who have been beaten up – and I hate spelling that has no graphical accents, which is similar to the straight spit that infuriates me, regardless of who is spitting. (Pessoa 1999)

Thus, the writer's declaration of love for his language, stating that he lives in and for this language, totally disconnected from a territory or a national identity, has been stripped of its meaning in countless speeches, articles, and, as below, blogs:

My homeland is the Portuguese language. Portuguese is one of the most widely spoken languages on the planet. It is spoken by more than *two hundred million* people throughout the world. Eight countries have Portuguese as their *national language*: Portugal, Brazil, Angola, Mozambique, Guinea, Timor, Cape Verde, São Tomé and Principe. *Portuguese* is also spoken in various regions throughout the world, such as Galicia (Spain), Casamance (Senegal), Goa (India), Macao (China), etc. Portuguese-language countries created a community, the CPLP [Community of Portuguese-Language Countries], which represents *an entirely common identity*. [...] *The Portuguese language is a homeland* and a common identity for many people spread across the world. [my emphases][22]

The lyricism of our bloggers merely neglects the Kristangs of Malacca (Malaysia) (Fernandis 2000), the Burghers of Sri Lanka (Jayasuriya 2000, 2005), the 'true Portuguese' of Bengal (Caixeiro 2000), the prayers recited in 16th-century Portuguese in Sulawesi and on the Isle of Flowers (Indonesia), all actual traces of an ancient colonial history that, nonetheless, do not constitute Portuguese, or even Lusophone, communities at all.

The fine expression thus becomes empire. 'My homeland is the Portuguese language' *for a particular writer* is reversed and becomes 'The Portuguese language is a shared homeland' *for the most diverse peoples*. Of course we will not deny that the common use of a language is a shared characteristic, but contemporary Lusotropicalist discourse popularises the idea that countries using the Portuguese language have a shared homeland, which is naturally a little bit Portuguese. It is also significant that the common language is referred to as 'national' (rather than 'official'), that Creole (Casamance) is confused with Portuguese,[23] and that the most hackneyed myths about the Portuguese language in Goa[24] and Macao are reused without the slightest sense of doubt about the Lusophony of Mozambique and Angola.

Social levels of language

Lusophony (in the same way as Francophony, of course) is a single blanket term that smothers some extremely different social realities and incomparable social statuses.

Language can be maternal or affective, that is, identity forming and founding. For example, for the majority of French, Quebecois (still known as French Canadians not so long ago) and Belgian Walloons (whose community is called French, not Francophone), the French language is a strong identity marker. It makes little sense to call them Francophone, as this would mean they are able to *hear* French (in the rather Portuguese sense of the word: *entender*). Of course they hear and understand it, but it is also their *identity forming language*.

This is not the case of conquered peoples that have kept their national languages. The new language is therefore either *second* or *foreign*. It is second in situations where it is not the mother tongue but nor is it felt to be foreign. This is the case of extensively Creole-speaking countries such as Cape Verde and São Tomé and Príncipe; no one speaks Portuguese in Cape Verde (not even ministers, except when they sit in council), but thanks to Kriol, everyone can understand Portuguese. This is not the case in Mozambique; in the census of 1997, 6.51 per cent of Mozambicans had Portuguese as their mother tongue (7.0% in urban areas, 2% in the country), 8.8 per cent had Portuguese as the 'language most commonly spoken in the home' (26.1% in urban areas, 1.4% in the country) and lastly 39.6 per cent considered Portuguese as a language that they understood (without further details about the level of comprehension) (72.4% in urban areas and 25.4% in the country) (INE 1997). Obviously, unlike Kriol, the Bantu languages are of no help in understanding Portuguese, which is a foreign language for the vast majority (91.2%) of the population.

In such cases the language is an instrument, one which probably has identity-forming effects, especially in the long term, but which does not found the identity of social groups on a given territory. A large number of Senegalese are true Francophones since they understand and can speak French; a large number of Angolans, particularly in Luanda, are true Lusophones for the same reasons. But they are still Wolof, Toucouleur, Peul, or Mbundu, Bacongo, and Ovimbundu.

These countries should not build the same socioeducational and sociolinguistic policies for populations that have such varied relationships with the colonial language. In particular, literacy learned directly in the colonial language can produce disastrous psycho-pedagogical results and can be one of the factors behind high failure rates at school. Children need to learn to read and write in their affective language, not in a foreign language. The diversity of African languages is often put forward as an argument in favour of a single language, but this is a technocratic argument corresponding to the interests of the elite. However, there is no need for these languages to be perfectly standardised and 'grammaticalised' for literacy to begin – especially as in most cases there are missionary materials available (dictionaries, lexicons, grammars) which, although old and imperfect, can still be used. But the argument also holds for the cooperation policies of former colonial powers; are the substantial sums allocated to disseminating the Portuguese (or French) language spent in the interest of the populations for whom the 'cooperation' is conducted? This policy is all the more counterproductive in that it has been proven time and time again that starting literacy learning in the affective language leads to better acquisition of the colonial language. The question is actually social (privilege of an elite) and ideological (the very idea of the nation and modernity). Many countries (including Mozambique and, more recently, Cape Verde) have passed laws allowing schooling to start in African languages. Aside from the fact that these languages are not always the mother tongue of the children themselves (as is the case of Kiswahili in Tanzania, Kenya, and Uganda), these laws are often improperly or inadequately applied or suffer from the fact that, for lack of political will, the financial means are not allocated and there is no long-term teacher-training effort. Parents then come to see the learning of the mother tongue as detrimental to the interests of their children – as was also the case in France with the patois spoken by our grandparents – and themselves identify with the colonial language. The very legitimate aspiration to social progress is assimilated with a certain postcolonial modernity. In the space of three generations a language can disappear, although the situations are highly diversified.[25]

More generally, language cooperation policies that do not take account of the diversity of the language's social status are a case of old cultural imperialism, sometimes with the best intentions. For example, around Christmastime 1999, shortly after the drama in East Timor, the Commission for Support in Transition to East Timor, a Portuguese interministerial body,[26] conducted a major fundraising campaign – with the sweet little face of a Timorese child on the prospectus, which bore the slogan '*Neste Natal, contribua para que os meninos de Timor aprendam a falar português*' ('This Christmas, please contribute so that the children of Timor can learn to speak Portuguese'). Where did the 'learn to speak *Portuguese*' come from?

In Africa the issue of language is very closely linked to the imaginary of the nation under construction. In a situation where the historical processes of identification are weakened by the non–socially promoting nature of the states, which are situated on the periphery of capitalism,[27] language is at the heart of a paradigm of authoritarian modernisation. This is by no means a case of a gradual process whereby ethnicities, although a long way from disappearing, nonetheless merge into a pan-identity of anterior identities, a nation of nations, in rather the same way that the British identity is a pan-nation of the English, Scottish, and Welsh nations. In Mozambique, Guinea, and so on, will Portuguese be the language of national unity (which is a nonpeaceful concept in exactly the same way one might say that English will be the language of European unification), or will it be one language among others, learned by pupils who are already literate in their mother tongue? The model applied in the PALOP followed the first rationale to the detriment of the second; the 'new man' had to speak Portuguese, build concrete tower blocks, have no ethnic group, and promote state farms with a high level of fixed capital. Socialism was accused, of course, but well before that there was the idea of the modern nation, European-style and, in the case of the PALOP, Jacobin-style; today the state farms have been privatised and the telephones are mobile, but the technocratic development model has barely changed and is not based on boosting the farming economy, crafts, and small industry, all of which are able to generate resources in the country itself. The paternalistic and authoritarian idea of 'modernising the people' in order to forge a nation – that is, by negating the African societies that were historically present in the border areas divided by colonisation – easily survived the so-called fall of Marxism. This shows that this was not a consequence; on the contrary, Marxism was a contextual instrument in subaltern Westernisation by the elite in these countries, the instrument of their 'nationism' (desire for a nation).

The Portuguese legacy – a linguistic legacy?

As far as I know, there is little in the way of long-term studies on the reasons why, after five centuries of colonisation, the Portuguese language has barely gained a foothold in certain territories, while after much shorter periods, it has survived, creolised, or even grown in others. Why does no one speak Portuguese in Goa; why was Portuguese barely used even in the time of Portuguese occupation? It is very possible that Goa was more Lusophone in the 18th and 19th centuries than in the 20th century. It is possible that the gradual economic decline of the Estado da Índia[28] encouraged a large proportion of its elite to emigrate to Bombay or elsewhere in British India, especially as the British were looking to recruit these Indians, who could use the Latin alphabet. This explains why Goans (generally not Lusophone[29]) were to be found throughout the British colonial administration in East Africa and why from re-emigration to re-emigration there have always been numerous, long-lasting Goan communities in London and Canada, while in Portugal they have disappeared through integration. But the premise holds true: the Portuguese language was not socially useful to these Goans in their professional activity or for their identity-forming cohesion.

The same can probably be said of Macao, a city in which the Portuguese language has never been more than a thin veneer. But what about Malacca, which was Portuguese only from 1511 to 1641 and was conquered by a troop of around a thousand Portuguese soldiers (or mercenaries serving Portugal) and a few hundred Chinese under the orders of Afonso de Albuquerque?

How can it be that a Portuguese settlement remained and that Papia Kristang (Portuguese Creole) survived until the first half of the 20th century? There is every reason to believe that professional (fishing community), religious (Catholic) and linguistic (Portuguese-based Creole) identification was at the root of the social cohesion of this very small group.[30]

As for Timor, there is not the slightest doubt that the Indonesian invasion did the Portuguese language a huge favour. Not only did the Timorese government declare Portuguese to be the official language (in 2002, along with Tetum, one of the local languages) as an independence tool against Indonesia and Australia, but the Catholicism / Portuguese language complex was undeniably a driver of cultural and social resistance against Indonesian oppression and the spread of Bahasa (Javanese) (Hattori, Gomes, Ajo, and Belo 2005; Hull 1998). But is it a legacy? Portuguese is not spoken much in Timor today, but still a lot more often than it was in 1975. There has been an expansion of the language of Camões owing to its social and political utility; it is the language of the Catholic Church and the main instrument of civil resistance.

Whether the language expands, declines, or disappears, what always comes back is not the linguistic aspect but the social utility criterion. Quite clearly, Portuguese was of no use to the Goans in upholding their social identity, which already included the Indo-Iranian language Konkani and then, as migrations came and went, English. Portuguese did not cement the Goans' economic and professional status, and the lethargic situation of Salazarist Goa (Bègue 2006) did not change things. However, while no one speaks Portuguese in Goa, not even the Catholic archbishop, there are other Portuguese legacies on every street corner: people's names, the architecture, Roman law, a higher percentage of Catholics than elsewhere in India, and alcohol consumption. In addition, there is a certain anti-English sentiment – a feeling of irritation towards the New Delhi Indians, who are all too keen to consider that the Goans have remained excessively Portuguese without wondering whether they themselves have remained somewhat 'English', as Portuguese is strongly felt to be a colonial language, while English is not.

In Bengali villages, the claim to 'Portugality' or Christianity (which are often linked) obviously serves to maintain cohesion among village communities with a distant Portuguese political ancestry – probably villages founded by descendants of Asian mercenaries working for the Portuguese in the 16th and 17th centuries (Caixeiro 2000). Yet these Bengalis are not distinguishable from other Indians in terms of language or religious rites (there are many Christians in Bengal). The same was probably not true of the Sri-Lankan Burghers, for whom the Creole language was linked to their Christianity in an otherwise Sinhalese and Tamil world. However, their demographic weakness was such that the process of their assimilation/disappearance is almost complete today (there are still a few dozen people with Luso–Sri Lankan Creole as their main language). When, in 1999, Ivo Carneiro de Sousa visited the communities of the Isle of Flowers (Indonesia), where prayers were still recited in a 16th-century Portuguese they no longer understood, the inhabitants were alarmed because they thought he was an inspector coming to check that they had remained 'true Portuguese', which they clearly were not. When asked the question 'Where is Portugal?' they were unable to supply an answer. An elderly man from a community near Djakarta gave a nice reply: 'Portugal is in the sky.'[31]

Lastly, let us mention those 'forgotten Lusophonies', the Agudas of Benin, Togo, and the Niger Delta. The Afro-Brazilian communities in this zone, descendants of slave traders who came over from Brazil (most notably Bahia) or of slaves themselves who came back to Africa in the 19th century, have not spoken Portuguese for decades, have in some cases even converted to Islam (although only a minority), and made a point of supporting the government against Salazar during the Fort of São João Baptista de Ajuda affair.[32] Nonetheless, the Afro-Brazilianity of the Agudas, with their own special religious parades, their Portuguese names, a certain level of endogamy, a rich architectural past, and a number of transatlantic trips to visit their Brazilian cousins, clearly serves to ensure the imaginary cohesion of this social milieu, only without the language.

In more directly political terms, we should also point out the legacy of the Portuguese national imaginary. Portuguese may be the mother tongue of only a tiny minority of Mozambicans today, but the idea of the nation as it was conveyed by the Marxist-Leninist Frelimo and in certain respects today by the neoliberal Frelimo, with the state as the main actor of the economy, the homogenous identity of the people, the single official language, union corporatism, the hypertrophied civil service, and so on, is all very Portuguese, not to say Salazarist. This is quite a sizeable national legacy.

Religious, legal, imaginary, and national legacies – in our deconstruction efforts here, we are not attempting to deny or even to minimise the legacies, but they are nonetheless more a case of Luso*topia* than Luso*phony*. The concept of Lusotopia was first put forward in 1992 by the French geographer Louis Marrou to describe all the spaces and communities which, irrespective of their past and present languages, have been more or less forged or fashioned by the history of Portuguese expansion. Naturally, the same can be said of the former French and English domains. But there is a specific Portuguese feature here, namely, a colonial domain that is more markedly ancient and that spatially grew larger more quickly[33] than those of the other European powers, a long development and a slow decline from the first colonial age, which produced more social milieus linked with this particular period of colonisation.[34] Lusotopia is thus more resonant than Francotopia or Anglotopia. But for all that, it does not provide the outline of an identity-forming or even linguistic space.

What Lusophony cannot be and can be

A purely linguistic view of the question results in the definition of a community according to a single identity marker, despite the fact that there are many others, and additionally without any concern for the social statuses of the language (maternal-affective, second, foreign). It more or less boils down to considering that contemporary Lusophony is nothing more than the end result of a historical process of dilatation of Lusitanity. In other words, it is merely a continuation of the imperial imaginary, albeit without colonialism as a policy but with colonisation as a sociocultural acculturation phenomenon.

This inclination, which we already noted in the phrase 'African countries of Portuguese expression', is an integral part of a Portuguese nationalist tendency which glorifies Lusophony in order to make up for the small size of the 'mainland rectangle', all the more so as integration into the European Union since 1986 has emphasised this smallness. Owing to its history, so profoundly rooted in the national imaginary, Portugal, unlike Belgium, Denmark, Switzerland, and Norway (4,640,219 inhabitants on 1 January 2006), is incapable of 'being peacefully small'. The expansion is no longer military, of course, but Portugality still needs a predefined, reassuring space upon which to project itself: Lusophony. It is an avatar of the old Lusotropicalist tendency, according to which the Portuguese people had the innate, hereditary gift of harmonious acclimatisation to other peoples, usually in the Tropics. The question that this imaginary never asks itself (it is true that imaginaries rarely ask themselves questions) is how the 'other Lusophones' feel about the Portuguese way. And yet one only needs to study the reactions in African countries to the creation of the CPLP [35] to see that all this is merely perceived as Portuguese old hat and that it does not help stabilise a healthy relationship with a country that, like it or not, has had its importance in the history of the new African states.

Lusophony was very interestingly defined by Eduardo Lourenço as a 'specific area of intersection with other identities'; it is indeed defined by a shared specificity, namely, the language, but this specificity is delimited and relative (according to the social statuses of the language). In the era of globalised merchandising, the fact that language has itself become a commodity through privatised media is a not insignificant factor.[36] But it is still only one factor. The Lourenço definition corresponds even better to Lusotopia: if absolutely no one either speaks or understands Portuguese on the Planalto Maconde (in Mozambique), in the New Conquests (Goa), in Macao, or on some of the Bissagos Islands (Guinea-Bissau), even the 'specific area of intersection' is no longer defined relative to the language.

Although the facile compilation of statistics on inhabitants of countries with Portuguese as the official language (rather than actual speakers) produces massive errors in terms of the number of Lusophones, it is still true that the majority of these inhabitants have at least a smattering of Portuguese. Furthermore, the other identity markers discussed earlier produce a certain identity-based feeling, with or without the language. Otherwise, why would the Mozambicans support the Portuguese or Brazilian football team during the World Cup? But this is what could be called a 'light identity', one which, moreover, is modulated according to social milieu. All else being equal, it could be compared with what used to be the Soviet identity. The USSR was never defined by its leaders as a nation (or even a nation of nations) but as the 'homeland of socialism', in which there were dozens of nations. People from the USSR felt first and foremost Russian, Armenian, Ukrainian, Chukchi, and so on, but they also had that Soviet light identity. Lusophony, Francophony, and even Anglophony (although in the latter case, the fact that it has an economic hegemony makes the question more complex) could all fall into the category of light identity.

As for the political leaders of the PALOP, who did not share the grandiloquent Luso-Brazilian discourse on 'shared origins' and 'centuries of conviviality', there is not the slightest doubt that for them the CPLP was just one political tool among others. Angola refused to join as long as Mário Soares was president,[37] Guinea-Bissau, Cape Verde, and São Tomé became members after first joining Francophony, and Mozambique after joining the Commonwealth (Cahen 2001a).

Lusophony is therefore most certainly not a cultural area but instead a specific postcolonial space, a 'relative space'. This in no way prevents it from working with, for example, the expansion of neo-Pentecostalism or priority being given to Brazilians when shops take on staff (in Porto for example) because, according to the Lusotropicalist myth, 'Brazilians smile' (Machado 2004). Of course, there are cultures within Lusophony but not at the global level of a Lusophone cultural community, unless this is reduced to just Portugal and Brazil.

All of the above naturally also applies to Hispanophony, Francophony, and Anglophony. However, in the Portuguese case the imaginary has been heightened by the frailty of mainland Portugal, which is incapable of forming a neocolonial 'backyard' of the French type (there is no 'LusÁfrica', no Portuguese version of 'FrançAfrique'). Angola and Mozambique do not view Portugal as a home country.[38] This absence of a neocolonial backyard is a good thing and may lead to a new type of North-South relationship. But for now, it merely feeds the Portuguese government's anxiety as other, better-financed powers encroach upon *África nossa*. And yet it is the absence of a LusAfrica which allows us to say that the Portuguese language has been decolonised; Portuguese languages are indeed used from Timor to Brazil via Maputo and Minho, but there is not a common linguistic homeland outside minuscule social milieus, which are globally 'Afro-Luso-Brazilian'.

The light identity of Lusophony, that supra-identity bolstered by the merchandising of language, is highlighted by people when it is in their interest to do so; this is the case with Brazilians or Cape Verdeans who immigrate to Portugal (often considering it to be a step towards 'real Europe'). Conversely, we can but observe the total absence, long-term, of any bonds or even convergences between the Brazilian Americans, Portuguese Americans, and Cape Verdean Americans (formerly 'brown Portuguese') of the United States. In France, Belgium, and Holland, countries where there are many Portuguese, Cape Verdean, and Brazilian communities, rarely do they get together, and there is no sense of a pan-community. Perhaps in Portugal there is a certain complicity, particularly musical, between Cape Verdeans and Brazilians.

Lastly, there is the generational factor. There is no doubt that the Portuguese youth of today seem to be more detached from the 'caravels' than their grandparents were in the Salazar era or even their parents at the time of the Carnation Revolution, the Third-Worldism of which fitted in perfectly with a modernised Lusotropicalism – Portugal could now have an 'exceptional relationship' with Africa, because with fascism dead, Portugal's smallness would always prevent it from being imperialist. However, it is not certain that the Portuguese firms based in Africa were more philanthropic than their French, American, or Brazilian counterparts. Nonetheless, this discernable distancing from the caravels by young people in Portugal has not yet led to a sea change in discourse on Africa or in the Portuguese grandiose rhetoric.

The light identity that is Lusophony is typical of the fluid situations that some people describe as postmodern. It does exist, but only relatively and contextually, and is profoundly affected by the persistence of history (Carvalho and Cabral 2004) in the heterogeneous spaces in which it has lasted. That is why it cannot be 'reified' into a unified human community.

Notes

[*] A previous French-language version of this article was published in Cahen 2007. Some amendments have been made to the text with a view to this publication, up to April 2011. My thanks go to A.-M. Binet and Presses Universitaires de Bordeaux for their authorisation to publish this later version.
1. In particular, see Léonard 1995 and 1998 and Cahen 1997.
2. It was far more complicated in reality, as certain Creole milieus were strongly anti-Portuguese. See Cahen 2001a. On the history of Creole milieus in Angola, see in particular Messiant 2006.
3. On the Brazilian imaginary in Angola, see Santil 2006.
4. PALOP is the Portuguese acronym for 'Portuguese-speaking African Countries'. In Portuguese, the acronym stands for Paises Africanos de Lingual Oficial Portuguesa, which literally means 'African countries with Portuguese as their official language'.
5. When the Portuguese regent Pedro (later Emperor Pedro I) refused to go back to Portugal, declaring, *'Fico'* (I stay), his statement was paradoxically emblematic of

this desire for independence without decolonisation: a native does not say 'Fico', because the idea of leaving does not even cross his mind, even to refute it.
6. Colonisation generates entire societies (not only classes) and there is nothing shocking about observing that even the black slaves of Brazil are part of the world of the Portuguese coloniser rather than that of the indigenous colonised people; they are the most exploited *class* in colonisation, but are exploited *within* the colonisation, and not as an outside society invaded by the coloniser. This also explains why there have been relatively few Indian/Black uprisings. Nowadays Brazilians descended from European migrants are not descendants of colonised people but of colonisers; and black Brazilians are descendants of slaves integrated by force into the coloniser's world, not the colonised world.
7. It is not possible in this article to describe the Lusotropicalist constellation. What we call Lusotropicalism is mainly neo-Lusotropicalism as it appeared in the 1950s, when Salazar retrieved the theorisations of Gilberto Freyre, with his full agreement. But while (and however open to criticism it might be) the original Lusotropicalism of Freyre in the 1930s made interbreeding and integration in the Tropics the basis for a new civilisation, the later Lusotropicalism made interbreeding a step towards 'whitening' and Westernisation. Lusophony understood as a dilatation of Lusitanity is clearly part of this late Lusotropicalism (see below).
8. On the paradoxical nationalism of the anticolonial fronts that did more for the Portuguese language than the coloniser had in five centuries, see Cahen 2001b.
9. The sweetness (or pleasure) of nostalgia.
10. Popular music, probably of slave origin.
11. A place of pilgrimage in memory of the anti-Bolshevik appearances of the Virgin Mary in 1917.
12. MPLA (People's Movement for the Liberation of Angola) one of the Angolan anticolonialist fronts, which came into power in 1975 in a one-party regime, then, from 1991, became an ultrahegemonic and endemically corrupted party system.
13. Unita (National Union for the Total Independence of Angola), an anticolonialist group that survived the MPLA counteroffensive and the Cuban troops in 1975–76 and became the main armed opponent to the regime, initially with the support of Maoist China and then with white South Africa. Since its military defeat in January 2002 and the Luena Agreements, Unita has become a legal political party.
14. MFA (Movement of the Armed Forces [previously the Movement of Captains]), responsible for the military coup which triggered the Carnation Revolution on 25 April 1974.
15. FNLA (National Liberation Front of Angola), the oldest Angolan anticolonialist front, responsible for the major uprising of 1961, backed by the Mobutu regime in Zaire and then by the USA. However, the FNLA did not survive the MPLA counteroffensive and the Cuban troops. It still exists today but as a minor opposition party.
16. The first two of Messiant's articles have been republished in Messiant 2008, pp. 131–174 and 175–199.
17. The French Cooperation Ministry is now part of the Ministry of Foreign Affairs. The two ministries had very different traditions, the first being 'populated' by former colonial-era staff and the second by diplomats.

312 *Michel Cahen*

18. Although the Portuguese were unanimous in 1999, this does not mean that the country was unanimous in 1975 in defending the independence of Timor. General Costa Gomes, for example, had always imagined that Timor should be returned to Indonesia, as Goa had been returned to India in 1961.
19. We should not forget the very difficult and bloody conquest of East Timor by the Portuguese (Pélissier 2000) and the repression of the 1959 uprising.
20. Portuguese right-wing party.
21. Coalition of small far-left parties.
22. Taken at random from the countless sites and blogs, the Lusitânia Portugal blog can be described as somewhat caricatured. But while this is true in many aspects (glorification of Portuguese history, etc.), its linguistic paragraphs do not detract from the usual Luso-linguistic ideological landscape in Portugal: http://groups.msn.com/smkq6tklbkrpsggg511l6n9287/aminhaptriaalnguapotuguesa.msnw
23. In 2004, there were around 1,700 people with Guinean Creole as their mother tongue in Casamance, or 0.28% of the Casamance population and 0.016% of the Senegalese population. About 20,000 Senegalese had French as their mother tongue, or 0.188% of the population. French is still a foreign language spoken by 15% to 20% of Senegalese men and barely 2% of Senegalese women. It remains the mother tongue of a tiny elite, probably because 55% of young Senegalese live in rural areas, and very few of them go to school (source: http://www.tlfq.ulaval.ca/axl/afrique/senegal.htm).
24. We should remember that the last Portuguese census in Goa (1960), before the Indian military intervention, produced around 1% of Goans with Portuguese as their mother tongue or the language most commonly spoken in the home. Nowadays no one speaks Portuguese in Goa, although the colonial legacy can be seen in many other features (Portuguese surnames, architecture, Roman law, percentage of Catholics, alcohol consumption, etc.).
25. Certain African languages such as Wolof, Lingala, and Kiswahili are expanding despite the prevalence of colonial languages.
26. *Comissariado para o Apoio à Transição em Timor-Leste,* http://www.comissariotimor.gov.pt/entrada/home.asp
27. In French history, for example, the fact that people from Alsace and northern Lorraine, who have a German culture, identify with France is due in large part to the legacy of the French Revolution: it was better for them to be citizens of the French Republic than subjects of the king of Prussia. A state bringing economic, social, and cultural progress will obviously have greater 'agglutinating power' than a predator state.
28. Official colonial name for Goa, whose capital is Panjim.
29. Not Lusophone in Goa, these émigrés had no reason to be Lusophone in British Africa. These Goans did however have a certain knowledge of Portuguese, and they maintained their Portuguese nationality. Portugal used them for decades, up to the 1960s, to staff its consulates and vice-consulates in British East Africa (Zanzibar, Mombasa, Dar es Salaam, Pemba, and so on) with vice-consuls and honorary consuls. The professional diplomats were only in Nairobi and Salisbury. See Margret Frenz's chapter in this book.
30. In 1999, I asked Gerard Fernandis, a Kristang intellectual, whether he thought his tiny community could survive. He was sure of himself on this question because, he said, 'Government understood it's good for tourism....'.
31. Conversation with the author.

32. Benin (formerly Dahomey) became a French colony in 1892, with the fort of São João Baptista de Ajuda remaining as a minuscule Portuguese property, totally surrounded by French territory and containing just one inhabitant, the administrator. When Dahomey won independence on August 1, 1960, the new government demanded that the fort be handed back. Salazar refused, ordering the administrator to set the fort on fire before the Benin troops could intervene (which he did not do, apparently). A compromise would certainly have been possible, making the fort an extraterritorial pocket under the responsibility of the Portuguese embassy. But Salazar would not hear of this, while the Benin government wanted to test the loyalty of the Agudas. Portugal recognised the annexation in 1985, allowing the start of restoration work by the Calouste Gulbenkian Foundation. On the Agudas, see Yai 1997, Guran 2000, Amos 2007.
33. Although this is not comparable to the 'effective conquest of territories' of the late-19th-century imperialist phase.
34. To specify: this fairly wide-scale production of social milieus related to the first age of colonisation does not mean that interbreeding was more prevalent in Portuguese colonisation *overall* than in the others. Some of these milieus could be totally Asian or Bantu. Also, if there was one colonial period when interbreeding was low key, it was the contemporary colonisation period, where the main priority was 'whitening' the colonies. The unrivalled interbreeding of Lusotropicalist myth was above all that of slavery. The Portuguese influence as regards the production of Creoles, by contrast, cannot be limited to the Portuguese territories. First, there are territories that were Portuguese that kept Creole (such as Fa d'Ambu, Annobon Island, attached to 'Hispanophone' Equatorial Guinea). But territories that were never Portuguese are also concerned. For example, Papiamento de Kòrsou, the main language of Curaçao, is based on African languages, Dutch, Spanish, and Portuguese, even though the island was not a Portuguese colony.
35. Or even resistance among a part of the Timorese youth to the Portugalisation of education. This youth, although anti-Indonesian, experienced the period of linguistic Javanisation.
36. It also produces religious vectors. For example, while the neo-Pentecostal churches are of North American origin, those that set up massively in Brazil (Igreja unida do reino de Deus, etc.) more easily 'leaped' to Angola, Mozambique, Portugal, and the Lusophone diasporas in Paris than in non-Lusophone areas.
37. Because of his supposed support for Unita.
38. This is perhaps less true of Cape Verde and Guinea-Bissau and does not prevent the Angolan oil nomenklatura from shopping in the luxury stores of Lisbon.

References

Amos, A. Meira (2007), *Os que Voltaram – a história dos retornados afro-brasileiros na África Ocidental no século XIX*. Tradição Planalto Editora, Belo Horizonte.
Bègue, S. (2006), *La fin de Goa et de l'Estado da Índia : Décolonisation et guerre froide dans le sous-continent indien (1945–1962)*, PhD thesis, Nantes University, Nantes.
Cahen, M. (1997), 'Des caravelles pour le futur ? Discours politique et idéologie dans l'institutionnalisation' de la Communauté des pays de langue portugaise,' in 'Lusotropicalisme' [dossier], *Lusotopie* 3, pp. 391–435.
—— (1998), 'L'Expo'98, le nationalisme et nous,' *Lusotopie* 4, pp. 11–19.

—— (2001a), 'Que faire du Portugal quand on est africain ?' in *Le Portugal et l'Atlantique*. Arquivos do Centro cultural Calouste Gulbenkian, Paris and Lisbon, pp. 53–70.

—— (2001b) 'L'Afrique "lusophone": Approche socio-linguistique,' in M. Cahen (ed.), *Pays Lusophones d'Afrique. Sources d'information pour le développement. Angola, Cap-Vert, Guinée-Bissau, Mozambique, São Tomé e Príncipe*. Ibiscus, Paris, pp. 21–29.

—— (2001c), 'Loro Sa'e, "soleil levant" archaïsant ou signe de modernité à l'ère de la modernisation ?' *Lusotopie* 8, pp. 125–134.

—— (2007), 'Lusitanité et lusophonie. Considérations conceptuelles sur des réalités sociales et politiques,' in A. M. Binet (ed.), *Mythes et mémoire collective dans la culture Lusophone. Eidôlon. Cahiers du Laboratoire pluridisciplinaire de recherche sur l'imaginaire appliquées à la littérature* no. 78, Presses Universitaires de Bordeaux, Pessac, pp. 127–146.

Caixeiro, M. C. (2000), 'True Christian or True Portuguese? Origin Assertion in a Christian Village in Bengal, India,' *Lusotopie* 7, pp. 233–252.

Carvalho, C., and Cabral J. de Pina (2004), *A persistência da História*. Imprensa das Ciências Sociais, Lisbon.

Fernandis, G. (2000), 'Papia, Relijang e Tradisang. The Portuguese Eurasian in Malaysia: Bumiquest, a Search for Self Identity', *Lusotopie* 7, pp. 261–268.

Freyre, G. (1940), *O Mundo que o português criou: Aspectos das relações sociais e de cultura do Brasil com Portugal e as colônias portuguesas*. Documentos Brasileiros no. 28, José Olympio, Rio de Janeiro.

Guran, M. (2000), *Agudás – os 'brasileiros' do Benim*. Nova Fronteira – Gama Filho, Rio de Janeiro.

Hattori, R., Gomes M., Ajo F., and Belo N. (2005), *The Ethnolinguistic Situation in East Timor*. University of Hawaii (International Graduate Student Conference Series, 20), Honolulu.

Hull, G. (1998), 'The Languages of Timor, 1772–1997: A Literature Review,' *Studies in Languages and Cultures of East Timor*. Vol. 1. Instituto Nacional de Linguística, Dili – University of Western Sidney, MacArthur, pp. 1–38.

INE (1997), *Censo Geral da População e da Habitação*. Instituto nacional de Estatística, Maputo.

Jayasuriya, S. de Silva (2000), 'The Portuguese Cultural Imprint on Sri Lanka,' *Lusotopie* 7, pp. 253–260.

—— (2005), 'The Portuguese Identity of the Afro-Sri Lankans,' *Lusotopie* 12, nos. 1–2, pp. 21–32.

Léonard, Y. (1995), 'La "Communauté des pays de langue portugaise," ou l'hypothétique Lusophonie politique,' *Lusotopie* 2, pp. 9–16.

—— (1998), 'La Lusophonie dans le monde,' *Problèmes politiques et sociaux*, no. 803, special issue.

Machado, I. J. de Renó (2004), 'Imigrantes brasileiros no Porto. Aproximação à perenidade de ordens raciais e colon iais portuguesas,' *Lusotopie* 11, pp. 121–140.

Manya, J. (1998), 'La vie quotidienne à Lisbonne au temps de l'Expo'98,' *Lusotopie* 5, pp. 633–637.

Messiant, C. (1997), 'Angola, entre guerre et paix,' in R. Marchal and C. Messiant, *Les chemins de la guerre et de la paix : Fins de conflits en Afrique orientale et australe*. Karthala, Paris, pp. 157–208.

—— (2000), 'Angola 1974–1999. De la guerre d'indépendance à la guerre civile et régionale,' in M. H. Araujo Carreira (ed.), *De la Révolution des œillets au IIIe millénaire. Portugal et Afrique Lusophone : 25 ans d'évolution(s)*. Éd. Université Paris 8, Paris, pp. 197–223.

—— (2004), 'Bicesse, Lusaka: À quoi a servi la "communauté internationale"?,' *Accord* 15, pp. 16–23.
—— (2006), *1961. L'Angola colonial, histoire et société. Les prémisses du mouvement nationaliste.* P. Schlettwein, Basel.
—— (2008), *L'Angola postcolonial. I. Guerre et paix sans démocratisation*, Karthala, Paris.
Pélissier, R. (2000), *Timor en guerre. Le Crocodile et Les Portugais (1847–1913).* Éd. Pélissier, Orgeval.
Pessoa, F. [Bernardo Soares] (1999), *Livro do desassossego.* Companhia das Letras, Lisbon.
Santil, M. (2006), '"Ce métis qui nous trouble". Les représentations du Brésil dans l'imaginaire politique angolais: L'empreinte de la colonialité sur le savoir,' PhD thesis, Université Montesquieu Bordeaux 4, Pessac.
Yai, O. B. (1997), 'Les "Aguda" (Afro-Brésiliens) du Golfe du Bénin. Identité, apports, idéologie : Essai de réinterprétation,' *Lusotopie* 4, pp. 275–284.

14
Conclusion: Decolonisation and Diaspora
John Darwin[*]

Our modern 'globalised' world was the unpredicted and unpredictable outcome of an extraordinary conjuncture. The collapse of the Soviet Union and its 'eastern bloc' clients; the opening of China; the financial deregulation of Western economies; the revolution in communications brought by the Internet and its humbler companion, the ubiquitous containership: all helped to create the unprecedented intensity of commercial and cultural connections between different parts of the world. But this globalised world was also the product of two other transformative changes, the key concerns of this book: decolonisation and diaspora. As earlier chapters have made clear, in the Portuguese case as well as in others, decolonisation and diaspora were not separate phenomena. The meaning of each was partly produced by the other just as the impact of each was magnified by the other. If we fail to observe the geopolitical context that decolonisation created, both the causes and character of our contemporary diasporas will remain deeply puzzling.

Decolonisation is conventionally thought of as a constitutional change: the acquisition of sovereignty by a former dependency. As a global event, it marked the transition from an 'imperial' world order to a 'world of nations'. But this is to take only the narrowest view of a much vaster process and to miss most of its meaning. For the end of the colonial or semicolonial order (where semicolonial describes cases of informal empire) brought about a wide range of 'knock-on' effects. The most obvious of these was the necessity of state building among the administrative fragments that colonialism so often bequeathed to its successor states. Some form of common identity and some sense of shared history were now urgently needed. People of alien origins could now be seen as a nuisance, perhaps even a threat. The expatriate presence in the state apparatus must be swiftly reduced or driven out altogether. The military arm of the state must be unswervingly loyal to the new ruling group, a result best obtained by applying ethnic or kinship criteria to their recruitment and leadership. The state must also control its economic inheritance to prevent both external and internal subversion and appease the demands of its impatient new citizens, especially their land hunger. It must make good its claim to be treated as an equal member of international society and resist any suggestion of deference to its old masters in Europe.

It is obvious that for many former colonies this was a hugely demanding agenda. It is equally obvious that, under actual conditions, its implementation was bound to be crude, violent, and often corrupt. The meaning of decolonisation for many among the liberated peoples was to reduce their security and damage their rights – if not to drive them out altogether. This was one way in which decolonisation was linked to migration. But decolonisation was not simply a matter of state building and its fallout. Nor was it primarily an economic transformation, in which the business interests of outsiders were now closely regulated or expropriated completely by new postcolonial regimes. For decolonisation must also be seen as a cultural, linguistic, and intellectual upheaval of global importance. In this respect, too, decolonisation and diaspora were closely entwined.

Culturally, decolonisation represented rejection of the achievements and values of the imperial world order. The European colonial empires had embodied a clear cultural claim. Other world cultures might be picturesque, exotic, and beautiful, but in terms of social advancement, they were so many dead ends. At best, they were stuck at a moment of cultural attainment that lay far in the past – the common European view of Islamic societies. They lacked the capacity to develop and make progress because the conditions required for social adaptation and evolution were invariably lacking. Only European cultures – and only some of those – contained the critical elements that interacted mysteriously to produce what the reports of the (British) government of India called 'moral and material progress'. Colonial societies had had to be rescued from chaos, stagnation, and even retrogression. Because their own cultures offered no guide to the future or even a sense of what the future might hold (this was the colonialist view), the new, foreign culture must be riveted on to them as far as was possible, politically and financially. (In practice, the concern for stability and the extreme shortage of cash made most colonial regimes very cautious indeed.) Western educated *évolués* who demanded their place in the colonial sun, had little choice but to echo the disparaging view of local cultural achievement that their masters asserted. Indeed, it is likely that they adopted it willingly since in certain vital respects the cultural values (but not necessarily practices) of the colonial state were deeply attractive: above all the stress on the individual and his (rarely *her*) freedom from the tyranny of tradition and custom.

Decolonisation required the public repudiation of this hierarchical (and implicitly racist) view of the relative standing of cultures. In western countries, the end of empire was rapidly followed by the public embrace (usually at an elite level only) of multiculturalism – sometimes in foolish and ignorant ways. Formally, all cultures were equal and (by necessity) incomparable.

Because making comparisons might throw up embarrassing results, it was best to avoid it. In practice, of course, the picture was more complicated. Western opinion went on believing that its political and cultural values (now suitably modified to erase imperialism and racism) represented the best to which humanity could aspire. So did many of the educated in the former colonies. Of course, new forms of periphrasis had to be found to avoid the imputation of racism. Moreover, while the struggle for influence in the ex-colonial world between the Soviet bloc and the West continued, it was wise to be discreet unless would-be clients and allies took cultural offense. But once that constraint was removed, as it was after 1990, the universal application of human rights and market economics was once more proclaimed in the West with quasi-imperial certainty. But this is not the whole story.

Although there was huge variation in the experience of different peoples and states, decolonisation was, almost everywhere, a remarkable moment of cultural 'mobilisation'. There were three main reasons for this. Firstly, when colonies became sovereign states in the hypercompetitive world of the Cold War era, they were exposed to the cultural competition that accompanied Cold War diplomacy. However jejune and exaggerated, a new sense of their place (and importance) in the world was encouraged. New external connections were made, and new opportunities for cultural travel (often as students) created. This was in most places an enormous transition from the cultural isolation that had afflicted all but the wealthiest of colonies. It was a powerful incentive to fashion new ideas of individual and collective identity, to invent a new history, and to 'showcase' in suitably accessible ways the indigenous cultures that became newly fashionable in the multicultural West. Secondly, there was an immediate local incentive to engage in culture building as part of state building. New states needed a history that supplied a usable past and discovered the 'link'(however implausible) between past modes of resistance and the achievement of statehood. They needed new symbols of their national identity: flags, buildings, monuments, ceremonials, and styles of dress. They needed cultural as well as political heroes. Thirdly, however, a more anarchic force was at work. Most colonial states had bundled together peoples of different religions and ethnicity and conspired in arrangements that gave some much more privilege than others. The promise of freedom that decolonisation brought thus had a double meaning in most colonial societies. 'Freedom for the nation' might be the headline. But it was freedom from the oppression of their indigenous fellow citizens that most concerned many newly liberated colonials. In the coming scramble for power in the new state, it was vital to mobilise by every means possible. That meant teaching and preaching the distinct cultural identity of different regions, ethnic groups, and communities and their claim to a share of the expected rewards that freedom would bring. Of course, this was not the policy of newly independent states, least of all that of the Portuguese ex-colonies, where it was a national identity and the creation of 'new men' on the Marxist-Leninist model on which state propaganda insisted. Nevertheless both within many new states, as well as in their external posture, 'identity politics' was the corollary of decolonisation. And just as in Europe's own history, identity politics was the spur to forms of cultural self-realisation, indeed to what might be called a type of cultural democratisation. We will see in a moment how this affected diaspora.

Decolonisation of the kind described here was the product of a particular conjuncture in modern world history between 1945 and the 1990. Diaspora, on the other hand, is a phenomenon as old as human history. Indeed the movement of peoples might be regarded as one of the great driving forces of historical change, along with the movement of goods and ideas. But diaspora has been given a remarkable new impetus in recent times by the effects, often unexpected and unintended, of decolonisation. Indeed, in many ways, the shift from a world of empires to a world of nations might have been expected to slow down migrant movements or stop them altogether. The history of the 19th century suggested in fact that migration was really a consequence of Europe's immense demographic expansion on the one hand and the needs of empire building on the other. Thus, the huge outflow of Europeans – very largely to the United States or to other temperate regions in South America and Australasia – was associated with a particular phase in Europe's demographic history that appeared to have largely ended in the 1930s – until given a vigorous new impetus by the Second World War, which created millions of refugees and displaced persons as well as inflicting a prolonged period of economic austerity on postwar Europe.(Indeed, Portuguese continued to emigrate to Brazil into the 1950s). The other forms of migration – whether the forced migration of slaves from Africa, the flow of indentured labour from China and India, or the free movement of Indians and Chinese into regions of European colonial rule (e.g., Kenya, Uganda, Burma, Malaya, and Trinidad) – seemed to depend upon the needs of colonial rulers or their willingness to sanction the growth of multiethnic colonial societies that were never expected to achieve national self-determination. By contrast a world of nations seemed to promise demographic stability or fixity. Once the necessary population transfers required to create 'mono-ethnic' nations had been completed, there would be little reason for further large-scale migrations. The planned economic development of ex-colonial territories might have been expected to reinforce this new demographic stability. The provision of infrastructure in previously backward regions and the creation of more diversified economies that offered industrial employment was expected to soak up the rural unemployment that had plagued many colonial societies in the Depression-hit 1930s.

Of course, this still left great uncertainty about the likely fate of the 'settler' communities in colonial territories, where the migrants formed a sometimes very small minority of the overall population. The expatriate Europeans who had provided administrative service or performed technical tasks in ex-colonial societies usually had no roots in the country and could be retained on contract or sent home in retirement, as the case might be. But for settlers who were born in the colony, who had come to settle permanently, who owned immoveable property such as farmland, and had children who had been brought up and educated there it was a different matter entirely. As late as the 1950s, it was widely assumed that the pace of political change would be slow in colonial Africa especially. Even when it began to speed up, schemes for power sharing and partnership reflected the assumption that settler communities would stay on, that their property would be safe, and that their economic contribution to postcolonial development would be valued – since in many cases they provided the bulk of the export commodities that earned foreign exchange.

However, these sanguine expectations were not borne out by events. In the Congo, the violence that accompanied independence led to an exodus of the Belgian population. Although some settler-farmers remained behind in Kenya after independence in 1963, their numbers dwindled, and provision was made to buy out their holdings in the so-called White Highlands. 'When I was in Kenyaah' began to be heard on hotel verandahs in Durban. There was a similar pattern among the white miners in Zambia, where independence arrived with the breakup of the white-ruled Central African Federation. The greatest exodus of all was that of the *pieds-noirs* from Algeria after 1962, perhaps one million altogether. In the 'white South' of Africa, white flight was delayed. In the case of Zimbabwe, although some whites had left during the long guerrilla war of the 1970s, it was only after majority-rule independence in 1980 that the white community began to shrink rapidly. In South Africa, where Afrikaans-speaking whites (some 60% of the white population) had no other homeland and were deeply attached to their Afrikaner nationhood, where a complex industrial economy contained many niches where whites could maintain a high living standard, and where the postcolonial regime made a virtue of racial reconciliation, there was no dramatic decline in the white population, but perhaps a gradual attrition over time.

But these movements producing minidiasporas of white Africans – sometimes back to their national homelands, sometimes to different but congenial destinations such as Australia, Canada, or the United States – form only one part of the migrational activity that decolonisation induced. Vastly greater in scale were three other sources of mobile humanity. Firstly, to an extent that those who looked forward to decolonisation had never envisaged, there was a tide of (nonwhite) refugees. The consolidation of new states, or the violent circumstances in which the transition to independence occurred, incited much ethnic conflict. The dependence of new regimes upon the support of one ethnic group and the identification of others with the ancien régime and its colonial masters were obvious sources of tension.

Where this translated into the partisan control of public goods or the harassment of communities who were not represented in the ruling group, exile or flight was likely to follow. Many postcolonial regimes quickly relapsed into authoritarian models of government. Opposition had to be carried on from a safe haven abroad. Sometimes, of course, what actually happened was an uncontrolled population transfer: in the Indian case, between the three different spaces of postcolonial mainland South Asia. Sometimes safety lay over the border. Palestinians were squeezed into Jordan or moved to other Arab states. Zimbabweans oppressed by the Mugabe's regime fled south into South Africa. But in many more cases, those driven out had no neighbouring refuge. Instead they created diaspora communities wherever they could. Catholic Vietnamese found their way to Quebec. East African Asians who were driven out of Uganda went (largely) to Britain. Congolese went to Belgium or France.

Secondly, to an extent that the policy makers never imagined, many new states displayed symptoms of breakdown. In some, such as Somalia and Sierra Leone, the eventual breakdown was extreme. In many others it was partial but sufficient to threaten the survival of large populations. Directly, this might be because of rebellions and wars such as those fought in Ethiopia, Nigeria, and the Congo. Indirectly, the breakdown of settled authority might bring economic collapse or the disappearance of infrastructure and vital public services (in health, for example), whose effect was to destroy even the basis for a subsistence economy. Long before that, those with transferable skills or the resources and contacts to arrange emigration were likely to find ways of removing themselves and their families from places of danger or dearth. Needless to say, however, these were conditions that did not arise only in the wake of decolonisation. The flight of Cubans, Iraqis, Iranians, and Afghans reveals a much wider pattern of forced diaspora when political oppression and economic disaster converged.

Thirdly, of course, there were vast population movements that were really economic migrations. Perhaps these should be seen as mainly the product of change in the global economy and the new opportunities created by economic globalisation. Thus, the astonishing growth of Internet technology – a key component of globalisation – has sucked many Chinese and Indians into California's Bay Area, just as the oil industry has drawn Pakistanis into the Gulf. What is the link, we might ask, between these flows of people and decolonisation? There are really two. Firstly, the cultural and normative aspects of decolonisation destroyed the moral basis for the racial exclusion of emigrant peoples. In old settler societies such as Australia, New Zealand, and Canada (a category in which the United States should also be included), it was no longer possible by the 1970s at latest to exclude on the basis of race. Indeed, a strong counterclaim was advanced for the moral and cultural benefits of admitting very different communities. It was also the case that the old imperial connection of nationally shared citizenship made it difficult to refuse entry to at least some categories of the formally colonised. So, quite unexpectedly, far from increasing the separation between mother country and colony, decolonisation quite often produced the opposite consequence – although, interestingly, not in the Portuguese case, with the exception of Cape Verde. Secondly, decolonisation in its cultural aspect helped to reinforce the diasporic ties between those who migrated and those who stayed at home. Why was this?

We have already begun to see why. If decolonisation had necessitated the fashioning of new national identities, it had also encouraged the cultural expression of innumerable 'sub-national' ones. This cultural expression had to be portable; that is, it had to be accessible and comprehensible to outsiders – whether local or international – if the economic and political claims it embodied were to stand any chance. It had to be literate (or suitably visual) and use a more or less standardised language-form. It had to incorporate some understanding of the modern technological world; a pristine traditional culture was of no use in the business of claim-making. Hence, vast numbers of people previously equipped only with a highly localised culture and an uncodified language without grammar or literature quickly acquired the basic techniques of preserving a distinct cultural identity in an alien environment. An infrastructure of culture building – religious associations, newsletters, cheap forms of literature, music, radio, and television – sprang up to promote it. It was easy for these to follow the migrant wherever he or she went. Far from encouraging those who migrated to adopt local customs and culture, this infrastructure relied upon promoting the opposite. More to the point, it played another critical role in shaping diasporic behaviour. Maintaining the cultural connection with the original homeland allowed the members of migrant communities to move easily to and fro, to extend family influence through new marriage connections in the homeland, and to add new recruits to their migrant establishment. Diaspora and decolonisation have thus interacted to create a degree of cultural diversity within the host states that was entirely unexpected and is (almost certainly) without historical parallel.

This is the larger background against which we should set the history of Portugal's imperial migrations, diasporas, and postimperial connections, fascinatingly chronicled in this book. One of the most striking features of Portuguese colonialism was the lateness of its settler migration, especially to Africa. In 1900, the white population of Angola and Mozambique was perhaps 15,000 to 20,000 – less than two per cent of that of South Africa's at the same period. The Portuguese state controlled out-migration much more rigorously than the British, partly because it feared the creation of new 'Brazils'. (the British Brazil – the United States – absorbed some 60% of British migration up to 1900, but no effort was made – nor could have been made – to restrict this great flow). Not until 1962 (the year of the white exodus from

Algeria) were Portuguese actually allowed to move freely into any part of the 'Portuguese economic space', even if the constitutional reform of 1951 and the Lei Organica do Ultramar of 1953 had already unified the national territory. The scale of the movement was certainly impressive; by 1973, the white population of Angola and Mozambique had surged up to 500,000, although this figure includes the military personnel that were sent there. But lateness was not peculiar to Portugal. The white population of the two Rhodesias (today's Zimbabwe and Zambia) also rose very rapidly after 1945, reflecting the boom in their extractive economies. In both cases, therefore, in the Rhodesias and the Portuguese colonies, the great bulk of white settlement was a very recent phenomenon. It was also heavily urban. We might be tempted to think that both these characteristics increased the likelihood of a rapid departure once the political conditions on which economic and physical security depended began to collapse. In that sense, there was little difference in the fate of white settler minorities in the British and Portuguese Empires. The peculiarity of South Africa, where (as noted above) the change in the white community's position has been much less dramatic, lay partly in its much more developed economy but also in the sovereign independence enjoyed by the dominant white nation practically from 1910, formally from Status of the Union Act in 1934.

Nor were the Portuguese colonies unusual in attracting non-European migrants such as the Ismailis and Chinese described in earlier chapters. Indians and Chinese migrated to British colonies both freely and as indentured labour. Indeed, Ismaili communities could be found in British East Africa, that is, Kenya and Uganda. The Ismailis form a specially fascinating case since they owed their primary allegiance to an expatriate religious hierarch, the Aga Khan, the descendant of one of Iran's great provincial notables, but by the mid-20th century usually resident in Europe. The Aga's authority over Ismailis worldwide and his right to levy a tax on his followers had been confirmed in 1864 by a British court in Bombay. Hence the status of Ismailis in Portugal's colonies was mediated by the 'special relationship' of the Aga Khan with the government in Lisbon; according to Nicole Khouri and Joana Pereira Leite, their early evacuation in 1972 was kept secret so as not to embarrass the Portuguese government. The Ismailis existed as a distinct settler or sojourner community. The Chinese in Mozambique managed their relations with the colonial administration through the Chinese Athletic Club in Beira. (It's intriguing to remember that the bastion of British Uitlander resistance to the Afrikaner government in 1890s Transvaal was the Wanderers' Sports Club). When Portuguese rule ended, the Chinese left quickly – not for Portugal but Brazil. The Goans, as described by Margret Frenz, also survived (in this case in British East Africa) as a separate group. They combined an increasing identification with British rule, choosing to become British subjects, with a preference for retaining a more than vestigial link with Portugal. They mediated their relations with the British authorities through the Goan consuls in East Africa. But perhaps the most fascinating group were the Cape Verdeans. As Alexander Keese shows, the metropolitan Portuguese regarded the Cape Verdeans with suspicion, fearing an uprising in the archipelago. As an intermediary group in the African colonies, their loyalty was valuable but also suspected. In fact, with few exceptions, they remained loyal to the empire. There is an interesting parallel with Britain's African colonies. The extension of British influence along the coast of West Africa had largely depended on the Sierra Leone Krios, many of them freed slaves of Yoruba origin who had been brought to the colony. The Krio elite was Anglophone, Christianised, and often highly educated. It created a merchant and missionary diaspora and sometimes called itself the 'black English'. It saw the construction of a British West Africa as a great opportunity and expected to be treated as partners and allies by the new British rulers. But the British resolved to govern their new inland empire after 1890 through so-called traditional elites and indirect rule. They sidelined the Krios and disparaged their claims. The result was the gradual disenchantment of the Krio with their English identity that promised so much and yielded so little and the turn towards an anticolonial nationalism that swept along coastal British West Africa after 1945.

But what of the white settlers who left Mozambique and Angola after 1975 (in Angola and Mozambique the white population had slumped to some 5,000 and 2,000, respectively, by the mid-1990s before rebounding sharply in recent years)? As Claudia Castelo points out, many of those who had gone to Angola saw it as much more dynamic and modern than their Portuguese homeland. This has its parallel in the attitude of Britons who went to the Rhodesias, South Africa, and Australia after 1945, when Britain itself seemed depressed and exhausted by war and austerity. It chimed with an older tradition in the white settlement colonies that saw them as more democratic and open societies than class-ridden Britain. So while some Portuguese who left Mozambique and Angola went back to Portugal and perhaps thereafter elsewhere in Europe (as well as to Brazil), others chose to go to South Africa, nearer and still – in the 1970s – an apparently successful economy. As Clive Glaser shows, by the 1990s persons of Portuguese descent formed some 10 per cent of the white population, although some were Madeirans and others had come directly from Portugal. In many ways South Africa was an obvious choice, as it was for former (white) Rhodesians. It more nearly resembled the colonial societies from which they had fled than anywhere else on the planet. But it was far from ideal. For the Portuguese as foreigners could not hope for public service employment. They were Catholics in a largely Protestant white community. They were unused to the rigidity with which apartheid was enforced in South Africa. And among South African whites, Portuguese were held in low social esteem, partly because of the widespread belief that many nominally white Portuguese were in fact of mixed race.

The second grand theme with which this book is concerned is the post-imperial survival of Portugal's influence: the idea of *Lusofonia*. It was hardly surprising that Portuguese governments and other Portuguese interests should have wished to maintain a special relationship with the former colonial territories. Both Britain and France had sought to do the same, mainly to prop up their claims to world power long after the economic and strategic resources for such a grandiose role had vanished. For Portugal, of course, world power ambitions were hardly appropriate, with or without a colonial empire. But there was an obvious utility in laying claim to a zone of exceptional influence. It eased the pain of imperial loss among some parts of public opinion. It might offer some commercial benefits to Portuguese trade and investment in the ruthlessly competitive world of globalisation. It raised the profile and enhanced the prestige of Portuguese language and culture. And once Portugal entered the European Union, it allowed Lisbon to claim (like Spain, France, the Netherlands, Belgium, and Britain) that it brought to Brussels a set of special connections between an expansive Europe and the non-European world. Since the European Union itself has (carefully veiled) quasi-imperial ambitions, this was not entirely fanciful.

It was obvious, however, that the special connection could not rely on a shared political outlook or a common political tradition, let alone recognition that the Portuguese head of state had a quasi-constitutional relationship with the former colonial territories. Here the contrast with the British idea of a commonwealth is striking. The core of the British Commonwealth was a group of former white colonies; in three out of four, the British queen remains head of state (as she does in several independent Caribbean nations). In the rest of the Commonwealth, where republics are the rule, the queen is styled Head of the Commonwealth – a personal though not hereditary status. Although much abused in reality, all the countries of the Commonwealth claim to respect the political values of individual freedom and representative government derived (sometimes obscurely) from their colonial connection with Britain. Of course, the original notion that the Commonwealth would serve as a vehicle for British influence in the world had all but collapsed by the late 1960s. Britain was too poor and too weak to provide the economic and strategic incentives that had once been expected to cement its postcolonial relationships in Asia and Africa. Yet the Commonwealth survived as a global association because its member countries (some 50 of them) found it a useful arena in which to seek influence and friendship as much with each other as with Britain.

The Portuguese case was bound to be different. The breakup of the empire created six new states – Angola, Mozambique, Guinea-Bissau, Cape Verde, São Tomé, and (after liberation from Indonesia) East Timor. What could hold them together in a globalised world? *Lusofonia* was predicated on a shared language and culture. But, as Michel Cahen points out with some vehemence, this was at best a delusion. In Cape Verde, no one speaks Portuguese.

In Mozambique less than 7 per cent of the population used it as their mother-tongue. Nor did the fact of having Portuguese as the official language of state promote any sense of shared cultural origins or a common history. Moreover, Guinea-Bissau, Cape Verde, and São Tomé became members of Francophonie, and Mozambique joined the Commonwealth before joining CPLP (the association of Portuguese-speaking countries). It seems wise to conclude with Michel Cahen that for all these states, their connection with Portugal is only one 'space' of several in which to conduct their external relations. Of course, although their shared interests are somewhat more evident, the same could be said of the Commonwealth countries.

Perhaps the real message of the chapters in this book is how much more there is to learn about the various migrant communities for whom empire in some form was an opportunity and a shelter. In the British case also, we have barely begun to probe the complex identities of superficially similar colonial populations. A huge work remains to be done on the origins and development of the wide range of minorities – European, Asian, African, and American (if we include Afro-Brazilians) – who filled critical spaces in colonial societies and economies and for whom decolonisation was such a traumatic event. For reasons described in the earlier part of this chapter, more and more of these stories are coming to light because of the ways in which decolonisation and diaspora have meshed and converged. In all the great empires (including the Soviet Russian) many more remain to be told. But for Portugal at least an excellent start has been made in the chapters of this book.

Note

* I am most grateful to the editors for their comments and advice.

Index

25 April 1974, see Carnation Revolution

abolition, l79, 125n1, 205, 249
abraço de Lusaka (Lusaka embrace), 278
Academia do Bacalhau, 228
Acto Colonial, see Colonial Act
Addis Ababa, 156
administration, 6, 14, 23n8, 75, 77, 107, 111, 118, 119, 120, 121, 129, 130, 133, 134, 137, 138, 139, 140, 141, 144n5, 152, 155, 156, 161, 170, 195–196, 198, 199, 205, 206, 208n4, 240, 242, 246–247, 267, 270–271, 272–274, 305, 323
 see also British administration, British colonial administration, central administration, civil administration, *Estado Novo* administration, Frelimo administration, local administration, native administration, Portuguese administration, public administration
administrator, 6, 86, 129, 130, 131, 137, 138, 142, 143, 170, 198, 199, 222, 313n32
 see also British administrator, Cape Verdean administrator, colonial officer
Afonso X, 99n4
Africa, 6, 8, 11, 13, 14, 15, 16, 17, 19, 24n17, 42, 45, 48, 57, 58, 59, 60, 63, 64, 66, 72, 74, 75, 79, 81, 82, 83, 85, 86, 88, 92, 93, 94, 97, 98, 100, 107, 108, 109, 110, 111, 112, 113, 114, 118, 120, 121, 122, 123, 125, 130, 133, 138, 168, 172, 176, 177, 178, 179, 181, 182, 184, 185n13, 193, 194, 195, 196, 197, 199, 200, 203, 205, 206, 207, 223, 239, 240, 241, 250, 252, 254, 265, 266, 267, 268, 269, 270, 271, 272, 275, 278, 279–281, 298, 299, 300, 304, 305, 307, 309, 310, 312n29, 319, 320, 322, 324, 325

África nossa (our Africa), 298, 299, 309
Africa of French expression, 299
African, 4, 6, 8, 12, 16, 17, 18, 20, 23n8, 24n18, 24–25n20, 31, 39, 40n36, 41, 45, 52, 53, 57, 58, 61, 68, 70, 72, 73, 74, 75, 76, 77, 78, 79–83, 84, 85, 86, 87, 88, 89, 90, 91, 92, 93, 94, 95, 96, 97, 98, 99n2, 99n5, 100n20, 107, 108, 109, 121, 122, 124, 126n15, 126n17, 129, 130, 132, 133, 138, 139, 142, 143, 150, 151, 153, 155, 159, 160, 161, 162, 163, 170, 171, 173, 179, 199, 203, 208n10, 223, 247, 253, 256, 257, 258n7, 266, 267, 269, 270, 275, 279, 280, 281n2, 289, 290, 298, 299, 300, 308, 320, 326
 see also Africans in Brazil, Central African, Luso-African, Sino-African, South African, White African
African American, 288
African authenticity, 298, 300
African colonies, 6, 16, 24n13, 53, 58, 97, 98, 108, 109, 200, 267, 277, 324
African élite, 95, 151, 163, 286
African former colonies, 299
African immigrants, 64, 67n125, 74, 96, 98, 99, 101
African language, 171, 303, 304, 312n25, 313n34
African Liberation Day, 293n21
African Liberation Support Committee, 293n21
African nationalism, 152, 159, 163
African society, 17, 24n20, 142, 219, 220, 224, 230, 232, 298, 305
 see also South African society
African woman, 40n36, 72, 92, 99n4, 247, 267
Africanness, 289
 see also blackness
Africans in Brazil, 8, 24–25n20, 39, 64
Afrikaans, 218, 229, 230
Afrikaans-speaking whites, 221, 320
Afrikaners, 216, 219, 221

327

328 Index

Afrique d'expression française (Africa of French expression), 299
Afro-Asian, 247
Afro-Brazilian, 58, 307, 326
  see also Black Brazilian
Afro-Brazilianity, 307
Afrocentrism, 288
Afro-Luso-Brazilian, 309
Aga Khan, 18, 168, 169, 173, 176, 177, 178, 179, 180–181, 185n13, 185n15, 186n22, 187n37, 187n38, 323
agriculture, 48, 54, 139, 200
Agualusa, José Eduardo, 276
Agudas, 8, 58, 307, 313n32
Albuquerque, Afonso de, 305
Albuquerque, Manuel Francisco de (consul in Zanzibar), 200, 201
Albuquerque, Mouzinho de, 81
Alegre, Costa, 77
Alegre, Manuel, 293n23
Algarve, 50, 76, 99n5
Algeria, 19, 107, 121, 267, 320, 323
Alto-Molocué, 151, 155, 156
Álvares, Afonso, 77
Amaral, Serafin Bruno (father), 250
Amaral and Co., 159
Ameal, João, 81
American Board Mission, 151–153, 158
American Presbyterians, 153
American whaling industry, 56
Anderson, Perry, 3, 4, 5, 268
Andrade, Freire de, 271
Andrade, Joaquim da Rocha Pinto, 141
Andrade, Mário [Pinto] de, 95, 132, 133, 152, 235n32, 260n31
Anglophony, 309, 324
Angoche, 169, 170
Angola, 5, 6, 8, 11, 15, 16, 17, 18, 20, 22, 24n19, 39, 57, 58, 61, 63, 76, 85, 87, 93, 107–126, 130, 133, 138, 139, 140, 142, 145n22, 198, 202, 222, 223, 225, 228, 251, 254, 260n32, 299, 300, 301, 302, 309, 322, 324, 325
Angolan, 14, 16, 58, 65, 67, 86, 93, 98, 109, 114, 120, 122, 133, 138, 139, 140, 141, 142, 143, 205, 223, 224, 225, 226, 250, 273, 275, 288, 299, 300, 301, 303
Angolan civil war, 301
animalised, 76, 90

Anjuna, 200, 201, 209n18
Annobon Island, 313n34
anthropophagi, 91
Anthropophagus, 82, 86, 87, 88, 90, 91, 93
anthropophagy, 84, 87, 88, 90, 91–92, 93–94, 100n14
anticlericalism, 158
anticolonial revolt, 131, 140, 143
anti-salazarist, 92, 95
April 25, 1974, *see* Carnation Revolution
Arab nationalism, 248
Arabic, 75
archetypes, 74, 77, 81, 90
Argentina, 42, 49–50, 50n63, 53
Arrentela, 288
articulation of modes of production, 2
artisans, 139, 215, 220, 221, 222
Ásia nossa (our Asia), 299–302
assimilados, 14, 126n15, 126n17, 208n16, 249, 266
  see also assimilated
assimilated, 7, 17, 73, 87, 93, 126n15, 216, 266, 304
Associação Chinesa (Chinese Association), 242, 244, 247, 248
Associação Cultural Chinesa do Paraná (Cultural Chinese Association of Parana), 240, 253
Associação da Colónia Portuguesa, 227
Atlantic Islands, 33, 38, 52
Atlantic World, 36, 37, 45
Atlético Chinês (Tung Hua Athletic Club), 239, 241, 242, 245, 246, 251, 254, 257
Australia, 18, 107, 240, 241, 252, 255, 306, 320, 321, 324
authoritarian modernization, 304
autochthonous, 72, 257
autonomism, 13, 14, 122
autonomy, 5, 22, 73, 85, 228
  see also economic autonomy, political autonomy
Aveiro, 118, 126n19
Azorean, 56, 70
Azorean communities, 53
Azorean emigration, 53
Azorean immigration, 34n14
Azoreanisation, 68
Azores, 53, 54, 56, 57, 83, 233n5

Index 329

Baartman, Saartaje, 83
Bacongo, 16, 303
Baixa de Cassange, 93, 138
Baixa de Cassanje, *see* Baixa de Cassange
Bakongo, *see* Bacongo
Bandeira, Sá da, 79
Bandeirante, 39
Bandung, 94, 248
Bandung conference, 94, 248
Banian, 184n1
Bantu, 313n34
Bantu language, 303
barbarism, 92
Bardez, 195
Barreto, Honório, 77
Bastide, Roger, 100n12
Batepá, 93
Beira (Mozambican city), 24n14, 120, 122, 126n16, 144n14, 152, 180, 239–260, 323
Beira (Portugal region), 8
Belgian, 303, 320
Belgian Congo, 114, 125n14
Belgium, 267, 308, 310, 321, 325
Bengal, 8, 9, 59, 60, 302, 306
Benguela, 122, 130
Benin, 58, 58n89, 307, 313n32
Berg, Henrique, 155
Berlin Conference, 79, 150, 271, 272, 281n7
Bissagos Islands, 308
Bissau, 93, 240, 300
Bissau-Guineans, 24n19, 86, 132, 133, 134, 135, 138, 142, 277, 312n23
black, 9, 13, 17, 24n20, 60, 72, 74, 75, 76, 77, 78, 80, 81, 82, 83, 85, 86, 87, 89, 90, 97, 99, 109, 114, 115, 121, 151, 152, 172, 186n23, 225, 234n25, 269, 288, 291n1, 298, 311n6
Black African, 82, 91, 126
black Atlantic, 265
black blood, 78
Black Brazilian, 311n6
see also Afro-Brazilian
black colour, 75
black consciousness, 288
black diaspora, 9, 12
black elite, 150, 151
Black English, 324
Black Fernanda, *see* Fernanda do Vale

black immigrant, 225
black intellectual, 152, 163n6
black labour, 109
black majority107, 222
black migrant, 226, 275
black people, 151
black population, 60
black Portuguese, 12, 54
Black Power Movement, 289
black race, 80
black rule, *see* black majority
black skin, 88
see also skin colour
black slave, 17, 24n20, 76, 99n5, 311n6
blackness, 12, 88, 219, 300
Bloemfontein, 217, 224
Boaventura de Sousa Santos, 3, 277
Bocage, Barbosa du, 77
Bombay, 184n2, 195, 200, 204, 205, 305, 323
Boror (*prazo*), 160
Boror, 150, 159, 160, 161
Boror Company, 150, 159–161
Bovay, Gustave, 159
Boxer, Charleson, 33
Braga, 44, 69
Bragança, 118
Brasileiros, *see* returnees
Brásio, António, 88
Brava, 54, 139
Bravas, 54
Brazil, 6, 8, 13, 15, 17, 18, 20, 22, 24n20, 25n23, 34, 35, 36, 37, 38, 39, 40, 45, 46, 47, 48, 49, 52, 53, 59, 67, 68, 69, 70, 86, 87, 108, 109, 110, 111, 112, 113, 119, 126n17, 179, 197, 208n9, 216, 239–261, 267, 298, 302, 307, 309, 311n6, 319, 322, 323, 324
Brazilian, 8, 16, 17, 21, 22, 39, 45, 46, 47, 48, 49, 58, 61, 64, 68, 69, 69n136, 122, 253, 256, 288, 298, 309, 310, 311n6
Brazilian Americans, 10, 311
Brazilian communities, 69, 275, 310
Brazilian diaspora, 69
Brazilian emigrants, 61
see also Brazilian Migrants
Brazilian emigration, 68
Brazilian empire, 108

330   Index

Brazilian immigrants, 10, 13, 15, 45, 46, 47, 48, 64, 67, 68, 70
 see also Brazilian Migrants
Brazilian immigration, see Brazilian migration, Brazilian immigrants
Brazilian intelligentsia, 298
Brazilian leaders, 298
Brazilian migrants, 69, 275
Brazilian migration, 49, 69, 70
Brazilian missionary, 155
Brazilian nationalism, 39
Brazilian politicians, 21
Britain, 5, 6, 194, 196, 198, 199, 267, 324, 325
British, 3, 4, 6, 23n6, 59, 123, 168, 169, 170, 194, 195, 196–200, 202, 203, 204, 205, 206, 220, 270, 271, 272, 273, 304, 305, 312n29, 317, 322, 323, 324, 325, 326
British Africa, 312n29
British administrator, 199
British (colonial) administration, 205, 206, 208n4, 305
British colonisation, 168, 169
British East Africa, 15, 59, 185n13, 193–210, 323
British Empire, 3, 15, 19, 193, 194, 199, 200, 203, 206, 207
British India, 194, 196, 199, 305
British Indians, 168
British officials, 195
British Raj, 199
brotherhood, 9, 76, 248, 249
Brown Portuguese, 54, 310
 see also Cape Verdean American
Brubaker, Rogers, 265
brutality, 81, 90, 93, 95, 162, 269, 270
Buenos Aires, 38, 42, 42n46
Bull, John, 82
burghers (of Sri Lanka), 302, 306
Burlin, Natalie Curtis, 151
Burma, 319

Cabral, Amílcar, 95, 99n6, 132, 133–134, 135, 136, 260n31, 279, 290, 293n23, 293n26
Cabral, Luís, 132, 134
Cabral, Vasco, 95
Cachéu, 99n6
Caetano, Marcelo, 222

caixeiro, 46, 47
California, 53, 54, 56, 58, 321
California gold rush, 56
Cameron, Verney Lovett, 272
Camões, Luís de, 32
Canada, 53, 56, 57, 62, 63, 68, 240, 241, 252, 305, 321
 see also Luso-Canadian
Canarins, 59
cannibal, 91
cannibalism, 92
cannibalistic acts, 94
cannibalistic practices, 90
cantinas, see retail stores
Canton, 244, 250
Cape Town, 213, 214, 216, 217, 224
Cape Verde, 20, 52, 54, 55, 64, 67, 86, 96, 130, 131, 132, 134, 136, 137, 139, 140, 142, 143n2, 144n14, 145n16, 145n17, 146n34, 303, 304, 309, 313n38, 322, 325, 326
Cape Verdean, 10, 14, 15, 16, 22, 24n18, 52, 53, 54, 55, 58, 65, 66, 70, 86, 97, 98, 101n21, 129–146, 275, 286, 308, 324
Cape Verdean administrator, 129, 131, 138, 143
 see also Cape Verdeans officials
Cape Verdean Americans, 10, 310
Cape Verdean emigration, 65, 138
Cape Verdean migration, 15, 52, 58, 66–67, 97, 98
Cape Verdeans officials, 129, 136, 138
 see also Cape Verdean administrator
Cape Verdeans settlers, 131, 138, 139, 140, 142, 143
capital, 13, 109, 119, 124, 126n21, 136, 154, 158, 159, 169, 171, 172, 175, 240, 293, 299, 305
capitalism, 2, 4, 5, 16, 44, 150, 157, 159, 304
capitalist world system, 4
Capuchins, 149
caravels, 299, 310
Cardoso, Luis, 276
Caribbean, 19, 50, 240, 266, 325
caricature, 78, 87, 93, 100n10, 269
Carnation Revolution, 4, 98, 125n2, 136, 173, 175, 178, 179, 186n23, 251, 252, 277, 279, 280, 287, 310, 311n14

Casa da Madeira, 227
Casa dos Estudantes do Império, 133, 144n6
Casamance, 302, 312n23
cashew nuts, 170, 172
caste, 10, 168, 185n7, 199
Castile, 4, 99n4
Catholic, 6, 7, 51, 56, 59, 64, 65, 66, 75, 149, 150, 157, 158, 163, 170, 195, 197, 198, 203, 205, 206, 207, 220, 226, 227, 231, 245, 250, 301, 306, 324
Catholic Church, 6, 51, 157, 158, 163, 226, 227, 250, 306
Catholic Goans, 59, 64
Catholicism, 7, 56, 149, 195, 206, 207, 250, 306
Cavaleiro da Ordem de Christo, 201
CEI, see Casa dos Estudantes do Império
Cela, 110
central administration, 130
Central African, 39
charter companies, 6, 108
Chee Kung Tong (Clube Chinês), 239, 241–242, 243, 247–249
Chiloane Island, 240
China, 240, 241, 246, 247, 249, 250, 253, 257, 259n12, 259n27, 319
Chinese, 11, 14, 15, 18, 21, 22, 60, 239–261
Chinese Athletic Club in Beira, 241, 242, 245, 257, 323
Chinese Christian, 245
Chinese Club, see Clube Chinês
Chinese nationalism, 241
Chinese School, 242, 243, 244, 248
Christian, 208n4, 245, 306
Christian anticolonialism, 301
Christian ideology, 3
Christian marriage, 75
Christian name, 75
Christian Protestant (missions), see Protestant mission
Christianised, 324
Christianity, 198, 306
Chuabos, 159
Chullage, 286, 287, 288, 289, 291
church, 6, 51, 149, 151, 153–155, 156, 157, 158, 162, 163, 206, 214, 226–247, 250, 306, 313n36

citizens, 20, 31, 61, 112, 122, 124, 129, 139, 193, 194, 196, 199, 200, 202, 203, 207, 208n16, 244, 246, 248, 249, 250, 252, 256, 266, 275, 288, 316, 318
citizenship, 121, 144n3, 194, 203, 207, 257, 287, 290, 322
civil administration, 111, 120
civil society, 299
civilisation, 21, 32, 77, 80, 81, 82, 83, 84, 86, 92, 110, 159, 249, 259n27, 270, 276, 311n7
civilisational, 75, 79, 82, 83, 86, 92, 276
  see also intercivilisational
civilised, 81, 83, 86, 94, 129, 271, 274
civilising, 85, 92, 111, 266
civilising action, 92
civilising effort, 92
civilising endeavour, 82
civilising factor, 109
civilising ideal, 247
civilising mission, 79, 83, 86, 92, 266
civilising worlds, 247
civility, 97
clandestine immigration, 44, 51
classification, 9, 72–74, 77, 80, 90
Clube Chinês (Chee Kung Tong), 239, 241, 243, 250, 255
clubs, 123, 223, 224, 227, 228, 229, 230, 239–261, 323
Coimbra, 118, 246
colonial, see ex-colonial, first colonial age, lusocolonial, semicolonial
Colonial Act, 13, 111, 209n31, 274
colonial administration, 23n8, 92, 119, 121, 130, 134, 137, 141, 152, 156, 170, 208n4, 240, 242, 246, 271, 272, 273, 305, 323
colonial army, 222
colonial capitalism, 150, 157, 159
colonial city, 195
colonial communities, 7
colonial companies, see charter companies, colonial enterprises
colonial culture, 81, 121
colonial domination, 72, 79, 107
colonial emigration, 17
colonial empire, 2, 31, 36, 60, 129, 130, 131, 135, 143, 240, 317, 325
colonial enterprises, 75, 159, 161

colonial exhibition, 83, 84, 85, 86, 100n13
colonial family, 222
colonial government, 15, 111, 133, 136, 193, 195, 196, 199, 204, 209n19, 271
colonial hegemony, 290
  see also hegemony, economic hegemony, imperial hegemony
colonial ideology, 83, 290
colonial imaginary, 249, 293n23, 298–299, 300
colonial immigrant, see immigrants
colonial language, 303, 304, 306, 312n25
colonial legacy, 312
colonial memory, 99
colonial migration, 19, 24n18, 107, 109, 111, 118–120
colonial minority, 17
colonial model, 23n3
colonial modernity, 255, 274
colonial mythology, 79
colonial narrative, 244, 275
colonial nation, 269
Colonial Office, 199
Colonial officers, 14, 15, 133, 136, 139, 271, 272
  see also administrator
colonial officials, see colonial officers
colonial order, 316
colonial past, 20
colonial people, 16
colonial period, 3, 14, 35, 64n113, 70, 72, 150, 157, 186n23, 243, 253, 259n12, 307, 311n17, 313n34
  see also first colonial age
colonial plan, 82, 84
colonial police, 137
colonial policy, 81, 172, 203, 246
colonial population, 7, 14, 16, 18, 326
colonial power, see colonial rule
colonial racism, see racism
colonial reality, 72, 79, 83, 92, 112, 143
colonial regime, see colonial rule
colonial relationship, 11, 266, 275
colonial representation, 79, 81
colonial rule, 86, 108, 124, 129, 131, 132, 135, 136, 137, 141, 144n14, 173, 182, 216, 259n12, 267, 268, 274, 281n5, 304, 317, 319

colonial science, 79
colonial settler, 17, 61, 170, 223, 253
colonial societies, 17, 22, 24n20, 35, 61, 107, 108, 122, 169, 172, 173, 175, 298, 317, 318, 319, 320, 324, 326
colonial state, 132, 136, 138, 142, 143, 200, 274, 317, 318
colonial struggle, see colonial wars
colonial subjects, 14, 15, 31, 59, 143, 194, 199, 278, 318
colonial system, 121, 123, 130, 142, 143
colonial territories, 20, 58, 319, 325
  see also colonies, colonised territories
colonial urban social groups, 73
colonial urbanism, 99
colonial wars, 24n17, 92–94, 95, 98, 112, 118, 124, 125n2, 154, 156, 158, 161, 178, 182, 203, 220, 246, 267, 278
colonial women, 35
colonialism, 3, 4, 5, 6–7, 14, 16–17, 19, 60, 73, 83, 93, 95, 108, 110, 123, 149–164, 168, 268, 269–272, 277, 288, 290, 298, 308, 316, 322
  see also Portuguese colonialism, subaltern colonialism, ultracolonialism
colonialist, 96, 109, 124, 157, 291, 293n26, 294n30
coloniality, 288, 291
colonies, 1, 3, 4, 6, 7, 8, 13, 14, 15, 16, 19, 20, 21, 22, 53, 58, 73, 78, 83, 84, 85, 86, 87, 93, 94, 95, 97, 98, 107–109, 110–112, 113–118, 120, 121, 122, 123, 124, 138, 186n23, 194, 197, 198, 199, 202, 223, 251, 266, 267, 268, 273, 277, 289, 299, 300, 313, 317, 318, 323, 324
  see also colonial territories, settler territories
colonisation, 14, 18, 32, 35, 57, 75, 83, 86, 94, 108, 109, 110, 111, 150, 160, 172, 293, 298, 305, 307, 308, 311n6, 313n34
  see also British colonisation, direct colonisation, first age of colonisation, five centuries of colonisation, Portuguese colonisation, settler colonisation, white colonisation

Index 333

colonisation policy, 114
colonised, 1, 2, 3, 6, 73, 81, 82, 87,
    281n5, 301, 322
    see also overcolonised, subcolonised
colonised cities, 120
colonised communities, 200
colonised condition, 149
colonised people, 3, 7, 14, 16, 17, 86,
    109, 311n6
colonised people, 7, 14, 16, 76, 86,
    109, 311n6
colonised population, 19
colonised societies, 17, 18
colonised subjects, 7
colonised territories, 182
    see also colonial territories, colonies
colonisers, 3
color, 74, 87, 88, 270
Columbia University, 37, 151
Commemoration of Portuguese
    Discoveries, 299
common origins, 298
Commonwealth, 25n23, 210n37, 276,
    278, 309, 325, 326
Communities, *see* Azorean, Brazilian,
    colonised, colonial, CPLP, creole,
    creolised, Goan, imagined,
    immigrant, Lusophone, migrant,
    Portuguese Canadian Community,
    Portuguese sending, Portuguese
    sojourner, Protestant, settler, South
    African, communities/community
Companhia da Zambézia, 161
Companhia de Moçambique (Mozambique
    Company), 6, 152, 240, 241
Companhia do Boror, see Boror Company
Congo, 85, 178, 270, 320, 321
Congolese, 82, 321
Congone (chief), 160
Congress of African Historians, 289
conscription, 220
construction, 49, 73, 74, 77, 79, 82, 97,
    98, 124, 173, 195, 204, 220, 221,
    241, 246, 249, 251, 265, 324
consul general, 201, 231
consul(s), 59, 133, 193–210, 324
consulates, 17, 25n22, 46, 200, 201, 202,
    203, 205, 217, 223, 228, 229, 255,
    256, 312n29
contratados, 16

conversos, see crypto-Jews
coolie, 240, 258n3
cooperation, 218, 304
Costa, Américo, 99n6
Costa, António, 280
Couto, Mia, 239, 257, 276, 277, 279
CPLP (*Comunidades dos Paises de
    Língua Portuguesa*, Community of
    Portuguese Language Countries),
    19, 20–21, 22, 25n23, 204, 206,
    258n2, 275, 276, 287, 297, 298, 302,
    308, 309, 326
Creole, 7, 13, 298, 302, 303, 306, 307,
    310n2, 312n23, 313
    see also krio, kriol
Creole communities, 7
Creole milieu, 13, 298, 310n2
creolised communities, 170
Crespo, Gonçalves, 77
crisis of 1929, 171
    see also economic collapse or crisis
Cruz, Gorgonio Tomaz Esperato da, 201
crypto-Jews, 8, 37, 38, 41, 42n46
Cuba, 67
Cuban, 321
Cuban troops, 311n13, 311n15
Cultural Chinese Association of Parana,
    see *Associação Cultural Chinesa do
    Paraná*
cultural values, 200, 201, 317, 318
Cunene, 110
Curaçao, 313n34
Curitiba, 18, 240, 243, 246, 249, 252,
    253, 254, 255, 256, 260n36

Dakar, 40n36, 133, 135, 136, 137
Daly, Charles P., 270
Daman, *see* Damão
Damão, 168, 195
Dar es Salaam, 176, 194, 200, 201,
    312n29
de Sousa, *see* Sousa, de
decline, 17, 56, 207, 300, 305, 306,
    307, 320
degradation, 79–81
dehumanisation, 76
Delagoa Bay, 169
Delgado, Humberto, 14, 24n14, 122
demographic character, 7
demographic characterisation, 118

334   Index

demographic conditions, 110
demographic data, 51, 58
demographic demographics, 44
demographic effect, 8
demographic expansion, 319
demographic history, 319
demographic phenomenon, 45
demographic point of view, 108
demographic pressure, 56
demographic role, 39
demographic stability, 329
demographic surplus, 110
demographic vulnerability, 216
demographic weakness, 306
demographical level, 13
demographics, 44
demography, 38n30
  see also demographic…,
  demographics, demographical,
  undemographic
departure, 2, 8, 62, 114, 116, 118,
  126n20, 155, 168, 173–174, 175,
  176, 177–179, 180–184, 186n18, 252,
  257, 286, 323
dependency, 6, 22, 287, 316
dependent, 139, 197, 198
devaluation, 73, 74, 79, 81
Devisse, Jean, 75
DGS (*Direcção Geral de Segurança*,
  General Security Authority), 174,
  175, 176, 177, 180, 182
  see also PIDE
Diamang, 6
Diário de Moçambique, 244, 245, 246,
  254, 260n37
Dias, José António Fernandes, 280
diaspora, 2, 7, 8–13, 14, 18, 21–22,
  31–71, 72, 124, 131, 182, 184, 206,
  215, 229, 232, 240, 247, 252–258,
  265, 289–291, 293n26, 316–326
  see also Global diaspora, Goan
  diaspora, Indian diaspora, Jewish
  diaspora, Lusophone diaspora,
  Portuguese diaspora
diaspora building, 18
diaspora communities, 7, 12, 13, 31,
  290, 294n30
  see also Lusophone diasporic
  communities
diasporic, 286

diasporic behaviour, 322
diasporic belonging, 265
diasporic condition, 291n4
diasporic consciousness, 288, 293n22
diasporic dis/articulation, 286
diasporic experience, 62
diasporic fragments, 12
diasporic group, 8
diasporic identity, 291
diasporic intellectuals, 290
diasporic man, 11
diasporic mobilisation, 290, 293n26
diasporic roots, 288
diasporic social formation, 11
diasporic studies, 312n2
diasporic ties, 265, 322
dictatorship, 15, 49, 79, 82, 122, 125n2,
  130, 256
direct colonisation, 24n16
  see also colonisation
discoveries, 85, 232n2, 273, 288,
  299, 301
discriminated, 94, 164n12
discrimination, 78, 87, 99, 121, 131, 152,
  153, 158, 172, 247
discriminatory, 93
district of Aveiro, 126n19
district of Beira, 244
district of Lisbon, 119
district of Lourenço Marques, 169, 244
district of Manica and Sofala, 151
district of Moçambique, 169, 178, 185n6
district of Quelimane, 150
district of Sofala, 240
district of Zambézia, 151
Diu, 168, 184, 188, 195
Diwane, Kibiriti, 153
Djakarta, 301, 307
Dom João VI, 197
Dom Pedro (Portuguese regent), 197
Dom Sebastião Soares de Resende
  (bishop), 250, 260n29
DuBois, W. E. B., 151
Dulaudilo, Alves, 154–155
Durban, 217, 223, 224, 233, 320
Dutch, 4, 170, 216, 269
dynamizing groups, 252, 260n35

Eanes, Gil, 129
Eanes, Ramalho, 277

Index 335

early modern, 43, 60
East Africa, 14, 15, 59, 60, 168, 185n13, 193, 194,195, 196, 199, 200, 202, 205, 206, 207, 208, 216, 240, 305, 312n29, 323, 324
 see also British East Africa, Portuguese East Africa, Southeast Africa
East African Asian, 321
East African Goan, 195, 205, 206
East Asia, 41
East London (South Africa), 217
East Timor, see Timor
East Timorese, see Timorese
Eastern Africa, 24n17, 178
 see also East Africa
Eça de Queirós, José Maria, 271
Ecaia (muene), 162
economic autonomy, 122
economic collapse or crisis, 17, 68, 114, 126n18, 152, 321
economic condition, 110, 197, 208
economic development, 110, 111, 120, 124, 319
economic expansion, 3
economic growth, 114, 185n9
economic hegemony, 309
 see also hegemony
economic integration, 46, 203
economic interests, 5, 112, 200
economic migrations, 321
economic opportunities, 54, 86, 206, 207
economic problems, 44, 141
economic progress, 109, 112
economic region, 158, 163
economic situation, 114, 168, 180
economic system, 113, 121
economics, 318
economy, 38, 44, 46, 68, 82, 96, 111, 114, 118, 143, 158, 169, 187n32, 199, 208n10, 217, 219, 220, 221, 270, 305, 307, 316, 319, 320, 321, 323, 324, 326
Eigenman, 159
elites, 10, 21, 23n6, 40, 46, 60, 65, 95, 119, 129–130, 131, 132, 134, 135, 138, 141, 142, 143, 144n5, 149, 151, 152, 153, 158, 163, 184, 186n18, 222, 223, 286, 303, 305, 324

emancipation, 76, 141, 249
emigrants, 35, 38, 44, 56, 61, 69n134, 70, 99n1, 108, 109, 112, 113, 114, 118, 119, 124, 290, 294n30, 321
emigration, 8, 13, 15, 16, 17, 36, 43–45, 46, 47, 48, 50, 51, 52, 53, 54, 59, 61, 62, 63, 65, 68, 86, 93, 97, 108, 110, 111–112, 113, 118, 119, 138, 140, 169, 215, 217, 220, 231, 305, 321
 see also Azorean, Brazilian, Cape Verdean, colonial, Madeiran, National Secretariat for Emigration, Portuguese emigration
empire, 1–9, 10, 12–16, 18–19, 21–25, 31, 34, 79, 98, 109, 143, 193, 194, 196, 265, 286, 298, 302, 316, 317, 319, 323, 324, 325,
 see also Brazilian Empire, British Empire, Portuguese Empire
empire building, 1, 319
Empresa Agrícola do Lugela, 150, 159, 161, 162
enclave, 215, 221, 223–224, 230, 293n28
English language, 36, 123, 171, 199, 206, 221, 223, 224, 230, 305, 306
Ennes, António, 80–81, 100n8
enslaved, 76
Equatorial Guinea, 25n23, 313n34
escravatura, 96, 292n10
 see also slavery
Estado da Índia, see Goa
Estado Novo (New State), 5, 8, 44, 49, 51, 53, 82, 83, 84, 109, 111, 112, 119, 122, 125n4, 129, 130, 133, 186n17, 197, 198, 203, 217, 267, 274, 278, 294n30, 298, 318, 319, 320, 321, 325
Estado Novo administration, 267
Estatuto Indígena, see Native Statute
Ethiopia, 156, 321
ethnic, see interethnic, multiethnic
ethnic club, 230
ethnic community, 57, 174, 227
ethnic discrimination, 152
 see also discrimination
ethnic diversification, 291
ethnic enclave, 221, 223
 see also enclave
ethnic group, 10, 126n16, 305, 318
ethnic identity, 12, 226
 see also pan-ethnic identity

ethnic institutions, 226
ethnic neighbourhood, 225
ethnic networks, 215, 219
ethnic past, 124n4
ethnic subject, 281n2
ethnicisation, 73
ethnicity, 73, 224, 247, 300, 304, 318
ethnographer, 76
ethnographic, 45, 68, 76, 274–275, 293n20
ethos, 21, 45, 245, 246, 250
EU-Africa Summit, 279, 280
Europe, 5, 15, 22, 50, 51, 59, 70, 74, 75, 76, 78, 79, 80, 83, 86, 88, 97, 97n5, 99, 112, 118, 123, 125, 197, 198, 200, 210n38, 231, 248, 266, 271, 275, 276, 277, 279–281, 299, 310, 317, 319, 323, 324, 325
European, 4, 5, 7, 12, 14, 17, 35, 51, 73–74, 79, 80, 81, 86, 87, 88, 90, 91, 98, 107, 108, 112, 113, 118, 121, 122, 129, 130, 138, 150, 172, 175, 181, 193, 197, 198, 216, 219, 220, 221, 227, 257, 267, 268, 269, 270, 271, 272, 273, 274, 275, 277, 279, 280, 288, 291, 299, 305, 307, 317, 319, 326
European expansion, 35, 87, 108
European imperialism, 2, 7, 269
Evangelical Church of Christ in Mozambique, 155
Evangelical Mission of Nauela, 151, 155–156, 158
evangelicals, 149, 235n31
Evangué, Castro, 154
Evangué, Ernesto, 154
Évolué, 73, 91, 317
exchange, 5, 113, 160, 170, 172, 185n7, 208n10, 320
exclusion, 22, 73, 77–79, 130, 321
ex-colonial, 225, 226, 227, 228, 318, 319, 320
Exhibition of the Portuguese World, 84, 86
exhibitions, 45, 83–86, 94, 100n13
exile, 8, 24n17, 34, 49, 83, 111, 135, 141, 144n14, 152, 208n9, 321
expansion, 2, 3, 4, 5, 7, 10, 87, 108, 114, 119, 172, 196, 253, 306, 309, 319

see also European expansion, Portuguese Expansion
exploitation, 100n8, 107, 109, 111, 121, 150, 159, 223, 288
Expo, *see* Universal Exhibition in Lisbon
export, 170, 171, 172, 233n4, 268, 320

Fa d'Ambu, 313
fado, 299
family, 36, 65, 66, 67, 70, 77, 119, 120, 124, 126n19, 139, 140, 160, 171, 174, 178, 182, 197, 200, 203, 208n9, 213, 214, 217, 224, 232, 241, 242, 246, 247, 251, 253, 254, 255, 257, 258, 277, 322
see also Portuguese families
family departure, 174, 178
family migration, 126n19
family of imperialism, 2, 7
Fanon, Frantz, 266, 279
FAPRAS, 228
farman, 181, 183, 184, 185n13, 187n24, 187n38
Fátima, 299
Federation of Rhodesia and Nyasaland, 243
Felipe, Prince Dom Luis, 160
female immigration, 48
Fernanda do Vale ("A Preta Fernanda"), 77
Ferreira, Vicente, 87
Figueiredo, Henry de Souza, 201, 209n27
filosofia portuguesa (Portuguese philosophy), 286, 291n2
first age of colonisation, *see* first colonial age
first colonial age, 307, 313n14
five century of colonisation (myth of), 94
FNLA, 250, 260n32, 311n15
Fogo, 139, 140, 142
Fonseca, Jorge, 99n2
Fonseca, Luís, 204
football, 227, 229, 231, 243, 309
forced labour, 24n18, 125n1, 161, 268, 278
forced labour migration, 53, 248
forced labourer, 16
forced migration, 34, 52, 58, 319

Index 337

formal empire, 22, 34, 316
  see also empire
Forros, 141, 142, 144n5
FrançAfrique, 309
France, 4, 11, 15, 17, 19, 23n9, 49, 51, 52,
  61, 62, 64, 108, 112, 119, 267, 276,
  299, 300, 304, 310, 321, 325
Francophone, 297, 300, 303
Francophony, 300, 303, 309
fraternities, 76
freedom, 122, 126n19, 199, 247, 317,
  318, 325
Frelimo, 149, 150, 151, 152, 153, 154,
  155, 156, 157, 158, 161, 162, 163,
  164n12, 173, 176, 186n18, 252, 256,
  260n37, 278, 307
Frelimo administration, 155
French, 6, 9, 19, 20, 51, 62, 69, 73, 129,
  169, 266, 273, 276, 288, 299, 300,
  303, 307, 309, 310
French colonies, 266, 300
French colonisation, 62, 144, 169
French Cooperation Ministry, 311n17
French Guyana, 25n20, 69
Frente de Libertação de Moçambique,
  see Frelimo
Frente Nacional de Libertação de Angola,
  see FNLA
Freyre, Gilberto, 39, 39n33, 83, 100n12,
  239, 246, 247–249, 258n2, 267, 294,
  301, 311n7
Funchal, 49n62, 50n64, 216

Galvão, Henrique, 85, 91
Geisel, Ernesto, 252
generations, 10, 11, 12, 13, 41, 66,
  107, 120, 169, 170–171, 173, 182,
  215, 218, 219, 221, 225, 226, 227,
  230–231, 232, 235n30, 241, 242,
  294n28, 304
Geneva, 161
Genoa, 4
German colonisation, 169
German Democratic Republic, 67,
  67n126
Germans, 6, 62, 62n104, 67, 162, 169,
  216, 220, 273
Germany, 62, 62n104, 207n1
Ghana, 152
ghetto, 287, 288, 292n11

Gilroy, Paul, 265, 281n1, 292n9
Global diaspora, 31, 40
globalisation, 61, 99, 184, 321, 325
globalised world, 61–70, 99, 184, 316,
  321, 325
Goa, 15, 34, 35, 59, 66, 70, 168, 172,
  186, 194, 195, 196, 200, 201,
  202, 203, 204, 205, 207n1,
  207n2, 302, 305,
  306, 308
Goa Medical College, 201, 209n20
Goan, 11, 14, 15, 40, 59, 60, 193–210,
  305, 306, 323, 324
Goan communities, 66, 194, 202, 204,
  205, 206, 207, 305
Goan diaspora, 59, 66
Goan identity, 66, 206
Goan immigration, 60
Gode (Ogaden), 156
Godinho, Magalhães, 33, 43
Godinho, Simoa, 77
Gomes, General Costa, 312n18
Gorgulho, Carlos, 141
Governo do Território de Manica e Sofala, 6
governors, 6, 170, 198, 251
Grant Medical College, 200, 209n21
Great Britain, 3, 6, 108, 119, 168, 272
Greeks, 14, 231
Grémio Negrófilo de Manica e Sofala,
  151, 152
Guadeloupe, 19
Guangdong, 240–241
Guarda, 118
Guebuza, Armando, 151, 152, 153
Guinea, see Equatorial Guinea, Guinea-
  Bissau, Guinea-Conakry
Guinea Coast, 38, 39
Guinea-Bissau, 14, 15, 16, 20, 23n13,
  24n18, 25n23, 52, 67, 86, 94,
  132, 133, 134, 135, 136, 137,
  138, 142, 267, 277, 300, 304,
  308, 309, 326
Guinea-Conakry, 133, 135
Guinean, see bissau-guinean
Gujarat, 60, 168–169, 170, 185n7
Gujarati, 59n90, 171, 187n24, 195, 196
Gungunhana, 81, 83
Gusmão, Pedro, 161
Guyana, 25n20, 50, 69
Gwenjere, Mateus, 158

338 Index

habitus, 246, 254
Hammond, Richard J., 2, 268
Hampton Institute (Virginia), 151
Hawaii, 54, 57
health, 139, 142, 157, 196, 199, 219
hegemony, 163
  see also economic, colonial, imperial hegemony
heritage, 1–2, 19–22, 47, 74, 291
  see also inheritance, legacy
heroes, 8, 81, 85, 100n9, 152, 153, 318
heroism, 81
hierarchisation, 77
hierarchy, 73, 74, 87, 271
Hindu, 42n43, 59n90, 60, 64, 168, 170, 171, 174
hip-hop, 287, 288, 289, 293
Hispanophony, 309
historical change, 319
historical legacy, 82
historical rights, 82, 92
historical trajectory, 9
historicity, 10, 12
historiography, 1, 3, 8, 57, 58, 74, 123, 152, 153, 156, 157, 232n2
history, 3, 5, 10, 11, 12, 13, 14, 16, 23n9, 31, 32, 34, 37, 45, 47, 48, 49, 50, 53, 55, 58, 60, 62, 66, 67, 68, 70, 73, 74, 77, 80, 81, 86, 98, 100n12, 155, 168–187, 196, 200, 229, 230, 266, 268, 277, 278, 279, 287, 288, 289, 290, 291, 302, 307, 308, 310, 312n27, 316, 318, 319, 322, 326
  see also oral history
Hong Kong, 241, 254
hybridity, 286, 288

Iberian Peninsula, 35, 74, 75
ICS (Indian Civil Service), 199
identification, 37, 73, 76, 87, 89, 181, 194, 201, 224, 230, 288, 304, 306, 320, 323
identity, 6, 9, 11, 12, 20, 31, 39, 40, 48, 52, 52n71, 57, 60, 61, 62, 64, 73, 76, 124, 133, 149, 150, 163, 206, 207, 223, 226, 227, 228, 229, 230, 231, 232, 256, 257, 266, 291, 301, 302, 303, 304, 305, 307, 308, 309, 310, 316, 318, 319, 322, 326

identity politics, 319
ideological, 4, 5, 12, 19, 22, 79, 81, 82, 83, 86, 108, 109, 110, 113, 123, 176, 202, 268, 287, 291, 294n30, 297, 298
ideologues, 73, 80
ideology, 2, 3, 13, 19–22, 32, 73, 83, 112, 121, 198, 203, 205, 231, 239, 268, 286, 288, 290, 301
idleness, 96
idolatry, 81
Ilha de Moçambique, 158, 169, 170, 185n6
illegal immigration, 56
illegality, 218, 231
imagery, 85
images, 48, 74, 79, 81, 82, 85, 86, 87, 88, 90, 93, 94, 98, 122, 123, 140, 163, 222, 226, 248, 254, 255, 277, 278, 287, 290, 299
imaginary, 72, 73, 74, 75, 81, 85, 87, 88, 257, 289, 298–299, 304, 307, 308, 309
  see also national imaginary
imagined community, 18, 20, 200, 201
immigrant communities, 9, 54, 62, 64, 70, 222, 232
immigrant invisibility, 62
immigrants, 10, 17, 45, 46, 48, 49, 50, 51, 54, 56, 57, 61, 62, 64, 66, 67, 68, 69, 70, 71, 74, 76, 98, 99, 169, 196, 214, 215–219, 220, 221, 222, 223, 224, 225, 226, 227, 228, 229, 230, 231, 232, 255, 294n28
  see also African, black, Brazilian, colonial, Indian, Portuguese, postcolonial immigrant
immigrated, 48, 97, 247
immigration, 13, 14, 15, 46, 47, 48, 51, 52, 53, 54, 56, 60, 62, 96, 97, 98, 118, 139, 140, 169, 216, 217, 218, 220, 221, 222, 223, 231, 232n1, 234n18, 290, 292n14
  see also Azorean, Brazilian, clandestine, female, Goan, illegal, internal dynamic, legal, Portuguese immigration
imperial, see postimperial, transimperial
imperial actors, 129, 193, 194, 206, 207
imperial apparatus, 14
imperial culture, 14, 194, 196
imperial discourse, 21

imperial ethos, 21
imperial hegemony, 4
  see also hegemony
imperial imaginary, 308
imperial (social area of) migrations, 2, 17, 18, 19, 25n24, 108, 322
imperial narrative, 265, 269, 281
imperial practice, 194, 196–200, 203, 207
imperial project, 4, 5
imperial space, 1, 3, 19, 21, 22
imperial territories, 17, 22
imperial world order, 316, 317
imperialism, 2, 3, 4, 5–7, 14, 21, 198, 268, 281, 304, 310, 313n33, 318
import, 170, 171, 287
indentured labour, 16, 319, 323
independence, 4, 6, 16, 17, 19, 22, 52, 79, 86, 93, 94, 95, 98, 108, 114, 132, 149, 151, 154, 155, 156, 157, 161, 163, 171, 172, 173, 176, 178, 194, 199, 201, 203, 207, 240, 243, 248, 250, 251, 252, 253, 256, 278, 279, 289, 298, 300, 306, 312n18, 320, 323
independence without decolonisation, 16, 298, 311n5
India, 39, 59, 64, 66, 168, 169, 170, 171, 186n23, 194, 195, 196, 198, 199, 205, 207, 248, 292n17, 305, 306, 317, 319
  see also British India, Portuguese India
Indian, 8, 14, 15, 17, 18, 23n8, 24n18, 59, 60, 114, 168, 169, 170, 172, 186n18, 186n22, 196, 199, 205, 207, 298, 312n24, 321
Indian Civil Service, *see* ICS
Indian diaspora, 23n8
  see also Goan diaspora
Indian High Commissioner, 205
Indian immigrants, 64, 196
Indian Ocean, 60, 60n94, 171, 204, 240
Indian traders, 60, 60n92, 114
Indian Union, 195, 205
Indígena, 16, 24n18, 274
  see also native, *Negócios Indígenas*
indigenato, 24n18, 125n1, 139, 248
indigenisation, 2
Indonesia, 301, 302, 306, 307, 312n18, 313n35, 325

Indonesian invasion (of Timor), 306
Indonesian massacres (in Timor), 300, 301
industrialisation, 168, 172, 199
industry, 14, 55, 56, 96, 98, 118, 217, 288, 289, 321
inferior, 7, 32, 80, 142
inferiority, 79, 80, 81, 82
informal British colony, 3, 4
informal colony, 3, 6, 23n4
informal empire, 316
informal settlement, 34, 42, 43
Inhambane, 99n6, 169
inheritance, 20, 21, 171, 316
  see also heritage, legacy
Inquisition records, 37, 41
Institut de Hautes Études Internationales (Geneva), 160–161
Instituto Camões, 287
integration, 5, 17, 19, 61, 63, 65, 67, 75–77, 79, 94, 96, 97, 112, 223, 229, 230, 267, 277, 290, 299, 308
inter-African migrations, 2
intercivilisational, 90
intercontinental migrations, 2
interethnic, 247
intermarriage, 235n31
internal dynamic [immigration dynamic], 43
interracial, 247, 267
invisibility, 62, 94–98, 156
Ireland, 199
irrational, 89, 268
Islamic organisations, 157
Islamism, 86, 170, 307, 317
Isle of Flowers (Indonesia), 302, 307
Ismaili, 11, 14, 15, 18, 22, 64, 168–187, 256, 323
Ismailism, 168
Italians, 14, 19, 23n8, 48, 273
Ivory Coast, 19

Jacobin, 305
Jesus, Madre Cecília de, 77
Jewish, 38, 38n28, 215, 231, 235n33
Jewish diaspora, 38
Johannesburg, 32, 218, 220, 221, 223, 224, 225, 226, 227, 228, 229, 231, 233n8, 234n14, 240, 243
Johannesburg Chinese School, 243

340   Index

Johnston, Harry, 273
Juntas Províncias do Povoamento, see Provincial Settlement Boards

Kalahari desert, 5
Kampala, 193, 194, 200, 209n27
Karachi, 204
Kenya, 107, 119, 121, 126n20, 178, 195, 199, 201, 205, 207n1, 208n8, 304, 319, 320, 323
Khoja, 168, 184, 186n22
Konkani, 66, 206, 306
Krio, 324
  see also Creole
Krio elite, 324
Kriol (language), 303
Kristangs (of Malacca), 302, 306, 312n30
Kuomintang, 240, 241
Kutchi, 171
Kwanza-Norte, 140

La Rochelle, 221, 224, 225
labour, 13, 24n17, 44, 46, 53, 55, 58, 64, 81, 98, 107, 109, 112, 113, 121, 140, 160, 161, 162, 199, 219, 220, 223, 248, 252, 268, 269, 278, 319, 323
Lagos, 99n5
Lançados, 39, 40n36
language, 2, 10, 20, 21, 42, 61, 75, 86, 98, 122, 151, 155, 171, 176, 200, 203, 204, 206, 207, 215, 217, 221, 229, 230, 243, 273, 276, 277, 280, 288, 297, 298, 300, 301, 302, 303–305, 306, 307, 308, 309, 312n24, 313n34, 322, 325, 326
Lanheses, 45
Latin America, 17, 49, 70
Latinophone, 300
laziness, 81
Leal, Cunha, 92
Lebanese, 14
legacy, 7, 12, 75, 278, 287, 300, 305–307, 312n27
  see also heritage, inheritance
legal immigration, 54, 56
Lei Orgânica do Ultramar, see Overseas Constitutional Law
Leite, Mário, 129, 143n2

Lêm Ferreira (suburb of Praia), 136
liberation, 14, 93, 95, 108, 124, 131, 132, 133, 135, 142, 149, 154, 158, 162, 163, 246, 278, 289
  see also freedom
liberation movements, 93, 133, 135, 142, 156, 158, 246, 278
liberation struggles, 14, 108, 124, 131, 135, 163
Liceu Gil Eanes, 129
Licungo (*prazo*), 159
Lima, Humberto Pinto de, 42
Limpopo, 110
Linder, Victor, 160
lingua franca, 206
linguistic, 22, 55, 75, 196, 206, 219, 277, 286, 300, 303, 306, 307, 309, 312n22, 317
linguistic legacy, 305–307
Lisbon, 6, 7, 11, 13, 14, 33, 34, 43, 44, 45, 49, 51, 53, 56, 58, 62, 65, 76, 77, 83, 84, 85, 86, 94, 95, 97, 108, 114, 118, 119, 122, 132, 133, 172, 174, 176, 177, 180, 216, 220, 222, 257, 271, 275, 279, 280, 287, 288, 289, 297, 299, 300, 323, 325
Little Portugal (Portuguese neighbourhood in South African cities), 221, 223, 224, 225, 227
Livingstone, David, 269, 270, 272, 273
Lobato, Alexandre, 11
local administration, 107
Lomué, see Lomwe
Lomwe (Lomué), 155
London, 7, 181, 217, 305
  see also East London
Lopes, Duarte, 100n14
Lopes, Óscar, 85
Lourenço, Eduardo, 308
Lourenço Marques, 11, 120, 121, 126n16, 130, 154, 157, 158, 169, 170, 175, 184, 216, 218, 222, 240, 241, 243, 252
  see also Maputo
loyalty, 160, 173, 184, 185n13, 202, 251, 313n32, 324
Luanda, 93, 122, 130, 138, 139, 222, 270, 300, 303
Lubango, 110

Index 341

Lugela, 151
Lugela Company, see *Empresa Agrícola do Lugela*
Lugela (*prazo*), 161–162
  see also *Empresa Agrícola do Lugela*
LusÁfrica, 309
Lusaka accords, 278
Lusaka, 161, 252, 278
Lusaka embrace, 278
Lusitanity, 298, 308, 311n7
Luso-African, 40n37, 67, 277
Luso-Asian, 40, 60
Luso-Canadian, 57, 63
Luso-Chinese, 239, 242, 247, 249, 250, 251
lusocolonial, 14 à compléter
Lusofonia, 265, 274–279, 286, 287, 289, 290, 325
  see also Lusophony
Lusophone, 2, 3, 8, 9, 10, 11, 21, 22, 25n24, 31, 32, 38, 43, 58, 64, 66, 68, 70, 133, 134, 230, 265, 266, 267, 276, 277, 280, 281, 286, 287, 290, 297, 302, 303, 305, 308, 309, 312n29
Lusophone community, 9, 20, 21, 279, 302
  see also CPLP
Lusophone culture, 287, 297
Lusophone diaspora, 10, 11, 22, 32, 33, 38, 43, 66, 70, 313n36
Lusophone diasporic communities, 31
Lusophone identity, 2, 20, 21
Lusophony, 21, 98, 286, 287, 288, 290, 291, 298, 302, 303, 308–310, 311n7
  see also *Lusofonia*
Lusotopia, 307, 308
Lusotropical repertoire, 21
Lusotropicalism (or Luso-Tropicalism), 3, 21, 22, 39, 58, 83, 92, 93, 100n12, 110, 125n4, 249, 258n2, 268, 286, 287, 290, 301, 310, 311n7
  see also neo-Lusotropicalism
Lusotropicalist (or Luso-Tropicalist), 239, 246, 247, 248, 249, 288, 291, 298, 302, 308, 311n7, 313n34
Lusotropicalist discourse, 298, 302
Lusotropicalist myths, 4, 299, 309, 313n34

Macao, 302, 305, 308
Machanga, 151, 152
Machel, Samora, 154, 158
Maconde (Planalto), 308
Macua, 170
Macuse (*prazo*), 159
Madal Company, 159
Madeira, 13, 49, 54, 119, 216–219, 227
Madeiran, 11, 49, 50, 216, 217, 218, 219, 222, 224, 225, 226, 227, 230
Madeiran emigration, 50
Madragoa, 76
MAEP (*Movimento de apoio ao emigrante português*, Support Movement for Portuguese Emigrants), 254
Maganjas, 160
Mahala (*muene*), 162
Maio, 129
Malacca, 302, 305
Malamulo mission, 153
Malanje, 99n6
Malawi, 153, 155, 272
  see also Nyassaland
Malaya, 319
Malema, 155
Mambone, 151, 152
mameluco, 39
Manchester, 83
Manica and Sofala, 6, 149, 151, 152, 153, 240, 247, 251
Manica e Sofala, see Manica and Sofala
Mantero, Francisco, 161
Maputo, 152, 153, 154, 157, 174, 176, 252, 260n37, 300, 309
  see also Lourenço Marques
Margarido, Alfredo, 99n2
Mário Soares, 277, 299, 309
Marist Brothers, 254
markers, 73, 81, 94, 206, 276, 303, 308, 309
Marmagoa, 204, 205
Marquis of Pombal, 12, 77
marriage, 45, 75, 77, 141, 219, 230, 232, 247, 322
Marrou, Louis, 307
Martinique, 19
Martins, Caetano Francis, 201, 209n26
Martins, Joaquim Pedro de Oliveira, *see* Martins, Oliveira
Martins, Oliveira, 43, 80, 81, 90

342 Index

Martins, Sousa, 77
Marxism, 305
Marxism-Leninism, 252
Marxist, 2, 9, 268
Marxist-Leninist, 155, 157, 307, 319
Massachusetts, 11, 54, 55, 63, 69
Mataca (chief), 160
Matos, Norton de, 109
Mbundu, 303
Melaka, 60
memories, 10, 11, 17, 74–75, 76, 122, 124, 141, 142, 174, 179, 183, 223, 230, 247, 254, 255, 257, 288, 290, 311n11
mestiço, 40, 52, 70
mestizos, 60, 74, 77, 78, 86, 94, 126n17
metropole (mother country), 1, 3, 4, 19, 87, 107, 108, 109, 110, 120, 124, 126n19, 196, 199, 200, 251, 267, 281n3, 293n26
MFA, 277, 300, 311n14
microhistory, 45, 50, 67
middlemen, 60
migrant communities, 54, 61, 275, 322, 326
migrants, 8, 10, 15, 17, 19, 25n22, 50, 56, 61, 63, 64, 66, 67, 69, 109, 110, 111, 112, 113, 114, 118, 119, 120, 169, 193, 200, 226, 275, 311n6, 319, 322, 323, 326
migrations, 1, 2, 6, 7, 8, 15–19, 22, 34, 38, 43, 44, 45, 46, 47, 48, 49, 50, 59, 61, 64, 65, 66, 68, 72, 107–124, 168–188, 193, 195–196, 204, 215, 216, 218, 220, 222, 232, 317, 319, 322
  see also Brazilian, Cape Verdean, colonial, economic, forced labour, forced, imperial, intercontinental, inter-African, Overseas, Portuguese, return, reverse, space of, settler migration
Miguel, Dom, 197
Milange, 153
military occupation, 111
Mindelo, 129, 130, 136, 137
Minho, 45, 92, 309
Ministério da Administração Interna, 291, 293n28

Ministry of Internal Administration, see *Ministério da Administração Interna*
minority, 17, 56, 69, 73, 107, 108, 120, 156, 219, 220, 223, 230, 235n31, 256, 307, 320, 323, 326
miscegenation, 37, 365
missionaries, 34, 82, 85, 86, 87, 149, 150, 151, 152, 153, 155, 157, 159, 162, 163, 195, 260n30, 269, 304, 324
Moçambique, see *Companhia de Moçambique, Diário de Moçambique*, District of Moçambique, Ilha de Moçambique
Mocambo, 24n20, 76, 77
Moçâmedes, 110
Mocumbi, Pascoal, 151
modern history, 23n9
  see also early modern
modern nation, 269, 275, 299, 305
modern period, 6, 18, 43
modern state, 157, 200, 274
modern time, 1
modern world, 259n27, 316, 319, 322
modernisation, 82, 304
modernity, 247, 255, 265, 268, 274, 291n2, 304
Mollat, Michel, 75
Molumbo, 153
Mombasa, 200, 201, 204, 205, 209n20
Mondlane, Eduardo, 99n6, 151, 152, 153, 158, 163n6, 268
Monsanto, 83
monstrosities, 79, 83
monstrous, 90, 91
Monteiro, Armindo, 83
Monteiro, Joachim John, 270
Montreal, 57
Moreira, Adriano, 125, 249
Morocco, 4, 43n47
Mossuril, 169
mother tongue, 20, 206, 300, 303, 304, 305, 307, 312n23, 312n24
Moutinho, Mário, 100
Movement of the Armed Forces, *see* MFA
Movimento das Forças Armadas, *see* MFA
Movimento Popular da Libertação de Angola (People's Movement for the Liberation of Angola), *see* MPLA

Index 343

Mozambican, 14, 16, 17, 58, 65, 86, 98, 122, 141, 142, 149, 151, 152, 153, 154, 155, 157, 158, 161, 163, 173, 176, 177, 186n22, 215, 220, 222, 223, 224, 225, 226, 227, 228, 229, 239, 247, 257, 273, 275, 276, 277, 278, 279, 297, 303, 307, 309
Mozambique, 6, 8, 11, 14, 15, 16, 17, 18, 20, 22, 24n18, 24n19, 57, 58, 59, 60, 61, 63, 67, 81, 94, 107–126, 136, 149–164, 168–187, 198, 216, 218, 220, 222–223, 225, 226, 228, 240–241, 243, 246, 247, 248, 251–258, 268, 271, 274, 276, 277, 278, 279, 300, 302, 303, 304, 308, 309, 323, 324, 325, 326
see also Moçambique
Mozambique island, see Ilha de Moçambique
Mozambique Liberation Front, see Frelimo
MpD (*Movimento para a Democracia*, Movement for Democracy – Cape Verde), 144n14
MPLA, 133, 260n31, 299–300, 311, 311n12, 311n13, 311n15
MUD (*Movimento de unidade democrática*, Movement of Democratic Unity – Portugal), 95
Mugabeque (*muene*), 162
mulattos, 46, 72, 73, 74, 77, 78, 79, 83, 87, 92, 96, 97, 98
multiculturalism, 293n28, 317
multiethnic, 319
multiracialism, 99n1, 203, 210n38, 239
Mundo Português (Portuguese world), 25n24, 84, 85, 86, 257, 259n27, 286, 291, 294n30
Murapa (*muene*), 162
music, 12, 75, 76, 227, 287, 288, 322
musical forms, 287, 288
musicscape, 287
Muslim, 60, 64, 66, 170, 171, 173
Mussoco, 159, 160, 162
Mutaca, Lourenço, 155, 156
Mutumula (*muene*), 162
Mutumula, Alberto, 154, 162
mythical, 94
mythification, 11
mythologies, 79, 81

myths, 4, 7, 10, 13, 17, 94, 132, 266, 267, 268, 275, 309, 313n34

Nacala-a-Velha, 169
Nairobi, 193, 194, 200, 201, 202, 203, 204
naked, 83, 86
Namagoa Plantations, 159
Nameduro (*prazo*), 159
Namibia, 217, 222, 234n21
Nampula, 155, 169, 180
Nangoma (*regedoria*), 154
national imaginary, 301, 307, 308
national language, 303
see also mother tongue
national liberation, 93, 108, 124
National Liberation Front of Angola, see FNLA
National Party, 248
National Secretariat for Emigration, 112
National Union for the Total Independence of Angola, see Unita
nationalism, 6, 14, 39, 66, 149, 152, 156, 159, 162, 163, 241, 248, 265, 277, 311n8, 324
see also African, Brazilian, Chinese, Arab, Portuguese nationalism, protonationalism, transnationalism, ultranationalism
nationalist, 6, 95, 110, 132, 136, 151, 154, 158, 220, 221, 227, 234n15, 241, 279, 290, 292n17, 294n30, 308
nationalist movements, 151
nationals, 3, 5, 7, 19, 20, 21, 22, 48, 64, 66, 73, 79, 86, 93, 95, 108, 109, 110, 112, 118, 120, 121, 123, 124, 132, 152, 172, 215, 228, 229, 230, 232, 246, 248, 256, 265–282, 288, 290, 291, 300, 301, 302, 303, 304, 307, 308, 318, 319, 320, 322, 323
nationism, 305
nations, 13, 24n18, 37, 45, 61, 73, 78, 84, 92, 99n1, 108, 124, 150, 198, 257, 266, 267, 268, 269, 271, 275, 278, 280, 281, 290, 299, 300, 301, 304, 305, 307, 309, 318, 323
native, 6, 7, 13, 15, 16, 21, 23n13, 24n18, 46, 73, 75, 81, 85, 86, 87, 107, 108, 121, 126n20, 129, 160, 249, 253, 259n12, 269, 270, 272, 273, 274, 298
see also *indígena*

native administration, 274
Native Affairs, 274
native labour, 81
native populations, 7, 86, 108, 121
Native Statute (*Estatuto indígena* or *regime de indigenato*), 13, 16, 24n13, 24n18, 248, 249
Ncomo, Tapera, 151
Negócios Indígenas, see Native Affairs
Negro language, 75
Negroes, 72, 73, 74, 75, 76, 77, 79, 80, 82, 83, 84, 85, 86, 87, 88, 90, 93, 94, 95, 96, 98
neighbourhood, 55, 67, 76, 126n19, 136, 221, 222, 223–226, 227
neo-colonialism, 292n10
neocolonialist, 286
neocolony, 17, 286, 290, 309
neo-Lusotropicalism, 311n7
  see also Lusotropicalism
neo-Pentecostal, 309, 313n36
neo-Pentecostalism, 309
Netherlands, 67, 325
Neto, Agostinho, 95, 99, 255
New Brazils, 13, 46, 110
New Christians, see crypto-Jews
New England, 53, 54, 55, 56
New State, see *Estado Novo*
New York, 68, 151
New Zealand, 18, 321
Niassa (Mozambican Province of), 153, 160, 164n12, 169, 170
  see also Nyassa
Niger Delta, 307
Nigeria, 321
Nihia, Eduardo da Silva, 155–156
Nkomo, Tapera, 153
Nogueira, Franco, 99n1
nonracial, 268
nonracialism, 268, 275
nonracialist, 121
nonracism, 269
North America, 18, 54, 59, 63, 70
Notícias da Beira, 244, 251, 254
Núcleo de Estudos de População (NEPO), 69
Nucléo Negrófilo de Manica e Sofala, see *Grémio Negrófilo*...
nudity, 92
Nyassa (Lake), 272
  see also Niassa

Nyassaland, 272
  see also Malawi

O Século de Joanesburgo, 229
objectified, 76
official discourse, 110, 176, 178, 268, 298
official documentation, 32, 172
official language, 20, 61, 276, 277, 280, 297, 306, 307, 308, 310n4, 326
official settlement schemes, 32, 33, 57, 120
officials, 13, 33n9, 129, 130, 131, 133, 134, 136, 137, 139, 143, 206, 218, 219, 271, 272
  see also British officials, Cape Verdeans officials, Portuguese officials, South African officials
Ogaden, 156
old colonies, 19, 120, 304
old settler societies, 321
old settlers, 13, 244
Oliveira Martins, see Martins, Oliveira
Ondjaki, 275
oral history, 48, 49, 55, 67, 131, 207n1
oral interview, 57, 143
Order of Homoudieh, 201
Order of the Brilliant Star of Zanzibar, 201
Other (the Same and the Other), 74
outlying district, 97
overcolonised, 7
Overseas Constitutional Law (or Organic law on Portuguese overseas Lands), 13, 83, 323
Overseas Development Plans (*Planos de Fomento do Ultramar*), 112
Overseas empire, 37
Overseas expansion, 34
overseas migration, 108–112, 114, 120, 126n19
overseas provinces (*Províncias ultramarinas*), 13, 86, 93, 99n1, 108, 109, 110, 111, 112, 114, 118, 126n19, 198, 202, 203, 209n31, 239, 241, 249, 268
Ovimbundu, 303

pacification campaigns, 81, 123
PAICV, 132
PAIGC, 132–137, 142

Paises Africanos de Lingual Oficial Portuguesa, see PALOP
Pakistan, 194, 199, 207, 321
PALOP, 20, 61, 276, 298, 300, 305, 309, 310n4
Pan-Arab nationalism, 248
pan-ethnic identity, 232
Papia Kristang (Portuguese Creole), 306
Paraná (state of), 240
Pardo, Domingos Loureiro, 77
Paris, 7, 49, 64, 83, 85, 300
Partido Africano da Independência da Guiné e do Cabo Verde, see PAIGC
Partido Africano da Independência de Cabo Verde, see PAICV
paternalism, 280
patriarchy, 219, 232, 267
Paulino, Pai, 77
PCP, 95s
Pemba (Mozambique), 312
Pemba (Zanzibar), 312
People's Movement for the Liberation of Angola, see MPLA
perception, 41, 52, 154, 174, 181, 184, 194, 199, 200, 206, 216
Pereira, Aristides, 132, 134
Persia, 168
petty Asians, 8
petty whites, 8, 172
Peul, 303
PIDE (Polícia Internacional e de Defesa do Estado, State and International Defense Police), 95, 133, 179, 187n27
see also DGS
Pidjiguiti, 93
pieds-noirs, 19, 320
Pigaffetta, Filippo, 100n14
Pimentel, M. do Rosário, 76, 99n2
Pinheiro, Bordalo, 78, 82
Pinheiro, Rafael Bordalo, 78, 82, 100n10
Pinto, Boaventura, 201
Pires, Armando, 155
plague, 201, 319
Planos de fomento do Ultramar, see Overseas Development Plans
Poço dos Negros, 99
poetry, 171, 289, 292n17, 299
Polícia Internacional e de Defesa do Estado, see PIDE

policy, 22, 35, 45, 48, 58, 108, 110, 111, 113, 114, 155, 156, 157, 160, 172, 173, 185n9, 195, 198, 199, 200, 202, 203, 216, 217, 233n7, 246, 265, 271, 280, 290, 298, 299, 304, 308, 318, 321
political autonomy, 107
politics, 8, 20, 21, 58, 87, 143, 194, 197, 201, 202, 216, 273, 289
see also identity politics
Pombal, see Marquis of Pombal
Pombaline era, 52
Port Elizabeth, 217
Porto, 11, 36, 44, 45, 46, 84, 85, 118, 309
Portugal, 1–25, 31, 33, 39, 43–53, 58, 61–67, 72–83, 85–87, 90, 94, 95, 96, 97, 98, 108, 109, 110, 113, 114, 118, 119, 120, 122, 124, 129, 130, 133, 135, 138, 139, 156, 159, 168, 174, 175, 176, 177, 178, 179, 182, 184, 186n23, 193, 194, 196–199, 200, 201, 202, 203, 204, 205, 220–221, 222, 223, 224, 225, 227, 229, 230, 231, 240, 246, 247, 248–249, 250, 251, 252, 254, 256, 257, 266, 267–280, 286, 288, 289, 290, 291, 297–313, 322–326
see also Little Portugal, postcolonial Portugal
Portugality, 306, 308
Portuguese, 1–25, 31–71, 72–101, 108–114, 118–123, 129–146, 149, 152, 153, 154, 155, 157, 159, 160–163, 168–174, 176–178, 180, 182, 186n23, 193–210, 213–235, 239–261, 266–281, 286–291, 293n23, 297–310, 316, 319, 322–326
Portuguese administration, 14, 133, 139, 141, 152, 161, 247, 270
Portuguese Africa, 24n17, 53, 72, 73, 99n1, 112, 118, 123, 125n13, 252, 266, 267
Portuguese Africa, 24n17, 53, 72, 73, 99n1, 112, 118, 123, 125n13, 252, 266, 267
Portuguese Americans, 10, 55, 63, 310
Portuguese Atlantic "nation", 37
Portuguese Canadian Community, see Luso-Canadian

346 *Index*

Portuguese Colonial Exhibitions, 84, 85, 86, 100n13
Portuguese colonialism, 3, 5, 60, 73, 93, 95, 110, 149, 152, 153, 162, 168, 268, 322
Portuguese colonisation, 24n17, 32, 43n47, 54, 83, 86, 122, 173, 174, 313n34
Portuguese Communist Party, *see* PCP
Portuguese corporate state, 43, 61
Portuguese corporatist state, 31
Portuguese decolonisation, 60
Portuguese diaspora, 11, 12, 31–71, 215, 229
Portuguese East Africa, 195, 196, 216, 218
Portuguese economic problems, 44
Portuguese economic space, 112, 185n9, 323
Portuguese emigrants, 38, 61, 109, 114, 119, 124, 254, 290, 294n30
Portuguese emigration, 13, 17, 33, 43, 44, 45, 48, 51, 61, 62, 63, 86, 108, 110, 112, 118, 125n13
Portuguese empire (or Portuguese African empire, Portuguese colonial empire), 1, 2, 3, 6, 7–12, 13, 15, 16, 21, 22, 24n17, 31, 32, 34, 36, 42, 53, 57, 60, 82, 108, 110, 129–146, 163, 168, 193–210, 281, 323
Portuguese empire, 1, 2, 3, 6, 7–12, 13, 15, 16, 21, 22, 24n17, 31, 32, 34, 36, 42, 57, 60, 82, 108, 110, 129–146, 163, 168, 193–210, 281, 323
Portuguese expansion, 5, 31, 32–43, 77, 80, 85, 86, 100n12, 196, 288, 307, 308
Portuguese families, 18, 36, 48, 54, 109, 214, 224, 239, 251, 258, 260n30
Portuguese fighters, 93
Portuguese genius, 98
Portuguese government, 13, 15, 23n6, 52, 95, 110, 135, 138, 161, 184n1, 185n13, 193, 196, 197, 200, 201, 203, 205, 208n9, 215, 223, 278, 299, 309, 323, 325
Portuguese Guinea, *see* Guinea-Bissau
Portuguese historiography, 74
Portuguese identity, 11, 39, 40, 57, 60, 224, 226, 227, 228, 230, 231, 233n3

Portuguese ideological discourse, 86
Portuguese imaginary, 289, 298
Portuguese immigrants, 17, 45, 46, 49, 50, 51, 54, 56, 57, 62, 67, 172, 220, 221, 222, 224, 226, 227, 229, 230, 231, 232
Portuguese immigration, 47, 48, 52, 54, 56, 221, 231, 233n2
Portuguese India, 168, 194, 196
Portuguese Indians, 168
Portuguese language, 10, 20, 75, 98, 185n13, 204, 205, 207, 226, 229, 276, 277, 280, 287, 297, 298, 301, 302, 305, 306, 309, 325
Portuguese legacy, 305–307
Portuguese merchants, 46
Portuguese migration, 17, 47, 51, 58, 65, 111, 122, 220, 222
Portuguese nation, 84, 108, 111, 124, 198, 266, 267, 281, 300, 301
Portuguese nationalism, 3, 268
Portuguese nationality, 97, 160, 187n23, 243, 253, 255, 256, 312n29
Portuguese nationals, 73, 109, 111, 208n16, 275, 301, 307
Portuguese officials, 13, 93, 133, 134, 138, 139, 141, 170, 195, 272
Portuguese people, 90, 93, 123, 281n3, 301, 308
Portuguese policy, 141, 173, 195, 271, 299
Portuguese population, 23n6, 79, 83, 85, 86, 96, 110, 232n1
Portuguese presence, 34n9, 42, 51n68, 57, 60, 85, 93, 195
Portuguese Republic, 194
Portuguese sending communities, 55
Portuguese settlement, 33, 35, 54, 306
Portuguese settlers, 32, 33, 58, 60, 99n1, 100n8, 109, 126n17
Portuguese social fabric, 87
Portuguese social imaginary, 72, 74, 75, 76, 81, 85, 87, 99n2
Portuguese society, 15, 45, 64, 66, 72–101, 108, 124, 126n18, 197, 223
Portuguese sojourner communities, 36
Portuguese soldiers, 81, 94, 300, 305
Portuguese universities, 77
Portuguese women, 36
Portuguese world, *see* *Mundo Português*

Portuguese-speaking African Countries, *see* PALOP
postcolonial historiography, 152, 153, 156
postcolonial imaginary, 293n23
postcolonial immigrants, 64
postcolonial nation-states, 31, 61, 290
postcolonial period, 144n7, 256
postcolonial Portugal, 62n100, 274
postcolonial studies, 12, 286
postcolonialism, 277
postimperial, 22, 281, 322, 325
postmodern, 310
Praia, 129, 136, 137
prazo system, 37
prazos, 37, 39, 159, 160, 161–162, 164n16
prejudice, 73, 74, 75, 77–79, 86, 89, 94, 95, 98, 99, 110, 221
Presbyterian Church, 149
Pretugal, 288, 291n1
primary school education, 171
primitive, 81, 85, 87, 89, 268
principle of effectivity, 272
Procter, John C., 155
protectionism, 274
Protestant, 149, 156, 157, 221, 235n31
Protestant Church, 151, 162
Protestant community, 156, 324
Protestant culture, 219
Protestant leader, 158
Protestant mission, 6, 149, 150, 155, 162, 163
Protestant missionaries, 149, 150, 163
Protestantism, 149, 151, 152, 156, 157, 163
protonationalism, 152
Provincial Settlement Boards (of Angola, Mozambique), 14, 112, 139, 140
Províncias ultramarinas, *see* overseas provinces
public administration, 77, 118, 119
Punjabi, 195, 196
push and pull factors, 45

Quaresma, Virgínia, 77
Quebec, 321
Quebecois, 303
Queen Victoria, 198
Quelimane, 150, 158, 160
Quilombo, 24n20

Rabelados, 137
race, 14, 52, 77, 80, 81, 87, 92, 119, 158, 183, 199, 230, 240, 247, 248, 260n30, 271, 273, 274, 275, 321, 324
racial, 60, 64, 65, 87, 94, 99, 111, 121, 123, 130, 143, 196, 199, 200, 203, 204, 210n38, 216, 221, 223, 231, 243, 248, 265, 266–267, 268, 269, 271, 274, 278, 320, 321
see also nonracial
racial discrimination, 87, 121
racialisation, 73
racism, 65, 68, 78, 83, 92–94, 96, 123, 170, 172, 268, 275, 288, 318
racist, 92, 94, 95, 99n3, 122, 123, 131, 157
rap, 288
Red Bull Music Academy, 287
refugees, 56, 98, 156, 214, 222, 226, 227, 228, 234n21, 254, 319, 320
regime de indigenato, *see* Native statute
Reis, Batalha, 272, 273, 281n9
Reis, Jaime Batalha, 272
religion, 21, 31, 75, 85, 86, 149, 150, 152, 155, 157, 158, 163, 202, 205, 206, 226, 318
religiosity, 53
religious, 11, 12, 34, 47, 62, 66, 70, 75, 76, 86, 136, 150, 152, 155, 156, 157, 168, 173, 174, 184, 291, 306, 307, 321, 322
remittances, 44, 108, 234n17
Renamo (*Resistência Nacional de Moçambique*), 187n32
Rendall, Luís, 146n35
representation, 3, 32, 48, 72, 73, 79–98, 99, 121, 173, 182, 194, 195, 196, 200, 201, 205, 206, 207, 240, 254, 281
repression, 76, 95, 96, 124, 130, 131, 141, 142, 220, 223, 312n19
repressive, 44, 137, 144n5, 214, 231
republican mindset, 81
Resende, *see* Dom Sebastião Soares de Resende
resistance fights, 81
retail stores (*cantinas*), 170, 171, 185n13
retornados, *see* returnees

348 *Index*

retornos, see returnees
return migration, 51, 68
returnees, 45, 48, 52, 124n18, 126n17, 177, 254
  see also refugees
Reunion, 19
reverse migration, 47
Revolution of the Carnations, *see* Carnation Revolution
Rhodes, Cecil, 82
Rhodesia, 16, 107, 108, 119, 121, 123, 126n16, 152, 158, 160, 240, 242, 243, 254, 323, 324
Ribeiro, Angela, 193, 201
Ribeiro, Rosendo Ayres, 193, 201
ridiculing, 87
ridiculous, 88
Rio de Janeiro, 45, 47, 254
ritual, 87, 91, 244, 247
Rodrigues, Nascimento, 144n8
Rodrigues, Sarmento, 239, 247
Roman, 75, 276, 306
rural unemployment, 319

Sá Carneiro, Francisco, 290
Saa, Mário, 78
SAGM (South African General Mission), 155
Salazar, António de Oliveira, 6, 73, 92, 95, 96, 99n1, 100n12, 109, 111, 112, 114, 172, 173, 185n15, 197, 198, 202, 203, 217, 220, 222, 231, 274, 275, 307, 310, 311n7, 313n32
Salazarist, 14, 92, 275, 294n30, 306, 307
  see also anti-salazarist
Salcette, 195
Sampaio, Jorge, 276
Santarém, 118
Santa-Rita, Augusto, 90
Santiago (Island, Cape Verde), 129, 136, 137
Santomean, 16, 24n18, 77, 86
Santos (port of), 253
Santos Machado Brothers, *see* Sonte Machado Brothers
São Gabriel de Munhamade (church), 153
São João Baptista de Ajuda, 307, 313n32
São Nicolau, 139

São Paulo, 18, 37, 46, 47, 48, 68, 69, 70, 260n36
São Tomé (city), 141
São Tomé (Island), 83, 93
São Tomé, or São Tomé and Principe (archipelago and country), 14, 15, 16, 22, 24n13, 25n23, 38, 52, 58, 85, 114n5, 138, 140, 141, 142, 161, 210n37, 271, 302, 303, 309, 325, 326
São Tomé e Principe, see São Tomé and Principe
São Vicente, 88, 129, 136
saudade, 299
Scandinavian Independent Baptist Union, 155
Scotland, 199, 272
second generation, 219, 221, 229, 230, 294n28
second Portuguese empire, 15
Second World War, *see* World War II
secondary education, 129, 130
secret, 130, 133, 135, 136, 141, 184
self-perception, 194, 200
semicolonial, 316
Sena Sugar Estates, 159, 160, 164n19, 164n22
Senegal, 25n23, 135, 138, 302, 312n23
Sephardic Jews, 37, 38
Sephardic studies, 38
Sepoys, 162, 172
sertão, 39
settlement, 14, 32, 33–35, 36n21, 38, 39, 42, 43, 45, 52, 54, 57, 76, 86, 92, 94, 107, 108, 109–114, 119, 120, 123, 124, 138–143, 169, 170, 173, 177, 178, 179, 180, 184n1, 241, 306, 323, 324
settler, 11, 13, 14, 22, 24n16, 33, 34, 38n30, 61, 93, 108, 109, 110, 119, 120, 121, 122, 123, 126n16, 130, 171, 250, 253, 323, 324
  see also Cape Verdeans settlers, old settlers, Portuguese settlers
settler colonies (model of), 107
settler colonisation, 18, 125n3, 130, 140
settler communities, 11, 17, 107, 121, 122, 126n16, 319–320
settler migration, 322
settler minorities, 323
settler racial attitude, 64

Index 349

settler territories, 124
settler's culture, 122
Seventh-Day Adventist Church of Munguluni, 151, 153–155, 158, 162
Seychelles, 201
Shangaan, 149
Shi'a Islam, 183
Shi'a Muslim, 186n22
Sierra Leone, 321
Sierra Leone Krios, 324
Silva, Adolfo Capristano, 137
Simango, Bede, 151
Simango, Kamba Columbus, 151, 152, 153
Simango, Sixpence, 151, 152
Simango, Uria, 152, 153, 156, 158
Simango, Uria Timóteo (father of Uria Simango), 152
Sinhalese, 306
Sino-African, 247
Sino-Asian, 247
Sino-Mozambicans, 252, 255, 256, 259n12, 260n36, 260n37
skin colour, 73, 94, 107, 130, 258
    see also black skin
slave trade, 8, 45, 52, 88, 110, 240, 299
slave traders, 8, 269, 307
slavery, 8, 12, 36, 73, 77, 79, 88, 96, 265, 299, 313n34
slaves, 17, 52, 75, 76, 77, 99n5, 272, 307, 311, 319, 324
smuggling, 218
Smuts, Jan, 216
social mobility, 22, 58, 120, 121, 206, 207
social networks, 50, 54, 223–226
social utility, 306
socialist state, 157
Sócrates, José, 279, 280
Somalia, 321
Sonte Machado Brothers (Santos Machado Brothers), 154
Sousa, A. C. L. de, 201, 209n21
South Africa, 11, 12, 15, 16, 18, 22, 32, 63, 107, 119, 121, 123, 126n16, 151, 158, 170, 171, 213–235, 240, 243, 271, 320, 321, 323, 324
South African communities of Portuguese origin, 12

South African General Mission (SAGM), 155
South African officials, *see* Union officials
South African society, 219, 232
South America, 42, 97, 319
South Asia, 194, 199, 207, 321
South Asian, 194
Southeast Africa, 279
Southeast Asia, 60, 241
Southern Africa, 169, 228
Southern Rhodesia, 16, 107, 108, 119, 121
Souza, Justiniano Baltazar de, 201
sovereignty, 107, 109, 111, 162, 272, 316
Soviet Union, 260n31, 316
space of migration, 1, 7, 18–19, 22
Spain, 62, 302, 325
Spanish America, 37
Sri Lanka, 59, 302
Sri Lankan, 306, 307
St. Vincent (Saint Vincent and the Grenadines), 50, 50n64
stagnation, 220, 317
state building, 316, 317, 318
Stucky, Georges, 160
Stucky de Quay, Joseph Émile, 159
students, 46, 68, 94–95, 96, 97, 132, 133, 160, 202, 223, 229
subaltern colonialism, 3–4, 6–7
subcolonised, 7
subcultures, 288
subject, 1, 7, 14, 15, 16, 17, 20, 31, 33, 36, 39, 49, 51, 55, 59, 60, 67, 84, 108, 137, 194, 196, 199, 202, 203, 204, 205, 206, 207, 215, 259n12, 266, 267, 268, 269, 270, 272, 273, 274, 275, 278, 281, 323
subject status, 194, 199, 207
Subrahmanyam, Sanjay, 33, 33n9, 41, 196, 269
Sulawesi, 302
Sultan of Zanzibar, 195
Sun Yat Sen, 241
Sunni, 170, 173, 174, 183, 186n18
Sunni Islam, 183
Suntak (China), 243
Swaziland, 180, 218
Swiss Colonial Bourgeoisie, 150, 159
Swiss communities, 149, 150, 162

350 Index

Swiss Mission, 149, 150–158, 162–163
Swiss Protestants, 149, 150, 163

Tacuane, 154
Tamil, 306
Tanganyika, 195, 201, 205
Tanzania, 156, 176, 178, 199, 304
Tetum, 306
third empire, *see* third Portuguese empire
third Portuguese empire, 8, 9, 13, 15, 18, 22, 25n24, 31, 57, 110
Third World, 3, 4, 277, 310
Thomaz, Américo, 268
Timor, 25n23, 84, 92, 301, 302, 304, 306, 309, 312n18, 325
Timorese, 276, 297, 300, 301, 304, 306, 313n35
Tirre (*prazo*), 159
Tiswadi, 195
Togo, 307
Toi San (or Taishan, China), 243
Tongas, 146n29
Toucouleur, 303
Touré, Sékou, 133
transimperial, 193, 194, 206–207
translocal, 193
transnational, 65, 66, 193, 232, 265, 288, 289, 290–291
transnationalism, 66, 265, 290
Transvaal, 217, 218, 222, 240, 323
tribalism, 73, 158
Trindade, 141
Trinidad, 319
Trinidad and Tobago, 50
Tropics, 4, 24n16, 92, 107, 110, 125n4, 308, 311n7
true Portuguese (of Bengal), 302
Tungululo, Abílio, 154, 155
Turkey, 4

Uganda, 178, 179, 195, 199, 201, 205, 304, 319, 321, 323
Uganda Railway, 195
Uíge, 140
ultracolonialism, 3, 5, 268
Ultramar, *see Lei orgânica do Ultramar*, *Planos de fomento do Ultramar*
UNAR (*União Nacional Africana da Rombézia*), 154, 164n12
Ultranationalism, 281n1
undemographic, 23
underdevelopment, 44
uneconomic Imperialism, 5, 23, 268
UNHCR (United Nations High Commissioner for Refugees), 156
União dos Povos de Angola, *see* UPA
União Nacional Africana da Rombézia, *see* UNAR
União Nacional para a Independência Total de Angola, *see* Unita
Union of the Peoples of Angola, *see* UPA
Union Officials, 218
Unita, 299, 300, 311n13, 313n37
United Church of Christ, 151, 153
United Kingdom, 3, 204
United Nations High Commissioner for Refugees *see* UNHCR
United States, 9–10, 11, 15, 52, 53, 54, 55, 56, 57, 62, 63, 65, 68, 69, 70, 107, 151, 234n15, 240, 248, 252, 310, 311n15, 319, 320, 321, 322
United States of America, 9, 10
Universal Exhibition in Lisbon, 299
UPA, 93, 94, 114, 140, 250, 260n32
see also FNLA
upheaval, 216, 317
uprisings, 159, 311n6, 311n15, 312n19, 324
upward mobility, 54, 219, 221, 234n16
urbanisation, 45, 120
U.S. Azorean Refugee Act, 56

Valdez, Pedro Campos, 159
Vanombe, Faustino, 153
Varela, Raul Querido, 136
Vasco da Gama (bridge in Lisbon), 299
Vasco da Gama, 280, 292n17, 293n23
Vasconcelos, José Leite de, 76
Velhos colonos, *see* old settlers
Venezuela, 49, 49n62, 50, 53, 175, 216
Vila Real, 118
Vincke, Edouard, 73
Vingoe (*muene*), 162
Viseu, 118
voluntary migration, 52
Vuilleumier, René, 161–162

Wales, 199
Walloon, 303

Index   351

Wanderers' Sports Club (Transvaal), 323
welfare, 139, 219, 228, 242, 291
West Central Africa, 45, 138
western, 4, 56, 73, 75, 98, 280, 316, 317, 318
westernisation, 305, 311n7
Wheeler, Douglas, 152, 268
White African, 320
   see also petty white
White Angolans, 17
white colonisation, 113
white community, 9, 11, 13, 323, 324
White Fathers, 79, 149
white immigration, 13
White Mozambicans, 17, 173, 186n22, 214
white people, 8, 15, 84, 86
white population, 14, 111, 112, 113, 114, 120, 123, 232n1, 322, 323, 324
White Portuguese, 11, 12, 13, 87, 94, 141, 324
white settlement, 108, 110, 111, 114, 123, 124, 323, 324
white settlers, 13, 93, 107, 124, 323, 324
White South Africans, 230, 231
white working class, 14
whiteness, 219, 234n15
whitening, 45, 48, 93, 125n4, 311n7, 313n34

William Ponty School, 129
Witwatersrand, 32, 213, 214, 215, 217, 225, 240
Wolof, 303, 312n25
world economic crisis, 114, 152
World War I, 6, 23n9, 113, 201
World War II, 8, 13, 24n17, 108, 109, 111, 114, 124, 130, 132, 138, 140, 171, 172, 197, 208n4, 319

Yao, 160
Yaos, 170
Yoruba, 324

Zaire, 311n15
Zambesi, 37, 39, 59, 60
Zambesia, 37, 39, 59, 60
Zambezia (Zambézia), 149, 150, 151, 153, 154, 155, 156, 158, 159, 160, 161, 162, 163, 164n16
Zambezians, 154, 156, 158
Zambia, 23n6, 278, 320, 323
Zanzibar, 59, 195, 200, 201, 207n1
Ziguinchor, 135
Zimbabwe, 16, 23n6, 258n5, 320, 323
Zimbabwean, 321
Zurara, Gomes Eanes de, 99